The Study of Chinese Society

The Study of Chinese Society

ESSAYS BY MAURICE FREEDMAN

Selected and Introduced by
G. WILLIAM SKINNER

STANFORD UNIVERSITY PRESS
Stanford, California 1979

Stanford University Press
Stanford, California
© 1979 by the Board of Trustees of the
Leland Stanford Junior University
Printed in the United States of America
ISBN 0-8047-0964-5
LC 78-65395

Acknowledgments

My heaviest and most deeply felt debt is to Judith Freedman for assisting me in myriad ways with characteristic generosity and devotion.

The Introduction to this volume draws in part on a short obituary written jointly by Arthur P. Wolf and myself immediately after Freedman's death (*China Quarterly*, No. 63 [1975]: i–iii) and on my subsequent full-length obituary (*American Anthropologist*, 78 [1976]: 871–85). I am indebted for biographical details and other assistance to Professors Donald G. MacRae, Stuart R. Schram, and Arthur P. Wolf. For bibliographic help I thank Giok Po Oey of the Cornell University Libraries, Howard Nelson of the British Library, Margaret I. Scott of the Cambridge University Library, and Mark W. Tam of the Hoover Institution. For assistance with the Character List, I am grateful to Emily M. Ahern, Hugh D. R. Baker, and John McCoy. I am happy, once again, to be able to acknowledge the editorial collaboration of J. G. Bell.

I am grateful to the publishers and organizations listed below for having given me permission to include the following 24 essays in this volume. The essays are numbered in the order in which they appear in this volume, but the titles in all cases are those under which they originally appeared.

1. The Chinese in South-East Asia: A Longer View. China Society Occasional Papers, 14. London: The China Society, 1965, with permission of the publisher.

2. The Handling of Money: A Note on the Background to the Economic Sophistication of Overseas Chinese. *Man* 59 (Article 89), 1959: 64–65, with permission of the Royal Anthropological Institute of Great Britain and Ireland.

3. The Growth of a Plural Society in Malaya. *Pacific Affairs* 33(2), 1960: 158–68, with permission of the publisher.

4. An Epicycle of Cathay; or, the Southward Expansion of the Sinologists. In *Social Organization and the Applications of Anthropology*,

Robert J. Smith, ed. (Ithaca, N.Y.: Cornell University Press, 1974), pp. 302–32, with permission of the publisher.

5. Immigrants and Associations: Chinese in Nineteenth-Century Singapore. *Comparative Studies in Society and History* 3(1), 1960: 25–48, with permission of Cambridge University Press.

6. Chinese Kinship and Marriage in Early Singapore. *Journal of Southeast Asian History* 3(2), 1962: 65–73, with permission of the publisher.

7. Colonial Law and Chinese Society. *Journal of the Royal Anthropological Institute* 80, 1950: 97–126, with permission of the publisher.

8. Chinese Family Law in Singapore: The Rout of Custom. In *Family Law in Asia and Africa*, J. N. D. Anderson, ed. (London: George Allen & Unwin Ltd.; New York: Praeger Publishers, Inc., 1968), pp. 49–72, with permission of the publishers.

9. Religion and Social Realignment among the Chinese in Singapore; with Marjorie Topley. *Journal of Asian Studies* 21(1), 1961: 3–23, with permission of Dr. Topley and the Association for Asian Studies, Inc.

10. Chinese Geomancy: Some Observations in Hong Kong (mimeo). Paper prepared for Seminar on Cognitive and Value Systems in Chinese Society, Bermuda, January 24–25, 1964, sponsored by the Subcommittee on Research on Chinese Society of the ACLS-SSRC Joint Committee on Contemporary China, 17 pages, with permission of the Social Science Research Council.

11. Shifts of Power in the Hong Kong New Territories. *Journal of Asian and African Studies* 1(1), 1966: 3–12, with permission of E. J. Brill, Leiden.

12. "Emigration from the New Territories" (Paragraphs 72–83 of A Report on Social Research in the New Territories, mimeo, 37 pp., Hong Kong, 1963). *Journal of the Hong Kong Branch of the Royal Asiatic Society*, 16 (1976), 1977, with permission of the publisher.

13. Rites and Duties, or Chinese Marriage. [Inaugural Lecture as Professor of Anthropology in the University of London at The London School of Economics and Political Science, January 26, 1967.] (London: G. Bell & Sons Ltd., 1967), 24 pp., with permission of the London School of Economics and Political Science.

14. Ritual Aspects of Chinese Kinship and Marriage. In *Family and Kinship in Chinese Society*, M. Freedman, ed. (Stanford, Calif.: Stanford University Press, 1970), pp. 163–87, with permission of the publisher.

15. The Chinese Domestic Family: Models. *In* VIe Congrès international des sciences anthropologiques et ethnologiques, Paris, 30 Juillet-6 Août 1960 (Paris: Musée de l'homme, 1963), Vol. 2, Part 1, pp. 97–100, with permission of the publisher.

16. The Family in China, Past and Present. *Pacific Affairs* 34(4), 1961: 323–36, with permission of the publisher.

17. Ancestor Worship: Two Facets of the Chinese Case. In *Social Organization: Essays Presented to Raymond Firth*, M. Freedman, ed. (London: Frank Cass & Co. Ltd.; Chicago: Aldine, 1967), pp. 85–103, with permission of the publishers.

18. Geomancy [Presidential Address, Royal Anthropological Institute, 1968]. Proceedings of the Royal Anthropological Institute of Great Britain and Ireland 1968 (1969): 5–15, with permission of the Institute.

19. The Politics of an Old State: A View from the Chinese Lineage. In *Choice and Change: Essays in Honour of Lucy Mair*, John H. R. Davis, ed., London School of Economics and Political Science Monographs on Social Anthropology, 50 (London: Athlone Press; New York: Humanities Press, 1974), pp. 68–88, with permission of the London School of Economics and Political Science.

20. On the Sociological Study of Chinese Religion. In *Religion and Ritual in Chinese Society*, Arthur P. Wolf, ed. (Stanford, Calif.: Stanford University Press, 1974), pp. 19–41, with permission of the publisher.

21. Sociology in and of China. *British Journal of Sociology* 13(2), 1962: 106–16, with permission of the publisher.

22. A Chinese Phase in Social Anthropology [Third Malinowski Memorial Lecture, October 30, 1962]. *British Journal of Sociology* 4(1), 1963: 1–19, with permission of the publisher.

23. What Social Science Can Do for Chinese Studies. *Journal of Asian Studies* 23(4), 1964: 523–29, with permission of the Association for Asian Studies, Inc.

24. Why China? [Presidential Address, Royal Anthropological Institute, 1969]. Proceedings of the Royal Anthropological Institute of Great Britain and Ireland 1969 (1970): 5–13, with permission of the Institute.

Contents

Introduction by G. William Skinner

PART ONE: *The Chinese in Southeast Asia*

1. The Chinese in Southeast Asia: A Longer View / 3
2. The Handling of Money: A Note on the Background to the Economic Sophistication of Overseas Chinese / 22
3. The Growth of a Plural Society in Malaya / 27
4. An Epicycle of Cathay; or, The Southward Expansion of the Sinologists / 39

PART TWO: *Chinese Society in Singapore*

5. Immigrants and Associations: Chinese in Nineteenth-Century Singapore / 61
6. Chinese Kinship and Marriage in Early Singapore / 84
7. Colonial Law and Chinese Society / 93
8. Chinese Family Law in Singapore: The Rout of Custom / 140
9. Religion and Social Realignment Among the Chinese in Singapore / 161
(*with Marjorie Topley*)

PART THREE: *Social Change in the New Territories of Hong Kong*

10. Chinese Geomancy: Some Observations in Hong Kong / 189
11. Shifts of Power in the Hong Kong New Territories / 212
12. Emigration from the New Territories / 223

PART FOUR: *Kinship and Religion in China*

13. The Chinese Domestic Family: Models / 235
14. The Family in China, Past and Present / 240
15. Rites and Duties, or Chinese Marriage / 255
16. Ritual Aspects of Chinese Kinship and Marriage / 273
17. Ancestor Worship: Two Facets of the Chinese Case / 296
18. Geomancy / 313
19. The Politics of an Old State: A View from the Chinese Lineage / 334
20. On the Sociological Study of Chinese Religion / 351

PART FIVE: *On the Study of Chinese Society*

21. Sociology in China: A Brief Survey / 373
22. A Chinese Phase in Social Anthropology / 380
23. What Social Science Can Do for Chinese Studies / 398
24. Why China? / 407

Notes / 425
References Cited / 445
Character List / 479
Index / 485

Introduction

Maurice Freedman wrote three books treating Chinese society and edited a fourth. This intellectual achievement secures for him an honored place in the annals of social anthropology and sinology. Yet both fields would be impoverished if the remainder of Freedman's sinological *oeuvre* came to be neglected. The greater part of it is contained in this book.

In this introduction, I mean to do three things: place the essays in this volume in the context of Freedman's career, review one aspect of their substantive contribution, and point up the significance of Freedman's work for both sinology and anthropology.

It was primarily an interest in race relations that led Freedman to enroll, in January 1946, as a graduate student in the Department of Anthropology at the London School of Economics and Political Science (LSE). This concern, which stemmed from his experiences as a British soldier in India (and, one may assume, as a Jew in English society), is evident from the title of his Master's thesis, "The Sociology of Race Relations in South-East Asia with Special Reference to British Malaya." Throughout his subsequent career he retained a lively interest in interethnic relations. Out of this general concern there crystallized a specific interest in the Overseas Chinese; and when it came time to undertake doctoral field research, he embarked on a study of Chinese family and marriage in Malaya.

Part of the attraction of the Overseas Chinese was surely the analogy with Jews (for a sophisticated treatment of that analogy, see Essay 4), but the influence of his mentors at the LSE is also apparent. China had penetrated British social anthropology a decade earlier. In 1936, when A. R. Radcliffe-Brown was lecturing in China, Fei Hsiao-t'ung was writing his celebrated village ethnography at the LSE under Bronislaw Malinowski's direction. In 1938, Raymond Firth published a paper in a Chinese journal (the issue was dedicated quite guilelessly to the "London School of Anthropology"), and during the 1930's and 1940's several Chinese in addition to Fei studied at the LSE, among them Francis L. K.

Hsu, Lin Yueh-hwa, and T'ien Ju-k'ang. Freedman's initial field research was part of a larger program, promoted by Firth, which saw the completion of two other studies of Overseas Chinese society, T'ien's *The Chinese of Sarawak* (1953) and Alan J. A. Elliott's *Chinese Spirit-Medium Cults in Singapore* (1955).

It was originally intended that Freedman's doctoral research should be carried out in the Federation of Malaya, with an initial inquiry in Malacca, but emergency conditions in the Federation led to a shift of venue to Singapore. There Freedman and his wife Judith, also a doctoral candidate at the LSE, conducted research from January 1949 to November 1950, he on the Chinese family, she on the Malay family. Both dissertations were subsequently published as monographs: Maurice's *Chinese Family and Marriage in Singapore* (1957a) and Judith's *Malay Kinship and Marriage in Singapore* (Djamour 1959). The Freedmans returned to Singapore briefly for additional research in 1962 and 1963.

Five of the papers in this book treat Chinese society in Singapore. One (Essay 6) investigates the changing nature of Chinese kinship and marriage during the nineteenth century, contrasting the "intermediate" society of the local-born Baba Chinese with that of China-born immigrants. Two others analyze Chinese family law, one (Essay 7) as it was at the time of the 1949–50 fieldwork ("in part Chinese, in part English, and altogether odd"), the other (Essay 8) as transformed by the Women's Charter of 1961. The paradox of the Charter, which Freedman was able to spell out by virtue of the 1962–63 research, rests on the fact that a largely Chinese revolutionary party, "under an ideological compulsion to raise the status of women from the lowly level to which . . . colonialism and feudal institutions had condemned them," threw out custom to claim the heritage of post-colonial modernism, thereby bringing "to full fruition the colonial introduction of English law." The other two Singapore papers, less closely related to Freedman's dissertation research, analyze the changing forms of Chinese voluntary associations in the nineteenth century (Essay 5) and of Chinese religious institutions in the twentieth (Essay 9).

Freedman's example attracted other anthropologists to the Overseas Chinese as a field of study, and throughout his subsequent career he kept in close touch with their work, which he greatly furthered by periodically reformulating the intellectual issues involved. This broader interest in the Overseas Chinese is represented here by four papers. Essay 1 provides an overview of the Nanyang Chinese. Essay 2 looks to the economic history of the particular regions in China from which emigrants hailed for a partial explanation of their economic success overseas. Essay 3 analyzes the effect of nationalism and political independence in creating pan-Malayan ethnic blocs from what had previously been merely categories, thereby sharpening the plural nature of Malayan society. Essay 4 disputes the thesis that the Nanyang Chinese represent merely the latest phase of the inexorable southward expansion of the Chinese colossus.

In his first book (1957a: 10), Freedman reports that after settling into a village near Singapore he was faced with a clear choice: to plumb the depths of a single village or to move beyond his village and conduct a study "as broadly based as I, one lone fieldworker, could make it." He chose the latter course. Looking back on his and others' research on the Nanyang Chinese, he drew the following lessons for anthropological methodology (1963a: 4):

> To delimit a "community" and confine one's attention to it would miss the very characteristic of the society which makes it interesting: its scale and its scatter. Trying to study the Overseas Chinese a man must find his anthropological prejudices corroded away. He must be mobile. He must learn to contain his impatience when he cannot see all his subjects acting out their many roles. . . . He must adjust his vision so that he may see behavior and ideas within the framework not only of the immediate locality but also of the society from which the migrants have come, of the largest territorial settlement within which they find themselves, and of the non-Chinese society in which they are embedded.

For Freedman the Overseas Chinese were also a window on China proper. As recounted later (1970: 8), he had striven passionately to see beyond the Singapore Chinese to the society from which they had come. The book that resulted from this "obsession," *Lineage Organization in Southeastern China* (1958), revealed an exceptional skill for recreating social institutions in the round from myriad facts and clues in the published literature. On the methodological side, it taught us how "to sit in archives (or at least in libraries) and interview the dead" (1963a: 5). On the substantive side, it drew, wherever appropriate, on the concepts developed by E. E. Evans-Pritchard, Meyer Fortes, and other Africanists, but went on to discuss topics that had no counterpart in the African kinship literature: social differentiation within the lineage, the relationship of lineage structure to political power and economic control, and relations between the lineage and the state. One chapter, on the family, was subsequently elaborated in two of the papers reproduced here. Essay 13 contrasts the long cycles of the rich and powerful, in which family division occurs at a high level of complexity, with the shorter cycles of the poor and lowly, in which division typically yields simple conjugal families. Essay 14 presents a more comprehensive treatment, summing up anthropological "knowledge" about the family in traditional China, under the Republic, and during the first decade of the People's Republic.

Soon after this initial work on family and lineage in China was undertaken "as an exercise in armchair anthropology," a stopover of a few days in Hong Kong persuaded Freedman that in the New Territories it was still possible to study traditional Chinese society "in action." There he found himself confronted by "the walled villages and localized lineages which hitherto had been merely the stuff of dreams" (1970: 8). That was in 1955, but the field research he then envisaged was to be realized only in 1963. Three of the essays reproduced here concern Chinese society in the New Territories, each demonstrating a sense of problem that had long since been finely honed. Essay 10, reporting his observations of geomancy in the early 1960's, is published for the first time in the present volume. Essay 11 traces local politics in the New Territories from late imperial times to the postwar colonial era. Essay 12 treats overseas emigration from New Territories villages and market towns.

The main significance of Freedman's research in Hong Kong, however, is its profound effect on the subsequent course of sinological anthropology. Having shown that we could learn about mainland Chinese society from the Overseas Chinese and from the archives, he now showed what we could learn from observation in what he later came to call "residual China," notably Hong Kong and Taiwan. Several of his students, e.g. Hugh D. R. Baker, subsequently carried out field research in Hong Kong or Taiwan. And together with students from American, European, and Chinese universities, they produced during the 1960's studies that in number and scope exceeded the sum total of the anthropological work done in China proper before 1949. Nearly all of this research was inspired by Freedman's work.

How the New Territories research affected Freedman's own scholarship may be glimpsed from the following account of his growing love affair with Chinese geomancy (1970: 10):

When I first got seriously interested in the subject I cannot now remember; it was certainly not during my field research in Singapore, although it was then that I must have read what J. J. M. de Groot has to say on the subject. . . . While I was writing my first book on the Chinese lineage . . . , I fastened on the evidence in de Groot's books and other sources that seemed to suggest that Chinese played out their rivalry for social status within the system of *feng-shui* by competing for good grave sites. It is clear from my notebooks that I had read a good deal of the relevant literature, and it astonishes me now that I made so little of what I read. It was the experience of a live system of geomancy in the New Territories in 1963 that forced me to think again and to formulate ideas on it to take back to London and to the books. The books began to yield.

And what a harvest we have had! Not only on geomancy but on every aspect of society on which New Territories communities and the libraries could be made eloquent. The first fruits were served up in Freedman's magnificent *Chinese Lineage and Society* (1966), and the subsequent bounty is reproduced here. Marriage rites are treated in Essays 15 and 16. Ancestor worship is examined in Essays 16 and 17, in which the geomancy of tombs is shown to be the *yin* counterpart of the *yang* cult focused on tablets. The geomancy concerned with habitations of the living, in contrast to those of the dead, is taken up in Essay 18. Essay 19 treats the role of the lineage in the interplay between local and bureaucratic politics. And Essay 20 confronts the totality of Chinese religious institutions and behavior, exploring the ways in which they may be said to constitute a single system.

The second lineage book and the subsequent papers reproduced here as Essays 15–20 were published during a dramatic decade in Freedman's professional career. At the LSE, where he had taught since 1951, he was made Professor in 1965; Essay 15 was his inaugural lecture. A preliminary version of Essay 16 was prepared for a conference on kinship in Chinese society in 1966, and the original version of Essay 20 was prepared for a subsequent conference in the same series. Essay 17 was Freedman's contribution to a volume he edited in Firth's honor, and Essay 19 was published in a similar volume honoring another LSE anthropologist, Lucy Mair. Essay 18 was his Presidential Address to the Royal Anthropological Institute.

In 1970 Freedman accepted the chair in social anthropology at Oxford, succeeding Evans-Pritchard. From then until his death in July 1975, he was Director of the Institute of Social Anthropology at Oxford and Fellow of All Souls College. During those years he became more and more interested in the intellectual history of sinological anthropology. This had been a long-standing concern. As early as 1961, he tracked down and interviewed Daniel H. Kulp, the American sociologist who had published the first ethnography of a Chinese village in 1925; and in 1969 he had confessed an abiding fascination with "the rhythm and pace of the anthropological studies of China." Now, as he read the lessons of false starts and lost opportunities as well as of critical turning points and intellectual breakthroughs, he became convinced that it would be worthwhile to push the story back from the 1920's to the 1870's. During his last few years he spent time in Leiden and Paris interviewing people who had known his distinguished predecessors, J. J. M. de Groot and Marcel Granet. Freedman's translation of Granet's classic study of Chinese religion (Granet 1975), with a long critical introduction, was published shortly after he died, and his papers include extensive notes on de Groot's life.

This aspect of Freedman's work is reflected in the final papers of this volume. Essay 20 treats, inter alia, the place of Granet and de Groot in the intellectual history of sinology. Essay 21 is a brief history of the sociology and social anthropology of China since the 1920's; and Essay 22, a Malinowski Memorial Lecture, draws from the first round of anthropological experience with Chinese civilization a number of lessons for both anthropology and sinology. In Essay 23, Freedman spells out various ways in which sinology stands to benefit from the work of social scientists. And in the final essay of this book, his second Presidential Address to the Royal Anthropological Institute, Freedman asks "Why China?" To that question this book as a whole stands as an eloquent answer.

Kinship and Religion

Freedman's brilliant work on Chinese kinship and religion has had the unfortunate effect of obscuring his excellent scholarship on other aspects of Chinese society, notably economics, politics, law, inequality, and ethnicity. We have space here, however, only for the areas that his work virtually transformed as fields of study: family and marriage, lineage and ancestor worship, and religion.

Family and Marriage. During the first fifteen years of his scholarly career, Freedman's chief concerns with the Chinese family were sociological. He strove to get control of the ethnographic facts in order to specify the relevant structural principles and jural rules and examine how those principles and rules shaped family interaction and composition. The results were presented in his book on Chinese family life in Singapore, in a separate chapter devoted to the family in each of his lineage books, and in four papers reproduced here as Essays 6, 7, 13, and 14. This first round of research initiated a period of lively ferment: a whole generation of sinological anthropologists entered the fray, and to Freedman's intense pleasure few of his early formulations survived their investigations unchanged, though none has been superseded.

Some examples may help to illuminate this debate on the sociology of the Chinese family. The first concerns the relation between paternal authority and fraternal solidarity. In Freedman's initial formulation everything hinged on the de facto power of the father in the exercise of his authority as family head. Where the father drew political and economic strength from outside the family, he could successfully enforce the obedience of his sons and suppress the competition among them. Where his social and economic resources in the community were inadequate, his sons could defy him either directly or by allowing their wives to sow dissension leading to family division. Margery Wolf (1972: 164–70) has challenged this view for its male-centeredness, holding that mothers are as strongly motivated as fathers (albeit for rather different reasons) to mute conflict among married sons, and better situated to do so successfully; and that women married to brothers have their own reasons for hastening division. Myron Cohen (1976: chap. 7) offers yet another view: married sons suppress their differences as long as it is in their economic interest to do so, and unleash their wives when continued cooperation is no longer economically advantageous.

Our second example is the debate over the idea that the Chinese family was an enduring corporation. Freedman argued that it was not. As he put it in Essay 17 (p. 304), "the Chinese family is a property-owning estate which dissolves on the death of each senior generation to reform into successor-estates, none of which can be said to have the identity inhering in its predecessors. As each son is born (or adopted) he is automatically endowed with a potential share in the family estate." Yes and no, replied Arthur Wolf (1974c: 129ff; see also Wolf & Huang 1979: chap. 5), pointing out that Freedman has reference here to the descent-group aspect of the family at the expense of its residence-group aspect. In Wolf's view, the Chinese family is an amalgam of two distinct institutions: the *chia*, the basic unit of production and consumption and a component part of the empire, and the line, property-owning descent group and the social unit responsible for domestic ancestral rites. Sons are born to *chia*, not to lines; but they are recruited to lines either through recognition by the line's head or by adoption. And both lines and families dissolve on division. Freedman admired this bold reformulation, but died before he could respond in print.

Our third example has to do with the relative social status of husbands and wives. In his description of marriage in Singapore (1957: 110), Freedman observed that in socioeconomic terms "some sort of parity is aimed at in matchmaking," but he also noted that in practice both men and women might rise in status by marriage. (Thus, for example, "a businessman in search of a useful son-in-law may prefer a bright ambitious lad of humbler family.") But in his survey of the literature on China Freedman found that whereas a first marriage might leave "the girl's family ritually and socially in a relationship of inferiority with the boy's" (Essay 16, p. 294) the reverse would never occur. Not so, says Emily Ahern (1974: 279). Arguing from her field data in Taiwan, she holds that "marriage creates a ranking in which wife-givers are distinctly superior to wife-takers. From the time of betrothal the bride's family is defined as ritually superior to the groom's, irrespective of the previous economic and social position of the two families." In his response, presented orally at a conference, Freedman argued that whereas her argument might be sustained for ritual superiority, it could not be correct for social superiority. As Arthur Wolf has pointed out (1974a: 15) this debate forces us to rethink what ritual statements say about social reality.

Meanwhile, Freedman's own work on marriage and the family had moved on to just such issues. Even as the controversies touched off by his sociological analyses raged, his research turned from structural principles per se to their symbolic representations and from jural rules to rites. The new subtlety and sophistication that accompanied this shift of emphasis is apparent in Essays 15 and 16. "Rites, as symbolic affirmations," we read in the second of these essays (p. 294), "are the opposite of jural rules. Jural rules rely for their value on their relative clarity; rites derive their strength from the poetic vagueness." A structuralist influence also became evident in Freedman's growing fascination with complementary dualism, both as an expository device and as a feature of Chinese cognition.

One of the most straightforward of the dualistic distinctions he draws is between the ancestral cult and the cult of the stove god (Essay 16, pp. 274–75). These two complementary aspects of the domestic religion, the first dominated by women and the second by men, link the household to different supernatural hierarchies. In the same paper (pp. 288–89) Freedman suggests the ways in which "ancestor worship and marriage rites form a balanced pair." Men are "endowed with forebears" but "must choose affines." Agnatic bonds are given and immutable, marriage ties contractual and potentially fragile. Rites for the ancestors are regular and continual, marriage rites irregular and intermittent. Differences between the two sets of rites systematically reflect these distinctions. Moreover, and more interestingly, because marriage is at once essential to agnatic continuity and a threat to agnatic solidarity marriage rites appear as "a structure of resonant ambiguity." The ideal state of agnation is clear enough, but "it remains for the rites of marriage to dramatize the indecisiveness of affinity."

Such dichotomies often raise questions about a potential *tertium quid*: thus one wonders, for example, how Freedman's dualistic formulation of domestic worship accommodates the patron deity of the household. In the case of agnation and affinity, Freedman himself examines a third category of relationship: the ties between men and the agnates of their mothers and wives. This tricky area, in which the struggle between agnation and affinity is too complex for the rites to resolve, is brilliantly discussed in Essays 15 (pp. 269–71) and 16 (pp. 294–95).

Lineage and Ancestor Worship. In moving from the family to the lineage, we encounter another of Freedman's dualisms—that between the cult of immediate jural superiors and the cult of descent groups. The former, the care and commemoration of forebears "as it were for their own sake," is a domestic cult associated with the family (or, as Arthur Wolf would have it, the line), whereas the latter, "a set of rites linking together all the agnatic descendants of a given forebear" (1966: 153), is associated with extrafamilial kin groups: clans, lineages, and lineage segments. Little was achieved in the study of Chinese ancestor worship until this distinction was clearly drawn by Freedman (1957: 218–23), and the continuing utility of the contrast is apparent in the extraordinary reformulation of ancestor worship included in this volume (Essay 16, pp. 274–88). Once again we see specialization by sex: women prominent in the domestic cult both in the home and at the graveside, men prominent in the cult of the descent group.

Both forms of ancestor worship, in turn, are crosscut by yet another dualism, in which tablets are counterpoised with tombs. Ancestors in their *yang* manifestation are given ritual care as tablets housed in domestic shrines or lineage halls, whereas ancestors in their *yin* guise are tended at their graves. In the domestic cult, ancestors slide over the horizon within a few generations; but a select few, those who "serve as points of reference for lineages and their segments," live on, the objects of ritual care at the hands of lineage elders, both at their tombs (or cenotaphs) and in the ancestral hall, where their tablets are placed on the top shelf of the altar. Whereas the domestic cult was very nearly universal, the cult of the descent group was absent whenever lineages were; moreover, where lineages or segments were unable to afford a hall, rites of descent-group solidarity were limited to those at the tomb. The manner in which these structural arrangements of ancestor worship are expressed in ritual activity, and the "argument" and symbolism of that activity, are laid out in masterly fashion at pp. 282–86 below.

"The study of lineage structure and organization is one of the main ways in which social anthropology has established itself within the general study of Chinese society" (1974: 68). We have Freedman alone to thank for that achievement, not to mention its obverse: the successful introduction of the Chinese case into the comparative ethnology of lineage organization and ancestor worship. Essay 19 recapitulates his main arguments concerning the lineage and updates some of them. One in particular deserves comment here: his 1958 view of lineage formation as a matter of segmentation: "a small agnatic group growing and gradually becoming differentiated internally by the emergence of new segments, and segments within segments." The pattern of irregular segmentation predicted by the model was amply confirmed by the work done by Jack Potter (1968) and Hugh Baker (1968) on Cantonese lineages in the New Territories of Hong Kong. However, Burton Pasternak (1968a, 1968b,

1969) and Myron Cohen (1969), working with Hakka lineages in Taiwan, produced a significantly different picture. There scattered groups of the same surname, with or without verifiable genealogical connections, had been brought together within the framework of a lineage endowed with an estate. Was it, then, a question of segmentation on the mainland (or among Cantonese) and aggregation in Taiwan (or among Hakkas)? In Essay 19 (pp. 343–46) Freedman tells us why he thinks not, providing yet another major reformulation of some critical issues in the study of lineage organization.

Religion. Freedman's interest in religion developed naturally out of his initial concern with kinship. His first publication in this field, a treatment of the sociology of religion in Singapore, is reprinted here in expanded form as Essay 9. The concern in this essay is basically sociological: from which social categories did different sects, temples, and religions draw their priests and their followings, and why? There are some fascinating findings. For example, in the Buddhist and sectarian institutions that attract mostly unattached women, the possibility is held out of reincarnation "as a member of the male (and therefore privileged) sex" (p. 182), and groupings of female masters and disciples, taking on some formal characteristics of the Chinese kinship system, address one another as *male* agnates (p. 183). Among the essay's virtues is its systematic comparison of religion in Singapore's Chinese community with religion in China, providing insight into both.

In a review of main trends in social and cultural anthropology (written for UNESCO in 1970–71 but still in press in 1978), Freedman wrote:

Some anthropologists have placed the accent on the pragmatic side of religious belief, to stress the support it may give to the arrangements of social life and to deprive it of its independence as a mode of experience and thought. In a narrow sociologism of religion the nuances and complexity of belief are lost to view, and the problem of striking deep into its roots does not present itself. In many areas of anthropology, the last decade and a half or so have marked a shift from religion as only an institution to religion as a way, however difficult of access, of knowing and apprehension. There has been a "religious revival."

He would, I think, place his own work within this overall trend. If in retrospect his initial analyses of ancestor worship and of public religion in Singapore are not wholly free of "narrow sociologism," his subsequent work took religious ideas more seriously.

Let me illustrate with his study of the geomancy of burial, where we confront yet another of the dichotomous mysteries of Chinese cosmology. The geomancy of tombs and ancestor worship are "but two faces of a single religious phenomenon":

Each dead forebear appears in two separate guises. . . . The ancestors as bones are *yin*; they are of the Earth, passive and retiring. The ancestors in their tablets are *yang*; they have affinities with Heaven and are active and outgoing. *Fengshui* [geomancy] handles *yin*; ancestor worship *yang*. . . . Each . . . presents a distinct configuration of attitudes towards the dead and has different implications for behavior between agnates. In the geomancy of burial what strikes us above all is that men are constantly striving to individualize their fate and better themselves at the expense of their patrilineal kinsmen.

But that is hardly the end of it. The geomancy of tombs also stands in complementary opposition to that of houses. The distinction here is between *yin* buildings (dwellings of darkness and of the dead) and *yang* buildings (dwellings of light and of the living), which are at once distinguished and linked together into a single system. Essay 18 is devoted to the geomancy of houses and settlements, and from it I may appropriately draw a point that serves to bring the subject around to ironic closure. Ancestral halls, dwellings of light, may be geomantically sited no less than the tombs of apical ancestors, dwellings of darkness. Thus, halls may be sited to the amoral benefit of individual lineage members even as the ancestral tablets they house interact in a system of moral causation with the fortunes of the lineage.

Freedman's work on marriage rites, in particular Essays 15 and 16, confronted him with "the rich symbolism—in word, action, and object— of which each significant step in the unfolding of the rites is composed" (p. 295). The study of this symbolism led to yet another line of his future work. In 1974 (Essay 20, pp. 367–69) we find him pointing up features of a theology that underlay both the pragmatic-agnostic interpretation of elite religion and the polytheistic religious world of the common people. In a structuralist mode he posits transformations that bridge the metaphysical gulf that has traditionally been held to pervade all spheres of Chinese religion.

Cognition, symbolism, and theology are identified in Freedman's UNESCO essay as the chief "styles" of the "religious revival" within anthropology, and he made it known in the spring of 1975 that divination was to be the subject of a forthcoming lecture series. It is not unreasonable to surmise that at the time of his death he was contemplating a full-scale analysis of Chinese religious ideas, an analysis that would "do justice to ideas while maintaining the study of the interaction between them and the social arrangements of the men who hold them." This project, if project it was, now becomes a charge and a challenge to his surviving colleagues and successors.

人類学 漢学
Anthropology and Sinology

Although Freedman's discipline was anthropology, his impulse was not to view China through the miniaturizing lenses that might make it accessible to traditional anthropological methods, but rather to reshape the discipline so that it might rise to the challenge posed by the world's largest society. Anthropology as well as China deserved no less. In Essay 22 he demolished the notion, prevalent among anthropologists in the 1950's, that the village was somehow a microcosm of the total society. As for the strategy of generalizing from a range of meticulously executed community studies, which he attributes to Radcliffe-Brown and Malinowski, it was the "most grievous" of "all the biases to which the anthropological approach has been subject" (p. 383). In general, he saw a practical danger in "the anthropological preoccupation with the small in scale: the risk of speaking generally of a society with the confidence bred of an intimate acquaintance with local communities in it."

But how then does one conceptualize the totality of a complex society? Freedman quickly came to distrust radically simplifying models that fix on certain cleavages to demarcate compartmentalized segments. Thus in Essay 3 he points up the deficiencies of Furnivall's plural-society concept with reference to Malaya. For China proper, of course, the dominant paradigm has been the distinction between the elite and the masses, or in Fei Hsiao-t'ung's terms the gentry and the peasantry, which draws inspiration in the cultural realm from Redfield's distinction between the Great and Little Traditions. In Freedman's view, however, far from raising the sights of anthropologists to incorporate the totality of civilization, Redfield's paradigm has been seized by most of them as a license for delimiting their domain to village communities and folk culture, and indeed has served to direct attention away from "the interpenetration of the cultivated and the popular, the high and the low, the gentry and the peasantry" (1975: 207). More fundamental difficulties arise from the arbitrariness of the scheme itself. Of all the many gradations of class and class-specific cultures in China, what is the rationale for singling out any particular horizontal line for dichotomizing the whole—or indeed for preferring horizontal ties to vertical, class variation over regional variation? With respect to China at least, "the intoxicating discovery by social scientists of a neat division between elite . . . culture and peasant . . . culture has been (or at any rate, ought to be) replaced by the further discovery that the first discovery is an illusion" (*ibid.*).

Freedman in his own writing presented not so much a paradigm as a conceptual framework. Implicit in his view of Chinese society were two kinds of hierarchy: that of community and region on the one hand, that of class and status on the other. What might be considered class subcultures were differentiated by territorial system, and what might be considered local and regional subcultures were differentiated by class. This realization grew out of his meticulous analysis of agnatic kin groups in China. The hierarchy of segments within localized lineages and of localized lineages within higher-order lineages was shown to be shaped by the differentiating forces of class, status, and power, whose locus was likely to be in other territorially based hierarchical systems. It is in this sense that he emphasized "the need to keep the study of the lineage within the framework of the study of *all* groups and relationships" (p. 345).

The vast array of subcultures associated with this structural complexity, in Freedman's view, drew their elements from a common fund—a cultural repertoire that informed the civilization as a whole. In Essay 19 (p. 340) he notes that "to move from countryside to town in traditional Chinese society was not to leave one social world and enter another." In Essay 18 he shows that geomancy is but one expression of a universal Chinese system of metaphysics. His survey of marriage rites in Essay 15 "confirms the oneness of the system": "Variations there are, but I believe that the Chinese marriage rites everywhere can be represented by one basic model" (p. 257). In Essay 16 (p. 288) he comments that the investigation of virtually every topic in the study of Chinese society "leads to numerous points in the total system of Chinese social behavior and the total system of Chinese ideas." And in Essay 20 he identifies himself with an intellectual tradition within sinology "that takes Chinese religion to be an entity." "Members of the elite might stand by a puritanical version of Chinese religion, and in that posture deplore the antics of the superstitious masses; but the elite as a group was bound to the masses indissolubly by its religious beliefs and practices" (p. 369). Of course, systemic integrity does not imply uniformity. Indeed, emphasizing the "variations in institutions and beliefs" that characterize Chinese society in time and space, Freedman calls, at the end of Essay 17 (p. 312), for a research strategy that capitalizes on them. "Well documented, China . . . could provide an admirable framework for testing, by a study of variation, the validity of an analysis proposed for one small set of data."

"Well documented"—it is an important qualification, central to Freedman's view of sinological anthropology. Anthropologists naturally "graze in the field," as he once wryly put it, but in studying China they must also learn to "feed on documents." Facts about the past need to be built into analyses of what is studied in the field, not just as "background to the present" but as "integral to the matter under study." China offers special opportunities not only for advantageous "interplay between the anthropologist as fieldworker and the anthropologist as bookworm," and not only for history-in-the-field, but also for historical sociology per se.

But is the past to be the only future for sinological anthropology? Can anthropologists—should they—contribute to the study of Chinese society in the People's Republic? Absolutely, says Freedman. Not only must the tools of sinological anthropology be kept sharp against the day when the anthropological study of mainland society is renewed in China itself (Essay 21, p. 379), but anthropologists must study the socialist transformation in China if they are to be true to their calling: "Social anthropology is not a mere search for scientific propositions, but an exploration of the realized possibilities of human action" (Essay 24, p. 421). Finally, we must study China because it is there (Essay 14, p. 254); even if "for the moment we cannot produce satisfactory answers, the habit of putting questions must be kept alive." Both the tone and the sentiment here are characteristic of the great anthropologist whose essays follow.

PART ONE

The Chinese in Southeast Asia

The Chinese in Southeast Asia: A Longer View

1964

Longer than what? And why? The subtitle of this lecture is an encourage-ment to try to avoid certain misunderstandings of the position of the Chi-nese in Southeast Asia. On the short view, our eyes myopically focused on the present day, the Nanyang Chinese, that is to say, those Chinese living in the region which stretches from Burma in the west to the Philip-pines in the east, seem to be some twelve million misplaced persons, a restless and insecure population acting as the markers of a vague outer frontier for a politically expansive homeland. This is the "present." The trouble with it is that it confirms the prejudices of both those who dislike or distrust the Chinese and those who worship them. Everywhere in Southeast Asia there are visible and viable Chinese communities, great and small, which serve at once as "proof" of the anti-Chinese contention that the Chinese are always alien and unassimilable entities, and as "evi-dence" in aid of a pro-Chinese thesis that Chinese culture is so superior in fact and in its evaluation of itself as to be able to withstand the impact of other Asian influences and of westernization.

Both views are wrong and unjust, as a longer perspective on Southeast Asian history will, I think, demonstrate conclusively enough. Chinese have certainly been assimilated in large numbers in various parts of the region and have effectively disappeared off the map of the Nanyang. And when they have not been so assimilated their specifically Chinese culture has often been weathered away. The present is deceptive because, al-though the chapter of Chinese immigration to Southeast Asia has been virtually closed since Communism conquered China in 1949, the effects of recent immigration are still clearly to be seen a mere decade and a half later; and because, while Portuguese Timor and British-protected Brunei

Lecture delivered on 17 June 1964 to the China Society, London, and separately published in 1965 as no. 14 of the Society's Occasional Papers. Reprinted in *Asian Review*, n.s. 3, no. 1 (1966), 24–38; and in Robert O. Tilman, ed., *Man, State, and Society in Contemporary Southeast Asia* (New York, 1969), 431–49. The original title showed "South-East" instead of "Southeast."

are now the sole remnants of foreign rule in the region, the colonial atmosphere still hangs about our thoughts. We live in a post-colonial era, but it is yet so new that we need to make a great effort of the imagination to come out from beneath the shadow of its predecessor. And it is important to add that, having made this effort and emerged, we run the further risk of being seduced by the new myths of latter-day nationalism, "neo-colonialism," and *le tiers monde*.

Let me try very briefly (and amateurishly, for I speak as an anthro-pologist, not a historian) to survey the story of Chinese movement into the area we have come, increasingly since the Second World War, to call Southeast Asia. The present Chinese diaspora known to us as the Nan-yang ("Southern Ocean") rests historically on early merchant ventures from southeastern China powerfully reinforced during the colonial period. The term Nanyang itself stresses the sea connection with China; in fact it originally meant the coastal area of Southeast Asia plus the islands of the Philippines group and the Indonesian archipelago. In ear-lier times Vietnam, Burma, and Thailand were reached from southeastern China by land routes. For the Chinese the Nanyang was in the first place an area for trade and only in a minor degree an arena for the exercise of political power (although the imperial might was more than once shown in Southeast Asian waters). Trade was encouraged by both official policy and official capital during Sung and Yüan times, and while the early Ming rulers put restrictions on the trade, their successors eased them in order to continue the commercial tradition laid down by the previous dynasties. At the turnover to the Ch'ing dynasty in 1644 the southern Chinese with Nanyang connections formed an important part of the resistance to the new regime, and it was then for the first time that the Nanyang came to be a significant factor in the political life of the empire. It is important to note that the Nanyang traders were concen-trated in the two southeastern provinces of Fukien and Kwangtung and that this region of China held out against the new Ch'ing rule until the 1680's. And even when open resistance had ended, anti-Ch'ing sentiment remained. It was institutionalized in the secret societies (the "Triad" and others) which came to form an important element in the social life of the southern Chinese who stayed at home and of those who moved over-seas. Ch'ing policy, based on a view of China as a land power and un-sympathetic to the attachment of the southeastern provinces to the sea, was set against ties with the Nanyang. But while overseas trade was hin-dered it was not stopped. Indeed, one of the unintended consequences of imperial action seems to have been precisely to promote the overseas settlement which it deplored; for Chinese traders, fearing the difficulties and dangers created for them at home by the officials of the new regime, now established themselves *in partibus infidelium* where formerly they had gone temporarily to trade.

In the course of the eighteenth century the Chinese trade with Southeast Asia became heavily dependent on Western enterprise as the European presence made itself increasingly felt in the region; and from this bracketing of the Chinese merchants with Western power springs the anti-Chinese view of the present day that Chinese economic dominance has been one of the attendant afflictions of Western imperialism. When the Dutch in the East Indies were the chief among the Western traders, the Indies were the center of Chinese commerce, but with the founding of Penang (toward the end of the century) and of Singapore (early in the nineteenth century) as British settlements, the Malay Peninsula came to the fore as the geographical focus of Chinese trading activity. (Originally a Portuguese acquisition and subsequently Dutch, Malacca was added to the list of British possessions early in the nineteenth century. With Penang and Singapore it came eventually to form the Straits Settlements, a British nucleus in the Peninsula from which has emerged in our own day the western part of Malaysia.) At the same time as Chinese commercial talent was being deployed in the East Indies and the Malay Peninsula, Chinese were making an economic niche for themselves in Thailand, although here independently of Western enterprise and influence. In this fashion the historical basis for the modern concentration of the Nanyang Chinese in the three countries of Malaysia, Indonesia, and Thailand was laid.

But it was not until well into the nineteenth century that migration from China took place on the grand scale, to man the modern agricultural and mining enterprises, to populate the growing cities, and to cover the region with a network of small businesses. Especially after about 1850 the Chinese overseas became preponderantly composed of poor working men, the coolie element (recruited from the peasantry of Fukien and Kwangtung in a drive which swept Chinese into the Americas and Australia as well as Southeast Asia) swamping the merchants who had hitherto characterized the Nanyang.

When, as a result of the Opium War, Hong Kong was established as a British colony and the first treaty ports of China were opened to the West, Chinese commercial enterprise in the Nanyang began to operate with securer bases at home, the final blow having been delivered to the Ch'ing policy of restraining ties with the non-Chinese world. Chinese business empires grew up which linked various parts of Southeast Asia with financial centers such as Singapore, the hub of the Nanyang, Shanghai, and Hong Kong. And with every advance of the frontier of Western control in Southeast Asia (for it is important to realize that the effective colonial government of the region did not reach its maximum extent very long before it was shattered by the Pacific War), the Chinese expanded their economic interests, until by 1941 a framework of Chinese commercial and industrial relationships covered the whole region.

As Ch'ing fortunes began to decline at home, the Nanyang Chinese repeated their role at the beginning of the dynasty by forming a base for revolutionary activities, and we have merely to remind ourselves of Sun Yat-sen's comings and goings in Southeast Asia to underline the significance of the Nanyang in the political life of modern China. Since the establishment of the Republic in 1911 until the present day the various governments of China (whole or divided) have sought in greater or lesser measure to watch over the interests of their overseas subjects (for a long time defined as *all* the descendants through males of men from China) and make use of their resources in capital and skill for China's economic development. During the rise of modern China, and under the encouragement of its government, the Chinese overseas became Overseas Chinese, having come to think of themselves as an entity with rights and duties vis-à-vis their homeland. In brief, China was their political focus and their cultural model.

The new nationalism (pride in their homeland and consciousness of their connection with it) was reflected in the modern education of the Nanyang Chinese. Even before the 1911 Revolution Mandarin had to some extent been taught as the national language among Chinese overseas. (Mandarin was of course a foreign tongue to people whose homes lay in the linguistically peculiar provinces of Fukien and Kwangtung.) It was not long before a Mandarin-speaking school culture was well established in the Nanyang. Post-imperial China as seen through the eyes of Overseas Chinese educated in the new schools became the yardstick for cultural judgment and the point of reference for political thinking. Political activity in the Nanyang, to the extent that it was ideologically inspired, was oriented to the homeland. Domestically, in each of the various countries of Southeast Asia, the Chinese were narrowly concerned with protecting their special interests. In the colonial territories of the region the Chinese were not typically anti-Western (except as they reflected China's radical rejection of its Western harassers), and this fact, coupled with the economic strength which the Chinese built up under the umbrella of colonialism, earned them the suspicion from local nationalists which still bedevils the position and security of the Nanyang Chinese.

I apologize doubly for the potted history. It is both inelegant and, although in this form necessary to the argument, inaccurate in its brevity.[1] I hope presently to redeem myself by going more deeply into the facts of the most important of the Chinese communities in Southeast

Asia. But before I do so we shall need to set out the basic population figures of the Nanyang as a whole. We have seen that there are some twelve million Chinese in the region (say, 5 percent of the total regional population). But what kind of a fact is this? It is the vaguest of statistical notions about a mass of people who are in some sense Chinese. What does "Chinese" mean? In one country it means anyone who says he is Chinese in answer to the census taker's question. In another country it means anybody who bears a Chinese name. The twelve million include Chinese who speak Chinese, are citizens of China, live in domestic surroundings similar to those to be found in southeastern China, wear clothes such as are worn in China, eat Chinese food . . . No problem about them. But in the global figure there are also people who do not know a word of Chinese, are citizens of the Southeast Asian country of their birth, and live, dress, and eat in fashions which would be intolerably exotic to a Chinese fresh from China. One may imagine the variations possible between these two extremes. "Chinese," therefore, begins to emerge as a label for some kind of political and social status (varying as between countries) and to recede as a name for a way of life or culture.

In Burma, the Philippines, Cambodia, and Laos Chinese numbers are relatively small. They are particularly small in the last of these countries, while they fall below half a million in each of the other three. There are getting on for a million Chinese in the two Vietnams. The giants, for historical reasons which we have already glanced at, are Malaysia, Indonesia, and Thailand. In the first of these countries, there are four million Chinese in the western part (that is, the Malay Peninsula including Singapore) and over a third of a million in the eastern (Sarawak and Sabah). The Malaysian figures are based squarely on census returns and we may assume that they account for virtually everybody who thinks of himself as a Chinese. In Thailand we may say that there are between two and a half and three million Chinese; it is a hit or miss figure for reasons which will become clear when we consider the Thailand case later on. The Chinese population in Indonesia was last counted by a proper census in 1930, and then by roughly the same principles as applied in Malaya and British Borneo; for recent times we have to rely on less satisfactory statistical sources. We may estimate the present-day Chinese population of Indonesia to be two and a half millions. It will be clear, therefore, that as far as our figures go, the three giants of the Nanyang account for some 80 percent of the Chinese in Southeast Asia.

We have established that not all the twelve million Southeast Asian Chinese are Chinese by culture. Not all of them are "racially" Chinese in the sense of being descended exclusively from Chinese forebears. Not all the people descended exclusively or partly from Chinese immigrants in Southeast Asia are accounted for in the twelve million Chinese. The Chinese cultural heritage has been whittled away. The Chinese biological heritage has been dispersed. Let us try to see how this has come about. I shall begin with the case of western Malaysia, which up to 1963 could be discussed as the Federation of Malaya and the State of Singapore. I shall refer to it simply as Malaya for the sake of convenience.[2]

As we have seen, Chinese settlement in Malaya began in Penang, Malacca, and Singapore. From these British bases Chinese moved out to trade and mine tin in the Malay States even before the extension of British rule to them, which began in the 1870's. Despite this earlier movement into independent Malay territory, however, we may say that the Chinese experience in Malaya was essentially a colonial one. As a result of this experience (the wielders of ultimate power being British) and of the fact that the indigenous people with whom they came in touch were Muslims, there was little inducement to the immigrants to stop being Chinese. It was open to them to be converted to Islam; as converted Muslims they were welcome in Malay society. And it is fairly clear that over the years men in a Chinese community very short of Chinese women sometimes found their way to a new religion and a wife. They entered Malaydom, as the Malay expression has it, and were lost to the Chinese. But the numbers of Chinese-turned-Malay were small; and in fact, the main infusion of Chinese "blood" into the Malay population has come about in a different manner: since the time when Chinese women have become more numerous, and right up to the present day, unwanted babies (nearly always girls) in Chinese families have often been sold to Malays to grow up as full members of Malay society.

In the early phase of Chinese settlement in the country there was a reverse flow of Malay "blood." The first Chinese merchants in Malacca took women from among the strange people in whose midst they lived. (The women were probably for the most part slaves and non-Muslim.) From these early unions there sprang a Chinese population to which the name Baba came to be applied. The significance of this population lies not in the fact that it was "racially" mixed but in the cultural amalgam for which it was responsible. Beginning in Malacca and thence spreading to other parts of the country, the Babas carried forward into our own day a Malayized Chinese culture which demonstrated that it was possible in the Malayan context to be unambiguously a Chinese without the full Chinese cultural apparatus which would have been demanded in China. The Babas spoke a dialect of Malay; their prayers, folklore, and literature were put into this dialect; their music, food, costume, and manners were all heirs to the Malay tradition. But the Babas were Chinese—and so much so that throughout the nineteenth century, although decreasingly towards its end, they were a dominant element in Malayan Chinese society, a kind of elite which enjoyed riches inherited from previous generations and could communicate with the Malays in Malay and with the British in English (for many of them took advantage of the first opportunities in Malaya to gain a Western education). Forming a superior stratum of Chinese society they attracted to them and absorbed ambitious Chinese immigrants ("Chinamen" they condescendingly called them) to whom they gave their daughters in marriage.

The first lesson the Babas teach us, then, is that Chinese culture does not in all circumstances enjoy the vitality and viability which many sinophiles lovingly attribute to it. But in fact there is an even more striking lesson to be learned from the history of the Malayan Babas: Chinese culture may die to be reborn again in a different guise. Having moved away from Chinese culture to Malay, all the while remaining Chinese, the Babas have in more modern times shifted back to the culture of the majority of the community of which they form part—having become Malayan. The Baba sector of the Chinese community was progressively reduced in size as more and more people came into Malaya from China; at the end of the nineteenth century the Babas formed perhaps 10 percent of the Chinese population in the Straits Settlements and certainly a smaller percentage in the Malay States. For a time they kept their lead of the Chinese community and its institutions, but economically they began to lose out to successful immigrants who were no longer willing to be absorbed by them; more women were being brought from China and a self-subsistent immigrant Chinese group became possible. During the early part of the twentieth century, although some Baba families retained their riches, the Babas as a whole declined to a less significant point on the economic scale and ceased to constitute an elite for the Malayan Chinese.

By this time Chinese culture in its modern nationalist form had entered the Malayan scene. True, one or two Baba intellectuals were already teaching themselves Chinese and trying to bring about a Chinese renaissance before the end of the last century, but for the great part of them it was the growth of the modern Chinese school system in the period between the World Wars and its florescence after the Second World War that turned them into Chinese speakers or at least gave them the feeling that they were heirs to Chinese culture. (Baba Malay literature passed out of existence in the late 1930's, as far as I have been able to judge. The costumes and ceremonies specifically associated with the Babas were still to be seen after the Second World War, but were clearly giving way before the competing symbolism of nationalist Chinese culture.) Of course, the Chinese language "reacquired" by the Babas was Mandarin;

it was not the Chinese spoken by their (largely southern Fukien) ancestors. The "folklore" they now assumed was that of Chinese nationalism; it was not the tradition of their forebears. But in the very process of becoming, so to say, more Chinese, the Babas were in fact fitting themselves for the latest phase of Malaya's history in which to be a Malayan a man must have an identity as a Malay, Chinese Indian, or Eurasian. The Malayized culture of the Babas had not made them Malay; to be Malayan they had to grow more Chinese.

The story of some of the leaders of present-day Singapore is in this connection illuminating. Baba in origin (although by their day, the name Baba having become pejorative, it had been replaced by "Straits Chinese"), they fought their way to the head of an overwhelmingly Chinese colony by identifying themselves with the hopes of the culturally aggressive Chinese. (To do this they learned Chinese and to think as nationalist Chinese, while using the skills taught them by their English education in order to operate within a British political framework.) From this position in the van of an army of enthusiastic Chinese they have sought to guide their followers into a Malayan (and subsequently Malaysian) nation which, ironically enough, must in the long run relegate the Chinese language to a poor third place behind Malay (the country's national language) and English, and put an ever-increasing distance between the culture of the Malayan Chinese and that of their congeners in China (a "homeland" of diminishing significance).

The growth of Chinese cultural nationalism in Malaya in the twentieth century was in one sense a response to the colonial situation; in order to react to colonialism, the Chinese, not being part of any local nationality, could respond only as Chinese. And as Malaya has emerged as an independent country Chinese cultural nationalism has declined. We can most clearly see the relationship between the two processes in the history of Chinese education. While Malaya was under British rule and the Chinese were regarded, and largely regarded themselves, as sojourners on foreign soul, their school system was as to form and content modeled on that of China. Chinese school culture then became one of the chief instruments in modern times for the expression of anticolonial sentiment, most dramatically so in Singapore where during the 1950's the Chinese schools formed a major center of ideological ferment and political action. But in independent Malaya, where the state can intervene more decisively in educational policy than its British predecessor and where a Malayan ideology can compete with Chinese, the old purely Chinese school system is already virtually dead. Again, the establishment of the Nanyang University in Singapore in 1956, which to its sponsors and supporters seemed to be the logical extension of the Chinese educational systems of

Southeast Asia and the final step along the road to Chinese cultural independence, a mere decade later already looks as though it will prove to have been at best a brave gesture. The splendid irony of change has been that, since the withdrawal of the British from Malaya, it has been English education which has begun to capture the allegiance of the Chinese.

In the old Malaya the Chinese were not assimilated by the Malays. They are not now being so assimilated although I should guess that Islam will seem to be a decreasingly difficult barrier to some Chinese ambitious to reach the peak of national power. But even if there should prove to be no absorption of Chinese into the Malay ranks, Chinese culture and Chinese views of themselves must undergo a radical transformation. Every new Malayan institution is an incentive to Chinese to act as Malayans and to abandon a parochial Chineseness. It is true, of course, that the network of Chinese commercial and industrial life, by means of which the Chinese play a dominant role in the Malayan economy, is an inducement to the Chinese to stay within an ambit which minimizes contact with people of other "races." It is also true that the constitution in certain particulars favors the Malays against Chinese, Indians, and the other ethnic groups and restricts the access of non-Malays to some central points in the bureaucracy. But within the framework of a political system which is seen to rest on the collaboration of the various "races" (a collaboration formalized in the dominant Alliance of Malay, Chinese, and Indian parties) the Chinese are constantly wearing down their particularity and moving toward a Malayan meaning of "Chinese."

Yet to the visitor to present-day Malaya, Chinese culture must seem very vigorous still. He should realize, however, that what he sees is not simply a straightforward heritage of the Malayan Chinese past. It is, on the contrary, a refashioned Chinese culture which took its standards from the homeland via the modern school system. That system, as we have seen, flourished up to the time of Malayan independence, increasingly affected by left-wing Chinese nationalism after the Second World War. For the young Chinese who had been through the system, what the Malays stood for was looked down upon, and to the extent that the new education promoted local political ambitions they were concerned with the assertion of Chinese (not general, Malayan) rights against the British rulers. But if we examine Chinese culture in twentieth-century Malaya a little more carefully we shall see something that at first sight seems highly paradoxical: while it rejected English (except for purely practical purposes in business and administration) and saw little to emulate in the behavior of the British on the local scene, it was in fact Westernized to a high degree. The Malayan Chinese of this century took their standards from China; China took many of hers from the West. For this reason, foreigners like myself who knew both Chinese-educated and English-educated Chinese in pre-independence Malaya were often more impressed by the former; through their Chinese culture they had a window on the world. They saw it distorted, no doubt, but at least they saw it. The English education provided in Malaya served to give Chinese a practical linguistic skill without arousing in them any great interest in things outside the range of their immediate experience.

Turning our attention to the most recent years, we see another twist in the fate of Chinese culture in Malaya. Chinese education, as we have noted, is beginning to decline. Elsewhere in Southeast Asia Chinese school systems have suffered some grievous blows from unsympathetic governments. That is not the case in Malaya. The government there has certainly not repressed the Chinese schools. Rather, as a postcolonial Malayan society has been taking shape, Chinese ambitions have been turning in directions to which "modern" Chinese education (now itself old-fashioned) is less relevant. By a wisely formed and executed policy, the Malayan authorities have stressed the importance of the national language (Malay) and of English, and have provided means by which the Chinese schools may be built into a national system of education, shedding their exclusive preoccupation with the Chinese language and things Chinese.

Malaysia (and with it Malaya) is, in the context of the Nanyang, a special case. The four million Chinese in Malaya are neither numerically nor politically a minority. They are 44 percent of the total Malayan population and fractionally more numerous than the Malays. They form a powerful economic and political bloc. It seems to follow that cultural pluralism is not merely the basis of Malaya's history but also its destiny, and no wise Malayan politician has ever tried to bring about a future in which the Chinese would cease to exist as in some sense distinct in their cultural heritage and social identity. It cannot be part of the idea of Malayan citizenship that those who bear it have a uniform set of values and a standard style of life. A rigorous attempt to realize in Malaya the nineteenth-century ideal of a coincidence of folk and polity would remove the possibility of a single society surviving within its present frontiers. The riches, the votes, and the organization of the Chinese assure them their survival as Chinese. What "Chinese" will mean in Malaya a generation or two hence we cannot now foresee, but it is at least certain that it will have little interest for sinologues in search of a "pure" Chinese culture outside China.

We have only to take a hint from current diplomatic practice and confront Malaysia with Indonesia to see how numbers matter, culturally as well as politically. The Chinese in Indonesia are well over half as numerous as those in Malaysia, but they are a mere fraction (between 2 and 3 percent) of the total population of the Republic.[3] Under Dutch rule the Chinese of the East Indies could hold their own; legally and politically a place was allotted them in the plural society which Furnivall and others have described for us; economically they were well entrenched. But in a nation-state which detests the stranger within the gates and believes its survival to depend on the elaboration of an indigenous culture, the Chinese as a minority are under the threat of cultural extinction. It would be foolish to imagine that the extinction will inevitably be consummated, but twenty years after the Pacific War we can already see that a great part of the Indonesian Chinese are moving toward a "nationalization" that empties the description "Chinese" of nearly all its cultural content.

Malaysia and Indonesia are not merely neighbors (and, for the moment at any rate, rivals); they have much of their history in common. Their Chinese communities grew up in much the same manner and went through similar processes of adaptation. Let us consider again the case of the Malayan Babas, this time in the light of the Chinese who parallel them in Indonesia, the Peranakans. As a result of the great flood of immigrants to Malaya in the latter part of the nineteenth century, the Babas came to form a small minority of the Malayan Chinese. When their economic fortunes declined relatively to those of many of the immigrants and when the Chinese nationalism of the twentieth century undermined their confidence in their own Malayized culture, the Babas began to move back into the Chinese cultural fold. The Straits Chinese, as they are now called, are still to some extent identifiable as a special area of the Chinese community, but one cannot drive a hard line through the community to arrange Straits Chinese on one side of it and "immigrant" Chinese on the other.

Yet something of the sort may be done in Indonesia, at least in Java, which is of course the heart of the country. Here the Peranakans, the analogues of the Babas (and often related to them across the international frontier by kinship and marriage) have managed to survive into our own day as a large, self-subsistent, and relatively independent Chinese community. The Chinese with whom we contrast the Peranakans are the Totoks, the "immigrants" (but not necessarily literally so, for many of them are Indonesian-born). In Java at any rate, they have emerged as a separate kind of Chinese, counterposed to the Peranakans, only in the twentieth century; for before then, the rate of Chinese movement into Java being relatively low and steady (and, as elsewhere, composed almost exclusively of men), the immigrants were absorbed by the Peranakans, as at one time the Babas ingested the immigrant Chinese in Malaya.

Again like the Babas, the Peranakans sprang from unions between Chinese and local women. A Peranakan culture was formed which was expressed in one or other of the languages of Java and in customs some of which are readily traceable to Javan origins. But it must not be supposed that the contrast between this culture and that of the Totoks in the twentieth century is a simple one between, say, half-Chinese and full-Chinese, for the word "Chinese" has here a slippery meaning. True, the Totoks, being of more recent derivation from China, were fully Chinese in their speech, their general mode of life, and their evaluation of things-Chinese-from-China. But they were "modern" Chinese and reproduced in Java many of the features of Republican Chinese society and its ideology; whereas the Peranakans (being from this point of view fossil remnants of imperial China) carried forward to our times many traditional Chinese characteristics within the framework of their Javanized culture. Paradoxically (and the point holds true *mutatis mutandis* for Malaya), the Peranakans are in some sense more Chinese than the Totoks.

I shall try to illustrate this paradox very briefly. Although the Peranakan system of family and kinship has been heavily affected by its need to adapt to local (non-Chinese) values and to new urban and economic conditions, Peranakan family affairs are conducted more conservatively and ceremoniously than those of the Totoks. Indeed, the family seems to carry more weight in Peranakan than in Totok social organization, while domestic ancestor worship (which we naturally think of as being a hallmark of Chinese culture) is apparently carried out by more families and more regularly among the Peranakans. Certainly, nobody who has seen a Baba wedding (and I assume the same to be true of a Peranakan wedding) and has been able to compare it with a wedding among the "immigrants," can fail to be convinced that in certain respects Baba-Peranakan culture is sinologically more interesting than the strident nationalist Chinese culture of modern times. At a Baba wedding one may feel that one has had privileged access to the Chinese past. At a "modern" wedding one is more likely to be impressed by the Chinese version of Western symbolism.

Peranakans and Totoks in Java have emerged as socially separate groups and culturally distinct entities of very roughly equal size. Yet—and the point brings us back to the strategic importance of formal education in the shaping of Nanyang destiny—the boundary between the two groups and their cultures has not been steadily maintained. Under the influence of nationalist enthusiasm in the early part of the century many Peranakan children walked the road to modern Chinese culture in the Mandarin-speaking schools set up in Java, their parents having been caught up in the movement, essentially Totok in inspiration, to unify the

Chinese in the Indies as a coherent group and to press for greater political privileges within the framework of the colonial society. At this stage of Peranakan development Dutch policy intervened sagaciously. From 1908 onward Dutch schools for Peranakan children were created by the government. And the Dutch accorded the Peranakans legal and political privileges which helped to steer them away from identifying themselves with the nationalism of the Totoks.

A second period of Peranakan-Totok rapprochement came during the Japanese Occupation and its aftermath. Chinese self-consciousness was heightened and an interest in Chinese education promoted. In Java the Peranakans continued their interest in Chinese education for some years after the end of the war; when in the uncertain years of the Dutch return it was not clear that they were soon to go for ever, many Peranakans were unwilling to make common cause with the Indonesians; and during the early years of the Republic there was enough in Indonesian behavior toward the Chinese to convince the Peranakans that they had little to gain by abandoning whatever they had of a Chinese heritage. But by the late 1950's the general situation had changed and we have since then been witnesses to a sharpened divergence between Peranakan and Totok. It would appear that at the present time only Totok children attend Chinese schools and that almost all Peranakan children are being educated in schools where the language is Indonesian, that is, the modern language of the Republic, based on Malay. (But these latter schools are for the most part run by the Peranakans themselves; the education is Indonesian but structurally separate.) Peranakans and Totoks have disentangled themselves from each other in fields other than education; above all in associational life, so that the two halves of Java Chinese society operate without a common leadership and with few relationships to tie them together. As G. William Skinner (1963: 110), our chief authority on the Indonesian Chinese, has it: "... today the chief links between the two communities are the now anomalous Chinese-educated Peranakans and the diminishing number of Peranakan women married to Totoks."

The wedge now driven between the Peranakans and the Totoks squeezes the former into closer and closer identification with the Indonesians and the latter into a sullen defense of their national and cultural integrity. "Indonesian" has two meanings. On the one hand, everybody who is a citizen of the Republic is an Indonesian; and, although the citizenship issue is fantastically complex, we may assume that most, perhaps nearly all, Peranakans are Indonesians in this sense. On the other hand, the word is used for the indigenous peoples of the country to the exclusion of such ethnic outsiders as the Chinese, who, in this context, are said to be not real (indigenous, *asli*) Indonesians. (There is less confusion in the parallel terminology across the water in Malaya, where "Malayan" or "Malaysian" describes citizenship and cannot be used to distinguish Malays from their fellow citizens of other "races.") We may say that the Peranakans, having become Indonesian in the first sense, are straining after acceptance in the second.

What makes their effort the more striking is that both official policy and public attitudes do not go very far toward matching their enthusiasm. Indonesian citizens of Chinese descent are discriminated against, above all in economic life, where the old Chinese dominance of local trade and some forms of industry is met by the preferential treatment (in the granting of licenses, credit, and so on) to "real" Indonesians. Of course, as elsewhere in Southeast Asia, the attempt by the government to gouge Chinese out of their economic niches and replace them by "true" citizens has had the effect of promoting alliances between Chinese capital and skill on the one hand and the licenses and contacts with officialdom of "true" citizens on the other. And the bonds so set up in economic activity between Chinese and non-Chinese are one basis for Peranakan hopes that they may be eventually accepted fully within the Indonesian fold. It would appear that at times when alien Chinese have been under attack (as was outstandingly the case at the end of 1959 when foreign Chinese were prohibited from engaging in trade in the rural areas, and in West Java were forcibly evicted from the countryside) the Peranakans have for the most part held themselves aloof, either having little sympathy for Totoks or at any rate not wishing to jeopardize their own *modus vivendi* with the Indonesians by demonstrating solidarity with foreigners.

"Assimilation" is now a plank in the Peranakan political platform. What this is meant to imply in the predominantly Muslim parts of the country (for not all Indonesian "Muslims" are in fact Muslim; some indeed are hostile to Islam) is not clear. But there seems to be no doubt that influential members of the Peranakan community foresee some kind of cultural merger, the first steps to which have already been taken. (It should be particularly shocking to cultural sinophiles that in recent years an increasing number of Peranakans have been giving their children Indonesian names and suppressing their Chinese surnames.) The voices raised in favor of "merger" are by no means all crying for the immediate disappearance of the Peranakans as a separate entity. Indeed, a policy of "integration" seems to command the largest following. The Chinese of Indonesian citizenship have in the last decade been organized chiefly within the framework of an organization known as Baperki, through which, and by taking part in politics acceptable to the rulers of the country, the Peranakans have achieved what appears to be a fairly stable relationship with the society englobing them. The Peranakans are therefore still a distinct and organized entity within Indonesian society. One day, possibly, they may cease to be. Meanwhile, contrasted with the Totoks, from whom they have been increasingly differentiating themselves in recent times, they show us a Chinese identity stripped of much of its Chinese culture.

In neither Malaya nor Indonesia have the Chinese in any considerable numbers been assimilated to the point of disappearing as Chinese, although in the latter country the thing may yet happen. Thailand, the third country I have chosen to talk about, illustrates the opposite case: mass assimilation has taken place. Just as Singapore or Kuala Lumpur looks like a good argument for assuming that Chinese culture has always flourished in Malaya, so Bangkok today seems to be certain proof of the persistence and viability of that same culture in Thailand. The common-sense inference happens to be wrong, for what we can now see in Thailand is the not yet assimilated portion of a much larger historical population of Chinese. This is a country which in two major respects stands contrasted with the others we have looked at: it was never a colony, and its dominant religion is Buddhism.

Once more we must have grateful recourse to Skinner's work. This careful student of the Chinese (both at home and overseas) asserts—and supports his assertion by a mass of sociological and historical evidence—that there has been a steady stream of Chinese into the Thai population since the eighteenth century. And it is probable that this old process will continue, perhaps to the point where all the Chinese landmarks, except for "archaeological" monuments and literary remains, will have vanished from the kingdom.

I must content myself with the barest outline of the facts. While Chinese newcomers to the country were free to build up for themselves an economic position which both local and international economic circumstances encouraged, and which their social organization and its values prevented the Thai from occupying, the Chinese were at the same time given a license to merge into Thai society, shedding their Chinese identity completely. Their economic roles, and the social organization created about them, made Chinese immigrants a distinct sector of Thailand society. But the descendants of these distinctive immigrants moved into general society with ease, more especially because they were children of the Thai women whom the Chinese immigrants found little difficulty in marrying. But immigration from China was not, of course, once for all; new Chinese kept coming into the country to take the place, so to say, of those who had disappeared from the ranks of a distinct Chinese enclave. Chinese society in Thailand was, as it were, a kind of staging post along the road from the society of southeastern China to the Thai-speaking Hinayana Buddhist society of Thailand.

In examining part of the history of the Chinese in Malaya and Indonesia we have had to take account, however cursorily, of the impact of the form of Chinese nationalism we associate with the rise of the Chinese Republic in the early years of this century. We must do the same in the case of Thailand, noting that in the same period Thailand itself was undergoing the experience of a modern nationalist awakening. The two nationalisms in interaction produced a sharper confrontation of Thai and Chinese on Thai soil, and the line between the two was further entrenched by the appearance of women in considerable numbers among the immigrants from China. Intermarriage, hitherto the order of the day, decreased in significance as a bridge over which Chinese might pass easily and fairly quickly into Thai society.

Once Chinese in Thailand were defined as foreigners (instead of being welcome strangers) they could be subjected to official pressures to curb their economic strength, their cultural idiosyncrasy, and their competing nationalism. The list of these pressures is a long one, and as tedious to recite as they were painful and offensive to the Chinese who experienced them. Certainly, the attempts made by the Thai government in modern times to hinder immigration, lever Chinese out of their economic strongholds, and suppress Chinese culture (notably by placing severe restrictions on Chinese schools) might seem to be unambiguous evidence of a serious anti-Chinese policy—a policy likely to make the Chinese close their ranks and resist the forcible assimilation to which it pointed. But there are two very important points to be borne steadily in mind when we try to interpret the history of the fate of Chinese in Thailand.

The first point is that anti-Chinese policy in many of its aspects was directed against organized Chinese society, not against Chinese as such. The numerous Thai of Chinese descent have not generally been made to suffer for their foreign antecedents. On the contrary, the definition of "Thai" being operatively cultural, Thai of Chinese ancestry have fared outstandingly well. Naturally, economic policy aimed at reducing Chinese strength bore heavily on individuals, but it does not appear to have been intended to starve the Chinese out.

The second point is that it is characteristic of the Chinese in non-colonial Thailand to look up to and not down on the "foreigners" among whom they live, in contrast to the behavior of their congeners in colonial Southeast Asia. The Thailand Chinese have been attracted to their hosts, who, being masters in their own house, have not labored under the disadvantages of Malays or Indonesians as subject peoples. Some Chinese in Malaya could aspire to behave like Englishmen and be socially acceptable to them: and there have been some fair Chinese imitations of Englishmen in Malaya. Some Chinese in the East Indies aimed similarly to consort with the Dutch; in modern times they could acquire certain legal privileges open to the "assimilated." But no Chinese could *become* an Englishman or a Dutchman. In Thailand a Chinese could become a Thai. And the repressive measures taken in Thailand to curb the Chinese seemed to have worked in the sense that they gave the Chinese an extra push in the direction of committing themselves finally to adopting a Thai identity. All in all, it looks as though anti-Chinese policy in Thailand may be interpreted to have been more halfpence than kicks.

At the present time the situation appears to be something after the following picture. There is a small Chinese "society" alongside the Thai society. (At its maximum extent this Chinese "society" cannot contain more than 10 percent of the total population of the country.) Each of the two societies is a crystalized entity. A Chinese may participate in both of them, assuming a personal name and language to suit his alignment and associations of the moment. Many Thailand Chinese of the second and subsequent generations move back and forth in this fashion, but the movement is in fact very sensitive to changes in national policy. In periods when the pressure is taken off, the movement is unhampered and a man does not need to throw in his lot finally with the Thai. But when repressive measures are applied he must make his choice. The whole time, whether or not the government of the country is being officially anti-Chinese, the process of assimilation goes on (although at differing speeds), and—which is particularly important and interesting—it serves to cream off the leaders of the organized Chinese community. It seems that once a Chinese gets to the top of the Chinese social hierarchy he is paradoxically in a fair way to being a Chinese no longer, for Thai society offers him great rewards of prestige to lure him in. And while he himself may never cease to belong to the Chinese community in some sense, his children will be more definitely committed to the dominant society. Perhaps the most illuminating single fact about the Chinese in Thailand is that, despite the unbroken history of Chinese settlement in the country since at least the fifteenth century, "even fourth-generation Chinese," in Skinner's words (1960: 86), "are practically nonexistent."

If it is true that assimilation is taking place with regularity, although at different rates at different times, then "the Chinese" cannot survive in Thailand, for here, as is the case generally in the region, the gates have been pretty well closed to immigration since 1949. It follows that the Chinese minority will be eroded away. Then—if we may toy with the fancy of being alive to witness this consummation—we shall be able to say "So much for the superiority and self-satisfaction of Chinese culture."

There is a final point to be made on the case of the Thailand Chinese. When in Malaya and Indonesia we think of the Chinese changing their culture (becoming acculturated, as some anthropologists put it), we can envisage the process as one in which Chinese grow less and less Chinese and more something else (although in Malaya, in contradistinction to contemporary Indonesia, that something else falls well short of a non-Chinese identity). And since the process will not operate at a uniform rate for everybody, and not everybody will have started to move along the path at the same time, some Chinese will be culturally less Chinese than others, the newcomer from China at one end of the scale and the modern versions of the Baba-Peranakan at the other. This kind of model will not take us far in perceiving the realities of the situation in Thailand as it exists today. There the terminal points for a scale of acculturation can certainly be found: the most recently immigrant Chinese from China and the man of Chinese descent in whom Chinese culture is barely perceptible. But the bulk of the Thailand Chinese cannot be strung along a line between the two points to form a scale, for they have that "double identity" which one of the writers on them, Richard J. Coughlin (1960), has chosen for the title of his book. Culturally, most of the people we call Chinese in Thailand are both Chinese and Thai, although with varying emphases.[4]

Thailand is by no means the only Southeast Asian country in which Chinese have been swallowed up in numbers, although it is the most dramatic case of such cultural ingestion, principally no doubt because of its exemption from colonial rule. But to attempt now to talk about Burma, Laos, Cambodia, Vietnam, and the Philippines would be very rash, not only because I should be abusing the hospitality offered by a single lecture, but also on account of the fact that the sociological groundwork for the study of these smaller manifestations of the Nanyang is for the most part yet to be done.

May I take the liberty of reminding you of the two points I have set out to argue? It is wrong to imagine, first, that the Chinese are an unassimilable lump in the digestive tract of every Southeast Asian country, and second, that Chinese culture is highly resistant to being worn down by other cultures. The clamorous (and to tourists colorful) "Chinatowns" are but one aspect of a long history of Chinese settlement in the Nanyang—and not necessarily its most significant. The twelve million Chinese in present-day Southeast Asia are of different nationalities, speak many languages, follow several religions, and live many styles of life.

And, as some of them have painfully discovered by going back to one of the two Chinas, many are so little Chinese in their outlook that they are foreigners in several senses in the land of their forefathers.

Yet it by no means follows that the Nanyang has completely lost its meaning in the 1960's, or that in the context of Southeast Asia the adjective "Chinese" has come irretrievably adrift from the noun "China." The Chinese in one Southeast Asian country are certainly aware of the fate of those in another; and the awareness may enhance or decrease their satisfaction with their own lot. They have a fellow feeling for their congeners dispersed about the region, and may sometimes indeed be related by family ties to many of them. And China itself, now occupying a position in world affairs which is at least unambiguous in its importance, stands for the inhabitants of the Nanyang as an ancestral land, however remote it may be in a distance measured by generations, knowledge, or political sympathy. These facts are not a discredit to the Nanyang Chinese, yet they often stand to their disadvantage. They make the Chinese seem to be rootless cosmopolitans in a world where narrow-minded nationalism requires a more straitened discipline of loyalty. It is true that some Chinese in Southeast Asia, being Communists, are doubly a risk to the countries where they live: they stand not only for Communism but also for a giant China. It is also true that some Chinese businessmen show a greater concern for their own commercial interests than for the economic policies of their rulers (although in this they are sometimes of greater benefit to the economy than are their rulers). But the longer view of the Nanyang for which I have tried to plead in this lecture should suggest that "Chinese" does not automatically mean alien, that the presence of Chinese in Southeast Asia does not entail the subversion of national integrity, and that—although in keeping my lecture close to the subject of changes in culture I have neglected this theme—the economic benefits, in capital formation and entrepreneurial skill, which the Chinese have brought to Southeast Asia would in a just world earn them more gratitude than jealousy.

The Handling of Money:
A Note on the Background to the
Economic Sophistication of Overseas Chinese

The vast majority of the men who left southeastern China in the nineteenth century to make their fortune overseas were peasants or artisans. In Southeast Asia great numbers of them took to business; many grew very rich. The general economic success of the Chinese abroad could not have been due to any special business training in China because the commercial class played too small a role in the emigration. The prosperity of a great many of the first generation of Southeast Asian Chinese rested on their industriousness. The peasant Chinese was almost proverbially a hard worker; his patient toiling habits were so often commented on that we can have little doubt that the capacity of Overseas Chinese for regular and sustained work was founded in a discipline acquired at home. But the will and ability of Chinese to work hard could not have been the sufficient cause of their progress in the amassing of riches. They accumulated wealth because, in comparison with the people among whom they came to live, they were highly sophisticated in the handling of money. At the outset they knew not only how to work themselves but also how to make their money work.

The Chinese peasant was not a hoarder who, so to speak, put his savings in a stocking under the bed. If he had money over and above his immediate needs he invested it so that it might grow. Some peasants took to trade, and if they were fortunate advanced from small beginnings to considerable riches. Some who had made money invested in land, which was likely to give a smaller economic return but was both more secure and a base for high social status. At a certain level of prosperity a man might also invest in education, for to move into the class of the scholar-

Man, 59 (1959), 64–65. Reprinted in Thomas H. Silcock, ed., *Readings in Malayan Economics* (Singapore, 1961), 38–42.

gentry was a possibility opened up by increasing riches (cf. Freedman 1958: 58–59). But even very small sums of money could be put out to fructify, for there was a constant drive to invest in credit. A considerable part of the demand for credit was met by landlords, pawnbrokers, and traders, but for small loans peasant could turn to peasant, the man with a temporary surplus placing it with a kinsman or neighbor who was for the moment below the line.

A missionary who seems to have been a careful observer of life in Fukien, one of the two provinces from which nearly all Overseas Chinese came, suggests how ordinary people were schooled by debt and credit, nearly all men being at one time or another debtors and many of them creditors. "The great mass of the Chinese people are in a chronic state of debt. It seems to be the natural and normal state in which a Chinese passes his life. He is born into it; he grows up in it; he goes to school with it; he marries in it; and he ultimately leaves the world with the shadow of it resting on him in his last moments." But if the opening paragraph of the Rev. John Macgowan's chapter on "Money and Money Lending" (1909: 171) inclines us to think that the Chinese were generally crushed by the burden of debt, the next sentence disabuses us. "This state of things does not seem to depress him in the least." Indebtedness was nothing to be ashamed of, was public knowledge, and was readily incurred.[1] Creditors were also widespread. "These money lenders are not a distinct class such as exist in England, but they are everyone who has any spare cash at his disposal." The servant woman with a spare dollar and the coolie who "finds himself with a surplus of three dollars" look around for debtors with whom to place their money. "The whole Chinese empire may be said to be in a perpetual state of borrowing and lending, and a large majority of its people are daily concerned with that most practical question how they shall pay the interest to the minority who have lent them money" (*ibid.*: 173).

If such a generalization cannot convince us that Chinese were generally put to school by experience to learn how to handle money, we can turn to another kind of evidence. Observers constantly refer to "money loan associations" which at first glance look like simple mutual credit clubs calling for the minimum of economic skill. When we examine them more closely we see that they must have taught entrepreneurial, managerial, and financial skills of considerable importance. The money loan associations were small groups of people who paid regular (usually monthly) sums into a pool which was placed at the disposal of the individual members in turn. The institution was so common that printed books were sold which set out the rules and provided columns for the necessary entries. The normal procedure was for a man or woman who wished to raise a sum of money to get together a number of people (commonly ten) who paid the desired sum in equal shares and then recouped themselves in turn at fixed intervals. The order in which the members, other than the promoter, drew the pool was determined either on the basis of chance (by lots or dice) or by means of tenders to forgo a proportion of the contributions due. (In a less usual version, the organizer did not start the scheme by collecting the total sum for himself but was paid for his services by receiving one-half of one individual contribution from each of the individual drawers of the periodical sums in turn.)

The members needed to trust both the promoter and one another not to decamp after drawing the pool. It therefore fell to the promoter to recruit his group in such a fashion as to inspire confidence. Even in a village community there was a risk that a man might default and run away. In urban conditions the risk was much greater and the burden on the promoter heavier; the members did not necessarily know one another or even meet, the promoter going the rounds to take bids and collect and distribute money. The promoter had to make a careful assessment of the risks of default and of the financial soundness of the members, because he was often bound to make good in some measure the losses resulting from a member dropping out. In return for the risks he ran and his services as an organizer, the promoter received a joint loan from the members which he repaid without interest in as many installments as there were members. (In many loan associations the promoter paid interest in the form of a feast which he gave at the first meeting; but he then benefited from the feasts which were given at each subsequent meeting by the individual members drawing the pool.) On their side the members were playing a careful financial game when they tendered for the pool. Each man had to weigh his desire to draw the pool early against his wish to pay the minimum interest. After he had drawn the pool, he had at each subsequent draw to pay a full contribution, so that the interest which he paid declined with the period for which he held off; the last man of all to draw paid in the least money in periodical contributions and took out the maximum amount.

Suppose that there were nine members and a promoter, the initial sum collected by the latter being $90. At the first meeting each member paid the promoter $10. At the second meeting tenders were submitted, the highest bid being $2. The successful bidder then collected $10 from the promoter and $10 − 2 = 8 from the other members. Suppose that at the third meeting the successful bidder offered to forgo $2.40; he then received $10 each from the promoter and the previous successful bidder and $10-2.40 = 7.60$ from each of the remaining seven members. The bids would probably rise at each meeting, but if for the sake of simplicity we assume a flat rate of bidding at $2 throughout, then the very last member (who of course made no bid) came away with $9 \times \$10 = 90$, having paid $74. If the meetings were at monthly intervals, the last member had invested $74 over a period of nine months and made a profit of $16 at the end.[2]

It was to the advantage of the men who could wait the longest for their money that the periodical bids should be high. People therefore often put in small bids, which they knew would not win, in order to frighten the members who really needed the money into bidding up. The tenders were written and sealed, or otherwise kept secret, so that a large number of bids seemed to indicate to the man who desperately wanted to draw the pool that he would need to forgo a large proportion of the contributions if he wished to ensure a successful tender (Ball 1904: 632ff; Kulp 1925: 189ff).

One way of looking at this institution is to see it as a means of procuring relatively cheap credit on a cooperative basis. The promoter paid no interest on what he borrowed, while the members paid interest at rates below those demanded by moneylenders and pawnbrokers. Writing of a Kwangtung village in the 1920's, D. H. Kulp said that "not infrequently interest rates on loans run as high as twenty percent per month" (Kulp 1925: 191). The legal maximum rate of interest in the nineteenth century was 3 percent per month, but because of various contrivances a peasant was probably not able to borrow at less than 5 percent per month (L. S. Yang 1952: 100−101). But this is to look at the advantage accruing to the member as debtor; the member as creditor also benefited. The interest that he earned was comparatively small, but the investment was probably more secure than in ordinary moneylending, it did not need to be assembled in one sum at the beginning, and it was more certainly to be recovered in a fixed time. We must see in the money loan association the drive to lend as well as the pressure to borrow.[a]

Shrewdness in handling money was an important part of the equipment which ordinary Chinese took with them when they went overseas in search of a livelihood. Their financial skill rested above all on three characteristics of the society in which they were raised: the respectability

[a] In the Chinese village described by Fei Hsiao-t'ung, the kind of uncommon and unpopular loan association in which bidding was allowed was "called Kwangtung Piao Hui, an auction system supposed to be originated in Kwangtung" (Fei 1939: 274). It may be that southeastern Chinese were particularly ingenious organizers of and hard bargainers in money-loan associations, but the bidding system was by no means confined to the provinces of Kwangtung and Fukien. See A. H. Smith 1899: 154ff and L. S. Yang 1952: 6, 77.

of the pursuit of riches, the relative immunity of surplus wealth from confiscation by political superiors, and the legitimacy of careful and interested financial dealings between neighbors and even close kinsmen.[3] The Chinese were economically successful in Southeast Asia not simply because they were energetic immigrants, but more fundamentally because in their quest for riches they knew how to handle money and organize men in relation to money.

The Growth of a Plural Society in Malaya

The idea of a "plural society" was formulated by a British student of the political economy of Southeast Asia (Furnivall 1939, 1942, 1948). It has come to irritate some sociologists and find favor with others.[1] In this article[2] I begin by assuming that we know roughly what is meant by the term, and after a brief analysis of the social structure of Malaya, I try to show how I look upon Malayan society as "plural."

Malaya does not form one political community, for it is divided into the Federation of Malaya (an independent territory within the Commonwealth) and the State of Singapore (an internally self-governing territory of the Commonwealth). Before the postwar changes the country fell into three kinds of political territory: the Straits Settlements (a Crown Colony), the Federated Malay States (four States under British protection), and five Unfederated Malay States (under British protection). Each Malay State was headed by a ruler (in most cases a sultan) and administered by a civil service staffed at its higher levels by officials from Britain and by Malays. The political pattern was colonial.

But the colonialism of Malaya was greatly complicated by its ethnic divisions. We can get some idea of these divisions by a glance at demographic history.[3] Today there are some 7,750,000 people in the country; before 1850 the total population numbered perhaps 600,000. Malaya began its modern history as a set of petty States populated (with the exception of the aborigines in the jungle) by Malays and small settlements of other Asians. Among the latter the Chinese were the most important; they formed both trading communities (largely urban) and groups of tin miners. From about the middle of the nineteenth century Chinese immigration increased sharply and continued up to recent years.

Pacific Affairs, 33, no. 2 (1960), 158–68. Reprinted in Immanuel Wallerstein, ed., *Social Change: The Colonial Situation* (New York, 1966), 278–89. Based in part on a paper submitted to the Fourth World Congress of Sociology, Stresa, 1959, and on a paper read in a series on Malaya in the Seminar on Constitutional Problems of Multi-Racial Countries, Institute of Commonwealth Studies, University of London.

Indian immigration began on a large scale as a result of modern rubber-growing. At the present there are in Malaya as a whole some 3,500,000 Chinese and about 850,000 Indians. The Malays have built up a modern population of roughly 3,400,000, partly by absorbing immigrants from the area we now know as Indonesia.

Already we are faced by two different patterns of immigration. The Chinese and Indians who arrived in Malaya have remained Chinese and Indians, not only in the eyes of census takers but also in culture, social organization, and political status. In contrast, "Indonesian" immigrants have found their way into that part of the population which British policy regarded as enjoying primacy of occupation and political rights. A Malay is an individual who speaks the Malay language, is a Muslim, and displays a culture which, for all its variations, is clearly recognizable. To be assimilated into this politically privileged part of the population a non-"Indonesian" immigrant had to abandon one way of life and assume a new one, of which the practice of Islam was an important element. A few Chinese and Indians have in the past crossed this bridge, and doubtless a few still do; their antecedents are no more significant for their present status as Malays than are those of the many Chinese babies adopted by Malays. But the movement across the line into Malaydom has never been considerable.

Malays, Chinese, and Indians together make up 98 percent of the country's population. The Chinese are more numerous than the Malays, but since the population of Singapore (about 1,500,000) is predominantly Chinese, the Malays are the largest ethnic community in the Federation. Partly because of the different age structures of Malays and Chinese, the latter are increasing at a higher rate, and it may be that after another generation the two communities in the Federation will be of equal numbers.

The plural society which has grown up in Malaya may be conveniently analyzed into four spheres: political, economic, social, and cultural. Again as a matter of convenience, we may speak of three "societies"— Malay, Chinese, and Indian. But these are merely preliminary to a more realistic view of Malayan society as a whole.

Malay society today can be traced back in a straight line to the characteristics it displayed when, in the last quarter of the nineteenth century, the British began to interfere actively in the affairs of the Malay States. (Before that period the British had for the most part remained politically within the Straits Settlements.) Each State was ruled by a member of a royal family who was "invested with attributes of supernatural power and dignity" (Gullick 1958: 21). He exercised very limited powers of central government. The State consisted of a number of districts, each ruled by a chief who came of a family long connected with the district. Together the district chiefly families "formed a more or less united ruling class of the whole State" (*ibid.*). Beneath the district chief and the class from which he came were the mass of the people, the peasantry; their inferiority was political, social, economic, and cultural.[4] (In these and the following generalizations I am greatly simplifying the facts and must therefore do violence to a complex reality, especially in regard to the State of Negri Sembilan, which was organized on the basis of matrilineal kinship groups with political functions.)

There was little marriage between the peasantry and the aristocracy (the chiefly class), except insofar as aristocrats took minor wives from among the people. The relation between the chief and his people was in principle one in which strong authority was matched by submission. The chief exacted *corvée*, was likely to help himself to any significant surplus accumulated by the peasant, and occasionally took village women for his household. Moreover, the chief kept up the numbers of his entourage (both for domestic and agricultural labor and for fighting purposes) by bringing men into a form of servitude known in English as "debt bondage." On the other hand, the economic and political realities of Malay life were set against a system of grinding oppression, for men who were pushed too hard could run away to establish themselves in the district of another chief or even in a different state. Land was plentiful, and since the wet rice fields relied upon rainfall and on merely temporary and simple irrigation works, there was little capital investment in land. A man could pull himself up and move without great economic loss. It seems likely that at this period of Malay history there was considerable movement of population.

Under British control the Malay States underwent an economic revolution, but while the Malays benefited from the development, they were only in small measure its direct agents. The reason lies, at least in part, in the way in which economic enterprise had been linked into the traditional Malay political and social system. The peasants lived in an economy in which money was used for some exchanges; they bought part of their foodstuff and a range of household necessaries; they sold some of their agricultural produce and materials collected in the jungle. But Malay trading on any considerable scale was conducted by the chiefs, who derived revenue from taxes imposed on goods in transit through their territory and, in some cases, from Chinese miners (at this time the main exploiters of Malaya's tin). Some chiefs entered into partnership with Chinese tin miners. There was very little investment by Malays in public works or productive enterprises, apart from what was staked in Chinese mining.

Beginning in the 1870's, British rule modified the political role of the chiefs; the economic aspect of their activity was accordingly reduced, and the Malays as a whole ceased to play a significant entrepreneurial part in the economy of their country.

British control bureaucratized the rulers and their chiefs. It raised the ruler from his traditional status of a chief among equals to that of an elevated king; at the same time it turned him into a kind of constitutional monarch. The chiefs were pensioned and some of them made administrative officers. State councils were set up. Courts of law were instituted under European and Malay officers. Public works were undertaken and an educational system devised.

Western and Chinese enterprise turned the country into a hive of economic activity, but Malays took no conspicuous part in it. They refused generally to sell their labor on mines and estates. But even so their role in the new economy was by no means unimportant; the peasantry adapted itself to producing cash crops (especially rubber and coconuts) on small holdings. By taking advantage of the limited educational opportunities offered, some peasants' sons were able to move into the lower ranks of the civil service and something like a rudimentary Malay middle class emerged on the basis of the administration. On the other hand, the traditional class system persisted in its main outline within the new framework. The old aristocracy was now the new administrative class, some of its former personal links with the people being transmuted into bureaucratic relationships. Since the Second World War the old aristocratic class has shown its leadership in the organization of Malay nationalism, within which Malays of all classes have demonstrated their attachment to their political privileges and their eagerness to keep the Federation in some real sense a Malay country.[5] The compromise worked out within the dominating political alliance in the Federation since Independence is an attempt to push these Malay nationalist ambitions as far as they can go without upsetting the communal balance. I return to this matter later.

In modern times Malaya has seen the rise of cities and towns, but except in the administrative section of urban life the Malays have not taken a great part in this new kind of society. They are to be found disproportionately in the less developed parts of the country. European control was first established along the western side of the peninsula and it was here that the greatest economic growth took place. Chinese and Indians are today overwhelmingly concentrated in a strip about fifty miles broad along the west coast. Here too there are many Malays, but their greatest concentrations are in the extreme northwest, where the Chinese west-coast strip thins out, and in the extreme northeast, where very few Chinese and Indians are to be seen. The vast majority of Malays are still villagers (cultivators and fishermen) and it is largely for the interests of countrymen that their leaders speak in debates on economic and political matters.

The cultural lines of demarcation have remained and, in some respects, been strengthened. The Malay language in its literary form is hardly known to non-Malays (except for a handful of Western Malay scholars); it is a possession which Malays have not abandoned in favor of English, despite the fact that Malay administrators have been educated in English. It may be that Malay will one day become the main cultural and political language of Malaya; for the moment, in its developed form, it is the mark of the Malays. Islam and the customary ways of Malay life (affected as they certainly have been by the modern world) are valued things which Malays see as central to their civilization and as indispensable to their survival as a people. Islam is certainly crucial to the solidarity of the Malays, having advanced both in organization and in intensity since the coming of colonial control. It has been bureaucratized and made sensitive to the currents of Muslim thought in the greater world. The Islamic orthodoxy which now begins to be seen as an important political factor has one of its roots in the pilgrimages and Muslim missionary activity conducted under the *pax britannica.*

The development of Chinese society and Indian society in Malaya has been very different. They are *nova,* lacking continuity with a Malayan traditional past. The Chinese population is by origin predominantly rural, but its pursuits in Malaya have been so commercial and industrial as to keep it either urban or, when rural, of a rather urban cast. Chinese filled the growing towns which were called into being by the expansion of trade, first in the Straits Settlements and then from the last quarter of the nineteenth century in the Malay States. They supplied skilled and un-skilled labor in enterprises promoted both by Western capital and the capital they themselves accumulated and invested. They set themselves up as the traders and shopkeepers of Malaya *par excellence,* collecting, distributing, and acting as sources of credit. Some of them became exceedingly rich, so that in purely economic terms the Malayan Chinese were diversified from millionaires to coolies.

The reasons why the Chinese have been economically successful in Malaya are complex. In the earlier immigration there were experienced traders who laid the foundation for the greatly expanded Chinese activity of later times. The great mass of the Chinese arriving in Malaya, however, have been farmers and artisans rather than men of commerce, and the business success which many of them enjoyed must have been due to their general understanding of the uses of money and the manipulation of men in relation to money (Freedman 1959a [Essay 2 above]). As immigrants they were inclined to be energetic and adventurous; when opportunities were created in Malaya, there were Chinese to seize them.

Chinese tin miners were present in considerable numbers when the British intervened in the west coast States. During the last quarter of the nineteenth century Chinese economic power in the Malay States was firmly based on the control of mining and a monopoly of the State revenue farms. In the present century many Chinese have prospered in the rubber industry. Chinese have penetrated into nearly every corner of the economy, being conspicuously absent only in rice cultivation and the higher levels of the administration. They are too large a part of the population to form a homogeneously middle-class group—unlike many of their congeners in other parts of Southeast Asia; during this century some three-quarters of them have been "working class," but the commercial and industrial middle class has been predominantly their preserve.[6]

The urban proclivities of the Chinese are marked. Nearly 54 percent of them were classed as urban in the 1947 census. Before the Pacific War there were Chinese on estates and mines, on rubber small holdings, on vegetable gardens, and, as shopkeepers, in Malay villages; the prewar depression drove larger numbers out into the countryside in search of a living, a movement which was intensified by the Japanese occupation. Many of these newcomers to rural life in Malaya, scattered here and there, remained beyond the scope of administration after the end of the war. When the Communist uprising began in 1948, Chinese in the countryside were widely involved in the moves and countermoves of the guerrilla fighting; a plan to resettle large numbers of them was drawn up, and by the 1950's the whole aspect of rural Chinese life in Malaya had been changed by the establishment of the so-called New Villages.[7] About one-sixth of the total Chinese population of the country was involved in this transfer. One of its social consequences was to produce, for the first time in Malaya, a series of nucleated Chinese villages. Behind the barbed-wire perimeters, clearly defined Chinese rural communities were forced into being. A political result of the change in settlement was that communications between the rural Chinese and leaders of the wider Chinese community were greatly facilitated, so that, while the security ends of the administration were served, a contribution was made to the development of pan-Malayan Chinese organization. It may well be that the New Villages have come to stay; if they survive, they will greatly help Malayan governments in their cultural and political control of the rural Chinese.

The Chinese did not arrive in Malaya in groups which could readily produce traditional leaders. Organizing themselves in relation to the economic roles for which they had been cast, they built up a social system in which leadership went to rich men and status depended directly on economic power. The Chinese evolved no class system comparable to that of the Malays. They were both physically and economically mobile. In any one area of the country they grouped themselves on the basis of interlocking associations which gave them the means of exercising control within their own ranks and of dealing with the outside world represented by Malay and British officials. During the nineteenth century their self-government rested primarily on secret societies, which brought Chinese into conflict with one another and at the same time held them together in the face of non-Chinese.[8] In more recent times the associations giving Chinese society its form and chains of command have been more various; among them, Chambers of Commerce, trade associations, and organizations recruiting on the basis of like territorial origin in China (a species of *Landsmannschaften*) have been the most important.

When the emigrants left China in the nineteenth century to go to Malaya and the other overseas settlements, they were not ambassadors of Chinese culture. They went generally against the wishes of the authorities at home and were fired by predominantly economic ambitions. If they had business dealings with Malays or Europeans, they acquired enough colloquial Malay to make these transactions possible. There was no place for them in the main political framework of the country, and its values and symbols remained largely alien to them. The Chinese were linguistically differentiated among themselves by the several (and for the most part mutually unintelligible) "dialects" of their language; and these linguistic divisions were built into the associations and groupings which came to constitute Chinese society in Malaya. A small section of the Malayan Chinese, tracing its origin to the early settlement in Malacca, into which non-Chinese women had been incorporated, has in modern times maintained a Malayanized version of Chinese culture and spoken a somewhat sinified Malay colloquial. It is an exception to the rule that, insofar as Chinese culture has survived in Malaya, it has preserved its essentially southern Chinese peasant character—despite the adoption of *Kuo-yü* and modern styles emanating from China.

Of course, social and cultural consequences were to flow from modern nationalism in China. The "homeland" became a focus of political interest. A modern school system was created by the Chinese themselves which adopted *Kuo-yü* (the Chinese "national" form of Mandarin) as its medium. Chinese in Malaya became conscious of forming part of a Chinese nation, both politically and culturally. It is one of the instructive paradoxes of modern Malaya that the nationalist "school" culture of the Chinese has been strongest in the very period when they have been preparing to take their place in a Malayan nation.

The education of the Chinese has not, however, been entirely Chinese. Many children have passed through the "English" school system which in modern times has culminated in the University of Malaya. It is wrong, nevertheless, to ascribe all the Westernizing elements in Malayan Chinese life to the "English" schools (for in one sense the Chinese schools have been more Westernized than their "English" counterparts, bringing in modern influences via China), and it is a mistaken view of Malayan Chinese society which makes a sharp division between the Chinese-educated and the English-educated sections of the community. The two forms of education overlap, often in the same family, sometimes in the same individual.

I have given drastic summaries of Malay and Chinese society in Malaya. If I am even briefer on Indian society, it is because the subject has been little explored rather than because I am trying to reduce a great body of knowledge to a simplified statement. The vast majority of Indian immigrants were Tamils from south India, brought over to work on estates. Historically and economically their place in Malaya has been bound up with the development of the rubber industry. Today Indians outnumber all other employees on rubber estates, and they hold a similar position on practically all other kinds of plantations. A common form of Indian local community in Malaya has, in consequence, come to be a body of workers on an estate, housed and supervised by an industrial concern. Indians are prominent in many other areas of the labor market. On the other hand, some south Indians as well as immigrants from other parts of India have taken on commercial roles in the Malayan economy which resemble some of those of the Chinese. Indian shopkeepers are to be found in Malay villages and a significant proportion of rural credit has come from Indian sources. There are large numbers of Indians in the towns, both in the trading middle class and among workers, skilled and otherwise. They have produced a number of professional men and many clerks, both in government service and private employment.

Some among the Indians (including those who may now regard themselves as Pakistanis) are Muslims. This has given them a ritual meeting ground with the Malays, and intermarriage has sometimes taken place as a result. But while Malay society has absorbed a few Indians in this fashion, the line between it and Indian society has remained sharply defined. Within the ranks of the Indians several Indian languages are spoken; these languages, and to some extent the cultures associated with them, have been perpetuated in schools specially provided for Indians or set up by themselves, the dominant language (for simple numerical reasons) being Tamil. As with the Chinese, however, significant numbers of Indians have gone through the "English" school system.

The Malayan Indian population is no longer dominated, as it was before the Second World War, by the coming and going of laborers from south India. It is now more highly stabilized in the country, politically as well as socially, the government of India having encouraged Malayan Indians to make their political home where they live.

We may now start to consider Malayan society as a whole, discarding the useful fiction that it is a plurality of societies. None of the individual "societies" has been politically autonomous; the British and the Malays have between them exercised the major political control, limiting one another in its application; Chinese and Indians have had to maneuver within the framework of overriding Malayo-British control. Nor can we continue to assume that each "society" has in reality constituted a unit. Have Malays, Chinese, and Indians been valid groups?

As far as the first two are concerned (for I am reluctant to commit myself on the Indians), we are certainly dealing with meaningful cultural categories, all the members of which regard themselves as belonging to a kind of ethnic community. But it does not follow that each community is an organized entity. In recent times the Malays, through the agency of a dominating political party, have built up a hierarchy of power within their own ranks which allows us to speak fairly realistically of a unified Malay group within the setting of national politics. This is the end-result of a process which began with the impact of colonialism on a set of independent Malay States. Before the Pacific War the Malay community, despite the early signs of pan-Malay nationalism, was essentially a plurality made up of units defined by State boundaries.

The Malayan Chinese have not attained the same degree of unification. The emergence of the Malayan Chinese Association notwithstanding, there is no single political party in the Federation which has welded all Chinese together. Structurally they are too loosely linked, economically and ideologically they are too diversified, to allow a single hierarchy of power to form among them. And yet today they are closer to unity than ever before. The resettlement in New Villages has simplified the lines of communication among a large section of the Chinese. The political developments of the last few years have rested on a widely accepted assumption that the first steps in Malayan democracy must be taken by means of an electoral alliance between the dominant Malay party (UMNO) and a single Chinese and a single Indian party (MCA and MIC). The rights of Chinese and Indians have had to be defended against both the nationalism of the Malay party forming the major unit in the alliance and Malay elements outside it which press for an Islamic and highly Malayized polity. These are conditions which favor a heightening of Chinese unity and a clearer definition of power within the ranks of the Chinese.

If, however, we ignore these recent developments and fasten our attention on the position as it was before the Pacific War, we see a different picture. The plural society then consisted not of ethnic blocs but of ethnic categories within which small groups emerged to form social ties inside and across ethnic boundaries. In any one locality a balance was struck between the interests of Malays, Chinese, and Indians. A rich and influential Chinese in one of the States, for example, maintained his position vis-à-vis Chinese and non-Chinese partly as a result of his relations with Malay power holders. Before the intervention of the British an agglomeration of Chinese power (as in the case of the tin-mining "wars" in Perak between rival Chinese camps) bore directly on the struggles between Malay contenders for power. The shifts of power within Malay ranks affected similar shifts among Chinese, and vice versa. The routinization of the political system brought about by the British prevented the repetition of such wide movements, but the continued interlocking of the interests of Malay and Chinese power holders forbids our looking at Malay and Chinese "societies" as though they were discrete entities, the existence of one failing to influence the fortunes of the other. The ties between local groups of Chinese and local groups of Malays could be determinants of the organizational features of both.

Malaya was and remains a culturally plural society. Paradoxically, from a purely structural point of view, its plural nature is more marked today than ever before. Nationalism and political independence in their early phases have tended to define, on a pan-Malayan basis, ethnic blocs which in former times were merely categories. Then the social map of Malaya was, so to speak, made up of a kaleidoscope of small culturally defined units rearranging themselves in accordance with local conditions. "The Malays" did not interact with "the Chinese" and "the Indians." Some Malays interacted with some Chinese and some Indians. But as "Malays," "Chinese," and "Indians" come to be realized as structural entities on a nationwide scale, they can begin to have total relations with one another.

The conservatism which predominates in the political life of the Federation (and which differentiates it from Singapore and other parts of Southeast Asia) is an aspect of the balance between the structurally defined ethnic groups. The compromise which has been worked out on the political plane between Malays, Chinese, and Indians within the Alliance puts a premium on caution in the manipulation of economic and social change. It encourages moderation and damps down an enthusiasm for radical policies. The threat to the present balance from the extremism represented by the relative successes of the Pan-Malayan Islamic Party in

1959 and from other stirrings of ethnic and ideological opposition could lead either to a determined effort to maintain the compromise (if necessary by a retreat from electoral democracy) or to a dismemberment of the Federation as we now know it.

The compromise in the Alliance has an important economic aspect. There is in Malaya no neat hierarchy of Furnivallian "orders" endowed with specific economic functions. The Asian "immigrant" population does not sit squarely in the middle of the occupational pyramid performing only intermediate economic roles. Chinese and Indians are distributed over a wide range of economic functions, while in the period since the end of the Second World War a sizable number of Malays have appeared in the ranks of industrial employees. On the other hand, capital and economic skill are highly concentrated in Chinese and, to some extent, Indian hands. Further economic development of the country is likely to strengthen the economic position of the non-Malays, unless some socialist formula is devised. Moreover, Malays wishing to enter more fully into the commercial and industrial life of the country come up against the difficulty of finding their way into networks of economic relationships which are composed of the personal ties between Chinese or Indians. Yet Malaya, when judged by Asian standards, is a prosperous country and it is conceivable that solutions to its economic problems will not appear so difficult as those to its political problems.[9]

The cultural face of the political compromise is, superficially at least, uncomplicated. Malay is ultimately to be the national language and is now to be taught in all schools. But the Chinese and Indian schools remain, although their curricula are Malayanized. There has been no attempt to "assimilate" the non-Malays; the emphasis has been put upon a common language (which will not exclude others) and a general minimum understanding of Malayan institutions. For the time being the cultural compromise appears to work.

One of the disadvantages of the notion of the plural society, as Morris (1957) has pointed out, is that it tempts us to argue from cultural and "racial" appearances to social realities. Through most of its modern history Malaya has shown important cultural and "racial" divisions, but these divisions had not created cleavages running the length and breadth of the society. The social ideals of Malays, Chinese, and Indians were different and their interrelations governed by narrowly defined political and economic interests; but there was no framework for the massive alignment of ethnic forces. In the Federation of Malaya the attainment of Independence has furnished conditions for such an alignment. Malays, Chinese, and Indians are forced to confront one another and pushed into speaking for their own ethnic communities on a national scale. But of course the ethnic alignment is not complete; there are other cleavages in the society (some within ethnic groups, to weaken them; others marking divisions across ethnic groups). The political compromise of the Alliance will presumably go on working as long as it can keep within bounds the realization of the principles on which it is based; it could be destroyed by the logic of the communalism which it imperfectly enshrines.

An Epicycle of Cathay; or,
The Southward Expansion of the Sinologists

"This conception of civilizations as recognizable objects in the landscapes of time and space coincides nicely with the conventional view of culture which the anthropologists have so thoroughly and, in my opinion, too successfully promulgated during the past thirty years, and which is by now so widely accepted that most of us use the term, it would be my claim, without thinking sufficiently about what its referents might be. ... Equipped only with the conventional cookie-cutter concept of culture, we find ourselves in grave analytical difficulties when we turn to Southeast Asia, lying between the great creative but self-producing civilizations of India and China. ... Though we know all too little about it, Vietnam in itself may perhaps be seen as a cultural continuum in time in the Brown, Reischauer, and Fairbank sense, a suborder within Southeast Asia; or, with more emphasis on space, simply as a branch of the great Chinese civilization extending southward as an intrusion into an adjacent region." (Sharp 1962: 4, 5.)

The scholar whom we salute in this book here speaks with nice caution, for, expert on "culture," he knows what many other such experts, anthropological and other, do not know: cultural boundaries are not unambiguously given in culture; they are chiefly the artifacts of our classifications. And of course our classifications change. But surely there can be no difficulty about seeing that Vietnam does not belong in Southeast Asia, where it is by convention placed, and that it ought to be put among the East Asian countries, the area of "Chinese" civilization?[1] Well, we might (especially under Professor Sharp's eye) want to hesitate before offering an answer, but while we are arguing or pondering the point we could consider how our redrawing of the cultural map might affect our

In Robert J. Smith, ed., *Social Organization and the Applications of Anthropology: Essays in Honor of Lauriston Sharp* (Ithaca, N.Y., 1974), 302–32.

vision of the political relations between China and Southeast Asia. If Vietnam is in that region, then any exercise of Chinese power within that country is an invasion, and a further proof that China drives south. If it is in East Asia, it may well mark the furthest southern limit of Chinese influence. Anthropological arguments and considerations aside, some people may sleep more peacefully for Vietnam's being classified in the region of Chinese civilization.

But the sinologues will disturb them. Just a little while before Professor Sharp delivered the presidential address to the Association for Asia Studies from which I have quoted, a symposium had been held in Hong Kong in the published proceedings of which we find a section entitled "The Southward Expansion of the Han Chinese in Historical Times." In that section there appears an abstract of a paper read by Professor F. W. Mote, the eminent sinologist, on "Cities in North and South China," where he says:

[China's] geographical South in the last thousand years has been absorbing Annam and Kwangsi, pushing into Southeast Asia, and crossing seas to the Philippines, Malaya and the Indonesian Archipelago. Despite Australia's immigration laws, Singapore's determination to become "Malaysian," and tensions of the Sino-Burmese and Sino-Indian borders, it is possible to imagine, or almost impossible not to imagine, the continued sinicization of Asia lying further to the South. For although most Chinese have not yet conceived of these regions as parts of China, in terms of the long and unabating Chinese advance, they clearly appear to be outposts like many others further north that China absorbed gradually throughout the centuries. (Mote 1967: 153.)

But there is a fuller and more recent version of the sinological thesis to tackle. I mean Professor C. P. FitzGerald's splendid new book, *The Southern Expansion of the Chinese People* (1972).[2]

I think it may be useful to begin with to try to site Professor Fitz-Gerald's thesis within the general tradition to which I believe it belongs. Of course, the view is by no means novel that Chinese culture and power drift (or drive) south, and the reappearance of a unified China (Taiwan aside) since 1949 has for many observers brought the southward movement closer to being resumed. With the thesis of the southward trend many people couple the thesis that in the Overseas Chinese, China has a ready-made spearhead or fifth column. Those Overseas Chinese are held, in the thesis, to be a people set apart from where they live, and in consequence, a guarantee of an effective intervention by China in the region. One remembers the argument as it has appeared in the newspapers from time to time, and in the books that bear some family likeness to the newspapers.

And one remembers it in its scholarly forms. In these latter, the thesis is, of course, hedged around with qualifications and made more subtle. One remembers Herold J. Wiens. His version of the southward drive from China is clear-cut. Having spoken of the "direct threat from the colossus of the north" as something being "graver than at any time in history, more serious than during the southward drive of the empire of Ghengis Khan," he goes on to plead for the cooperation of the Southeast Asian countries with the "Free World nations" (how quaintly it reads) "that lead the vanguard of the opposition to Communist enslavement" (Wiens 1967: 351). Yet his view of the role of the Overseas Chinese in the great drive is mild: "Thailand, which aside from Vietnam, perhaps has the closest historical ties with China, at the same time fears the influx of the Han-Chinese the most. And well it might, when it reviews the historical pressures of the Han-Chinese upon their [sic] cultural forefathers from the days of the Ch'u Kingdom down to the present" (Wiens 1967: 345). That from a geographer.

A sociologist writing upon the Chinese in Thailand and explaining very well how in one sense they are assimilated and in another sense not, concludes his book with a section entitled "China's March South" where he speaks of the growth of the population of China and the likelihood that that country will "turn to Southeast Asia for living space, for markets, and for raw materials and food." "Historically," he proceeds,

the lands south of China have served as outlets for China's population. . . . Because of their fear of overseas Chinese economic and political influences, all Southeast Asian governments, Thailand included, have erected immigration barriers against the Chinese. None welcomes the revitalization of its Chinese communities by a new wave of immigration. But one must ask whether small nations like Thailand can resist the tremendous pressures exerted by China's expanding population, and if that, whether they can also resist the extraordinary cultural dynamic that China represents in Asia today. . . . Perhaps it is more realistic to think of China assimilating all the lands to the south, with a gradual, but determined penetration, the first stage of which is now taking place. (Coughlin 1960: 204–5.)

The chief features of nearly all versions of the theory is that China is a menace (Dulles and dominoes . . .) and that the Overseas Chinese in Southeast Asia, willingly or unwillingly, act as agents of (to borrow Wiens's language) the colossus of the north. But it is not necessary that the theory be anti–Overseas Chinese, although it is usually so: a moving and generous plea in the Philippines for a fairer treatment of the Chinese in that country falls within the range of variations of the theory. That cry in defense of the Philippine Chinese says that unless they are better treated and so encouraged to identify themselves more closely with the country where their home is, they may align themselves with the enemy without.

The dilemma of the rich Chinese has always been whether to integrate with Filipinos and not be really accepted by them or to stay as they are, aliens forever. We must solve the dilemma not for some but for all. We have caused them to coalesce by discrimination and, particularly, by legislative discrimination. That discrimination must be removed. . . . Our country now faces the possibility of an armed invasion. In 1946 the communists were at Mukden. . . . Today, they are at the outskirts of Saigon. At this rate, it is no exaggeration to say that in the next few years, we ourselves may have to face them. When the time comes, union shall be essential. We cannot afford to have the Chinese portion of our population disloyal and ready to give aid to the enemy. (Felix 1966: 11.)

Against this background Professor FitzGerald's version may be a surprising variation. For him of course China is hardly a menace, and he does not fear an imminent burst of Chinese power into Southeast Asia. The two elements in his general argument (eloquently set out in his new book) that bring it fully within the compass of the present are: (1) the stress put upon the southward movement of Chinese culture; and (2) the contention that the presence of large numbers of Chinese in the Nanyang (Southeast Asia) will in the long run involve the government of China in that region, Chinese power being extended perhaps even with the greatest reluctance. If the other versions may be said to represent China as a fire-breathing dragon, Professor FitzGerald's seems to suggest a huge but mild-mannered dragon unwillingly stirred to action. We may call this latter a "left" version to match the more common "right" one.

Professor FitzGerald writes as a historian, but to the extent that as anthropologists we approve his work we may want to claim him as one of us. And we should be in part justified in doing so. As a matter of fact, his anthropological interests are chiefly represented by the book he wrote many years ago on the Min Chia of Yunnan (1941), the fieldwork for which was done after he had been taught by Malinowski at the London School of Economics. And now in his new book we can see how important a role Yunnan plays in his thinking about the spread of Chinese culture. That province and Vietnam are for him two key variations on the theme of sinification. Yunnan is now in China, Vietnam now out of it. The former is in a sense less Chinese than the latter. While China now looks from north to south across the frontier between the two, it once looked north from a "Vietnam" (a fraction of the present country of that name) in China to a "Yunnan" (Nanchao) outside it.

These captivating paradoxes spring, to speak very briefly, from the following historical circumstances. The kingdom of Nanchao, roughly on the site of the present-day Yunnan, and the Tali kingdom that succeeded it in the tenth century, had come under heavy Chinese influence and included Chinese (Han) people within their frontiers. But partly sinicized, Nanchao/Tali lay outside China until the Mongol conquest in the middle of the thirteenth century, undertaken in a movement to outflank the Sung empire, brought it within its great neighbor's frontiers, where it was to stay. On being hauled into China it was an ethnically mixed country, imperfectly sinicized; and so in some measure it has remained to this day. Vietnam, in contrast, had been thoroughly sinicized during a long period of Chinese rule before it broke free in the tenth century; and never again to come under the rule of China for any great length of time, it was not until the present day to abate its Chinese culture.

Yunnan and Vietnam furnish us, on Professor FitzGerald's reasoning, with models of two quite different processes of cultural and political domination by China. In the first model, Yunnan, we have a territory holding a population of mixed origins which acquires some Chinese culture before it passes under Chinese rule. It makes a nuisance of itself to China, and in the end is forced to join it. (The Mongols captured it and left it to a China that would not part with it.) The second model, Vietnam, involves a country which, although it has a tribal population, is overwhelmingly of one ethnic group. It receives Chinese culture, but few Chinese people. Having at last attained independence from China, it refrains from harassing its erstwhile ruler, now its suzerain. Indeed, it turns into a sort of miniature copy of its great neighbor and begins its own march to the south, having to clear out of the way and expropriate, or absorb, great numbers of Chams and Khmers before it reaches the modern limits of the country.

The People's Republic of China has pushed Han civilization and control outward from "China Proper" toward the corners of the vast territory bequeathed to it, at one remove, by the Ch'ing dynasty, although of course some of the Ch'ing lands (much of Mongolia among them) have been lost. Far-flung as they are, the modern frontiers of China might well have been more extensive. They might have included a large area to the south and west if, for example, the naval power culminating in the Ming ventures of the early fifteenth century, and which made possible the magnificent expeditions as far west as the east coast of Africa, had not been dispersed.[3] And even if we suppose that the territory ruled over by China had not been extended by the maintenance of great sea power, then at least we may assume that that power would have changed the relations between China and the many countries lying near it. As things turned out, Ch'ing China looked upon many of its neighbors as tributary states, and they performed the rites required of them in that status; but its political influence upon those states which lay to the south was on the whole weak. And when the West set out to drag China screaming into the nineteenth century, she was left defenseless for lack of strength at sea.

It is a commonplace of the writing on Ch'ing China that that dynasty principally faced north, whence it had come.[4] And it was precisely when official Chinese eyes were turned away from the Nanyang that for the first time large groups of Chinese began to build up in that region. Of course, Chinese had settled in places in Southeast Asia before Ch'ing times, but never before that dynasty had they settled in large numbers, and never before the middle of the nineteenth century had they emigrated (mainly from the southeastern provinces of Fukien and Kwangtung) in a flood. The Western occupation of Southeast Asia which at its fullest extent (attained early in the twentieth century) covered the whole of the region with the sole exception of Siam, created the conditions for a massive "diaspora" of the Chinese. Indeed, the rulers of China began to take official cognizance of its emigrants only in the very last years of the dynasty, and then partly under pressure from the Western powers.[5] We have reached the modern world into which the Communist regime of China was soon to enter.

Professor FitzGerald's new book opens: "Chinese influence, Chinese culture and Chinese power have always moved southward since the first stage of which we have historical knowledge" (1972: xiii). What he appears to mean is that when Chinese culture overflows the edges of China, Chinese power is likely in the end to be dragged in to regulate the consequences. "It is rather a pattern of seepage, of slow overspill from the great reservoir which was China" (1972: xxi). Of the two models proposed to us, Yunnan and Vietnam, the former exemplifies the process; and we can begin to see from this point how the model may be used to illuminate the Nanyang as we now know it. Once more (the sinologue says), as in the kingdom of Nanchao, there now exists "a large Chinese population established in an alien land." Once again "the rulers of this region are rather more hostile than friendly to the government of China." Once more the local Chinese "have developed the economy and brought a great increase of trade and prosperity." And, as in Yunnan, "the majority of the immigrants have taken to urban life and occupations, leaving the ownership and occupation of the land to the natives" (1972: 183f). This comparison of the Nanyang and Yunnan culminates in the assertion that "the immigrant community, at first poor, unsophisticated and often illiterate, has . . . been culturally enriched both by its own growing prosperity and by the advent of a significant number of Chinese of the educated classes" (1972: 184).

I am not concerned in this essay to argue out fully the political implications of Professor FitzGerald's analysis and projections for the future; but I need briefly to say, as a preliminary to what follows, that I do not accept the argument that China may expand into Southeast Asia as a direct result of the presence there of Overseas Chinese. Expand it may, especially if it recovers the sea power it once gave up, but, in my opinion, the Overseas Chinese will have nothing or very little to do with it.[6] To see why that is so we need to abandon the base in China from which the sinologists have been working and examine the Nanyang Chinese from much closer up.

They have been examined by some very distinguished historians and social scientists—one's mind jumps at once to Professor Wang Gungwu and Professor G. William Skinner. As for the anthropologists, it is now becoming easy to overlook the fact that for the longish period between the end of World War II and (to fix upon a date which I shall not attempt to defend here) 1958, the Overseas Chinese were, or appeared to be, the only sort of Chinese among whom anthropologists might practice their traditional craft of field work. (Of course, although the study of Overseas Chinese was not confined to those in Southeast Asia, it was concentrated on them.) I said "appeared to be" in the sentence before last because I have in mind the possibility that Hong Kong and Taiwan could have been exploited much earlier than they in fact were; academic blindness as well as political myopia must be held to account (cf. Freedman 1970 [Essay 24 below]: 8–9). Whether the anthropologists were justified in looking upon the Nanyang as a substitute for a China from which the international situation had excluded them may be interestingly debated.[7] But I do not think it could be reasonably argued that they brought to their perception of the Overseas Chinese a model of Chinese society and culture into which the Nanyang data had to be forced. On the contrary, it is chiefly to the anthropologists, although not to them alone, that we owe our realization and understanding of the extent to which Chinese culture has been whittled away in Southeast Asia and how great numbers of people of Chinese descent have been totally absorbed into non-Chinese society. It would be interesting to speculate on the reasons why the anthropologists in the Nanyang showed themselves to be considerably more history-minded than those who had preceded them in the study of China and, more strikingly, than those who were immediately after them to study the "residual China" of Hong Kong and Taiwan. Indeed, one begins to wonder, as the prospect of field work in

TABLE I
Chinese Population in Southeast Asia, 1972
(Estimated in thousands)

Country or territory	Chinese population	Chinese as % of total
Portuguese Timor	5	1
North Vietnam	200	1
Philippines	450	1.5
Burma	400	1.5
Laos	45	2
Indonesia	2,750	2.5
South Vietnam	850	5
Cambodia	430	7
Thailand	2,600	8.5
Brunei	25	26
Malaysia	3,300	35
Singapore	1,400	75

mainland China itself seems to get closer, whether one ought to view it with some alarm, instead of with the more usual messianic enthusiasm; perhaps the harvest will prove to consist of quite unhistorical and very old-fashioned "community studies." But let that pass.[a] We must turn to the data on the *hua-ch'iao* (see Nevadomsky and Li 1970), "the Chinese sojourners overseas," as the Chinese term prejudicially calls them.

In one sense there is an entity to be called the Nanyang Chinese; in another sense, no such entity exists. Let us begin with the latter assertion. If we list the countries/territories of Southeast Asia as they are at the present time—Burma, Thailand, Malaysia, Singapore, Indonesia, Portuguese Timor, Brunei, Cambodia, Laos, the two Vietnams, and the Philippines—we shall discover that they all number Chinese people in their populations, the proportions formed by these Chinese varying enormously. Consider Table 1,[8] in which the territories are arranged in order (lowest to highest) of the percentages formed of their populations by the Chinese. If we rearrange the territories by the size of their Chinese populations (greatest to least) we get: Malaysia, Indonesia, Thailand, Singapore, South Vietnam, the Philippines, Cambodia, Burma, North Vietnam, Laos, Brunei and Portuguese Timor. In only one country, Singapore, are the Chinese in the majority. In two others, Malaysia and Brunei, they

[a] Of course, the prospect may be a mirage. Perhaps the time will never come. The barrier that came down in 1949 might be said to have restored a normal state of affairs that had been merely interrupted for the previous hundred years. China does not know the tradition of freely opening its social life to close inspection by the outside world (Dawson 1967: 167–68), and it may well be that the students of China who have been perfecting the techniques of study at a distance are better advised than the optimistic field-workers who imagine that before long (I write in mid-1972) the barrier will be raised.

form very substantial minorities. Elsewhere their minorities are small, some very small indeed. Political accident and political design (for the latter one thinks of Singapore) have produced an enormous range of percentages.

But that is merely the beginning of the variation. The name "Chinese" does not carry the same meaning throughout the table: one is in the grip of a spurious category if one supposes the contrary. Obviously, if one starts from a legal point of view then one notices at once that in each country "Chinese" includes people of Chinese nationality/citizenship (but not just of *one* China) and those of the relevant local nationality/citizenship (cf. Coppel 1972)—not to mention those holding the passport of some third country. But there is far more to it than that. In any one country some of the people listed as Chinese are, in terms of their culture (and perhaps their descent), likely to be more Chinese than others so listed; and the gap between the extremes may be very great, a point we may illustrate by the distance between a Malay-speaking Baba Chinese in Malaysia or Singapore and his Mandarin-speaking compatriot. And if there were such a thing as—in cultural terms again—an average Chinese in each country, then he would not be the same from country to country. Countries differ in their non-Chinese respects, and their Chinese with them. Countries contain and condition their Chinese.[9] That is a fact that observers afar (especially from China perhaps) find it particularly difficult to assimilate. And they find it hard partly because there is also a Chinese Nanyang although we can see that there are in fact separate Chinese communities scattered through Southeast Asia. The Chinese Nanyang manifests itself in part in the interconnections among Chinese in the different countries of the region, in part in the organizations that purport to speak in the name of the Overseas Chinese of the region or in that of some special interest group among them, and in part in the attempts by various Chinese governments to treat the Chinese in Southeast Asia as a whole.

The international character of the Chinese in the Nanyang has clearly been an important feature of their lives and a crucial element in their commercial success. Links across frontiers of family and kinship, as well as of common origin in China, have made them quick to receive economic intelligence and to respond to the opportunities it might suggest. And perhaps Professor FitzGerald is right to give importance (1972: 165) to the fact that in their written language the Chinese in Nanyang have a special instrument for the "coded" transmission, in their newspapers, of information of commercial value. But these are matters that belong to the past more than the present. In pre-colonial and colonial times the barriers between countries were for the most part more permeable than they are now, when nationalism has taken frontiers and turned them into formidable obstacles. One has observed during the past twenty years or so how the growing individuation of the countries of Southeast Asia has progressively isolated from one another their Chinese communities. Of course, the process does not go so far that all links are severed; and in favorable circumstances (as is at the moment the case with Chinese in Singapore and Indonesia in the important role they play in the trade between their countries) older ties may be reactivated. Certainly, enough of the old internationalism of the Nanyang Chinese survives to lend color to the accusation made against them that they lack a full commitment to the countries where they live. A former strength is a present weakness.

Now, it will have been seen from the summary offered earlier in the essay of Professor FitzGerald's application of the Yunnan model to the Nanyang that it supposes in the latter a culturally vigorous Chinese community—or, more correctly, a series of such communities. It would be grossly unfair to Professor FitzGerald to suggest that he has shown himself unaware of some of the important differences among the Nanyang Chinese groups and of the fact that assimilation, in varying degrees, has taken place, sometimes in its extreme form on a large scale. But it is fair, I think, to say that he has not brought his awareness of these differences into harmony with his general propositions. The sketch of Yunnan-in-the-Nanyang demonstrates that defect. Professor FitzGerald considers it possible that China will one day need to intervene in Southeast Asia precisely because there are Chinese there, not necessarily because they stand in need of succor: He suggests the possibility that a flourishing alternative "China" in the Nanyang (Singapore—where else?) might provoke from China a hostile intervention (1972: 209). And the general argument assumes that somehow the Chinese in Southeast Asia will have grown more Chinese than they are, just as they are now more Chinese than they were. The assumption follows from Professor FitzGerald's version of the history of Chinese emigration.

In the beginning the emigrants were humble, poor, and often illiterate. (So far so good. That will certainly do for a generalization.) But as they grew richer, their Chinese cultural standards rose: "As the Overseas Chinese steadily become predominantly native born, and immigration ceases the level of transplanted Chinese culture has risen, not fallen, so that communities which were mainly illiterate only a century and less ago, are now steeped in the culture of their ancestral homeland, and unwilling to forego this heritage" (1972: 119). The *hua-ch'iao* were helped in the attainment of these new standards by small numbers of educated emigrants who came over to raise the general level. One can suggest how in this Professor FitzGerald has been forced into his version of Nanyang history by his attachment to his (seductive, one may freely admit) Yunnan model. "In Yunnan these latter [i.e. a significant number of Chinese of the educated classes] were more often political exiles sent to the remote province by the government of the day; in the Nanyang they are more likely to be exiles who have preferred to live abroad rather than remain in, or to return to China under Communist rule" (1972: 184).

This view of the history of the Nanyang is difficult to reconcile with the evidence normally considered. In the first place, such elevation of Chinese cultural standards as occurred (by the spread of Mandarin and the nationalist culture that went with it) happened in the first half of the twentieth century, and precisely before China turned Communist. Since that great event, the parallel rise of nationalist regimes in the Southeast Asian countries has generally led to a decline in what I suppose Professor FitzGerald would regard as Chinese culture; certainly, at the present time in the Nanyang there must be less Chinese-language education and less use of the Chinese language for literary purposes than in 1949. (Professor FitzGerald is aware [p. 119] that English is a challenge to Chinese; but he clearly underestimates the extent of the challenge. Perhaps however, since English is widely used as a practical, not literary, language, Professor FitzGerald would not want to allow it within the limits of his somewhat austere definition of "culture.")

One wonders too about the political exiles said to have been cultural leaveners, and one might suspect that there is in the analysis some confusion of social status and level of culture, whatever that latter may mean precisely. There is no doubt that the intensification of Chinese culture among the Nanyang Chinese at various times from about the beginning of this century, which produced among other things the resinification of some highly acculturated Chinese in Malaya (cf. Freedman 1965 [Essay 1 above]), has made for a strengthening of bonds with China. But the bearers of the means of cultural renewal were by no means generally of high social standing. For many decades they were for the most part poor and socially depressed schoolteachers and, in more recent times, often poor and socially depressed university teachers (from Taiwan). It is true that there is now in the Nanyang a higher regard for education-without-riches than there used to be, but it still seems to me to be a distortion of Nanyang life to give the impression that educated newcomers from China have appeared to their overseas fellows as a sort of wondrous cultural saviors. The sociology of Chinese culture in the Nanyang is far more complex than Professor FitzGerald's formulae allow for.

We must recognize the break between the system of social stratification in China and that developed in the Nanyang. *Shih, nung, kung, shang*:

scholar-administrator, farmer/peasant, artisan/worker, merchant—that idealized hierarchy represents for traditional China the differential worth of occupational groups in terms of the distribution of the values of civility and productivity. Civility marked off *shih* from the rest; productivity ranked *nung* before *kung* and *kung* before *shang*. The hierarchy does not represent the distribution of power within traditional Chinese society, for it is obvious that *shang*, a category embracing everybody from petty trader to great merchant, could not be at the bottom of a scale of power. The hierarchy rejects in *shang* the value of what is taken to be unproductive, uncivil, and possibily luxury-inspiring activity.[10] By this formula moral and political leadership is to vest in *shih*. We may see at once that *hua-ch'iao* society must by its arrangements contradict the ancient formula. It lacks *shih*. Leadership falls (or at any rate fell until quite recently) to *shang*.[11] A traditional hierarchy is then stood on its head when the few *shih* who find themselves in the Nanyang are treated as mere instruments (schoolteachers, clerks) of the *shang*. If we ignore the small farming population among the Overseas Chinese, we might go so far as to say that the Nanyang hierarchy came at times to be *shang, kung, shih*. And even when, in more recent decades, one has been able to detect a more traditionally arranged system of occupational statuses, such that educated men stand at the top and take on positions of leadership (professionals: lawyers, doctors, and the like), they have by no means been the sort of men that Professor FitzGerald seems to have in mind. (Cf. Wang Gungwu 1968, esp. pp. 209–13.)

The Chinese "wherever they have settled, have brought with them their own culture, at first in simple forms suited to a mainly illiterate migrant population, but as the level of their wealth and standard of living rose, they turned without hesitation to the more sophisticated art and literature of their ancestral land" (C. P. FitzGerald 1972: 138). Did they? Much depends upon what is meant by "they turned without hesitation to." The outward signs might be displayed without attachment on the part of their displayers to the artistic or literary values they might be thought to enshrine. I remember, from British Malaya, one of the richest men in the country (of distinguished Baba lineage), who knew no Chinese, assuring me that the splendid calligraphic scroll that hung upon his wall had been done entirely by hand. And in the past one has watched the surprise on the face of newcomers when first in the presence of what they soon learned to categorize as nouveau riche style. It is not for the anthropologist to pass judgment: his point must be that Overseas Chinese culture, varied as it is from time to time and place to place, is not a mere approximation to the culture of the homeland. It grows from its special social circumstances, and none of these predisposes it toward the progressive adoption of the "higher" cultural values and styles of China. Professor FitzGerald's argument will be seen to rest fundamentally upon the supposition that Chinese culture is endlessly viable. That is an assumption that must certainly come very naturally to a sinologue and sinophile. The Chinese in China (there is no secret about it) have a very high opinion of their cultural achievements and of their general superiority to the peoples around them. And sinologists often take on the prejudices of what they closely study. Indeed, to go by the advice offered by Professor Owen Lattimore in his Inaugural Lecture at Leeds in 1964, "the student of modern China, even when doing his research and teaching outside of China, should cultivate an intellectual method of seeing China from within, and looking from China outward at the world" (Lattimore 1964: 2). Well, anthropologists will be among the first to recognize the methodological desirability of working outward from the categories of the people they study, insofar as that task can be achieved without abandoning categories which make sense of more than one society. They may be suspicious of a sinological aim to pose the student on one spot; in assimilating the Chinese point of view he may easily come to forget that there are others.

That China has been and will almost certainly continue to be one of the great civilizations is indisputable. Only a shortsighted peering at the century following 1840 could explain the failure to see that truth. But it does not follow that Chinese emigrants and their descendants must forever reflect the glory of their homeland or neglect to take advantage of the cultural and political opportunities open to them where they live. In the course of living outside China many have in fact already disappeared as Chinese, and many more will surely go the same way. We cannot predict exactly how Chinese the Nanyang Chinese will be in, say, twenty years from now; but, short of an effective presence of China itself in Southeast Asia, the chances are that there will be less Chinese culture than there is now. The continued creaming off of Chinese leaders in Thailand, when there can be no accession of new cultural strength from China (Skinner 1968: 203); the erosion of Chinese culture in Singapore under the stern antichauvinist policies of Mr. Lee Kuan Yew's government (so much so that the only possible candidate for the position of a China-outside-China seems likely to manage in the end with only a residual Chinese cultural apparatus); the destruction of Chinese cultural institutions in Indonesia—all these point to a desinification in the Nanyang. I should add, to avoid a common misunderstanding, that the acculturation to which these facts point is by no means to be taken as a sign of increasing social and political adjustment; the Chinese in Malaysia and Indonesia, for example, may well find that their relations with their respective compatriots get worse as they come more and more to resemble them in their cultural lives. But that is another matter.

Professor FitzGerald's view that the fate of Southeast Asia is that of Yunnan and not Vietnam can be turned on its head: we may say that if Chinese culture is to come to dominate in (parts of) the region, then it will be because of conquest by China. The correct model will have proved to be not Yunnan but Vietnam (*absit omen*). Violence will have led to Chinese culture, not Chinese culture to violence.

But as the argument progresses one grows uneasy with the word "culture," and one's mind returns to Lauriston Sharp's words quoted at the beginning of this essay. We know, as long as we remain reflective anthropologists, that *a* culture is a classification that we impose upon the data. Vietnam is in or out of China depending upon the arrangement we choose to make at different times of the facts at our disposal. Certainly, whatever else it may be, a culture is not a homogeneous substance with the power to spread, like butter or treacle. But that is how Chinese culture seems to be presented in the arguments for its inevitable expansion—except that Professor FitzGerald allows for the possible dilution of the culture as it moves: "The March to the South [by the Vietnamese], especially in its later phases when some proportion of the conquered population was assimilated into the victorious Vietnamese people, had the effect of diluting and subtly altering the character of the Chinese culture which the northern Vietnamese had so long adopted" (1972: 31).

Consider other statements, already quoted in this essay: southern expansion "is rather a pattern of seepage, of slow overspill"; "Chinese influence, Chinese culture and Chinese power have always moved southward." We were invited by language of that sort to accept a physical (sometimes hydrographical) theory of Chinese culture. And if we have before us in our mind's eye a wall map of Asia, north conventionally at the top, we may be tempted to imagine Chinese culture oozing and dribbling down under the pull of gravity. Our anthropological defenses lowered, we may be lulled into the confident belief that we are the recipients of a great key to human history.

Of course the frontiers of Chinese power and culture have advanced southward, the two frontiers not always coinciding (Vietnam and Nanchao/Tali). Of course vast tracts of territory and huge numbers of "barbarians" have been made Chinese[b]—some of them in fact were probably ancestors of the Overseas Chinese we are now discussing among whom many have desinified themselves. But are we obliged to believe that the

[b] Cf. Miyakawa 1960, especially perhaps the delightful expression of the Confucian point of view at p. 31. "An important way in which Confucianism civilized the southern natives was by improving their marriage systems."

process of southward movement must continue? Obviously not. There is
no inevitability about it. Population pressure could conceivably make
China turn hungry eyes upon empty spaces in Thailand, where there is
an opportunity to reproduce a Chinese agricultural way of life—there
being few other candidates in the south. But in fact, within the frame of
the political conditions that we can envisage for Asia in the near future,
Chinese power is more likely to manifest itself in the revived form of a
Chinese suzerainty that, in the abnormal conditions of the last hundred
years, we have tended to forget.

China is not simply *chung-kuo*, a state/country with clearly drawn
boundaries, but also (in one sense of the term) *t'ien-hsia*, All-under-
Heaven, a civilization (*the* civilization in its own estimation) embracing
its neighbors without imposing its culture upon them. At the center of
t'ien-hsia stood the bureaucratically controlled state presiding over the
area of intense Han life and culture. Around this area were arranged
others where control was exercised through a more personal form of
rule,[12] the emperor acting now as overlord to local chiefs and rulers. At
the periphery of this outer part of the civilization we find territories and
rulers whose obligations were no more than to acknowledge the overlordship of the emperor and to send envoys who would make obeisance
to him. The characteristic of the central area, China Proper, was that it
was an agricultural country whose inhabitants were preferably engaged
in administration and farming. Beyond the edges of the central realm lay
barbarous peoples whose economic life was opposite (pastoralists,
nomads), in which case they were unassimilable to Han culture, or similar but rudimentary, in which case their primitive forms of tilling the soil
made them potential recruits to that culture. To the north and west the
central realm could not traditionally expand; to the south it might. But
the total range covered by the imperial overlordship could more easily
be enlarged; and when relations were established with Western powers
within the only system that traditional China could recognize, the list of
tributary states could include some in the West, although because of their
bases abroad, they might be thought of as being closer to China. The roll
of regular tributary states given in the 1818 edition of the *Ta-Ch'ing
hui-tien*, administrative statutes of the Ch'ing, reads: Korea, the Ryu-
kyus, Annam, Laos, Siam, Sulu, Holland, Burma, Western Ocean (Portu-
gal, the Papacy, England).[13] Out of context, that list looks comic, but it is
far from being so. And one may imagine a new context in which the list,
suitably modified, would resume its meaning . . . indeed, take on more
meaning than the Ch'ing, in their preoccupation with the north, were
able to give it. Chinese culture may have attained its furthest geographical limits; Chinese political influence may yet have a great distance to go.

If the Chinese survive in the Nanyang until the time when such a re-arrangement of the political map appears likely—and China is seen to be on the point of becoming the great patron to a collection of Southeast Asian client-states—then obviously their position will be peculiar. One hesitates to say "privileged" because they might then be so different from the Chinese of China as to make them to the latter a dubious asset. But, more important, the imposition of such an order in Asia would in no way depend on there being recognizable Chinese in the Nanyang. The government of China seems intent, as the recent book by Dr. Stephen Fitz-Gerald (1972) cogently argues, on desinifying the *hua-ch'iao* by a combination of integration overseas and, if necessary, repatriation to China (cf. Freedman 1972a). There could come a movement of Chinese power to the south, but Professor FitzGerald notwithstanding, if it does come, it will not have been caused by a drift of Chinese culture. The sinologist may be tempted to make culture the pioneer dragging politics in its train. The anthropologist (is it a paradox?) puts politics in the van, culture trailing.

But it is not only "culture" that creates difficulties for us in our attempt, as anthropologists, to assess the value of the various models used to explain the position of the *hua-ch'iao*. If Professor C. P. FitzGerald's Yunnan model links the fate of the Overseas Chinese too closely to China, another model, which also makes a fleeting appearance in his new book (1965: 84), may put too much emphasis upon the permanent marginality of the *hua-ch'iao* as an explanation of their position. I refer to the model called "the Jews of Asia." Professor FitzGerald sums up a good deal of the Jewish analogy when he writes: "Situations comparable to the Middle Eastern conflict of Arab and Jew would have been more than possible. . . . It is no accident that King Rama VI of Thailand and other sharp critics of the Chinese in the Nanyang had described them as "the Jews of the Far East." (Cf. Purcell 1965: 120–21 and Skinner 1957: 164f.) It is also perhaps no accident that the rulers of the new Republic of Singapore, when seeking instructors for its new armed forces, found Israelis to their liking" (1972: 197). (One might have supposed that Israeli military expertness of a special kind had something to do with it.) Of course, the Jewish analogy is everywhere found in the literature on the Overseas Chinese; it is a tribute paid by the East to the West; and one may be forgiven for being so bored with it that one has forgotten to submit it to scrutiny.[c]

[c] But see some sensible remarks in Heidhues 1968: 339–40. I must confess that I myself appear to have been guilty of slapdash thinking on the subject: Freedman 1959b: 68. But I stand by the statement made there: "What things are common and not common to Jews

When Professor W. F. Wertheim, the eminent Indonesianist, published a newspaper article on the ejection of Chinese from the West Java countryside, it appeared under the title "Exodus der Joden van het Oosten" (1960).[14] In his collection of essays *East-West Parallels: Sociological Approaches to Modern Asia* (1964) we find one entitled "The Trading Minorities in Southeast Asia," which is mainly concerned with the people "of Chinese ancestry, who are . . . a 'homeless' minority within most of the Southeast Asian states, and who, largely as a consequence of their dominant position in trade, today present a series of social, economic, and political problems in most of the countries of that area" (1964: 41). Although (he argues) not all Chinese are traders, yet in the crowded rural areas where many of them settled they filled an occupational gap corresponding to that which accommodated the Jews in medieval Europe; and "they have still to bear the odium attached to the trading profession by a rural society in which aristocratic and feudal values are still strong" (1964: 44). More generally, the Chinese in the Nanyang have got themselves into an awkward marginal position, and the root of their difficulty is to be found in the "economic competition between adjoining social groups. . . . The present outbursts of violence or organized discrimination on a mass scale are not comparable with the occasional pogroms or riots in past centuries" (1964: 76). For we are now in a transitional phase in which the new independent countries are trying to transform their societies. In this phase the Chinese find themselves faced by economic rivals from among the indigenous population. Thus it "is not cultural divergence which is at the root of the tensions. The movements become virulent precisely at the moment when the cultural differences are waning to such an extent that competition becomes possible. Lack of assimilation . . . provides an excuse to select a special group of 'foreigners' as the target. . . . It appears to me that a similar line of reasoning could be applied if we wish to explain the emergence of anti-semitism and some changing attitudes and inconsistencies throughout European history" (1964: 79).

What Professor Wertheim says is obviously in part true. The competitive frictions between ethnic groups must increase when non-Chinese aspire to the economic roles and positions hitherto monopolized by the Chinese, and that increase has long been foreseen. But one might wish to quarrel with Professor Wertheim over his apparent determination to find an economic cause of both anti-Semitism and anti-Chinese action in Southeast Asia. After all, the real problem (although it may not appear so

outside Israel and Overseas Chinese would make an interesting and instructive study—if there is a scholar who commands the literature on both." Who does?

to the victims) is to discover not so much why they are envied occupants of valued economic niches, as why they are still classified as aliens to justify their being made legitimate targets. (In the national language of Indonesia the problem is well stated by the division within the general category of "Indonesian citizen" between Indonesian citizens who are indigenous, *asli*, and those who are not.)

But though we may fault Professor Wertheim's analysis by saying that it does not go deep enough, we of course recognize in it a serious and scholarly effort to pursue an analogy as far as the evidence will take it (cf. Eitzen 1968). The less thoughtful versions of the model rest upon a much broader conception of what is common to Jews and *hua-ch'iao*, or at least they are apt to excite in the reader's mind a fuller range of such common features. Jews/Chinese wander about the earth; they are people of an ancient culture; for the most part they work their way into intermediate positions in economy and society, constrained to do so by the restrictions placed upon them; they are disliked and persecuted; and, rootless cosmopolitans, they look to Zion/China. . . . We get back to Professor C. P. FitzGerald's speculations. In another context he possibly refers to the Jews without mentioning them: "The existence of discrimination in some degree in all the Nanyang except Singapore tends to make the Chinese, no longer 'alien' nor 'transient,' into a peculiar people, a separate nation within the nation" (1972: 191). Is one justified in hearing in this passage some resonance from Deuteronomy 14: 2? "For thou art an holy people unto the Lord thy God, and the Lord hath chosen thee to be a peculiar people unto himself, above all nations that are upon the earth." Well, the analogy has of course broken down at that very point. The Chinese are not a chosen people. They have in fact no Almighty God to choose them. In reality they have not wandered the earth for centuries bereft of a home and keeping themselves to themselves in the name of a religious duty. The people who left China centuries ago have few descendants now who think of themselves as Chinese. The Chinese "diaspora," by comparison with the Jewish, is an illusion created by a mere hundred years or so of history. It has no deep roots and may indeed soon fade away. Certainly, we must expect to see "Chinese" survive as the name for a political bloc in Malaysia, and as the label of small ethnic minorities in many other Southeast Asian countries. But there may be no "diaspora" of the Chinese, organized and oriented to China.

Interesting and illuminating as they are, neither "Yunnan" nor "Jews" can in the last analysis help us to a complete understanding of the fate of the Chinese in Southeast Asia. As anthropologists, we know that in trying to study one complex phenomenon from all sides we are forced in the end to acknowledge its uniqueness. Perhaps we shall never succeed in fully understanding the Overseas Chinese, try as we may. But in making the effort we may be able to clear a number of intellectual errors out of the way (some of them may be bound up with our use of "culture"), and with the aid of such salutary cautions as that with which this essay opened we may learn to be critical of the most pleasing of the solutions offered to us.

PART TWO

Chinese Society in Singapore

Immigrants and Associations: Chinese in Nineteenth-Century Singapore

The society built up by Overseas Chinese in Southeast Asia has always been remarkable for its wealth of voluntary associations. In the various historical and sociological studies of Southeast Asian Chinese which have appeared the importance of associations has been duly stressed, although in respect of only two settlements have we been given full treatment of their structure and significance.[1] In this paper I shall consider the associations which Singapore Chinese created and modified in the course of the nineteenth century. Studying this earlier period of Singapore history we can see how the Chinese members of the colonial society adapted their social organization to the conditions of a trading settlement in which, while they often amassed great riches, they were not their own political masters. At the end of the paper I shall consider the Singapore evidence within the wider setting of Southeast Asia and put forward certain general conclusions which may be taken up in other papers on the same theme.

Chinese in Singapore in the Nineteenth Century

When Raffles acquired Singapore for the East India Company in 1819 the Chinese numbered a mere handful in a total population which was itself tiny. By the end of the century the Chinese were more than 70 percent of a population of over a quarter of a million, having begun to outnumber the non-Chinese in the 1840's. The mass coolie traffic developed in earnest about the middle of the century, and Singapore as the main Malayan port of entry took in great numbers of Chinese many of whom remained for some time in the settlement. Certainly, before modern times the Chinese population had a markedly transient character. At the end of

Comparative Studies in Society and History, 3, no. 1 (1960), 25–48. Reprinted in Lloyd A. Fallers, ed., *Immigrants and Associations* (The Hague, 1967), 17–48.

the century about 10 percent of Singapore Chinese were locally born and only a fifth of the total Chinese population was female. During the period we are discussing Singapore Chinese were preponderantly ablebodied men; women, girls, boys, and old men were relatively few in number. The Chinese who found their way overseas were nearly all either peasants or small businessmen and craftsmen from the countryside. To get the numbers of emigrants demanded by the labor market in Southeast Asia the recruiters scoured the rural area; the urban concentrations of poor people were too small to act as adequate reservoirs. From the countryside of Fukien and Kwangtung, Chinese left to find a living overseas— as refugees from official displeasure, as banishees from their local communities, as captives in "clan" wars sold to dealers, as free emigrants seeking their fortune, and as contract coolies.

The organized coolie traffic led Chinese from narrowly defined areas of the homeland to concentrate in particular parts of Malaya. Singapore, however, was not a mining territory, while the plantations played only a small part in its development; as a result it was rarely the final destination of the coolies brought over by recruiters. At the crossroads of Southeast Asia Singapore built up a very heterogeneous population of Chinese. Within this population were found speakers of all the dialects of Fukien and Kwangtung, and on the basis of differences in their spoken language the Chinese in Singapore, as elsewhere, proceeded to organize their social life. Writing of his fellows in the middle of the century a prominent Singapore Chinese (Siah U Chin 1948: 290) divided them into six categories: Hokkien, Teochiu, Malacca Chinese, Cantonese, Hakka, and Hainanese. In 1881 the official census (Straits Settlements 1881) broke down the Chinese population of the settlement in the following manner:

	Males	Females	Total Chinese
Cantonese	9,699	5,154	14,853
Hokkien	23,327	1,654	24,981
Teochiu	20,946	1,698	22,644
Hakka	5,561	609	6,170
Hainanese	8,226	53	8,319
Straits-born	4,513	5,014	9,527
Not stated	259	13	272
TOTAL	72,571	14,195	86,766

The Malacca Chinese referred to by Siah U Chin in 1848 and the Straits-born Chinese enumerated in the censuses between 1881 and 1901 were people otherwise known as Babas. Although not a dialect group in any literal sense, they formed a distinct element of the Chinese population both in respect of their cultural differentiation and their economic and social position. The Malacca Babas were Chinese in their social identity, but in language and some other cultural respects they resembled the Malays among whom they lived. Many of these Babas moved into Singapore on its establishment as a British possession, and there, joined by recruits from the general Chinese population, they continued their distinctive way of life. During the nineteenth century the great dearth of women in the non-Baba section of the Chinese population ensured that a large proportion of those born in the settlement were in fact born into Baba families.

When the Chinese went to Singapore they were in search of a livelihood. They found it in the growing of gambier and pepper, in the practice of labor and crafts which were necessary for the building up and maintenance of the new settlement, and in various forms of trade. For the most part, these economic activities kept Chinese in the town, but some of them established clearings in the wild countryside which was remote from British authority in the early period. When the Chinese population later increased by leaps and bounds and the growing of pepper and gambier ceased to play an important part in Singapore's economy (as it began to do in the 1860's), the role of the agriculturalist in Singapore Chinese society declined. Trade, the pursuit of crafts, and the performance of unskilled labor characterized a largely urban economy.

The commercial economy provided ample opportunities for immigrants to make money, and many of them succeeded handsomely. Immigrants found themselves in a free economy by means of which some of them managed to climb to the top. Throughout the nineteenth century, however, the Malacca Babas, their descendants, and those who had become assimilated to them appear to have maintained a consistently high position in the economic scale. From Siah U Chin's data for 1848 we can see that the "Malacca Babas," as he calls the whole category, were predominantly traders and businessmen and lacked the working-class elements strongly represented in the other dialect groups. The dominance of Baba culture in the nineteenth century was due not simply to the passage of wealth from generation to generation, but also, and perhaps mainly, to the absorption of successful immigrants into Baba society. The poor newcomer in an overwhelmingly male society could hardly find a wife in Singapore; the successful immigrant could secure a wife from among the Straits-born. So preponderant was the influence of the Babas, at least in Western eyes, that as recently as 1913 an observer could regard them "as the most highly educated and the most influential section of the Chinese community in the British possessions . . ." (Shellabear 1913: 52). On the other hand, as time went on the Babas tended also to concentrate on "safe" clerical jobs and withdrew from economic enterprise, so that at the end of the century their status as a whole was in fact declining.

In a society based economically on business and recruited largely from peasant China, social differentiation was geared very closely to the distribution of wealth. Men who made money moved up in the social scale, and those who lost it declined. Except at the end of the century when cultural nationalism promoted studies in Mandarin among a few Chinese, and except for the Babas who went to English schools, little attention was paid to education. Not only was it uncalled for in a political system which did not recruit administrators from among the Chinese, but it was also largely unnecessary, except in a rudimentary form, for the kinds of economic activity in which Chinese engaged. (The imperial examination system of China provided Singapore Chinese with something to gamble on at the end of the century, but it did not attract them to classical studies.[2] Their ambitions were channeled along commercial lines.) The poor immigrant was at a disadvantage in lacking capital, but once he had amassed some he could go ahead without fear that his lack of education would prevent him either from exploiting his economic position fully or from reaping the social benefits of economic success. The power and prestige of the illiterate or half-literate rich man were not challenged by Chinese bearing the stamp of the cultivated gentry.

The men who acquired riches and came to occupy positions of power sought to differentiate themselves in a number of ways from their humbler fellows. In 1869 "a circular was issued by some Chinese requesting their friends to draw a line between the higher and the lower classes of the Chinese community by the wearing of stockings" (Song 1923: 153). Some Singapore Chinese availed themselves of the opportunity to buy imperial degrees when in the last decades of its existence the Manchu dynasty was especially given to raising funds in this manner.[a] Club life and the lavish celebration of weddings, birthdays, and funerals were other means by which the rich could at once display their wealth and validate their status. The speculative nature of the business in which many rich men engaged did not ensure for them a safe place at the top of their society, nor was wealth so regularly and securely transmitted down the generations as to procure a class system based on descent. The class of rich and influential Chinese established itself early in the history of

---

[a] But it would seem that imperial honors were sometimes forced upon Singapore Chinese. Large sums of money were subscribed during the war with France, in some cases because the Singapore Chinese feared reprisals on their families in China. See the *Straits Settlements Government Gazette* [hereafter *SSGG*], 12 Feb. 1886: 131.

Singapore,[b] but it was a class the personnel of which appears to have been subject to constant change.

Certain social correlates of Chinese economic life in Singapore are clear. The individuals and organizations controlling the "pig business" (by which laborers were shipped from China and distributed to the Southeast Asian markets) were well situated to exercise power within the Chinese ranks. The clipping together of riches and social status (with no intermediate qualification), and the reliance by the Singapore authorities on rich Chinese to be spokesmen for their fellows, produced a structure of control in which the relations between employer and employed and between creditor and debtor were likely to be political as well as economic. Moreover, these political and economic relations might be expressed in the setting of voluntary associations, so that various forms of ritual and secular solidarity could enter into the ties between men unequally balanced in wealth and status.

One further aspect of Chinese social organization in Singapore must be considered before we can understand the significance of voluntary associations. The Babas built up a system of family, kinship, and marriage which tied them into a wide network of social relations. Some of the immigrants married into the Baba camp, but for the great mass of the China-born, Chinese family and marriage played a relatively small part in the ordering of their lives. Certainly, the immigrant was not likely to have a wife and children in Singapore. Whatever residential, economic, and political framework he succeeded in fitting himself into he was not likely to find himself mainly in the company of kinsmen. Although men sometimes grouped themselves in voluntary associations on the basis of surnames, the major structural features of Singapore Chinese society were generally remote from kinship.

Secret Societies

One of these structural features was the secret society.[3] In comparison with other matters touching the social life of the Malayan Chinese in the nineteenth century, there is a considerable body of writing on the secret societies, not only because they were important in determining the behavior of Chinese, but also because they offer more dramatic and colorful material than other facets of Chinese social organization. One can scarcely assert that this literature affords us a satisfactory account of the

---

[b] Cf. Raffles's statement in 1822 that the Chinese were roughly divided into three classes: those who gained their living by handicrafts and personal labor, a "higher and more respectable class engaged in mercantile speculations," and cultivators. See Song 1923: 11–12.

secret societies and their role, but at least we may expect to find in it some important clues to their structure, working, and significance.

The society or group of societies known as the Triad was especially associated with the provinces of Fukien and Kwangtung, where by the nineteenth century it had come to play an important part in the political relations between the people and the state (Freedman 1958: 117ff). Emigration to Southeast Asia took it overseas to enjoy a major role in Chinese social life and prove a source of dismay to colonial administrators. It is even possible that after the end of the Taiping period in China the main center of Triad activity lay overseas (cf. Giles 1880: 27). Singapore, at the hub of the region, must have been the scene of many secret society meetings and decisions which affected a wide area.

We may begin with a very brief chronological survey of the data on secret society activity in Singapore. We know that secret societies were established there at a very early date. In an eyewitness account which probably relates to 1824 Abdullah Munshi, Raffles's tutor, gives us a picture of a secret society meeting held in the interior of the island (Hill 1955: chap. 21). By the 1840's the secret societies had won a reputation for lawlessness and were said to number perhaps 10,000 members (Read 1901: 91) when the total Chinese population of the settlement was some 20,000. At this period the "Tean Tay Huey" (that is, the Heaven and Earth Society, an alternative name for the Triad) was thought to be governed by a council of four officers, each of whom represented a "tribe": Amoy (that is, Hokkien), Kheh (Hakka), Teouchoo (Teochiu), and Macao (that is, Cantonese) (Buckley 1902: 365ff). We catch a glimpse of the pervasiveness of the secret societies at this time and of the cleavages within their ranks from a statement made in China by a Chinese who had been in the Straits for many years. "Secret societies have risen up in all the settlements. But they are all emanations of the *Triad Society.*" There were two great societies, the *"hae-shan-hwuy*, 'the sea and land society'; and the *e-ching-hwuy*, 'the righteous rising society.' These two associations are scattered over all the settlements. . . ."[4] As soon as a newcomer arrived in the Straits he was invited to join. If he refused he was at once persecuted. However, the two societies often wrangled, "and if you belong to the one and not to the other, you are equally persecuted" ("Chinese Emigrants" 1833: 230–31).

In 1851 secret society men attacked Chinese Roman Catholics living in the interior, when over five hundred Chinese were said to have been killed,[5] and in 1854 there was a ten days' riot which accounted for some six hundred dead (Read 1901: 92). (J. D. Vaughan [1879: 92–93], writing of the 1854 riot a quarter of a century later, asserted that it was a fight between natives of Fukien and Kwangtung and had nothing to do with the secret societies.) There were further riots in the 1860's. The Governor, Sir Orfeur Cavenagh, and a large section of the European population were in favor of submitting the secret societies to strict control. In the first year of his governorship Cavenagh wrote:

There is no doubt that the Societies do lend themselves to the obstruction of the course of Justice, and it is generally believed that they are ambitious of drawing all criminal cases among their countrymen to their own tribunals. In civil matters their settlement of disputes is looked upon rather with favor than otherwise, and to their apprehensions, their claim to adjust criminal cases is equally well grounded ... Murder and kidnapping are said to be of frequent occurrence in order to remove obnoxious witnesses out of the way, but there is probably some exaggeration in the reported frequency of such crimes. (Straits Settlements 1858–59: 53.)

The only way in which Cavenagh and his colleagues could hold the societies in check when trouble broke out was to swear in their leaders as special constables and parade them up and down, in order, as Cavenagh says with nice irony, "to entice them to take a warm personal interest in the preservation of the peace."[6]

The mounting official resentment over Chinese brawls finally found its way on to the statute book in an ordinance aimed at suppressing dangerous societies which was brought into force in 1869. Under this ordinance began the registration of secret societies.[7] In 1876, the year before he was appointed the first Protector of Chinese, W. A. Pickering (1876: 440) wrote that the registration of the secret societies was a farce because their real leaders kept out of the limelight, but after a little experience in his new office he appeared to believe that the society leaders were generally cooperating with the government and that the system was working well.[8]

In 1879 the official register of dangerous societies showed a total membership of nearly 24,000, the societies appearing individually as follows:[9]

	No. of office-bearers	No. of registered members	Subscribers
Ghee Hin (Hok Kien)	187	4,291	3,380
Ghee Hin (Tie Chew)	45	1,453	1,187
Ghee Hin (Hailam)	60	1,576	1,156
Ghee Hok	304	4,728	3,234
Ghee Sin	61	1,212	972
Ghee Khee Kwang Hok	61	2,331	1,377
Hok Hin	92	3,109	1,575
Kong Fooy Sew	55	1,576	1,026
Song Peh Kwan	40	2,224	1,160
Haisan	19	1,358	821
TOTAL	924	23,858	15,888

In Vaughan's list of the secret societies, which consists of the same as those given in the official register, the name Ghee Hin is extended to the Kong Fooy Sew and the Song Peh Kwan, which are regarded respectively as the Cantonese and Hakka branches of the Ghee Hin. Vaughan (1879: 108) says further that the Ghee Hok, Ghee Khee Kwang Hok, Hok Hin, and Ghee Sin were branches of the Ghee Hin but now at odds with it. Pickering's Annual Report for 1878[10] supports the thesis that all the societies (with the apparent exception of the Hai San) were organizationally connected, for he writes: "In cases when the headmen of a lodge offend against the general laws of the Ghee Hin (or mother) Society, they are tried at the Rochore Kong-si house, before a general council of the nine branches. . . ." In 1881, when the total male Chinese population of the settlement was 72,571, the secret society books showed 33,103 members, of whom 16,195 had actually paid their subscriptions in that year. It is clear from this and other evidence that the influence of the societies was widespread.

An effect of registration and supervision by the police and the Chinese Protectorate was to keep the headmen in check and to prevent quarrels between societies from being realized to the full. At the same time the superimposition of an outside power weakened the headmen vis-à-vis their followers and sometimes affected their ability to keep order within their own ranks.[11] Increasing governmental control of the societies curbed what seemed to be their undesirable activities but loosened their internal disciplinary force, so that registration was not entirely successful. Authority had to be taken to suppress a dangerous society (in 1882 the Hai San met this fate), while locally born Chinese were forbidden to be members of the societies because the weapon of banishment could not be used against them.

So-called Friendly Societies also began to be registered as dangerous societies because of their obnoxious activities; some of them were later suppressed, as were several of the secret societies. Difficulties were brought to a head in 1887 when Pickering was attacked by a man said to have been incited by the headman of the Ghee Hok society. Pickering now thought the time had come to bring about a gradual abolition of the societies,[12] and on the first day of 1890 a new ordinance came into force which suppressed them altogether. From this date the secret societies began to decline to the status of small-scale criminal organizations as we have known them in more recent times. Once removed from the political plane they became, insofar as they survived, small groups without a larger framework of organization. (Cf. Comber 1956: 155.) At 1890, therefore, we may draw a line across the chronological narrative and try to analyze the evidence on the secret societies during the first half of Singapore's history.

In the first place, it is apparent that although all, or nearly all, the secret societies in Singapore continued to operate under the anti-Manchu banner which had furnished them with their *raison d'être* in China, and retained an elaborate ritual of initiation which enshrined this political purpose, their activities overseas—except when they supported rebellion in the homeland[13]—were not really concerned with anti-dynastic policy. When the Manchus were finally overthrown in the twentieth century the secret societies continued underground in Singapore much as before; and we may argue for the nineteenth century that once the anti-dynastic apparatus was moved overseas it adapted itself to new aims. These aims included the assertion of the independence of the Chinese in territory under the control of "foreigners" and the building up of some kind of community organization to meet the needs of new settlements.

While the anti-Manchu aspect of the secret societies in Singapore was unimportant, their general political aspect was not, for they were for a long time the means by which control was exercised within the Chinese fold by Chinese and a way of regulating the contact between the mass of the Chinese and the "alien" administration. We should remember that, although clandestine in China, where to belong to one was treason, the secret societies were not really secret in Singapore (except in a ritual sense) until the suppression of 1890. The leaders were usually well known to the authorities. Failing to establish an administrative system by which the Chinese were brought under British control by orthodox means, the Singapore authorities found themselves making use of the secret societies as an instrument of government.

From the foundation of British Singapore in 1819 until 1826 the Chinese were put under the jurisdiction of a *Capitan China*; Raffles set out to induce the non-Malay settlers to police themselves under the supervision of the authorities (Song 1923: 7–8, 13). But the system was short-lived; the Chinese were left largely to their own devices, and from 1826 until the establishment of the Chinese Protectorate in 1877 there seems to have been no official institution for administrative contact between the government and the Chinese.

There were of course points of contact between the Chinese and the Europeans on both commercial and political grounds. The Singapore Chamber of Commerce was from its creation in 1837 until 1860 open to Chinese. (The Chinese Chamber did not come into existence until 1906.) It is clear that business made a number of Europeans familiar with Chinese affairs. An eminent Chinese businessman was made a member of the

Legislative Council in 1869 and a few years later an extraordinary member of the Executive Council; during most of the years which followed this man's death in 1880 a Chinese member sat in the Legislative Council. The first Chinese Municipal Commissioner was appointed in 1870. A number of Chinese were appointed as justices of the peace and as jurors. Throughout the century the revenue farms provided another important connection between the administration and the Chinese.[14]

But despite these many contacts there was no recognized system for consulting Chinese opinion at large or passing down information in a systematic fashion. Three rich Chinese appear to have acted during much of the century as unofficial "Captains of the Chinese." "Though possessed of no legal power, they exercised very considerable control over their countrymen, and on several occasions rendered important services to Government" (Song 1923: 174). Yet certainly by the 1870's the Europeans were greatly dissatisfied with the independence of the Chinese. Proposals were several times made to put the Chinese under recognized leaders who would be responsible for them (*ibid.*: 166, 174; Pickering 1876: 443). By the time the Chinese Protectorate came into being (1877) the Chinese population of Singapore had had over half a century in which to build up political institutions of their own devising, and these institutions seem to have been very intimately connected with the secret societies.

Looked at from one point of view the secret societies were criminal gangs rather than what we are used to thinking of as political groupings. Mills's description (1925: 203) of the secret society as a Pirates' and Robbers' Cooperative Association could be supported by much evidence of piracy, armed robbery, assault, and murder. It is possible that some of the societies were at an early date what all of them were later to become: criminal groups whose overriding aim was robbery and extortion. But the majority of them seem to have had a weightier significance. They set up mechanisms of "law" within the Chinese community. They provided immigrants with an organized group in which they could find a place for themselves in the absence of traditional territorial and kinship systems. They distributed political power among the Chinese in such a way as to harmonize with the economic system which grew up.

Before we go any further, we must satisfy ourselves about the nature of the units which are spoken of in the literature as societies, lodges, and branches, and we must examine the correspondence between these units and other types of alignment in Singapore Chinese society. All or nearly all the secret societies in Malaya about which we know employed some version of the Triad ritual and were anti-Manchu.[c] Historically, that is to

[c] Comber (1959: 147) asserts that the Triad society was the "common ancestor of all Chinese secret societies in Malaya . . ." Another view was put forward by Wynne (1941).

say, they were closely connected. But there seems to be no reason to suppose that there was ever a single secret society in Malaya with which all other societies were organizationally linked.[d] At any given point in time some of them might be banded together, but the principles of alignment do not seem to have been constant.

As far as Singapore itself is concerned, the Ghee Hin group of societies appear to have been part of one organization for a considerable time. In 1872 a house was bought to serve as the "mother temple" (Ward and Sterling 1925: 13ff); here the "nine branches" of the Ghee Hin (that is, all the societies listed in the register for 1879 less the Hai San) foregathered for twice-yearly rituals (Pickering 1879: 2). The temple remained the center of Ghee Hin life until the suppression of 1890, for, although there was often conflict between the "branches,"[15] they were ritually bound together in respect of the "temple," where in addition the settlement of their differences was supposed to take place and in fact was sometimes achieved.

What was the basis of the rivalry between the various societies composing the Ghee Hin group? Five of the nine societies in the list for 1879 were apparently single-dialect organizations: Hokkien, Teochiu, Hainanese, Cantonese, and Hakka. But these five societies accounted for only about a half of both the registered and the subscribing members. The other half of the Ghee Hin membership was distributed over four societies which were probably each heterogeneous in dialect. In 1887, when the Teochiu Ghee Hin was no longer legally alive, the four remaining dialect societies numbered some half of the total Ghee Hin membership and somewhat over half of the subscribing membership. The lines between the various Ghee Hin societies, then, were not simply the lines between dialect groups. We might suspect that when members of one dialect group appeared in two or more societies, those in one society in fact belonged to a particular subdivision of the dialect group, so that a correspondence was maintained between the two kinds of alignment. But there appears to be no evidence which suggests this; the destruction of the secret society records in 1889–90 may prevent us from ever knowing the facts.

Yet it is more plausible on sociological grounds to argue that the two

---

Wynne's thesis was that there were two groups of secret societies, always at loggerheads, one deriving from the Triad, the other from the "Han League." The fact that the Hai San society stood apart from the Ghee Hin group for a long period may perhaps mean that some variation of Wynne's thesis may prove on further investigation to be valid.

[d] Comber (1959: 149) seems to think that the various societies were coordinated, for he speaks of the Triad society in Malaya and Thailand having a headquarters which "only moved to Singapore about 1850."

kinds of alignment cut across each other.[e] For although there was violence enough, there might well have been more if societies had always
been ranged against one another in such a way that there were few ties
between members of different societies. Writing in the 1870's, Vaughan
(1879: 93) asserted that in several of the riots the opposing parties were
not secret societies but provincial or dialect groups. "The solemn obligations of the secret societies were cast to the winds. . . ." If opposition
could switch from one principle of alignment to another, there was less
risk that Chinese society in the settlement would break into segments
irreconcilably hostile to one another.

If dialect affiliations were not unambiguous pointers to membership,
what determined that a man should join this and not that society? It
may be that some societies exercised territorial jurisdiction, so that a
man's residence brought him within the sphere of control of a particular
society. And because there was a tendency for people of the same dialect
group to cluster in special parts of the town,[f] some societies may have
been able to establish themselves on the dual basis of locality in Singapore and place of origin in China. On the other hand, in the first year
of his Protectorship Pickering seems to imply that the individual societies
were dispersed in their membership, for he reports that in the new registers "the members have been entered according to districts under the
Headman in charge of each district. . . ."[16] There may have been occupational and commercial homogeneity in society membership, societies
sometimes grouping men according to their economic interests, but there
could have been no neat and regular division of the societies by the economic role of their members.[17]

Obscure as these matters are, the general significance of the societies
for the steady stream of newcomers from China is quite clear. His secret
society provided the *sīn-khĕq*, the greenhorn, with something equivalent
to a local community. It furnished him with assistance when he was in
need, organized funerals, defended his rights, and established a focus for
loyalty in a social setting far removed in its structure from the kind of
society he had known at home.

The means by which societies maintained their position were of course
often poorly regarded by the non-Chinese observer, but it is difficult for
us to see how far the immigrant ensconced within a society looked with
disapproval on the "protection rackets" and exploitation of brothels and

[e] There is one fact on record (Song 1923: 175) which shows that even the gulf between
the Hai San and the Ghee Hin group could be spanned by one dialect group. In 1874
a street fight took place which arose from a dispute between the two as to which should
carry the coffin of a man who had a son in either camp.
[f] This pattern is still discernible at the present day in the old quarter of the town. See
Hodder 1953.

opium dens. Some societies at some time certainly oppressed the newcomers. Societies appear to have been intimately concerned with the importation of coolies in the "pig business" in the latter part of the century; and the thugs used as "police" and the barbarous practices often employed in disposing of the newly arrived labor could hardly have commended themselves to those who suffered from them.

The sanctions at the disposal of the societies for coercing men into membership and holding them to the rules once they had joined seem to have been drastic. Violence (sometimes assassination) was a real threat. But physical force and self-interest were evidently not the only means of ensuring adherence and loyalty. In the records of the Triad initiation ritual which have come down to us[18] we find good evidence of the religious pressures working to produce a faithful brotherhood. Two opposite and equally incomplete views of the Triad ritual have been held by Westerners. Ward and Stirling thought that the ritual was essentially apolitical and mystical (Ward and Sterling 1925: iii). Purcell speaks of the "wealth of mumbo-jumbo with which these hoodlums and gangsters surrounded their conspiracy to suck the life-blood of the community" (Purcell 1948: 167). Perhaps the elaborate esoteric ritual was so much empty noise and movement to the ruffians who, in the days after suppression, formed the membership of the Triad societies. Doubtless too, the moral and mystical significance of the ritual was at times of great importance. But the ritual of initiation as we know it from the literature and as we know it was practiced—Abdullah Munshi witnessed an initiation in 1824 and Pickering saw a similar rite in its entirety in 1878—was also clearly a religious means of forging loyalty to a political group. The ritual practiced in Singapore was not of course devised for overseas circumstances; it was in essentials the same ritual as that used by the Triad societies in Fukien and Kwangtung. But while its elements were not always adapted to local conditions, its creation of a sworn brotherhood and the repetition of solemn oaths served to bind men together in ritually sanctioned solidarity.

Politically the secret societies broke up the Chinese population into groups which furnished their members with economic and "legal" facilities. Within this framework certain men raised themselves to positions of power, perhaps making use of the societies to aid them in their amassing of riches, probably converting wealth into prestige by their exercise of leadership. Miss Campbell cites the case of a Penang secret society headman who was a powerful broker and took charge of all the coolies landed in Penang until they were disposed of. "It is no doubt true that the Sinkhehs were unaware of the existence of any other institution of Government in the Straits Settlements" (Campbell 1923: 8). A fluid and commercialized society threw up men who united political and economic power by controlling their fellows through the secret societies and acting as their representatives to the government. By 1889 the unruliness of the Chinese in the Straits Settlements had grown to a point where the authorities would no longer tolerate it; then the secret societies really became secret by being put down. From "communities" the societies changed into purely criminal associations. New forms of grouping and leadership emerged among the Chinese, while the government came to make its influence more directly felt.

Voluntary Associations

The secret societies were sometimes more than voluntary associations. They were not always voluntary and they covered a far greater area of the social lives of their members than is implied in the word "association." Alongside the secret societies there existed voluntary associations of a less ambiguous kind. Two of the principles on which these associations rested sprang directly from the nature of the society from which the immigrants had come. Solidarity could be created or strengthened overseas between men bearing the same surname and between men originating from the same area or dialect group in China.

To some extent at least, as we have seen, the dialect principle determined the inner division of the secret societies; outside the secret societies this principle served to construct a number of associations which, in common with those recruiting on the basis of surname, were often regarded by the Singapore authorities as harmless benevolent organizations. On the other hand, the government was aware that voluntary associations of this kind were sometimes powerful enough to make trouble. A decade before the suppression of the secret societies Pickering wrote that even if these societies were done away with, "there are several large clans in this Colony, which would readily take the place of the present secret societies, and would perhaps cause even more trouble." [19]

In an account written by an anonymous Straits Chinese nine years after the banning of the secret societies we learn that each dialect group in Singapore maintained one or more organizations based, at least in name, on religious worship. The Hokkien people were grouped in one large body centered on a famous temple, but divided the town into five wards in connection with the annual and triennial ceremonies. The Teochiu people were organized in a similar way. The Hainanese were also grouped in a single organization, but both the Cantonese and Hakka were broken up into a number of bodies according to territorial divisions in the homeland (A Straits Chinese 1899: 43ff).

From the same source we can extract a Chinese view of the surname associations of the nineteenth century. "Taking advantage of the clannish spirit inherent in the Chinese race, . . . powerful families . . . form themselves into organisations for mutual protection and aggrandisement. So influential were these associations that even during the existence of the dreaded Triads they were able to hold their own in their struggle with each other." These surname associations were formed for the worship of ancestors and for rendering mutual assistance at weddings and funerals, but they interfered in quarrels and lawsuits and opposed government measures. Although regarded as friendly societies, both dialect group and surname associations were really obstructive (*ibid.*: 44–45).

In a number of respects the associations which were recruited on the basis of like surname or territorial origin in China resembled the secret societies. But, unlike the secret societies, the associations continued legally to exist after 1890. From this date it was the associations which provided the major framework of "mutual aid" for Singapore Chinese. Ceasing to be overshadowed by the secret societies, they became the only "community" organizations which Singapore Chinese could devise.

A man was free to belong to both kinds of association, surname and territorial or dialect. Why did they emerge in this form? The territorial association was not invented overseas. The "guild" of fellow provincials living in a strange part of China was called by the same name as that applied to territorial and dialect associations in Singapore: *hui-kuan*. In foreign parts the Chinese grouped themselves on the basis of much smaller territorial units than in China itself, but the overseas groupings were essentially of the same order as those found in the large towns of China, where people from other areas congregated for trade, work, or, in the case of the capital, examination-taking. To some extent the groupings by territorial origin corresponded to a grouping by economic interests; this was so both in China and overseas. A pattern of economic specialization by dialect group was apparent from the early days of Singapore Chinese history, and it clearly persisted in part through the nineteenth century.[20] But whether or not territorial and dialect associations functioned directly as traders' or workers' organizations, they were economically important in providing financial help to their members, especially at times of bereavement and in cases of destitution. They acted as what we should nowadays call social service agencies, providing shelter, religious worship, and fellowship for men thrown down in a strange environment.

It is not so immediately understandable why the surname principle should have been brought into play. Yet if we consider the role of the surname in the homeland society, we can see that it could enter upon the Malayan scene in two different ways. First, if in fact any association was built on the basis of membership of a single-lineage village in China, then what from one point of view was a territorial association was at the same time a surname association. Second, the structuring of the homeland society by the lineage system and the dependence of an important part of the religious system on agnatic grouping clearly induced Overseas Chinese to use surnames as bases for cooperation, both secular and religious. In reality, because no doubt of its very heterogeneous Chinese population, Singapore does not seem to have produced many surname-village associations in its earlier period. The surname associations which grew up recruited from among men coming from a wide area of country in the homeland, and the agnation implied by like surname was more general in its nature than the agnation inherent in the lineage structure of local communities in China. But just as at home similarity of surname could link lineages together in wider patrilineal groupings, so in Singapore it could bring together men who came from widely separated communities in China.

Under the new law which suppressed the secret societies the voluntary associations were allowed to continue provided that they were registered. By the end of the century 68 associations were registered in Singapore, all but 13 of them probably being Chinese; the 51 associations for which membership figures are given total over 13,000. In addition, there were at least 31 Chinese associations on the list of bodies so innocuous as to be "exempted from registration" (Straits Settlements 1900: 318ff). In this period the territorial associations were probably the main controlling bodies of ordinary Chinese in Singapore. They sometimes behaved like the old secret societies and incurred the displeasure of the government in arrogating to themselves the right to try crimes. (See, for example, Straits Settlements 1898: 224.)

The purposes of territorial and surname associations were expressed largely in welfare and ritual terms. Whatever direct intervention they may have made into the business or labor world, their functions were not generally intended to be of this order. That is why there existed alongside these voluntary associations bodies which determined their membership by the nature of their economic aims. The account of Singapore associations by the anonymous Straits Chinese mentions industrial guilds and commercial organizations.

"Carpenters, builders, blacksmiths, tanners, shoemakers, tailors, and barbers organize themselves each under its exclusive guild and its own patron-god" (A Straits Chinese 1899: 45). The guilds furnished mutual aid and set out rules for the training of apprentices and for regulating the wages of trained men. The writer says that the best known of the commercial organizations were the Gambier and Pepper Society and the Sago Dealers' and Pineapple Preservers' guilds, the main aim of the traders being to prevent "illegal" sales by planters in their debt. There is also mention of a recently expired guild of passage-brokers which had attempted to keep up the price of fares. Bodies of this kind tried to restrict particular fields of activity to their members and to maintain economic order within these fields. The strength of the economic controls so set up clearly disturbed British administrators, who thought them unfair. Of the Gambier and Pepper Society the Protector of Chinese wrote that it "arrogated to itself the combined powers of a ruling sovereign and the Supreme Court in that it collected revenue on imports by means of custom officers, imposed fines and ordered confiscations after enquiry."[21]

The author of "Local Chinese Social Organizations" also refers to money loan associations and friendly societies (A Straits Chinese 1899: 45). The former were of a kind well known from the literature on China (e.g. Lien-shang Yang 1952: 72f). They were small ad hoc groupings of people for short-term credit and investment. Friendly societies assumed welfare functions also performed by territorial, surname, and economic associations: primarily the provision of death and funeral benefits. Friendly societies, at least in form, were indifferent to the surname and territorial origin of their members, although the social ties which preceded their formation and the limits naturally imposed on the area of recruitment doubtless produced some significant degree of homogeneity in the membership. (Cf. Song 1923: 29, 264.)

The nameless Straits Chinese writer makes no mention of the social clubs which were already a fairly important kind of grouping among the Chinese in Singapore. These clubs were probably modeled on those maintained by the Europeans. While they were not likely to embrace more than a small part of the Chinese population, they served to add to the complexity of its organization. In the eyes of the administrators the clubs were perhaps most significant as scenes of gambling (Straits Settlements 1897: 285).

"A Straits Chinese" concludes his article with a general reflection on the place of associations in Singapore Chinese life. In China the care of the sick and the indigent and the provision of education were "usually left to the family, the guilds there being merely supplemental in their operations. In the different conditions under which the Chinese live in this colony, these organizations should therefore rightfully supply the shortcomings of their family arrangements" (*ibid*.: 47). That is to say, the structure of Chinese society having changed overseas, essential welfare functions had to be transferred from one type of grouping to another. When the secret societies flourished these functions together with the political organization of the Chinese were left mainly in their hands. After 1890 the network of voluntary associations gradually expanded, providing a loosely knit Chinese society with some means of political coordination and a measure of social insurance. From this time, in fact, we begin to see Singapore Chinese society in its modern form.

Discussion

By confining our attention to the nineteenth century we are able to study Chinese associations before they were affected by modern political and cultural developments. We can see them more clearly in relation to the conditions of an immigrant settlement in which the Chinese were ultimately controlled by a colonial authority.

The Chinese in Singapore were overwhelmingly composed of immigrants throughout the nineteenth century, and in this fact we look for our first clue to the importance of associations. When immigrants are thrown down in a strange setting where they must make their social life among themselves, they are likely to divide into units which express the solidarity of homeland ties. The village, the county, the prefecture, and the dialect area provided overseas Chinese with lines along which to organize themselves. On these lines they constructed their *Landsmannschaften*. Dialect grouping became the major frame of organization, but an immigrant might belong to a territorial association which mediated his ties with the dialect association which stood above it. Instead of being an anonymous individual the immigrant was organizationally a man from, say, such and such a county and then from such and such a dialect area. Grouping themselves in this fashion the Chinese in Singapore established their rights vis-à-vis one another and attempted to deal with non-Chinese authority.

Dialect grouping was everywhere in Southeast Asia a framework for Chinese social organization, for it was a "natural" way of differentiating immigrants into units which defined and protected rights. In Indo-China the external political authority actually seized upon the dialect grouping of the Chinese as a means of formal control. The French took over from the Annamite imperial government the system of grouping Chinese in *bang*. Under the French the Chinese in every province were normally grouped in *congrégations* according to their dialect, the headquarters of each *congrégation* being in the provincial capital. The system was political, fiscal, and judicial. The heads of the *congrégations* helped in the assessment and gathering of taxes, in the policing of their members, in the regulation of their disputes, and in the dealings between their members and the administration.[22] Elsewhere in the region dialect grouping was less formal, but at least in the earlier phase of settlement it always placed the individual immigrant in such a way that there was a small group which claimed his loyalty and attached him to the wider society.

The surname associations of the Chinese in Singapore did not necessarily cut across territorial and dialect associations; they usually restricted their membership to men from particular areas in China. The surname became the basis for formal associations in Singapore because it was in fact the only way in which large numbers of kinsmen could be brought together; the ideology of agnatic kinship remained important, while the kinship arrangements of the homeland could not be reproduced overseas.

After the suppression of the secret societies in 1890, territorial-dialect and surname associations emerged clearly among the Chinese in Singapore. They did so precisely because the solidarities which they enshrined were not sufficiently expressed in the other arrangements of social life. The secret societies had gone (at least as far as the mass of the Chinese were concerned); men originating from the same parts of southeastern China were often dispersed in Singapore; people of the same surname were not likely to live near one another; mobility in economic life had made it less usual for men of like origin or surname to work or trade together; the solidarities of origin and surname were not sufficiently caught up in the run of ordinary social life. From these conditions flowed the formal associations based on territory or dialect and surname. If we compare the situation in Singapore with that in Sarawak we see how the formal associations fail to emerge when the solidarities to which they are devoted are otherwise expressed.

In his study of the Chinese in Sarawak in modern times T'ien (1953) makes a basic distinction between the social organization of the rural and the town-dwelling Chinese. In the countryside social and economic relations are based mainly upon "clanship," that is, identity of surname (p. 21), and there is a tendency for people of the same surname and deriving from the same locality in China to cluster together (p. 31). Apart from, as T'ien put it, enjoying an irreducible value of its own, "clanship" in the rural area is the framework on which economic relations are hung. The rubber smallholders, permanently in need of credit, are tied to shopkeepers, who are to a very great extent their fellow "clansmen" (pp. 33–45).

In the countryside people in one area tend to be of the same dialect group. In the town, on the other hand, there is a multiplicity of dialect groups, and there we see the emergence of a close relationship between dialect group (or territorial origin) and economic pursuit (pp. 45−57). Not only is there a close correspondence between the type of business or occupation engaged in and dialect group, but in the all-important rubber-dealing business, for example, different dialect groups can be shown to cluster at different levels in the hierarchy, so that dialect groups are differentiated economically both in type and status (pp. 54−68).

Voluntary associations appear in this general setting, but they differ significantly from those of Singapore. In the Sarawak countryside surname ties are implemented in everyday life, economic and otherwise. In the town, since there is a tendency for particular surnames to predominate in each group (pp. 17−18) and there is a close relationship between dialect group and economic life, formal expressions of the surname tie appear in associations which are not specifically concerned with surname solidarity. In 1947 there were only five surname associations among 156 Chinese associations in Sarawak (pp. 10, 24). As T'ien shows, in the majority of these associations there is a close interweaving of solidarities and shared interest on the basis of both provenance and occupation. "As we have seen there is no way of differentiating sharply between associations based upon shared dialect, shared locality, shared clanship, or even, as a rule, shared occupation. All these primary social relationships tend to overlap, so that many of the members of an Association organised on the basis, say, of locality, may be expected to be related also by clanship, and most of them will also share the same occupation. Obviously, too, they will be speakers of the same dialect" (p. 19). If we take Sarawak as the model of a simple and relatively small-scale overseas settlement, we may assume that in their earliest phase the Singapore Chinese bound all their solidarities together in a similar fashion, the secret society acting as the knot. In later times increasing complexity and growth of scale forced individual principles of grouping to crystalize in different types of association. Later Singapore is presumably the model of the most developed form of immigrant Chinese settlement in Southeast Asia. In contemporary Singapore the network of territorial-dialect and surname associations can be shown to be relatively independent of economic groupings and to some extent of political groupings (see Freedman 1957a: 92ff).

Through most of the nineteenth century Singapore Chinese were dominated by the secret societies. Why did the internal control of the Chinese community take this form? Perhaps we can approach this question best by looking at the evidence on the Chinese in West Borneo (see Groot 1885, Schlegel 1885, B. E. Ward 1954b, and Purcell 1951: 489−94). In this area we find Overseas Chinese setting up a self-contained political system modeled fairly closely on the homeland pattern; secret societies apparently came into being among the Chinese here only when this political system was destroyed.

When the Dutch established their control over the Malay principalities in West Borneo in the nineteenth century there had for long existed independent Chinese local communities, which are referred to in the literature by the Hokkien name of *kongsi*. Only one of these *kongsi* survived the Dutch conquest of 1854; this was the Lanfong *kongsi* over which the Dutch allowed its own chief to rule until 1884 (Groot 1885: 1–2). The Lanfong *kongsi* had been founded in Mandor in the late eighteenth century by a Hakka who had emigrated to the gold lands of Pontianak, taking with him over a hundred kinsmen.

Although de Groot is at pains to stress the basic similarity between the *kongsi* and the Chinese village community from which its members derived, the Borneo local settlement was much more complex than the village at home. The Lanfong annals say that its members numbered 20,000 at the end of the eighteenth century (*ibid*.: 21), while at the beginning of the nineteenth century it could put 6,000 fighting men in the field (Purcell 1951: 491). The Lanfong *kongsi* appears to have been organized at three territorial levels: the *kongsi* as a whole, the district, and the settlement. There seem to have been eight districts, including the headquarters district, when the *kongsi* was at its widest. Before the advent of the Dutch each district had a complement of four officials. The men in each settlement elected their local officers, who in turn elected the district and *kongsi* officers (B. E. Ward 1954b: 365ff). The settlement enjoyed autonomy in the regulation of disputes among its members and in respect of certain minor offenses.

When the Dutch assumed direct control of the Lanfong *kongsi* in 1884 they encountered great resistance, as they had done earlier when the other *kongsi* had been destroyed. De Groot (1885: 172–93) concludes his monograph with some pertinent thoughts on the relation between the *kongsi* and the troublesome secret societies with which other writers had linked them. His thesis in brief is that if immigrant Chinese are not allowed to exercise some measure of political independence, secret societies will spring up. When the *kongsi* in West Borneo were put down secret societies emerged; they had not been heard of before. If the historical facts are correct, we may conclude that secret societies were likely to appear only when the Chinese were faced with a challenge to their control of their own affairs. The "challenge" may of course need to be loosely interpreted, because it may not amount to more than the relatively mild interference of an authority trying to maintain public order. (De Groot's remarks [p. 177] on the emergence of secret societies in the Straits Settlements from *kongsi* which had been suppressed by the British are wide of the mark.) Let us say that secret societies were a response to external government.

It then becomes easier to understand why the Triad flourished in Southeast Asia when anti-Manchu sentiment was hardly relevant to the local situation. The Triad was an instrument forged in China to oppose central government; it was a rebellious and not a revolutionary movement (although it came later to be linked with the republican overthrow of the empire). It expressed a solidarity of opposition to the state which cut across the opposition between communities. (See Freedman 1958: 119ff.) In Singapore the constituent units of Chinese society were not local communities but rather dialect groups; these groups opposed one another and yet were linked together in the face of the external authority. The Ghee Hin group of societies in Singapore were ritually connected and yet fought bitterly among themselves. Their determination to settle accounts in their own way was an aspect of their unity against colonial claims to rule them.[g] Moreover, secret society alignment did not exactly coincide with dialect grouping,[h] so that overlapping ties were likely to reinforce the solidarity of the Chinese vis-à-vis the outer world even as they temporarily weakened a dialect group or secret society by distracting the loyalty of some of its members.

The secret societies were able to keep their hold on large numbers of Chinese in Singapore because of the constant flow of immigration. In this immigration the secret societies to some extent participated, because their leaders were sometimes principals in the "pig business." The poverty-stricken newcomer without kinsmen or protectors was peculiarly subject to a discipline which rested not only on the exercise of force but also on appeals to primary loyalties and ritual sanctions. Furthermore, while it may be true that many "respectable" Chinese in Singapore held themselves aloof from secret society activities, the very principles of status in a commercial society drew rich men on to validate and exert their authority within the institutions which dominated social life. At home in Fukien and Kwangtung rich merchants put their sons into the public examinations in order to turn them into gentlemen and officers of the state;[23] money could be converted into political strength and the high social status which flowed directly from ties with the bureaucracy. In Singapore rich men might sometimes dress themselves up in the (purchased) robes of a mandarin, but in fact the marks of the cultivated gentry of China were largely irrelevant to the local system of stratifica-

---

[g] Skinner (1957: 141) puts great emphasis on the "divisive force" of the secret societies in Thailand; I am suggesting that there is another, and opposite, aspect of secret society conflict.

[h] Cf. *ibid*.: "Membership was almost exclusively along speech-group lines. . . ."

tion. Money was turned into political power by being invested in relations with Europeans (which required no education) and with humbler Chinese who could be controlled by a mixture of protection and thuggery.

The most general conclusion from this analysis is that in the study of Chinese associations in Southeast Asia—and perhaps also in other parts of the Chinese diaspora—we are likely to find two major regularities. First, the associations which in a small-scale and relatively undeveloped settlement express social, economic, and political links in an undifferentiated form tend, as the scale and complexity of the society increase, to separate into a network of associations which are comparatively specialized in their functions and the kinds of solidarity they express. Second, secret societies came into being in the pre-modern era as a means both of insulating the Chinese from outside interference, and of balancing the relations between the segments of a relatively closed Chinese community.

Chinese Kinship and
Marriage in Early Singapore

When the history of Chinese social institutions in Malaya comes to be written it will, I suspect, be especially difficult to construct a picture of the life associated with the domestic family and ties based upon common descent and marriage. The sources of material on these matters are likely to be very limited, at least in regard to the nineteenth century. Yet, as a social anthropologist I shall draw attention to a number of facts drawn from published material on nineteenth-century Singapore, hoping to show that there are some interesting problems in the analysis of the Chinese kinship institutions of the period and that, however hard it may be to come by the data, a worthwhile task awaits the historian with some sociological insight.

It will be useful to begin by considering a section of the Chinese population which, because it was demographically balanced and relatively settled in Singapore, needed to build up a local system of family and marriage. The Baba Chinese of Malaya sprang from unions between Chinese men and Malaysian (probably non-Muslim) women.[a] As a result of these unions there grew up, first in Malacca and later in other parts of the Peninsula, a Malayized form of Chinese culture which marked out a distinct part of the Chinese population.[1] When Singapore was founded as a British settlement in 1819 Babas were among its first inhabitants, and they occupied throughout the nineteenth century a prominent position in local Chinese society, maintaining leadership within it by virtue of their commercial success and by absorbing ambitious immigrants from China into their ranks.[b] Owing to the constant flow of newcomers, the Babas

Journal of Southeast Asian History, 3, no. 2 (1962), 65–73.

[a] The name Baba is Malay, being written in Chinese with a specially made up character. The women of the Babas were known as *nyonya(h)*, also a word of non-Chinese origin.

[b] As recently as 1913 a Western observer of the Babas in the Straits Settlements (Shellabear 1913) could regard them as the "most highly educated and the most influential section

were in a minority. In the last decades of the nineteenth century they probably formed about 10 percent of the total Chinese population of Singapore.*c*

Among the early immigrants there were very few women, so that nearly all the Chinese born in Singapore in the first part of the nineteenth century and a large proportion of those born there in the later part of the century were Babas by birth. Of the marriage system which the Babas developed we are able to gather a few hints. It was to a considerable extent a system in which bridegrooms went to live in the houses of their wives' parents. In technical language, the virilocal system of the Chinese homeland (in which brides normally took up residence in their husbands' houses) was partly replaced among the Babas by an uxorilocal system. A description of a Singapore Chinese wedding in 1835 (Tracy 1836) tells of the nuptials of a daughter of one of the principal merchants in the settlement; it was evidently an uxorilocal marriage. Thirty-five years later we find a general account of Chinese marriage customs in the Straits, according to which parents tried to marry their daughters off when they reached the age of fifteen, commissioning a friend or relative to act as go-between; if when the horoscopes were exchanged they agreed, "the interested parties hold a consultation to ascertain whether the bridegroom is to take his bride home, which is called *China bo*, . . . or to go in her home, called *Chin choe*; the latter mode is generally adopted by 'Babas' whose parents are dead or by Chinamen whose relatives are in China, for by this arrangement the bride's parents have to do everything for the bridegroom" (Minchin 1870). The expression *China-bo* is evidently composed of the Malay word *China* and the Hokkien word *bò*, meaning wife. *Chin-choe* is the Hokkien term (*cìn-cuĕ*) for a form of marriage in which the husband goes to reside with his wife's people without prejudicing his rights as father of his future children.[2]

---

of the Chinese community. . ." (p. 52). Shellabear says (p. 51) that Baba Malay was the business language of Singapore, Penang, and the Federated Malay States. Some idea of the extent to which Baba culture was dominant at this period may be gathered from the fact that when in 1906 discussions took place in the Hokkien Temple in Singapore on the reform of religious festivals, Baba terms were apparently used. The seventh moon masses were referred to as *sembayang hantu*, a Malayism which would have been unthinkable in more modern times in any gathering other than one composed only of Babas. See Song 1923: 407ff.

c In the 1881 census (Straits Settlements 1881) there were 4,513 "Straits-born" men in a total Chinese male population of 72,571 and 5,014 "Straits-born" women in a total Chinese female population of 14,195. Siah 1848: 290 shows 1,000 "Malacca Chinese (descendants of Hokien immigrants)" as against 9,000 Hokkiens, 19,000 Teochius, 6,000 Cantonese, 4,000 Hakkas, and 700 Hainanese; the figures are of gainfully occupied men only, but they still seem to underestimate the size of the Baba component, Siah was himself a Teochiu.

Uxorilocal marriage has persisted to the present time as a common form of marriage among the "Straits-born" Chinese. The children of such unions take their father's surname and inherit property from him in the normal way, but they are raised mainly among their matrilateral kin (people related to them on their mother's side) and in houses which tend to pass down the generations through women. The Babas did not, of course, invent the institution of *cìn-cuĕ*; the term is genuinely Chinese; but they made greater use of it than their forebears in China. It seems likely that the widespread practice of uxorilocal marriage among the Babas had its origin in the frequent marriage of their daughters to immigrants from China with no home of their own; but why the institution continued to flourish when the Babas married largely within their own ranks is a problem which will be answered only when we have a proper study of the Baba way of life.

The wedding practices and ceremonies as they developed in Baba hands remained manifestly Chinese, although carried out largely in a foreign language and augmented by a number of features peculiar to the Straits. (According to Minchin [1870: 85], nearly 80 percent of the Singapore and Malacca Babas were unable to speak Chinese properly. "It is a strange fact," he comments, "that when any real Chinaman is married in Malacca or Singapore, he is obliged to talk Malay to his wife in order to be understood.") Minchin speaks of the payment of *Pien Kim* (i.e. *phièng-kîm*, bride-price), "a sum of money from sixty to one hundred dollars," and details the first, second, third, and twelfth day ceremonies of marriage more or less as we know them from the traditional wedding in China. He mentions (p. 82) the *Cheo' tow* ceremony (i.e. the rite of *chiū:-thaú* which precedes the joining of husband and wife) and the worship before the table known as *San kia to*, by which he means *sām-kăi* (H. 'trinity') *toh* (Malay 'table'), the table for the worship of the trinity of Heaven, Earth, and Man (cf. Freedman 1957a: 134ff). The use of the betel nut mentioned in the account of the 1835 wedding in Singapore (Tracy 1836) and Minchin's details (1870: 82ff) on the wedding processions of his day, which included "Klings" (South Indians) as bearers, are hints of the Malayanization (if the term be not anachronistic) which the Baba wedding ceremonial had undergone. In the evidence taken in 1925–26 in the Straits Settlements by an official committee we find a good deal on Baba marriage practices;[3] it makes a fairly consistent picture which tallies with Minchin's account half a century before and shows continuity with the marriage customs of the homeland. On the habit of Babas reverting to more purely Chinese ways of behaving on the occasions of marriage and death we may quote the Victorian censure by the young Lim Boon Keng (1897: 56): at weddings the "Mandarin or official —the stiffest form of etiquette is observed, and instead of the simple uncovering of the head or genial shaking of hands, the rules of propriety are followed. The horrid red table cloth replaces the pleasing snowy cover that speaks at once of good taste and cleanliness, the simple chopsticks play the part of spoons and forks as in an orthodox Chinese dinner, and lastly the dishes are prepared and served *à la Chinoise.*"

The Babas took on many foreign habits, in speech, clothing, food, and so on; but they retained certain fundamental principles of Chinese social organization. They preserved their Chinese surnames in the Hokkien version, although, because they abandoned the Chinese system of writing, they were sometimes confused about different surnames which were similar in their romanized forms, and, of course, they could easily be mistaken about surnames as they were spoken in dialects other than Hokkien.[d] On the whole, the Babas appear to have maintained the bar on marriage between people of like surname which they inherited from their south Chinese ancestors.[4]

The language which the Babas evolved was predominantly Malay in vocabulary but heavily influenced by Chinese (Hokkien) in construction and idiom (see Shellabear 1913 and Chia 1899). Its orthography largely followed that of romanized Malay. The language produced a small literature of stories translated from the Chinese and some original compositions partly modeled on Malay forms. Baba Malay literature continued to be printed in Singapore until about the Second World War. In relation to certain important institutions the Babas retained a Hokkien-derived vocabulary. This is strikingly the case with the terms used for naming kin relationships.

Among the kinship terms which are Malay in origin we find *mak* (mother), *adek* (younger sibling), *abang* (older brother), and *mertua* (father/mother-in-law) (cf. Shellabear 1913: 54, 59ff); but the Baba *mak* may perhaps come from a Hokkien *mà*, the word *abang* did not entirely displace the Hokkien-derived terms *hiâ:* and *ng-kou*, and words of Hokkien origin were also used for parents-in-law. (The syllable *ng, n,* or *m* which forms the first part of a number of kinship terms in Baba Malay is a version of *ng*, the vocative particle in the Changchow subdialect of

---

[d] Note Tan 1924, a book on the Chinese surnames evidently published for the guidance of puzzled Straits Chinese. Tan refers, p. 3, to the misunderstandings which may arise because of the different pronunciations of the same surnames. Stressing the difficulty of dealing with the dialectical variations, Tan says he persisted in the arduous task he set himself out of "love and moral compassion for the ever-increasing number of the Straits-born Chinese who are always found to be lacking in the light of Chinese virtue, the knowledge of the Chinese surnames and their proper use."

Hokkien; the earliest Hokkien emigration to Malaya being from the Changchow area, its speech determined the pattern of Hokkien words in the Baba language.)

In general, Malay words were used for junior relative and Hokkien-derived terms for senior. And this usage appears to correspond with that of the analogues of the Babas across the water in Java, the Peranakans, among whom both Malay and Javanese terms come into play for junior relatives. The Baba kinship terms of Hokkien origin, although used as terms of reference (i.e. in such contexts as "my father," "your older sister," "his grandfather") are often couched in the vocative form. That is to say, the Baba system seems to have taken over the terms of address only (as when I say "Father!" "Older brother!"); and we know that the Chinese vernacular system of terms of address does not include terms for relatives junior to the speaker, who are addressed by name. (Cf. Freedman 1957a: 83.)

The discrimination made in the Baba terminology between certain relatives traced agnatically (i.e. exclusively through males) and non-agnatically (for example, *ng-cêk*, father's brother, as against *ng-kū*, mother's brother) could not have been preserved if the Malay terms, which fit a kinship system which does not separate out agnates, had been taken over completely; and we may infer that these discriminations were important in the Baba system.

The persistence of the ancestral cult in some form among the Malayan Babas is attested at the present day by the ancestral houses (known in Baba Malaya as *rumah abu*, "ash houses") to be found especially among the well-to-do Straits Chinese in Malacca. To what extent Singapore Babas attempted to set up houses of this kind it is difficult to know, but, of the three cases mentioned by Song Ong Siang (1923: 14, 30, 100) in which rich men tried to tie up property for the purposes of ancestral worship, one certainly relates to a Baba. Choa Chong Long, who was born about 1788 in Malacca, was a rich Singapore Chinese who, dying in 1838, left a will containing "a devise for ever of certain properties for 'sinchew' [i.e. *sīn-cù*, ancestral worship] purposes. . . ." Choa's was probably the first Chinese will which the local courts had to judge on the point of tying up property. It was declared void, as were later all such provisions coming to the attention of the courts. Of course, it by no means follows that because the colonial legal system refused to allow the construction of perpetuities for the ancestral cult none was successfully carried on. We may suspect with Napier, writing at the end of the century, that "in many cases family arrangements are come to, and forced on unwilling members, whereby the rules of the English law are evaded."[5] But the maintenance over a long period of ancestral houses, where tablets were stored and regular rites were performed with income derived from tied-up property, must have depended on the persistence of agnatic lines; and it is difficult to see whether in fact such a degree of continuity was achieved by many Singapore Babas.

As for the non-Baba Chinese of Singapore, the chances that normal family life developed among them were, for demographic reasons, low. Marriage and family for them were largely matters pertaining to the homeland rather than their life overseas; many had married in China and left their wives there. The immigration figures show how few were the Chinese women arriving in the Straits in the last century. By 1881 there were 9,000 non-"Straits-born" Chinese females to 68,000 non-"Straits-born" males in Singapore, but this was a high proportion of women in comparison with previous decades. In 1860 there had been a mere 3,250 females in a total Chinese population of 50,000, and presumably some of the women were prostitutes. It was especially unusual for the better-off Singapore Chinese to bring their families out of China.[6] Some of the immigrants, as we have seen, married Nyonyas, and, as long as they remained in Singapore, conformed to Baba ways of life.[e] A number of the immigrants who married overseas already had wives in China, but, since the China and Singapore wives were rarely confronted with each other, problems of their relative status hardly arose. In any case it came to be accepted that, despite the fact that traditionally a Chinese might have only one principal wife at a time, "in the Colony there is a custom to take more than one principal wife, subject to the proviso that they must not be taken in the same place" (Braddell 1931: 85; see Freedman 1950: 102).

The institution of double principal wives quite apart, some immigrant Chinese who managed to amass riches engaged, as did the Babas, in plural marriage. We have the evidence of the courts of law that Chinese in the Straits sometimes married not only a "wife" but also one or more "concubines" (Freedman 1950 [Essay 7 below]: 101), or, in sociologically more satisfactory language, both principal and secondary wives. In some cases both kinds of wife were kept under one roof in a manner resembling the gentlemanly polygyny of the homeland.

We have seen that there is evidence of ancestral property being set up among the Babas in the Straits. Of the three attempts to tie up property for ancestral worship mentioned by Song Ong Siang (1923: 14), one was definitely, and a second possibly, made by an immigrant. Tan Che Sang, born in Canton about 1763, died in Singapore in 1836, leaving a

[e] Cf. Minchin 1870: 86. "The maiden 'Nonias' at any of these places prefer the 'Babas' as husbands to the pure Chinese; when they get the latter as husbands . . . they force them to wear the tight sleeve jackets usually worn by the 'Babas' in order to make them appear as such."

will which directed that a block of his land "should be kept for the joint concern and reserved for ever as an ancestral heritage and should not be turned into money for appointment nor sold nor alienated." But this part of the will was annulled by the courts in 1880. Chee Teang Why, who died in Singapore in 1861, left a will in which properties in both Malacca and Singapore were to be set aside "not on any account to be sold or mortgaged but were to be reserved for ever as 'ancestral heritage,' and the rents and profits thereof were to be applied towards paying the expenses of sacrificing to the sinchew or tablets of himself and his deceased ancestors from time to time 'agreeably to the custom of the Chinese.'" This provision was overturned at law in 1908.[7] It is possible that a number of well-to-do immigrants tried to do in Singapore what would have been right and proper for them to have done in their home villages: endow an ancestral hall which would establish a new segment of the lineage (or clan, as it is often called).[8] That they failed in their plans was not due solely to the English law against perpetuities, which in any case had to be invoked by dissatisfied descendants. It was unlikely in the fluid society of Singapore that agnates would continue over several generations to congregate to perform ancestral rites. The structural forms of the homeland society were not so easily to be reproduced in the alien conditions of Singapore.

It is clear, at any rate, that while it was possible for the Baba section of the Chinese population of old Singapore to build up a system of marriage and family, no analogous system could surround the ordinary immigrant. As far as his life in Singapore was concerned, he was likely to be without a wife and children.[f] Whatever residential, economic, and political framework he succeeded in fitting himself into overseas he was not likely to find himself in the company mainly of kinsmen. The major structural features of his society were a different order. Secret societies and other more or less voluntary associations based on a number of principles of recruitment were the dominant groupings of social life.[9]

Yet kinship must to some degree have entered into the field of extra-familial social organization. The immigrants came from a part of China where agnatic lineage very often coincided with local community, and, although the Singapore Chinese population was, because of Singapore's special position as a port of entry and redistribution, much more heterogeneous than that of other places in Malaya, people of like agnatic

---

[f]His sexual needs were, however, partly cared for. Lim Boon Keng, quoted by Song (1923: 125–26), says that 1863 saw the first recorded importation of Chinese prostitutes; but there must have been facilities before this time. Vaughan (1879: 8) darkly hints at less conventional methods of sexual satisfaction. Reference is made to quarrels over catamites in the secret society oaths given in Ward and Sterling 1925: 65.

descent and from the same small locality in China must have clustered together. It is usually overlooked in discussions of Chinese migration from Fukien and Kwangtung that in fact there was no area from which migrants evenly came; within a general emigrant area some villages sent men overseas and others did not.[10] (How the emigrant villages came to be selected—or selected themselves—and what consequences flowed from the selection seem to me matters which should stand high on a list of priorities in research on Overseas Chinese questions.) Both free choice and the policies of labor recruiters in the latter half of the nineteenth century led to there being small groups of men in Singapore who were members of single lineages at home.

In the nature of things these men could not reconstitute lineages in Singapore, but they often associated with one another, sometimes setting up special places of worship. On the other hand, as soon as immigrants from different places in China were thrown together in Singapore they began to recognize a bond implicit in the sharing of a common surname, so that not only did men associate because they came to the same lineage but they also formed wider groupings on the agnatic principle of common surname. The members of a formal surname group might be limited to men coming from a particular area of Fukien or Kwangtung or speaking a particular dialect. Doubtless, the range of recruitment fluctuated with changes in migration, the building up of alliances, and internal disputes.

In the earlier phases of Singapore Chinese history, the solidarities springing from like agnatic descent seem to have been caught up along with other kinds of solidarity (like territorial origin in China, like occupation, like place of residence in Singapore, and so on) in the network of relationships governed by the secret societies. And clan (surname) associations were not a prominent feature of society until after the suppression of the secret societies in 1890. But they certainly existed to some extent even during the heyday of the secret societies. "Taking advantage," wrote an anonymous Baba in 1899, "of the clannish spirit inherent in the Chinese race, such powerful families as the Tan, Lim, Chua, Ong, Li, etc., form themselves into organisations for mutual protection and aggrandisement. So influential were these associations that even during the existence of the dreaded Triads they were able to hold their own in their struggle with each other."[11]

We are left with a very vague and imperfect picture of Chinese kinship and marriage among the Singapore Chinese in the last century, but the attempt to fit the few pieces of data together suggests a number of interesting problems for future work. How, for example, did the surname groupings respond to changes in the composition of the population and to shifts in alignment within local Chinese society? What continuity was in fact achieved over the generations by the establishment of ancestral property, and what implications did such property have for economic cooperation between persons descended from the ancestor who set up the property? How far did ties of kinship and marriage enter into commercial operations? Was Singapore Chinese society so fluid, and individuals within it so mobile, both physically and socially, that the obligations of kinship counted for relatively little in the pursuit of riches and power?

Colonial Law and Chinese Society

I set out in this paper to do two things: firstly, to answer the question "What is the family law applicable to Chinese in the Colony of Singapore at the present time?" and, secondly, to discuss the problem of the relationship between "government" law in Singapore and the customary law of the Chinese.

By law, in this context, I mean: the rules and procedure of the courts set up in the framework of the colonial administration of Singapore; the rules and procedure of the government agencies in Singapore, dealing with Chinese disputes, which exist outside the judicial system properly so-called; the rules and procedure of courts established in politically constituted society in China, both in the past and the present; the rules for the regulation of betrothal, marriage, separation, divorce, adoption, and inheritance which Chinese hold, or have held, to be binding on them, and the procedure they have adopted to implement these rules when they have had no recourse to politically organized courts. I imply in this a pragmatic definition of law, which, while it certainly takes in a wider field of behavior than many anthropologists can tolerate under a single label, allows me to make under one heading comparisons between the sets of rules, procedure, and sanctions which merge and conflict around some of the crucial events of Chinese family life.

What follows is based upon documentation collected and observations made during a period of fieldwork in Singapore, 1949–50, under the auspices of the Colonial Social Science Research Council.

The Chinese in Singapore

Modern Singapore began its development in 1819 under Sir Stamford Raffles and the East India Company he represented, as a virtually deserted tropical island. The new trading settlement quickly attracted Chinese merchants and laborers. Today in a total population of over a mil-

Journal of the Royal Anthropological Institute, 80 (1950), 97–126.

lion, the Chinese are some three-quarters of that number. They are a homogeneous group in the Colony only in the sense that they are usually treated as a legal and statistical entity by the government and regard themselves as a "national" community in opposition to other "national" communities: Malays, Indians, Europeans, and Eurasians. Seen in isolation the Chinese are distributed over a very wide range of wealth and occupation, greatly differentiated in education, and broken up into several loosely constituted dialect groups. Despite a Chinese history of settlement over a century and a quarter, the great majority of Chinese in Singapore today are of not more than two generations' standing. Broadly speaking, this factor of length of settlement has differentiated a small group of long-established Chinese, in some ways culturally assimilated to Malays, from the remainder of the community.

For the first seven years of Singapore's existence the Chinese population was indirectly controlled by the British through a system of headmanship by *Capitans China*. Under this form of loose supervision the only legal rules and mechanism applied to the Chinese were of their own choice and devising. In 1826 the jurisdiction of the Penang court was extended to Singapore and Malacca, these being now the three British settlements in the Malay Peninsula. Penang, which had been founded in 1786, had received its first set of legal regulations in the form of a Charter of Justice in 1807.[1] This Charter, according to the first Recorder, "secures to all the native subjects the free exercise of their religion, indulges them in all their prejudices, pays the most scrupulous attention to their ancient usages and habits" (Purcell 1948: 49–50). The subsequent Charter of 1826 took up the same attitude to native custom, but the extent to which English law was to be modified to pay this respect to local usages was not clear. The third Recorder of Penang held that the Charter of 1807 applied the law of England, as it then existed, only to criminal cases, and that civil law was to be administered by the canons of native custom. Sir Benson Maxwell, in his well-known judgment in the case *Choa Choon Neoh* v. *Spottiswoode*, 1869, said:

In this Colony, so much of the law of England as was in existence when it was imported here and is of general (and not merely local) policy, and adapted to the conditions and wants of the inhabitants, is the law of the land; and further, that law is subject, in its application to the various alien races established here, to such modifications as are necessary to prevent it from operating unjustly and oppressively on them. (Braddell 1931: 62; Straits Settlements, Supreme Court, 1885: 221.)

From the time of the establishment of a system of law on the English model there came a series of judgments in civil suits which frequently refused to allow Chinese custom in the realm of family matters. Napier (1913: 146), writing in the last year of the nineteenth century, gave three main points on which "the wholesale introduction of English law has disappointed Chinese expectations and ideas," of which the first was the nonrecognition of adoption. The other two points were "its giving the wife and the daughter a large, and in the case of the latter an equal share with that of the sons, and . . . the impossibility of tying up property for several generations with a view to the due performance of the 'sinchew' or ancestral worship." On this last matter Napier (*ibid.*) comments significantly: "I have sometimes wondered that the Chinese have not made the attempt to get these decisions reversed by the Privy Council, but I suspect that in many cases family arrangements are come to, and forced by Chinese opinion on unwilling members, whereby the rules of the English law are evaded."

From the abandonment of indirect rule in 1826 until the present time the colonial[2] courts have wrestled with the problems of the incorporation of Chinese customary law into an essentially English legal system. I shall attempt at the end of this paper to assess the total effect of this process, but it is necessary to point out here that, historically, it is probably only since the last quarter of the nineteenth century that government intervention in Chinese affairs has had any great influence. With the disappearance of the *Capitans China* the internal affairs of the Chinese community largely passed out of the purview of the British administration. Legally and politically the Chinese contrived to maintain their own world. The few civil cases which came up for judgment before the courts had only a limited significance for the Chinese community as a whole. During the half-century before the growth of a system of direct control of Chinese affairs the codes by which Chinese regulated their family affairs and the bodies to which they resorted in cases of dispute were beyond the reach of the government. It was during this period that the secret societies flourished as instruments of political control and courts of law within a closed Chinese society.[3] Legislation to register associations (as a measure of control over obnoxious societies) was passed in 1869, and eight years later the first Protector of Chinese, Pickering, was appointed. He was followed by a long line of British experts in Chinese language and affairs who supervised the Chinese community on behalf of the government. In 1877, also, an attempt was made to control the coolie immigration into the Colony. The Protector came to take statutory powers under such legislation affecting the Chinese as the Societies Ordinance, the Women and Girls Protection Ordinance, and the Labour Code. His general function was to effect liaison between the government and the Chinese population, or, perhaps more correctly, between the authorities and the poorer and more newly immigrant sections of the Chinese. Outside the limits of his statutory powers he exercised a wide quasi-judicial function by keeping disputes among Chinese out of the courts and settling them by judgments enforced usually by nothing more than the prestige and implicit power of his office.

Besides the Protectorate there have been other means by which the British administration has brought itself into closer relationship with the Chinese. These have been the establishment of the Chinese Advisory Board, the entry of some Chinese into the Colonial legal and administrative services, and membership by Chinese of the Executive and Legislative Councils. With the growth of this direct contact between the authorities and Chinese, "government law" has assumed an increasing importance.

The Law of China

The provisions of the Charters required the modification of English law to take account of native custom. What was Chinese custom? The courts had access to Chinese *law* in the sense that they could consult the code of laws in existence under the Manchu dynasty (1644–1911), which was available in English translation (Staunton 1810; Hare 1904; Jamieson 1921; Möllendorff 1896). In addition to these literary sources they called for the testimony of Chinese consuls, Protectors of Chinese, and local Chinese of standing.

These several types of information, however, did not together provide a very satisfactory guide to the courts. What was found in the so-called textbooks were general statements covering the whole of the Chinese empire, while the colonial courts were directly concerned with the practices of people coming from two particular provinces (Fukien and Kwangtung) of southeast China. And even within the Chinese community of the colony it was evident that there was considerable variation in practices springing from local differences within the home provinces. Such customary variations in the several regions of the empire had legal significance in the sense that they might be enforceable in the courts of that country. The nature of Chinese law was such that the codes embodied a set of models for ideal behavior rather than a system of absolute rules, and in the performance of their duties local magistrates in China were able to exercise considerable discretion in the extent to which they might incorporate local custom into the law they were to administer.[4]

How the judges of the colony were confused by the conflicting evidence which their varied sources of information provided may be illustrated by the following extract from a judgment given in 1926, in a case

where a decision had to be made as to what constituted the proper ceremonies for the marriage of a "principal wife." The judge[a] said:

> Before leaving the question of the so-called usual and essential ceremonies for
> the wedding of a principal wife, I would like to observe that the whole matter
> is in my opinion most unsatisfactory and vague. There seems to be no real and
> final authority at all as to what are the actual essentials of the marriage. . . . A
> consideration of various text books—van Mollendorf [*sic*] and Jamieson—and a
> number of decided cases leads me to the conclusion that these ceremonies differ
> in different parts of China and again differ here in Singapore. The expert witness
> Mr. Stirling [Protector of Chinese] was quite vague as to the essentials, so are von
> Möllendorff and Jamieson and the expert witnesses.

In more recent times a further complication has developed. The Manchu code passed away and was replaced by a modern compilation of
laws. From the birth of the Republic of China legal reformers made successive attempts to codify and "modernize" family law. The culmination
of these efforts was the Civil Code which came into effect in 1931 (Valk
1939: chaps. 5–11).[5] The essential characteristics of this new code were
that it set up a concept of law independent of the *li*; it ignored the cult
of the ancestors; it protected the rights of individuals against those of the
family; it established the principle of the freedom of marriage; and it
removed "unjust discrimination between men and women" (*ibid.*: 57).

There seems little doubt that the new code was rarely applied outside
the cities of China. It embodied the ideas of an elite of legal reformers
and made little headway in reshaping the principles of Chinese society at
large. But, from the point of view of those outside China, the new code
was the law of the land. By the time of its appearance, however, the
courts of the colony had already laid down in a series of precedents
the main lines along which the law of China was to be taken into account. The reforms of the Republican law could find no significant place
in a colonial legal system erected in pre-Republican times.[b] It was in the
realm of the ideology of social reform that the new law made its mark
among Singapore Chinese. For those Overseas Chinese affected by the
political and social idealism of Chinese nationalism the 1931 Code, how-

[a] Chief Justice Murison in the case *Woon Kai Chiang v. Yeo Pak Wee and others* (*Straits
Settlements Law Reports* [hereafter *SSLR*] 1927: 33). A source of confusion of which the
judges were not probably aware was the disparity of "class" between the Chinese population within their purview in Singapore and the social order in China to which the elaboration of ceremonial set out in the "textbooks" really applied. I discuss this problem of
"peasantry and gentry" in the final section of this paper.

[b] The rules of the 1931 Code, however, are applied in the colony in certain matters of
inheritance. If a man of Chinese domicile dies in the colony, the division of his estate follows the principles of the Code. Again, the real property in China of an intestate of colonial
domicile will be disposed of by the rules of the Code.

ever dimly and inaccurately conceived, represented a charter for modernism. To illustrate this type of legal idealism I refer to an article published in Singapore in 1940[6] (Kuan 1940) in which the author draws a comparison between Straits Settlements law and the 1931 Code in the provisions they make for marriage, inheritance, and will-making. Largely misrepresenting Colonial law, he eloquently argues its inferiority to the new law of China. What is perhaps most striking in the article, however, is not so much the evaluation of the provisions of the Code as the strong plea for the application of the new rules to Overseas Chinese. The Code may never have been enforced in the courts of China to any considerable extent, but it can be used as a device for impressing Overseas Chinese with the inescapable nature of their ties with their homeland.

More recently still, a third code from China has made its impact on Overseas Chinese. In April 1950 the Singapore Chinese press carried the text of "The Marriage Laws of the People's Republic of China" which had just been proclaimed.[7] A comparison between the provisions of the Communist legislation and the Kuomintang 1931 Code shows that there is in fact no revolutionary development in the former. The possible real difference between the two codes will, ultimately, be in the extent to which they will have been enforced. While the 1931 Code largely slept on the statute book, the Communist rulers of New China are showing a determination to realize their reforms.

Betrothal and Marriage

In this section and the three that follow it, I propose to examine the four topics of betrothal and marriage, separation and divorce, adoption and the position of children, and inheritance and rights to property. For each subject I shall indicate the way in which Colonial case and statute law have dealt with Chinese customary conceptions, and show the manner in which the law of China itself has changed.[8]

The law relating to marriage as it stood in China before the modern changes may be briefly summarized as follows. The actual act of marriage, in which the two immediate parties were brought ceremonially together, had to be preceded by a valid betrothal which involved the use of go-betweens and the exchange of horoscopes, deeds, and presents. Betrothal could be arranged at any age of the couple, but strictly speaking the engagement of unborn children was disallowed. In fact, such antenatal betrothal was practiced.[9] The negotiating and consenting parties in betrothal were not the future husband and wife, but their paternal grandparents and parents. Betrothal validly carried out established a relationship between two families which was tantamount to marriage. The fiancée was virtually a daughter-in-law from the moment of engagement, and withdrawal from the obligation to fulfill the contract of marriage was possible only in very rare circumstances. The death of either fiancé could dissolve betrothal, but the girl could enter her late fiancé's household as his widow if she wished (Doolittle 1865: vol. 1, 98).

Marriage, in its narrowest sense, was with a "wife." The taking of a wife involved, apart from the formalities of betrothal, a series of ceremonies, the most important of which were the formal invitation of the bride, her passage to the house of her husband's father, and the introduction of the newly married couple to the household gods, ancestors, and living persons of authority in the groom's home. A woman married in such a fashion occupied the unequivocal position of a wife. The taking of a concubine, in contrast, could be conducted with little ceremony. A concubine was "bought" rather than taken to wife. Hare (1904: 4–5) says: "A Chinese may *ts'u* . . . or marry only one *ts'ai* . . . or wife. . . . A Chinese may *lap* . . . appoint, *mai* . . . buy or *chi* . . . acquire by purchase one or more *ts'ip* . . . or concubines."

The ideology of concubinage was that it was an institution to insure against the extinction of the male line of descent. If the wife failed to produce a male child the husband brought in a concubine in the hope that she would make up the deficiency. The wife's consent for the introduction of a concubine was necessary, and the concubine lived in the house of her husband in the position of one subservient to the wife. But there is evidence that the ideology of concubinage did not find its exact counterpart in reality. Lack of sons was not the only circumstance in which a concubine was taken, nor was she always kept in her husband's house along with his wife. Nevertheless, the essential characteristic of Chinese polygyny was that it was a system in which socially inferior women were brought officially into a man's household (main or subsidiary). Any children the concubine bore him were legitimate. The concubine was not a "mistress" in the sense of a "kept woman."

The Chinese terminological distinction between a wife and a concubine, and the sociological differentiation in rights and status, greatly exercised the wits of the colonial courts obliged to hear cases in which claims on intestate estates were in dispute. Sir Benson Maxwell, Recorder in the Supreme Court, in 1867, started off a series of legal judgments which ruled the Chinese to be polygamous. He said in the course of his judgment:[10] ". . . I had to consider the question some years ago, in Penang, and I was of the opinion that a second or inferior wife was to all intents and purposes a lawful spouse and was entitled to share with the first or superior wife in the property of her deceased husband. . . ." In the case he was hearing at the moment he observed:

The first wife is usually chosen by her husband's parents of a family of equal station, and is espoused with as much ceremony and splendour as the parties can afford; while the inferior wives are generally of his own choice made without regard to family connection. But that they are wives not concubines seems to me clear from the fact that certain forms of espousal are always performed, and that, besides, their children inherit in default of the issue of the principal wife,[c] and that throughout the Penal Code of China they are treated to all intents and purposes as well as the first.

When Acting Chief Justice Law delivered judgment in the so-called Six Widows Case in 1908 he was able to cite a list of previous cases in which the Chinese had been held to be polygamous.

On the whole, in view of the statements referred to above [i.e. as to the position of concubines in Chinese law], that in the case of secondary wives, as I will call them, some sort of ceremony is usually required, and that they were regarded as belonging to the family of the man they lived with, in view of the law that these secondary wives cannot be divorced except for the same reasons as a first wife, in view of their right to maintenance on the death of the man they lived with out of his estate, just like a first wife, in view of their right to apply to the Court to secure such maintenance, and in view of the other points already referred to above, I think that in regard to these secondary or inferior wives (or concubines as they have been called), though socially their position is no doubt very inferior to that of the first wife, yet legally their position more nearly resembles that of a wife where polygamy is allowed than it resembles anything else: and I think myself, though I do not think the matter is free from doubt, that Chinese marriage must be regarded as polygamous as Sir Benson Maxwell held and as Sir Theodor Ford and other Judges have taken to be the case. . . . I believe myself that there are other cases besides those to which reference has been made, where plurality of wives among Chinese has been recognised in the Courts here, but of course cases of this sort would not be reported indefinitely, and it must be remembered that a very great number of those who can afford to support more than one wife have disposed of their property by will, and that the question we have been considering may thus not arise.[11]

Linked with the ruling that the Chinese are polygamous has come the decision that, in view of the difficulty of establishing the exact nature of the forms of "secondary marriage," "the doctrine of presumption of marriage now applies to the Chinese" (Braddell, 1931: 82). "A ceremony is, of course, essential to the taking of a first wife . . ." (*ibid.*), but in 1926 Chief Justice Murison, in a context already referred to, observed:

I am not so sure that some day the Courts here will not have to hold that the only real essential of the Chinese marriage of a principal wife is intention; and that it is a question of fact in each case whether or not there has been a per-

[c] This is inaccurate; the sons of concubines inherit with the sons of a wife.

formance by the parties in this Colony of so much of the ceremonies usual in Chinese principal marriages as would justify the Court in finding that there was an intention to perform a principal marriage, and that therefore such a marriage has taken place.

The whole question, in the absence of legislation, must, I think, be considered to be in the melting pot, and after the lapse of years the crystallisation of essentials in the accurate sense of the word may eventuate. In my opinion there is no such accurate category in Singapore yet.[12]

In Chinese law a man could not take more than one wife at the same time. The marriage of a second wife during the lifetime of the first was bigamous. (But there did exist the possibility of taking two wives of approximately equal status in the case where a man was required to carry on two lines of descent—his father's and his father's brother's—at the same time.) In 1901 a Chinese was sentenced in Malacca to three months' simple imprisonment after being found guilty of going through two similar forms of marriage with two women, the second union taking place while the first wife was still alive. Chinese residents of Malacca and the acting Chinese Consul-General in Singapore, called to give evidence, stated that a Chinese can have one wife only. The Consul-General insisted that a concubine is not a wife and should not be so called.[13]

Again, in deciding the Six Widows Case, Acting Chief Justice Law upheld the decision of Mr. Registrar Velge that one of the unions of the deceased Choo Eng Choon was bigamous. However, Braddell comments:

Despite the above judgment, it is submitted that the doctrine of bigamy is at this date inapplicable to non-Christian Chinese, for amongst many Chinese domiciled in the Colony there is a custom to take more than one principal wife, subject to the proviso that they must not be taken in the same place. This custom was proved by sworn evidence in *Cheang Thye Pin v. Tan Ah Loy and Others* . . . though it does not appear in the report of that case.[14]

The effect of these various judgments, then, has been to establish a legal situation in which at this time in Singapore Chinese marriage is held to be polygamous in the sense that a man can have one "principal" wife and any number of "secondary" or "inferior" wives. In this way Colonial law has followed the Chinese social discrimination between a wife and a concubine. But since the courts have held that a "secondary" marriage may be established merely by evidence of cohabitation and repute, Colonial law may appear to have moved away from the traditional position in which a concubine was a woman recognized as a part of her husband's household. It is true that in Singapore today a number of well-to-do Chinese keep several "wives" in one house in such a fashion as to correspond with the old organization of concubines under the control of the wife. On the other hand, it is very common for a married man, if he wishes to take more than one wife, to keep a woman or women tucked away in a corner of the town out of the purview of the main family. Such subsidiary unions vary in their degree of permanency. Chinese sometimes refer to women maintained in this way as "kept women" rather than concubines. But whatever the common conception of their status, these women might be able, on the intestate death of their husbands or "keepers" to prove a secondary marriage "by cohabitation and repute." The question arises: What constitutes repute, and how strong an element is it in the presumption of marriage?

The only postwar case I have been able to find bearing on this problem actually puts little stress on repute and locates the establishment of marriage in the realm of consensus. In 1949 Chief Justice Murray-Aynsley (Singapore, Law Reports 1949: 172) found that a plaintiff, claiming a share in her husband's estate as a "t'sip," a secondary wife, was entitled to such a share on the grounds that, although the deceased man had kept his marriage to the plaintiff a secret from his family, "the law of this Colony merely requires a consensual marriage . . ." Ending his judgment the Chief Justice observed[d] (*ibid.*: 174):

After considerable hesitation I come to the conclusion that the plaintiff had acquired the status of a t'sip, as it has been declared by Courts composed of lawyers versed in English ideas. This conception is now part of the law of the Colony. It is now too late to reopen what has been decided in the Six Widows Case and subsequently to reduce the matter to one of Chinese custom.

The exaltation of Chinese concubines to the status of secondary wives, in which process they have acquired rights in intestate inheritance unknown in old Chinese law, may, if this last judgment becomes current, be matched by an even more significant shift of a class of women from the status of kept mistresses to that of secondary wives. One wonders whether future decisions in the courts will follow in this direction.[e]

[d] It is of interest that in a very similar case heard in 1947 in Penang—which has the same legal background as Singapore, although the two settlements no longer belong to one political or judicial unit—the judgment went in exactly the opposite direction. As in the Singapore case, the evidence indicated that the deceased man had kept his union with the plaintiff a secret from the rest of his family, and had not introduced her to his wide circle "of distinguished friends." Despite the fact that cohabitation and intention to form a more or less permanent union were established, the case failed for lack of "repute." The judge commented: "When one appreciates that a secondary wife may be acquired with so little formality and when acquired, she and her children, if any, in the event of an intestacy, share in the estate of the late husband, there is, if marriage is to remain a recognised honourable estate, an urgent necessity to ensure that a mistress or kept woman and her children, if any, should not step in to minimize the shares on distribution of the legal wives and children of the deceased." Malayan Union, Supreme Court, 1950: 72–79.

[e] The general position as it stood in the 1930's is stated succinctly in Payne 1932: 24–25,

The cases which have in this way established the status of Chinese wives have all been judged in the realm of intestate inheritance. Magistrates have sometimes been called upon to decide the validity of secondary marriages when hearing applications for maintenance,[f] but the law has been made by the higher courts in dividing disputed estates. In no other respect have the courts passed final judgment on the nature of Chinese marriage. In 1924 a woman obtained from the Supreme Court a declaration that she was a man's secondary wife (she was attempting to obtain maintenance from him), but on the appeal brought by her "husband" it was ruled that: "The Legitimacy Declaration Act of 1858 is not law in the Colony. The Supreme Court has no jurisdiction to entertain a suit for the declaration of the validity of a marriage. . . ." [15]

The realization that the successive rulings on Chinese marriages were unsatisfactory in a number of ways, and that there was no legal machinery for dealing with marital disputes, led the Government of the Straits Settlements to appoint in 1925 a committee of which the terms of reference were as follows:

To report on the customs, rites and ceremonies, relating to marriages observed by Chinese resident in the Straits Settlements and to submit, if thought desirable, proposals for legislation as to what forms or ceremonies should constitute a valid marriage and as to the registration of such marriages . . . To enquire and report whether legislation in respect of dissolution of marriages contracted according to Chinese rites and ceremonies by persons domiciled in the Colony and other cognate matters, such as decrees of nullity, of judicial separation and of restitution of conjugal rights is necessary or desirable; if so, to recommend the grounds

---

n. (q): "It is often a matter of difficulty to distinguish between a secondary wife or *t'sip* and a mere concubine or casual mistress, and in doing so the Court, following the judgments in the cases cited above, will consider such questions as the intention of the parties to form a permanent union, the length and nature, e.g. living in the same house as the rest of the family, of the association, whether the association was severed, the recognition by the intestate of any child of the union not per se evidence of marriage since according to Chinese law this can be done without legitimisation of the woman as a *t'sip*; . . . the performance of any ceremony by the parties (not however essential to the validity of a secondary marriage . . .), the recognition of the marriage by other members of the family, and the expressions used by the intestate in any deed or document, or upon any tombs or ancestral tablet."

[f] The law provides in the Married Women and Children (Maintenance) Ordinance, 1949 (and before this under section 37 of the Minor Offences Ordinance), that a married woman may sue her husband for maintenance of herself and their children, and that an unmarried woman may sue the father of her illegitimate children for their maintenance. In 1948 there were about one hundred such cases in Singapore in which Chinese women sued. Only in one or two cases were illegitimate children involved. In determining the validity of Chinese marriages magistrates appear to be satisfied with the evidence of a ceremony or the production of a marriage "certificate," and in default of such proof they seek evidence of repute. They do not seem to concern themselves with the third element in the trinity, intention.

upon, and the conditions and restrictions subject to which orders should be made. (Straits Settlements, Chinese Marriage Committee 1926: 1.)

The Committee was composed of the Secretary for Chinese Affairs, eleven Chinese gentlemen, and three Chinese ladies. It took evidence from forty-three Chinese and one European. Further, it received a total of two hundred and eighty-one letters from Chinese associations and individuals.

The Committee sat at a time when marriage procedure among the Chinese was changing. From the very first years of the Chinese Republic legal reform was in the air and changes in marriage custom developing at the same time were affecting Overseas Chinese groups. Evidence before the Committee showed clearly that two general types of marriage were current in the Colony at the time. In the first place, there was marriage in the old style; in the second, a new form involving a public ceremony and a "certificate" of marriage. The Committee, like the judges in the courts, found themselves confronted with evidence of considerable variation in the ceremonies held to constitute a valid union in the old style.

We have found it impossible to submit proposals for legislation as to what forms or ceremonies should constitute a valid marriage, because the evidence disclosed the fact that there were no essentials for Chinese marriages in the old style common to all the Districts of South China or to the locally-born descendants of emigrants from these Districts, while the new style of marriage does not require any particular form (*ibid.*: 11).

(In fact, an analysis of the statements made before the Committee shows that evidence on the essentials for an old-style marriage was taken from only just over a third of the witnesses. Summaries of these statements would show a quite considerable agreement on certain main features which might be held to be the sought-after "essentials." Three of these features are: (1) prior arrangement of the match (usually with the use of go-betweens); (2) the exchange of presents; and (3) the formal introduction of the bride to the groom's house (or vice-versa in the case of matrilocal marriage) by the worship of the household gods and the family's ancestors, and the reverencing of the seniors of the house. To these might be added the exchange of documents (consisting of horoscopes and papers setting out the names of all persons concerned in the match), the ceremony of dressing the hair during the night preceding marriage, and the formal passage of the bride to her groom's house. These ceremonies are, of course, for the taking of a wife. Witnesses were not in agreement on the necessity of any formality in the acquisition of a concubine.)

Assuming that the essentials were not in evidence, the Committee made certain recommendations for legislation which may be summarized as follows:

(1) A law should provide that the courts recognize unregistered marriages in the new style, both past and future, provided that such unions were willingly entered into, were with the consent of parents and guardians (where such consent was required by the draft Civil Code of China), did not infringe the prohibitions on marriages of persons within certain degrees of consanguinity, and were not contracted when an impediment to marriage existed.

(2) In each of the Straits Settlements a Registrar of Chinese Marriages should be appointed to keep separate registers for the voluntary registration of old- and new-style marriages.

(3) For the registration of old-style marriages it should be sufficient that a declaration made before a Justice of the Peace be handed to the Registrar. This declaration should contain the names of the parties to the match and their parents or guardians, and include a statement "that the ceremony was carried out with all the essentials required by custom in the District of China from which the bridegroom and bride or their ancestors came, or by such modified custom observed by the Chinese resident in the Colony from that District" (*ibid.*: 10).

(4) Licenses should be given to approved temples, schools, and associations to allow new-style marriages to be conducted on their premises, one of the provisions of such licenses being that a copy of each marriage certificate should be passed to the Registrar.

(5) New-style marriages carried out before such legislation came into effect should be capable of being registered by a declaration filed with the Registrar.

(6) Provision should be made for the annullment of a marriage in the case of a false declaration.

The Committee designed in this way a system of voluntary registration, eschewing compulsion on the grounds that their evidence showed strong resistance to the idea. "The opposition among Chinese aliens to registration of Chinese marriages of any kind is practically unanimous; Chinese British Subjects were divided in their opinions on this matter; ... the supporters of compulsory registration consist chiefly of Chinese ladies and a limited number of Chinese gentlemen of advanced views" (*ibid.*: 4). The two most powerful causes of the opposition to compulsory registration were dislike of government interference in private affairs, and the fear that registration "would involve monogamy in the future" (*ibid.*: 4).

None of the Committee's recommendations was ever put into effect.

Today, non-Christian Chinese marriages in Singapore, whether old- or new-style, are still conducted outside any scheme for compulsory registration, and largely outside the official provisions for voluntary registration. The latter category has grown up in the following manner. Up to January 1, 1941, a Christian Marriage Ordinance was in force, which governed the solemnization of marriages to which at least one party was a Christian. Under this Ordinance a Marriage Registrar was appointed before whom a Christian marriage could take place. In 1941 a new Christian Marriage Ordinance was brought into effect which removed the Registrar from the list of persons able to solemnize a Christian marriage. At the same time a Civil Marriage Ordinance was introduced which set up a Registrar before whom monogamous marriages could be performed. In such marriages it was required that neither party should have previously contracted a valid marriage "under any law, religion, custom or usage" and be still so married, and further, that after civil marriage neither party could contract a valid marriage with a third party. The new Ordinance, par. 6(i), also provided that if a man married under its provisions "contract a union with a woman which but for such marriage would confer rights of succession or inheritance upon such woman or upon issue of such union, no issue of such union shall be legitimate or have any right of inheritance in or succession to the estate of such male person, and no such woman shall have any such right by reason of the death intestate of such male person."

In this way, any Chinese man who marries before the Registrar deprives himself of the right to take a secondary wife. The extent to which Chinese in Singapore have availed themselves of this system of voluntary registration is set out in the following table:

Year	Number of marriages		Year	Number of marriages	
------	Chinese with Chinese	Chinese with non-Chinese	------	Chinese with Chinese	Chinese with non-Chinese
1941	247	12	1945	369	8
1942	407	18	1946	169	34
1943	821	13	1947	286	40
1944	886	13	1948	329	25

By way of comparison I give for the same period the numbers of Christian marriages.[16]

Year	Number of marriages		Year	Number of marriages	
------	Chinese with Chinese	Chinese with non-Chinese	------	Chinese with Chinese	Chinese with non-Chinese
1941	223	17	1945	140	12
1942	298	18	1946	186	24
1943	226	14	1947	212	28
1944	173	17	1948	225	25

The total of these figures for monogamous registered marriages represents, of course, only a small part of the number of marriages into which Chinese have entered during the period.[17] The great majority of marriages have been either old- or new-style unregistered by government. Old-style marriages have clearly declined in popularity since the time of the Chinese Marriage Committee. They are still occasionally to be seen, but the form of marriage which is in a sense standard today in Singapore is that in which the couple are brought together in a public assembly and a certificate signed. The performance of such a ceremony does not, of course, exclude the possibility of carrying out also some of the older customary rites, but the new system does shift the crucial point of marriage from prior negotiation and the passage of the bride, to the time when a man and a woman are publicly joined.

The kind of marriage certificate in use in the 1920's is reproduced in the *Proceedings* of the Chinese Marriage Committee on page 23, and reference is made on page 6 and at other places to booklets which set out the manner in which new-style marriages are to be conducted. I give here a translation of the standard type of certificate sold in Singapore bookshops at the present time. These certificates are highly decorated documents, made up either mounted on cardboard and folded like a book, or rolled and contained in cardboard or metal tubes. They are sold in pairs, the price ranging from about $1.50 for the cheaper varieties to about $7.00 for the better kinds.

The certificates read as follows:

MARRIAGE CERTIFICATE. [Groom] _____, born in _____ District, _____ Province, on _____ day, _____ month, _____ year, _____ at the _____ hour. [Bride] _____, born in _____ District, _____ Province, on _____ day, _____ month, _____ year, at the _____ hour.

Through the introduction of Mr. _____ the wedding ceremony is hereby held at _____ [place], at _____ [time], on _____ day, _____ month, _____ year of the Republic of China.

Mr. _____ has been respectfully invited to officiate at the wedding ceremony. Two families are joined in marriage, making a contract in the same hall. Look upon this day: "brilliant are the peach-blossoms, [the bride] ordering well the chamber, ordering well the house." We may confidently anticipate that in years to come "long drawn-out will be the stems of the gourds" and they will be "resplendent and prosperous." We put down on this paper the wish of growing old together in order that our oath of red leaves may be clearly recorded.[18]

Bridegroom _____ (signature)
Bride _____ (signature)
The person officiating at the ceremony _____ (signature)
The Introducer [go-between] _____ (signature)
The Guardians [i.e. Fathers or other guardians] _____ (signatures).

The above certificate is signed on _____ day, _____ month, _____ year of the Republic of China.

With some of the certificates are included slips of red paper which set out the form the ceremony is to take. Translated, the slips read as follows:

Program of a Wedding Ceremony

Wedding Ceremony.
Music.
Guests take their seats.
Guardians take their seats.
The Introducer takes his seat.
The Person Officiating takes his seat.
The Best Man and the Bridesmaids
  lead the Bride and the Groom to
  their positions.
Bride and Groom stand up facing one
  another and bow three times.
They return to their positions.
Person Officiating at the Ceremony
  reads the Certificate.
Bride and Groom exchange
  ornaments.
The Groom puts his seal.
The Bride puts her seal.
The Guardians put their seals.
The Person Officiating puts his seal
  (The Master of Ceremonies should
  remind the Person Officiating to
  apply his seal over the revenue
  stamp).

Music.
Speech by the Person Officiating.
Speech by the Introducer.
Speeches by the Guests.
Replies by the Guardians.
Replies by the Bride and Groom.
The Bride and Groom bow to the
  Introducer to thank him.
The Introducer retires.
The Bride and Groom bow to the
  Guardians to thank them.
The Guardians retire.
The Bride and Groom bow to thank
  the Guests.
The Best Man and Bridesmaids lead
  the Bride and Groom into the
  Bridal Chamber.
Music.
The Ceremony completed.

Ceremonies of marriage in the new style in Singapore at the present time follow the set program substantially. (The speechmaking is usually curtailed, and music is not a necessary feature. Since many of the new-style marriages are conducted in some public place, leading the bride and groom into the bridal chamber may just mean taking them out to their car.) [19]

At the time of the Chinese Marriage Committee the validity of a new-style Chinese marriage had not, within the knowledge of the Committee, been in question in the courts. The Committee asked Mr. (now Sir) Roland Braddell, the only non-Chinese witness, his opinion on this point. He indicated the difficulty that, if both husband and wife were alive, the court would have to decide whether the new style was within the meaning of the expression "religious customs and usages." After the death of the husband the matter would be simpler since marriage could be established by cohabitation and repute (Straits Settlements, Chinese Marriage Committee 1926: 151–52). I have been able to find only one reported case bearing on this problem.[20] A woman applied for maintenance in the District Court, Singapore, from a man she alleged to be her husband. She claimed to have married him in 1923 in the reformed style of marriage. The District Judge said: "I am unaware of any decision on the subject of Chinese marriages, solemnised in the reformed style. And Counsel could refer me to no case exactly on point." The Judge finally ruled that the couple had contracted a valid marriage, the woman being *at least* a secondary wife. By this he did not imply that she was not a first wife, for the question of relative status did not arise in this case. There seems to be little doubt that the courts at the present time would accept a marriage in the new style as valid. However, it is unsettled whether the new-style ceremony is sufficient for the marriage of a "principal" wife.[g]

The two chief characteristics of the new form of marriage are the use of a standardized document and performance in public. Such a marriage is often performed in the club-hall of one of the numerous territorial or clan associations, the local school, a hired public hall, or the Chinese Consulate-General. It may take place in a private home, but even there the element of publicity may be introduced.

If the marriage is conducted in the Consulate-General it takes on the further characteristic of being registered. (I was informed at the Chinese Consulate-General in 1949 that, contrary to general opinion, only about fifty to sixty wedding ceremonies were conducted there in a year, and that, apart from these marriages, only a few others were registered.) Correlated with publicity is the presence of an officiator, who tends to be a man of standing and influence in the Chinese community.[21]

Quite apart from weddings in the old and new styles, there is a further form of marriage which is of far less general significance. By this method a man and a woman simply come together to cohabit and publish a statement in the newspapers to this effect. As far as I can judge, this declaratory form of union is very rare and is confined to intellectuals. The only case personally known to me is that of a primary school principal and his teacher wife. The form of the announcement in the newspapers, as I judge from cuttings made from the Singapore daily *Hsin-chou jih-pao* during 1949, is as follows. It is headed either Announcement of Marriage

[g] Magistrates certainly accept evidence of a new-style wedding as proof of marriage but they are not concerned with discriminating between principal and secondary wives.

or Announcement of Cohabitation. It is signed by both parties to the match and states something in this manner: "We agree to be partners for life and to live together from such and such a date." Sometimes a prior introduction by friends is mentioned; often the phrase "with the permission of our parents" is included. The declaratory form of marriage does not appear to have ever been in question in the courts.

I shall now summarize as briefly as possible the law of marriage as set out in the 1931 Code (China [Republic], Laws, statutes, etc. 1931). Book IV of the Code is entitled *Family*. The Code assumes the normal practice of betrothal before marriage and sets out the requirements for such betrothal (*Code*: Arts. 972–9). However, it departs radically from the old law in two respects. Firstly, it does not require betrothal as an essential preliminary to marriage, whereas "The old law did not recognise the validity of a marriage without a previous betrothal." [22] Secondly, it requires that "An agreement to marry shall be made by the male and female parties of their own accord" (*Code*: Art. 972). An agreement to marry does not allow an absolute demand for the completion of the marriage from either side. Conditions are set down in which breach of the agreement is held to be justified (as when, e.g., the other party enters into another agreement to marry or in fact marries), and compensation may be claimed by the party who is so injured. Similarly, compensation may be claimed by one party when the other party breaks the engagement without justification.

Articles 980-1,003 of the Code deal with the Conclusion of Marriage. Marriages cannot be performed by a man under eighteen or a woman under sixteen. There is no explicit provision that marriage shall be concluded by the two persons immediately concerned of their own accord, but Valk (1939: 78) argues that such provision is implied. Bigamy is not allowed. "A person who has a spouse may not contract another marriage" (*Code*: Art. 985). One of Valk's (1939: 79) comments is very relevant to "South Seas" problems:

Marriage concluded abroad after marriage had been legally concluded in China has the same value, and the person who marries a second time afterwards, before his previous marriage is dissolved, commits bigamy. This case occurs sometimes nowadays, when Chinese, having married at a very early age in their own country, marry a foreigner abroad and find this marriage annulled after their return to China.

Marriage prohibitions are set out as follows:

A person may not marry any of the following relatives:
   (1) A lineal relative by blood or by marriage.
   (2) A collateral relative by blood or by marriage of a different rank (i.e. gen-

eration), except when the former is beyond the eighth degree of relationship and the latter beyond the fifth.

(3) A collateral relative by blood who is of the same rank and within the eighth degree of relationship but this provision does not apply to "piao cousins" (i.e. "cousins" of a different surname). (*Code*: Art. 983.)

In the traditional Chinese system marriage prohibitions followed two principles: firstly, ban on marriage between persons of the same surname; secondly, ban on marriage between related persons of different surnames and not of the same generation. The post-revolutionary legislators were concerned to remove from the law the structure of the ancestral cult with which these two prohibitory principles were closely linked. In fact, as far as the first principle is concerned, they have left it intact, except that outside the eighth degree of relationship one may marry one's clanswoman.[23] The old ban on intergeneration marriage is partly removed by the provision that a man may marry a relative of a different generation as long as she is beyond the fifth degree of relationship in the case of an affinal relative, and beyond the eighth degree in the case of a relative by blood. The Central Political Council stated in 1930 the principle adopted in reshaping the bars on marriage: "Where formerly in our country no prohibition existed we do not, as before, impose any prohibition.... Where prohibitions extended too far, their extent has been restricted...." (Valk 1939: 184.) The form of marriage is briefly given as follows: "A marriage must be celebrated by open ceremony and in the presence of two or more witnesses." (*Code*: Art. 782.)

No provisions are made for the drawing up of any marriage documents, nor does the code mention registration. However, the Law of the Register of Families, in operation from 1 July 1934, obliges parties to a marriage to ask the Registrar of Families to register their marriage within fourteen days (Valk 1939: 85). (One wonders how far such registration has actually been carried out.) Valk points out that the form of marriage so instituted removes the possibility of secret marriages.

There is not a word on concubinage in the whole Code. The lawmakers, throughout their draft codes before the final one, had struggled with the problem of concubinage, which they wished to see eliminated and yet were forced to take account of as a rooted Chinese institution. Up to the Nanking Draft of 1928 concubinage was recognized. This draft and the 1931 Code, however, give equality to men and women in the matter of divorce on the grounds of adultery (Valk 1939: 114), and presumably a woman can sue for divorce if her husband takes another woman. But she cannot delay too long in such action, for ". . . the wife cannot apply for a divorce, when her husband has taken a concubine and she has expressly or tacitly recognised it" (Valk 1939: 115). The protection of a concubine's children is partly provided for under the Code by the process of legitimization by recognition. The Code, then, went some of the way toward making possible the eradication of concubinage, but its provisions by no means justify an opinion, which I found current in Singapore, that concubinage is nowadays "illegal" in China.[24]

Articles one to six of the 1950 Marriage Law of the People's Republic of China set out the new legal conditions for marriage. Developing the modernist trends of the 1931 Code, the new compilation finally disposes unequivocally of the problem of concubinage,[h] and goes one step further in increasing the range of relatives within which marriage is permitted. The primary intention of "custom shall rule with regard to the prohibition of marriage between collateral blood relatives within five generations" (Article 5, section 1) is probably to allow intrasurname marriage except between persons of close kinship. "Collateral blood relatives" not of the same surname were marriageable under the traditional law provided that they were of the same generation; under the new rules a man may, presumably, ignore the generation difference in marrying a relative of a different surname as long as they are not related within five generations. The concession to custom in the retention of these minimal marriage restrictions is conspicuous in a code which sets out to abolish "the feudal system of marriage."[i]

It would seem from Article 6 that registration is a necessary element in the formation of marriage, but the nature of the ceremony of marriage is not indicated.[25]

Separation and Divorce

The 1926 Marriage Committee found "that there is practically unanimous opposition among Chinese residents born in China to any divorce legislation, which is shared by many Chinese born in the Colony" (Straits Settlements, Chinese Marriage Committee 1926: 4). Chinese ladies of Penang were the only group solidly in favor of divorce, "as a means of obtaining the prohibition of concubinage." There is, indeed, a very strong emotional resistance among Chinese in Singapore today to the

---

[h] But it should be noted that children born illegitimately have, by the provisions of Article 15, economic claims on their father, which again affords some protection to their mother. Much turns upon the interpretation of "Children born out of wedlock shall enjoy equal rights with children born in wedlock." It is of interest that while the new laws forbid concubinage the Shanghai People's Court has apparently tried to prevent even the most informal types of polygamous unions.

[i] The "hard core" of five generations—implied also in the Kuomintang 1931 Code—may be adjusted to the smallest exogamous patrilineage found in China. For some parts of the country intra-surname marriage is tolerated beyond the five-generation group. Cf. Fei 1939: 84, 86.

idea of divorce (and Malays and Europeans are derided for their recourse to this practice), despite the fact that a process of separation tantamount to divorce is generally recognized.

Under the old law this type of separation by mutual agreement was acknowledged. Repudiation by the husband was possible, but hedged about by limitations. A husband could repudiate his wife for any of the following faults: adultery or the commission of some serious offense against property; ill-treatment of children or disobedience to parents-in-law; insanity or leprosy; fraudulence in marriage; unjustified refusal to live with him; failure to bear children.[26] But, except in the case of adultery, repudiation could not be effected "if the wife had no family of her own to which she could return, if she had mourned for her parents-in-law for three years, or if her husband's family, formerly poor, had become rich in the meantime" (Valk 1939: 22). On her side, the wife could obtain divorce only in exceptional circumstances. The law made no explicit provisions for the divorce of a concubine, but it is probable that such a woman could be discarded without much formality.

As in the case of marriage, Colonial courts have dealt with Chinese divorce mainly in the context of disputed rights to property.

Giving evidence before the Chinese Marriage Committee, Mr. Braddell said:

So far as divorce is concerned the only case I have ever heard of in the Supreme Court was a recent one, in which Sir Walter Shaw held that a secondary wife who had been turned out by her husband had been divorced by that very turning out, and he made a declaration to that effect. I have myself always understood that so far as divorce is concerned, it is a very doubtful matter and that the exact method of divorce amongst the Chinese themselves is far from settled, at all events, in this Colony. (Straits Settlements, Chinese Marriage Committee 1926: 140.)

In Penang, in 1861, the Recorder had to determine, in an action concerning ejectment from land, whether a Chinese woman had in fact been divorced by her first husband, as she claimed. "Chinese witnesses were examined on the subject of Chinese law, but their evidence showed that their information was of the slightest character. On that point, however, the learned Recorder relied wholly on Staunton's Translation of the Chinese Penal Code."[27] He found the divorce clearly established, and went on to rule that a Chinese woman after divorce is free to remarry (arguing from Staunton), and that at such remarriage the presence of a guardian to give the woman away, although a necessity in Chinese law, was not to be accounted an essential in colonial law.

The Six Widows Case, 1908, had recognized the possibility of the divorce of a *ts'ip* or secondary wife, and the case of *Cheang Thye Pin* v. *Tan Ah Loy*, 1916, gives the same ruling (*SSLR*, 1933: 541). In 1924 the case *In the Estate of Sim Siew Guan Decd.*, to which Mr. Braddell referred before the Chinese Marriage Committee, reaffirmed this possibility. Chief Justice Shaw had the evidence of the then Acting Consul-General for China, who said

that customs in China as to divorce were more or less alike. He stated that a Chinese man could divorce his *t'sip*, or secondary wife, if she were disobedient to the orders of the first wife, or if she violated the rules of the family. . . . Asked as to whether there was any formality, Mr. Tsing replied that the prevailing custom was for the man to declare to his clansmen that he had divorced his *t'sip*. Clansmen should be called together, and the declaration made to them publicly. Otherwise he could call his near relations together and declare that he did not want his *t'sip*. (*SSLR*, 1933: 540f.)

The Judge in this case found a valid divorce of the secondary wife.

The question of divorce was gone over again in the case of *Lew Ah Lui* v. *Choa Eng Wan and others*, in 1935. The Judge said: "Now on the subject of divorce expert evidence was given by Dr. Tyau, Consul-General of China. He was asked "can a man divorce his concubine?" In reply he said: "Since my arrival in Singapore questions of this nature have frequently cropped up. I find the general opinion here with regard to concubinage is not quite the same as held in China. A concubine here has been given a position far higher than in China." And later he said: "As to Singapore, I cannot give a decided opinion, but if they follow Chinese custom it should be the same. A Chinese Magistrate never interferes with a divorce arranged by mutual consent—it was recognised." (*SSLR*, 1935: 177.) Because of the doubt on the Chinese custom of divorce and the changed status of secondary wives in the Colony, the Judge preferred "to consider how far divorced has been recognised in location decisions" (*SSLR*, 1935: 177).

After examining previous judgments he said: "I accept with respect the reasoning of C. J. Shaw that just as in the case of the formation of a secondary marriage, its dissolution can be proved by intention and repute." (*SSLR*, 1935: 179.)

In this way the Supreme Court has recognized the divorce of secondary wives, but it is not altogether clear exactly in what circumstances such a divorce will be upheld. (In the case of *Khoo Hooi Leong* v. *Khoo Chong Yeok*, for example, the Privy Council, in 1930, accepted the evidence of Mr. Beatty, as an expert on Chinese custom, that a secondary wife who has borne a son cannot be put away.) (Great Britain. Parliament. House of Lords 1930: 353.)

Legal provisions for the settlement of matrimonial disputes in Singapore are very scanty. In 1871 a Chinese woman applied to the Supreme Court for restitution of conjugal rights, and the finding was that "The Supreme Court has no jurisdiction either on its Civil or Ecclesiastical side, to entertain a suit for restitution of conjugal rights among non-Christians" (Straits Settlements, Supreme Court 1885: 236). There is no judicial divorce for the mass of the Chinese in Singapore. The Divorce Ordinance, as amended in 1939, provides for divorce only "where the marriage between the parties was contracted under a law providing that or in contemplation of which marriage is monogamous."[28] The law has regulated the financial aspect of separation in that under Section 37 of the Minor Offences Ordinance a woman, during the lifetime of her husband, has been able to sue him for maintenance. If the woman refuses to live with her husband, the court has power to enforce maintenance if it is satisfied that the man "is living in adultery or that he has habitually treated his wife with cruelty," provided that the wife herself is not living in adultery. (Since August 1949 a Married Women and Children (Maintenance) Ordinance, No. 26 of 1949, makes the same provision in this matter.) The provision for maintenance has certainly been applied to secondary wives, but there appears to be considerable doubt whether it was intended to do so.[29]

While the law has taken little part in Chinese divorce and separation, a government agency, acting without legal sanction,[30] has been handling Chinese matrimonial disputes for many years. The Women and Girls Section was set up very early in the history of the Chinese Protectorate, but since the war has formed part of the Department of Social Welfare. The Section deals with various aspects of the welfare of women and girls. In the case of husband and wife quarrels, officials of the Section attempt reconciliation or agreement as to the extent of maintenance to be given to the wife by the husband. Whatever results are achieved must rest on agreement. If the husband refuses to pay his wife maintenance the case must pass from the Section to the magistrates' courts. In a number of cases separation is agreed upon and a document is signed which is popularly referred to as a divorce. The standard form which such an agreement takes is as follows:

I, XYZ (f), x years, Hokkien, of _____ do hereby agree to separate from my husband ABC (m), y years, Hokkien, of _____, on this day, the z day of _____, nineteen forty-nine (_____ 1949) and will have no further claims on him in future. ABC is free to remarry if he so wishes.

Explained by me: FGH.   Signed: XYZ.

In the presence of IJK, Supervisor, Women and Girls' Section, Department of Social Welfare, Singapore.

I, ABC (m), y years, Hokkien, of _____, do hereby agree to separate from my wife, XYZ (f), x years, Hokkien, of _____, on this day, the z day of _____, nineteen forty-nine (_____ 1949) and will have no further claims on her in future. XYZ is free to remarry if she so wishes.

Explained by me: FGH.   Signed: ABC.

In the presence of IJK, Supervisor, Women and Girls' Section, Department of Social Welfare, Singapore.

Singapore _____ 1949.

If there are any children, then details of custody are added thus:

It is also hereby agreed that I should have the custody of our daughter, XLM, aged q years _____.

I also agree to let ABC have the custody of our daughter XLM, aged q years.

The difficulty arises that, while such a document is proof of intention to separate, it is not on a par with a judicial decree of divorce. The Chinese Marriage Committee said: "It is within the knowledge of members of this Committee that persons so separated have remarried. Nevertheless in other cases a wife so separated has successfully claimed a share in the estate of her original husband" (Straits Settlements, Chinese Marriage Committee 1926: 4).

The Japanese destroyed practically all the records of the Chinese Secretariat in Singapore, and for statistical evidence of the recourse to the Women and Girls Section we have only postwar figures. I set these out here:[j]

Year	Number of Family Dispute cases	Number of separations signed	Number amicably settled
1947	c. 150	?	?
1948	488	75	94
1949 Jan. to Aug.	415	66	105

The Women and Girls Section is not the only organization which sees to the drawing up of agreements to separate. This Section is, in fact, an agency which meets the needs, generally speaking, of the poorer and less educated members of the community.[31] The Chinese Consulate-General also acts as an informal court for family quarrels. (The Consulate-General informed me in 1949 that, while a number of matrimonial disputes were regularly brought there for settlement, only a mere handful of divorces by mutual consent were actually signed—perhaps a dozen a year. These divorces were only those involving principal wives, I was

[j] Nearly all Family Dispute cases are of the type of husband and wife quarrel. They are also nearly all Chinese.

told, since the Chinese Government did not recognize the institution of concubinage. In contrast, the separations signed in the Department of Social Welfare are often between a man and his secondary wife.) Better-off Chinese call in lawyers to draw up separation agreements. From time to time notices appear in the newspapers giving the substance of a mutual separation.

An examination of English-language newspapers in Singapore from January to August 1949 shows the occasional announcement of dissolution of marriage in two cases. I find only one case of a dissolution by mutual consent. It runs:

Notice of Dissolution of Marriage

Notice is hereby given (1) that the Marriage between Dr. ABC of No. x _____ street, Singapore, and Madam XYZ of No. y _____ road, aforesaid, has been dissolved by mutual consent pursuant to a Deed of Dissolution of Marriage dated _____ day of _____, 1949, and (2) that the said Madam XYZ will in all respects provide and pay for her own maintenance and support and (3) that as from the said _____ day of _____, 1949, the said Dr. ABC will no longer be responsible for his wife's debts whether contracted before or after the said dissolution of Marriage.

Dated this _____ day of _____, 1949.
Signed: Dr. ABC.
Signed: Madam XYZ.

In the other class are a few notices which appear to be unilateral repudiations of marriage from the side of the wife. Thus:

Notice

Notice is hereby given that Madam XYZ of _____ Singapore, has on the _____ day of _____, 1949, left the care and protection of her husband and henceforth she does not regard herself as the wife of the said ABC.

Dated this _____ day of _____, 1949.

ooo
Solicitor for Madam XYZ.

Such a withdrawal from marriage by the wife has, of course, no sanction in general Chinese custom and could hardly be held to constitute a valid divorce in colonial courts taking that custom into account. Notices by husbands are also published, but they do not mention divorce, being concerned only to announce that, as a result of desertion by his wife, the husband no longer holds himself responsible for her acts or debts.

Announcements in the Chinese newspapers usually take the form of notices of divorce by mutual consent. They are headed Divorce Announcements. The possibility of remarriage by either party is sometimes mentioned. I have come across only one repudiation by a woman. This was inserted by a woman in Johore and headed Severance of Marriage Relationship. The woman announced that she was repudiating the marriage on the grounds that her husband had married another woman. The Civil Code of 1931 provides for the dissolution of marriage in two classes. Firstly, it sanctions divorce by mutual consent. Such a divorce must be effected in writing in the presence of at least two witnesses. Secondly, it provides for judicial divorce, at the instigation of either party, on various grounds. These grounds are: bigamy, adultery, ill-treatment, ill-treatment of the wife by husband's "lineal ascendants" and vice versa, desertion in bad faith, attempt on the life of one spouse by the other, incurable loathsome disease, incurable mental disease, uncertainty for over three years whether the other party is still alive, and sentence of the other party to not less than three years' imprisonment or imprisonment for "an infamous crime" (*Code*: Art. 1,052).

Action for bigamy and adultery must be taken within two years of the occurrence of the guilty act, or within six months if the innocent spouse had cognizance of it. If the innocent party consented to or condoned the act then no remedy can be sought. There is provision for awarding damages to the innocent party.

The Code gives effect to the principle of the equality of the sexes in divorce, allowing the same grounds to either side, but, as was pointed out earlier, cohabitation with a concubine is still possible as long as the wife does not take rapid action for remedy.

The rules for divorce given in Articles 17–19 of the 1950 Marriage Law further reduce the judicial element. For not only is there divorce by mutual consent, as in the 1931 Code, but also, when unilateral divorce is applied for, the court's function is not to decide the justice of the claim but merely to attempt a reconciliation between the spouses. If the reconciliation fails the court grants the divorce.

Adoption and the Status of Children

The gulf between the Chinese and English legal conceptions of a "child" has been commented on many times in the courts. The basis of the disparity is that, while in English law a man's child is one born of the lawful wife (or of an unmarried woman and subsequently legitimized by marriage), the Chinese attitude is that any child of a man, whatever the status of its mother, is his fully legal offspring as long as he recognizes it as such. English law rests on legitimate birth, Chinese law on recognition of paternity.

From the acceptance by the colonial courts of the fact of Chinese polygamy has followed the necessity of treating the offspring by a man's secondary wife as equally legitimate with the children of his principal wife. In cases of intestacy a person's claim on his father's estate rests entirely on the validity of the marriage of his parents. In colonial courts, evidence of recognition, however strong, carries no weight. A man may be publicly acknowledged as a son, enjoy all the privileges and perform all the duties of a son during his father's lifetime, and have his name inscribed on his father's gravestone, but, if there is no proof of the marriage of his father to his mother, he cannot successfully claim in the courts for a share of his father's intestate estate. However, the courts will recognize legitimation by subsequent marriage (Braddell, 1931: 87–88).

Similarly, in the colony adoption confers no rights on the adopted child to claims on his adoptive father's intestate property. In traditional Chinese law the process of adoption, an essential feature in a social system requiring the continuance of a family line even in cases of childlessness, confers on the adopted child rights similar to those of a begotten child. Under the traditional law an adopted son suffers only the disability that he ranks after a begotten son, despite the latter's juniority in years, in the succession to the ancestral cult and the inheritance of an extra share of property that goes with this succession. Even if a boy were adopted for charity's sake, and not to be a possible successor to the cult, he has certain rights (Valk 1939: 23).

In Malacca, in 1858, *In re Chee Siang Leng's Estate*, it was ruled that "Adopted children of a Chinese [are] entitled to joint administration of his Estate in preference to his nephew" (Straits Settlements, Supreme Court 1869: 11). But this decision was overruled, and the judgment in the case of *Khoo Tiong Bee and another v. Tan Beng Gwat*, 1877, firmly set Colonial Law against the admission of the claims of an adopted child. Acting Chief Justice Ford said in this last case:

The circumstances of inconvenience or injustice in declining to recognise this practice of adoption, does not seem to me sufficiently grave to call for the modification of English law, as sought. Indeed with an absolute testamentary power, and that full knowledge of the terms under which Chinese settle in this Colony, which this and previous decisions may be supposed to give, it will be hard to make out much semblance of their existence. (Straits Settlements, Supreme Court 1885: 417.)

But the disinheritance of adopted children has certainly been looked upon by the Chinese as an injustice. Napier (1913: 146) in 1899 drew attention to this fact, and the Chinese Marriage Committee in 1926 exceeded its terms of reference to record its opinion "that the adoption of sons should be legalised in accordance with law and custom in China. . . ." (Straits Settlements, Chinese Marriage Committee 1926: 10.)

Braddell (1931: 88) points out that the exclusion of adopted children "has been applied even in the case of a Chinese domiciled in China." The 1931 Code takes account of legitimation by recognition and provides for adoption (*Code*: Arts. 1,056, 1,072–83). However, an adopted child in inheritance has only one-half of the share of a begotten child if true lineal descendants exist. Unlike the old law, the Code ignores the ancestral cult, and does not, therefore, distinguish between a boy adopted to succeed in the cult and a boy or girl adopted for other reasons. Adoption of children of either sex is of one kind and establishes relations similar to those between parents and their begotten children (Valk 1939: 134).

The 1950 Marriage Law devotes much of its space to the legal rights and position of children. There is clearly the attempt, in the first place, to put illegitimate children on a favorable footing. Article 15: "Children born out of wedlock shall enjoy equal rights with children born in wedlock. No person shall harm or discriminate against them." Provision is made for the payment of maintenance by the father of an illegitimate child. Similarly, the only reference (Article 13) to adopted children seeks to equate their status with that of begotten children. Articles 20–22 state the rules for the maintenance and care of children after divorce.

In Singapore at the present time adoption of one kind and another is very common. Since 1939 there has existed an Adoption of Children Ordinance (number 18 of 1939), "to make provision for the adoption of infants," but the registered form of adoption which it established is expensive, as a legal process. Recourse to it has been very small. Figures supplied to me by the Registrar of Births and Deaths, Singapore, show that for the years 1940–49 inclusive the total number of Chinese children adopted under the Ordinance has been twenty-one, while only eighteen of the adopting parents have been Chinese. It is as well to note, in referring to the neglect of the Ordinance, that it does not remove the disabilities in inheritance of children adopted under its provisions. Paragraph 6 (2) of the Ordinance says an adoption order does not deprive the child of any rights or interests in property which it would have enjoyed but for the adoption, and further, that it does not confer on the child "any right to or interest in property as a child of the adopter." The Ordinance also disallows payment for the child beyond what the court may sanction.

The forms which adoption takes in Singapore among the Chinese may be given as follows: (1) adoption of a son; (2) adoption of a daughter; (3) adoption of a son-in-law; (4) adoption of a prospective daughter-in-law; (5) *mui tsai*. I propose to deal with each of these forms in turn.

    1. *Adoption of a son*. A basic principle of adoption among Chinese is

that it is a transaction involving the passage of money. There is a great discrimination in "price" between boys and girls to the advantage of the former, and the transfer of boys is on a much smaller scale than that of girls. Chinese will often dispose fairly freely of their daughters to other Chinese, or even to non-Chinese,[k] but comparatively few Chinese parents will part with a boy. It is possible to get a baby girl by paying the lying-in expenses of a Chinese mother; for a boy one must expect to pay several hundred dollars. A Chinese man will generally adopt a son only when he has given up hope of having one of his own. When such a boy, however, is adopted, he is treated as a son and enjoys all the privileges of a begotten son. He takes the surname of his adoptive father and continues his line. Under the old Chinese law, a man seeking to adopt a son was obliged to look first among possible agnates of a lower generation, then among other boys bearing the same surname, and then among related boys of a lower generation bearing different surnames.[32] In Singapore today it is evident that a considerable proportion of boys adopted are nonrelated persons who have been procured from destitute parents.

Further, in some cases, boys are not adopted to fill a gap in the descent line but merely as "children." Often it is lonely women who do this. In these cases considerations of proximity in descent do not apply.

All the abuses in the adoption of children to which the Colonial government has given its attention in the past relate to girls. It has never been suggested that any special measures be framed to regulate or supervise the adoption of boys. Apart from the precautions taken in the employment of boys in theatrical troupes, transferred boys come no more under the eye of the law than boys living with their parents.

2. *Adoption of a daughter.* When a girl is adopted she is not taken out of consideration for descent. She is adopted simply as a daughter who can work in the house and who will, in time, leave the house as a bride. The adoption of girls as daughters is on a smaller scale than that of prospective daughters-in-law. While a girl can be got at little expense, she is the same kind of liability as a real daughter, "goods on which one loses."

3. *Adoption of a son-in-law.* Like polygyny and the adoption of sons, the institution of the adopted son-in-law is a device for ensuring the continuance of the line of descent. It is recognized clearly in the 1931 Code under the name of *chui-fu*. The Code states that the domicile of a *chui-fu* is that of his wife and that he prefixes his wife's surname to his own (*Code*: Arts. 1,000, 1,002). The institution is established in Singapore. It is necessary, however, in the context of the "South Seas," to distinguish clearly between a man who enters his wife's home to carry on the

---

[k] There is a steady flow of Chinese females into the Malay and Arab communities.

line of his parents-in-law from the man who merely takes up matrilocal residence. The strong Chinese tradition of patrilocality has been considerably modified in practice by conditions of migration, and it is well known that many men who have come to the "South Seas" have been taken into the homes of their wives. At the present time, Penang is the area in Malaya where matrilocal marriage appears to be practiced most extensively.

Sometimes Chinese make a further distinction between a man who enters his wife's house and agrees that one or two of his future sons shall carry on the line of his father-in-law, and a man who sells himself and his surname outright. The latter type of person is contemptuously said "to sell his great lantern," the reference being to the lantern hanging outside the house which bears the family name.

4. *Adoption of a prospective daughter-in-law.* What in the Hokkien dialect is called a *sīm-pŭ-kià:*, a little daughter-in-law, is a girl who, usually at an early age, is brought into the house with a view to her later marriage to a son. It is usually said that a *sīm-pŭ-kià:* is taken for a particular son and that the institution is merely a system of betrothal in which residence begins in the man's home at betrothal instead of at marriage. But in fact there may not be any stipulation as to the exact man the girl will marry, and I know of cases where prospective daughters-in-law did not marry any of the sons of the house. It is also a possibility that the status of the girl may actually be left undefined at the time of the transfer, so that if there is no son for her to marry she can be treated as a daughter and either be married out in the normal way or have a "son-in-law" brought into the house for her.

Families take prospective daughters-in-law because they are cheap brides and a source of domestic help. This does not at all imply that they are necessarily ill-treated. They are not to be confused with the girls who form the fifth class of adoption, the *mui tsai*, although in any particular case there is the possibility that a *mui tsai* is being held in the guise of a "little daughter-in-law." (The institution of the prospective daughter-in-law is not referred to in the 1931 Code, but Valk (1931: 76 ff.) states the effect of case law. An agreement to marry, according to a decision of the courts, is considered to have been concluded. But since it is concluded by a parent on behalf of a minor child, the latter has the right to repudiate it later.)

5. *Mui tsai.* The whole question of young girls transferred to work as domestic servants[33] has been thoroughly gone over by an official report published twelve years ago. A commission of three persons, headed by Sir Wilfrid Woods, made on-the-spot inquiries in Hong Kong and Malaya in 1936, and their report, *Mui Tsai in Hong Kong and Malaya*, was pub-

lished by the Stationery Office the next year. Very summarily I give some of the leading findings and recommendations of the Majority Report by Sir Wilfrid Woods and Mr. C. A. Wills (Great Britain, Colonial Office, Mui Tsai Commission 1937: 113).

The adoption of girls is common. . . . In the great majority of cases it is for a perfectly legitimate purpose. . . . In Southern China the domestic servitude of girls (the Mui Tsai system) has been a recognised institution of Chinese life . . . , involving valuable consideration on this as on every other occasion of a child's transfer. . . . The Mui tsai system is essentially a system of domestic service. It is not a system of exploitation of a girl's sex and does not ordinarily expose her to moral dangers.

The practice of the *mui tsai* system was not expressly forbidden in the Straits Settlements until the introduction of Ordinance number 5 of 1932 (in force on 1 January 1933) which forbade the acquisition of *mui tsai* and required the registration of those *mui tsai* held at the time. In 1933, 706 *mui tsai* were registered in Singapore, and by 1936 their number had dropped to 367 (112 having been married, 98 ceased to be *mui tsai*, 30 returned to their parents, and 36 admitted to the government home of protection (p. 313). The Commission (p. 114) found that "the registration of existing *mui tsai* . . . was seriously incomplete [and] the prohibition against the acquisition or employment of *mui tsai* has not been strictly enforced."

The registration of all transferred girls was ruled out by the Commission, and they made various recommendations (pp. 116 f.) for the improvement of the machinery for eradicating the system of *mui tsai*. However, the Minority Report, by Miss E. Picton-Turbevill, expressed concern at the exploitation of young girls, and pointed out the difficulty in distinguishing between different kinds of transferred children. It recommended the wholesale protection of girls who had left their parents before the age of twelve (pp. 245–48).

In 1939 the Government of the Straits Settlements introduced an Ordinance (number 17 of 1939) which embodied the main recommendations of the Minority Report. It required notification to a Protector of present and future transfers of girls under the age of fourteen. This Ordinance, however, was never gazetted as coming into force, and on 27 May 1949, a further Ordinance, called the Children and Young Persons Ordinance, was brought in. This latter legislation came into force at the end of 1950. Among other things, the Ordinance sets up a system for the supervision of girls under the age of fourteen other than the following: those who are living with either of their parents, with a grandparent, with a brother or sister (whole or half), or with the brother or sister (whole) of a deceased parent; those who are over twelve years of age and living with their husbands or the parents or grandparents of their husbands; those who have been adopted by a written law and are living with the adopter; those who are living with a guardian appointed lawfully by deed or will or by a competent court of law; those who are living with a person in pursuance of an order made by a court; those who are inmates of institutions or boarders at registered schools; those who are regularly attending registered schools and living with relatives or friends of their parents or guardians.

These provisions will bring within the scope of supervision most girls of the status of prospective daughter-in-law and adopted daughter. As far as *mui tsai* are concerned, the Ordinance 9 (1) and (23) rules that no child under the age of eight years shall be employed in any form of labor, and that no child under the age of twelve shall be employed in any employment

except agricultural or horticultural light work carried on collectively by the family of the child or by the local community, or on light work of domestic character in the household of a natural parent or legal guardian of the child.

After the commencement of this Ordinance every person who has or intends to have a transferred child [i.e. a girl under the age of 14] in his care, custody or control in the Colony, shall forthwith notify such transfer or intended transfer to the Protector (14(1)).

The Protector will have the discretionary powers to refuse to allow the transfer and to accept notification of the transfer on condition that the person receiving the child furnishes a security. If thoroughly enforced the new legislation will provide an index to the extent of the adoption of young girls in Singapore.

It is made an offense under the Ordinance to pass or to accept valuable consideration in the transfer of children, except in any cases of transfer in contemplation of or pursuant to bona fide marriage or adoption, where one at least of the natural parents or the legal guardian is a consenting party to the marriage or adoption.[34]

Property Rights and Inheritance

In traditional Chinese law a basic principle of property rights was that such rights were vested primarily in males. On inheritance property passed to a man's sons. A man could attempt to will away his estate from his sons, but such a will would be upheld in the courts only in most exceptional circumstances (Hare 1904: 16).

If a man's estate was divided after his death it was shared equally among the sons, except that the eldest son, charged with the perpetuation of the ancestral cult, received an extra share to part of which his own eldest son was entitled. Adopted and begotten sons ranked equally for inheritance, except that an adopted son, where begotten sons existed, could neither succeed to the cult nor take the extra share associated with that succession. Wives and concubines did not inherit, but were entitled to maintenance from the estate, wives having a voice in the management of that estate. Daughters, if married, received nothing. If they were unmarried they were entitled to maintenance until marriage and to a sum for their expenses on marriage (Hare 1904: 16–17, 21).

Book V of the 1931 Code is entitled *Succession*. It establishes equality of the sexes in inheritance. A person's spouse holds the dominant position. After the spouse heirs are ranged in four orders: (1) lineal descendants by blood; (2) parents; (3) brothers and sisters; (4) grandparents. Adopted children rank with begotten children except that if begotten children exist an adopted child's share is one-half that of a begotten child. Several heirs of the same order inherit in equal shares. Among persons of the first order the persons nearest in degree of relationship come first as heirs. A spouse's "successional portion" is the whole estate if there are no heirs of any of the four orders, two-thirds if he (or she) inherits in conjunction with heirs of the fourth order, one-half if he inherits with heirs of the second or third orders, while if he inherits with heirs of the first order his share is equal to that of one of those heirs (*Code*: Arts. 1,388–44).

A person can will his property within limits. A spouse cannot be deprived by will of more than one half of his (or her) successional portion, a lineal descendant of more than one-half, a sibling and a grandparent of more than one-third (*Code*: Art. 1,223).

There are no clearly defined rules for inheritance in the 1950 Marriage Law. While Article 12 states that "Husband and wife shall have the right to inherit each other's property," Article 14 gives the same principle of reciprocal inheritance as holding for parents and children.

In Singapore a person can dispose of his property freely by will. A man may disinherit his sons, which runs counter to Chinese custom, and his wife, which is not allowed under the modern Code. If he dies intestate domiciled in the colony his estate will be divided, if the division is left to the courts, according to the Statute of Distributions modified to take account of polygamy and legitimation by subsequent marriage (Payne 1936: 218–19). Illegitimate and adopted children do not inherit.

As the Statute of Distributions operates, the estate of a Chinese man dying intestate is divided in the following manner. If the intestate leaves a widow and children or lineal descendants of children, the widow's share is one-third, and if he leaves a widow and no descendants her share is one-half. Co-widows share the widow's share between them equally. Children take equal shares, and where they have to share with descendants of a dead sibling the division is *per stirpes* and not *per capita*. Where there is no issue, the first next-of-kin to inherit is the intestate's father; after him the intestate's mother, who will, however, share equally with any siblings of the intestate. If neither parent of the intestate is alive and

the next of kin are brothers and sisters and children of deceased brothers and sisters, they are entitled to share in the estate *per stirpes* where there is at least one brother or sister living. If there be no such brother or sister, their children, that is the nephew and nieces of the intestate, will have the estate distributed among them *per capita* . . . (Payne 1936: 169).[35]

The estate of an intestate married woman passes wholly to her husband. Separation of the married couple does not affect the husband's rights, but where a judicial decree of separation has been obtained (but this, of course, cannot apply to the great majority of Chinese) all property acquired by the woman after the decree passes as though the husband were dead (Payne 1936: 160).

Administration of an intestate's estate may be given to the surviving spouse or next-of-kin at the discretion of the court. Since joint administration is possible it has happened that two Chinese widows together have been granted Letters.

It is assumed in the compilations of old Chinese law that women do not hold property in their own right. They merely have interests in the property of their own family and that of their husband's family successively. The 1931 Code lays down elaborate regulations for the safeguarding of a married woman's property rights. On marriage, unless the couple adopt by contract one of the contractual regimes provided for under the Code, the Statutory Regime governs their property (*Code*: Arts. 1,004–5).

The statutory regime is the union property regime. It embodies two principles, separation of property, as both husband and wife keep their own property; on the other hand a community system as community property is created.

In principle liabilities remain separated: the husband is responsible for his debts incurred before marriage, the wife for hers. At the dissolution of the marriage the wife takes back her own property. (Valk 1939: 101.)

The contractual regimes are three in number. The Community of Property Regime makes the property of both spouses "a legal unity instead of merely an economic one . . ." (Valk 1939: 105). On death, half of the common property goes to the other spouse and half to the heirs.

The Unity of Property Regime transfers the wife's property to the owner-ship of the husband. The Separation of Property Regime leaves each spouse in sole management and ownership of his or her property (Valk 1939: 109ff).

In the first Article of the 1950 Marriage Law are laid down the princi-ples of "equal rights for both sexes," and "the protection of the legiti-mate rights of women and their children." The Communist reformers have been greatly concerned with the status of women in Chinese society, and this preoccupation is well reflected in their legislation. "Husband and wife are partners in a common life." The wife has equal rights with her husband in the possession and disposal of property. On divorce the woman takes away from the union what property she brought to it and has a claim, in her own interest and that of her children, on the family property (*Code*: Art. 23).

In 1902 a Married Women's Property Ordinance was introduced in the Colony (number 11 of 1902) which was based on earlier legislation in England. The Ordinance set up the separate property rights of a married woman. A married woman is defined in terms which include customary marriage, and the legal capacity of a married Chinese woman to hold and dispose of her separate property is thereby established.

The coming of English law to the Colony meant a clash with Chinese practice in the matter of the tying-up of property indefinitely for the purpose of endowing ancestor worship. In 1869 Sir Benson Maxwell ruled that perpetuities were not valid in the Colony (Braddell 1931: 63), applying the English Common Law to Colonial conditions on the grounds of public interest. Setting aside the property for ancestral wor-ship was held not to be charitable, but, at the same time, the courts have not ruled this practice "superstitious," and a will reserving certain prop-erty for the uses of ancestor worship for a limited period will stand.[36]

The Development of Law and Its Problems

It has been necessary in this paper to examine four different systems of formal law, each of which has some significance for the regulation of family affairs among Chinese in Singapore. Two of these systems are modern codes, worked out to reflect certain modernist ideals of indi-vidualism and sexual equality and designed to help shape Chinese society in accordance with those ideals. Another system is made up partly of an older codification and partly of a none-too-well defined body of custom. The fourth system is the product of the attempt by Colonial courts to give force to such parts of pre-revolutionary Chinese law as were held not to conflict with English principles.

This system is by its nature anomalous. It is, as judges and commentators have frequently observed, neither Chinese nor English. It has been described as an unfortunate hybrid developed to the detriment of Chinese interests. While in a sense it has grown up haphazardly, passing from precedent to precedent with occasional statutory modifications, its development has been governed by two basic principles. These are the absence of fundamental legislation and the failure of the initial Charters of Justice to make unambiguous provision for the application of Chinese custom. With only the vague injunction to modify English law, the judges have felt themselves obliged to apply the rules of the Statute of Distributions in cases of Chinese intestacy (while adjusting them to take account of polygamy), to disallow perpetuities, and to refuse to acknowledge the status of adoption in inheritance. The "injustices" of the resulting system follow from the principles upon which it is based and are not the product of attempts by colonial judges to build an arbitrary family law from their own uncontrolled opinions and preferences.[37]

It has, of course, occurred to jurists and administrators in the Colony from time to time that the legal process has moved far from Sir Benson Maxwell's interpretation of the Charter to mean that "the law is subject, in its application to the various alien races established here, to such modifications as are necessary to prevent it from operating unjustly and oppressively on them." From 1869 to the present the tolerant spirit of the Charters has been invoked in the courts, but the results have often appeared inconsistent with the aim. Consequently, from time to time attempts have been made to right matters by drafting legislation, but these efforts have never met with success. In 1901, for example, when there was public comment on the contradiction between granting several co-wives shares in their husband's intestate estate and prosecuting a Chinese for bigamy, Napier asked in Council whether the government would legislate to place the law of Chinese marriage and inheritance on a satisfactory basis. Government, government-like, replied, "that the matter was one of considerable importance and delicacy, and it was giving the question of legislation on the subject serious consideration" (Song 1923: 392–93).

The failure to draw up suitable legislation has been attributed to the indecision of the Chinese themselves. Writing in 1921, Braddell said:

What they [the judges] have done has resulted in very fair justice and those who readily clamour for legislation on the subject of Chinese marriage would do well to remember that several of the best lawyers we have had have tried their hands on the subject and dropped it. The plain unvarnished fact that governs the whole matter is that the views of the Chinese of this Colony are so very divergent that legislation is practically impossible. (Braddell 1921: 165.)

Again:

No one pretended that this decision [in the Six Widows Case] was in accordance with Chinese custom, and proposals were made from time to time to introduce legislation more in accordance with Chinese ideas. It appeared, however, that the Straits Chinese themselves were not altogether agreed as to what legislation was required, and accordingly the law was left as it was. (Terrell 1932: 63.)

The situation is one, then, in which the lack of a unified public opinion among the Chinese has contributed to the permanence of an unsatisfactory legal system. This diversification of attitudes toward the theme of legal reform can be analyzed into a number of factors.

In the first place, at no period in its history has the Singapore Chinese community been recruited from a single dialect group from China. There has always existed a medley, in varying proportions, of the major groups, Hokkiens, Cantonese, Teochius, Hakkas, and Hainanese, with some smaller groups in addition.[38] Although virtually all the Singapore speakers of these several dialects have originated from the two adjacent southeastern provinces of Fukien and Kwangtung, and from some points of view display characteristics as a whole which might be called a regional complex, nevertheless, between the dialect groups, and often within them, there is evidence of such diversity of custom as to prevent us assuming a unified attitude to family law. The institution of the prospective daughter-in-law, for example, does not have a uniform distribution over the dialect groups. Certain details in the ceremonial of the old-style wedding vary from group to group. More strikingly, one subgroup even traditionally practices junior levirate, an institution rigorously prohibited under the imperial codes.[39]

This last example raises the question of "class." The analysis of Chinese society must take account of the divergence in behavior between "peasantry and gentry," to use the current terminology. Professor Fei Hsiao-t'ung (1946) has argued this discrimination forcefully, and modern sociological work on China appears to accept it as an analytical device. Already in earlier European studies of China there is much to validate the concept. From the point of view of family law, it is the at least ideal behavior of the Chinese gentry which is reflected in the imperial codes and the general statements of family patterns and ways. There is much to show that the peasantry has widely diverged from these gentry norms, and that certain values (such as the chastity of widows), ritual elaborations (as in marriage), and types of organization (the large joint family, for example) have been largely confined to the gentry.

In Singapore we are concerned with a Chinese population which has been recruited with few exceptions from the "peasantry" of Fukien and

Kwangtung. This "peasantry" has at times included elements, some of them urbanized, not based economically on the land, but still sharing that "lower class" culture which is generalized as "peasant." The small merchant section of the overseas migration was never assimilated to the gentry class, which, literate (in the Chinese sense) and securely established, remained aloof from the largely disreputable movement to foreign parts. It follows that much of the evidence sought and taken by colonial courts on Chinese family practices has in fact related to ideals of gentry behavior which have never been current in the mass of the population.[1] The position in Singapore, however, has been complicated by the growth of "gentry-consciousness" among those Chinese who, by rising up the ladder of wealth, have considered themselves to constitute in a sense the "gentry" of overseas society. Up to the foundation of the Chinese Republic well-to-do Overseas Chinese "bought" from the Imperial government the right to the status of mandarins, and portraits of their suitably adorned persons hanging in their family houses contradicted the other evidences of their humble origin and lack of education. Large-scale concubinage, the keeping of *mui tsai*, attempts to maintain large households, and efforts to build a secure cult about their memory by the endowment of ancestral worship, were the chief means by which pre-twentieth-century Singapore Chinese established their class position in the realm of family matters. In modern times, while polygamy still survives as a class index, the other means have become greatly attenuated.

Factors of education, religion, and nationalism can conveniently be grouped under the heading of "modernism." Living in a British colony brought Chinese into contact with foreign religions and exposed some of them to a Western education. Only a very small percentage of Chinese have adopted Christianity[40] and limited numbers have been through the "English school" system, but contact with the Christian philosophy of marriage and Western ideas of the relations between the sexes has played some considerable part in the general process of modernization. Paradoxically, at first sight, the most potent source of "Westernizing" and "modernizing" has been the postrevolutionary system of Chinese education. Here, in a milieu built on models and principles constructed in latter-day China, large numbers of Chinese have been familiarized with the

---

[1] I may illustrate briefly some points of divergence. "*Usus* is undoubtedly the commonest form (of marriage) amongst many of the lower classes, and receives the sanction of law when the *usus* can be proved by litigants. . . . The strictly ritualistic marriage is only performed in its complete integrity amongst the wealthier classes, though fragments of it are frequently introduced into the lower marriage ceremonies" (Werner 1910: 28). De Groot (1894: 760) points out that among the poor the remarriage of widows during the mourning period for their husbands was done in the region of Amoy, in Fukien province, and winked at.

essentially Western ideas of sexual equality, courting and free choice in marriage, and monogamy. Chinese nationalism has gone hand in hand with this educational system. It has provided it with a language and a set of political and social ideals. At the present time the social reformism implicit in the New Life Movement of the Kuomintang has largely given way to the more extreme ideology of the People's Republic. From the older nationalism sprang education for girls and the new-style marriage; the newer version sets up the ideals of absolute monogamy and sexual equality.

Division into dialect groups, class differentiation, and the influence of "Western" and "modern" ideas upon certain sections of the community, together prevent the development of a homogeneous public opinion toward problems of family law. If, for example, the government were to make one more attempt to establish the law of Chinese marriage and divorce on a statutory basis, it would be faced with a contrariety of attitudes which might successfully defeat it once again. On the single question of the registration of marriages alone one could foresee a bitter debate.

It will be recalled that the Chinese Marriage Committee of 1926 found sufficient support for the recommendation of a voluntary system of registration. Since that time the demand for the security which such a procedure gives has certainly increased. Although it was administratively an absurd request, on the occasion of one of the Mass Weddings in 1949 the organizers sent a letter to the Registrar of Marriages in the Colony asking him to attend the ceremony and register the unions made there. Registration is closely linked with monogamy, and polygamy to some considerable extent is a "class" interest. At the simplest level the well-to-do might line up against the "modernists." But in fact the division could not be so elementary, because many "upper class" Chinese, themselves often polygamous, would have to take their stand with the "modernists" for purely political reasons. And, moreover, one particular dialect group, as a result of the political commitment of its formal leadership, would be the most disposed to throw its support publicly on the "modernist" side.

Publicly displayed loyalty to one or other set of legal ideas is not a safe clue to the actual rules by which people conduct their own family affairs. The eloquent speechmakers in favor of the new Chinese regime and the reformist notions it propagates may be observing rules of private conduct which would fall into the Communist category of "feudalism."[41] They may be polygamous, grant little independence of movement to their daughters, arrange their sons' marriages, and even keep *mui tsai*. This is not simply an illustration of the usual divergence between ideal and actual behavior, but an example of the acceptance of different norms at different levels of social activity. The demands of political life require adherence to one set of rules, the operations of one's private life permit another. There may have been a time when the cry for legal reform in the colony meant simply the recognition by the courts of something that might be said to be the de facto law of the Chinese. Today, acceptance of the demands for reform would contribute to the reshaping of social behavior in conformity to the doctrines of "modernism."

Colonial law purports to govern Chinese family affairs along certain lines. It recognizes polygamy and raises the status of a secondary wife very nearly to that of a principal wife. It grants rights in intestate inheritance to widows and gives daughters equal rights with sons. It disallows the rights of adopted children and children born out of wedlock recognized paternally as legitimate. It accepts the unilateral divorce of a secondary wife, but is doubtful on the validity of a divorce by mutual consent and silent on the unilateral divorce of a principal wife. It allows a married woman control of her own property. It grants absolute freedom in testamentary disposition. It prevents a man from tying up his property indefinitely for the performance of ancestral worship. What influence, in fact, has this "government law" had upon Chinese family life?

There was a time, before the coming of the novel legal ideas of the Republic of China, when colonial law was, by Chinese standards, an advanced system in many respects. Chiefly, it enhanced the legal status of women. It protected them as wives, concubines, inheritors, and adopted "daughters." It is of the greatest significance that the main principles of Chinese family law laid down by the courts in the colony arose directly from disputes over inheritance. Chinese women were ascribed rights unknown in traditional law and many of them took advantage of this acquisition. In modern Singapore the daughters of wealthy families and the secondary widows of rich men are not slow to press their claims where there is no will. In fact, a good deal of "modernization" has been achieved by the "government law." In its prohibitory aspects the law has, by statutory means, made the keeping of *mui tsai* very difficult and certainly contributed to the decline of this institution. In refusing inheritance rights in intestacy to adopted sons and "illegitimate" sons recognized by their fathers it has caused resentment; but a Chinese of foresight can provide for these children by will. It is doubtful whether, under the mobile conditions of Overseas Chinese society, the law against perpetuities has decisively affected the continuance of ancestor worship; the disintegration of family worship in Singapore can be explained in other terms.

Partly because of its concentration around problems arising from inheritance, the law of the Colony is silent on some points of Chinese family law which are of importance. One of these is the traditional prohibitions of marriage between certain relatives. Surname exogamy is very nearly universally observed by Singapore Chinese, despite the relaxations granted by newer conceptions. It does happen from time to time that two people of the same surname marry, but they are never of the same known descent, and the exceptions they constitute are significantly interpreted by Chinese at large as the extreme form of modernism. The ban on sexual relations between two persons of the same surname, for the mass of Singapore Chinese, is a law, but it is a law without legal sanction. The courts cannot enforce it, and no organized action by Chinese can be taken to punish its contravention (as would have been done traditionally in China). Public opinion and private punishment may act as sanctions, but the anonymity of city life allows escape from both. That surname exogamy persists so hardily is evidence of the powerful sanctions of moral conviction and fear of ritual punishment.*m*

In a similar way the minimum ages for marriage are not laid down in the Colonial legal system.*n* There does not appear to have ever been a tradition among the Chinese to marry very young girls, and child betrothal did not lead to sexual relations until the wife was mature. The setting of the minimum ages at sixteen for women and eighteen for men in the 1931 Code would not, if applied in Singapore, have been a restriction. The new Communist Marriage Laws, however, raise these ages to eighteen and twenty and would run counter to some practice. It is significant that there was much Chinese support and no Chinese opposition to recent legislative proposals in Singapore for the imposition of a minimum age of sixteen for the marriage of women. Opposition from Muslims to this proposal was loud and effective.

In constructing rules for the reciprocal rights and duties between parents and children Colonial law has confined itself largely to the protection of the children. In imperial China a local magistrate could be invoked to punish a son for unfilial conduct, and it will be noted that the new Communist Marriage Laws specify that children are obliged to support their parents. In general in Singapore, Chinese assume this obligation in the order of things. Many grumble at the burden imposed on them, but the complaint is against the particular misfortune and not the principle of filial duty behind it. When I teasingly told a young Chinese

m While sexual relations between persons of the same surname is in Chinese eyes incest, colonial law defines incest in Western terms. See Section 376A of the Penal Code.

n It seems to follow from Section 375 of the Penal Code, however, that thirteen years of age is the lowest at which a woman can fully enter a state of marriage. If she is below that age her husband commits rape in having sexual intercourse with her.

that Europeans abandon their parents, he protested strongly: "What nonsense? They bring you up, and you don't feed them when they are old?" But against the nonconformers to this rule no legal sanction can be invoked. What moral values and public opinion cannot enforce must go uncorrected.

Since the courts deal with only a tiny number of Chinese divorces official intervention in questions of the custody of children after divorce is to be seen in the working of the Women and Girls Section of the Department of Social Welfare. But in this agency divorces are arrived at only by mutual consent, and the question of to which party the children are to be given in custody has to be settled by compromise between the two parents. Traditionally, except in the adopted son-in-law system, the children of a marriage "belonged" unequivocally to the husband and his paternal ascendants. If the marriage was broken the children remained in their father's house. But in modern disputes in Singapore the "ownership" of children is frequently conceded to the wife by the husband as part of the bargaining process leading up to the final signature of divorce papers. Colonial law, by its concept of illegitimacy, even provides a woman who is determined to gain exclusive control over her children with the means of doing so by denying marriage with their father. If a magistrate is satisfied that in fact there was no marriage, he can make an order against the father to pay a certain sum monthly for the support of the illegitimate children; but this maintenance confers no rights on the father over the children. In any dispute before them concerning the custody of children the Colonial courts will pay great attention to the interests of the child and will prefer the claim of a parent to that of a remoter relative.[42] In this way, old people whose widowed daughter-in-law takes away their grandchildren have no remedy against her; by custom the children are theirs, but they cannot enforce this right in Singapore.

Except that the divorce court will take adultery as a ground for divorce in the case of a monogamous marriage, this misdemeanor receives no recognition in Colonial law. But in Chinese eyes adultery committed by a woman is a heinous crime. In imperial law it was severely punishable. Even the Republican government had great difficulty in carrying through its modernist ideology into this field; while, on the one hand, it created symmetrical rights in divorce for men and women, on the other hand it was at one point nearly forced to provide for the punishment of adulteresses only in the Criminal Code.[43] In Singapore a Chinese husband has no legal right to punish an unfaithful wife and if he throws her out she is still married to him unless she is willing to sign a divorce.

I have so far considered three general categories of factors contributing to legal change in the realm of the Singapore Chinese family: the colonial legal system, the impact of new legal ideologies from China, and the heterogeneity of Overseas Chinese society. The emphasis has been placed upon the rules of family life, that is, the content of law. Equally important is a study of changes in the institutions which enforce the law. I have pointed out that the significance of "government" law begins about the last quarter of the nineteenth century; at that time the self-sufficiency of Singapore Chinese society began to break down, and internal organizations which could control the behavior of Chinese without interference from outside gradually disintegrated. In recent times there have been no Chinese organizations which can be said to have seriously competed with the colonial courts or government agencies in the regulation of family affairs.

In the first place, there are no Chinese organizations in Singapore of a specifically legal character. In the second place, where organizations exist which appear to have a legal aspect, their regulation of family matters is very small. Today in Singapore there are more than a thousand Chinese associations which function with the sanction of Government. They are organized on a variety of principles of which the more important are kinship and quasi-kinship, territorial origin in China, and professional interests. Many associations explicitly set up "courts" for the settlement of disputes between their members and make provision for the protection of members' interests against members of other associations. But in effect family matters are very rarely raised for such adjudication. One might have expected that associations recruiting on a kinship principle at least would play a part in the settlement of family difficulties and quarrels. The explanation of their failure generally to do so lies in the structure of such associations and the nature of their functions.

What are called clan associations in Singapore are groups of men (with the odd appearance of women in some cases) who bear the same surname. Possession of the same surname for Chinese constitutes a blood or quasi-blood relationship because of the ideology that each surname originates from one ancestor and is handed down from father to child.

As a result, however widely two men may be separated by their places of origin in China and by the dialects they speak, the single fact of the same written surname sets up a kinship relation between them.[ο] At the

---

[ο] The same surname may be pronounced very differently in the various dialects. What is *Hsü* in Mandarin is *Khoù* in Hokkien. In this matter of claiming kinship on the basis of surnames we have a very simple and striking example of the influence of written language on social organization; had the Chinese character system of writing been replaced by a phonetic script the notion of a kin link between Mr. Hsü of Peking and Mr. *Khoù* of Amoy would have probably long since passed away. Some evidence from the old established Overseas Chinese in Southeast Asia also suggests that reliance on a phonetic script may lead to the merging of surnames which in character are distinct.

very least, such a relation prevents their children from marrying one another. Many clan associations do in fact recruit people of the same surname without consideration for place of origin. Others may confine their membership to those of the same surname belonging to one dialect group. It is only when we come to associations formed by overseas persons from single localized lineages in China or linked groups of such localized lineages that we have something approaching genuine kinship organizations. A large proportion of the villages in southeastern China appears to consist of single lineages or of single dominant lineages with minor extraneous elements.[44] Despite the fact that these village lineages present the appearance of classical anthropological lineages in which there is segmentation at various levels of the genealogical structure and ancestral cults about the focal points of such divisions, there is much to be said in support of Fei Hsiao-tung's (1946) suspicion that clan villages are in reality local rather than kinship organizations. In particular, when members of such lineages group themselves together in Singapore they do so as much on the basis that they come from one village as because they are of the same kinship organization. The village association in Singapore stands not only at the base of the complex of clan associations but also at the base of the associations recruiting on a territorial principle. Discrimination between generations and lineage segments is not used significantly in village associations; the body of members is not divided along such lines, and leadership follows the same principles as govern prestige and control in practically all forms of Overseas Chinese organization: namely, wealth and high status in the community at large. In home conditions the village lineage is large—it may run into several thousands—and differentiated in wealth, occupation, and social status. It is by no means a simple face-to-face group with homogeneous interests. In overseas conditions the heterogeneity of the village association is even more pronounced, and, furthermore, it is a nonresidential and noncommunal organization. It meets for certain narrowly defined purposes at certain times. Like most other Chinese associations it makes the collection and distribution of funeral benefits a central concern. It organizes so-called ancestor worship once or twice a year. Affiliated to some larger organization of clansmen it may take some part in the regulation of graveyards for clansmen and the publication of a magazine concerned with home conditions and the doings of outstanding members in the "South Seas."

The limits to the social effectiveness of village associations apply, *a fortiori*, to clan associations recruiting on a wider basis. A member of a clan association is reluctant to bring a family dispute before such a body for two reasons: firstly, because the sanctions it can apply are very restricted, and secondly, because there is "shame" in washing one's dirty linen before a tribunal which is in a sense public. The clan association is not the immediate group of kinsmen who would fall within the category of private. Such a "private" group could be defined, in the vast majority of cases, only in terms of small single households and groups of households (by no means physically near one another) related by the closest of kinship links—father-son, brother-brother, father-daughter, for example. And such shapeless kinship units do not see the emergence of a pattern of authority which could settle serious disputes without recourse to some external agency. When a squabble develops over inheritance or "unhappy differences arise" between husband and wife, some outside person or body has to be invoked if settlement is to be reached. Very often, as I have indicated, the outsider is "government law." But there are, in addition, other agencies which might all be grouped under the general heading of "prestige arbitrators." Certain individuals of high wealth and social status, or of high social status alone, are known as arbitrators. When a family quarrel is afoot one of them may be called in to adjudicate or make a compromise. Some of these arbitrators are persons in highly institutionalized roles: the Chinese Consul-General (but the last incumbent of that post assured me that only a small number of disputes were brought to him), lawyers, pastors and priests of the Christian churches (in the case of Christians), important school principals; but a great number are of merely a generalized high position in the community by virtue of their wealth or social prominence. However, as far as one can judge, the arbitrator system does not cover a large part of the process of peacemaking. It is rather a makeshift device and operates without adequate sanctions. The law of the Colonial courts has explicit sanctions; the Women and Girls Section has the implied power of government behind it.

There remains the question as to why, if "shame" can detract from the effectiveness of clan associations as legal mechanisms, "shame" should not prevent recourse to such outsiders as the "government" and arbitrators. There is no doubt, of course, that the publicity of the courts and the newspaper accounts that may follow are very embarrassing to Chinese. If they put up with this uncomfortable procedure it is because other considerations weigh more heavily with them. (The courts wield the final authority in that they alone can apply absolute legal sanctions.) What I have called prestige arbitration and the Women and Girls Section, however, are different. There is no public scrutiny of the procedure. If a party in a dispute has to lose face, then he loses it either before an arbitrator who can be avoided in any future dealings, or before an official of the Department of Social Welfare who, although usually a Chinese, represents a level of society, the government level, which has no day-to-day relevance to his ordinary life.[p]

"Government law" comprises the major legal mechanisms in the field of the regulation of Chinese family affairs. These are, from one point of view, substitutive mechanisms in that they have replaced legal procedures indigenous to Chinese society. What were the procedures in the homeland? Our knowledge of peasant society in south China is slight but there are scraps on which we can base some sort of a hypothesis.[45] In the first place, we have to distinguish between mechanisms in the village community and those provided by a centralized government. The former may have arisen from the lineage structure in that genealogical seniors acted as arbitrators and judges, or from a combination of lineage and such other types of village leadership as that of the wealthy, the literate, and the elderly. The sanctions at the disposal of such judicial persons might in extreme cases be those of physical force; in breaches of the incest taboos defaulters could be chased out of the community. More typically the sanctions were of public reprobation and moral pressure. In a large village community justice at the highest level might be concerned mainly with the adjustment of interests between warring segments; conflict between sublineages is a frequent enough theme discussed by Overseas Chinese.

Over and above the structure of communal justice presided the formal courts of the centralized government. The mandarinate was likely to be invoked in a dispute between two communities, although group self-help might be resorted to and one village attack another. But even within the village the local mandarin could be appealed to when indigenous mechanisms had failed to provide a solution.[46] How the balance between community and official ways of control has varied from place to place and from time to time is a problem to be looked into. The evidence, such as it is, seems to suggest, for example, that in Republican times the magistrate has not taken over in rural conditions much more of the control of family affairs than its imperial predecessor. That is to say, "government law" in China has remained up to now largely above a system of indigenous mechanisms. Like court law in Singapore it has represented, in the last resort, the only authority with full legal sanction; but below it other solutions to problems have been worked out by other means. As a hypothesis we may say that the comparative weakness of kinship and local organization in overseas conditions has thrust more of the burden

---

[p] And, moreover, the officials in the Women and Girls Section are mainly Chinese *women*. The association with government overrides their social inferiority.

of control of family affairs on the superimposed "government law" than its analogous institution, the mandarinate, bore in the homeland. Paradoxically, the alien legal system assumes greater importance than the Chinese.

It has followed from my initial definition of law in this paper that certain laws among Singapore Chinese have no legal sanction. If two people of the same surname marry or a son allows his father to die of starvation no strong forces can be marshaled against the offenders which will effectively discipline them and deter others from committing the same misdemeanors. In any colonial context such a situation may arise; the superimposed legal system may construct new rules and back them with sanctions and leave traditional rules unenforceable. Whether we are to persist in calling the older rules "law" or to classify them rather as rules with only the sanctions of moral conscience, or ritual, or public opinion, can be made to depend on the status such normative rules have in the total system of social regulation. Since surname exogamy and filial duty are crucial elements in Chinese society and are generally accepted by Chinese as rules which command conformity they ought perhaps to be called "law"; at least, they ought to be called "law" when we are discussing other crucial norms which differ only in that they have the sanctions of a legal system. Otherwise we should have to speak of "the rules of family life" instead of "family law," keeping "law" for what political society sanctions. Consequently, I have preferred here to classify all rules and mechanisms touching the regulation of the major aspects of Chinese family affairs as "law." In Singapore an alien legal system permeates Chinese society disturbing the dividing lines between types of sanction. As a body of rules for the regulation of an institution there is an entity to be called "Chinese family law"; but the law of the courts covers this entity imperfectly.

Chinese Family Law in Singapore: The Rout of Custom

The Situation Before 1961

Since 1961 there has been no special Chinese family law in Singapore. The Women's Charter of that year subjected all non-Muslims resident or domiciled in the State (which is now a Republic) to a set of family rules that cannot in any sense be described as Chinese. Yet the Chinese form some nine-tenths of the non-Muslim population of Singapore (and about 75 percent of the population as a whole), and it follows that, while there is no longer any specifically Chinese family law, there is a new body of family law for a predominantly Chinese population.

And yet, in the most literal sense of the word "Chinese," there was no Chinese family law in Singapore before 1961 either. If we look at the Chinese diaspora we can, for the purpose of our present inquiry, divide the countries where Overseas Chinese are domiciled into three classes. In the first (the outstanding example of which is Hong Kong) the family law governing the Chinese is the law of China—at least, as that law was before the Republic. In the second class, Chinese are subjected to a general family law that takes almost no account of their ethnic peculiarities. England is an obvious example. In the third class (to which the Singapore of pre-1961 belongs) Chinese family law as a whole is not admitted, but many principles peculiar to the Chinese are taken into account. We shall now see that, before the enactment of the Women's Charter, Singapore Chinese were governed by a family law that was *sui generis*, being in part Chinese, in part English, and altogether odd.

It developed in this fashion.[1] Founded as a British settlement in 1819, Singapore joined Penang, and was a few years later joined by Malacca, to form the trio that was eventually to become the Colony of the Straits

In J. N. D. Anderson, ed., *Family Law in Asia and Africa* (London, 1968), 49–72.

Settlements. And for this reason we have, up to the Second World War, to treat Singapore law as part and parcel of the law of the Straits Settlements. The lawmakers and judges of these Settlements found themselves dealing with people of many religions and national traditions: Chinese, Muslims (chiefly Malays, Arabs, and Indians), Hindus, Christians, Parsis, and Jews. The list could be extended. It was natural, therefore, to suppose that each religious or ethnic community would be governed as to its family law by its own traditions. The Penang Charter of Justice of 1807, in the words of the first Recorder, "secures to all the native inhabitants the free exercise of their religion, indulges them in all their prejudices, pays the most scrupulous attention to their ancient usages and habits."[2] But as the business of the courts built up on the basis of the Second Charter of Justice, 1826, it became clear that the judges thought themselves obliged to apply the law of England, although in such a way as to deal fairly with native custom. In a famous judgment of 1869 (*Choa Choon Neoh* v. *Spottiswoode*) Sir Benson Maxwell said: "In this Colony, so much of the law of England as was in existence when it was imported here and is of general (and not merely local) policy, and adapted to the conditions and wants of the inhabitants, is the law of the land; and further, that law is subject, in its application to the various alien races established here, to such modifications as are necessary to prevent it operating unjustly and oppressively on them (Braddell 1931: 62). The term "alien races" applied to all the non-English,[3] but one section of the population had some claim to be considered indigenous: the Malays. And when British rule was extended from the Straits Settlements to the Malay States in the last quarter of the nineteenth century, the special position of the Malays came to be reflected in the Colony. It is for this reason that Islamic family law became established almost in its entirety in the Straits Settlements and that it is now the only special family law left in Singapore (see Ibrahim 1965a). The Chinese, unambiguously immigrant, were subjected to English law modified to accommodate certain features of their institutional life.

No statutes were enacted to lay down what that accommodation was to be, and it was left to the judges to make the law as they went along. They made it, to summarize its main points, by finding that the Chinese were polygamous, that widows and daughters were entitled by English rules to shares of an intestate's estate, that adopted sons were not entitled to such a share, and that property could not be tied up indefinitely in order to provide for ancestor worship.

The chief concession to Chinese principles was to acknowledge that they were polygamous. But that polygamy so sanctioned was not in fact an institution that the Chinese could recognize as their own. For the law of the Straits Settlements turned concubines or secondary wives into spouses of virtually equal status with major wives. The rulings arose chiefly when decisions had to be made on the disposal of intestates' estates.

By the application of English law a widow on her husband's intestacy was granted a half or a third share of his property, depending on whether he left issue. This certainly was not Chinese law, for under that law a widow had no claims to an outright share, her rights being restricted by the fact that family property vested in males. And having admitted the wife to this right, the judges opened the same door to concubines, the widow's half or third share being divisible equally among all widows. Sir Benson Maxwell appears to have begun the series of relevent judgments in 1867. He said:

The first wife is usually chosen by the husband's parents of a family of equal station, and is espoused with as much ceremony and splendour as the parties can afford; while the inferior wives are generally of his own choice made without regard to family connection. But that they are wives not concubines seems to me clear from the fact that certain forms of espousal are always performed and that, besides, their children inherit in default of the issue of the principal wife, and that throughout the Penal Code of China they are treated to all intents and purposes as well as the first.[4]

By the time of the spectacularly named Six Widows Case of 1908 there had been a series of judgments in which the Chinese had been held to be polygamous in this sense.

But how was a concubine to be distinguished from a mistress or (in the language of the Straits) a "keep"? Rich men were sexually active; they made informal liaisons that were often fruitful of children. From the Chinese point of view, the legitimacy of offspring depended on a man recognizing them to be his children, and such recognition said nothing about the status of the mothers as the man's consorts. But to find that a child was a legitimate heir the Straits courts had to find that his mother was a wife; and while the judges seem to have begun by demanding that a marriage be proved by evidence of some ceremony, they finished up in recent times by accepting that a secondary marriage could be found where there was merely intention to form such a union. In the 1930's the general test of a secondary marriage appears to have been whether there was cohabitation and repute, but since the Second World War intention has come to be taken as the crucial element. In 1965, when Singapore was still part of Malaysia (into which country it had ventured in 1963), the Federal Court upheld a Singapore judgment to the effect that, in order to prove a Chinese secondary marriage, it is necessary to show only that there was a common intention to form a permanent union as husband and wife and the formation of the union by the man taking the woman as his secondary wife and the woman taking the man as her husband. And that is how the law will presumably continue to be applied until all the secondary unions formed before 1961 have been exhausted by time.

But the doctrine of consensual marriage has not been confined to secondary unions. In the beginning the courts assumed that a primary marriage was formed by means of a complex series of rites; and as long as the Chinese in the Straits kept to some version of the traditional marriage procedure no serious problem could arise. But when the Chinese Empire came to an end and new forms of marriage ceremonial were copied from China by people in the Straits, it became less certain that the courts could with ease arrive at decisions about what was to constitute a primary marriage. Against this confused background, the Government of the Straits Settlements appointed a Committee in 1925 which reported the next year. The Committee was invited to submit *inter alia* "proposals for legislation as to what forms or ceremonies should constitute a valid marriage and as to the registration of such marriage . . ." (Straits Settlements, Chinese Marriage Committee 1926: 1). But the task proved very difficult. The evidence before them, in their view, disclosed to the members of the Committee that "there were no essentials for Chinese marriages in the old style common to all the Districts of South China or to the locally-born descendants of emigrants from these Districts, while the new style of marriage does not require any particular form" (p. 11). The new-style form of marriage referred to was one in which, whether the wedding was held privately or publicly, a so-called wedding certificate (an unofficial document to be bought at a stationer's shop) was signed by the parties to the match, by their guardians, and by their "Introducers" (p. 23; see also Freedman 1950 [Essay 7 above]: 105).

The Committee recommended legislation to provide that the courts recognize marriages in the new style (on certain conditions), and a system of voluntary registration of both old- and new-style marriages (pp. 9–10). Compulsory registration was out. "The opposition among Chinese aliens to registration of Chinese marriages of any kind is practically unanimous; Chinese British subjects were divided in their opinions on this matter; . . . the supporters of compulsory registration consist chiefly of Chinese ladies and a limited number of Chinese gentlemen of advanced views" (p. 4). Among the reasons for opposition the two most powerful were dislike of government interference in private affairs and the fear that registration "would involve monogamy in the future."

The Committee's recommendations were not acted upon and, in the same year in which it reported, the Chief Justice observed in court:

I am not so sure that some day the Courts will not have to hold that the only real essential of the Chinese marriage of a principal wife is intention. . . . The whole question, in the absence of legislation, must, I think, be considered to be in the melting pot, and after the lapse of years the crystallization of essentials in the accurate sense of the word may eventuate. In my opinion there is no such accurate category in Singapore yet.[5]

Chief Justice Murison was right in his first prediction: since the Second World War it has been established in the courts that the doctrine of consensual marriage applies to all marriages among the Chinese (Freedman 1950 [Essay 7 above]: 120). Meanwhile, however, the forms of Chinese marriage had increased. To the old and the new style had been added a still newer form in which the marriage was made by a statement of intention placed as an advertisement in the newspapers (*ibid.*: 107).

But if the law of marriage was obscure, what of the law of divorce? The Chinese Marriage Committee found (p. 4) that there was "practically unanimous opposition among Chinese residents born in China to any divorce legislation, which is shared by many Chinese born in the Colony." Chinese ladies of Penang were the only group solidly in favor of divorce "as a means of obtaining the prohibition of concubinage." Yet the Chinese knew and practiced divorce, and the courts were forced to take some account of it. In 1861 the Recorder had to decide in Penang whether a Chinese woman had been divorced, as she claimed to have been. The report says: "Chinese witnesses were examined on the subject of Chinese law, but their evidence showed that their information was of the slightest character. On that point, however, the learned Recorder relied wholly on Staunton's translation of the Chinese Penal Code."[6] He found the divorce proved. The Six Widows Case, 1908, recognized the possibility of a concubine being divorced, and the matter arose several times in later years. The position on the eve of the coming into force of the Women's Charter in 1961 was that, in the eyes of the courts, a Chinese secondary marriage could be terminated by the husband repudiating the wife. In 1935 a judge said: "I accept with respect the reasoning of C. J. Shaw that just as in the case of the formation of a secondary marriage, its dissolution can be proved by intention and repute."[7] There was no test case to decide whether the repudiation of a primary wife or the agreement to divorce between a man and such a wife was acceptable in law. And yet we know that divorces by mutual consent were quite common, some of them in fact being concluded with the help of a government agency—the Secretariat for Chinese Affairs, and, more recently (up to about 1954), the Department of Social Welfare.

The baroque muddle illustrated by the law of marriage and divorce could be elaborated by our considering the law of succession to property, adoption, maintenance of wives and children, and the tying-up of property for ancestor worship. Fortunately, I lack the space to go into these complications, for they would confuse my account intolerably. I shall close this section of the paper with a few general observations on the law as it existed up to 1961.

Some of the muddle arose from the attempt to adapt English law to certain Chinese principles. That is obvious. But some of it was due to the difficulty of knowing what precisely those principles were. During the nineteenth century and the early years of the twentieth, the courts sometimes looked at Staunton's translation of the Ch'ing Penal Code (a translation which is incomplete) and various digests of the law of China prepared by Westerners. In addition, evidence as to this law was taken from experts, both Chinese and British. No coherent and accurate picture of the law of China could be extracted from these sources. In the first place, the written sources, to be fully intelligible, would have needed to be subjected to a keen analysis, informed by sinological as well as legal skill, a point amply illustrated by Mr. McAleavy's work (1963) on the parallel situation in Hong Kong. In the second place, it cannot be taken for granted that the customary law which the parties to, and witnesses in, particular cases thought appropriate coincided with the written law of China. The Singapore Chinese were not all from one part of China (although nearly all came from the southeastern provinces); local customs differed. And when the Chinese twentieth century opened, as it did in 1911, new legal ideas and new social rules were projected onto Singapore from China. The culmination of this source of confusion came in the 1950 Marriage Law of the People's Republic, which, as we shall see presently, was in part responsible for the Women's Charter eleven years later.

But we are not to assume that the confusion in the courts was exactly mirrored in the social life of the Singapore Chinese. For the great majority of them the law of the courts was irrelevant; they married, divorced, adopted, and disposed of their property according to the rules they recognized. When large properties were left by an intestate, some dissatisfied widow or child could invoke the law of the courts to secure a share; but most of the time family disputes were settled outside the framework of the legal system, narrowly defined, and by principles that the courts might well have refused to accept. It was only when law began to be thought of by Singapore Chinese as a desirable instrument of social change, and when law as an instrument of politics was placed in the hands of Singapore Chinese, that a new chapter opened in the history of family law.[a]

The Women's Charter, 1961

In the constitutional changes made after the Second World War, Singapore was separated from the rest of Malaya. In 1959 it graduated from the status of Colony to become an internally self-governing State. In its new form the State began life under the administration of the People's Action Party led by Mr. Lee Kuan Yew. Mr. Lee and his party may now seem to us no further to the political left than Mr. Harold Wilson and the majority of the Labour Party, but at the time of Singapore's independence the PAP was radically left, including in its ranks men and women for whom Communist China was a social model. When the Women's Charter Bill was introduced for the first time in 1960 one major change had already been made in Singapore family law; the Muslims Ordinance, 1957, had made provision for a Shariah Court and prohibited the registration of divorces other than those by mutual consent except by order of this Court. And in 1960 the Ordinance was amended severely to restrict Muslim polygamy (Djamour 1966: 26ff). Muslim family law having been put on the map of social reform, it was now the turn of the rest of the population, some nine-tenths of whom were Chinese.

The legal background of the proposed reform of 1960 has already been sketched in, but one further set of facts is required to make the provisions of the new Bill comprehensible. In 1960 many Chinese were already contracting registrable and monogamous forms of marriage. Since 1898 Christians had been barred from polygamy and obliged on marriage to enter monogamous registered unions—although the law was not as clear on this point as my summary makes it (see Buxbaum 1963). In 1960, 426 Chinese couples were married as Christians. In addition, it had been

---

[a] It is interesting in this regard to compare the somewhat hesitant attitude expressed by Mr. Lee Kuan Yew in 1957 (the context being a debate on proposals to register Hindu marriages) with the stand taken by his party a very few years later. After referring to the "curious spectacle" in Singapore "of the English law of intestacy of the eighteenth century embellished and embroidered to fit the polygamous institutions of China of the eighteenth century" Mr. Lee went on: "This is a matter which should receive comprehensive review. No single political party could brave the storm of religious protest and resistance, but if we made a serious attempt to reconcile religious practices with modern-day needs in a modern-day world, we might then first decide whether omnibus legislation covering all religions, except the Muslim religion which is an almost established church in the Federation (of Malaya), might not be a better answer than the proposal of the Member for Seletar" (Singapore, Legislative Assembly, 1957: 53–54).

possible since 1941 for people to form monogamous unions under the Civil Marriage Ordinance; and in 1960, 3,082 Chinese couples married in this fashion. The total figure for monogamous Chinese marriages in 1960 was therefore 3,508. In 1941 it had been 470, in 1948 554, in 1957 1,751, and in 1959 2,490.[8] But a caution must be entered. By no means all the Chinese marriages registered in these years were, so to speak, fresh unions. Many involved couples already married by custom; and as the debates leading up to the new marriage law created a greater public awareness of the significance of registered marriage (for example, it was fairly clear that many Chinese women were under the impression that, once married in this form, they could get their husbands punished for keeping a mistress), the recourse to civil marriage increased. Of the 3,500 registered Chinese marriages in 1960 it would appear that about 1,000 were of couples already married by custom.

The 1960 bill was not made law. It had been sent to a select committee and the Assembly prorogued before any further action could be taken. It was reintroduced the next year, sent to a second select committee, and enacted. During the whole period of the debate there was no opposition to it in principle in the Assembly and little sign of public resistance. One or two voices were to be heard expressing themselves in favor of allowing polygamy to continue, but there was no serious protest. At neither of the two select committees did any effective opponent of the bills put in an appearance, although a few representations were made which opposed certain aspects of the new law. It was not a time to be in favor of keeping the clock from turning forward.

The Women's Charter Bill was deliberately so called in order to convey the impression that a new deal for women was to be enacted. There was to be monogamy and judicial divorce for all (except Muslims); women's property rights were to be strengthened; and—which accounts for the curious fact that both civil and criminal provisions were made within one Ordinance—firmer measures were to be taken to protect women and girls against sexual exploitation. I propose now briefly to survey the second bill as it passed into law.

Part II of the Ordinance deals with monogamous marriages. It begins (s.4) with the provision that nobody who on 2 March 1961 is lawfully married "under any law, religion, custom or usage to one or more spouses" may, during the continuance of any such marriage, validly contract a further marriage. Polygamists are called to a halt. For people marrying after 2 March 1961 there will be monogamy. And (s.6) penalties are laid down for bigamists. Henceforth (s.7) every marriage shall continue until it is dissolved by death or by a judicial decree.

In Part III the Ordinance deals with the solemnization of marriage. Marriages may be solemnized by the Registrar of Marriages or by any person to whom an appropriate license has been granted. Parties to a marriage must be eighteen years of age or older unless a special authorization is granted. The degrees of relationship within which marriage is prohibited are set out (s.10); they are virtually the prohibited degrees of English law. But, by s.10 (5), the Minister may in his discretion grant a license for a marriage to be solemnized "notwithstanding the kindred or affinity of the parties, if he is satisfied that such marriage is valid under the law, religion, custom or usage applicable to the parties" (a curious provision, it has been pointed out (Athmulathmudali and Bartholomew 1961: 320), since it seems to presuppose the continuing validity of systems of marriage which the Ordinance otherwise wipes off the slate). The remainder of Part III deals *inter alia* with the consent to a marriage required in the case of a minor, the notice required for a marriage, and the form of the marriage ceremony. Every marriage must be solemnized in the presence of at least two credible witnesses. The person solemnizing the marriage must be satisfied that both parties freely consent to it. No further ceremonial requirements are made, except that a form of marriage is laid down in the case where the Registrar performs the marriage. And it is provided that religious rites may be added at will. Finally, it is lawful for a religious rite of marriage to be performed when a person "is under the expectation of death," but such a rite "shall not be deemed to be a solemnization of marriage for the purposes of this Ordinance."

Part IV opens (s.24) with the provision that every marriage solemnized henceforth must be registered. Methods of registration are laid down. But an escape clause is inserted: "Nothing in this Ordinance or rules made thereunder shall be construed to render valid or invalid merely by reason of its having been or not having been registered any marriage which is otherwise invalid or valid." To round off the provisions for registration and its effects we may jump to s.166 in Part XI, a section which provides that nothing in the Ordinance affects the validity of marriages created before 2 March 1961, and that such marriages if valid under the law, religion, custom, or usage under which they were solemnized shall be deemed to be registered and shall continue until dissolved by death or by a judicial decree. Taking Parts II and III together with s.166 we can see that it is the intention of the Ordinance that all future marriages should be registered, that they should be solemnized only by people licensed to do so, and that all past extant marriages should be treated as though they had been registered.

Part V makes certain provisions for the solemnization and registration of marriages. I need draw attention only to s.35 where freedom of marriage is entrenched by the rule that "Any person who uses any force or threat (a) to compel a person to marry against his will; or (b) to prevent a person who has attained the age of 21 years from contracting a valid marriage" commits a punishable offense.

Let us jump to Part IX which deals with divorce. Roughly, this Part extends the provisions of the now repealed Divorce Ordinance (which applied only to monogamous marriages) to all marriages registered or deemed to have been registered, including polygamous unions formed before 2 March 1961. The English derivation of the provisions is plain in nearly every section, and is made explicit in s.81 where it is laid down that, subject to the provisions in this Part, "the court shall in all suits and proceedings hereunder act and give relief on principles which in the opinion of the court are, as nearly as may be, conformable to the principles on which the High Court of Justice in England acts and gives relief in matrimonial proceedings." By s.83 a petition may not normally be presented until three years after the marriage. Before determining an application for an early petition, the court may refer the parties to a Conciliation Officer. (Mention of this officer is first made in s.46, where it is provided that the Minister may appoint as Conciliation Officers such public officers as he thinks fit, and that where there are differences between spouses one or both may refer the differences to an Officer for his advice and assistance.) The grounds for divorce (s.84) are adultery, desertion for three years, cruelty, and incurable insanity. These grounds are common to husband and wife, but the wife may offer two further grounds: that since her marriage her husband has gone through a form of marriage with another woman, and that since her marriage her husband has been guilty of rape, sodomy, or bestiality. Now, the first of these two additional grounds at first sight seems otiose, but it would appear to have been inserted to make it possible for a woman married before 2 March 1961, whose husband validly contracted a further marriage before that date, to petition for her own marriage to be dissolved. Thus, if a man was married to several wives before 2 March 1961, all of them except the last now have grounds for divorce.

At s.91 we come to nullity suits. I shall comment on only one of the many grounds specified. S.92 (1)(c) provides that a decree of nullity may be made on the ground that "the former husband or wife of either party was living at the time of the marriage and the marriage with such former husband or wife was then in force." *Prima facie*, the last of the wives of a polygamous husband validly married before March 2, 1961, who cannot, like her co-wives, sue for divorce under s.84, can, under s.92, sue for a decree of nullity. S.92 specifies for some other grounds set out, but not for this one, that a decree shall not be granted unless *inter alia* the petitioner was at the time of the marriage ignorant of the facts alleged.[b]

Petitions for judicial separation and for restitution of conjugal rights are dealt with in ss.96–104. We may now turn back to Part VI. It opens at s.45:

> (1) Upon the solemnization of the marriage the husband and the wife shall be mutually bound to cooperate with each other in safeguarding the interests of the union and in caring and providing for the children.
> (2) The husband and the wife shall have the right separately to engage in any trade or profession or in social activities.
> (3) The wife shall have the right to use her own surname and name separately.
> (4) The husband and wife shall have equal rights in the running of the matrimonial household.

It seems very doubtful whether any specific legal rights and duties flow from these provisions—at least in the case of (1), (2), and (4); and the right asserted in (3) seems to be legally established quite independently of this Ordinance. The legislators had their attention drawn to the vagueness of the section; perhaps the fact that it has passed into law is a sign that the Women's Charter was intended to be a demonstration of sexual equality even in realms where that equality was unenforceable.

S.46, as we have seen, provides for Conciliation Officers. The remainder of the Part deals with the property rights of married women, generally reenacting the provisions of the repealed Married Women's Property Ordinance.

Parts VII and VIII provide for the maintenance of wives and children and for the enforcement of maintenance orders. Here the general effect is to reenact the provisions of the repealed Ordinances dealing with maintenance, but there is an important difference in the new treatment of illegitimate children. Whereas in the old legislation a limit was fixed in respect of the maintenance that could be awarded for illegitimate children, under s.62 legitimate and illegitimate children are treated alike (the court having discretion to decide the amount); and the assimilation of rights seems to have been prudently enacted when, by the banning of polygamy, the Women's Charter may be expected to increase the population of bastards.

It is worth pointing out that a possible measure to provide for wives and children is conspicuously absent from the Ordinance: no restraint

---

[b] As far as I know, however, no divorces have been sought on the ground mentioned at the end of the last paragraph and no petition for nullity has been made on the ground mentioned in this paragraph.

is placed on a married man willing away his property. So while wives and children are protected during a man's lifetime, his widow and orphans are not. An attempt to remedy this defect was made in 1963 when the Inheritance (Family Provisions) Bill was given a second reading; but this piece of reform got lost during Singapore's membership of Malaysia, and has only just now (March 1966) reappeared. The Bill, which seeks to enact the provisions of the English Inheritance (Family Provision) Act, 1938, as amended by the Intestates' Estates Act, 1952, gives the court the power to vary dispositions of property in order to provide for the maintenance of dependents. It will not apply to Muslims.

Part X of the Women's Charter generally reenacts the repealed Women and Girls Protection Ordinance; it is concerned with criminal offenses (prostitution and traffic in women and girls) of no relevance to family law. As for Part XI, the only section of interest to us, s.166, has already been discussed.

The Discussions Regarding the Women's Charter Bills

The atmosphere in which the Charter was brought to birth and the attitudes and considerations motivating its sponsors and supporters are conveyed by the debates in the Legislative Assembly and the discussions with witnesses before the two Select Committees. I think it is worth referring to these valuable historical sources. They reveal, in the first place, that for many of the legislators the Charter was an important first step toward the good society in which women would be placed on a basis of equality with men. Full equality would come only with the consummation of a socialist society; meanwhile, as much as possible was to be done, even within the limits of a still backward community, to secure a good measure of female emancipation. Listen to the words of Miss Chan Choy Siong (translated from Chinese):

This Charter as drafted has incorporated some of the provisions of a number of Ordinances. It has also adopted those of the existing laws of China which have some merits. . . . The marriage system provides for monogamy to enable both the husband and the wife to enjoy equal status in their matrimonial life. The previous evil custom will vanish with the coming into operation of this Charter. The passing of this Women's Charter will not only enable women to be safeguarded in law but will also bring about a revolutionary change in society on a practical basis. . . . The problems of women are the result of an unreasonable society. Men take women as pieces of merchandise. The inhuman feudalistic system has deprived women of their rights. In a semicolonial and semifeudalistic society, the tragedy of women was very common. Man could have three or four spouses. Men are considered honorable, but women are considered mean. It was common in those days to regard having more than one female in a Chinese family as being very despicable. Women in our society are like pieces of meat put on the table for men to slice. The PAP Government has made a promise. We cannot allow this inequality in the family to exist in this country. We will liberate women from the hands of the oppressor.[9]

The indignation at the abuse of women was probably coupled in the minds of many radicals with a puritanical resentment of the opportunities afforded to men in Singapore to exercise their sexual capacities to the full. Dr. Lee Siew Choh expressed the point with elegance.

. . . as our country is just on the threshold of a new era and will need all the energy and help from all quarters—male as well as female—in the gigantic task of nation building, it might be advisable for those who are blessed with more zest and vitamins in their system than may be good for them to rechannel their exuberant energy into other socially useful and non-population-increasing types of productive occupations. The practice of the noble art of sexual sublimation will serve as a shining example for our future generations and will also lighten very much the burden of the Family Planning Association. It is a long cry, sir, from primitive communism and polygamy as has been practised throughout the ages in various parts of the world. Customs die hard but, in all progressive countries, the one man one wife system of marriage is the recognized social order.[10]

But alongside the left-wing ideological pronouncements there lay technical discussions on matters of detail and procedure. I shall deal with three such points: the registration of marriage, the rights of husbands and wives, and the rules of divorce. The first matter arose because, while in the charter as it passed into law all extant marriages formed before 2 March 1961 were deemed to have been registered, in the 1960 bill they were required to be registered. Within a fixed period of the new law all marriages not already registered under some previous ordinance were to be reported to a Registrar, upon whom was to fall the task of deciding in each case whether a valid marriage existed. An appeal was to lie to the High Court. It emerged that certain major disadvantages attached to this procedure. First, the administrative burden would be very heavy indeed, for nearly every existing marriage would need to be registered and there was likely to be a great number on which the Registrar would have to spend time before pronouncing on their validity. Second, from the point of view of the public, wholesale registration would be a great nuisance: many men would be embarrassed to report their plural marriages and some women would be too shy to come forward to register marriages that their husbands had neglected to report. But there was more to it than that: the post-registration of customary marriages was likely in the most dramatic fashion to highlight the conflict between the stand taken by case law on the nature of Chinese polygamy and the attitudes and values of a great part of the Chinese population.

Let me cite the evidence given before the first Select Committee by Mrs. Lee Cheng Hiong, the Chairman of the Singapore Women's Council. Mrs. Lee suggested that a separate register be kept for concubines. The Chairman of the Select Committee asked Mrs. Lee what she meant by a concubine, and she replied: "When a young man has a first girl friend and they get married, then that girl is considered to be the legal girl. And the women in any subsequent marriages of this man are termed 'concubines.'" The Chairman: "But before this Bill was introduced, it was a recognized thing, shall we say, for the Chinese to have more than one wife; is that correct?"—"We do not have the phrase 'more than one wife' in our vocabulary. If there is more than one woman, we call her a concubine. According to Chinese custom, there is only one wife." The Chairman: "Is the Women's Council then suggesting that a man, who now has five wives (using the term 'wife' in that sense) has, in effect, in the eyes of the Women's Council, one legal wife and four mistresses? Is that what the Council means?"—"Yes. We do not consider the mistresses as wives." The Chairman: "If you understand me, of course, that is against the common law as we find it in Singapore. Do you understand that our courts have, in fact, recognized that these other wives are, in fact, secondary wives and not mistresses? Do you realize that?"—"The men who have more than one wife say that those women are their wives. But according to proper Chinese custom, such women cannot be called wives. That is impossible" (Singapore, Legislative Assembly 1960, cols. 13–14).

It then became clear that the ladies represented by Mrs. Lee wanted to deprive the concubines of rights to their intestate husbands' estates; in other words, virtually to make the monogamy rule retrospective. It was the cruel plight of the wife that apparently weighed with Mrs. Lee, not that of the deprived concubines (*ibid.*, cols. 15ff). "My suggestion is to protect those women who are on the legal side. They are the righteous and decent ones. You cannot protect such women as well as those women who are on the wrong side. There must be some difference" (*ibid.*, col. 20). And since the Charter as it has become law dispenses with post-registration, only a few disputed marriages will ever come before the courts (although in somewhat greater numbers than before, because the new divorce provisions now embrace past customary marriages), and Singapore was spared the spectacle of numerous wives contesting the claims of their husbands' concubines before a harassed Registrar.

We have seen that in the Charter s.45 sets out the rights and duties of husbands and wives under four heads. The last head in the first bill read:

"The husband and wife shall have equal rights in the running of the matrimonial household and in the ownership and management of the family properties." The clause as a whole came under fire, but subclause 4 was shown to be particularly weak. In the Assembly Mr. Rajah confessed himself not to understand it. He went on: "The implications of this subclause could be very drastic. Some of the phrases used are such that they cut across the whole conception of property and operation of law in Singapore." He then quoted the subclause, asking what it meant. (A member interjected: "Half the bed!" [11]) In this debate the clause was defended (it was said to be taken from the Swiss Civil Code[c]), but in the end subclause 4 was modified, "as it was suggested that it might be inconsistent with the provisions relating to the property rights of married women." [12] The legislators had found themselves torn between giving married women securer rights to "family property" and protecting their rights as individuals.

We come to the question of divorce which, as we have seen, now rests on English principles ("framed on the basis of Protestant theology," as a lawyer critic asserted before the second Select Committee) (Singapore, Legislative Assembly 1961, col. 12). A case was put by witnesses before both Select Committees for introducing divorce by mutual consent; and it was inevitable that somebody should cite the model of the new law in mainland China (or rather, what that law was taken to mean) (Singapore, Legislative Assembly 1960, cols. 55ff; and 1961, cols. 8ff). At the first Select Committee, the Minister for Labour and Law, Mr. Byrne, said that he and his colleagues had taken a close look at the Chinese law, concluding, first, that it had been made in conditions very different from those in Singapore ("there were a lot of forced marriages in China") and, second, that it appeared that it had become very difficult to obtain a divorce in China in respect of marriages formed after the installation of the new régime (Singapore, Legislative Assembly 1960, col. 63). And in the final debate Mr. Byrne said:

The Bill is not as revolutionary as some people would like it to be. In particular, the provisions relating to divorce follow closely similar provisions in the English Divorce law. . . . It was felt, however, that to allow a marriage to be dissolved by mutual consent or under the Chinese custom by a unilateral public act by the husband would be to defeat the basis on which the Women's Charter was framed. The Bill seeks, on the one hand, to make it as easy as possible to enter into the contract of marriage and, on the other hand, to make it as difficult as possible

---

[c] There is in fact a strong resemblance between the first subclause and Article 159 of the Swiss Civil Code, but it could hardly be the case that the second, third, and fourth subclauses were modeled on anything in that Code.

to contract out of it. It is especially necessary, in a situation where existing polygamous marriages are recognized and where monogamy is to be enforced for the future, that the institution of marriage should be safeguarded and that too easy divorces should be prevented. For otherwise, it would be very easy for an unscrupulous husband to divorce his existing wife or wives and take for himself another wife. Thus the very basis of the legislation would be demolished and instead of raising the status of women, the Charter would further lower it. It may be that when the women of Singapore are more advanced and more aware of and more in a position to exercise their rights, it would be possible to go further in liberalizing the law of divorce—but for the present it is felt that it would be better to work on the existing law, which has been in force in Singapore since 1912, and which has been found on balance not to have operated unsatisfactorily.[13]

It will by now have become clear how paradoxical the Women's Charter is. A left-wing political party felt itself under an ideological compulsion to raise the status of women from the lowly level to which, according to the then current political analysis, colonialism and feudal institutions had condemned them. At the same time the new legislators were working within British parliamentary forms and on the basis of an English legal system, so that the reforms had to be couched in an idiom which was far from being revolutionary. Indeed, we may say that the Women's Charter brought to full fruition the colonial introduction of English law by making the law of marriage and the family a close replica of the relevant law of England—divorce law and all. The courts and the legislators of the Straits Settlements and colonial Singapore had in some measure respected Chinese custom; on independence a largely Chinese party threw out custom to claim the heritage of post-colonial modernism: English law justified by the principles of Asian socialism.[d]

The Consequences of the Women's Charter

It is clear that the legislators responsible for the Women's Charter looked to it as a means both of propagating new norms (that is to say, new ideal standards of conduct) and of enforcing new rights by legal sanctions. At the same time, they obviously recognized that rule-making in a complex society is not simply a matter of positive law but also of education in the broadest sense. The State has in fact forgone the opportunity to press home by penal action a crucial reform: to date (March 1966) there has

[d] It is possible (as has been pointed out to me) that an important reason for introducing the Women's Charter may well have been the growing need in a modern state to ensure clear definitions of the status of wife, husband, and children. In taxing and providing social services, a modern bureaucracy must know the precise standing of its citizens.

not been a single prosecution for the irregular solemnization of marriage.[e] It was assumed, perhaps, that the new law would gradually take root by the operation of self-interest.

As was to be expected, registered marriage, which was on a steadily rising curve before the Women's Charter came into law, has climbed higher still since 1961. Registered Chinese marriages for the years 1961 to 1964 were respectively 3,508, 4,229, 4,769, and 5,476. And these figures have increasingly represented new marriages; in 1963 the four and three-quarter thousand registered Chinese marriages included only fifty-five marriages of couples already married by custom. The problem is how to interpret these figures. The population increased from just over a million in 1957 (when Chinese registered marriages numbered one and three-quarter thousand) to about a million and a third in 1964 (when Chinese registered marriages were five and a half thousand), and some of the rise in registered marriage must be attributed to the growth in the numbers of young people reaching marriageable age. Clearly a great number of marriages must still be taking place outside the provisions of the new law. When I wrote about the Singapore Chinese as I knew them in 1949–50, I hazarded the guess that a total of 7,000 primary marriages were formed each year (Freedman 1957a: 114), registered marriages making up about 8 percent of them. (The population was then just over three-quarters of a million.) Can we now assume that some 12,000 marriages are taking place annually? If so, only a half are being registered.

There are in fact some indications that the couples entering registered marriage come disproportionally from the richer and better educated elements in the population. In a sample drawn from marriage licenses taken out by Singapore Chinese in 1962, a sociologist (Yeh 1964: 104) found the mean ages of brides and grooms to be 24.25 and 28.35 respectively;[f] and these figures suggest that we are dealing with a biased group. Of the 1,335 husbands only sixty-one had had no education, and a total of 535 had been educated at the secondary level (Chinese or English) (*ibid.*: 108). Again, only 518 husbands were in unskilled and semiskilled jobs, while 367 were in superior occupations and 459 in skilled jobs (*ibid.*: 109).[g]

[e] And there have been only six prosecutions for bigamy in the years 1961–65 (nine cases in all having been reported). Of course, the lack of prosecutions for the irregular solemnization of marriage may perhaps have been due to a difficulty lying in the term "solemnization." Many Chinese marriages, it might reasonably be contended, are formed without elements of such rites as are implied by the English word "solemnization." Can a marriage made by a declaration be said to have been solemnized?

[f] The average ages of brides and grooms in *all* registered marriages in 1963 were 23.9 and 27.6 respectively.

[g] There is a peculiar feature of the figures for registered marriages. The Women's Charter

Yet I think we may assume that there is steady progress toward universal registered marriage. It was already clear to me in 1949 and 1950 that Chinese were making increased use of civil marriage because of pressure exerted from the bride's side: after such a marriage there was no possibility of doubt about the woman's status and no means by which the husband could legally take a concubine. The insistence on civil marriage was part of the bargaining leading up to a match and sometimes the price paid for domestic peace by a man who had been party to a customary marriage. It is in the interest of women and their protectors to seek registered marriage, and the man as husband loses out to the man as father or brother of the bride. In a very few years from now, even without penal action by the State, nearly all new Chinese marriages will probably be registered.

One of the consequences of wholesale registration is that, in the eyes of the law, no Chinese marriage is dissoluble except by a judicial process according to English principles. In the old days several hundred Chinese marriages must have come to an end in any one year. In 1951, 143 divorces (nearly all Chinese) were signed in the Department of Social Welfare by the informal procedure then current (Freedman 1957a: 182). At the same time many divorces (but how many it is impossible to say) were signed with or without the help of lawyers (*ibid.*: 183–84). And some marriages simply ended by one spouse quitting the other. There has certainly been a rise in the number of divorce petitions before the court in recent years, but it is equally evident that since 1961 Chinese marriages have not been legally dissolved in anything like the same proportion as in the earlier decade. In 1963, having the opportunity to go through the divorce files in the Supreme Court, I found that in the years 1959 to 1962 the numbers of petitions involving marriages both parties to which were Chinese were 40, 54, 54, and 72; they led to the following numbers of decrees: 35, 47, 49, and 48. In the first seven months of 1963, 64 Chinese petitions were before the court. Since that time the total number of petitions presented has gone up, the figure for 1965 being 156, but in this number Chinese cases are merged with all non-Muslim cases. Legal aid is available,[14] but there must still be some economic deterrent acting

provides for two kinds of marriages: in the Registry and by a person licensed to solemnize a marriage. We find that of the total of registered marriages in 1963 (the latest year for which I have the figures) 4,416 were solemnized in the Registry, 848 in churches, 51 in Hindu temples, and 51 in "various other places." The implication is that the Chinese are not taking the opportunity of converting the former "new style" weddings (often held in public buildings or club premises) into registered marriages by getting the heads of associations and other leaders licensed as solemnizers. But is the heavy concentration on Registry weddings a cause or a consequence of the failure of large numbers of Chinese couples to marry by the rules of the Women's Charter?

along with the formidable obstacles set up by a divorce system working by English rules. As the Minister of Labour and Law said in 1961, an immediate aim of the Women's Charter was to make marriage difficult to get out of. Clearly, the point was to prevent husbands shedding their wives; one may ask whether wives are not also being prevented from ridding themselves of undesirable husbands. Of the 220 Chinese petitions presented in the years 1959–62, 145 were petitions by wives.[h]

Of course, the new law of 1961 was concerned above all with sexual equality, and the extirpation of custom was to be a means to procure that equality. It was, after all, a Women's Charter. New nations emerging from the status of British possessions tend to carry into their new lives political and legal assumptions which, deriving from the institutions of modern Britain, presuppose enfranchised, property-owning, literate, independent women. In the case of the Singapore Chinese, high modernity has been inspired not simply by the direct British model, but also, and more importantly, by the version of Western ideals created in China during the past half-century. We come now to the sociological problem. What social conditions will facilitate or impede the realization of the ideals of sexual equality?

In fact, Singapore seems to enjoy the basic conditions likely to allow institutions to respond to the call of the new ideals. It is a country made up very largely of a city and dominated by urbanism. Its old economic function as a center of trade and small industry is being partly replaced by the function of a large-scale manufacturing center. Education is highly developed. Family planning is publicly and officially accepted as a means of limiting fertility. At the time of the 1957 census (which is the most recent) nearly a quarter of all Chinese women over the age of 14 had worked more than fifteen hours during the so-called "reference week," only an eighth of these working women being "unpaid family workers," and a half of all these working women being married. The literacy rate (per thousand) for Chinese females in the age group 10–14 was 580 and in the age group 15–19 496. The foundations of what passes for sexual equality in a modern society seem to have been laid. And I think we may safely assume that since 1957 the economic, political, and social roles of women outside the domestic sphere have both multiplied and been more largely filled.

[h] It will be recalled that the Women's Charter made provision for the appointment of Conciliation Officers, to whom the divorce court might in certain cases refer couples. There was one such officer in mid-1963 (when I was in Singapore), but no case had been referred to him by the court. On the other hand, conjugal disputes are still brought to the Counselling and Advice Section (which in this matter is the successor to the Women and Girls Section) of the Department of Social Welfare.

What the precise implications of these general changes have been I cannot say, for I have not been able to repeat the observations I made in 1949–50 (my study in Singapore in 1963 was brief) and, although some other studies have been published,[15] they are neither comprehensive enough nor sufficiently up to date to make it possible for us yet to assess the manner in which the new law has meshed with general social change. We are left with a set of unanswered questions. Has polygamy declined *de facto*? Are the rich still able to maintain several households and procure their acceptance as Chinese families by drawing on the reserves of traditional attitudes and values? As Mrs. Wee (1963: 401ff) has pointed out, for many educated young women secondary marriage to a rich man has hitherto been an honorable estate.[i] Has the Women's Charter for them constituted a repeal of status? Is there now even less of a distinction in Chinese eyes between a concubine and a mistress? In the traditional Chinese view, as we have seen, the legitimacy of children depended upon their being recognized by their fathers. Has the new law led to a shift in values such that henceforth only the children of monogamously married wives will be socially acceptable? In a word, how are the norms enshrined in the Women's Charter being translated into the values and expectations of ordinary people?

In Singapore the norms of family life in a modern society have been stated in order to induce that family life. Industrialism and education may well push society along the road to the fulfillment of the new ideals, but it would be dangerous to assume that they will inevitably succeed in all particulars. It is true that the institutions of family and marriage all over the industrialized world tend to take on a common pattern; yet it would be unwise to imagine that every detail of the Chinese tradition will be flattened by the steamroller of modernity. Is it likely, for example, that the ideal of monogamous devotion (that we, looking out from Britain, take to be the hallmark of stable and satisfying family life) can be established where male sexuality has traditional license and the women are categorized into humdrum mothers and alluring playmates? The left-wing puritanism that inspired the Women's Charter is not a set of religious values permeating society. It can dominate politics and law, as new economic opportunities can help women assert the rights that new ideology and new law create for them; but the responses of a complex society to legal and economic changes are not to be foretold by a few simple rules of prediction. It is certainly a pity that, as an anthropologist taking

---

[i] Nobody knows how widespread has been the practice of plural marriage by the Chinese in Singapore; but it has certainly been fairly common, and not confined to the rich, although most noticeable among them. Cf. Freedman 1957a: 119ff.

part in a legal symposium, I have had to pontificate on the law and be very hesitant about the fate of social institutions. Yet at least I shall have demonstrated how much remains to be done in the study of the politics and sociology of family law in Singapore. And, by implication, I am arguing the case for wider and comparative study.[j]

[j] It may be worth adding that I once looked forward from my experience of the Singapore Chinese in 1949–50 to the legal reforms that were yet to come. Happily, I made no predictions but, addressing myself to the colonial government of Singapore, I referred to three "delicate" matters in the realm of Chinese marriage on which I was prepared to make recommendations. The first of these matters was secondary marriage. I wrote: "There is a possibility, I suppose, that public and official opinion might eventually move against Chinese polygamy . . . ," but I was not very sure about it; and I went on to recommend some legal definition of secondary marriage in order to prevent "a mistress slipping over the line into the territory of the wife." I then made a case for the compulsory registration of Chinese marriages. Finally, I asserted that Chinese divorce required some proper basis in law. I wrote: "With or without the aid of registration and with or without the intervention of the courts, it should be possible to legislate for some certainty in this field." (Freedman 1957a: 218–19.)

Religion and Social Realignment Among the Chinese in Singapore

WITH MARJORIE TOPLEY

The social organization of the Chinese in Singapore is so complex that many studies of it will have to be made before we can understand it as a whole. Three anthropologists and one sociologist have worked among the Singapore Chinese, two of them concentrating on religious organization.[1] In this essay we try to give an outline of the sociology of Chinese religion in Singapore, making use of our incomplete knowledge and pointing out what seem to be reasonable conclusions from it.[2]

In 1947 the Chinese in Singapore numbered three-quarters of a million. They then formed nearly four-fifths of the population of a British colony made up of very diverse ethnic elements. Despite their preponderant numbers, the Chinese constituted in political terms a "minority," for they exercised little direct power in the government of the Colony. They maintained institutions within their own ranks which marked out a relatively independent although loosely organized community. The political changes of more recent years have accustomed us to thinking of the Chinese in Singapore as the leading figures in the assault on a colonial bastion, but we should remember that the translation of a numerical into a political majority is a new phenomenon the general social consequences of which are by no means yet clear. Today Singapore is a self-governing State, so far as internal affairs are concerned; the Chinese are the most prominent element in its political life; but the social and cultural aspects of this modern phase have not so far been explored.

When the settlement of Singapore was founded by the British early in the nineteenth century, Chinese from the southeastern provinces of China went there to trade, plant cash crops, and provide a growing commercial center with various kinds of service. As the settlement emerged as the chief trading point in the area, the Chinese increased their numbers

Journal of Asian Studies, 21, no. 1 (1961), 2–23.

by a constant flow of immigration. By origin the immigrants were predominantly rural (although in Singapore they concentrated in the town) and were drawn from the peasant and petty trading strata of the home society.[3] Many newcomers acquired great riches in a largely commercial colonial society, the Chinese as a whole becoming widely diversified in wealth and occupational status. In the social atmosphere of Singapore economic success was treated as perhaps the greatest end of human ambition and as one of the major rewards to be received at the hands of the gods. Many men failed in the quest for riches, but all appear to hope that their turn would come. In a society ranging in economic status from coolie to millionaire, and detached from the bureaucratic structure on which the class system of the homeland had greatly depended, social position rested primarily on wealth.

Nearly all the Singapore Chinese came from the provinces of Fukien and Kwangtung. They spoke a number of different dialects of Chinese. The differences in spoken language became a basis for alignment within Singapore Chinese society in that speakers of one dialect tended, especially in the early days, to cluster residentially, form voluntary associations, worship in the same temples, and (when Chinese women began to immigrate in considerable numbers) marry one another.

The Chinese shared Singapore with British administrators; European traders of various nationalities; Hindus, Muslims, and Sikhs from India, who spanned a wide range of riches; Muslim Malays, who rarely reached the higher parts of the economic pyramid; commercially successful Arabs; and numbers of other Asian peoples. Except insofar as their business required otherwise, the Chinese kept socially very much to themselves. A small number of them, who derived from the older settlement at Malacca, were the products of early intermixture between Chinese men and Malaysian women. They spoke a version of the Malay language, and were in other ways culturally akin to Malays; but even this minority, whatever its cultural adjustment, was still socially Chinese. The great majority of the Chinese spoke one or more of the Chinese dialects at home, even though some of them learned English at school and sometimes used a simplified form of Malay for business purposes. A negligible number were converted to Islam. Christianity, despite its strategic position in the educational system, attracted only a small Chinese following.[a]

Maintaining in Singapore a version of the (mainly "lower class") culture of the homeland, the Chinese remained a cultural appendage of

---

[a] In recent times Chinese Christians (the greater part Catholics) have probably not numbered more than about 25,000, while there have been only two or three hundred Chinese Muslims. That is to say, Chinese positively belonging to a non-Chinese religion account for only some 3% of the total population of Singapore. Cf. Elliott 1955: 29–30.

China. Politically they have taken their standards from China since the establishment of the Republic; before the rise of parliamentary government in Singapore, political groupings within the Chinese ranks were directly connected with movements and alignments in China. In respect of political and cultural innovation, Singapore Chinese society has stood to China much as a province to a standard-setting metropolis.

The Chinese in Singapore lived within a double framework. They were dependent both on China and on the colonial plural society of which they were numerically the greater part. (They have constituted more than half of the local population since about 1840.) In discussing their religious practices and ideas we shall need to bear this double framework in mind. The Singapore Chinese have maintained in foreign parts a religious system which we at once recognize as characteristically Chinese and which we can see to have been affected by religious changes in the homeland. Yet we can also judge how the structure of Singapore society has varied the Chinese religious system in accordance with the special circumstances of overseas life. The religious tradition carried over from China has come to be internally rearranged and modified as a whole.

Religious Aspects of Territorial and Kinship Grouping

In southeastern China the village as a local unit found its religious center in a temple (or, in smaller villages, a shrine), which housed gods who might be ritually subject to gods in temples belonging to higher territorial units. The agnatic lineage of which the village or village-section was composed expressed itself ritually in an ancestral hall, while segments of the lineage might be grouped in relation to lesser ancestral halls in such a way as to produce linked hierarchies of segments and halls.[4] It was from a social and religious background of this kind that the majority of Singapore Chinese originated.

In Singapore there are temples bearing the same name as those associated in China with fixed social units, and which may seem at first glance to serve as ritual foci for determinate social groups on a local basis. These are the temples known in the town as those devoted to the God of the Ramparts and Ditches, and in the countryside as those devoted to the Earth God. While the gods of these temples have jurisdiction over a more or less fixed area, and in consequence may be called upon to protect people living within their purview, the "congregation" of a temple is not drawn from a defined area. Owing to specialization in dialect, rites, and paraphernalia, a temple may principally attract people from one dialect "group," but individuals may and do worship in any temple they choose. The "community" which supports and runs a temple may well be an ad hoc collection of people living within an ill-defined range of it. The members of the temple committee, formally elected each year by means of divining blocks from among subscribers to the funds, are not in urban conditions officers in a clearly marked out local community. In fact, many temples in the town are run by individuals or small groups operating on a business basis and taking their profit from subscriptions and the sale of ritual paraphernalia. In the countryside a local temple is likely to stand in a more determinate relationship to the people who live near it, but even there, owing to the dispersed and continuous form of rural settlement, the population is not always clearly segmented in respect of its temples.[b] (Cf. Elliott 1955: 40–41). In brief, what we may call the general "nonlocal" character of Chinese social organization in modern Singapore is reflected in the status of temples.

Chinese in Singapore have not formed local groups on the basis of agnation, and when what appear to be ancestral halls are found they turn out to be the premises of associations which recruit from among men bearing the same surname. All men of a single surname are agnates, but since the number of surnames is fairly small—there are probably no more than a little over two hundred Chinese surnames represented in Singapore[5]—and since the members of one so-called clan association are likely to be drawn from a wide area of southeastern China and live in different parts of Singapore, the overseas ancestral hall is socially of a different order from its model at home. The Singapore halls are not connected with a localized group of people. Membership is entirely voluntary. The ancestors served stand in a relation to the living which is different from the relation between the ancestors and the living in the halls maintained in China.

In the homeland a domestic unit set up a tablet or other ritual instrument for each socially mature man and woman who died. When a household divided, the tablets passed into the keeping of the senior son. A tablet was kept until it was three to five generations away from the oldest living generation; it was then destroyed or buried near the grave of the individual for whom it stood. For the man or woman superannuated in this fashion from domestic worship a different kind of tablet might be made to be installed in the lineage hall (if there was only one) or the hall belonging to the segment of the lowest level maintaining one. There were,

---

[b] At the time of the 1947 census 537,000 of the total Singapore Chinese population lived within the boundaries of the Singapore Municipality. This figure is only a rough guide to urbanization, because some parts of the Municipal area were semirural in character, while there were small urban settlements outside the Municipal area. Some of the Chinese in the countryside were fishermen, but the most characteristic rural occupations were vegetable gardening, fruit growing, and the raising of pigs and poultry.

then, two structurally distinct phases of ancestor worship in the homeland. They were associated with different social units, different ritual instruments, and different shrines. In one phase the congregational units were individual households or groups of households resulting from recent division. In the other, the units were lineages or their segments.

In Singapore the ancestors are not regularly promoted from one type of shrine to another. In the household the immediate ancestors are represented mostly by plaques of red paper which, owing to the discontinuity of much of the Chinese settlement, preserve the names of only one or two generations. After a time these instruments may be moved to one of a number of public shrines. Moreover, tablets and plaques are sometimes deposited in a public shrine immediately on the death of the people they stand for, so that there is no promotion from house to "hall." The shrines may belong to clan associations, to associations formed on the basis of like territorial origin in China, to temples, or to cemeteries. Once in a public shrine the tablets and plaques are cared for in return for a fee. Sometimes a tablet is set up in a hall in the village in China. In other words, the dead as represented in instruments of worship outside the household are not grouped systematically in relation to their living descendants.

In Singapore we do not find the rhythm to be detected in China by which households divide their hearth and property and yet remain bound for a time in one religious unit in respect of the tablets kept by the senior brother. Overseas the individual household emerges as the only regular ancestor-worshiping unit. Because the instruments in public shrines in Singapore are scattered and form heterogeneous collections, any worship at one of them is not the expression of a fixed social unit. The clan associations, of course, come closest to providing the setting for the collective worship of the ancestors of a fixed social unit, but even there the ancestors represented in the shrines are grouped unsystematically in relation to the membership. We certainly may not say of the ancestors whose memory is perpetuated outside the household that they have ceased to be important for their descendants. The very fact that signs are set up for them is a measure of their significance. But we can see that the changed structure of kinship grouping in Singapore has led to corresponding changes in the grouping of ancestors vis-à-vis the living. Ancestors survive as individuals in what we may call a memorialist cult (Freedman 1957a: 218–19), but beyond the household they cease generally to be foci for clearly marked out groups of kinsmen.[c]

---

[c] It should not be supposed that all the arrangements for ancestor worship in Singapore are without precedent in the big cities of China itself. Note Parker 1879: 71–72: "In the

Temples and Organized Religion

The religious life of any Chinese in Singapore may be limited to his participating, directly or indirectly, in the rites conducted at the shrine in his house, where both a chosen god or gods and the immediate ancestors are served (see Freedman 1957a: 44ff). If, however, he is involved in the voluntary associations thrown up by the "nonlocal" and differentiated nature of his society, he may be a member of groups which in principle at least practice rites before a chosen deity. In former times, when the Chinese population of Singapore was smaller, the main dialect and subdialect "groups" formed associations clearly centered upon particular temples (A Straits Chinese 1899: 10, 43 – 44). Nowadays, while some of the large dialect "group" associations remain linked with and control temples, the numerous territorial associations which recruit from localities and counties in China generally keep their religious symbols and conduct their worship on their club premises. Similarly, many of the numerous commercial, occupational, and other types of association carry out worship of a patron god. In general, when Chinese band together within a traditional setting and for a serious purpose (as opposed to mere entertainment), they set up common worship.

In addition to the religious worship in which he is involved by his belonging to certain social groups, a Chinese may choose to avail himself of the services of the many temples in Singapore. Some of these are the quasi-local temples already discussed. Others are noted for the efficaciousness of their gods, their peculiar sanctity, or their success in conferring special kinds of benefit. Some are the centers of the spirit-medium cults with which we deal later.

Mahayana Buddhism and Taoism are represented in Singapore by separate priesthoods, the specialists of both religions placing themselves at the disposal of anyone who will pay their fees. Their services are in demand mainly for funeral rites. On the other hand, the two religions are not so clearly distinguishable in temple organization. The strictly Buddhist temple is a rarity in Singapore. In most temples both Taoist and Buddhist images are likely to be found, although usually in different rooms or shrines. Taoist priests in Singapore mostly belong to subdivisions of their religion which allow them to marry and lead ordinary lives. Buddhist monks and nuns, in contrast, are people who have "left the

---

provincial Metropolis of Canton there are Ancestral Shrines open to all persons in the Province who bear the same surname, and have contributed to the general fund, irrespective of race or origin (i.e. Hakka, Punti, etc. etc.). Tls. 200 are frequently paid for the privilege of placing a tablet therein, and grand sacrifices and feasts are held in the spring and autumn of each year."

family"; they need monasteries and nunneries. There are two kinds of monastery. The "monastery for all the world" is open to any ordained monk who chooses to stay there. It is only in an institution of this kind that monks and nuns can be ordained. Singapore has only one such monastery, although in fact no ordinations appear to be performed in it. The other kind of monastic institution is for "sons and grandsons." It consists of a Buddhist "family" made up of a master and his (or her) disciples. In practice, a Singapore monastery or nunnery of this sort usually has in it members of more than one "family." However, there are very few nunneries whose inmates are all nuns in the strictest sense (that is, women who have been fully ordained and whose heads are shaved). A nunnery usually has both nuns and other women who have entered the Buddhist faith by taking a teacher and certain vows which bind them to sexual abstinence and a vegetarian diet.[6]

To the ordinary man or woman religion is not a matter of being born into or joining an organized faith. But some people enter Buddhism by taking vows and adopting a special way of life, and there are certain institutions, most of them residential, some connected with Buddhism and others with sects of a syncretic religion, which make it possible for people to adopt a specific faith and, as it were, to opt out of the vague and relatively uninstitutionalized religion to which the mass of Singapore Chinese are committed.

Spirit-Mediumship

Chinese spirit-medium cults are common in Singapore. Recourse to them is widespread. In the main branch of mediumship people consult a god or goddess who has taken possession of a medium in some more or less public setting. The questions put are very largely about illness and other forms of misfortune (Elliott 1955: 161). The medium is occupied with personal and private matters and is not a figure of a public nature expected to settle public issues or help in formulating general opinion. Nor does he stand at the center of a fixed social group of which he might be said to be a permanent functionary. Quite apart from the fact that medium cults in Singapore are transitory, they are nearly always of the nature of enterprises which in effect purvey a service to a relatively undefined public in return for gifts which amount to fees.

A minor branch of mediumship is primarily concerned with communicating with the dead. Here the purpose of the consultation is not so much to solve problems or reach decisions as to learn about the welfare of the recently dead. Seances are completely private to the kinsmen of the dead person contacted.

Where else should religion as business flourish if not in Singapore? But we need to step warily. The evidence on spirit-mediumship in China is ambiguous. It is said to be very general there (e.g. Harvey 1933: 127) and de Groot's monumental researches on religion in southeastern China reveal more or less the same constellation of facts as we can study in Singapore.[7] Yet de Groot's work was done almost entirely in the port town of Amoy and his records as a whole may have little to do with rural conditions. Similarly, Gray writes of what he saw in Canton (J. H. Gray 1878, vol. 2: 22ff) and Doolittle of his experience in Foochow (Doolittle 1868: 437ff). Nor can we appeal to the evidence from the Singapore countryside; the fact that mediumship is well known there by no means conflicts with a hypothesis that a fluid and disturbed society lends itself to the flowering of this kind of religious practice. On the evidence we have we should be rash to commit ourselves to firm views on the differential incidence of medium cults among Chinese. But the fact that both in China and overseas mediumship concerns itself mainly with disease and personal problems, rather than with revelation and spiritual advice to the public,[8] may well suggest that there is nothing special about the widespread recourse to it in Singapore. Yet there is one further fact which must not be overlooked: in one or two medium cults and in other forms of occult practice in Singapore the purely utilitarian limit is exceeded, and people begin to produce utterances from the gods which have a general moral meaning. We shall refer to these unusual pronouncements later.

State and Religion in Imperial China

Many of the facts we have so far brought forward might plausibly be just as true of an urban setting in China as they are of Singapore. But as soon as we think of Singapore as a polity based upon principles different from those which have regulated society in China, we see corresponding differences in Chinese religious life. The Chinese who came to Singapore in the nineteenth century left a country in which their religious activity was both stimulated and checked by the ideology and practices of officialdom. They found themselves overseas in a political system in which their new rulers concerned themselves with the purely religious activity of Chinese only when it caused an obstruction in the traffic or made too much noise.

It may be true, as some writers assert (e.g. Chan 1953: 9–10), that Confucianism cannot be said to have been the state religion of China; but it was certainly the basis of an official religion of which the rites and beliefs enjoyed a special position in Chinese society.[9] Public acts of worship were the principal cult of this religion. Its beliefs were concerned with the maintenance of harmony between society and the universe and between men in politically organized society. Mahayana Buddhism and Taoism exerted considerable influence on the ideas and acts of Chinese at all levels of society, but from the strictly official point of view they were generally, at least in more modern times, to be tolerated and controlled rather than respected (cf. A. F. Wright 1959).

The state was above all suspicious of secret societies with religious elements and of certain heretical religious groups which grew up outside the limits of the sanctioned institutions of Buddhism and Taoism. These religious groups and the sects to which they belonged appear to have been common enough. In their rites and ideas they were syncretic, having made of elements taken from both Buddhism and Taoism systems different from either. They were in many ways unlike the two tolerated religions in their organization.[10] In regard to the syncretic religions and their sects, China was far from being the religiously tolerant state it is often supposed to have been.[d]

Especially in the nineteenth century the southeastern provinces of China showed themselves restive under Manchu rule. Rebellious associations and movements harassed the state. Quite apart from the Taiping revolution in the middle of the century, which nearly brought the dynasty to grief, secret societies and secret or near-secret syncretic religions involved the bureaucracy in a constant campaign of repression.

The secret societies were primarily political in intent and appear to have accounted for by far the greater part of the unrest in southeastern China. Anti-dynastic in their professed aims, they were pledged to rebellion and the replacement of the ruling house by a native dynasty. Their religious ideas, which we are able to study the more easily because they were set out in documents collected by Western students,[11] were preoccupied with sanctifying political rebellion. Their chief ritual was an elaborate and dramatic initiation suffused with elements drawn from a wide range of Chinese religious traditions.

[d] The great work on this subject is of course Groot 1903–4. Records and tables of religious leaders kept in Singapore show that many of the sects described or enumerated by de Groot were offshoots of a widely ramifying religion called Hsien-t'ien Ta-tao, the Great Way of Former Heaven (which we later often refer to simply as the Great Way). Information gleaned from newspapers published in the People's Republic of China shows that syncretic religion is still so much alive as to need repressing. Some of the sects named in the newspaper are offshoots of sects known in imperial times. One sect, T'ung-shan She, was established in 1917. Another, I-kuan Tao, was founded in imperial times but changed its framework of ideas during the republican period. Both these sects belong to the Great Way.

Syncretic religions, such as the Great Way of Former Heaven (Hsien-t'ien Ta-tao)—to name one of the more important—were not primarily directed to political or rebellious ends. Their fundamental concern was spiritual: their members strove to achieve Buddhahood (sometimes within one lifetime) by the cultivation of spiritual powers attained by performing yoga-like practices and reciting secret sutras and incantations. These activities were tied to a number of religious ranks, only individuals of higher rank being able to reach Buddhahood and immortality. However, some of the merit acquired by holders of high rank by means of their religious practices could be transferred to members of lower rank although, at least in the Great Way of Former Heaven, merit could not be passed, as was the case in Buddhism, to people outside the religion. Lay members could not hope to become Buddhas or acquire supernatural powers, but the merit they received was thought to enable them to be born in a future life in conditions more conducive to "realizing the Buddha nature."

On the face of it, then, these religions seemed to have consisted of innocuous groups of people seeking a path to salvation. De Groot's thesis, expressed in a fine fire of Protestant indignation, starts from this general assumption, and proceeds to the conclusion that uprisings were the direct result of the persecution to which they were constantly subject. It is certainly true that the state condemned syncretic sects for activities which were regarded as being contrary to Confucian notions of propriety and moral conduct. Men and women worshiped together. They lived somewhat like monks and nuns in their own homes. In the "vegetarian" (*chai*) sects of the Great Way rank was open only to those who undertook to refrain from sexual intercourse. Members wore no special form of religious dress (at least openly), recruited their members and met in secret, and so doing did not lend themselves to control. Partly on these grounds the state proscribed the sects and tried to stamp them out, often in the face of great resistance.

One might suspect, however, from the literature on messianism in China that the heretical religious movements came into conflict with the state not only because they were persecuted but also because they were positively against the state for some ideological reason. The documents kept by Singapore sects of the Great Way suggest that they took part in, or instigated, political uprisings not only to protect themselves but sometimes also because they thought that the dynasty was "unorthodox": it lacked Heaven's mandate—which the leaders of such religions themselves claimed to hold. They believed that state unorthodoxy would lead to a catastrophe in the form of fire, water, or wind, in the same way as "incorrect teaching" of religion produces disasters.[e] Sometimes floods would be pointed to as "water catastrophes" which indicated the end of a period of incorrect teaching and the beginning of a new era.[12]

The participation by a sect of the Great Way in political rebellion was usually connected with the belief that its leader was an incarnate Buddha, an individual who had reached Buddhahood on earth by means of esoteric practices. As in Mahayana Buddhism, Maitreya, the Buddha To Come, is the figure chiefly associated with salvation. When a religious leader claims to be Maitreya on earth and when natural disasters are interpreted to mean that the end of incorrect teaching, or unorthodox government, is at hand, salvation may come to be seen in more practical terms. The leader, or teacher-patriarch, as he is known in many of the sects of the Great Way, controls religious policy. The religion has as its supreme object of worship a female deity known in many sects as Venerable Mother. The leader often receives the most important orders on religious policy from this goddess. One sect records an occasion in the mid-nineteenth century when a certain incarnate Maitreya claimed to have received a message from Mother ordering him to start a rebellion. Some present-day offshoots of the Great Way came into being when high-ranking members refused to believe that the message was really from Mother and declined to take part in the uprising.

Perhaps the Chinese sectarian organization best known in the West is that commonly called the White Lotus. Its resemblance to the religion of the Great Way is apparent. Information gathered from documents and statements made by sectarian leaders in Singapore suggest the possibility that the two religions were connected. According to Singapore sources, White Lotus is not the name of an organization but a term which indicates the work of the sects of the Great Way at a certain time. One set of names given by the sects to the three cycles of Buddha influence is: Blue, Red, and White Lotus cycles. In the White Lotus cycle, which is the final one before the end of the universe, Maitreya will appear seated on a white lotus and lead all members to salvation. The religious "work" being carried out by a sect of the Great Way is named after the color

---

[e] An important idea of the Great Way is based on a Buddhist theory of cycles of Buddha influence (*kālpa*). In the Great Way three major cycles are recognized. These are associated with different Buddhas. Each cycle is divided into three periods. In the first there is perfect teaching: that of the Buddha himself. In the second there is "counterfeit" teaching based on correct teaching but gradually moving away from the truth. The final period is one of decay of the doctrine; it is followed by a catastrophe. Two complete cycles are believed to have already passed. The final cycle, believed by some of the sects to have now begun, is the one in which Maitreya, the Buddha To Come, teaches the doctrine. This too will eventually end in a catastrophe unless a revival of correct teaching can be brought about.

of the cycle. "White Lotus work" appears to be conducted when a leader claims to be an incarnate Maitreya. (The nature of the work is obscure.) One sect with a branch in Malaya has at the present time an incarnate Maitreya as leader; it says that it is undertaking the final work of the religion. It believes that an emperor will soon appear on the Dragon Throne in China and that he will be head of the religion. Soon after he will lead all to salvation, whereupon the world will undergo a wind catastrophe in the shape of an atom bomb. This will mark the end of the cycle of the White Lotus.

Political Aspects of Chinese Religion in Nineteenth-Century Singapore

In Singapore the relation between the Chinese and their political masters was not expressible in religious terms. In some respects British officials were assimilated in Chinese eyes to mandarins, but however far the analogy was pushed the colonial official and the system of which he was a part were beyond the range of Chinese religious activity.ᶠ The Government of the Colony imposed no state cult and saw no link between political order and religious orthodoxy. It left the Chinese completely free to organize their religious groupings and express their religious beliefs in any way they chose, manifesting an indifference to religion which amounted to a tolerance not provided in the Chinese homeland.

The Chinese who went to Singapore could draw on a rebellious tradition linked in a number of ways to religious beliefs and practices. But although sects and secret societies which had been associated with political movements in China were imported into Singapore, they were not normally used to oppose the colonial administration. Moreover, the balance between secret societies and religious sects was different in Singapore from what it had been at home. In nineteenth-century Singapore the sects played a relatively insignificant role in the life of the Chinese. The political secret society, in contrast, came to assume in Singapore an importance which outstripped that of any other Chinese institution in the Colony.

The cradle of many sects of the Great Way of Former Heaven was Szechwan. They do not appear to have reached southeastern China until about the 1860's, when they spread into Fukien and Kwangtung. According to records kept in Singapore, branches of one of the sects began to move overseas about the year 1868, the religion not establishing itself

---

ᶠ Although there have been a few examples from Malaya and Hong Kong of British officials being invited to open religious festivals for gods of the kind which in China were associated with the official religious system, we have come across no similar cases in Singapore.

firmly in the Colony until the late part of the century. The sects were administered through institutions called *chai-t'ang*, a term we may conveniently translate as vegetarian halls. The first sectarian hall of this kind in Singapore appears to have been established in 1880.

Since the higher ranks in the sects are reserved for men, the founding halls in Singapore were all male establishments. Several halls were later set up for the use of female members of the religion. There is little on record of the early development in Singapore of the various sects of the Great Way.[g] Although it is possible that they retained an interest in political affairs in China, their activities in the Colony must have been innocuous; at least, their existence remained unnoticed by the British administration. Their vegetarian halls are today thought of generally as being just another sort of Chinese temple.

The Singapore halls of the sects were associated with different dialect "groups," the majority of the members of a hall appearing to have come from the district in China where the Singapore branch of the sect originated.

In the nineteenth century the main concern of the Singapore sects seems to have been to provide occasional accommodation for working members and permanent living quarters for elderly retired members who did not go back to China.[h] The female establishments catered both for young women who wished to live in on a permanent basis and for elderly women. Although at that time there were few women likely to avail themselves of these facilities, the provisions for women were to prove important in the expansion of the sects in the 1930's.

The secret societies had come to Malaya and Singapore long before the sects of the Great Way reached southeastern China. The social conditions of Singapore were well suited to the development of the secret societies from subversive movements into large-scale communal organizations. The Singapore authorities did not concern themselves unduly with the anti-dynastic activities of the Chinese within their jurisdiction. Apart from a short-lived attempt in the early years of the settlement to work a system of indirect rule through Chinese headmen, the Chinese in Singapore were left politically very much to themselves. Within the ranks of the Chinese the commercial system threw up men who, having acquired great riches, proceeded to exercise authority in the setting of various kinds of association. The continuously fluid and immigrant society, in

---

[g] The Great Way appears to have been the first of the syncretic religions to reach Malaya and Singapore. More research will have to be done before this can be stated with certainty.

[h] We gather from elderly informants in Singapore that among the first members of the local sects were men of high rank who had devoted the greater part of their lives to the religion and gone overseas to escape official persecution.

which there were very few women and little domestic organization, lent a special importance to bodies which undertook to provide a protective milieu for newcomers. In such circumstances the secret societies, still ritually anti-dynastic and ritually secret, evolved until by the late nineteenth century they had come to engross the majority of the Chinese population and to provide for it a series of political instruments by means of which both the internal affairs of the Chinese and the relations between the Chinese and the Singapore authorities were largely regulated.

All, or nearly all, of the secret societies in Singapore were "branches" of the Heaven and Earth League, usually known as the Triad Society. Consequently they used the same basic ritual. But although for a considerable period they maintained a central meeting house, they were not always organizationally coordinated. To some extent, as in the case of the syncretic sects, the various societies specialized in dialect "groups," although secret society alignment and dialect "group" loyalties often cut across one another. Residential and occupational principles underlay the structure of some of the societies.

From time to time the various societies came into open conflict. The bloodshed and uproar to which their quarrels gave rise led the government first to try to control them by a system of registration (1869) and finally to suppress them (1890). Then the secret societies really became secret. Yet even after their suppression they do not appear to have taken an essentially anti-British turn. In ritual terms their hostility was directed against the Manchu dynasty. Having generally no ambitions in regard to the political control of Singapore as a whole, the Chinese in the last century kept their ideological weapons aimed at their rulers at home.[13]

From 1890 the secret societies began to decline in membership and to move toward the status of small-scale criminal combinations. The revolutionary activities connected with Sun Yat-sen at the end of the century and during the early 1900's brought some of the Singapore secret society world into the field of politics,[14] but generally in the last fifty years or so secret society and political activity have not greatly overlapped in Singapore. Immediately after the Second World War, Triad organizations in Malaya assumed political importance for a time. In north Malaya they became involved in the struggle between the Kuomintang and the Communists. In Singapore, apart from an abortive attempt in 1947 to introduce a branch of the China Triad Democratic Party, the Triad movement showed little sign of political ambition (see Blythe 1950). It may be of course that democratic institutions in a self-governing Singapore will furnish the secret societies with profitable opportunities for intervening in political life; but it is still too early to write on this subject.

Modern Religious Changes in the Homeland

The advent of the Chinese Republic brought religious changes to China and a rearrangement in the political sentiments of the Chinese in Singapore. Now Overseas Chinese began to identify themselves with the government at home, instead of opposing it, and to find that nationalism secularized their political activities. To the body of voluntary associations among the Chinese in Singapore were added some which were linked with political aims and activities in the homeland. The new associations based on political and cultural nationalism, being devoid of religious purpose, introduced into Singapore Chinese society a completely secular type of organization which, in the serious matters of social life, it had not known before.

But modern nationalism was not simply indifferent to religion; it was sometimes opposed to it. The religious skepticism and distaste for superstitious practices which had been common among Confucian gentlemen in China now began to find their way into Singapore Chinese society via modern nationalist education. Attempts in China to rationalize and secularize social life were sometimes imitated in Singapore. Yet religion by no means suffered an eclipse. Political life was, so to speak, deritualized, and nationalism dictated that some social occasions be given secular rather than religious expression. But outside the field of political activities modern secularism rarely found complete victory.

The trend of Republican China was, however, by no means consistently against religion. The syncretic movements of imperial China have had important heirs in recent times. Some of the new movements, led by men who had held official positions in Manchu days and were opposed to the tendencies of political life in the Republic, were considered a sufficient threat to new ideas to be proscribed when Chiang Kai-shek eventually formed a national government. State orthodoxy having been abolished and the elite of the country greatly disturbed by the revolutionary changes after 1911, there emerged in China new mystical religious organizations.

Some of the new movements consisted of groups of laymen interested in esoteric Buddhism (cf. A. F. Wright 1959: 114ff). Others were either new syncretic religions or sectarian offshoots of older religions. Still basing themselves on highly eclectic beliefs brought together within a general salvationist framework, they now began to look beyond the field of traditional religious ideas for new elements. Christianity and Islam were laid under contribution. Like their Buddhist counterparts, the sectarian organizations tended to emphasize charitable works as ways to spiritual advancement. The Fellowship of Goodness (T'ung-shan She) [15] was a new offshoot of the Great Way of Former Heaven. It was particularly influential during the heyday of warlordism and developed into an organization with branches in all parts of China.

The programs of religious movements evolving in the Republican era were partly extensions of changes in religious ideas and organization during the nineteenth century. In Chinese Buddhism salvation was thought to depend on the accumulation of merit by special earners and its transfer to other sentient beings. Although merit was to be gathered by the performance of charitable deeds, its greater part was earned by members of the Buddhist Order. Before and during the nineteenth century action by the state to control and limit the monastic Order seems to have produced a general fall in the religious respectability of its members. Numbers of "unofficial" monks and nuns appeared, living beyond the control of orthodox monasteries and nunneries. Among the laity the belief that monks and nuns could earn merit on behalf of humanity at large appears to have been weakened by these developments. At any rate, the laity began to assume an importance which it had not had before. Lay men and women entered the Buddhist system, taking vows previously reserved for the clergy. They also took over certain ritual functions which had previously been the exclusive right of the Order, and organized societies for the study of doctrine and the practice of "self-cultivation." Moreover, Buddhist vegetarian halls were set up for the benefit of laymen wishing to practice self-cultivation in a monastic atmosphere without actually entering a monastery. And as the functions of the Order were in part transferred to the laity, so greater emphasis came to be placed on charitable and welfare work as means to accumulating merit. Numbers of lay-sponsored schemes for social improvement began to appear.

In one at least of the older syncretic religions changes were also taking place. The early sects of the Great Way had been vegetarian—like Buddhism they had emphasized vegetarian diet and sexual abstinence as ways to spiritual enlightenment. Rank in the religious hierarchy had depended on taking vows to observe these abstentions. But gradually, from being centered on the home the sects became organized around vegetarian halls whenever they could remain undetected by officialdom or there was a lull in state persecution.

However, during the nineteenth century annd later some new branches appeared which placed less stress on abstinence as qualifications for rank. They did not set up vegetarian halls but rather declared themselves to be Confucian and anti-monastic. As a result they began to attract a new kind of recruit. The organizers of the nonvegetarian sect T'ung-shan She were "Confucians"; they were conservative members of the upper class who were unlikely to favor anything so subversive of family life as sexual abstinence, while a vegetarian diet would have greatly discommoded them in their public life. The intellectual invigoration of T'ung-shan She and the importation of ideas from Islam and Christianity into I-kuan Tao, another nonvegetarian sect of the Great Way, were clearly results of the appearance of scholarly kinds of men in the field of syncretic religion.

Some of the new religions emerging in this century have, like Buddhism, engaged in charitable works as means to accumulating merit. One of them, Tao Yüan, better known to the West under the name of its department of charitable works, the Red Swastika Society, was established in China in 1921, some years after a magistrate and his friend had claimed to receive messages from various spirits (ultimately from the Creator Himself) in the course of their experiments with automatic writing; a popular pastime among the gentry. Its purpose is set out in a booklet printed in Singapore (Tao Yüan, Singapore Branch n.d.). The Great War had produced much suffering. The world had become increasingly materialistic, and the Chinese religions of Buddhism, Taoism, and Confucianism had been "slandered and ridiculed" and said to be the cause of the "weakening of our nation." This religion was to prevent mankind from being plunged into the "very depth . . . of materialism." Its further purpose was to eliminate the confusion caused by the divisions between sects and denominations. Tao Yüan was five religions in one. Taoism, Buddhism, Confucianism, Christianity, and Islam were all regulated by the great *tao* from which they had sprung. The Red Swastika Society was open to all who sympathized with its work, including those who were practicing members of one of the five religions incorporated in the Tao Yüan. The Red Swastika Society was the "outer works" department of the religion. Membership of the "inner department" was confined to people who were not exclusive believers in one of the five religions. The founders of these five religions were successive human transformations of the Divine Spirit: the Venerable Patriarch or Creator. "Members of the 'Tao Yüan' who do not understand . . . or make a distinction among the five religions will then keep themselves to their own particular religion, thus they will misunderstand the particular merit of each religion, and thereby [cause] the danger of dividing opinion among the people" (Hou Su-shuang n.d.).

The new religious movements of this kind clearly rested to a great extent on the reaction of educated and upper class people to the problems of their day, and on their desire to raise Chinese religion from the level of what was thought to be popular superstition. Politically the leaders of the movements were often conservative. Quite apart from seeking in the mystical movements some purely spiritual satisfaction, they doubtless strove to use the new religions as ways of shaping and controlling public opinion. The role of religious organizations in the political affairs of Republican China would not seem yet to have been properly studied. The material on T'ung-shan She suggests that it was linked with the rise to power of Tuan Ch'i-jui after the brief period in 1917 when the Manchus were reinstated. It is believed that Tuan was behind the founding of the sect; certainly, the T'ung-shan She was opposed to Kuomintang ideals and melted away as an open organization as the Nationalists moved north in the years 1926–28 (De Korne 1941: 18–19, 73ff).

Modern Religious Developments in Singapore

Buddhist lay organizations as they had developed in China were paralleled in Singapore, while the new religions sent branches to the Colony. But there were marked differences between China and Singapore in the organization and activities of both Buddhism and the syncretic religions.

A "Forest of Laymen" was formed in Singapore in 1934. It was responsible for founding several other Buddhist bodies. During the Japanese Occupation (1942–45) it carried out charitable work under a Buddhist Relief Association. The Forest of Laymen is not, however, an exclusively Buddhist organization. In 1955 its members included many sectarians, some of them holding important positions. We must explain why members of syncretic religions should (on the face of it, very strangely) play an important part in Buddhist life in Singapore. The freedom enjoyed by sectarianism in Singapore, and the absence of any Confucian elite to pronounce on its unorthodoxy, have enabled it to earn a reputation among the local Chinese which it could never have acquired in China. The priests and priestesses of Singapore sects of the Great Way are accepted generally as a recognizable type of religious practitioner; i.e. they offer ritual services to the public in competition with Buddhists and Taoist priests. Members of the vegetarian sects have aligned themselves with Buddhists because of their similar interests in accumulating merit and self-cultivation. Indeed, these people often refer to themselves as "lay Buddhists." Some of their ritual is similar enough to that of the Buddhists for the practitioners of both kinds of religion to work together professionally, although cooperation of this sort is still rare. Finally, since many sectarians are influential, owning religious establishments which are popular with the public and in good economic shape, they could not be left out of an important religious organization in a religious atmosphere where business success counts for more than orthodoxy.

A more recent Buddhist body is the Singapore Federation of Buddhists, officially inaugurated in 1950. It arose from the Forest of Laymen. One of its declared aims is to purify Buddhism in Singapore, and to some extent it may be regarded as a movement to establish a religion enjoying the respect attaching to a regulated and organized faith, since to many Muslim and Christian observers the Chinese do not appear to have what they recognize as a religion. Once again the sectarians have not been left out. Moreover, the Federation includes all manner of temples and even vegetarian restaurants, and it is somewhat difficult to see how relevant the reform of Buddhism is to its organization. Although in 1955 its secretary was a Westernized Buddhist laywoman genuinely interested in reform, the Federation cannot be seen as a movement stemming generally from Westernized Chinese. Many of its ordinary and some of its committee members are uneducated women of peasant origin who manage either their own vegetarian halls or the halls to which they have been appointed by officials of their religion. All, however, are influential in religious circles, and some have grown rich from their business interests in religious organization. One advantage of belonging to the Federation is undoubtedly the opportunity it affords to engage in charitable activities which attract publicity. Although the Federation professes to include all Buddhists, whatever their ethnic attachments, it is in reality a thoroughly Chinese organization, stressing Chinese patriotic sentiments and the contribution made by the Chinese to the development of Singapore.

The Regional Center of the World Fellowship of Buddhists appears to some extent to be a rival to the Federation. In 1955 its president was the secretary of the Federation and its headquarters were situated in a Buddhist school of which she was headmistress (and which was founded by prominent members of the Federation and the Forest of Laymen). A notable characteristic of Chinese religious organizations in Singapore is the way in which they overlap and interpenetrate one another. One organization throws off others; committees interlock; a key man in one organization is often in a position to exert influence over a very wide field.

The three Buddhist organizations just discussed are general bodies which do not take account of dialect grouping. There are, however, a number of other Buddhist organizations recruitment to which rests on like territorial origin in China. These organizations shade off into others primarily concerned with providing funeral benefits.

There are two Singapore branches of modern syncretic religions about which we have some information: the Tao Yüan (with the Red Swastika Society) and the T'ung-shan She. The Singapore Tao Yüan is the main Nanyang branch organization of the religion. It was brought to Singapore by a group of (mainly Cantonese) men who had become interested in the religion during a visit to China. The Tao Yüan and the Red Swastika Society exist openly in Singapore, being recognized by the government. They have male and female branches, most of the members being Cantonese and Hainanese of, roughly, middle incomes. Although its charitable works are adjusted to the needs of overseas Chinese society, the Tao Yüan remains interested in affairs in China. The Red Swastika Society carried out medical and relief work during the Japanese Occupation of Singapore, and in 1955 it was continuing to give free medical treatment in both Chinese and Western traditions. Like the Buddhist Federation, it stresses the importance of Chinese civilization and advocates various methods for promoting Chinese cultural activities.

The T'ung-shan She in Singapore goes under the name of the Nan-Yang Sacred Union. It appears to have been set up by a man who is now the leader of a different Malayan sect of the Great Way. He was for many years a member of the T'ung-shan She in China, and in his background appears to be typical of the more intellectual followers of the religion. He was educated at military schools and had studied political economy in Japan. He held political and military appointments during the early years of the Republic, and apparently quit public life after a disagreement with the government. Having reached fairly high rank in the T'ung-shan She he applied to its headquarters for the next highest rank and was refused. Well past middle age he went to Singapore in 1928 (by which time the religion had been proscribed in China) and there founded the Nan-Yang Sacred Union as an overseas branch of the sect. But his organization was not recognized at home. After a while the Union began to attract considerable interest from Singapore Chinese, and branch organizations of the T'ung-shan She came to look upon the Singapore "branch" with jealous eyes. As long as the Union remained unrecognized none of the money coming in, from fees and as payment for the ranks bestowed, could be claimed for the "work" of the religion in China. (In the sects of the Great Way the lesser branches are supposed to hand over a certain proportion of their income to higher branches to be used for expanding activities.) Meanwhile the organizer of the Union had become interested in a rival sect in Malaya and had gone over to it. The headquarters of the T'ung-shan She, fearing lest the Union pass to another sect, gave it official recognition and placed the direction of its affairs in the hands of the Kwangtung branch.

Like the earlier vegetarian sects of Singapore, these later Buddhist and syncretic organizations have—or at least had up to 1955—taken little interest in local political developments. Insofar as they had political concerns they concentrated their attention on the homeland. The type of individual who is attracted to mystical and salvationist pursuits in Singapore is very rarely the politically frustrated intellectual of conservative outlook whom we have seen to have been associated with the modern syncretic movements in China. Chinese society in Singapore was not likely, by its nature, to throw up men of this kind in any significant number. The parallels sometimes drawn by sectarian religions between religious virtue and success in leadership are not apt to fire the imagination of the Singapore Chinese who in recent years have been politically ambitious.

Whom, then, do the organized faiths attract? Let us consider first of all the vegetarian sects. As we have seen, these sects opened vegetarian halls in which their members might practice self-cultivation. The halls became the basis of sectarian organization. They offered accommodation to members and sometimes to other people who were prepared to observe the necessary dietary and sexual rules while in residence. Buddhist halls began to offer similar facilities. However, in the earlier phase of their existence the halls did not attract great numbers of immigrants in Singapore. The newcomers to the colony were predominantly men, for whom there were already available the resources of other kinds of organizations. Moreover, in their eager pursuit of riches immigrants were probably more easily attracted to religious practices (such as those associated with medium cults) which emphasized material welfare and progress. Certainly, vegetarianism and sexual abstinence could not have exercised great appeal.

The vegetarian sects did not in fact expand their activities to any considerable extent until the 1930's when Cantonese women began to come to Malaya in large numbers. They arrived looking for work and, in the main, without families or husbands. They were to become the chief supporters of the halls, finding in them both economic and religious satisfactions. The work of the sects in Singapore thus became chiefly the provision of home and security for independent women. From a few halls at the turn of the century (the founding halls and a few female establishments) the number grew until in 1955 there must have been between 250 and 350.[16] The majority were for women. Although they included some Buddhist halls, sectarian halls predominated.

The women came from Shun-te and nearby districts of Kwangtung. They were socially unattached in one of two ways. First, there were widows and wives who had been separated from their husbands; many came into Malaya in this period precisely because immigration restrictions prevented their menfolk from entering the country. Second, a certain proportion (how big it was we cannot say) were spinsters who had vowed not to marry and women who were married "in name only." The latter had never cohabited with their husbands and had no intention of returning to them, except possibly when past childbearing. These women were associated with an anti-marriage movement which originated in the last century in Shun-te and spread to adjacent areas.

The Cantonese women immigrants generally sought work in Singapore as domestic servants, an occupation they still follow. While working they usually sleep in their employers' houses, using the halls for temporary accommodation only. In old age they go to live in the halls for good, knowing that when they die the mortuary rites will be properly executed for them. A few nonreligious cooperative lodging houses (*kongsi*) cater for such women during their working lives, but do not meet the needs of sick and retired women; consequently they hardly compete with the halls. We should note, furthermore, that the halls characteristically recruit women coming from the same village or larger territorial unit at home. Even sects originating in other parts of China now have numbers of halls attached to them which cater for women from Shun-te and its vicinity.

We should not try to account for the popularity of the vegetarian halls entirely in terms of ordinary economic advantage. The fact that almost the only organization to cater for the needs of unattached immigrant women in Singapore is a religious one is significant.[i] The salvationist religion of the halls seems to have a particular attraction for Chinese women not living normal family lives. Both the sects and Buddhism offer opportunities for rebirth as a spiritual being or at the least reincarnation in a more attractive setting and, according to popular belief, as a member of the male (and therefore privileged) sex. The religions also offer transport to a paradise in which men and women are of equal status.

Unattached women are especially suited to acquire the spiritual rewards offered by salvationist religion. They already fulfill one basic condition for self-cultivation, because they do not engage in (at least conventional) sexual activity. Two classes of self-cultivation have come to be recognized: the "pure happiness" cultivators, who have never had sexual experience, and the "half-life" cultivators, who have broken off sexual activity. Because merit can be transferred and self-cultivators are specially equipped to gain merit and pass it to others, the religious ritual they perform is particularly powerful. On retirement many domestic servants arm themselves with this kind of religious skill, while some per-

---

[i] Lang (1946: 109) notes that numbers of women who had taken part in the anti-marriage movement in Kwangtung had, as they became older, posed a problem for the provincial authorities, who had to provide special homes for them. In Singapore, however, there were few homes for the aged run by public bodies or private non-Chinese organizations; and those which existed did not seem to attract women of the kind we are discussing here.

form professional religious tasks on a part-time basis even while still in service.

In the hall and the religion to which it belongs a woman has opportunities to gain high status. Women often rise to positions of authority in the religious system, and so achieve a standing which contrasts sharply with their lowly station, as domestic servants and unattached immigrants, in secular society. By taking rank in a sect a woman can be put in charge of a hall. In both Buddhism and the sects of the Great Way she can become a religious master of others, sometimes being placed in authority over women who in ordinary life might be her employers. Advantages such as these are often hinted at in the vast body of religious literature known as "precious volumes" or "good books." These contain stories chiefly about women who take up the religious life and achieve mastery over their husbands, other members of their family, and princes. The stories are very popular with Cantonese women (who have their own variety known as "wooden fish books"), and most halls possess collections of them.

Another advantage of belonging to an organized faith is the opportunity to become a member of a religious "family." In both the Buddhist and sectarian religions recruits are grouped in relation to the master (who may be a woman) through whom they join the religion. Groups of masters and disciples have taken on some of the formal characteristics of the Chinese kinship system. Kinship terms express the relations between the members of the group, who, even if they are women, are treated terminologically as male agnates. Generation names are introduced into personal names in a manner which resembles the traditional system of secular naming in the lineage. The "families" trace their relations to common "ancestor" masters and practice "ancestor" worship, although the Buddhist "kinship" system tends to be shallower than that of the sects.

The "family" provides an additional bond between fellow members of a hall, and is an effective method of forming new social relationships with numbers of co-religionists living in, or otherwise connected with, other halls. Women in domestic service have few opportunities to make friends; for the unattached immigrant woman membership of a "family" is of considerable importance. The "family" gives an added interest to the everyday life of the hall. It involves members in a number of anniversary celebrations, which include dinners and visits to "kinsmen" in other establishments. It provides a body of mourners, "kinsmen" to care for the ritual needs of the dead, and "descendants" to carry out "ancestor" worship.

The vegetarian sects have attracted few men, either as lay members or rank-holders. Many holders of rank joined the religion as children, often in China; few were born in Singapore. These sects are generally regarded by more educated Chinese as intellectually unsound and inferior in every way to Buddhism and the modern syncretic movements. They are said to be "women's religions" (which indeed they largely are) and, as one young Buddhist put it, "peasant organizations coming from the countryside." The less sophisticated man who might possibly be attracted to sectarian religion by its secrecy and economic and social opportunities is likely to be put off by the restriction on sex and food.

The modern syncretic groups, which can offer no facilities comparable to those of the vegetarian sects, continue to attract men rather than women, although of course the number of men involved is very small when measured against the total population. If we may generalize from the few individuals we have known among the members of the T'ung-shan She and Tao Yüan, we should say that the men who take part in syncretic religious activities of the modern kind are either traditionalists or, if modern in outlook, find their models in pre-Communist China rather than in the events and leaders of the Singapore society around them.

We still do not know enough of the whole range of esoteric religious beliefs and practices among the Chinese in Singapore. But what we do know of salvationist elements suggests that in conditions of increasing social disturbance the tide of secularized politics may not go unopposed by religious movements. The old vegetarian sects in their rebellious periods in China were forward-looking, seeking to establish a new order. The new syncretic movements looked backward, striving to preserve the older society and its values. They were alike in one respect: they believed the moral order was in danger. A characteristic of the syncretic religions is to predict (usually by revelation) the likely future of mankind if it moves too far away from the "natural order of things" and if leaders are not virtuous men and lack the mandate of Heaven. They place importance on the need for spiritual cultivation for all those who would rule themselves and other men. Even spirit-medium cults, normally preoccupied with private problems, occasionally produce divine utterances of a broad moral significance. "Life is short, life is short," asserts one god through his medium, and urges people to think of the future life. "That which you enjoy in this life is only transient. . . . Good man, cultivate the lasting spiritual life" (Elliott 1955: 172–73). Buddhist tracts, and the "precious volumes" and "wooden fish books," besides indicating the material advantages of the religious life, make similar moral statements. The Tao Yüan points out that the development or expansion of religion has often taken place during a period of disaster: ". . . the upper classes acted without the principles of Tao and the lower classes had no respect for the laws. . . . If mankind is . . . to be saved and peace brought to them . . . the way by which salvation [can] be attained is by means of the 'Tao'" (Tao Yüan, Singapore Branch n.d.). Although salvationist religions in Singapore have so far displayed little interest in local political activities, we should not forget the history of their political involvement in China and the possibilities which their ideas afford for militant interpretation. The sects, the modern syncretic movements, and even the spirit-medium cults may come to assert a resistance to political pressure in a way we have so far not known in Singapore. We should remember that as the government of Singapore has become increasingly Chinese and decreasingly colonial, it has come more effectively within the range of Chinese religious weapons. We know that sectarian religion has survived to this day in China; there is little reason to suppose that it will vanish from Singapore.

PART THREE

Social Change in the New Territories of Hong Kong

Chinese Geomancy: Some Observations in Hong Kong

Introduction

From early February to early May 1963 I was roaming the New Territories of Hong Kong, planning research and collecting material for a report to the New Territories Administration on the possibilities of developing field studies. A practical problem preoccupying N.T. administrators, as I found, is *fung shui.*[a] I was pleased to have my growing interest in Chinese geomancy reinforced by the interest—I had perhaps better say "concern"—shown by the District Officers whose views on and reactions to *fung shui* beliefs and practices are an essential element of the system to be analyzed.

I realize that this paper is not well tailored to the needs of a seminar on cognition; my field data are more "sociological" than "psychological"; but I shall try here and there to point out what problems relating to cognition could usefully be looked into. My paper is further limited in its range by my field observations being confined largely to the countryside; but, again, I shall try to show where the analysis could be pushed further by taking urban conditions into account.

For the benefit of people who know little about Hong Kong, I must set out some basic features of the general situation which my account of geomancy assumes. The N.T. were leased to Britain in 1898, and when, in 1899, the British began to administer this accession of 100,000 people they were faced by a new problem: how to govern an established rural population. In fact, up to the 1950's the N.T. were lightly administered

Previously unpublished paper prepared for the Seminar on Cognitive and Value Systems in Chinese Society held at Bermuda, 24–25 Jan. 1964, under the auspices of the Subcommittee on Research on Chinese Society of the ACLS-SSRC Joint Committee on Contemporary China.

[a] I follow Hong Kong practice in giving Chinese terms in their Cantonese form in accordance with the modified Eitel/Dyer Ball system that is more or less official there.

and half a century of British rule had not brought many major visible changes to the countryside. In the last decade, however, the population has greatly expanded by immigration (the figure now stands at roughly half a million), the urban area of Hong Kong has engulfed parts of the countryside, market gardening and industry have become important features of the N.T. economy, and the Administration has intensified its activities. Now the N.T. are divided into five administrative districts, each with a District Officer and a large staff. (Under Ch'ing rule the area was some three-fifths of a county, the capital of which lay outside the territory acquired to form the N.T.). Public works are the order of the day.

The Nature of Geomantic Beliefs

Some of us will recall an earlier discussion on geomancy during which Marion Levy stressed the point that *fung shui* could not be made consistently to work if people were generally cynical in their claims. He was of course right, and I shall open my discussion with the assertion that any view of the situation in the N.T. is misguided which starts from the assumption that their inhabitants are parties to a conspiracy seeking to exploit the tender concern of the Administration for the religious susceptibilities of its charges. This is a view held by many city people, who, in a mixture of envy and condescension, gaze on their country cousins from afar, and by some outsiders in the N.T. whose distance from the local people is to be measured socially and not in miles. True, the Administration has shown itself to be zealous in protecting Chinese religion (and of course more tolerant of it than the preceding Chinese regime, whose officials were required to suppress unorthodoxy); and there are undoubtedly cases where a government with a less tender attitude might with impunity have overridden geomantic objections which, in the event, have cost the Administration time, annoyance, and money. But in fact the success of many country people in getting their way in *fung shui* matters has necessarily rested on their belief in it; for were they to be generally cynical the system would break down. And precisely because faith is general a few people can manipulate it to their advantage. Contact between government and people is maintained through the so-called Village Representatives; some of them may disbelieve in the claims made by their constituents and yet press them for political reasons, or cynically put forward claims for which they can summon up the necessary backing of popular faith. They thus pay tribute to general belief and help support it.

In fact, disbelief may appear to be more general than the preceding argument supposes, and it is not too difficult to collect evidence which suggests that a great many people think that *fung shui* is nonsense. But every field-worker knows that beliefs and disbeliefs are expressed in a context, and one can too easily fall into the trap of gathering evidence in contexts of skepticism. Let me offer an illustration. Early in my field study I found myself, during a visit to a remote coastal village, a fellow guest at lunch with two building contractors engaged in some local works. The conversation at table turned to *fung shui*. One of the contractors spoke English, as I discovered when he addressed me across the table to lament the nuisance caused by geomantic beliefs. I guessed that he had had or was having trouble with *fung shui* obstruction, and I read into his final remark on the subject an envy for a world where people would not be allowed to raise geomancy against builders; the talk at table had turned to how the authorities across the border in China had cast out *fung shui* along with the rest of traditional religion, and the contractor cried: "Yes, they have canceled [*sic*] all that bloody nonsense." (If his companions at lunch had understood what he had said, they would doubtless have been shocked, for they had been giving me an enthusiastic account of *fung shui* and its benefits.) Some weeks later I came across this contractor again, this time in the area where he lives, and, since I was already on good terms with members of the circle within which he moves, I was able to discuss with him many aspects of Chinese religion. I discovered in him a passionate interest in and devotion to *fung shui*. It is not necessary to conclude that he was deceiving me on the first occasion. He had then perhaps been irritated by the consequences of the *fung shui* beliefs of others. Or he may have been lining himself up with me as a European in opposition to country bumpkins. Again, one of my informants, a devotee of *fung shui* and a constant client of geomancers, quite sincerely and without any sense of strain condemns the foolishness of people who raise *fung shui* objections to government works designed to benefit them. Contexts differ.

Geomancy is a belief which entails certain actions. And in acting on their belief people often make economic sacrifices. Graves and dwellings are moved and altered. In former times (I know of no very recent case) whole villages were abandoned. How can we define this belief and account for its potency? *Fung shui* is in fact a complex of beliefs concerned with a central theme in Chinese metaphysics: man's place in nature and the universe. In the Chinese view Man stands with Heaven and Earth to form the three primary powers of the cosmos, for, although he may not be as important as Heaven and Earth, he is an essential element in the trinity.

We may say, using a Western idiom, that *fung shui* is the craft of adapting the abodes of men (buildings and graves) to the landscape. But while it may be perfectly true that geomancy has produced in the Chinese a sharpened aesthetic appreciation of their natural surroundings and led to superb techniques of landscaping, it is not, in fact, the physical landscape which is directly in question in *fung shui*. I have heard people in the N.T. commenting enthusiastically on the prospect from geomantically favorable sites; but their appreciation is grounded in their feeling for the virtues flowing from the harmony between the site and its owners. Man is involved in his surroundings; in some places he feels at ease and at peace—*shue fuk*, he is content. It is for this reason that English-speaking Chinese will often say that *fung shui* is psychological; they do not mean, as one might superficially conclude, that geomancy is an illusion; what they are asserting is that a man's mind is responding to a mysterious field of forces set up in a given place. He need not know very much about the details of *fung shui* as a craft or body of esoteric knowledge; it is enough to be conscious of the few hints contained in the landscape—a stretch of still water, an arc of hills—to be soothed and protected. "You," living or dead, "are content." That is the heart of the matter.

Fung shui: winds and waters . . . The Breaths (*hei*) which constitute the virtue of a site are blown about by the wind and held by the water. If the wind is high the Breaths will disperse; if the water moves fast the Breaths will be drawn away. Hills must protect a site against the wind; places from which streams and rivers flow must be avoided. An ideal site is one which nestles in the embrace of the hills standing to the rear and on the flanks; it is then like an armchair. Deficiencies in the line of hills can be made up by trees or, in extreme cases, by walls. The hills behind the site support it; they give it strength. Those to the left, as the site faces its unshielded fourth side, are the Azure (or, as it is more usually translated in Hong Kong, the Green) Dragon (*ts'ing lung*); those to the right are the White Tiger (*paak fu*). The Dragon is not a dragon; the Tiger is not a tiger. The former is a beneficent force (one comes fairly close to Chinese conceptions, as Chinese themselves sometimes do, in speaking of it as an electrical or magnetic force) which animates the hills and spreads itself in the approaches to the site. (Moreover, a *loi lung*, an Advancing Dragon, may come from the rear to pour its virtue into the site.) The White Tiger is a force of danger (white because it bears a patch of that color on its forehead, a sign of fierceness) which protects only as long as it is in complementary relationship with the Azure Dragon. Dragon and Tiger must be present in the right proportions. The Dragon must stand higher than the Tiger to ensure a proper balance of forces between them. The one is *yang*, the other *yin*; the one is spring, the other autumn;

the one is civil, the other military. They are opposite and complementary, neither by itself providing benefit and together in the correct ratio ensuring the concentration of the Breaths.

This last paragraph expresses the core (and merely the core) of the ideas entertained by experts. For them the entities involved in geomancy are metaphysical. The statement remains true even when the hills look like a dragon, a resemblance made the more likely by the use of the word *lung* for any long and sinuous object—a queue of people, a railway train, a trail of smoke. Other creatures, human among them, and objects may be detected in the landscape, conferring benefit on the site. There is a grave in the N.T. (I have discovered the existence of another such in Fukien) which lies in the crutch of a naked woman. There are forms of animals and deities. These things are not there physically and literally, and experts consider Europeans naive for supposing the contrary. They are signs. The Dragon has sinews and veins which may be cut; its blood may flow. But Sinews, Veins, and Blood are mystical, even though we may see them (as in the earth exposed by a road-cutting). The question arises (and Marjorie Topley has put it to me forcefully) whether the metaphysical view taken by the experts is matched in more general belief. Are ordinary people more literal-minded in their perception of geomantic objects: dragons, tigers, coffins, birds, Goddesses of Mercy, or whatever they may be? I say not. To posit an entity (dragon or tiger) because a site cannot be thought of without it, or to infer an entity from the resemblance between a natural feature and a being or object is a way of imputing certain characteristics to a landscape; it is not evidence that people are incapable of distinguishing between, say, real tigers and those crouching in the hills. The latter are certainly dangerous (that is why they are called tigers), but the fact that people believe them to be capable of acting on human beings proves nothing more than that mystical forces are credited with potency. The nouns used in such geomantic statements as "That is a coffin," "That is a Goddess of Mercy," and "That is a White Tiger" are the names of mysteries with recognizable characteristics of benevolence or danger.

This leads us on to another question. There is presumably some limit to the number of names used. Dragon and Tiger are part of the basic grammar of geomancy, but even in the system of resemblances, in which people detect forces by what they can perceive in the landscape, there is clearly no tendency to perceive just any old thing. We may very well guess that the range of objects is limited. A study of the range (never yet undertaken, to the best of my knowledge), or perhaps better still the ranges to be found in different communities, might allow us both to see some order in what at the moment looks like a very mixed collection of objects and to link up geomantic entities with entities of significance in other parts of Chinese belief.

But *fung shui* is not just a matter of winds and waters and beings and objects detected in the landscape. Other principles are involved. The stars are taken into account. The geomancer's compass shows, according to the number of rings on it, a given sum of criteria by which a site is to be selected and oriented. Over and above this there comes from the tradition of the *I Ching* an idea of the cosmos in a perpetual state of flux; that which is so at one point in time is not so at another. Things, and the fortunes of men with them, change. So that within cycles of time, definable by well-recognized principles (the sexagenary system of "stems and branches" among them), the virtues of any site may change, however expertly it was chosen in respect of its landscape. Geomancy, then, becomes a body of learning the complexity of which is represented to the layman by the compass, the books, and the experience of the practitioners. Ordinary men know a little, and they know that they do not know enough to rely in important matters on their own judgment. The geomancer enters the scene. (This is the *fung shui sin shaang*, who behind his back may be referred to by the distinctly less complimentary title of *fung shui lo*.)

The complexity of *fung shui* is a guarantee of its continued credibility. If it works, well and good. If it fails to work, a neglected principle, an ignorant geomancer, an undetected alteration to the landscape can be held responsible. From the point of view of the outsider, geomancy seems completely irrational, but once grant that man, dead or alive, is part of a universe with which his fortunes are inextricably woven, and the reasoning of geomancy can be seen to fall into a logical pattern. And the surviving strength of the appeal of *fung shui* to the minds of sophisticated Chinese rests precisely on what seems to them to be its reasonableness— the more rational the minds the greater is the degree of rationalization produced to support what only extreme rationalism rejects. *Fung shui* is not like most of the rest of Chinese religion; no reliance on the will of a deity is involved; there are no gods to serve and placate; it is not superstitious, for it is based on self-evident propositions; the principles which regulate the cosmos are fixed, known, and subject to exact treatment by experts who, in the performance of their duties, are like scientists or technicians.

From this view of *fung shui* there follow two consequences. One is that geomancers are held in an esteem not shared by other practitioners of Chinese religion. They are gentlemen, unlike priests (*naam moh lo*), spirit-mediums, and Buddhists who perform ordinary rites for laymen;

for these, whatever the need for their services, are looked down upon as being disreputable. Some geomancers are, in fact, gentlemen in a very specific sense; they do not make their living by their craft but practice it as a learned hobby (albeit a rewarded one on occasion). The Colony is the home of many weekend geomancers. It is highly respectable to be a *fung shui sin shaang*, and it is a matter for pride to be known to seek their company and profit by their learning. The second consequence is that a Chinese may cease to believe in and practice his traditional religion without abandoning his faith in geomancy. Be he Christian or atheist, *fung shui* retains its meaning and appeal. Geomancy is "science" for those who would have it so. The Administration, to my knowledge, has had to contend with *fung shui* objections by Christians; perhaps also by atheists.

Fung shui presupposes a certain view of the universe. It also assumes something about the nature of society. *Fung shui* is primarily concerned with siting graves and houses, but not all graves and houses are geomantically placed. *Fung shui* is a preoccupation with success, and, since an appetite for success must be stimulated by a taste of it, those who lack hope are not involved in geomantic striving. In other words, *fung shui* is not for the very poor. It is when a man begins to think of the possibility of increased success for himself and his issue, a measure of prosperity already having been achieved, that he takes to a concern with geomancy. On their side, those who are already successful cannot afford to ignore the need to ensure their continuing prosperity by taking geomantic precautions. Underlying *fung shui* is a fundamental assumption of Chinese society: all men (i.e. all Chinese who are fully accepted within society—not boat people or other marginal elements) are in principle equal and may legitimately strive to improve their station in life. The peasant in his cottage has as much right to hope for advancement as the mandarin in his yamen, or, to take a more contemporary and relevant example, the big businessman in his mansion. There can be no doubt that whatever different views we may have on the extent of social mobility in China, in the kind of Chinese setting of which the N.T. are a twentieth-century sample, men were morally entitled to take steps to raise themselves and their descendants—by scholarship, by the accumulation of riches, and by the religious pursuit of good fortune.

The Geomancy of Burial

When someone dies he is first buried in a rough grave from which, after a few years, his bones are removed to be placed in an urn. All, or nearly all, men and women pass through the cycle of burial and disinterment up to this point. The urns are stored in the open air, near the fields or on a hillside, but those belonging to families for whom geomantic burial has become important and possible are at some point put into new graves. These are the omega-shaped tombs which are so prominent a feature of the southeastern Chinese countryside. They are constructed according to *fung shui* and may take years to prepare, because the choice of a good site may call for a protracted search, and the correct time for entomb-ment may be long delayed by both practical difficulties and religious restrictions. The geomancy of burial is concentrated about this second interment, for although *fung shui* may certainly enter into the selection of the first grave and the siting of the urn, it is then of secondary impor-tance, since virtue flows essentially from that which is intended to be a permanent habitation. (The same principle applies to houses: a man's permanent residence is where he will concentrate his geomantic efforts, but he may also take some *fung shui* precautions in houses where he is temporarily lodging.)

Sooner or later the geomantically sited grave will bring prosperity to the descendants of the man or woman buried in it. "Sooner or later": the geomancer is not usually prepared to tie himself down to a guarantee of quick results. Indeed, with that keen selective skepticism marking the way in which they scrutinize their religion and its practitioners, Chinese joke about the latitude that geomancers allow themselves. "Like a geo-mancer," a Cantonese saying goes, "who cheats you by predicting within eight or ten years." (If one's own ancestor's grave shows results in, say, five years when the geomancer has stipulated a waiting period of ten, it is a matter for self-gratulation and gratitude; but somebody else's pa-tience with the passing of the years may be a matter for jest.) The lapse of years is necessary for the collection and concentration of the Breaths. They settle in the bones, and in a particularly successful case cause them to glow. (So that glowing bones in an unburied urn demonstrate that a good geomantic site has been hit upon.) From the bones the virtue passes to the living descendants, but not in any physical sense: nobody considers the possibility of a mechanism for such a transfer. Filial children benefit from the virtue of their parents' graves; how is a mystery. If they live close enough they must tend the graves, but their separation from them by mere distance is no bar at all to their receiving the virtue. Of course, not all attempts at geomancy work, even if people are patient. Once they have made up their mind that something is wrong, they may alter the site in some way or even move the grave.

Few people seem to doubt that descendants are affected by *fung shui*. But there is also a popular belief, not shared by some geomancers, that the virtue stored up in a grave can be tapped by strangers. And from this idea stem the attempts at poaching on sites, attempts, that is to say, to bury one's dead in the immediate neighborhood of a grave which has demonstrated its efficacy. Geomancers arguing against the wisdom of this course of action may say that the virtue is confined to one tiny spot in the grave, the site having been chosen to accord with the special characteristics of its occupant, and that the area round the grave will avail nobody else. On the other hand, they will also certainly say that a new grave close by the old may well destroy the latter's virtue by altering the conformation of the site. So that poaching is a serious offense and may be the cause of bitter disputes. I came across no such case myself, but there is evidence that quarrels of this sort have been known in the N.T. (In fact, the Administration introduced a system of grave registration in 1909 to overcome difficulties of the kind, but it has not lasted.) Generally, people in the N.T. are able to protect their graves against encroachment, and it is only in special cases that one sees the effect of the belief that the virtue of a site may be tapped. In a valley overlooking the sea near Kowloon there is a large unofficial cemetery which appears to have come into existence because it contains the tomb of Sun Yat-sen's mother. Here many townspeople are buried. Sun's success is attributed in Hong Kong to this grave; in consequence it has attracted to it a host of other graves, despite the prohibition placed by the Administration on burial there. (Sun's failures as well as his successes can be read from his mother's grave, as I shall show presently, but people who acquire plots in the cemetery—they appear to "buy" them from the villagers within whose area the cemetery lies—are presumably not concerned with this qualification.)

In addition to this famous cemetery there are a few other places in the N.T. where one may see graves clustered together to form graveyards; but they nearly always turn out to be the last resting-place of immigrants. N.T. people scatter their tombs. Geomancy in the open countryside entails dispersed burial. Each new omega-shaped tomb involves the search for a new site. An N.T. man with a parent to rebury and with the resources to back up his ambition will look far and wide for a good site, not necessarily confining his search to the neighborhood of his own village. The poor cannot indulge themselves so; but they are unlikely in any case to reach the point of looking for reburial sites, and the bones of their dead probably remain forever in the urns where they were deposited after the disinterment of the first grave. There is no dearth of evidence that urns lie neglected for many years, at the end of their career spilling their contents on the ground. For the humble, that is to say, geomantic burial plays a small role. Among the proud and the aspiring the hunt for the

Dragon, a never-ending search for advancement and security, leads people in a competitive race over the hills. *Fung shui* in this context represents the right of individuals to outstrip their neighbors.

Success which flows from *fung shui* raises a moral problem, for it is not a reward for merit. If the geomancer has done his job correctly, the Breaths will concentrate automatically, whether the descendants be good men or bad. Geomancy explains why some people succeed and others fail —or rather, it is one of the explanations for their success and failure— even when they have the same advantages and appear to have the same chances; but, at least at first sight, it seems to obscure the role in success which may be played by moral worth. The problem is in fact raised in some of the *fung shui* stories current in the N.T. They show that in reality the evil cannot expect to prosper by *fung shui*, however much they may appear to benefit by it in the short run. The universe is a moral entity; principles of right laid up in Heaven are not to be negated by the workings of Earth.

I heard one story in two different versions; here is a summary of its main points. A poor duck-breeder one day secretly observed a geomancer at work. The geomancer stuck a bamboo pole in a muddy duck pond and left it there. During the night it flowered. The duck-breeder stole it and replaced it with another bamboo pole, to the disappointment next morning of the geomancer, who had expected to find his pole flowering. He tried again and once more was foiled by the wily duck-breeder and was forced to abandon what he had thought to have proved a magnificent *fung shui*. The duck-breeder, equipped with the stolen knowledge of the site, ordered his wife to bury him in the crucial spot when he should come to die, which in good time she did, wrapping him in a mat, since she was too poor to pay for a coffin. Time passed and their son grew up to become a great scholar. Summoned by the Emperor to Peking, he made the long journey north. On the way the boat he was traveling in got into difficulty but was saved by the god in a nearby temple. The people with whom the young scholar was traveling honored the god for his aid, but he refused to do so, going so far in arrogance as to strike the god on his head with his fan. Eventually he reached the capital and after a while returned home in triumph. There he showed himself so overbearing, especially in his behavior toward his maternal uncle, that his mother was forced to rebuke him, reminding him that his father had died a humble death and had been buried in a mat. The scholar agreed to rebury his father in a fitting manner, but when he came to search for the body he could not find it. While men were fruitlessly hunting for it round the spot indicated by the widow, the god whom the scholar had insulted appeared in the guise of a stranger and advised him to throw lime into the pond, whereupon the body would emerge. The advice was taken. The body rose to the surface, but along with it came nine dead fish, only one of which had its eyes open. . . . Nine bright possibilities, that is to say, had been stored away in the *fung shui*; one of them had been realized in the success of the scholar—and that was now at an end; the other eight were ruined. (When I recounted this story to a Chinese friend in Singapore, he capped it with a Fukienese story in which a passing scholar, on being told of the enormous success of a family which had stolen another family's *fung shui* and acted cruelly toward its members, sat down by the stolen grave to lament. If such people could prosper by the principles of Earth—which, incidentally is an alternative name for *fung shui*—where were the principles of Heaven? He had hardly spoken when lightning smashed the tomb before his eyes to put an end to the fortunes of the wicked family.)

In *fung shui*, prediction and results are, so to say, in a strange relationship of mutual causality. Geomantic siting produces results. The existence of "results" implies the preexistence of *fung shui*. "That chap, X," one of my friends said to me of a policeman, "has just got promoted. Y," here he named a geomancer, "and I are going to look at the grave he built last year to find out what's so good about it." Retrospective *fung shui* is, in the nature of things, much more convincing; reasoning from effect to cause, one can make a compelling case. Let me illustrate from an analysis of the grave site of Sun Yat-sen's mother. I was taken to see it by a part-time geomancer. (He looks like an old-fashioned scholar. In his youth he was a graduate student in economics at a famous American university, although he has now virtually forgotten his English—and perhaps his economics, too, although this is one of the subjects he makes his living teaching.) This is the bare bones of his analysis of the site. The high peak at the rear is excellent; it stands for authority and power. The front aspect is also very good; the tomb looks down over the open sea, and sea in geomancy is reckoned as "static" water. The Azure Dragon is satisfactory, but the White Tiger is imperfect; there is a break in the line of the hills through which too much wind can pass. So that the whole configuration, while being good, falls short of being a perfect embrace. For that reason Sun enjoyed power, but not for long. A stream runs down the valley robbing the grave of its virtue in respect of money; Sun was poor. In the sea below there are several small islands which are to be taken as warships, some of them sailing out into the open sea; they show Sun's desertion by his armed forces. Finally, there appears in the distance, just over the line of the White Tiger, the peak of another hill; such a feature means robbery; Sun was kidnapped. The site explains Sun's career (or some version of it) and justifies the geomancer who is alleged to have predicted that Mrs. Sun's son would be a king.

This case illustrates two systems of analysis being employed together: the system of metaphysical forces composing a site, expressed in the balance between wind and water, Dragon and Tiger, and the system of resemblances, the latter being invoked to interpret the islands. But the chief interest of the case lies in the example it offers of retrospective interpretation. Geomancy is a self-reinforcing system of ideas. What is predicted is nearly always likely to be justified, because what is foretold is vague, or inevitable, or subject to frustration which deny a part of the system or the competence of a practitioner without damaging the system as a whole. Retrospectively it can invariably be demonstrated to be valid because the material can be read in a number of different ways to justify any collection of events. Moreover, the existence of prosperity by itself presupposes that it has been produced by *fung shui*, and failure to detect the precise reason why the *fung shui* has operated so well leaves it in the realm of knowledge which in principle can be obtained but remains inaccessible for the moment because of the lack of expertise. (One geomancer told me that Mao Tse-tung's mother is buried in a good *fung shui*. And, he added, perhaps for political symmetry, that Chiang Kai-shek also enjoys geomantic benefits, the fall in his fortunes being due to the operation of the cycle of time, which turns the wheel on all affairs.) Retrospective *fung shui* is illustrated also in the traditions of the Tang group of lineages in the N.T.; the Tang lineages were the most powerful local communities in pre-British days, although by national standards they were relatively small beer—a point made in the following story. When the Sung princess who married a Tang in the twelfth century grew old (the marriage is probably a historically true event), a famous geomancer chose a *fung shui* for her which resembled a lion, asking her whether she preferred to be buried in the lion's head or tail. "She asked what difference it would make, and she was told that if her grave was on the head her descendants would be very great men: but if on the tail they would be more humble people, perhaps officers of low degree, and, although prosperous, none would succeed to high rank" (Sung 1936: 34–35).

Political, Domestic, and Urban Fung Shui

The term *fung shui* is often used to mean simply a grave, and there is no need to labor the point that burial is the heart of geomancy. But in fact *fung shui* covers all aspects of men's dwellings on earth. Every territorially defined unit of society has its *fung shui*, from the household up to the state. The residence of the head of the state affects the prosperity of the country. (For this reason great emphasis is often laid on the geomantic excellence of Government House.) The fortunes of cities, towns, and villages depend on their physical disposition and their dominating buildings. Political units take their fate from government offices. (A new District Court had recently been built at Fanling when I arrived in the N.T.; it impressed many of the locals by its *fung shui*.) The *fung shui* of an ancestral hall determines the fortunes of the members of the lineage. (For this reason such a hall is rarely to be found inside a walled village; it must have free access to its site.) A house shapes the destiny of its master and those for whom he is responsible. Consequently, geomancers are often employed to advise on the siting, orientation, certain architectural features (especially height), and work- and opening-dates of domestic and other buildings. Indeed, there appears to be some specialization among *fung shui sin shaang* in the N.T., some of them putting themselves out to be experts on graves and others on buildings.

Burial and the *fung shui* associated with it differ markedly in city and countryside. Only the rich among the people in the urban area can afford to escape the regimentation of their dead in cemeteries—"They queue up to be buried," one of my N.T. informants said contemptuously of the urban dead being brought to a large government cemetery—and seek geomantically favorable sites in private plots. (Some urban Chinese of course are members of N.T. communities and can make a claim to be buried on village land. Others, lacking the connection, acquire the right to bury their dead in land forming the traditional preserves of N.T. villages. They may have to pay dearly for the privilege. Along one of the main roads in the N.T., there stands a pavilion, now many years old, which was put up as part of the compensation to the local people for the geomantic disturbance caused them by the burial in their area of a rich man from the city.) Similarly, the *fung shui* of buildings plays a less important role in the urban setting. There are naturally severe limits to what can be done in the city to extract the best possible geomantic possibilities from a given site and to avoid places which have been labeled bad *fung shui* risks. By and large, I think we may say that in the city *fung shui* is a retrospective explanation of fortune rather than a prediction of it, and that in urban conditions far more reliance is placed on the dominant geomantic effects of crucial sites (government offices and other public and semipublic buildings). City dwellers conducting a stranger around their streets point out to him the residences of rich men which have brought them fortune and the houses which, because of their unfavorable sites, have exerted a malignant influence on their occupants. (A new road, pointing like a deadly arrow at Mr. A's house, brought him disaster. Mr. B. enjoys the protection of wind excluded and static water.)

In the countryside, in contrast, the geomancy of buildings is both for-ward- and backward-looking. The height of a new village house must take into account the height and position of the ancestral halls and other houses, in order that the fortunes of other people may not be prejudiced by one's efforts to improve one's own. In a remarkably interesting case being argued out during my time in the N.T., a disproportion in the two halves of the roofs of new houses was the cause of an agitation which cost the people responsible for building the houses much money and frus-tration. It was held that, the front sections of the roofs being longer than the rear, the future of the occupants would be cut short. The houses were redesigned at great expense to make the back sections of the roofs equal in length to the front. As for retrospective geomancy, misfortune—dis-ease, death, lack of sons, poor harvests, and so on—may come to be at-tributed to faults in *fung shui* which are then put right. The main gate in the village wall may need to be protected by new "arms" or skewed to alter the orientation of the whole village. A building thought to be too high may be lowered. Again, good or bad fortune may be attributed to earlier *fung shui* actions for which, in fact, there is no evidence. It is a common feature of N.T. village organization that communities which are now composed solidly or predominantly of one lineage were in time past made up of several. (There may, in fact, have been cycles of lineage homogeneity and heterogeneity.) The disappearance of the weaker lin-eages, through emigration or the failure to reproduce, is often said to have followed from their geomantic indiscretions or, as in a case which has impressed itself on me, from the superior geomantic techniques of the survivors. In this case the sole lineage occupying the village point to the ruined ancestral halls of their late rivals and ascribe their own good for-tune to the cunning of their ancestor, who, at the time when the village ancestral halls were being built in a line, surreptitiously made a slight alteration to the direction in which his own hall was to face. If ever there was such an incident, which I take leave to doubt, the alignment now to be seen bears no trace of it. Nor can the jubilant survivors detect it; they merely assume it to be there.

Just as the *fung shui* (and in consequence the status) of people may be attacked by poaching on their grave sites, so conflict can arise over the *fung shui* of buildings. X's attempt to build higher than my house is an affront. I say he is ruining my *fung shui*, and perhaps I am implying that he has no right to put himself above me—in both senses. Y has pierced the wall of his house to make a new window. It has caused sick-ness in the village. We protest against his lack of consideration, for at the very least he should have taken ritual precautions. Perhaps we are also saying that he should not have done what others do not do. And *fung shui* objections become intensified when those who are held to be at fault are outsiders: strangers or the government. For then the community as a whole can be united in its determination to defend its interests.

A village is not just the ground on which its fields are made and its houses stand. It is the whole area which, by custom, falls within the control of the community. When the British arrived, they acknowledged rights not only to building sites and cultivations, registering these rights in the land records, but also to a wider village territory within which the local people had certain privileges: burying their dead, grazing their cattle, and collecting fuel. Villagers stand by these rights; they resent intrusion and try to make trespassers pay for their boldness if they cannot or if it is not desirable that they be excluded. The immigrant vegetable grower or poultry farmer may think he has the right to put up a shack, but he may find himself the center of a dispute from which he can extricate himself only by paying a sum of money. An industrialist may have all the necessary permits, but he may be forced to come to terms with the people in whose area he wishes to operate. The prudent immigrant and the prudent industrialist make their terms before they begin to build. Similarly, the government undertaking public works may fall foul of objections couched in *fung shui* language. A hole is being drilled in the road; a child falls sick; the work must stop. A road is being cut through a hillside; it disturbs the Dragon; the evil to follow must be averted ritually. And so on.

It is nothing new for the government to encounter *fung shui* difficulties. It has faced them from the very beginning, when police posts had to be put up and roads made. In 1899 Lockhart (the official mainly responsible for the administration of the newly acquired territory) received a petition from a group of "elders" praying that another site be selected for a proposed road, because if plans were carried out, the new road would traverse "the geomantic line along the hill at the back of petitioners' ancestral temple." Lockhart told the "elders" that, while the British government was always prepared to respect the beliefs and customs of the people, it would not tolerate agitators making an improper use of popular beliefs in order to obstruct public works and welfare. And he went on to warn them that the agitators were working for their own private ends (I admire his certainty) and would be severely dealt with if they persisted. The Governor, in correspondence with Lockhart, suggested a different approach, proposing a "judicious arrangement" with the geomancers which might be made "with a small expenditure." Lockhart demurred: "If the geomancers were paid, they would become more troublesome than they were already, as they would discover that the creating of trouble is a paying game." [1] Ever since then the Administration has been faced with the dilemma of yielding to *fung shui* objections (every act of tolerance being a pledge to further acts) or resisting them, and running the risk of being accused of denying the original undertaking by the British Government to respect local beliefs and customs. It is not to be wondered at that present-day administrators sometimes appear to be reluctant protectors of popular faith. They probably feel themselves caught in a situation where they are being exploited by the unscrupulous for the regard they show for their religion.[b]

I have been wondering how the predecessors of these British mandarins would have handled the problem. Did Chinese officials take close account of popular *fung shui* objections? Given the lightness of the traditional administration and the narrow range of its functions, would

[b] In February 1963 there was a *fung shui* dispute in the Ping Shan area of the N.T. The following newspaper reports (all from the *South China Morning Post*) illustrate what can happen when villagers oppose development. "Villagers of X . . . threatened to use force yesterday to stop workmen from erecting buildings on a piece of land adjoining their settlement because of Fung Shui. But before they could resort to physical demonstration, about a dozen of them, mostly women, were taken into 'preventive custody' when they refused to heed a police warning to disperse. . . . The trouble started three years ago when a preserved food factory bought the plot and intended to build structures on . . . the site. The villagers raised objections, contending that the buildings would constitute an 'interruption' of Fung Shui, thereby bringing bad luck and calamity to the village. The factory delayed action for some 10 days, when workmen chopped away a barrier of bamboo trees on the perimeter to begin construction. The villagers also objected to this, claiming that they had planted these trees 'long, long ago.' Yesterday, officials of the District Office, Yuen Long, went to the site to negotiate with the village representative, and a settlement was reached by realigning the building site 'a little to the right' so as not to cause any obstruction or interruption of Fung Shui. A village elder explained yesterday that bad luck would visit the village if the alignment between the village and the knoll was interrupted. The knoll, he said, was the Golden Arm Chair embracing the village, giving it protection from ill luck. More than 100 years ago the villagers buried two of their dead on this knoll and there followed a calamity as death visited the village and took away many inhabitants, the village elder said. A Fung Shui master advised them that there must be no burial on that knoll and there must be also an uninterrupted view between the Golden Arm Chair and the village. The graves were removed. Then about 30 years ago the owner of the land buried on the knoll two urns containing the ashes of members of his family and again catastrophie [*sic*] struck, this time claiming more than 10 deaths in as many days until the urns were traced and removed." (16 Feb.) "Three villagers from X village, arrested last week following a disturbance on a building site over Fung Shui came before Mr. A at Fanling Court yesterday on a charge of disorderly conduct. [They were two men and a woman.] The two men also faced two charges of criminal intimidation and disorderly conduct by issuing threats. They denied the charges. . . . It was alleged the three were among a crowd of villagers who stopped a building gang from working on a construction site. A construction company foreman testified that . . . the two men threatened to kill him if he did not stop work." (22 Feb.) "Three villagers from X village yesterday reversed their plea . . . and were bound over to keep the peace. . . . Mr. B told the court that the villagers had tried to stop the factory from building their premises because of Fung Shui. But, he said, the management had consulted a geomancer who contended that the structure would not disturb the Fung Shui of the village. This contention had not been challenged. Nevertheless, the factory management had conferred with village representatives and had realigned their factory site." (23 Feb.)

many cases have cropped up? Surely, the intensity of governmental action in the presentday N.T. and the well-established tradition of paying due respect to local custom have produced a Leviathan vulnerable to geomantic attack. In the full flood of rural development, traditional rights are bound to be increasingly affected. The system of geomancy is so complex, the alternatives in interpretation so numerous, that a *fung shui* case can be made against anything at all that meets with the disapproval of the country people. Any work undertaken by the Administration can be said to be harmful in geomancy. But (an alternative usually ignored by observers) it can also be judged to be geomantically beneficial if local opinion is in favor of its practical worth. I know a village in the N.T. where a proposed new road is being welcomed precisely on the grounds that it will help remedy a defect in the geomantic conformation of the front aspect of the village. But it is not to be assumed that people are making a coldly rational translation of their practical wishes into the language of *fung shui*. They may be rationalizing, but they are not hypocrites.

Faced by its dilemma, the Administration must fall back on what it considers to be a practical formula: *fung shui* objections will be heeded if they are "reasonable." What is a reasonable nonrational objection? A Chinese official who shared his people's ideas could consult his own judgment. A British official cannot; nor could he take professional advice. (There have been very few Chinese District Officers in the N.T. One of them was a Catholic and did not know very much about geomancy until, having a case on his hands, he got the subject up out of books in the Hong Kong University Library; but significantly, when he cowed a geomancer by displaying his superior—and newly acquired—knowledge, the villagers who had retained the geomancer cast him aside and called on the District Officer to ask him to be their future *fung shui* adviser.) As far as I can see, a case is thought to be reasonable if the objectors appear to be sincere (i.e. they believe what they assert) and are telling the truth about things which are objectively verifiable (e.g. about the ownership of graves).[c] Once a case is judged reasonable, the officials yield, and a project is abandoned or means are provided for effecting

[c] In *fung shui* a government which does not share the ideas of the governed has trouble countering nonrational objections. Here is another illustration of what can happen when officials are faced with the practical consequences of religious ideas they do not share: "Government has granted permission for Buddhists to exorcise the spirits reported to have been haunting Murray House. Does this then indicate that Government recognises the existence of ghosts there?" "Not necessarily," a Government spokesman told the *China Mail* today. "The fact that permission was necessary was because the building is a Government Department and whether Government believes in ghosts or not is irrelevent [*sic*] to the issue," the spokesman explained. (*China Mail*, 9 May 1963.)

a ritual remedy. (In a recent case the government set up bamboo screens to shield from the eyes of the ancestors in their hall the sight of Dragon's Blood flowing from the wound inflicted by the cutting of a new road.) But it is not necessary for the Administration to yield: a tough policy would almost certainly work, in the sense that objections would grow fewer and people grow accustomed to the fact that they are no longer in a position to get their way. There must have been times in the history of the N.T. when a firm resistance was put up by the Administration. Reporting on the first phase of British rule, an administrator wrote that *fung shui* objections had been made to the proposed routes of roads and the railway, "but it is characteristic of the Chinese folk that their superstitious fears have always yielded ultimately to the needs of a progressive age" (Hong Kong, Legislative Council 1912: 47). One senses the toughness in this bland officialese. Today there is a softer policy.

Will *fung shui* last in the N.T.? I suspect that from the very beginning officers of the Administration have detected signs of growing skepticism —they can always be found, for reasons I have already suggested—and confidently awaited the spread of modern enlightenment. Contemporary officials are probably less tempted to the facile optimism of their predecessors of a generation or so ago (we are all nonrationalists nowadays), but one can hear it asserted that the young people of the N.T. today no longer believe in geomancy. If this were so, the Administration could look forward to a surcease of its anxiety. But why assume that modern education by itself deals *fung shui* a deadly blow? Metaphysical beliefs supported by social props are not easily wafted away by the book learning of schools. There are certainly unbelievers in the N.T., but their skepticism, if it is at all thorough, probably stems from their having been prized loose from the grip of their traditional society. Urban Chinese can easily stop paying attention to *fung shui* if they choose, because they are free from the social pressures which, in a rural community, they would be forced to take into account. Living in a city, people are not so closely dependent on one another that the actions of one can be held to have an intimate effect on the lives of others; and townsmen can more easily escape the consequences of neighborly disapproval. In a village which is still a relatively self-contained community, people are tied together in a complex web of obligations. Conformity is produced as a response to a multitude of loyalties and sanctions; it is not the mere reflection of a simple mechanical uniformity. One has to live fully within a village or get out. If, therefore, I am accused of harming my neighbor's *fung shui* and he is supported by others in his contention, I must give way. If my fellow villagers think generally that some outsider has encroached upon our geomantic privileges, I must join in the reaction. And every response of this kind reinforces us in our faith. (I may believe that in my own case I have been hard done by, but my faith in the assumptions from which my neighbors are working is not undermined.) As long, then, as village life remains the kind of relatively closed community life it has traditionally been, *fung shui* is likely to continue undiminished. (Indeed, for a time it may even come to be more in evidence as the tempo of rural development increases.) But in fact life in the N.T. cannot remain unchanged; industrialization and the blurring of community limits by the penetration of newcomers have already gone too far. So that there is a prospect that, just as in the city today, so in the N.T. tomorrow, geomantic ideas will survive (affecting the behavior of people striving for enhanced status and providing a retrospective explanation of fortune and misfortune) without involving everybody in a sharp geomantic response to a challenge to his rights.

The Rituals of Geomancy

If *fung shui* is detrimentally disturbed, not only may compensation be demanded but a ritual remedy may be sought which often takes the form of a *tun fu* (sometimes *tan fu*; there seems to be a case for considering this a Hakka term applied to a Hakka rite, both term and rite having been taken over by the Punti). *Tun fu* is in fact a series of rites to cure misfortune. *Fung shui*, I have contended, is a sort of "science," its principles working automatically and without the agency of anthropomorphic supernatural entities. (To some anthropologists it will look like a textbook case of magic.) But some *fung shui*, even undisturbed, give off a malign influence, a Killing Breath (*shaat hei*) for which the remedy cannot be sought within *fung shui* itself. Rites become necessary. That is to say, although *fung shui* is riteless, it is part of a wider religious system of which rites are an intrinsic part. If *fung shui* is "magic" it depends on "religion."

Rites call upon supernatural beings (as opposed to forces) and characteristically require the services of men who, being "priests" and not "technicians," stand in contrast to geomancers. In reality, the contrast is imperfect, for some geomancers apparently undertake to perform *tun fu*, but the "pure" *fung shui sin shaang* will not meddle with such things, saying that a Deadly Breath will never emanate from a properly constructed *fung shui* (i.e. one he has himself made) as long as it is left undisturbed, and that the remedy for a disturbed or imperfect one is the province of religious practitioners from whom he is careful to dissociate himself. *Tun fu* are typically performed by *naam moh lo*, although other kinds of ritual specialist (e.g. spirit-mediums) may be involved. A *tun fu* invokes a range of deities, both general and local, to counteract the malignancy and ensure peace. Among the deities called upon, some will decide that the work falls within their province and take appropriate action. *Tun fu* by its initial rite imposes a special ritual embargo on the action of the evil influences and by its final rite (the two may be a year or more apart) removes the embargo when peace and security seem to have been assured.

These rites are complicated and expensive. When outsiders (including the Administration) are required to pay for them, the suspicion arises that the money handed over in payment covers more than the expert's fees. Perhaps indeed a profit is sometimes made; but I do not think this is so important a feature of the system as people imagine. The victory scored over the "intruders" by the very fact that they have been forced to acknowledge their "trespass" and make it ritually good is in itself a magnificent compensation, for a vital claim has been vindicated.

Discussion

This paper is based on preliminary observations, gathered incidentally to a wider inquiry, and its conclusions are tentative. Several problems occur to me. One of them, as I have already suggested, is the order underlying the choice of entities in the system of resemblances; and I would add here that the topic of the Chinese Dragon by itself, although much written about, merits a thoroughgoing reappraisal, for it is a symbol which directly links geomancy with a chain of political and religious meanings. A second problem is the relationship between *fung shui* as an explanation of fortune and other parts of Chinese religion. People who believe in *fung shui* also worship their ancestors and take part in domestic and temple rites; they may also be members of special and particular cults. Is geomancy all the more workable and credible for being merely one among several ways of accounting for fortune? I raise the general question but consider only one aspect of the link between *fung shui* and others parts of Chinese religion.

Geomancy and ancestor worship interlock. Graves stand at the center of geomantic attention, and graves are the abodes of the ancestors. Just as the system of admitting tablets to the ancestral halls preserves only certain forebears, so the pattern of burial ensures that only some ancestors will be guaranteed a long memory. Undistinguished progenitors—or rather, the progenitors of the undistinguished—are never honored by tablets in hall-shrines and pass into an anonymous eternity as bones in a decaying pot. But in fact are we dealing with the same ancestors in both *fung shui* and ancestor worship? In the latter we are in touch with fore-bears whose merits affect our lives; we reap what they sowed. More-over, as benevolent guardians of their descendants, the ancestors can be expected to exert such supernatural influence as they have to promote the interests and soften the hardships of their living issue. The ancestors in their graves, in contrast, are the passive vehicles of impersonal geomantic forces. Provided we are filial—and no other moral standard is applied to us—we can make them do what we want done, and they can do nothing for us that we do not make them do. In ancestor worship our forebears are active and we are passive; in *fung shui* we are active and they are passive. So that, while *fung shui* appears to rest on the assumption that fortune is rigidly determined, in fact it presupposes that men will actively intervene in their own fate to shape their destinies. And I think it follows from this that geomancy plays a larger part than ancestor worship in explaining fortune and that, for all the profound significance of ancestor worship in domestic and lineage organization, on the plane of ideas it pales before *fung shui*. Geomancy explains more and better than ances-tor worship. Consequently (and for other reasons too), I am skeptical of attempts to make ancestor worship the central feature of Chinese religion.

There is another difference. The ancestors to whom we pay attention in domestic and hall shrines are determined by our membership of par-ticular groups, and we are involved in their worship as we are involved in a hierarchy of groups. The ancestors in their graves who interest us are less regularly arranged. Why do I take particular notice of certain graves? In principle all ancestral graves are geomantically relevant, but my impression is that the further distant a grave is in time and genealog-ical space, the less significant it is. And in fact, when we examine *fung shui* preoccupations in action, we see people worrying about their par-ents' and paternal grandparents' graves—i.e. those from which they can hope to extract some advantage for themselves and those very closely related to them. Geomancy is an aspect of competition, and, since com-petition between kinsmen is legitimate, near ancestors in their graves be-come points for developing individual interests and for differentiating the paths taken by agnates.

This last point may go some of the way to explaining why mothers' graves seem to play so prominent a role in *fung shui*. In a patrilineal and polygynous society, women are important points of segmentation, for, in the simplest paradigm, I am differentiated from my father's other sons by the fact of our having different mothers. On the other hand, I imagine that women's graves feature so prominently in *fung shui* because, in addition, they add to the number of "chances" that each individual can take. If he expands his range of "chances" by including the graves of remoter ancestors, he is involving himself with too many fellow descendants—he must get their approval to move or otherwise interfere with a grave and he will be benefiting them into the bargain. If he confines himself to near ancestral graves, he then needs the female half of them to raise the number of his "chances." As far as I know, there is no rule which says that the grave of a father is worth more than that of a mother, or that of a father's father worth more than a father's mother's. I may try my luck with all of them and hope that at least one will bring me the success foretold by geomantic technique.

People say that only agnatic ancestors count in *fung shui*. It is what we should expect. But one of my informants spent a lot of time worrying about his wife's parental graves and certainly with the interests of his own immediate family in mind. But he was not any longer a villager, and it is possible that we may regard his family life as being so different from that of the community he had abandoned that he was justified in a different view of kinship and its geomantic implications: his children have ceased to be merely the agnatic descendants of his parents and have become in addition significant grandchildren of his wife's parents. I wonder what other modifications in kinship patterns are reflected in geomancy and how far the structure of "chances" varies with the structure of kinship and affinity.

The final question I raise is the extent to which what can be seen in the N.T. is characteristic of China, in respect of both its nature and its general importance. As to its nature, I suspect that a survey of the voluminous treatises and handbooks as well as of genealogies, gazetteers, novels, and other writings which provide incidental and illustrative material would establish a hard core of basic notions and techniques corresponding very closely to what can be derived from N.T. data.[2] And in this regard I would seriously call in question the first half of C. K. Yang's assertion (1961: 34) that geomancy "was partly a means of averting possible evil influence from the dead upon the progeny as well as being a means of inducing the supernatural influence of blessing." But the importance of geomancy in China as a whole is a more difficult problem. Are we to attach significance to the minor place allotted to it in general works on Chinese religion and to the incidental manner in which it is introduced into descriptions of particular communities? The N.T. data suggest to me that, whatever the enhanced importance given to *fung shui* in the special conditions of a British colony in the full flood of rural development, its meaning in relation to ancestors and ways of explaining fortune has been overlooked or underplayed elsewhere. But at this point I drop the matter for the time being.

In conclusion I offer three summary points.

(1) *Fung shui* is, in one respect, an assertion of rights: to home territory and to individual access to rank and riches. Rights of course can conflict: the right of the community may be in conflict with the right of an individual member of it, and the right of an individual member may conflict with that of another. Consequently, geomancy may appear to suppress claims as well as support them—as in accusations that a neighbor's house has been built too high.

(2) *Fung shui* is an amoral explanation of fortune lying alongside a moral explanation: Earth against Heaven, good luck against merit. So that Heaven and Buddhist ideas of retribution and reward, as well as notions of agnatically transmitted reward in ancestor worship, are balanced against the automatism of geomantic determinism.

(3) *Fung shui* is an intrinsic part of the cult of the ancestors but is in fact the opposite of ancestor worship. In geomancy the ancestors have no moral status but are pawns in a game played by their descendants. In the long run, morality may prevail, but for as long as possible men seek to evade the principles of Heaven by recourse to the principles of Earth.

Shifts of Power in the
Hong Kong New Territories

Hong Kong is now one of Britain's few remaining colonies. It could conceivably be its last. Doubtless, many anthropologists pray that its life may be long, for, paradoxically enough, it provides them with one of their two remaining opportunities—the other being Taiwan—to study traditional forms of Chinese social organization on its home ground. In Hong Kong it is possible to study, among other things, the preservative effects of a vanishing empire on a residue of one already long since vanished.[1] In 1842 Britain took full legal possession of the island of Hong Kong. Eighteen years later it acquired similar rights in the tip of the Kowloon Peninsula opposite the island. Up to this point in the Colony's history British administrators were engaged in fostering and governing a commercial and essentially urban Chinese settlement; they were not in the position of heirs to the government of China. But in 1898, for reasons of Western rivalry in China, a treaty was negotiated with the Chinese government which made over to Britain for 99 years some three-fifths of the country of Hsin-an (in the province of Kwangtung), of which Hong Kong island and the Kowloon Peninsula had formerly also been part. This accession of territory carried British rule well into the countryside, and, with a long established rural population of some 100,000 to govern, the administrators of Hong Kong were now forced to step into the shoes of the Chinese mandarins.

The New Territories, as the leased area came to be called, were created to be a buffer to the island colony, and the British administration designed for them was not concerned in the first place with development. The first consideration was to suppress disorder (partly traditional, partly

Journal of Asian and African Studies, 1, no. 1 (1966), 3–12. A preliminary version was delivered under the title "Changing Leadership in the Hong Kong New Territories" in Section N of the annual meeting of the British Association for the Advancement of Science, Southampton, 26 Aug.–2 Sept. 1964.

arising from the change of government itself) and ensure a continuing peace. The new subjects of the British Crown were to be governed, as far as was consistent with British principles, by traditional means. But, of course, the fact that the new rulers succeeded fairly quickly in bringing peace to the countryside, that they put up police posts and began making roads (there had only been paths before), and that they had to modify traditional social arrangements (especially in land tenure) to make them amenable to a new kind of bureaucratic control, meant that the greater part of Hsin-an county was inevitably to undergo a change more substantial than one in name.

Hsin-an was in most respects a typical part of southeastern China.[2] From a political point of view we may say that its outstanding characteristic was that the governed both resisted government and relied on it for their power to resist. The paradox lies in this. Powerful leaders in the countryside were able to exercise local control and rally local support against government interference because, culturally and socially, they were on a footing with, and were created by the same mechanism as, the governors. The county was administered by a mandarin whose offices were in the county seat, and three subordinate mandarins posted to different points in the county. These men came from provinces other than that in which Hsin-an was situated, and were bureaucrats who had been created through a system of examinations or one combining examinations and purchased ranks.[3] The people of Hsin-an were (except for a small minority of so-called boat people; see B. E. Ward 1954a and 1959) free to sit the same examinations and so acquire the titles and status hungrily sought by ambitious men. Once suitably qualified, a Hsin-an man could be a mandarin in another province. The population of the county must have been about 200,000 during the nineteenth century, and at any one point in time in the latter part of the century there were probably some 150 men who had qualified in the first important set of examinations (held in the prefectural capital) or had acquired equivalences. (These were the people to whom the Western commentators of the period referred as the "Bachelors of Arts"; some of them would move on to become the "M.A.s" and "Ph.D.s" created by the provincial and national examinations respectively.) They were publicly recognized scholars who enjoyed high standing with the government and prestige in the eyes of the populace.

In fact (as one might have expected) the county scholars came from a few local communities. In general terms, these were the largest and the richest in the county; they were situated in the fertile rice plains and had built up both large numbers and great wealth. Like many of the communities in the area, these favored ones were single patrilineages: groups of men (together with their unmarried sisters and their wives) who traced their descent through males to a common ancestor and formed corporate entities (see Freedman 1958 and 1966). The biggest of them numbered several thousand. They dominated the smaller communities in their immediate area, sometimes collecting "taxes" from them on their land. They exercised control of some of the market towns (of which there were about forty in the county), and generally acted as arbiters of local affairs. On the other hand, they were not in absolute control of the weaker communities, for many of the latter formed unions to protect themselves, sometimes playing off one more powerful lineage against another.

Political activity took place within a context of violence or the threat of it. Many of the local communities, especially the biggest and richest, were in moated and walled settlements; and while this warlike architecture (much of which is still to be seen in the New Territories today) may have been due in part to the brigandage and piracy for which the region was well known, it also played a role in the fighting between lineages. Recourse to arms was a recognized mode of settling disputes between members of different lineages. The richer communities had cannon and other firearms at their disposal; swords and spears served the martial needs of the generality. Between some of the communities there were vendettas, and violent death was a risk men had commonly to run. The more important the community, the more likely it was to use violence to defend or extend its privileges. And leading roles in collective acts of violence were sometimes taken by those very scholars who by education and standing were in theory dedicated to preserve the peace of a bureaucratic state. The scholars did not, of course, take up arms themselves; they encouraged and organized their humbler lineage mates to do so.

One might very well ask what government amounted to. At least during the second half of the nineteenth century, the mandarins appear to have done very little apart from collecting land taxes and making arrangements for men to take the periodic state examinations. The county magistrate rarely exercised his judicial functions; disputes were usually settled either by local mediation or (in cases involving people from more than one lineage) resort to arms; the state rarely hauled a malefactor into court on its own initiative. Krone (1859: 92), the missionary who has given us a description of Hsin-an county in the middle of the nineteenth century, says of one of the mandarins that he "had not, as far [as] I know, during a period of several years, more than one case brought before him for decision; in this instance he was both plaintiff and judge—the criminal being a youth who was caught stealing fruit in his garden."

There were about a thousand troops stationed in the county. They were largely ineffective in controlling banditry and could have been of small use in restraining the settled population scattered in perhaps a thousand villages and hamlets. It was, of course, the duty of the mandarins to keep the peace, but in practice they rarely intervened in local disputes, and even when they did so they were unlikely to make much headway against determined opposition. On the whole, people paid their taxes (the poor and the weak paying relatively more than the rich and the strong), and the mandarins were normally prepared to leave it at that. Order was produced by mechanisms of control within each local community, by mediation and controlled fighting between communities (controlled because neutral communities and organized neighborhoods of communities prevented long disturbances of the local peace), and by the desire on the part of the ambitious inhabitants of the county to stay on reasonable terms with the mandarins in order to keep them in check and ensure free access to the examinations. It would seem that the most effective sanction the county mandarin could apply to the lineages of high social status was to prevent their members going forward to the prefectural examinations. It has often been said that at the end of the nineteenth century the government of China was weak. True, but it by no means follows that it was a negligible element in the maintenance of order, for at the very least its officers were symbols of an awe-inspiring stratum of Chinese society and it had rewards of prestige and power to offer to the cooperative.

Violence could also appear in the relations between members of one local community, but at this social level it was not allowed to go far before being brought under control by leaders of recognized community institutions. Let us assume for the sake of simplicity that village and lineage coincided. (They often did.) Two kinds of leaders were to be seen: ritual headmen and village governors. Since a lineage, its segments, and in some cases segments of these segments were definable as ancestor-worshiping units, there was a hierarchy of ritual headships filled according to principles of seniority in generation and age. Associated with the ancestral halls belonging to these units, but especially with the hall of a lineage as a whole, there were councils, the membership of which was not regulated by any simple principle of seniority. The lineage council was the chief organ of lineage government. To it gravitated the men who for one reason or another were capable of exercising political leadership; they were the governors. Certainly, some of them were old and might well be ritual headmen; long life by itself was a sign of moral fitness; but relatively few old men were otherwise qualified, while young titled scholars were sure of a place, as were any men whose riches and outside connections gave them a voice worth heeding. In this council rules were drawn up and from time to time revised for the conduct of lineage affairs, provision was made for the management of lineage property (common land, schools, fishponds, and so on), and disputes and infractions of the lineage peace dealt with. Here was lineage power; here were the political leaders of the lineage—a small elite, and most literally so when, the lineage being large and heterogeneous in its composition, the chosen few were socially and culturally distanced from most of their fellows.

In each village there was a *ti-pao*, a kind of constable. He was the only official link between the village and the bureaucracy. But it must not be supposed that the position carried any prestige. On the contrary, precisely because the *ti-pao* was the routine channel for government instructions in one direction and information about the village in the other, the role was held in contempt. If representations needed to be made to a mandarin on behalf of the community, some village member of standing would be chosen for the task. If he could be a titled scholar, so much the better. As a matter of fact, the office of *ti-pao* was in the late nineteenth century a residue of a complex official system of grouping the local population into units for administrative purposes; but in the period we are concerned with the aggregation of villages into the neighborhoods fell outside the official system. Probably, to follow an argument recently advanced for China as a whole by G. William Skinner (1964), we must look in many cases to the lesser market towns as the foci of local organization above the village level. In these towns, tied to their dependent villages by economic, political, and ritual bonds, a local public opinion was formed and local leaders, over their bowls of tea, worked out solutions to parochial problems.

When the New Territories were created, one of the earliest acts of the British administration was to register all landholdings. In the process certain powerful lineages were deprived of the "taxing" privileges they had previously enjoyed over the land held by others. It was the first step in the decline of the few key lineages in the region. Although they took some years to put a final stop to banditry, the new rulers were enabled by their relatively efficient police force and better communications to suppress fighting between communities. Local power could no longer be backed by violence or the threat of it. Finally, by imposing an alien administration, the chief officers of which were outside the range of Chinese ideas and influence, the new regime broke the link for the Chinese between education, bureaucratic service, and high social status.

Paradoxically enough, despite—or rather, because of—their strangeness, the British officials soon found themselves taking a larger part in social control than their Chinese predecessors would have dreamed of assuming. People came to the new administrators with all manner of disputes for settlement. In the 1850's a mandarin in Hsin-an county had told Krone (1859: 73) that he had nothing to do but eat, drink, and smoke; half a century later British officials were busy not only with work of their own making (being driven on by political motives very different from those of their Chinese forerunners), but also with the affairs brought to their attention by country people. Now, it is interesting to note that the new administration had started off with the idea (based in part at least on its own rapid surveys of local life and customs) that the people would be able to manage their own affairs and settle their minor disputes within the framework of their traditional institutions; and in 1899 a Local Communities Ordinance was brought in which gave the Governor of the Colony powers to divide the New Territories into "suitable Districts and Subdistricts," to appoint committees for these units, and to establish District and Subdistrict courts exercising both (minor) civil and criminal jurisdiction. These provisions were never fully implemented, for it became clear that the committees and courts would not work (at least as they were expected to). In 1912 the District Officer reported (Hong Kong, Legislative Council 1912: 45):

Reference should be made to the waning influence of the village elders throughout the Territories. It was the intention of Sir Henry Blake [the Governor of the Colony, 1898–1903] that "existing village organisations should be maintained and utilised," and that the village tribunals should continue to decide local cases. But it soon became clear that the authority of the village elders was of no account, with the stronger authority of the Magistrates so easily accessible, and the idea of local tribunals had to be dropped. Under Chinese rule, the remoteness, the danger and the expense of the central courts had left much authority to local elders, and especially to those entrusted with powers of collecting taxes: under British rule their authority naturally decayed, though they have continued sometimes to be the medium of dealings with villagers.

In fact, however, the undermining of the tax privileges of certain "elders" could have been only part of the story. I suspect that the British administration made mistakes in the way in which it divided the area into Districts and Subdistricts; these were probably not always the units within which local cooperation had traditionally been expected. More important, however, the new regime was making false assumptions about the nature of traditional local government, and perhaps, too, confusing "elders" who were merely ritual headmen in the lineages with "elders" (village governors) who might be expected to be effective political leaders. The lineage councils, as we have seen, had been rule-making bodies, had managed lineage property, and generally presided over lineage affairs by taking what we should classify as executive and judicial action;

but they had never been convened and conducted according to bureaucratically formulable rules. The making of general decisions and the settlement of disputes had been a complicated and subtle matter, involving much mediation and argument and coming and going. Still less would it be realistic to think that there had been highly organized bodies regulating the affairs of units wider than a single local community. Political and social control had been the product of a vastly more complex system of relationships. Under the changed conditions of British rule, when an impartial official, standing outside the field of local push and pull, was prepared in certain cases to pronounce a decision fairly quickly and back it with his authority, he did not lack for custom, even though he could not possibly have attracted to himself more than a mere fraction of the cases generated in so large a population.

The first years of colonial rule brought important political changes, but in fact the New Territories for long remained a kind of traditional Chinese hinterland to urban Hong Kong. Administration was not, by British standards, intensive; changes were not rapid; and before the Second World War there could have been, but for the guarantee of peace, little difference in conditions and atmosphere between the New Territories and the China across the border. But in recent years matters have taken a sharper turn. The crucial year is, of course, 1949. Since Communism has come to mainland China the Colony has become jammed with refugees, many of whom have gone into the New Territories. This is not the first time that the New Territories have received refugees from China, but the new influx and the new economy which has its roots in the same event that flooded the Colony with refugees have changed large parts of rural Hong Kong into a different kind of "China." There have in fact been two economic revolutions in the Colony, one industrial (and fairly well known to the world outside), the other (much less commented on) agricultural (see e.g. Szczepanik 1960 and Topley 1964). The former has pushed out the urban frontier into the New Territories, scattered a few factories in the hinterland, and provided work for village women at home (needlework and the assembling of plastic flowers, for example). The agricultural revolution shows its effects more widely. Refugees have turned large areas of land into market gardens, changing the landscape with their crops and huts, and to some extent the newer agricultural pattern has been adopted by the long-established population.

There are now getting on for half a million people in the New Territories, the population having increased nearly five times since the beginning of British rule. The indigenous New Territories people have not grown very much in numbers in that period. In the last census (1961) only about a third of the people enumerated in the New Territories gave

Hong Kong as their ancestral "place of origin." In other words, the present-day descendants of the people who came under British rule in 1898 are probably only a quarter again as many as their forebears. There has, of course, been emigration, especially to urban Hong Kong, the West Indies, and, in recent years, to Britain. (In 1963 there were between twenty and thirty thousand New Territories people in Britain, mostly engaged in the Chinese restaurant business, and remitting perhaps more than £2,000,000 to their families at home.)

In the 1950's, when it was clear that the nature of New Territories society was being radically transformed, the administrative system was increased in size and complexity and an attempt was made to build up a framework of effective local representation by elaborating a Rural Consultative Council that had been set up thirty years before. There are now about 900 Village Representatives, nominated or elected. From these men are recruited the Rural Committees, of which there are twenty-seven. The chairmen and vice-chairmen of these Committees, together with certain other men, form the Rural Consultative Council. At all levels the men in the system have only advisory functions and are unpaid. From the official point of view, the Rural Committees act as spokesmen for local public opinion, mediate disputes, and provide a bridge between the people and the administration. But each of the four District Officers is also charged with mediating disputes, and it is fairly clear that the Village Representatives and Rural Committees of today are no more capable than were the "elders" of half a century ago of damming the constant flow of quasi-legal business to the offices of the British mandarins. (I say "quasi-legal" because recent legislation has stripped away the District Officers' judicial powers which are now vested in courts independent of the administrative system.)

In present-day conditions the most characteristic feature of New Territories leadership is a negative one: the old scholar-gentry has no cultural successors. Leadership and learning have been divorced, for, although there are some schoolmasters among the New Territories elite, the predominating element is commercial. In recent years education has flourished, and in some places the demand for it seems to exceed the supply. But unlike the school and tutoring systems of the nineteenth century, the modern system leads to a creaming-off of the local talent instead of, as was the case in the past, to a reinvestment of it in local leadership. For many parents the schools are potential avenues of escape for their children from a rural way of life that has lost its self-evident validity and attraction. The education horizon has moved outward to embrace foreign universities, but, apart from the odd graduate who comes back to teach school, the educated elite of the New Territories is lost to it.

Who would be a Village Representative? He draws no pay and belongs to a Rural Committee which has no formal powers. But in fact candidates for office are forthcoming, and there is evidence that many men are willing to work hard when they are appointed. They win prestige, and if they are ambitious enough they may reach the Rural Consultative Council. Certainly, Village Representatives give the impression of being very busy men, running constantly to the District Office, mediating between the administration and their constituents, and consulting with one another. From the government's point of view, Village Representatives are what their name implies, but it is a matter of view, Village Representatives are what their name implies, but it is a matter of common observation that in their communities they are called Village Headmen. What power do they have in effect? They are not a sole channel through which the transactions between villagers and administration flow, for any individual may approach the District Office or one of its staff in the field, and many people exercise this right freely, especially in areas where communications are good. But a villager's claim on the attention of officials is strengthened when he has his Representative to speak for or stand by him, and from this position the Village Representative is able to extract a power advantage which in reality raises him above the status of a mere mouthpiece for his constituency. Again, when he is called upon to express to the administration the state of opinion in his community on a particular issue or to aid in conveying to the community an instruction from the administration, the Village Representative can to some extent shape the reactions of his people, perhaps sometimes for his own ends, but more generally to suit his own view of what is desirable. On the other hand, precisely because he is a politician (which he was certainly not created to be) he must maneuver within the limits of what he assesses village wishes and demands to be. So that there are occasions when, in order to retain his position, he must take a stand that is not the one he might himself have chosen.

Let me illustrate from what is sociologically perhaps the most interesting practical problem in the present-day New Territories: geomancy. An administration extremely considerate of the religious beliefs and practices of its charges is finding itself constantly vexed by village claims that either the government itself or some private individual or group has infringed local geomantic prerogatives: a new building, road, or excavation may be held by local opinion (not necessarily on advice from expert geomancers) to have damaged the mystical properties of the landscape in which the village is embedded. (And since the government does not share the religion of the people it governs, it cannot manipulate their beliefs or counter them, so to say, from within. Chinese mandarins were able to talk back in the language of geomancy. British mandarins cannot.) In the full flood of rural development it is inevitable that such infringements of geomantic integrity will be common. A Village Representative may think that a claim on the grounds of geomancy made by his constituents is unwarranted or at least ill-advised; he may take a longer economic view than his fellow villagers (the building or road being seen to promise benefits); but if he is to maintain himself as a political figure he may need to support the claim and press it hard enough to assure his constituents that he is acting as their leader.

Power also comes to the Village Representative from the position he occupies in relation to the outside world. He confers with other Village Representatives and may be sought out by men who have conceived some economic interest in his village, from the humble immigrant who would like to establish himself there on a plot of land to grow vegetables (and whose chances of success in getting himself accepted may depend directly on what the Village Representative is prepared to do for him) to the land dealer who may need to rely both on the Village Representative's detailed knowledge of the complex land tenure of the village—some Village Representatives are considerable authorities on the records in the Land Office —and on his good will and help in securing what he wants.

The geographical range within which any Village Representative works is a function of his business interests and his position in the hierarchy of leaders. At one end of the scale we see men who deal only with other Village Representatives in the small area covered by the Rural Committee. At the other end, there are a few men with economic and physical bases in the city. The higher the leaders climb, the closer their relations seem to become with the businessmen in the city; and since the New Territories are growing as an area of interest to urban investors and industrialists, the local politicians widen their external contacts. It has always been true of rural Chinese society that people placed higher in the social scale have had more extensive contacts with the market towns and the cities. What is comparatively new about the situation in the New Territories is that the initiative for making social change in the countryside lies increasingly with urban capital.

What we can now see in the New Territories is the result of the impact of British colonial administration and economic change on a sample of traditional Chinese society. In many respects the New Territories remain traditional but, especially since the 1950's, their political shape has been altered. Curiously enough, the old *ti-pao*, the humble village constable, has been revamped into a new kind of leader, the Village Representative, who has in many cases taken the place of the gentry mediator between state and people. The local man who has standing in the eyes of the government is often now the man who deals with the government in a routine fashion. It is of course a different kind of government from what it was; it is positive, headed by foreigners, orderly, and impartial. It is capable of intimate concern with the affairs of the people just because, in its foreignness, it is far more immune than its predecessor to sectional and private pressures. In the context of the present-day international situation, Chinese nationalism has little political significance within the framework of Hong Kong politics, and leaders in the New Territories are unlikely to be able to make political capital out of being anti-government, even though they may challenge the government on particular issues. They take their strength from their success in handling the administration and promoting the economic well-being on which all eyes seem to be fixed. It has been said of Hong Kong that it is a bit of China under British management. That management has certainly preserved much of the traditional China for anthropologists (and tourists) to observe, but the distribution of power is so different from what it was that the New Territories today are neither the old China preserved nor either of the two modern Chinas in a state of arrested development.

Emigration from the New Territories

It is generally assumed that there are some 20,000 Hong Kong men in the United Kingdom at the present time, most of them in the restaurant trade. (The figure may be larger; the head of the biggest travel agency in the New Territories puts it at 25,000.) Most of these men are from the New Territories. In addition, men have gone to other parts of the world to seek a living. It is known that the money remitted home is a sizable portion of the annual income of the New Territories. I write without a copy of the 1961 census before me and I am unable to calculate very accurately how large a proportion the emigrants must form of the relevant sector of the population; but if we remember (a) that very few of the emigrants are men from the city, (b) that nearly all of them hold British passports and may be assumed to have been born in the Colony, and (c) that they are practically all men of working age, then we may conclude that they represent, very roughly, perhaps a third of all the men in the New Territories who were born there and who fall within the economically active years of manhood. Since, furthermore, there are certain areas of the New Territories from which emigration has been especially heavy, despite the fact that men from all areas have participated in the movement, there are grounds for assuming that the effect of migration must in places have been extremely important.

The scale and direction of the emigration of the last few years are novel, but they rest on a tradition which reminds us that in this, as in many other respects, the New Territories are geographically and culturally part of southeastern China. For, especially since the middle of the last century, the coastal regions of the provinces of Kwangtung and Fukien have served as a reservoir from which many countries, above all

Excerpt (numbered paragraphs 72–83) from *A Report on Social Research in the New Territories* (mimeo., 37 pp.), submitted in 1963 to the New Territories Administration of Hong Kong. The first sentence of paragraph 72 has been omitted here. The entire report has now been published: *Journal of the Hong Kong Branch of the Royal Asiatic Society*, 16 (1976), 191–261.

in Southeast Asia, have drawn population. Emigration to California and Australia—the "gold mountains"—was noted by the first British administrators of the New Territories (for they spoke of loan associations got up to finance men wanting to go to these two countries), but there are hints in the early census reports that New Territories people were scattered more widely. The 1911 census shows a handful of Chinese in the New Territories to have been born in Annam, Hawaii, the Philippines, the Straits Settlements, Siam, and Australia. In 1921 the countries which appear in this context, again with reference to very small numbers, are Annam, India, Japan, British Borneo, France, Italy, the U.S.A., and Mexico. The list for 1931 reads: Indo-China, British North Borneo, Malaya, Netherlands East Indies, Siam, Canada, the U.S.A., Cuba, Panama, Guiana, Peru, England, and Holland. There were, in fact, two kinds of emigrants: landsmen who went overseas to make a living in a particular country, and seamen who, whether legally or not, left their ships to try their luck in places to which they had been carried. The establishment of Hong Kong as a British settlement in 1842 created a demand for local seamen, many of whom were recruited from the Chinese villages lying near the new center. Men from Lamma Island and from Lantau Island seem at an early date to have taken service in British and other ships.

Early in the British period in the New Territories a considerable movement took place to the West Indies, especially from the Sha Tau Kok and Shap Sz Heung areas. After the Second World War the opportunities for overseas migration were much reduced both because of restrictions imposed in many countries and on account of the failure of the local shipping industry to reestablish its demand for seamen. New Territories men were casting about for new overseas openings; a few discovered the opportunity created by a demand for (what passes for) Chinese food in Britain, where there had been for many years a small but prosperous Chinese restaurant trade run mainly by Chinese from the New Territories and the area adjacent to it across the border in China; and within a short space of time a new emigration was under way, haphazard to begin with but becoming well organized as its economic possibilities were realized by entrepreneurs. San Tin, whose men now bulk very large in the ranks of the emigrants, appears to have been a pioneer; one of the oldest Chinese restaurants in London was started by a man from this settlement. (I have a figure, which I have not been able to check, of 520 San Tin men in the United Kingdom in February of this year.) The movement to Britain was already well marked in the early 1950's; it began to increase sharply in 1956 and reached its peak figures in the years 1958–62. In the last few months, for reasons to be discussed presently, emigration has fallen away, so that 1963 may well prove to be a year in which the movement to the United Kingdom can be definitively studied. The New Territories demand for overseas work has also been met in part during recent years by the opportunities for contract labor in Borneo and Nauru and Ocean islands. The figures for this emigration are given in the New Territories Administrative Reports, but it is a movement about which I know very little and on which I propose to say nothing more.

The ability of the Chinese restaurant trade in the United Kingdom to expand by tapping the New Territories for its workers has rested on the enterprise of a few men who organized an efficient method of recruiting, financing, and conveying would-be hands once it became clear that considerable profits were to be made. The early traffic was by sea. For a time charter flights took men over to London (and brought some of them back) at £90 a head. More recently the airlines have offered special migrants' fares at £85. Much of the recent financing has been done through a travel agency with its main office in Tai Po which, since 1960, has arranged loans for the bulk of the fare, the travelers being required to pay a small deposit and discharge the balance of the sum out of their earnings abroad over a period of one or two years. (There is a close relationship, evidently, between migration to the United Kingdom and the rise of banking in the New Territories. Banks are now to be seen everywhere, but the first to open began business in 1960.) To incur an expense of about $1,500 and pay off the bulk of this sum at interest in the course of working in Britain has not, in general, been a heavy burden, since earnings in the restaurants have been fairly high, even for the lowly dishwasher. But the initial capital outlay, amounting perhaps to only a few hundred dollars, has represented a barrier to many would-be emigrants, and it is clear that there have been many men who wanted to go but who could not, either in the form of cash or security, put down the starting sum. Naturally, before 1960 the problem of raising the fare was even more difficult. It follows from this that the poorest layer of the population has not been very much affected by the movement to Britain. True, some poor men have managed to get away, but they have done so because they were members of families or communities in which men of means were willing to stand behind them. In one of the villages I got to know, the Village Representative some years ago put up a sum of money ($7,000) to encourage workless men of his community to emigrate. Repayments of loans were made to a revolving fund from which further emigrants were financed.

Earlier forms of emigration, because they were largely bound up with seagoing (a man might make one trip and then jump ship), seem to have drawn on the poorest areas and communities of the New Territories. The modern movement to the United Kingdom, while certainly being general and in many cases recruiting in the communities from which men used in the old days to go as seamen, seems to have been biased in favor of the better-off settlements, pumping money back into communities which to begin with were the ones suffering the least economic hardship. Traditionally the large and powerful Punti settlements were not emigrant areas; now their men play an important role in the restaurant trade in Britain. It may seem to us that to be a waiter or dishwasher in a restaurant is no advance in social status on being a small farmer, but in fact the incentive to undertake strange and menial tasks has lain in the prospect of starting up in business. The hundreds of Chinese restaurants now in Britain (there are well over a thousand) began from a very small nucleus. Men started as workers, saved a little capital, joined with a few friends or relatives, and opened their own establishments, town after town being drawn into the network (so that, as one of my undergraduates in London put it to me last year, there has been created a provincial tradition for chop suey and chips). In its expanding phase the business could justify a claim to offer opportunities to all; now that its peak has passed it can no longer exert the same attraction.

Statements have appeared that the new law in Britain to restrict the entry of people from the Commonwealth has had a decisive effect in restraining migration from Hong Kong. I am under the impression, however, that the causes of the recent sharp decline in the movement to the United Kingdom have been more complicated. If the new law has in fact cut down entry from Hong Kong it is partly, it would seem, because misconceptions have arisen in the minds of restaurant owners about their responsibilities toward the men to whom they have offered jobs; I have been told that they wrongly suppose themselves to be the legal sponsors of the immigrants and have accordingly become reluctant to allow their names to appear on newcomers' documents. (When I began my inquiries in February this year, the new legislation did not appear to be having much effect; entry could be obtained for men who wanted to go.) But I am inclined to think that the basic reason for the closing of this chapter in New Territories emigration lies in economic conditions in Britain. The demand for Chinese restaurant food has probably been overmet; there have been unemployment and underemployment in the business. Some of the New Territories emigrants have only part-time jobs; others have been reported to be working only for their keep. Moreover, there is evidence that many have taken up work in different fields: as waiters in ordinary restaurants, as servers in fish-and-chips bars, and as barbers, some of them in these lines working in new ventures financed by New Territories capital and enterprise.

The New Territories restaurant business has not been confined to Britain. From there men have branched out into Europe, setting up shop in Holland, Belgium, France, and West Germany. But these outliers can never, presumably, compensate for a decline in the United Kingdom demand, for at the very least immigration restrictions on foreigners will block any spectacular expansion. It may be that New Territories Chinese in Britain will gradually diversify their occupations—they have begun to do so—finding their way step by step into a multitude of industries and jobs. And it is possible that a disintegration of the restaurant pattern of settlement will have important consequences for the assimilation of the migrants and their ties with home. So far the tendency has been for the unsuccessful to lose touch with their people at home (by failing to send money back and to return), and for the successful to maintain close ties. A man works a few years, sending money home, especially when his fare has been paid off, and saving for a trip back to Hong Kong. He then goes home for a while. If he is unmarried he uses his holiday as an opportunity for getting a wife. The break over, he returns to the United Kingdom to resume work. (I have seen emigrants' passports which show this pattern of work and return. Now that passports have to be produced in Hong Kong in connection with applications to be admitted to the United Kingdom it would be a comparatively simple matter for the authorities to keep statistics showing how long men stay abroad and where they have been. It would be very useful information.) The restaurant business itself acts as an insulation between the migrants and the people among whom they make their living. They are caught up in their own forms of social grouping (domestically and otherwise). Many of them return to Hong Kong knowing no more than a few words of English (as kitchen workers they will not have needed to speak to a non-Chinese); most of them cannot conduct a conversation in that language. A few hundred young women have gone to Britain from the New Territories in recent years to join their men (I have been given a figure of 300), so that a measure of isolation is assured for even some of those who set up family life. A few men have married, some bigamously, or formed liaisons with local women in Britain. If what is true for many minority groups in present-day Britain holds also for the Chinese, then such unions are not necessarily a link with the wider society, for the women often become a part of the small social island into which they have moved without throwing a bridge across to the mainland.

I have heard speculations about the role to be played by returned migrants in the social life of the New Territories. There is talk of their being so worldly-wise and sophisticated that they may come to form a difficult category of people to deal with. My impressions do not support this view. Certainly, in line with the traditions of their society, the successful make themselves prominent. They build new houses or renovate old ones; they contribute to communal works; they make their voices heard in local affairs, moving, if they were not already in it, into the small elite of "elders." But their experience of the world is in fact generally very limited, and the social ideas they bring back with them are largely the ones they took away. They tend to be traditionalists whose traditionalism has been strengthened by their newly acquired power and prestige. They seem to me, to take a telling case, enthusiastically for *fung shui*. So that if they appear to be outstanding and exceptionally difficult it is precisely because they have acquired so little from their experience. Riches and high status have come to them, but it might as well have come from other sources. (There are a few men who have added to their education in Britain, but all the evidence points toward the great majority of them showing little interest in the new culture around them while they are away. Alongside the restaurant migration, however, there is a small movement of New Territories boys and girls to the United Kingdom for further education. But the two migrations are closely connected, and it is not uncommon for the profits being made in the restaurant trade to be used in part for keeping members of the family at technical and commercial colleges in Britain.)

The economic consequences of the movement have been great. The data on postal and money orders cashed in the New Territories show that money has been sent back on such a scale as to form one of the major sources of New Territories income. The remittances have been mounting on an extraordinarily steep gradient during the last five years, roughly doubling themselves from one year to the next, and reaching the sum of $16 million in 1962. Some three-quarters of this money was sent from the United Kingdom. But they tell only part of the story. Considerable sums have been coming in through the banks in the New Territories since 1960. Cash has been sent home in the post. Money has been brought back by returning migrants. Travelers' checks, not always presented personally, have been used. I was alerted by a chance encounter to another way in which incoming money in the form of United Kingdom postal and money orders may be left unaccounted for by the available statistics: on a visit to a New Territories branch of my bank I saw one of my acquaintances paying in a thick wad of £5 orders; these will presumably have been sent into town by the bank to be cashed through a city post office and, along with orders actually presented at city post offices, fail to appear in New Territories figures. The indications from the travel agencies in the last month or so of my stay in Hong Kong were of few men going to Britain; the main agency has almost stopped any new business; and it seems unlikely therefore that remittances will increase further. On the contrary, the probability is that after a while they will fall as men remain away longer, their ties with the New Territories being reduced and their commitments abroad increased. And the question will arise whether hardship will result for the New Territories. It is not simply a matter of people being deprived of extra money; if there is any resemblance between the New Territories and the emigrant areas of Fukien and Kwangtung in respect of their economic response to overseas migration, then we should be prepared to find that economic standards and activities have become so adjusted to external income that its falling away occasions disruption and distress.

It is of course artificial to treat the matter of overseas migration apart from the movement between the New Territories and the urban areas of the Colony. The city has always attracted New Territories people to it and provided the countryside with an income. It would be extremely interesting to have material showing where absent members of a village are at a given time and what they are doing for a living. I discovered that on one of the islands a local committee was keeping records on emigration and I was able to obtain the data which are presented below. They can have no general value for the study of the problem as a whole, but they suggest the possibility that some Rural Committees have gathered information of this sort and that others might be encouraged to do so. The total number of emigrants involved in this case is 183. Of these 62 are overseas and the remainder in the urban area of the Colony. Of the 62 overseas, 33 are seamen, 23 are in the United Kingdom, 5 in the U.S.A., and 1 in Borneo. All these are men, but 22 of the 99 people in the urban areas are women. Of the 23 men in Britain 5 are in their twenties, 7 in their thirties, 9 in their forties, 1 in his fifties, and 1 in his seventies. Of the 5 in the U.S.A. 2 are in their forties, 2 in their fifties, and 1 in his sixties. The sole man in Borneo is in his thirties. Over a dozen communities are involved in these figures. The distribution of overseas migrants and seamen among them is very irregular, even when allowance is made for the differences in size between the communities. There are clearly specializations here, and sets of comparable statistics for other areas would be a necessary preliminary to a study of why, despite the fact that overseas migration has been very general in the New Territories in recent years, some communities have not contributed to it or done so on a very small scale. This problem has often been raised in studies of emigration from southeastern China, but it has never been thoroughly gone into, and it would be a pity if the opportunity to study it in the New Territories were missed.

Why do people emigrate? New Territories men do not go abroad to make a new life or even, it would seem, to see the world. They, like millions of men from Fukien and Kwangtung before them, have sought a way of earning a better living; they have not intended to settle abroad (whatever later circumstances and opportunities may have suggested or dictated) and have hoped to be able to return home with enough money to sweeten their old age. Although, as we have seen, a few hundred New Territories women have gone to the United Kingdom to join their men, the general character of the migration has been male. In an ideal pattern, men go abroad, earn, remit money, and return. But a large-scale exodus of ablebodied men entails some serious consequences for the social and economic life of the people left behind. In some areas of the New Territories the absence of young and middle-aged men is so striking as to be obvious even to the casual observer. Inferences from the census data are not easy to draw, because the absence of men from the old-established communities may be masked in the figures by surpluses of men among the new population, but the 1961 data show significantly that of the five Districts Sai Kung has the lowest ratio of males to females (951: 1,000) and that, within the Tai Po District, Sai Kung North and Sha Tau Kok stand out very sharply as areas with low ratios (794 and 782 respectively, whereas the ratio for the District as a whole is 1,019). Moreover, Sai Kung has had a low ratio over a long period (859 in 1921 and 800 in 1931).[1] Large numbers of ablebodied men being away, the women must assume new or at least increased responsibilities. Now it would seem that New Territories women, both Punti and Hakka, play a very active role in agricultural life. (It was not so everywhere in China, nor even throughout the southeast.) And it may be that their agricultural skill is not only a consequence but a cause of the absence of the men. (I also raise the question whether in the past the agricultural roles of women were more noticeable among the Hakka than the Punti, and whether, in turn, male emigration was in earlier times promoted more strongly among the Hakka by sucn a difference.) But however competent the women, a heavy draining away of male labor, when it cannot be replaced with hired hands, must impose a considerable strain on the women who stay at home. To see a woman plowing the fields with a baby at her back suggests many questions about the conduct of her domestic affairs. But it is not simply a matter of her economic duties being increased; if men are away some reallocation must take place in the social roles of the household; family life is affected; even the control of community affairs may pass partly to women. One study in the New Territories (Pratt 1960) has already approached this subject, but it is a fit topic for several detailed inquiries, for, apart from the theoretical problems it raises in sociology and demography, it has many welfare aspects—in the field of marriage, the care of children, and social control.

It seems to me to be important to study both ends of the movement to the United Kingdom. The migrants there are very far from being cut off from people at home, and their problems have a direct bearing on New Territories life. Stories of gambling losses and debt circulate widely. Talk of unemployment and the abuse of labor by restaurant owners upsets families with young men away. How the Chinese in Britain organize themselves, adjust themselves to their strange surroundings, and make use of the opportunities open to them are questions which deserve careful study. I have a Chinese graduate student under training in London who is interested in the problem, and if all goes well he should be able to produce a valuable study of it. As for the New Territories themselves, I think that the best material will come from community studies, because the effects of migration need to be studied in the round and not treated simply as a general topic that might be generally surveyed. On the other hand, there is certainly a need for basic data on the New Territories as a whole, some of which, as I have already suggested, might be gathered through the Rural Committees. I hope that it may be possible in a few years' time to have a clearer idea of such crucial questions as the uses to which emigrant money is being put, the role of the returned migrant, the social and economic adjustments of communities from which migration has been heavy, the reasons why particular communities have held aloof from the movement, and the part played by emigration in changing the status of individuals vis-à-vis the wider society (especially in the case of the Tanka and Hoklo who have been abroad).

Chinese abroad

PART FOUR

Kinship and Religion in China

The Chinese Domestic Family: Models

The conditions which I take for granted in this paper are roughly those of the last hundred years of the Ch'ing dynasty and the Republican period until the advent of the Communist regime. By means of a model I hope to throw into relief some of the principles which underlay the conformation of the domestic family in China and its movement as a unit through time.

Let us assume, to begin with, that every son on reaching marriageable age is given a wife and that he continues as a member of his father's domestic group as long as his father survives. A family with many sons will then greatly increase in numbers by the begetting of children, daughters lost in marriage being offset by wives acquired. If he lives long, the head of such a unit can expect to preside over as many as three generations of lineal descendants. The family will occupy one set of buildings and form, from an economic and legal point of view, one estate. Here is the Chinese large joint family.

Did it exist? It cannot have existed as a common form of the family because of the statistical fact that the average size of the domestic family was between five and six souls. But this figure, despite the inferences which have been drawn from it, is ineloquent. It does not say what proportion of families were close to the average and it conceals the numerical aspect of the process by which smaller families could become bigger, and bigger ones smaller, over time.

Let us assume instead, therefore, that married sons break away from their living parents, the estate being partitioned. It then becomes possible for an independent family to consist of a young man, his wife, and their children; or, an old couple with one of their sons and his marital family; or even the old couple by themselves. And these alternatives do not exhaust all the possibilities. If we now focus our attention on the young

Paper delivered in Aug. 1960 at the Sixth International Congress of Anthropological and Ethnological Sciences, Musée de l'homme, Paris. Published in VIe Congrès international des sciences anthropologiques et ethnologiques (Paris, 1963), vol. 2, part 1, 97–100.

man who sets up with his wife and children, we can follow his domestic career along a path which perhaps ends in his being left in his old age alone with his wife.

All this is obvious. The problem is to find out at what point partition took place and why—a problem which is economic, legal, moral, religious, and, in a restricted sense, psychological. It is also a demographic problem, because it is ideally necessary to get some idea of the chances of a family having the components without which partition would be uncalled for; but to evaluate the data on such questions as the chances of a young married man having a surviving father to live with, or the most general age at which heads of family die, or the probability of there being more than one son, would be too difficult in a summary paper such as this. On this point I shall merely say that I think that demographic questions of this kind are capable of being given some sort of answers on the basis of, first, various statistical inquiries made during the twentieth century, and, second, the analysis (now being increasingly pursued) of genealogical registers.

I turn to the problem of why partition occurred. Everything hangs on the relation between father and sons. This relation is overtly one of severe subordination of the sons and of correlative authority on the part of the father. In law a son cannot separate himself from the estate against parental wishes. But a relation of this kind is in a sense self-defeating as soon as the junior party to it assumes a role which makes his position ambiguous—and this happens when the son marries and begets children. Once *pater* he is potentially *paterfamilias*, but he can realize his position to the full only at the expense of his father—either by breaking away or by superseding him.

But his ability to dominate the father while staying with him depends on his relations with the other sons of the father. It might seem at first sight that the hierarchy of seniority among brothers would allow an oldest son to retain full authority over the younger sons even as he assumed the role of family head. But in fact another element enters: the fraternal relationship is one of solidarity vis-à-vis the father, but it is one of internal competition, and potentially of a fierce kind. So that a man is unlikely to be able to assume the role of family head in relation to his married brothers.

The competition between brothers is economic; they have almost equal shares in the family estate and they are jealous of their individual rights. It is domestic; but here it is their wives who, so to speak, compete on their behalf. The quarrelsomeness of Chinese women is in part a reflex of their position as the representatives of their husbands in inner-domestic life. But it is more generally a product of the completeness with which the rights of and in a woman are located in the house of her marriage. When she fights, she fights on behalf of her husband and their children, as well as on her own account. The differentiation between brothers rests in part on a differentiation between women. Brothers are, so to say, disentangled from one another by the fact of their being married to different women. They may also be differentiated by having different mothers. The great moral tract, *Sheng-yü* (known in English as "The Sacred Edict"), recognizes this fact by preaching against its consequences. "Even if brothers are not born of one mother yet they are the bones and blood of one father. It doesn't do to say, 'They are not of the same mother,' and accordingly regard them as of a different stock." [1] It is important to note that the differentiation introduced by women is the more thorough for their being diverse in their local and kinship origins; the marriage system does not consistently bring into one house women from the same unit.

By a superficial paradox, marriage is a threat to the family. But the events which precipitate the partition of a family may be remote in time and causation from any marriage. We know that some complex families held together for a long time. Why? The first thing to establish is whether such families are significantly different in some other respects from the common run. They are, in that they are rich. There is a steady correlation among rural families between the size of landholdings and family size, and while this is from our present point of view partly a kind of optical illusion in that more people mean more land (i.e. with a uniform per capita distribution, bigger families would have larger farms), it is to some extent due to a connection between comparatively great riches and family complexity. But it is not just a question of wealth. We are dealing with a society differentiated into classes, in which high standing is evidenced, in part, by the maintenance of complex families.

Professor Francis L. K. Hsu has quarreled with me in print (1959) over an earlier attempt of mine to interpret the significance of this class difference, and I take this opportunity of clarifying my view of the main issue at stake. Professor Hsu has argued that the "social ideal" of "the glorification of the father-son relationship" is realizable only among the rich; in poor families the solidarity between husband and wife asserts itself at the expense of the filial tie. My argument is that the matter should not be left there. Various implications must be teased out. One of them is that the power accumulated in the hands of the head of a rich family of high standing is a counterbalance to fissiparous tendencies. Another is that the greater involvement of the poor man with his wife and her interests is an aspect of his lesser involvement in extra-familial social relations; the completest segregation of the roles of the sexes, and the least solidarity between them, can take place only at the higher levels of the society. A still further implication is to be looked for in the relationship which completes the triangle we are concerned with: the relationship between brothers. To cleave to one's wife is to be alienated from one's brothers; the distance between brothers is made possible by the lack of a strong father. Now it would seem that the strong father among the rich people of high standing produces an opposition between the generations which is itself a kind of guarantee of their cohesion; sons stand together over against their father and are tied to him by this very opposition. By the same token, the sons of a poor and socially ineffectual man are highly individualized *inter se* and relatively independent of their father. The argument can be summarized by saying that three crucial relations vary together: father-son, brother-brother, and husband-wife.

It now becomes clear that a single model of what is now often called the domestic developmental cycle (see esp. Fortes 1958) will not do for China (or for any other highly differentiated society). Two models can represent the range of reality. We may start with the model of a rich family of high standing.

In this model each marriage of a man adds to the membership of the group. Conjugal families multiply. Each is a potentially new estate, but they cohere, drawing benefit from the corporation of which they are members and adding to its political and economic resources by means of many activities (public service, moneylending, acquiring land, perhaps trading). If the family head lives to old age, the partition of the estate at his death (although the partition may be postponed until that of his widow) will lead to new families which are themselves relatively complex. If the formula of one partition per generation continues, no elementary family is likely to emerge as a separate estate. Here in skeleton is the mechanism for the persistence of "joint families."

The model at the opposite pole is one in which elementary family estates emerge rapidly from more complex units. The cycle of development is short. One married son stays with his father; other sons depart. When the old man dies (or again, on the later death of his widow) a generation is cut off without any great reduction in complexity. In an even simpler version, all sons go off, leaving the elderly couple alone. The economic estate in such cases is very small, so small that some sons are extruded from it by poverty; they seek other ways of making a living.

Families corresponding to these two distinct models must differ greatly in their numerical variation. A family on the first model may consist at one point in time of, say, eighteen souls, be reduced to sixteen by the passing of the oldest generation, and then split into two families, one of ten and the other of six. Each of these will then gradually build up its numbers again. A family on the second model is likely to be at its largest extension at eight souls, and can be reduced to two (and in extreme cases one, when a widow or widower is left alone).

The model families must move within numerical ranges of these two different orders. But a real family can, as it were, commute between the ranges when it is moving up or down the social scale. As it grows richer and more powerful, having begun as a fairly simple unit, it can realize the complexity for which it has the children. Contrariwise, a move downward can shatter a complex unit into many new and simple ones. To put the matter another way, the time which is intrinsic to either of the two models measures no change, but only the unfolding of processes inherent in stable social and demographic circumstances. Even if we construct a model to take account of social mobility, time may still be regarded as intrinsic, despite the fact that from close up social change appears to be taking place.

One can go on complicating the models in the interest of greater realism, but this would be to defeat one's own purpose. The point of making a model is to escape from reality long enough to be able to grasp its underlying principles. The model refreshes reality, it does not blot it out.

The Family in China, Past and Present

The Western literature on which we draw for much of our knowledge of the family in China[1] is full of variations on the theme that the family was the basic unit of Chinese society. In one sense the statement must certainly be true. In any society the family is the group which produces the personnel to man the wider institutions; and in the process of generating social beings it impresses on them certain principles of conduct which have a bearing on the way in which they discharge their general tasks. The family is therefore basic. But this is not significantly truer of China than of most other societies, and what people usually appear to mean when they assert that the family was the basic unit of Chinese society is one of two things: either that the family provided the model for the society as a whole, such that even the total polity might be regarded as one massive family, or that family relationships predominated in their potency over all other kinds of relationship.

There are both naive and sophisticated versions of these views. A simpleminded account of China treats the emperor as the patriarch of a blown-up family formed by the empire as a whole. On this view it is possible to ascribe to the Chinese polity a benign authoritarianism exercised over a mass of patient and pious children by a stern yet considerate father. In more technical discussions the dominance of Chinese society by the family is expressed by assigning to it a strength which inhibits men in their dealings—say, their economic transactions—with members of other families.

Behind the confusion lies a failure, in the first place, to distinguish between family as a specific social group on the one hand and kinship on the other. We can show without much difficulty that kinship bound together large numbers of people in Chinese society and exerted an impor-

Pacific Affairs, 34, no. 4 (1961), 323–36. Reprinted in Albert Feuerwerker, ed., *Modern China* (Englewood Cliffs, N.J., 1964), 27–40; and in H. Kent Geiger, ed., *Comparative Perspectives on Marriage and the Family* (Boston, 1968), 12–26. A slightly different version was delivered as a University Lecture at Cornell University on 16 Mar. 1961.

tant effect on their political, economic, and religious conduct at large. Family is another matter. Essentially, its realm is that of domestic life, a realm of co-residence and the constant involvement in affairs of the hearth, children, and marriage. Kinship is something different. Outside his family a Chinese was bound by rights and duties to people related to him through ties of descent and marriage. The relationships traced exclusively through males, as a special set of kinship relations, might be so extensive and organized as to form patrilineal descent groups. These groups are often referred to in the literature as clans, but it is becoming more common nowadays to give them the technically more satisfactory name of lineages (cf. Freedman 1958).

Localized lineages were in some parts of the country (especially in the southeast) so wide in their extent that they encompassed large villages and sometimes even towns. Almost inevitably, some of their members were rich and others poor. Some might well be scholars, others illiterate. Some could move with ease in the wider political society; others were simple countrymen, deprived of influence. Yet lineages are sometimes represented as though they were families. People who make the mistake of thinking of them in this fashion may well be puzzled by the unfamily-like behavior shown by, say, a rich man squeezing his debtor-kinsman or an elder forcing his kinsman-inferior to pay him the deference due to one standing high in the general system of status of the society. A lineage is no family.

But let us assume that the problem is to decide what strength of potency lay in kinship relations as a whole. We may take China as it was in the last hundred years of its existence as an imperial state. The question resolves itself into an analysis of how the solidarities and values of kinship were enmeshed in a political and economic order which required of individuals that they owe allegiance to a state and participate, despite the dominance of agriculture, in a wide-ranging economic system.

From the point of view of the state, a man's obligations to it were in fact both qualified and mediated by his kinship relations. They were qualified in the sense that obligations springing from filial piety and mourning duties were held to modify duties owed to the state. An official who lost a parent was supposed to retire during his mourning. People related to one another in close bonds of kinship were so far regarded by the written law to require solidarity among them that the Code provided that certain relatives might legitimately conceal the offenses of one another (except in cases of high treason and rebellion), either escaping punishment altogether or suffering a penalty reduced in accordance with the closeness of the relationship; and that it was an offense generally for close kinsmen to lay even just accusations against one another. There was built into the system the principle that close patrilineal kinship set up special rights and duties standing apart from the rights and duties between man and the state. The structure of these privileged rights was conceived in terms of mourning duties, the relations between two kinsmen being expressed as a function of the mourning ritual due between them. For this reason the Code specified the grades and duration of mourning and the ritual costume associated with them.

In the eyes of the state, then, a man stood posed against it in a network of primary kinship duties. But the state also regarded kinship units as part of its system of general control, so that a man's duties to it were mediated through his membership of these units. The family is the clearest case. The Confucian emphasis on complex families and the legal power vested in the head of a family to prevent its premature breakup are aspects of a total political system in which some authority is delegated from the administrative system to what, in a metaphorical sense, we may call natural units. The Confucian moralizing about the family, the stress put upon filial piety and the need for solidarity among brothers, the underlining of the importance of domestic harmony—these reflect a political view in which units standing at the base of the social pyramid are expected to control themselves in the interest of the state.

But the family is not the only case. It was morally right for men to align themselves on the basis of their common patrilineal descent and to form lineages. Lineage organization implied ancestor worship, a Confucian value of high order. It implied the promotion of schools and mutual help; in these the state could take pleasure. It implied, finally, an organization which could be used by the state for political and fiscal control. And at once we can see the dilemma faced by the state when it tried to make use of the lineage and encourage its prosperity. To be of use to the state the lineage must be organized and strong; but strength might grow to the point at which what was once a useful adjunct of government now became a threat to it. Where the lineages grew in numbers and riches they fought with other lineages. This was objectionable enough, but clearly what frightened the central administration more than anything else was the tendency for patrilineal organization to snowball. A lineage was justified by a genealogy; people began to produce longer and wider genealogies to justify more extensive groupings, going so far— and this "excess" excited very great official indignation—that attempts were sometimes made to group together in one organization all the lineages in one area bearing a common surname. It is important to realize that genealogical rearrangement and the grouping together of lineages make perfect sense given the logic of the patrilineal system, and that the objections raised by officialdom, although they might be couched in terms condemning the falsification of genealogies, were essentially political. That is to say, strong nuclei of local power were being created which constituted a threat to state authority.[1]

From the political point of view, then, kinship organization entailed a balance of forces with the state. By incorporating in its ideals a high value set upon family and kinship and by attempting to make use of their institutions, the state involved itself in a struggle to keep them in check. Indeed, one aspect of a political system which might appear to be arbitrary and oppressive is that it called into being forces which negated its tendencies to be just that.

On the role of kinship in economic life we have no systematic and large body of information on which to rely, but we can make a general argument. If we start from the assumption that kinship relations and values predominate in the conduct of economic affairs, we must expect that enterprise will take the form of what is often called the family business. Now, of course, there is plenty of evidence to show that Chinese economic enterprise has tended strongly to be organized so that people associating their capital, or capital and labor, are related by kinship or affinity. But what is the real significance of this fact? Is it that the moral imperatives of kinship impel people to seek out kinsmen with whom to work? The answer is no. Given the nature of the capital market, given a legal system which offers little protection to business, given the tendency to rely on people with whom there is some preceding tie, we should expect that kinsmen would be associating with one another in economic activities. What is really involved is that these activities are made to rest on highly personalized relationships and that a man's circle of relatives is likely to contain the greater number of individuals apt for selection. It is important to remember that, outside the family, a kinsman has few specific economic claims, that he can be approached as a landlord or creditor as any other landlord or creditor, and that in general we must not look to see preference being show to a kinsman in economic matters on the grounds simply that he is a kinsman.

We have so far been concerned with the question of how far the family in "pre-modern" China can be said to have been the basic unit of society. The argument has taken the form that family and kinship together provided one method of balancing the power of the state and that kinship was not *in principle* basic to economic life. If we confined our attention to the family in the strictest sense of the term, we might be able, by noting how much of the ordinary individual's life is lived within it, to assert that we were dealing with something fundamental. But in doing this we should be ignoring the whole range of wider institutions without which the family can in fact have little meaning.

We must now turn to the inner structure of the Chinese family before modern times, placing emphasis on two things: first, the nature of the tensions inherent in it, in order to see whether they can help us in our understanding of modern developments; and second, the linkages between the family and the wider society, so that we may look for changes in the family which may correspond to changes in society at large.

The experts have been insisting for the last twenty years that it is incorrect to say that the Chinese family in traditional circumstances was big. We need not, therefore, put much stress on the fact that average size of the family was five or six persons, but rather consider why it was that some families were very large and others very small, with many gradations between these extremes. Let us go back to the political point that the state looked to the family as the first unit of social control. The ideal family from this point of view was one in which large numbers of kinsmen and their wives were held under the control of a patriarch imbued with the Confucian values of propriety and order. Some families came close to this model, several generations living under one roof. They were powerful families. We may consider the power they wielded in terms both of their control of economic resources and of their command over other people. They were rich. They owned much land and other capital resources. By renting land and lending money they could exert influence over other people. They could afford to educate their sons and equip them for membership of the bureaucratic elite. They often (perhaps usually) entered into the life of this elite, making use of their ties in it to control both less fortunate families and their own subordinate members. Such a family may be looked upon as a large politico-economic corporation with much power vested in its chief member. But this corporation could not grow indefinitely in membership, for with the death of its senior generation it split along the lines laid down by the constitution of the next generation, every son having a right to an individualized share of his father's estate on that man's death. However, despite the partition which took place every generation, high-status families were able to remain large. The passing of the senior generation was likely to take place at a point when the men in the next generation were themselves old enough to have descendants sufficient for complex families of their own. At this level of society fertility was relatively high, the chances of survival were higher, adoption was easy, the age of marriage was low, and plural marriage was possible.

At the other end of the social scale the family was, so to speak, scarcely Confucian. Poverty and powerlessness produced, instead of a strong patriarch, a weak father. He could rally no support from outside to dominate his sons. He had few resources to withhold from them. In fact, he might well have only one son growing to maturity. If, however, he had two or more sons reaching manhood, only one would be likely to stay with him, and perhaps even this one would leave him too. Demography, economics, and the power situation at this level of society ensured that families of simple structure were a constant feature of the landscape.

Changes in social status promoted changes in family structure. Upward social mobility was partly a matter of increasing the complexity of the family, both because changing demographic, economic, and power conditions entailed complexity and because the ideal Confucian family was a model toward which people strove when they were moving upward. And we should note that downward social mobility brought with it a corresponding decline in complexity.

The relations between the sexes and between the generations were dependent on differences in family structure. It will be convenient to start from a feature of Chinese family life which has always attracted the attention of outsiders: the unhappy position of the daughter-in-law. She may be looked upon from three points of view: as a woman, as a member of the family by incorporation, and as a member of a junior generation. It needs no stressing that being a woman was a disadvantage. Every aspect of her society and its values left the Chinese woman in no doubt on that score. In the family into which she was born she might indeed be well and affectionately treated, but this favorable treatment rested on the paradox that she was merely a temporary member of it. Certainly, her marriage would call upon the family's resources, for it would cause her father to assert his status by sending her off in such a manner as to narrow the status gap between him and the father of the groom. But her marriage cut her off economically and as a legal person from her own family and transferred the rights in and over her to the family receiving her. In this new family she was at once a stranger and a member—the former because she was new and the latter in that, henceforth, the rights and duties in respect of her would lie with her husband's people. From the day of her marriage she must begin to think of her interests as being inevitably involved in those of her husband and the members of his family. She had no secure base outside this family from which to operate, because, while she might try to bring in support from her family of birth to moderate oppression, she could not rely on it. To a large extent physically and in all degrees legally, she was locked within her husband's gates.

Her husband's mother was her point of contact with the new senior generation to preside over her—whence her tears, for she had to be disciplined into a new role in a new family. In fact, however, the difficulties faced by the daughter-in-law were only one aspect of a broader configuration of difficulties. Men in Confucian morality were urged to reject the claims made by their wives on their attention and their interests, and to stand by their brothers against the threat posed to fraternal solidarity by their wives. Women were troublemakers, partly because they were strangers. Her mother-in-law represented for the wife the female half of the family into which she was firmly thrust if her husband refused to come to her aid. Mother-in-law, daughters-in-law, and unmarried daughters formed a battlefield on which any one daughter-in-law must fight for herself and, later, for her children.

Now if in fact the married brothers in a family did stand together, refusing to listen to their wives' complaints, it was because they were posed against their father. And this father was a strong figure whose power rested on the economic resources he controlled and the command he could exert on the world outside the family. It will be seen, therefore, that we have been dealing with the characteristics of a family of high status. Because of riches, life might in one sense be easy for the married woman (she had servants and other luxuries), but she was distant from her husband and at the mercy of the other women in the house until she was herself senior enough to pass from the dominated to the dominators.

In a family of low status and simple structure the elemental relationships of father and son, brother and brother, and husband and wife formed a different pattern. The father's control was weak and the brothers highly individualized among themselves. Each brother stood close to his wife, so that while the wife might be made miserable by poverty and hard work, at the lower levels of society she had greater strength as an individual. Here she was far less likely to need to cope with other mature women in the house.

From this summary analysis we may conclude that the probability of tension between the generations and the sexes increased with a rise in social status, and we may look forward from this point to the attempts made in modern times to remedy what seemed to be the difficulties and injustices of the Chinese family system.

In the years following the 1911 Revolution changes in ideas and law reflected a lively preoccupations among intellectuals with problems of family reform. Let us take a single example, chosen partly because of the way in which sociology is called in to support reformist arguments. In an early paper, Quentin Pan (1928), who at the time was much concerned with problems of this sort, proposed a basic reform in terms of the "optimum family." In such a family the women, as in tradition, would be sent out on marriage, but "any male will have to start a family of his own as soon as he marries and is able to be self-supporting." When there was more than one son "the parents may live with each in turn at allotted intervals." In other words, the brothers should divide while making provision for the maintenance of the tie between the generations. "The 'greater family,'" Pan goes on, "is obviously a sociological mistake." It is numerically unwieldy, it suppresses individualism, and leads to psychological difficulty and discord. "If the greater family is a sociological blunder, the smaller one is a biological one." That is to say, the complete rejection by married sons of their parents means a lack of reciprocity between the generations; those who are cared for in childhood do not care later on for their parents. "Suffer your aged parents to stay with you and your children so that there will be constant association and interchange of sentiments. . . ." In effect Pan proposes that each complex family should give way to a series of elementary families (married couples and their children) and a "stem" family in which the old people would be living with one of their married sons.

In its naive way this statement makes an analysis of the problems inherent in the high-status family. What is more interesting, it puts forward a remedy which was in fact represented in reality by the family system of the greater part of the population, for whom the unwieldy family suppressing individualism was ruled out by poverty and lack of power.

The intellectual urge to reform was not, needless to say, inspired by inspection of the advantages enjoyed in family life by the lower orders. It stemmed in large measure from Western notions of modernity and progress. Somehow family institutions were to be reshaped to fit an imminently new form of society. One way of procuring this end was to legislate for it. After many years of debate a Civil Code dealing with many aspects of family life was in 1931 put on the statute book. One may well question the seriousness of the Code as a political attempt at social reform, but even if we regard it in much the same light as its imperial predecessor, that is to say, as a general statement of models of behavior rather than a body of detailed rules to be closely applied, it is still important because of the ideological investment made in it by the intellectuals of the day (many of whom looked upon it as a beacon of light) and because of the nature of the sociological insight employed in its construction. In fact, the Code turned out to be far less revolutionary than a superficial impression would convey. As scholars have pointed out, the provisions of the Code are rather conservative in the compromise reached between the needs of tradition and the call for modernism. Yet, for all its conservatism, it marked a major step in Chinese history. Before it was produced the republican courts were still bound by rules springing from the old order and might be forced to give recognition to practices likely to raise eyebrows in the world at large. In 1919, for example, in a case arising from a man's selling his wife, the Supreme Court ruled that the "purchase of a woman for the explicit purpose of begetting children is justifiable and not invalid" (China [Republic], Supreme Court Cases, 1922: 138).

The new Code's provisions have accumulated around them a considerable literature of scholarship, and there would be no point in trying to spell out details here. Broadly, the woman as child and wife acquires an enhanced status in the crucial spheres of property, marriage, and divorce, such that her rights are made more symmetrical with those of a man. Monogamy is established, but it is a monogamy which, given the tacit consent of the wife, allows a man to set up permanent relationships with other women from which legally recognized children may issue. The Code assumes an essentially patrilineal and patriarchal family, but it restricts the rights exerted over immature children and asserts the rights of mature children to go their own way. Yet rights to maintenance from children and grandchildren are written into the law. In effect, we have a set of rules which in many respects support the kind of family system envisaged as ideal by Quentin Pan: patriliny is preserved, but the ground is cut away from beneath the complex domestic unit.

The patrilineal configuration of rights and duties in traditional law is changed in the Civil Code into a system of reckoning kinship according to the Roman Law system. Yet in both Civil and Penal Codes something remains of the traditional solidarities expected among close kinsmen. The old absolute prohibition of marriage within the patrilineal *wu fu* (that is, with all cousins bearing the same surname closer than fourth) reappears, although obscured by the new legal language. In the Penal Code the "penalties for maltreatment, for unlawful confinement, false accusation, and murder are heavier when these offenses are committed against parents, grandparents, or great grandparents . . . the penalty for theft from relatives having joint property and living in the same house can be suspended, and no one can be prosecuted for theft from relatives within the fifth degree of relationship (by blood) and within the third degree by marriage without the victim's complaint . . ." (Lang 1946: 118). In other words, we are still in a Chinese world where reform has not yet tried to destroy, even at the symbolic level of the law, some of the most fundamental principles of cohesion in the family and among close kinsmen. In the eyes of the state the family continues to be an essential element of the total social and political order.

When we turn to the new state established in mainland China since 1949, we may begin by making the opposite assumption. The family is to be destroyed. How far will this take us in understanding what is afoot in Communist China? We may start by looking at the Marriage Law of the People's Republic, for this, despite its narrow title, constitutes a code for the regulation of family matters, and we may safely assume that it represents a far more serious attempt to change society than its Nationalist predecessor, at least by virtue of the positiveness with which it is applied. It is couched in very general and vague language, and its exact import in regard to particular matters could be gauged only from a study of the cases to which it has given rise. Yet the essential purposes to which it is directed are very clear. Marriage is to be a free contract between individuals, and one which, in the last resort, may be broken at the will of one party. The family vanishes as a party to marriage. An almost perfect symmetry of the rights of men and women is erected—in property, residence, choice of work, and control of children. Indeed, one might argue that the new law is concerned basically with only one question: the procreating, raising, and care of children.

There are, however, two features of the new rules which speak for the legal survival of tradition. The first is a clause which adds a prohibition to the bar on marriage between lineal kinsmen and between brothers and sisters: "The question of prohibiting marriage between collateral relatives by blood within the fifth degree of relationship is to be determined by custom." We are back to the patrilineal *wu fu* and provided with some evidence that society is not to be remodeled, at least not for the present, in every minute detail. The second aspect of traditionalism lies in the treatment of the duties of children toward their parents. "Parents have the duty to rear and educate their children; the children have the duty to look after and assist their parents. . . . Neither the parents nor the children shall maltreat or desert one another. . . . Parents and children shall have the right to inherit one another's property." Something of the old system is to be left.

But what does the remnant amount to? The concession to custom in the marriage prohibitions is a temporary affair. Given the nature of the Communist economy, what property claims on children would be important? Given the political nature of the new state, what is likely to amount to a child's desertion of his parents? Our initial assumption that the family is to be destroyed seems to be borne out. The old kinship system, which elaborated patriliny into corporate units of social structure, has been washed away. There is no room in a Communist polity for such nuclei of power. Devolution of power there must be in any political system, however tyrannical, but it cannot be reposed in units which by their very nature may turn it against those who have conceded it. The Communist rulers of China are not likely to fall into the dilemma of their imperial predecessors, who from time to time were embarrassed by the resistance set up in areas of society which they themselves supported by their Confucian regard for kinship values. From land reform to the establishment of the communes the society has passed through a process in which principles of local aggregation and leadership have been thoroughly made over. Even if in terms of population a lineage still occupies the same area, its erstwhile leaders now lack the economic resources and power, the ritual authority, and the external political support and connections to allow them to continue to have meaning. And beyond the range of the single lineage, the lateral bonds of clanship, uniting lineages in their common interest, are broken by the lack of ritual centers and the confinement of social relations within units laid down by the state for the benefit of its system of control.

China is now more bureaucratic than ever before. In the old days bureaucracy was checked both because its officers stopped at the county seat and because ambiguous loyalty was institutionalized. Up to a point a man was expected to work against the interests of the state in the cause of his kinsmen. Even as it tried to check nepotism, the state promoted it. But the new bureaucracy works on a purer model. Loyalty must have but one focus. Bureaucratic influence must reach down right into the affairs of the smallest units of society. Certainly, children must respect their parents, but a parent disloyal to the state must run the risk of seeing his child cast his own loyalty to the state against that to his parent.

The family now lies open to the state. It has little property to hold it together. Its ritual bond has been removed. Its head can call on few sanctions to support him in the exercise of authority—his wife can divorce him, his children defy him. The allocation of tasks in economic life is not now in any important respect a family matter. The whole range of activities once covered by the family is now reduced to a narrow field in which husband, wife, and children associate together in the interstices, so to speak, of large institutions—the work group, the dining hall, the nursery —which have taken over the functions of economic coordination, housekeeping, and the rearing and education of children. The family has become an institution for producing babies and enjoying the leisure time left over from the major pursuits of everyday life.

Now, as soon as we formulate our account of the contemporary Chinese family in this fashion—and of course the account may well be overdrawn, which in fact strengthens the argument to follow—we can no longer rely on the assumption that the family is to be destroyed. The more we look at this picture the more familiar it will seem to us, for it contains features from the Western experience of family life. For most of the inhabitants of an industrialized society the family is a small residential group from which many of the major activities of life are excluded. The factory, the office, and the school separate the members of one family for many hours of the day and provide them with different ranges of relationships and interests. What they unite for as a family is a restricted number of activities of consumption, child care, amusement, and emotional exchange. True, if we are to believe what we are told, the Chinese family in the commune has gone further in reducing the minimal functions we associate with family life, but it has not necessarily departed in principle from a pattern which we know to be intrinsic to the modern form of society.

If we begin a discussion of whether the family now exists in China with a definition of the family which lists a number of functions, it is possible that we shall deny it to present-day China, just as some people have denied it to collective settlements in Israel. If instead we look in the family for a configuration of relationships between spouses and between parents and children, a configuration standing out from the other patterns of relationship in which people are involved, then we should have little difficulty in satisfying ourselves that the Chinese family has survived.

But there is more to it than that. We can argue that the family has survived not *against* the wishes of the people responsible for policy in Communist China but rather in accordance with their desire to see the institution persist and flourish. The persistence is of course on their terms, but what they may seek to perpetuate is necessary for the orderly working of their society. Marriage may be potentially fragile, but marriage there certainly is. Its purpose is to provide a locus for the raising of useful citizens. Children are not going to be produced on an assembly line; they must be linked to parents before they can be linked to society. In the early years of their control the Communists gave the appearance of waging a war on the family. Since about 1953, the war having been won to their satisfaction, they have been at pains to stress such of the value of family life as they regard as important in the institution as it now is. Old people must be looked after by their children; the young must be respectful; there must be a harmonious relationship between husband and wife.

It would appear that the form taken by the family in recent years is essentially the same as that which we have seen to have characterized the greater part of the Chinese population before any of the modern trends began. That is to say, the family is either a unit of parents and their immature children, or it includes in addition to these people the parents or surviving parent of the husband or the wife (of the former rather than of the latter). The "solution" produced by the Communists is in reality an old one, and in arriving at it the Communists were continuing a process of change which had started many years earlier at the higher levels of Chinese society. In fact, it could be argued that just as the Communists worked on peasant hunger for land to bind the mass of the people to them in the early days of land reform, so they commanded the allegiance of many people by playing on the stresses inherent in complex family organization. The resentment of the wife and the son, and the strains between the sexes and the generations were material on which politics could work to create opinion favorable to its general aims. The Communists made Quentin Pan's "optimum family" universal; it brought them allies. They fulfilled the ambitions of the Westernizing intellectuals even while damning what they were attacking as "feudal" and "bourgeois."

There is little in what has so far been said that is not already well known. There are many good analyses of the traditional family in China; there have been valuable discussions of modern changes both before and after the Communist revolution. We have only to think of the names of such sociologists as C. K. Yang and Marion J. Levy and of such anthropologists as Francis L. K. Hsu and Morton H. Fried to remember that a body of scholarship on these themes is well established. But it is no disrespect to these scholars to assert now that their work is incomplete. It is in fact incomplete over the whole historical range skipped across in this survey. In other words, it is not merely the Chinese family since 1949 that we are ignorant about. Political and emotional barriers separate us from the Chinese mainland at the present (and the "us" includes the British as well as the Americans, for the former have no more access to hard data than the latter); there are other barriers between us and the China of the past.

An essential barrier is the fiction by which scholars convince themselves that they are treading the path of duty: discipline. We keep within our academic frontiers. Now, I am not advocating what is often in the United States called interdisciplinary cross-fertilization—and in conservative Britain is sometimes sourly referred to as interdisciplinary cross-sterilization—if by that term is meant a jumbling together of disciplines to the point where nobody knows who he is any longer and what he is supposed to be about. Academic disciplines maintain intellectual morale and keep people thinking in manageably defined fields and their hands in practice at well-tried techniques of research. They are vital, but for certain problems and topics they may be a nuisance. Such a topic is Chinese family and kinship.

Family and kinship are the anthropologist's bread and butter. Nothing is more striking in the modern history of social anthropology than the constant advance of theoretical ideas in this particular field. The historian of China is unlikely to know that, when he is tackling problems of family and kinship—for tackle them he often must, since they spring out of the picture the Chinese have made of their own society—he is dealing with a particular case of a large class into which anthropologists have been delving for a long time. Or take the student of Chinese family law vis-à-vis the sociologist. The former runs the risk of ignoring many interesting problems which the latter could bring to his attention. Conversely, the anthropologist and the sociologist are often unable to benefit from the knowledge and ideas of the sinologues—and China has much to contribute to comparative studies of society.

What is needed is the promotion and exchange of ideas between followers of different disciplines, not under the stimulus of the political cry that we must know our Cold War enemies, or under the financial sanctions of foundations which, by their mixture of open-handed generosity and narrow-minded business, would have us multiply the Malthusian profusion of books pressing upon limited natural resources of patience, but under the spur of intellectual curiosity and the challenge of unsolved problems. I shall take the liberty of suggesting a few of these problems.

Take the treatment of family, kinship, and marriage in the imperial Chinese codes. What is the inner logic of a system of prescriptions and proscriptions which defines the mourning duties for special classes of kinsmen and affines, applies punishments for incest with different relatives, prohibits certain marriages, and lays down the variability of offenses according to relationship? How will this system help us to understand other systems of patrilineal kinship?

What accounts for the peculiar distribution of wide-ranging lineage organization in China? What variations in structure can be detected in the family in different ecological areas of China, in cities, towns, and the countryside, and in "classes" and status groups? What demographic data can be marshaled to throw light on such differences?

All these problems are either purely historical or are capable of being tackled by a combination of historical inquiry and field investigation in those parts of the Chinese world still open to us—Taiwan, Hong Kong, and, to some extent, Overseas Chinese settlements. But there are also problems of the present mainland. Here the data are difficult to collect, biased, and discontinuous. But let us take what we can get hold of and submit it to close questioning. Does the system set up strains for married women when they are at one level treated as the equals of men and at another level as more responsible than men for household affairs? Are the tasks allocated to women in communal living of a sort that merely generalizes their inferiority? Given freedom of marriage and divorce, what patterns of selection will emerge? What frictions are introduced into a system of bureaucratic and "universalist" recruitment to offices and tasks by the persistence of kinship loyalties? Can these loyalties reassert themselves in some covert form? Does social promotion entail re-making kinship links? Do people change marriage partners as they move socially?

We can go on feeding scraps of information into a gradually expanding picture, knowing full well that until we can see mainland China for ourselves we are hardly likely to have firm answers to our questions. But it is not so important for the moment that we cannot produce satisfying answers. The habit of putting questions must be kept alive.

Rites and Duties, or Chinese Marriage

"So Sidney has been planning to persuade the other trustees to devote the greater part of the money to encouraging *Research* and Economic study. His vision is to found, slowly and quietly, a '*London School of Economics and Political Science*' a centre not only of lectures on special subjects but an association of students who would be directed and supported in doing original work. Last evening we sat by the fire and jotted down a whole list of subjects which want elucidating—issues of fact which need clearing up. Above all, we want the ordinary citizen to feel that reforming society is no light matter and must be undertaken by experts specially trained for the purpose." The passage is from Beatrice Webb's diary. It forms part of the history of the founding of the School as it has been told, Director, by you (Caine 1963: 2). "Last evening we sat by the fire. . . ." My generation, recreating the Webbs after their image in the picture that hangs in the Founders' Room, may think of them everlastingly before their fire, brooding on schemes for the improvement of society and knowledge.

I have chosen to begin with the Founders in an effort to attach myself ritually to the School. I hold the title of Professor, but do not occupy a chair. Or, if I have a chair, it is a "personal" one and too metaphysical to be sat upon. In this position I succeed nobody and have no office to transmit. Deprived of professorial ancestors I am correspondingly free of the duty of praising predecessors and can launch myself straightway into the subject of my inaugural lecture. But I feel myself to be a son of the School (even though I came to it only as a graduate student), and my sense of solidarity with it has been increased not only by its having done me the honor of calling me a professor, but by the sense of crisis marking our thoughts as we face the world which the School's founders helped to

Inaugural Lecture as Professor of Anthropology in the University of London at the London School of Economics and Political Science, 26 Jan. 1967. Separately published in 1967 by G. Bell, London.

shape. What surprises have the Treasury, the D.E.S., the U.G.C., and the S.S.R.C. yet in store for us?

Sidney Webb's motives for creating the School were complex, but it is obvious from the records that he thought, among other things, that fundamental research, conducted by scholars of different political views, would help to better society. The name he gave to the School spells out his conception of what was important, but under that name (even more misleading when it is shortened) a wide range of social sciences was soon to be taught. How anthropology came to be included has been told by Professor Firth in the brief history of the Department he published in 1963 (Firth 1963–64).[a] In writing that history Professor Firth was careful to point to the role played in it by applied anthropology. Of the distinguished scholars who have been associated with the Department I cannot think of a single one who did not or has not spoken up in favor of applied anthropology. If (to confine myself to the dead) I mention Radcliffe-Brown, Malinowski, and Nadel, it is to show how theoretical and practical anthropology have gone hand in hand. The Webbs could not reproach the anthropologists in their School for failing either to conduct fundamental research or to keep in mind the links between this research and the world of practical affairs.

Yet, if the Webbs were somehow to get wind of the lecture I am now giving, they might well be displeased with it. I shall be talking about China. Knowing that, they would probably expect some analysis of the dramatic changes taking place in that country, and perhaps even count on hearing about another "new civilization." In fact, I am proposing today to ignore the more modern China and, instead, to be deliberately antiquarian in talking of things that, on the Chinese mainland itself, are dead. I have adopted this stance because, on a privileged and ritual occasion, I want to make propaganda for a disinterested anthropology, well enough endowed to follow where its curiosity leads, untroubled by the fear that in a society which appears to be striving after the realization of part of the Webbian dream, resources will be found only for what is immediate, practical, and useful. Whatever else the universities may do, they must produce intellectual pleasure. That is perhaps a tactless thing to say, for the support of pleasure—even intellectual—on a large scale out of the public purse cannot be expected to commend itself to all our policy-makers.

Anthropology has many faces and many pleasures. Of the latter, one

[a] Lord Beveridge (1949: 50) threw some disconcerting light on the early days when he wrote of Webb bringing anthropology into the School "despite the doubts of an old guard who wondered why a School of Economics should concern itself with the 'nasty habits of dirty savages.'"

of the keenest is the contemplation of another society, the experience of analyzing ideas and institutions in another tradition, the leap of imagination across the gulf between us and different symbols and customs. The great men of social anthropology command our respect not only because they state problems, make theories, and engage in comparative studies, but also on account of the opportunity they afford us, through their theories and studies, to share in the experience of penetrating exotic ways of life.

On and off over most of the years I have been at the School I have been thinking about the society of China. (But let me not provoke the U.G.C. into asking me to estimate the percentage of my time so spent.) It seemed to me that I might try today to discuss the beginnings of an attempt to seize the meaning of one segment of traditional Chinese culture. As my title indicates, I am concerned with both rites and duties. And by taking Chinese marriage rites as my theme, I hope to be able to suggest some possible relations between rites on the one hand and claims and obligations on the other. In the exercise, I shall, as it happens, be bringing together two important strands in modern social anthropology: the study of things jural and the study of rites and symbols. The intellectual genealogy of my central theme runs from Van Gennep's classic on *rites de passage* (1909) to the present-day work best exemplified perhaps by the volume of essays published in 1962 by Professors Forde, Fortes, Gluckman, and Turner (Gluckman 1962).

The fact that China has a common literary tradition (in which books on family rites and etiquette play an important part) raises the presumption that we are dealing with marriage rites that form a homogeneous entity, despite the vastness of the country. My survey of these rites confirms the oneness of the system. Variations there are (I shall speak briefly about some of them), but I believe that the Chinese marriage rites everywhere can be represented by one basic model. Incidentally, I might add a word on the sources of my material for they cast a sly glance at anthropology. The subject matter I am concerned with calls for the most meticulous recording of words and acts. The notebooks of those who have done anthropological fieldwork in China, both Chinese and foreigners, must surely be full of the minute details I have been trying to track down; but for the fullest accounts of the marriage rites I have had in fact to turn to the missionaries and sinologues, for they, unlike the anthropologists, have published what they have collected. The pursuit of one kind of excellence in anthropology (analysis) has often precluded another (description).

The unity of the marriage rites stems from the unity of the family system, and that is where we must begin. We are dealing with a family that owns property as a joint person. In this regard the family is composed only of males: in the simplest case, a man and his son or sons. By being born or adopted into a family a man is immediately endowed with a claim to its property. He benefits from it generally while it is held intact, and takes from it a separate share when it is divided. The division can come about in different circumstances. A member of a senior generation can prevent a lineal descendant from taking out his share, and the ideal seems to be that partition will occur only as each senior generation dies off, the men in the next generation sharing the property between them. That is to say, they divide up the land and other assets, usually in equal shares, and set up separate cooking stoves and living quarters, either isolating themselves completely in their domestic arrangements, or, at the most, continuing to maintain in common the main hall of the house. Some part of the joint estate may be reserved as a collective holding, in which case it may develop into the property around which a lineage segment will come to be organized. However, a married son is sometimes permitted to take out his share while his father is still alive, so that the process of division is speeded up. And, at the other extreme, the process may be slowed down by fatherless brothers continuing their joint life. Yet the latter solution is unstable. A man cannot legally prevent his brother or a descendant of his brother removing his share; and the strains built into the fraternal relationship ensure that the complex family lacking a head in a superior generation will not last long.

In this thumbnail sketch I have seriously misrepresented only one thing: while it is true that men are the sole members of the joint person that owns the estate, certain claims fall to women. Before her marriage a woman is of course entitled to support; at marriage she must be endowed with a minimum of household equipment, clothing, and jewelry to take with her to her new home. And it is likely that she will get as much as her family can afford, because the men who send her out in marriage would not wish to demean themselves before the other family (to which, as givers of a woman, they are already, in the Chinese system, inferior) or, more generally, in the eyes of the public in whose presence the marriage rites are played out. Entering her new family, the married woman comes armed with her trinkets and perhaps a store of money; this is her individual fortune, to which she may add as time goes on by private earnings from work (such as sewing) done over and above her normal household duties. In some areas, indeed, women from well-to-do families may be given land as part of their marriage portion, either as an outright endowment or for life-use. In addition to her exclusive claims to her own wealth, a wife has claims to two other kinds of property. In the first place, the furnishings and trappings of the bedroom in which she begins her conjugal life, and which remains the private domain of the married pair within the larger domain of the family, are vested jointly in her and her husband. Second, in certain circumstances she has a claim to control and manage her husband's part of the family estate. Once she is the mother of a son she shares with her husband the privilege of preventing that son taking out his portion, and she can act alone in this matter when she is a widow. Again as a widow, she can manage the joint estate of the family in which she is the senior member.

Even if you have read a good deal on China, some of these points may surprise you. Many of the data for a reappraisal of the roles and status of the Chinese woman have long been on record; it has needed some fresh minds (notably those of British and American graduate students of anthropology) to put them together. Interestingly enough, there has been a convergence on the point from anthropological and legal directions. For example, both Mr. Myron Cohen, the anthropologist at Columbia University, and Mr. McAleavy, the lawyer at the School of Oriental and African Studies, have recently underlined the paradox that, since men are always in principle members of property-holding units, their earnings being absorbed into these groups, women are the only individual property owners in Chinese society. It is true that Mr. Cohen's material was in the first place drawn from his fieldwork in Taiwan. Mr. McAleavy's, however, comes from the voluminous sinological literature in Chinese and Japanese, a precious store which the anthropologists have hardly yet begun to rifle.

The complex claims and duties of women as property holders force us to think again about their position in family life. Often the eye of the observer is caught by the harsh and humiliating treatment of the young daughter-in-law. But after all, she is only at the beginning of a career in her new family, the climax of which is the solid matriarchy of old age and widowhood. Indeed, the forcing of the Chinese material into the mold of patriarchy (done in the nineteenth and early twentieth centuries largely under the influence of the analogy with Roman law) has introduced some false perspectives on the Chinese case. It has often been pointed out, for example, that a paternal imagery runs through Chinese expressions of authority; but the colloquial term for an official (*fu-mu-kuan*) means literally "father and mother officer," and the linking together of father and mother in the tracts on filial piety and in the rites of ancestor worship should encourage us to speak of parentalism rather than patriarchy.

Yet this view of the honor accorded to Chinese women is in itself partial, for it derives from our seeing them primarily as mothers. If now we look at them as wives, we shall find that they attract some of the most defamatory descriptions of which Chinese society is capable. Women are by nature quarrelsome, jealous, petty-minded, and preoccupied with the interests of their own husbands and children at the expense of the wider family. That is a Chinese view, and it is material to our interpretation of the rites of marriage.

I am using the word "wife" in its narrowest meaning. The woman whom a man marries as his major wife (usually, but not necessarily, his first) is *the* woman of his immediate family and of the house when he is the senior man in it (unless, of course, there is a widow in the generation above). In many respects the major wife is ritually and legally the mother of all the man's children, whether borne by her, by secondary wives, or by outside women. The rites of marriage to which I shall presently be turning relate to the major wife alone. Moreover, I shall be assuming for the sake of simplicity that the husband is marrying such a woman for the first time and that the marriage is of what we may call the standard kind. That is to say, a virgin is taken from one family and married into another, there to pass the rest of her days. With other forms of marriage I shall not be concerned, but I must stress that they exist. One of the commonest variants brings immature girls into the households of their prospective husbands; in fact, as "little daughters-in-law," they may be said to have parents-in-law before they have husbands. Again, many marriages, so to say, reverse the sex of the incoming partner to forge female links in the patrilineal chain, the husband being brought into the wife's family. Complicated substitutions may be made for people who die or are missing, the ingenuity of which has sometimes excited the admiration of Westerners. One of my favorite missionaries could exclaim "*Che bella combinazione!*" (He was a Frenchman.)

When we study the rites we shall see that certain rules of marriage are implied. Where are they stated? The Chinese empire had a sophisticated legal system, although its share of social control was much smaller than its elaborateness might lead one to suppose. In the so-called Penal Code of the Ch'ing dynasty we can study the rules of marriage, while records of legal decisions throw light on these rules. But the official legal system itself took cognizance of local custom, and we know that beneath the official system what we may call customary law regulated most of the behavior of most of the people. For material on customary law the anthropologist obviously turns to the field studies made in the 1920's, 1930's, and 1940's. But there have been surveys of customary law, the most important being the compilation made in the 1920's and published by the Ministry of Justice in 1930, the first complete translation of which into a European language has just started to appear.[1] The basic rules of marriage are everywhere the same, but there are enough variations to raise problems in the interpretation of the rites. It is a matter I shall come back to briefly.

The Chinese rites of marriage are lengthy, elaborate, and dense with esoteric meaning. Were I to set out to deal with them in their entirety, tracing their connections with the total Chinese language of customs and symbols, I should be writing a large book, not giving a lecture. I am going to concentrate on a very few points chosen for the light they may throw on the ritual conception of duties and their implications.

We may begin with the proposition that marriages are made in Heaven. This the Chinese assert, and one of the first steps taken in making a match presupposes the preordainment of a completed marriage. It is a remarkable feature of the documents drawn up in the course of a marriage that the most important are the so-called "eight characters," that is, the horoscopic data of the boy and girl. Indeed, when people are very poor and remote from the services of penmen, the "eight characters" may be the only documents used. The horoscopes worked from the basic characters are subjected to analysis to determine whether a proposed union is in accordance with Heavenly intentions. If, quite artificially, we narrow our vision of the ethnographic data, we shall see expert diviners measuring the compatibility of horoscopes by strict and impartial rules, confirming some proposed matches, rejecting others. In fact, some observers of the Chinese (usually not Chinese themselves) leave us with the impression that they think that, to use a contemporary image, there is a sort of celestial computer which, fed with horoscopic punch cards, delivers itself of an answer to the question put.

But of course it is not like that at all. The rules for divining are complex and to some extent arbitrary; two diviners may well give different answers. A diviner is quite capable of giving a client the answer he wants. Moreover, technical divination is not always resorted to; instead, the horoscopes may be laid on the house altar for a period of three days during which the absence of any physical or moral disturbance (for example, broken crockery or tempers) marks approval. At this stage negotiations are confidential, and unwanted proposals can be politely rejected. Proposals turned down are supposed not to lead to hard feelings.

I shall go so far as to assert that horoscopic matching introduces no element of randomness whatever—or, to put it as a Chinese might, it affords no insight into the matrimonial plans of the Old Man under the Moon. And yet ritually a match agreed upon is a match ordained. The same idea recurs in the wedding rites when it is embodied in the red thread used for linking the cups out of which the new couple drink and for tying together the candlesticks on the altar. Why are the shrewd calculations of social, economic, and political advantage that go into the making of a match smothered in the illusion that Heaven has spoken? Marriage is by far the most important contractual relationship in Chinese society. On it turns not simply the happiness of a husband and a wife, but, much more significantly, the successful absorption of a "foreign" woman into the family and the smooth regulation of the ties created between two sets of kin. (Let us note, by the way, that the betrothal, as we may very roughly call it, itself establishes the bond of affinity between the respective relatives of the boy and girl.) Knowing what is in store for the new bride, the domestic difficulties that flow from the creation of a new conjugal unit within the family, and the precarious balance of the relationships between the two blocks of affines, we can see that the doctrine of predestined marriage relieves men of a frightening burden of responsibility. Fate does not force them to a course of action; it helps to reconcile them to its almost inevitable failure.

The prevision of failure is implied in another aspect of the first phase of the rites. From the outset all negotiations are carried on by one or more go-betweens. "Without clouds in the sky," runs the Chinese proverb, "there is no rain. Without go-betweens there is no marriage." Now, it is obvious that in marriage, as in numerous other aspects of Chinese life, intermediaries are required to allow negotiations to proceed without loss of face to parties with conflicting interests. But the go-between is not a man (or woman) of one role. He may also be a broker in the marriage market: it is his business to know which boys and girls are available for matching and how the parity of "gates and doors" of different families allows them to be linked. In addition, the go-between, in return for his fees and commission, is held accountable for the quality of the brides and grooms and for the success of the marriage, at least in its initial phase. It falls first to the go-between to get back a young bride who absconds. But there is more to it than that. Chinese distrust, and even hate, this most necessary of men. Any Chinese community is full of stories about go-betweens who cheat by matching one-eyed girls or idiot husbands. These tales are myths which underline the fact that marriage is attended by terrible risks. In reality, few families are foolish enough to rely solely on go-betweens for their information; any obvious physical or moral defect in a proposed bride or groom will not easily escape gossip or the test of inspection, however surreptitious. A family does not take a new member blind, nor does a family marrying off its daughter cast her into the completely unknown.

According to the rites, new affines avoid one another, and the bride and groom at least have seen nothing of each other before the point in the wedding when, for the first time together, the husband lifts the bride's veil to look upon her face. But what the rite implies is not simply that they have hitherto been complete strangers (which may or may not be true), but that on this day there has been brought to pass what Heaven without consulting man has planned and the go-betweens realized. One does not curse Heaven for one's misery or blame one's parents; the go-between is near at hand. Here is one disappointed husband.

When I married that fright in our kitchen, as soon as I removed the veil from her face, how I was disappointed! That go-between, that liar of a Wang, had told me that she was very beautiful! I trembled from head to foot, and he, blinking his eyes, said not a word. How could he not know that he was peddling so bad a woman? During the prostrations [to the family and the guests], my heart full of anger, I cursed him terribly in a low voice: busybody, procurer! I suffered horribly when I made my three prostrations to him. If I hadn't been frightened of people laughing at me. . . .[2]

It may well be that this miserable husband had not clapped eyes on his woman before the wedding day; but we may safely assume that his parents or their trusted representatives had, and that they had chosen her for qualities other than her looks. But it is the go-between who must bear the brunt of the complaints.

The chief parties to a marriage are the most senior direct agnatic ascendants of the boy and girl. It is likely, but not necessary, that the giver or taker in marriage will be the head of the household. In most cases it is the fathers who assume the responsibility. Through the go-betweens they negotiate, among other things, the transfer of gifts. These prestations are an essential element in the making of a marriage, sometimes standing without any documentary transaction (other than the exchange of horoscopes) as the seal of a match. At the betrothal substantial gifts are passed from the boy's to the girl's family in the form of clothing, jewelry, food, and (sometimes) money. Some part of—perhaps nearly all—these gifts may later on find their way back to the groom's house in the bride's dowry and trousseau, but it is central to the transfer that it embodies the notion of an acknowledgment to the girl's family of their having brought her up. Countergifts are made immediately, but they are usually of small value in relation to what has just been received.

Since the betrothal may take place when the boy and girl are mere children, many years may pass before what we should call the consummation of the marriage. But in the Chinese view the marriage begins with the betrothal, which creates the tie of affinity, and which can be broken only by mutual consent or of the order of a court. The death of the boy or girl releases the family of the survivor, but a bereaved partner may go through the main wedding rites with his or her dead spouse, and a widowed girl may insist on being received into her late husband's house. This last is one of the ways in which her family can add to its glory, for they can then procure the setting up of an honorific arch (it is not really an arch) to a chaste widow.

What I shall call the main wedding rites occupy several days of intense activity in the course of which the bride is transferred to her new house, there inducted, and then temporarily returned to her original family as a visitor. In this time the rites indicate both what the rules of marriage require and what they may imply.

In the days before the transfer (usually the day before) the boy and girl, each in his own house, is initiated into adulthood. The girl has her hair ritually put up, the boy is said to be ritually "capped" or given a courtesy name. These (or rather their antecedents) are ceremonies of high antiquity which formerly had no immediate connection with marriage, being performed years in advance of it. In modern times they are still recognizably distinct rites, and yet they are made to fall within the ambit of the wedding, so that adulthood is made an immediate precondition, not for being married (for that the couple have been since their betrothal), but for assuming the full duties of the married state. The wedding is a limited emancipator. By being set up with a bride in a room of his own the young man has taken the first step along the road that will lead him, if Heaven wills, to the headship of a house. On this journey, bit by bit, he will assert the independence of his immediate family in relation to the unit within which it is embedded, and assume more and more of the domestic authority that lies with his father at the beginning of the marriage. For the girl the emancipation must seem more paradoxical, for it consists in her subjection to a new family. But we must grasp what her role in that family is to be. As quickly as possible she must bear children. (Many of the wedding rites underline this necessity, but in my summary account I neglect them.) Then, as wife and mother, she is the ally of her husband in the unceasing struggle for the autonomy of a new family. In connection with this dramatic change of status from girlhood to womanhood, let us note the change in her appearance. Not only is her hair put up in the initiation, but either at home just before she sets out or in her new house soon after her arrival, her forehead and temples are depilated to produce the clean hairline of the mature woman.

The preparation of the bride for her transfer is long and painful. For some days she may be put on a special residue-reduced diet and on the last day given medicine to suppress her urine, in order that she may stay the journey and the main rites in her new house without having to answer the call of nature. She is wept and howled over by her kinswomen and friends and must herself sorrow at the imminent parting. At the final leave-taking the women set out for her in their songs the duties to which she is now called, and the trials and pains of her new life. The songs can leave her in no doubt about the discipline to be imposed on her as a daughter-in-law and the burden of responsibility she will bear to acquit herself of all her tasks in order to preserve the good name of the family that gives her away. She will work hard, cooking, sweeping, and washing; she must not complain. She will be rebuked; she must not answer back. The prospect is painted in somber colors.

Between the betrothal and the wedding there are several exchanges of gifts. Some of the gifts are made in connection with the ritual arrangements for the dates and timings of all the ceremonies. They are fixed in consultation with a diviner who, in addition, often lays down the classes of people and animals which must be excluded when the bride leaves her house and enters her husband's. Cats and dogs, for example, must be kept out of the way, as must people who are horoscopically incompatible with the bride. The diviner will also bar the deformed, the barren, the widowed, those in mourning, and the "four-eyed." The last are pregnant women (and sometimes their husbands)—two eyes in the head and two in the belly. They form a class apart from the others (except for the horoscopically incompatible) because they not only harm but are harmable. As in the case of the other things most highly valued in Chinese society— riches, rank, and honors—progeny are thought of as a scarce good supplied to men in fixed quantities, such that one man's gain is another's loss (a sort of mystical mercantilism). The confrontation of a pregnant woman and the bride (whose first job is to get herself pregnant) may prejudice the chances of one or both producing satisfactory offspring. Similarly, ritual precautions have to be taken if two bridal processions meet, as well they may, given the fact that wedding days are chosen in accordance with a universally accepted almanac.

When the bride leaves she is being separated from her family. What must she take with her, what leave behind? Her trousseau and dowry (sometimes dispatched before her) are ritually cleansed to rid them of any noxious influences that may adhere to them. In a similar fashion the bride herself must be cleansed. In other words, it is the responsibility of those who give her to hand over a pure and innocuous bride of whom it could not be suspected (although of course it probably will be) that she has introduced poverty or sickness from outside. At the same time, the bride-givers must consider their own interests: the bride must not be allowed to take with her anything that would unduly benefit her new family at the expense of her old. And the rites usually include some gesture to indicate that, as the bride leaves the house, food and riches remain behind.

From the moment the bride is veiled she enters a phase of transition from which she will emerge only in her bridal chamber at the end of the journey. She is borne out of the house into the sedan chair, or if she walks to it, then her feet must not touch the uncovered ground. The chair has been carefully inspected to ensure that it contains no evil, and as she is installed the bride carries some object (often a metal mirror, sometimes an almanac) to ward off the malevolence to which she is now especially exposed. The sedan chair is sealed and borne off on a journey that must take several hours (in the course of which the bride may be half-suffocated and rocked into seasickness by the motion of the chair). In nearly all marriages the spouses come from different villages, but if the villages are close, or the wedding one of people who live as neighbors in a town, the procession takes a circuitous route; for the phase of transition must be well marked by duration. The phase is highly dangerous *and* it must not be cut short. Of all the accounts I have read I have come across none more dramatic in this respect than that which shows the bride to be in a state of possession by the God of Happiness for the whole of the phase (Frick 1952: 51–52).

During the procession the "wrong" people and animals may gaze upon the chair, while tall buildings (especially pagodas), bridges, and wells make mystic hazards. Against these threats the bride is protected by the heavy veils she wears and the ritual objects she carries. In some places she is further encased within a box inside the chair. To lessen the risks, the procession may move at night.

The special character of the transition is marked by another feature: as the procession moves off, as it arrives, and sporadically along the route, firecrackers are let off. Now, it is a curious feature of the West's acceptance of things Chinese that firecrackers, seeming as natural to the civilization as chopsticks or bird's nest soup, excite little intellectual curiosity. Inquiries into their use have typically stopped short when, in answer to direct questions, Chinese have said either (which is the usual reply) that the crackers scare off devils and ghosts, or that they express joy. And with such answers we can be no more content than with the old reply to the China hand's question why some junks have eyes painted on them: "No got eye, how can see? No can see, how can savvy?"

I do not pretend that I have yet got to the bottom of the mystery of the firecrackers, but I can summarize certain provisional conclusions. Crackers in China are part of a series of noise producers which stretches from the salt in the fire at one end to the cannon at the other. Noise is used as a marker. It punctuates approaches to and separations from humans. And in these contexts neither the fear of evil spirits nor the expression of joy need be in any way relevant. The marker is, so to say, neutral. But noise, as a symbol, can be linked to light and fire; crackers are all three. Noise and fire are purifiers. Noise and bright light are signs of joy. It then becomes possible to analyze the use of crackers in the bridal procession in different ways. Let us note that, although crackers may be exploded at many other points in a wedding, their use for sending off and receiving the bride seems to be a sort of irreducible minimum. They mark the beginning and the end of the most salient transaction of the wedding. But that they are also fired quite haphazardly en route suggests that the associations of crackers with fire and light are in play. The bride is in a dangerous phase and must be protected, and the character of the crackers as demonifuge is strengthened by the noise produced by the bands of musicians which accompany the procession. Light is provided not only by the crackers but also by the gay lanterns in the procession (which are *de rigueur* even in daylight). The "redness" of the sedan chair and of the clothing of its contents is an adjunct of both light and fire. From which I conclude that the use of firecrackers at this high point of the wedding brackets it off and stamps it with the features of danger and joy that would seem to be its natural attendants. Marriage is a "red" event, a joyful conjunction of Heaven and Earth, of male and female, a fulfillment of natural duty, a necessary stage in the continuation of descent. But it is also dangerous, attracting to its main participants the envy and spite of beings both human and supernatural, threatening the bride's family with losses even greater than that of a daughter, warning the groom's family of the frightening consequences of admitting the necessary stranger.

When she arrives at her new home the bride is subjected to a ritual treatment—the flashing of mirrors, purification by smoke—that brings her in as free as possible of the evil adhering to her. Her husband may have gone to fetch her or waited at home to receive her; whichever the case, the couple are now for the first time ritually conjoined. Within the next twenty-four hours or so (the timing varies) the pair worship Heaven and Earth, the ancestors, and (usually) the Kitchen God. The first of these acts of worship generally takes place very soon after the bride's arrival. It is performed at a special altar either set up in the open air or near a window in the house. There is a sense in which the worship of Heaven and Earth is the central act of religious devotion in the marriage, for although in real life it always forms part of a series of rites, it appears in fairy stories as the sole means by which mortal men marry female spirits. (It is only in fairy tales that men and women give themselves in marriage;

in society they should be married off by others.) The invocation of Heaven and Earth is crucial because it caps, and in a way resumes, every dual combination in the whole series of rites, which are shot through with the motif of paired balance. One go-between is paired with another; representatives in the negotiations are balanced in number and sex; there is a symmetry in the escorting parties of groom and bride; and so on. Marriage is pairing: Heaven and Earth, dragon and phoenix, mandarin drake and duck, wild gander and goose. It is a duality within unity—*yin-yang*: the one is made by the complementarity of the halves.

Before I come to the remaining rites, I want to make a marginal comment that applies to the whole series. The Chinese language is a natural for punning. In English (for those who like them) puns belong to the realm of wit, being prized for their inventiveness and spontaneity. In Chinese they are eminently ritual. Moreover, they are by no means confined to speech, for an object can be made to stand for a homophone of its name—a bat, to take the commonest case, representing happiness because the words are pronounced alike. And students of Chinese art (procelain, textiles, and so on) are soon made familiar with the way in which visual puns of this sort are combined into rebuses; that is, whole sentences made up of objects. For example, green-colored cups supported on clouds, as part of the design on robes, can be read as "may honors and riches be lofty."[3] It is elementary caution in the study of Chinese rites to examine every object used for the possibility that its presence is accounted for, at least in part, by some homophone of its name. The need for the caution is the more important in that the different spoken languages obviously produce their own stocks of puns. But the punning may go further than the production of rebuses: it may lead to charades, in which objects are manipulated to suggest meaning.

In the wedding rites (to take a widespread example) brides are brought into conjunction with apples. They are sometimes made to carry them, sometimes to bite them. Where animal transport is common, we find that as the bride arrives she is made to step on or over a saddle. Under it there is often an apple. The charade in the last case (apple plus saddle) is peacefulness. But apple and saddle each by itself can carry the same meaning. What begins by being very mysterious turns out to be yet another statement by the bride that, stranger that she is as she first comes through the gate, she nevertheless promises tranquillity to the house that receives her.

The bringing of the couple into their wedding chamber highlights a further anxiety. As they are ushered through the door, their respective escorts shove them forward in the hope that the one who gets in first will be the dominant partner in the union. Alternatively, as they take their seats on the bridal bed the groom tries to get his robe to rest on his bride's, and she counters his move. Chinese may hope that their brides will be meek, but they fear that they may not be. Apart from the feasting, it is in the bridal chamber that the remaining great event of the first day takes place. The bride is put on show, and for a few hours before bedtime, in the company of her husband, she is delivered up to the ritual hubbub which is often too mildly translated as "teasing the bride." In these few hours (although in places the license may be extended over a much longer period) two rules of propriety may be (are usually required to be) broken: the rule that seniors must not behave informally with juniors, and the rule that bars the expression of sexuality in the house. Senior men and women may come into the room to fling idle remarks at the couple. Old and young make pointed remarks on the bride's appearance. Bawdy rhymes are often recited—some of staggering and ingenious obscenity. The couple are required on pain of forfeits to perform ridiculous maneuvers and repeat tongue twisters. It is a test of the bride's fortitude (for she must never complain or lose her composure), and a dramatic inversion of the domestic life to come. In those hours, which immediately precede the bride's bedding, much that is henceforth to be forbidden is licensed. It is a ritual mockery the point of which is clinched when we know that the greater the hubbub and excitement, the more secure domestic harmony is thought to be. As a matter of fact, a distinction is made between strong and mild versions of the rite; indeed, the Buddhist terminological division between meat and vegetarian foods is sometimes used; the organizers of the wedding choose one or other according to whether they are persuaded more by the ritual benefit of the strong (meaty) version than by their fear of the consequences of a near-riot.

On the second day of the wedding, having been successfully deflowered, the bride makes her obeisance to the seniors among her affines and is inducted ritually into the kitchen. It is usual on the third day for the couple to be invited to visit the bride's family, this being the first of a series of visits during the early part of the marriage.

We have so far seen little of the kin relationships involved in the wedding, although some hint of the tension between the two sets of affines has been given. The bride's family are the losers, for, apart from anything else, they are likely (unless they are poor and humble) to be out of pocket on the economic exchanges. They are very touchy in the negotiations, and will not hesitate to make a row if the gifts from the groom's family do not match their expectations. And it is part of the go-between's job to smooth over these contretemps. Yet we cannot adequately deal with the link between the two families unless we examine the further links that tie together the parties to those marriages in the previous generation that have made the present marriage possible. The mothers of the bride and groom are each linked to kinsmen who have an interest in the new marriage. In the rites in the bride's house and in those in the groom's their respective mothers' agnates (represented chiefly by the senior maternal uncles) play crucial roles. And the implication of the nonagnatic relatives may be carried back a further generation by the involvement of the agnates of the fathers' mothers. The part of the senior mother's brother is especially conspicuous in the groom's house where he takes the seat of honor at the main feast.

The extent to which the bride's kin appear at the wedding in the groom's house varies from one area of China to another. In some places the bride's parents and others of her kin are received at a feast in the groom's house; in others they are rigidly excluded. In the latter case the bride is almost the only member of her family to take part in the wedding in her new home. I say "almost," because, on the evidence I have been able to collect, her younger brother (or younger agnatic cousin in lieu) is nearly always assigned some role as link between the two families. In some places he travels with the bride to her new home; in others he appears only later on to invite the bride and groom to visit his house. Now, the groom uses one kinship term for mother's brother and wife's brother, and in the Hokkien "dialect," through which I made my first venture into the study of Chinese society, the senior maternal uncle and the bride's younger brother are nicely balanced in the terminology: *tuǎ-kū* against *kŭ-à*. The former is "great *ku*," the latter "little *ku*." The senior of the pair has, as it were, furnished the bride of the senior generation, the junior of the junior. The first is a realized mother's brother, the latter a potential one. The two "uncles" can be classed together as representatives of the groups from which the groom's family has taken wives. (Of course, the bride's younger brother may or may not be the oldest of her brothers. If he is not, he is not the strict counterpart of the groom's oldest maternal uncle, for he will not be the senior mother's brother to the children of the present marriage. But it is easy to see why, when he is the sole representative of the bride's family at the wedding in the groom's house, he must be junior to his sister.)

The rites, then, suggest that relationships through mothers and wives hold a continuing significance. Brothers are in some sense protectors of their sisters and of the sons of their sisters. Maternal uncles make the ideal mediators among their nephews and between their nephews and their paternal uncles, especially in cases of disputed inheritance. Brothers show a ticklish honor if their reputation is attacked by the maltreatment of their sisters. The implication of these men in the fate of their sisters is brought out forcefully when the latter die; for at this point the brothers arrive, first, to see that death has not been the result of foul play or suicide, and, second, to ensure that the obsequies are conducted on a scale commensurate with their own standing. This last fraternal role can be documented widely in China. But I had not realized, until I came by serendipity upon a paper dealing with Chinese in Tsinghai province, that the post-mortem intervention could be ritualized to the extent that mock trials of the sister's children might be organized. In these trials, which in the case of a dead man are conducted by his mother's agnates and in that of a dead woman by her own agnates, the judge berates the kneeling defendants for their shameful neglect of their late parent and may deliver himself of great bitterness before agreeing to be reconciled (Ternay 1952).

Let me approach my conclusion. The legal rules and the rites of marriage are related in different ways. Some of the rites, seen from outside as mere events, are evidence of a marriage having taken place; and one could develop an instructive argument on the precise legal significance, from this point of view, of the various steps in the rites from betrothal to the wedding. It is not a matter I am able to go into today. In the second place, what the rules of marriage lay down as the essential feature of the institution are spelled out in a dramatic and straightforward manner in the rites. One family gives a woman to another in the expectation that she will stay permanently in her new home, bearing children to her husband's name, and submitting to the authority of her new family. It is quite simple.

And yet it is not. We have seen that the rites bring out the relationships through wives and mothers. They also place some emphasis on the continuing tie between the married girl and her natal family. And at this point we begin to see how the rites are commenting on aspects of marriage that are left ill-defined in the rules. I must concede that our (or at least my) inadequate knowledge of customary law may make the rules seem vaguer than they are. Certainly, in the matter of the role of the married woman's family, the rules vary from place to place, and it may be that the rites in different places vary in harmony. But I think that there is a general lack of definition in Chinese society of the norms governing the relations between affines and between a married woman and her agnates; and I suggest that the uncertainties to which this vagueness gives rise are played upon in the rites. One of the most poignant ritual acts I have seen on record (Serruys 1944: 117) brings out the ambiguity in the bride's status with some force. It is said of one area that when the girl leaves her natal home she drops a lock on the ground which is then attached half open to the door to signify that while she has been sent away the house is not completely closed to her. (What the informants actually say is that she can always come and visit her mother.)

But if the rites play upon those relationships which are ill-defined, they also exploit the implications of rules which are perhaps only too well defined. The wife has privileges and obligations in her new family which, as she exercises and fulfills them, lead on to clearly foreseeable and detested consequences. It is a joy for a family to take a woman in marriage, for she will produce the children it must have. And yet she is an enemy within the gates, because as she performs the duties of wife and mother she will be strengthening her husband's position as the nucleus from which will grow a new family pressing for the dissolution of the old. The more successful the wife is as a producer of children and cherisher of her husband's interests, the more dangerous she becomes. Taking all the rites together, we may say that under the threats from outside (from the wife's agnates) and the threats within (from the wife herself) marriage is shown to be an impossible institution. Men are made to fear what they know they must want and to be wary of all the failures implied in their best intentions.

Of course, the rites do not speak as clearly as that. If the rules of marriage are prose, the rites are poetry. They are a structure of resonant ambiguity. Some people may perhaps be completely deaf to them. To different ears they may give different messages. And at the very least, leaving aside all considerations of idiosyncratic sensitivity and experience (which are perhaps none of the anthropologist's business), we must expect that the performers of different roles in a marriage will be the receivers of systematically different messages. To put it simply, does the groom hear what the bride hears? But for such questions to be answered we must wait; for, although the religion and rites of China are dead where Communism has come to rule (or at any rate they are dead to us), they survive in Taiwan and Hong Kong. And these are places where, by the efforts of British and American anthropologists, the study of Chinese society has begun a new life.

We have been taught to see in *rites de passage* ways in which men are made to come to grips with the duties of the new roles they assume. But I think that the rites also mystify these duties, creating about them an air of uncertainty and ambiguity, so that the incumbent of a role faces his new responsibilities with suspicion as well as knowledge, bewilderment as well as confidence. I may be wrong in this proposition, but at least I am giving a correct report of the experience of one man undergoing a *rite de passage*—if you can call this a rite.

Ritual Aspects of Chinese Kinship and Marriage

Rites are a variety of heightened behavior. In this essay I try to summarize what we now know about Chinese rites in the contexts of ancestor worship and marriage, linking the poetry of symbolism and religious belief to the prose of social institutions. There are obviously many ways and contexts in which Chinese family life and kinship can be seen to be implicated in total systems of religion and rites; calendrical domestic rites alone form a vast panorama of activity, and the rites of birth, sickness, and death are as theoretically interesting as those of marriage. I have chosen to discuss ancestor worship and marriage mainly because I know most about them and think myself more capable of raising important issues in those two fields than in any other.

I write as an anthropologist, drawing in the main on my own experience of Chinese life (in Singapore and Hong Kong) and on the experience of my colleagues.[1] I do not involve myself in complex historical questions, nor can I, a non-sinologue, use extensive Chinese (and Japanese) documentation. Nevertheless, I assume that we may usefully generalize about key modes of behavior in Chinese society, huge though it is, and I venture to speak as if I could support my general statements with data from all parts of China and recorded at many points in time during the last hundred years. This essay suggests models of ancestor worship and marriage rites. The models feed on the evidence as I know it; they are not intended to masquerade as substitutes for evidence. They may turn out to be bad models as we come to know more and more about China, but they are intended as hypotheses about some significant features of Chinese ritual life and about the connections between that life and characteristics of the institutions of family and kinship.

In Maurice Freedman, ed., *Family and Kinship in Chinese Society* (Stanford, Calif., 1970), 163–87. The original version was prepared for the Conference on Kinship in Chinese Society held at Greyston House, Riverdale, New York, 15–18 Sept. 1966, under the auspices of the Subcommittee on Research on Chinese Society of the ACLS-SSRC Joint Committee on Contemporary China.

Ancestor Worship

Little was achieved in the study of Chinese ancestor worship until it was made clear that there are two distinct kinds of worshiped ancestors: domestic and extra-domestic. The universality of ancestor worship among the Chinese is the universality of the domestic cult, which, even when it dispenses with wooden tablets, always entails the representation of dead forebears and their ritual service. As we shall presently see, household ancestor worship is not the Chinese domestic religion *par excellence*, but from several points of view it is the more important half of the total cult of the ancestors. The part of the cult centering on lineage ancestors (the dramatic and awe-inspiring parade of ritualized piety) cannot be universal, for lineages are not everywhere found in China. Where they exist, and consequently both parts of the cult are present, the two parts differ in the ancestors they serve, the attitudes maintained toward them by the worshipers, the role ascribed to the ancestors, and the rites performed. The halves of the cult each belong to different phases of group life and have different implications for our understanding of Chinese social organization. This first formulation of the two classes of ancestors will, however, need to be modified a little later on, when we come to consider the possibility that ancestors are worshiped who are neither domestic (although they are in domestic shrines) nor the apical members of clearly structured lineages and their segments.

The domestic religion of the Chinese has many facets, but there is a sense in which the supreme domestic cult is that of the so-called Kitchen God, Tsao Chün, for in his worship each household (i.e. each unit defined in relation to its separate cooking place) stands out as a distinct religious entity.

In the village, the god, besides the ancestor spirits, who receives sacrifices most frequently is the kitchen god—his wife being sometimes included. The kitchen god . . . is the supernatural inspector of the household, sent by the emperor of heaven. His duty is to watch the daily life of the house and to report to his superior at the end of each year. . . . Based on the report, the fortunes of the household will be decided. (Fei 1939: 99–100.)

It is a picture familiar to anyone who knows Chinese home life. We can see that each Kitchen God shrine (which, however, need not be more than a place where incense sticks are put up) is the defining focus for a household in respect of its commensality. As separate household usually has a separate kitchen, and its Tsao Chün shrine is physically distant from those of related households; but two or more households may in some circumstances share a kitchen, and then the cooking place with its own shrine becomes the locus of differentiation. (It is clear that Stove God would be a better English name for Tsao Chün.) By the worship of this deity the domestic unit is linked into the hierarchy of groups with gods that gives Chinese bureaucracy its religious aspect.

This clear ritual segmentation of households does not coincide with the segmentation of units based on ancestor worship. Every house has an altar in its main hall (or at least in its main room when it cannot rise to the luxury of a hall); in it are set both the images of the gods that the household chooses to worship and its ancestor tablets (or substitutes). The household may be both wider and narrower than an ancestor-worshiping group. Not every member of a household is necessarily the descendant, or the wife of a descendant, of a dead forebear represented on the altar. The unit defined by a collection of ancestor tablets may include people distributed over several households. Imagine a house in which, by family partition, the immediate families of different brothers severally occupy distinct living quarters and yet maintain the hall of the house and its altar in common—by no means a rare pattern. Each household will keep a Tsao Chün shrine, for each eats separately; but the brothers, their wives, and their children will as a group collectively worship the ancestors on the altar.

Just as the household is tied into one religious hierarchy through Tsao Chün, so the family, whatever its precise constitution, is linked at least in principle to a ritual hierarchy of nearer and more distant ancestors. When each socially mature man or woman dies, a tablet is made for him and placed on the domestic altar. The qualification for being so treated is the attainment of parenthood, whether actual or merely potential, as when a man posthumously acquires an heir through an adoption; parenthood may also be only nominal in the sense that members of a junior generation accept the responsibility for caring for the tablet. A boy or girl of marriageable age dying single may be posthumously married—even perhaps to another dead mate—in order to establish a place on the altar. What the system rigidly excludes is the immediate entry of the tablets of dead children, for they are not considered potential ancestors and have committed an unfilial act by the mere fact of dying young. (Yet it may be possible after the lapse of a generation or more for the restless spirit of such an unfortunate and wicked child to be appeased by his being married off in a ghostly union so that he may join the ranks of the honored dead on the altar.) The tablet of a dead man rests (if for the moment we exclude the possibility of uxorilocal residence) on the altar that houses his father's, unless of course his family has by now moved from the place where that altar is kept. A married woman's tablet is installed in the altar belonging to her husband's family. A spinster is not supposed to die in her paternal house; if she is to stay unmarried even after death, then a nondomestic shrine must be found to accommodate her tablet, if indeed she is to have one.

As the generations unfold, new tablets are added automatically to the domestic stock, but old ones are being removed, for only some three or four generations are characteristically represented. A superannuated tablet is burnt or buried near the grave of the person for whom it stands. In principle, then, domestic ancestor worship works on a cycle in which the youngest living generation worships before an altar that houses the tablets of ancestors some four generations above it—a religious correlate of the Chinese abstraction that the core of agnatic kinship is formed by those related within the patrilineal *wu-fu*, the five mourning grades. (See Freedman 1958: 41ff, 93ff.) But for several reasons a particular domestic altar may not present so orderly and self-limiting a set of tablets.

In the first place, the agnatic thread linking any set may be broken. If a man enters into that form of marriage in which he lives uxorilocally and fathers children to his wife's surname, both he and his wife come to rest as tablets on an altar that will now contain parents-in-law and son-in-law and parents and daughter. Moreover, it is possible for a set to include the tablet of a non-agnatic relative or even a non-relative when that person has been a member of the house and has nobody outside it ritually to serve him. This apparent anomaly raises a crucial question (that we shall examine later) about the nature of the ritual tie between living and dead.

Second, tablets cannot build up in a regular pattern when one or more of a group of brothers move out of the house. In a new house a fresh stock may begin when the most senior member dies off; his descendants there may worship him yet still go to the old house to take part in worship, within a wider group, of more senior generations. On the other hand, especially when a new house is set up at a distance from the old, the new stock may begin with a "general" tablet on which are recorded the details extracted from the individual tablets left behind; thus worship in the new house may be addressed to the same collection of ancestors as is worshiped in the old house.

Finally, by an extension of the principle that families resulting from a recent division may come together at the altar maintained by one of them, one such altar may continue over many generations—well beyond the "standard" four—to house tablets serving as the focus for a large group of agnates scattered over numerous houses. Such an altar is physically domestic, and it is ritually domestic for the people in whose house it stands; but, acting as a ritual center for a long line of agnates, it has become akin to the altar constructed in an ancestral hall.

Before we turn to the matter of ancestral halls, however, we ought to consider an aspect of the character of ancestor tablets and the manner of their keeping. An individual tablet is usually "dotted": it has a red dot (ink or blood) imposed on it to establish a *hun* (soul) of the dead person in it, or at least to provide the *hun* with a place to settle. That ritual act sets up one instrument and distinguishes it from all others that may come to be made for the same person. As far as domestic worship is concerned, the "dotted" tablet should act as the focus when all those who are the descendants of the person for whom it stands wish to serve it jointly. In theory, a stock of tablets passes down the generations by primogeniture, and it is in connection with his right-duty to maintain the stock that the oldest son may claim and get an extra share of property when a patrimony is divided up among brothers. It follows (again in theory) that when a domestic shrine serves as the ritual center for a large nondomestic group of agnates, that shrine will have been transmitted from oldest son to oldest son, younger sons having established their own domestic altars. In reality, however, the primogenitory rule may have been broken, and the chief altar may have passed down a line that excludes some oldest sons.

We may now make the transition to ancestral halls. When a domestic tablet is destroyed or buried, having served its tour of duty, that event may mark the end of the ritual memory of the person for whom the tablet was made. And indeed, most Chinese pass into oblivion in this fashion, a similar process of erosion taking place in the treatment of tombs, as we shall see. Appearances to the contrary, the Chinese have never overburdened themselves with ancestors. But another tablet may be made for the same person and installed in an ancestral hall; once in such an altar, the tablet will remain as long as the hall stands. Often, in the cities when a tablet is similarly deposited in a club building or temple for safe and ritual keeping, it escapes the annihilation to which a normal domestic life, so to speak, would have condemned it. But it cannot play the role in an agnatic community played by a tablet in an ancestral hall, except possibly where it has been placed in a shrine belonging to a clan association.

Ancestral halls must be clearly distinguished from temples and from domestic shrines. Temples are devoted to gods, even though some urban temples may accommodate ancestor tablets. As ancestral hall is a building put up and maintained by a patrilineal group to house their ancestor tablets and serve as the center of their ritual and secular activities. Though it may display one or more deities in side-shrines, it is dominated by the symbols of ancestors. It is physically quite distinct from any normal living accommodation. The commonest form of ancestral hall is

that which belongs to a lineage, but any such lineage that is finely segmented may contain a hierarchy of halls, each of them the ritual center
of a segment. A hall requires for its building and its maintenance and
for the upkeep of its rites that it be endowed; hence, a hall is a mark
of riches, and a segment that enjoys the ownership of a hall is a rich unit
within a community of units.

The segments that form within a Chinese lineage are based on some
sort of income-producing property, most commonly land. Some segments are not rich enough to build a hall, and so find their ritual foci
in the tombs (they may in reality be cenotaphs) of the apical ancestors
from whom they trace their origin or in the shrines incorporated in domestic altars. The segments lowest down in the hierarchy (that is to say,
of the shallowest genealogical depth) are almost certain to own no ritual
center other than such a tomb or shrine. It becomes clear, then, that
whereas from the point of view of traditional Chinese, domestic ancestor
worship is a necessity, ancestor worship in halls is a luxury, expressing
and reinforcing the honor of a segment but not resting on an absolute
religious obligation.

The segmentary order of a Chinese lineage, as we now know, is typically asymmetrical. Segments well enough endowed to own halls stand
out against both coordinate segments that cannot afford halls and groups
of agnates that lack the means even to be organized into segments. Social differentiation is given one of its ritual faces. The factors that will
explain why deep lineages appear in some parts of China and not in
others (Freedman 1966: 159–64; Potter 1970: 130–38) will also explain why hall worship is found unevenly in the country. What accounts
for differing degrees of genealogical elaboration will help us understand
why nondomestic ancestor worship is differently elaborated.

The ancestral hall contains in the place of honor the tablet of the
founding ancestor. Logically, if the segments tracing their origin to the
sons of the founder also have their several halls, we should expect to find
no other tablets in the main hall. But that situation we do not in fact
find. The only lineage halls with a single tablet would appear to be those
belonging to Hakka (or at any rate those in the southeastern part of the
country) in which the solitary tablet is not that of the first ancestor but
a general tablet for agnatic ancestors as a group (see, for example, Aijmer
1967: 57)—the hall equivalent of the general tablets we sometimes find
in domestic shrines. It would seem that families will install a tablet for
one of their dead members not only in the lowest segment hall to which
they belong, but perhaps also in every higher segment hall of which they
are members and in the lineage hall. In this way, one tablet becomes
many. (The installation does not, however, have necessarily to wait upon

a man's death; living men sometimes have their own tablets put on an altar where they will stand, for the time being, shrouded auspiciously in red, eventually to merge into the general company of the dead.) Indeed, if we reflect for a moment on the significance of hall tablets, we see that the duplication makes good sense. The installation of a tablet is the assertion of the prestige of those descended from the person represented or of the person himself if he installs his own. That prestige, though desirable enough in the lowest-level hall, is yet more desirable in the halls to which larger groups of agnates have recourse. Of course, in the old days when tablets could be entered in the lineage or some other high-level hall only when the descendants were titled scholars or were for some other reason thought worthy of the privilege (perhaps hard cash being paid for it), many tablets found in the lower halls were not duplicated in the halls at or near the summit of the system.

I think it is useful at this point in the argument to examine the best ethnography we have to date on the distribution of tablets in ancestral halls. The new information was collected in the early 1960's in one of the great lineages of Hsin-an county, Kwangtung—since 1899 living under British rule in the Hong Kong New Territories. The village of Sheung Shui (the Cantonese form of its name) is traditionally the settlement of a single lineage bearing the surname Liao. Numerous "trusts" or estates held jointly (Freedman 1966: 33ff) have evolved at various generation levels, but only three ancestral halls now result from them: the lineage hall, a hall in the fourth generation, and one in the seventh. (See Baker 1968: 114, fig. 7.) The main ancestral hall—the lineage hall—houses three groups of tablets, of which the most important (and centrally placed) consists of the tablets of certain ancestors senior to the lineage founder, of the founder and his wife, of his only son and that man's wives and three sons, and, in addition, six tablets of the fourth generation, four tablets of the fifth, and one of the fifteenth (this last something of a puzzle, unless the fact that it belongs to a man who was a "Battalion Second Captain" has something to do with his inclusion in the main group of ancestors). The next most important group is formed by the tablets of ancestors "of particularly high academic success": two tablets for *chü-jen*, provincial graduates. The final group is of 156 tablets belonging to men who subscribed money at various times to restore the hall; there are tablets for members of each generation from the sixth to the eighteenth, the latter generation flourishing about the beginning of the present century. It is interesting to note that when in 1932 the hall was last restored and partly converted into a school, an entirely different method of rewarding donors was resorted to: their framed photographs were put up, but not to be worshiped or tended—apart from anything else, it would be awkward to treat them ritually, for the photographs include two of men who are not members of the lineage (Baker 1968: 54–60).

The lineage has three primary segments, stemming from the three members of the third generation (the founder, we recall, had only one son). None of these segments, however, has a hall. The second hall in Sheung Shui defines the segment springing from a fourth-generation ancestor: the older of the sons of the founder of the second primary segment. In this hall there are again three groups of tablets. The central group (of 139) consists of a "composite" tablet for the first three generations of the lineage and individual tablets for the apical ancestor of the segment and his wife, the remainder being tablets each of which stands for a man and his wife or wives. These last include men from the fifth to seventeenth generations, several tablets being duplicated in the lineage hall; it is not at all clear why these tablets appear on the central altar. The second group is made up of three tablets of men of high honor. The final group is of 115 tablets for men who donated money for the building and the restoration of the hall; the men are drawn from the thirteenth to the nineteenth generations (Baker 1968: 103–8).

The third hall has as its apical ancestor a man of the seventh generation, a descendant of the brother of the apical ancestor of the second hall. Here there is only one group of tablets, 70 in all, some of them duplicated in the lineage hall. The group consists of individual tablets for the apical ancestor of the segment, his wife, and their sons and wives; for the ten men of the next generation, the ninth; and for various men of the tenth to fifteenth generations, some sort of merit having apparently decided their entry. All these tablets seem to have been installed when the hall was built in the early nineteenth century. Well endowed, the segment to which this hall belongs apparently has not needed to solicit donations against the privilege of setting up tablets (Baker 1968: 110–11).

Few of these facts are in conflict with my earlier general statements; we see in Baker's admirably collated and analyzed data the duplication of tablets in halls and their roles as points of reference and markers of prestige. But Baker stresses in relation to my earliest treatment of the subject (Baker 1968: 61–62; Freedman 1958: 82ff) that there is in his material on Sheung Shui no support whatever for the view that ancestors in their tablets can be promoted from domestic to hall shrines, "the only way of securing a place there being to be alive (and sufficiently wealthy) at the time the hall is restored" (Baker 1968: 62). As a matter of fact, this last statement can apply only to the groups of tablets that represent donors in the lineage and fourth-generation halls; the evidence shows that the tablets of the earliest generations in the main altars of all three halls must have been installed after death, and it seems to me that this may well have been the case with more recent tablets in the central altars of the lineage and fourth-generation halls. As for the domestic cult, Baker says (1968: 62) that ancestors are worshiped "for a much longer period" than is provided for in my model, "many homes having paper 'tablets' representing 'all the ancestors of the Liao surname,' while others have paper 'tablets' recording the names of individual ancestors of ten generations or more (wooden tablets have disappeared from the home)."

Now, men installing their own hall tablets (and leaving them auspiciously shrouded while they live) certainly will not have prevented their tablets being put up in the houses where they die; thus for some generations at any rate such men will be worshiped both in the hall and in a domestic shrine. But nobody lasts indefinitely in a domestic shrine (except in the vague sense that he is embraced in a "general" tablet of the kind Baker describes: "all the ancestors of the Liao surname"), and a man's only chance of a posthumous installation in a hall lies in his descendants' procuring his admission, on some ground of eminence, to one or more of the central altars of the halls. Such an installation is no longer possible; but that may be because for the last generation at least the system has declined; certainly no new ancestral hall will now or in the future come into existence to make it possible for people to establish their ancestors in a permanent shrine belonging to a segment.

In Sheung Shui, as we have seen, individual tablets (in reality just sheets of red paper) may be kept in domestic altars for "ten generations or more." Two questions arise. First, has this lengthy retention something to do with the fact that eminent ancestors can no longer be put into hall shrines? Second, and more important, are some of the remoter ancestors kept in domestic shrines because they are in fact the foci of large and nondomestic groups of agnates? In connection with this second question I refer to other present-day evidence, drawn from a village study made in Taiwan. In Hsin Hsing there is a multiplicity of agnatic groups, none of which is very large. It would appear that only one of them has collective property and none an ancestral hall (Gallin 1966: 132–37). Yet the *tsu* (as they call themselves, using the term we normally translate as "lineage") participate in the common worship of ancestors on their death-dates, as do lesser groups within the *tsu*, the loci for such worship being domestic shrines (*ibid.*: 247–48). The relation between domestic worship proper and worship at a domestic shrine by some nondomestic group is indicated in Gallin's statement (p. 248): "Generally, a single ancestor is worshipped for about two or three generations, or as long as someone remembers him in his lifetime. When no one remains who remembers him alive, he, together with other more or less forgotten ancestors . . . is worshipped only on one designated day of the year, and then perhaps by the *tsu*." In cases such as this we are witnessing the bringing together, within the context of a domestic shrine, of ritual attitudes and practices that are clearly segregated when hall and house worship are independently developed.[a]

Ancestor worship in China is not confined to shrines, the tablet being only one of two localizations of an ancestor. The other is the grave. Lineages and segments that maintain halls may, by means of their economic resources, keep up grand tombs for apical ancestors and may conduct periodic communal worship at them. Lacking ancestral halls, lineages and segments may fall back on tombs as the only places for their joint worship. Just as a distinction is to be made between worship at domestic shrines and worship in halls, so it can be made in the worship at graves: families cherish the tombs of their more recent forebears, gradually abandoning them as they recede in time; the graves of remoter ancestors are tended only when they serve as points of reference for lineages and their segments. As Baker puts it for Sheung Shui (1968: 62):

> The most distant ancestor's grave known by me to be worshipped was that of a great-grandfather of the youngest agnatic descendant present. . . . Beyond this limit in generation depth graves are not worshipped by individual families, *but* grave-worshipped ancestors may be "promoted" to communal grave-worship and thus saved from extinction of memory, in much the same way as are the tablet-worshipped ancestors of Freedman's account.

Up to this point we have mapped out what might be called the general structural arrangements of Chinese ancestor worship. Now we must explore the nature of the ritual activity associated with those arrangements, beginning again with domestic worship. On any domestic altar there may be two kinds of tablet: individual and collective, the latter designating "all the ancestors." This possible combination helps us to see that domestic worship has two sides: on the one hand a family addresses itself on the major annual festivals to its ancestors and reports to them as a collectivity; on the other hand, individual ancestors are tended on their death-dates, perhaps with their favorite food being set before them and the family as a whole paying its respects. The distinction between the two classes of devotion does not, however, depend on there being two differ-

---

[a] In view of the clear differentiation between domestic and hall tablets, one might expect to find a vocabulary that reflects it. The common term for ancestral tablet is *p'ai* (*ling-p'ai*). Baker says that in Sheung Shui domestic tablets are *shen-wei* and hall tablets *shen-chu* (1968: 63). Shryock (1931: 170), on the other hand, gives *shen-wei* as the term for hall tablets, domestic tablets being *shen-chu*, although sometimes *shen-wei* in the case of great men. Addison (1925: 32) sets out a different use of the terminology: the front inner surface of the tablet bears the characters for *shen-chu*, the front outer surface those for *shen-wei*. There is, therefore, no consistent terminology, but the distinction between the two classes of tablet is often linguistically marked.

ent kinds of tablet. Ancestors as a collectivity can be worshiped in the absence of any tablet that represents them as such, and individual ancestors do not require individual tablets to insure that they are worshiped on their death-dates. (Some families keep sheets of paper or boards on which important death-dates are recorded as a guide.) Yet, although these two aspects are present, it is the worship of individual ancestors that is the more distinctive of domestic worship. Indeed, it is the highly individualizing and personal character of ancestor worship in the house that marks it off sharply from worship conducted by nondomestic groups.

Although the head of a family should formally put himself in charge of the rites conducted before the ancestors, whether at the festivals or on the death-dates of particular ancestors, the routine tendance—the daily offering of incense and the special offerings made on the first and fifteenth days of every lunar month—is carried out by women. Everywhere in China, at least outside the families of the small Confucian elite, the routine care of ancestors falls essentially to women—as indeed does nearly every part of domestic religion. On their shoulders rests the responsibility for remembering the death-dates of the ancestors for whom the family is concerned; it is they who are likely to pray to the ancestors for well-being and peace; and, as I have argued elsewhere (Freedman 1967a [Essay 17 below]: 97–98), to the limited extent that ancestors can intervene detrimentally in the lives of their descendants, it is women who are probably the agents for the unfavorable interpretation of ancestral behavior. There are enough hints in the literature that in many places in China the most conscpicuous role of men in domestic religion is in the conduct of the main rites for the Kitchen God. (See Freedman 1967a: 97; Eberhard 1958: 18; Maspero 1932: 292; Tun 1965: 64; Körner 1959: 35; and Bredon 1930: 13.) It may seem highly paradoxical that in the ritual sphere men should emerge as leaders of the household and women generally appear as prime agents in the rites of the family, but we might suggest that on the one side men are appropriately associated with the kind of domestic discipline for which Tsao Chün stands, and that on the other side they cannot be in too intimate a relationship with domestic ancestors because of the latter's potential power to inflict harm.

From the point of view of men, ancestors are essentially benign (Freedman 1967a: 93ff), their kindliness perhaps springing from the gradualness with which a son takes over responsibility from his father (for him the key domestic ancestor). Despite the ritual primacy of the oldest son (which we have already seen to be expressed in his custodianship of the family's stock of tablets and his right to an extra share of inheritance), there is, in real life, equality between brothers and no transfer from father to son of a power to control the other mature sons. The head of a family does not draw from his ancestors the capacity to punish by nonhuman means; he does not stand before the other members of the family with an array of disciplinary ancestors behind him. The ancestors represent protectiveness and solicitude. And yet they have rights—chiefly, to be served on their death-dates and provided with agnatic descendants—which, if they are denied, may lead them to cause sickness or some other discomfort to the living. The punitive element in ancestral behavior is a minor one, but (we may argue) it is of sufficient importance to make it difficult for men to deal closely with their dead forebears, that role being assumed by women. On marriage women are estranged from their own ancestors and placed under their husbands', to whom they now have special access and from whom they hope for protection and blessings even as they fear possible retribution.

The interpretation may well be wrong, but the evidence for the crucial place of women in domestic ancestor worship is accumulating. I was struck by the prominence of this womanly role in Singapore (Freedman 1957a: 45); Gallin (1966: 148, 247) records it; and a Chinese writer has recently done the same in respect of another village in Taiwan, although he appears to treat what he has seen as a sign that men have abdicated their role in favor of women in recent times. He writes of the village of Chin Chiang Ts'o that he and his colleagues did not see a single case in which a male *chia-chang* (family head) led his sons and grandsons in domestic ancestor worship. Men (he goes on) have become indifferent, have neglected their responsibilities, and are now represented by women (Ch'en Chung-min 1967: 174). I prefer to accept the observations and not draw any moral about modern social change.

We have seen that a collection of tablets in a domestic shrine may include a tablet of a non-ancestor, and the presence of such an outsider, who will automatically share in the general offerings made at the altar, forces us to examine the implication of statements that Chinese worship their ancestors. Some Chinese writing about peasants (e.g. M. C. Yang 1945: 90) deny that "worship" is the right word, and it hardly needs to be said that Confucian agnosticism has made it possible for the educated elite to look upon (or at least to present) their reverential treatment of their ancestors as a form of decorous ceremony. I think that Yang (1945: 90) is unjustified in asserting that Chinese "do not worship their ancestors in the way the gods are worshiped," for it can be shown for the mass of Chinese that first, the same ritual elements enter into the approach to ancestors as in that to the gods (offerings, libations, incense, and so on), and second, both gods and ancestors fall into the category of *shen*, "spirit." (It does not follow, of course, that ancestors and gods are treated exactly alike. In an important paper entitled "Gods, Ghosts, and Ancestors" [1974b] Arthur P. Wolf discusses the differences in ritual treatment on the basis of his Taiwan field data.) But a difficulty seems to arise from the fact that Chinese also speak of their actions for the dead as commemoration. In Singapore I found (Freedman 1957a: 219) that Hokkien Chinese most commonly used the term *kĭ-liãm* (Mandarin: *chi-nien*), "to commemorate," in the context of domestic ancestor worship, and it is clear that the desire to keep a person's memory green is a crucial element in the total system of ideas. The ancestral portraits of former times and the photographs of today are by themselves evidence of that notion: they are in no sense worshiped (except when photographs have been inserted into tablets or placed on altars as substitutes for them). As a Chinese, a person feels under an obligation to perpetuate the memory of somebody with whom he has lived. At the same time, the further obligation is incurred to prevent him from going unfed, whence his share in the offerings made in general at the altar. That is to say, the presence of outsiders on an altar highlights the fact that domestic ancestor worship is compounded of memorialism, devotion to the needs of the dead, and subjection to their vague authority.

Shifting our attention to the rites conducted in ancestral halls we see at once that we are dealing with a different kind of ancestor. There is a sense in which there are now no individual ancestors but rather a sort of ancestral collectivity, the common spiritual property of a corporate group. True, the names of key ancestors are picked out in the grand rites and people may decorate (and even perhaps pay private attention to) the tablet of some ancestor for whom they are specially concerned; but the atmosphere in the hall is overwhelmingly one in which a group of male agnates (or at least their elders and elite on their behalf) dramatize their existence by praising and sacrificing to a body of ancestors that they hold in distinction from other gruops of like order. The twice-yearly rites and festivities are a manifestation, to both the worshipers and those from whom they are differentiated by those acts, of a claim to a special standing and distinction bound up with the reciprocal relationship of honor between living and dead. Men glorify their ancestors and parade them as the source of their being. For their part the ancestors bask in the glow of the solidarity and achievements of their descendants.

This is a world of men. Their wives enter the hall only as tablets—a dumb and wooden fate. And even then, they are rarely admitted in the same numbers as men, for as we have seen in the case of the Sheung Shui halls, the wives of the most senior ancestors are likely to be represented, but not those of the men who have been installed on account of their special honor or generosity. The ancestral hall is not merely the site of agnation; it is the locus of the political life of the agnatic community, and in that life women can have no public place. The contrast with domestic worship is sharp: that sphere belongs above all to women; the ancestors are capable of some immediate intervention in the lives of their descendants; it is a realm of personal relationships between living and dead. In the halls the ancestors are raised by men to a plane from which notions of punitive behavior are excluded, whence only pride and generalized benignity flow.

The very same systematic difference is to be seen between the rites performed at the graves of recent forebears and those at structurally significant tombs of remoter ancestors. When family parties go out to the graves (ideally sited in the hills) to care for and make offerings at them—which they do at least at Ch'ing-ming—they enter into the same kind of relationship with individual forebears as we find in domestic worship. The women are prominent; personal appeals to the dead may be made; the delicacies offered are likely to be adjusted to the tastes of the departed. But the rites at the great tombs of distant ancestors are all pomp and splendor, a kind of alfresco version of what (if a group has a hall) will have taken place indoors, perhaps with chants of praise and bursts of music.

Yet as soon as we begin to consider the role of tombs in ancestor worship, we are forced to recognize that the term "ancestor worship" cannot embrace all that the Chinese do ritually to make their ancestors significant in their lives. When they worship at the graves they address themselves to entities that are identical with, or at least of the same order as, those tended in domestic shrines. (The distinction depends on the analysis one makes of the *hun* elements of the nonphysical personality; see Freedman 1967a: 86.) But in this context the buried ancestor is presenting only one of two sides of his nature, for he is not merely a disembodied soul but also a mystified set of bones. As the former he is attached to a tablet and hovers above his grave; as the latter he is permanently in the earth, where his relationship to his "physical" surroundings has a direct bearing on the fate of his descendants. We are now in the realm of *feng-shui*, "geomancy," the mystical determination of fortune by the acts of men on their environment. (See Freedman 1966: 119–42; 1967a [Essay 17 below]: 87ff; and 1969 [Essay 18 below]: *passim*.)

In the *feng-shui* of graves (that is, of *yin* habitations)—as distinct from that of buildings (*yang* habitations)—men seek to site their tombs where the "winds and waters" are most favorable; they look to this siting as a means of establishing or maintaining good fortune—riches, rank, and progeny—and they expect the ancestral bones to respond to the treatment to which they subject them. The worship of ancestors, which hinges on the moral duty of *hsiao* ("filial piety"), is counterbalanced by the "dis-respect" of ancestors implied in the *feng-shui* of graves.

We have seen that tombs may be used as foci of lineages and their seg-ments, either supplementing or replacing halls; and in the context of ancestor worship these graves are symbols of agnatic solidarity. But in geomancy the tombs mean something different, introducing fine points of differentiation among agnates. A man seeks to site a grave in such a way that the benefit it is designed to produce will flow to him alone or to him in the company of close patrilineal kinsmen. The benefit resulting from good siting ramifies along the lines of agnatic descent from the man or woman buried in the grave (a woman's agnatic descendants being her own children and the patrilineal issue of her sons); the remoter the buried ancestor, the wider will be the spread of beneficiaries, so that it becomes part of the strategy of choice in *feng-shui* to fasten onto a near ancestor in order to restrict the range of the people with whom one will be forced to share the benefits procured. The great tombs of apical ancestors yield geomantic profits of too general a character; agnates differentiate them selves by exploiting the *feng-shui* of their proximate forebears.

The point that in geomancy competition between agnates is of the es-sence is brought home most dramatically by the behavior of brothers, among whom in the Chinese system there is a built-in tendency to be rivalrous when they are adult. All brothers must of course benefit from the geomantically sited tomb of a common parent, but in fact the rules of *feng-shui* presuppose that they will not profit equally, for it is laid down that it is virtually impossible so to site and orient a tomb that all children will enjoy a like happiness. The evidence is abundant that broth-erly squabbling attends the attempt to get agreement on precisely where, in which direction, and at what time to bury a parent. By *feng-shui* men seek to individualize their fate, pressing individualism to the point where each can strive to climb above his fellows, and at their expense, for one man's gain is seen as another's loss.

Ancestors in their tablets and as they receive offerings at their graves are *shen* and their affinities are with Heaven (*t'ien*). Men cannot expect them to pour out their blessings without reciprocity; the ancestors are moral beings. Ancestors as bones, on the contrary, partake of the nature of Earth (*ti*); they are morally neutral, and the benefits of which they are the vehicle are amoral. Men use their buried forebears for their selfish ends, manipulating in the context of *feng-shui* the ancestors whom they revere in the realm of worship. It is a remarkable feature of Chinese re-ligion that the ancestors can be shown, in segregated spheres, to be sym-bols of authority and honor on the one hand and symbols of the satis-faction of greed on the other. That latter aspect of the treatment and conception of ancestors is poorly reflected in the literature. Is it because the *feng-shui* of graves is a kind of negative ancestor worship about which Chinese writers themselves are uncomfortable and which the foreign observers of China have been unable to see, partly perhaps by their being overpersuaded by the Confucian models set before them?

The brief excursion into geomancy in turn suggests the possibility that there remain much wider fields within which to inquire into the symbolic roles of Chinese ancestors. In this connection I may cite the pioneering work done in the last few years by Aijmer. In a recently published paper (1968b; and see Aijmer 1964: esp. 84ff, 92ff) he has sketched out a set of ideas that explore the *yin* aspects (other than that revealed in *feng-shui*) of the ancestors, particularly in regard to their agricultural role in the underground, and has looked at the various key festivals of the Chinese year as forming a system of alternating visits between the living and their ancestors in both their *yin* and *yang* guises. He writes (1968: 96):

During these festivals, *Qingming*, *Duanwu*, and *Chongyang* [Ch'ing-ming, Tuan-wu, and Ch'ung-yang], there appears to be no particular concern about the ancestor tablets. New Year seems to be the big event for them. Thus *Qingming* implies a visit to the *yin* ancestors and *Duanwu* a return visit from the latter. *Chongyang* implies a visit to the *yang* ancestors and New Year a return visit from them.

I leave the subject at this juncture. As with every other topic in the study of Chinese society, when we begin to systematize our understanding of it, the investigation branches off into directions—perhaps unforeseen at first—that lead to numerous points in the total system of Chinese social behavior and the total system of Chinese ideas. About these systems we have at the moment only general notions.

The Rites of Marriage

Ancestor worship and marriage rites form a balanced pair. They show the ritual treatment of the fixed bonds of agnatic kinship and the contractual ties of marriage. Marriage is an essential part of the making of kinship, but men are endowed with forebears and must choose affines. They are never relieved of the burden of dealing with their ancestors; they have only at irregular intervals to cope with the problem of taking in strange women. In the language of medicine, ancestor worship is chronic, marriage acute. The rites of marriage are, as I shall try very briefly to show, an extended commentary on the joy and trauma of forming new bonds of affinity. As in the case of ancestor worship, I shall assume that a general model of the rites can be constructed; in fact in this field we are on surer ground, for the descriptive literature is copious, and there is reason to suppose that there is a greater constancy over the whole of China in the institutions of primary marriage than there is in those of agnatic kinship. In view of the comparative richness of the sources I can afford to write more briefly in this part of the essay than in the first.[2]

The rites enshrine a single form of marriage, even though marriage is of different kinds, and it is to the one form that I shall confine the discussion: a man marries a virgin bride who is at that point brought into his paternal house as a primary wife. To Chinese, this is "marriage" in the abstract, and it is the norm from which all other forms of marital union are deviations, however significant they may be in real life. Men take secondary wives; widows marry; men marry into the houses of their fathers-in-law; girls are married in the houses to which they were given some years earlier in anticipation of marriage—sometimes these forms are statistically of great importance, but for the Chinese themselves their ritual expressions can never displace from its central position the set of rites that dramatize the movement of the virgin bride to her affinal family, there to occupy the status of her husband's major wife.

A marriage in this form transforms an immature girl under the authority of her agnates into a wife and potential mother within the control of her husband's kin. In moving from one family to another, a bride brings with her new sets of relationships for her affines, and in the transmutation of her own status from mere daughter to daughter-wife there begins a new traffic between two groups of agnates of which she is seen as the vehicle. For its continuity a family must have brides; the taking of them creates bonds of affinity that, from two points of view, provide uneasy benefits. To have affines is for a family to have potential friends and enemies. Especially when the status and rights of a married woman are at stake, the people who gave her in marriage may interfere intolerably in the affairs of those who received her. In the second place, the bride herself, the indispensable instrument for the perpetuation of the family and potentially an honored ancestress in it, is a menace to the very group she is summoned to serve, for she is an outsider who, in alliance with her husband, will form a nucleus from which will grow a new family pressing against the old—a new marriage in a new bedroom pointing toward a new stove. The doubtful profit from acquiring a bride and daughter-in-law and the relationships that adhere to her is a central preoccupation of the rites.

Before we turn to a brief summary of those rites (see Freedman 1967b [Essay 15 above] for a fuller account and analysis) it may be worthwhile emphasizing one contrast between them and those associated with ancestor worship. The main dimension through which the ancestor rites move is time. Agnation is, so to say, a vertical extension; the rites look backward and forward in time, and with respect to place stress immobility. Families and lineages are conceptually anchored in space; they move forward along time. In the rites of marriage time recedes, for what is crucial is physical movement, symbolized above all in the transfer of the bride but realized also in the many comings and goings between the two houses that both precede and follow the central event. Space is now of the essence. It is no wonder, then, that in the People's Republic, in the face of fierce attacks against superstitious ceremonialism, people persist in practicing the central rite of the traditional wedding (the transfer of the bride in her sedan chair) by conveying her on a bicycle. Walking, even when practical, is just not good enough; a dramatic movement must be made.

The so-called "Six Rites" of marriage of the canonical *Li Chi, The Record of Rites*, lie at the base of the modern system, having been reworked at various times in dynastic codes and handbooks of rites and etiquette. The sequence of events laid down in the "Six Rites" is essentially the structure of all Chinese marriage in its preferential form, however modified and embellished by custom. Inquiries are made in a girl's family by a go-between sent by a family seeking a bride; genealogical and horoscopic data are sought by the go-between; the girl's horoscope is matched with the boy's; the betrothal is clinched by the transfer of gifts; the date of the wedding (that is, the transfer of the bride) is fixed; the bride is moved. (See, for example, Chiu 1966: 4ff.)

We need to fasten on one sociological feature of this sequence before considering its ritual expression. What for the sake of convenience we call "betrothal" is in reality the first step in the marriage itself, in the special sense that it establishes the bond of affinity between two families, the personal bond between the two parties most closely affected being fashioned later by the transfer of the bride. After betrothal a marriage exists that can be broken only by death or a negotiated rupture; but if one of the two parties dies, the marriage may still be carried to the second stage by the surviving girl proceeding as a widow to take her place in the boy's house or the surviving boy going through the final rites of marriage with the dead girl.

The "Six Rites" are not concerned with one essential feature of modern Chinese marriage: "initiation." The canonical rites keep that event quite distinct, but we know it as an intrinsic part of the rites immediately preceding the transfer of the bride. Each in his own house (usually the night before the day the bride is to be conveyed), the girl has her hair ritually put up, the boy is "capped" or given a courtesy name. By that solemn act the married pair are rendered fit to enter into the conjugal tie of marriage, both having been made ready for the circumscribed emancipation that the transfer of the bride will bring. Once placed side by side and installed in their bedroom (their private quarters), the couple form a unit endowed with its own economic personality and a promise of greater independence to come. It is one of the striking features of Chinese family organization that while a man has little in the way of individual property rights until he eventually takes out his share of the family property on division, when he marries he becomes part of a conjugal property-owning unit endowed with furnishings of the bedroom brought by the bride and paid for to a large extent out of the money earlier passed from the groom's family to the girl's. Within the conjugal unit the bride herself holds as her own property such personal wealth (jewelry and cash, but even sometimes rights to income from land) as she has acquired on her own as a maiden or been presented with by her family and friends. A new family has begun to grow within the bosom of the family that calls it into being.

The "Six Rites" begin with the tentative investigations preceding marriage and emphasize the exchange of genealogical and horoscopic details and the role of the go-between. The data on the two families are required for the proper matching of families of like social status and for determining the position of the boy and girl each in his own family; in real life they may be dispensed with. Horoscopes and go-betweens, on the other hand, are crucial, and we are able to see part of the reason why as soon as we realize what hopes are staked in marriage and what is feared from it. The Chinese say that marriages are made in Heaven, and the horoscopes are examined to discover who has been prematched with whom. Yet we know in fact that they are merely a ritual mechanism for confirming the matches already hit upon, even when the actors are unaware of procuring the supernatural confirmation of what they desire. (See Freedman 1967b [Essay 15 above]: 10–11, and Eberhard 1963.) Heaven must be made to speak, and yet people are bent on realizing the benefit of their careful calculations of social, economic, and political advantage. I think that Eberhard is wrong to suggest (1963: 55) that in this context people do not believe in "fate," the treatment of horoscopes seeming to be "a manipulation which normally is more or less playful or 'ceremonial,' but which can be used to call off marriage talks. . . ." The forms of divination used are far from playful; the belief in fate is, I suggest, genuine. Both the sanction of fate and the achievement of self-interest are sought; they can be reconciled by multiple divinations. The belief in the preordaining of a match (symbolized in the rites by using red threads to tie together documents, candlesticks, and cups) is part of a system of ideas that recognizes the appalling dangers and risks of marriage. As I have put the matter elsewhere (Freedman 1967b [Essay 15 above]: 11), "the doctrine of predestined marriage relieves men of a frightening burden of responsibility. Fate does not force them to a course of action; it helps to reconcile them to its almost inevitable failure." More is hoped for from any marriage in the way of fruitfulness and peace than the system can produce. As for the go-between, whatever else his functions may include in the way of negotiating delicate transactions, if he is a matchmaker he stands as an external agent who can be blamed for disappointments and disasters that follow a marriage.

The main body of rites constituting a wedding segregate the girl from her ordinary life in her natal house, prepare her for the pains and duties of her married life, transfer her in a state of marginality to her new house, and begin the process by which she will be incorporated there. Consider as an illustration some of the data drawn from a study made in Tungkuan, Kwangtung. A month before she is due to leave for her wedding, the girl is confined to one part of the house, where she is accompanied and comforted by girls of about her own age. They sleep with her at night and work with her in the day. "During the night she wails very loudly, and as she wails she cries one by one the names of her parents, her brothers and sisters, paternal uncles and aunts, and similarly close and intimate relatives and friends. The words she uses are like those of a sad song of parting." (Liu Wei-min 1936: 85.) The texts of such songs are given in the source. There are also on record lamentations and songs sung for the girl by her relatives and friends that set out the duties she is about to assume and the tribulations of her new life. (See Frick 1952: 27–28, 33 ff; and see Yang Pi-wang 1963 and Highbaugh 1948: 47–49 for English translations of marriage songs.) The preparation, which in most cases culminates the "initiation" rite of putting up the hair, is both a dour instruction in the domestic and marital discipline to come and a rupture of the relationship between the bride and those among whom she has grown up.

When at last the girl is dispatched to the husband's house we see in action the most complex set of symbols and ritual prescriptions and proscriptions, a very few of which we may note. To reach the sedan chair that awaits her (and which, coming from the other house to fetch her, has perhaps met with opposition and delay), the bride must either be borne out of the house or walk upon the covered ground. Again, when she leaves the sedan chair at her destination her feet must not touch the bare earth—between one house and the other she is, so to speak, in a state of suspense. The journey, a transition at once physical and social, must be lengthy; for this reason, if the two houses are close together (although that is unlikely to be the case in the countryside, since women usually marry out of their own villages), the procession with the sedan chair as its center must take a roundabout route. Sealed inside the chair, which has been inspected before her installation in it to insure its freedom from evil, the bride sits armed with instruments to ward off malign influences and with symbols of peace. The world of humans, spirits, animals, and things is replete with threats to her and her fertility.

Once in her new house, the bride is treated ritually (mirrors are flashed, for example) to cleanse her of the evil adhering to her before she is led for the first time to her bedroom. It is clear that in the period from her dispatch to her reception she has undergone a radical transformation as a person and as a vehicle of social relationships. When her family sends her off she becomes to them an outsider, moving from the status of cherished daughter to that of potential enemy: ritual acts are performed to prevent her taking away any of the prosperity of her natal house, and behind her the doors are shut to insure that its fortune does not follow her. In the new house, by the time she has been stripped of the malignities she may have brought with her and made by rites to express her promise to produce peace, she is on the point of being bonded to her husband by their joint worship of Heaven and Earth, the ancestors of the house, and the Kitchen God.

These religious acts are coupled with the grand feasting and "the disturbance of the room" to form the core of the rites that see the bride wedded and bedded. "The disturbance of the room" calls for some comment. It is the bride's last great public ordeal. She must submit herself to being exhibited in her bedroom in the company of her husband, exposing herself to boisterous and even obscene teasing from all comers, young and old. It is a climax in the rites in which the curtain of domestic discipline is temporarily raised to be decisively dropped forever. For during the rowdy display, and never again, the barriers between young and old are lowered and sexuality is given open expression.

If the rites so far described take place on the same day as the bride's transfer (and this is commonly the case), the next day sees her introduced formally to the seniors among her affines, and she is ritually inducted into her kitchen duties. A few days later, usually on the third day after the main wedding events, the couple go on a formal visit to the bride's natal house, where she is received as a guest. At this point, although further rites in the sequence may be found, we may say that the marriage is completed.

Ritual Aspects of Chinese Kinship and Marriage

This is the barest sketch of a very few points in the sequence, which I now leave in order to explore some of its implications.[3] The rites of marriage demonstrate that the bride's body, fertility, domestic service, and loyalty are handed over by one family to another. To her natal family the loss is severe, both emotionally and economically: a member of the family is turned into a drain on its resources and a potential foe. On the other hand, the natural duty of marrying off a daughter is fulfilled and a bond of affinity is established with members of another family and community, a bond that, even as it leaves the girl's family ritually and socially in a relationship of inferiority with the boy's, provides it with a tie that in some circumstances may be worth exploiting. Economic and political relationships across communities may flow along the channels of affinity. For its part, the boy's family, while acquiring major rights in the girl and potential economic and political benefits parallel to those of the opposite family, must reckon with the possibility that the bride will become a focus of disruption within their own ranks and, never completely severed from her own kin, an occasion for unwanted interference in their affairs by their new affines. The rites presuppose what in reality may be quite untrue: that before "betrothal" the two families are unknown to each other. They emphasize the formality and distance between the families, mediating their relations through go-betweens, heightening their conflicting interests, and segregating them in the main events of the sequence from proposal to completion.

We may read the rites so openly, but they are not to be taken as simple statements capable of being given clear and unambiguous meanings by those who participate in them. Rites, as symbolic affirmations, are the opposite of jural rules. Jural rules rely for their value on their relative clarity; rites derive their strength from their poetic vagueness. Indeed, when the jural rules are themselves lacking in clear definition and are internally contradictory, then the rites exploit them by exaggerating their ambiguities and discrepancies. It seems to me that the Chinese rites of marriage above all stress the ambiguity of affinal relationships. Agnation has its problems, but both in ancestor worship and the rites of marriage clear enough leads are given to its ideal state; it remains for the rites of marriage to dramatize the indecisiveness of affinity.

The contrast between agnation and affinity leaves out of account the *tertium quid* of kinship through women. Yet it is precisely in this third category of relationships that we see at work the struggle between the first two. Affinity has a double aspect: from one point of view it is a bond between groups of agnates; from another, it is a tie between men and their mothers' agnates. As a man sees it, his mother having been incorporated into his family and placed in the company of his ancestors, is a member of his agnatic group; yet to her agnates he is both a kinsman and an affine—they are at once his matrilateral relatives and the group connected to his own by marriage. A man's wife and through her all her kin are his affines, but from the standpoint of the wife herself the relationships into which she was born are transmuted at the time of marriage into ties that take on the color of affinity; she is now a member of a group to which her natal group is linked by her marriage. (For the change made by marriage in a woman's mourning duties for her own kin, see Freedman 1958: 101.) It is in this ambivalence that we can detect uncertainties in the required behavior between affines and the playing out of the ambiguities in the rites of marriage.

The rites pose a problem and leave it unresolved. How is a woman to reconcile her duties as wife and daughter-in-law with those she has as sister and daughter? How are a group of agnates to reconcile their independence with the need to form ties by marriage? The bride's solemn send-off from her natal house is not a complete termination of her filial and sibling ties, for the rites also establish her as a married daughter with claims on her parents and brothers. (See Freedman 1967b [Essay 15 above]: 23.) Her family retains an interest in her well-being, most dramatically stated in the rites at the end of her life, when her brothers arrive to insure that her death is natural and that her funeral is lavish enough to reflect their own standing. (See Freedman 1967b: 22.) These interfering men are affines to the bereaved family, and yet they are also mother's brothers, in which role they are affectionate protectors of their sororal nephews and often sought by them to act as mediators among themselves. They also occupy a chief place in the marriage rites, appearing in the rites performed in the bride's house and in the groom's; in the latter the maternal uncle is given the seat of honor at the feast. But the ritual involvement of ties through women does not end there, for the bride's younger brother (a mother's brother in the making) is usually given some special role to perform in the house to which the bride travels. (See Freedman 1967b: 21–22.) Groom's mother's brother and bride's brother are ritual evidence of the non-agnatic links forged by a family in two generations—kindly matrilateral kinsmen on the one side, and troublemaking affines on the other.

This account of the marriage rites touches on the main line of the "argument" that runs through them; it ignores almost totally the rich symbolism—in word, action, and object—of which each significant step in the unfolding of the rites is composed. These symbols are of course not only related among themselves to form the "argument," but are each part of wider fields of symbolic discourse in Chinese culture. In the last analysis, then, we cannot fully understand what goes on at a Chinese wedding until we have studied all the realms of symbolic meaning that bring their significance to this one set of rites. Once again we have to end one study by saying that it is merely the beginning of another.

Ancestor Worship: Two Facets of the Chinese Case

The Chinese, for example, keep their clan and lineage interests, and also maintain their moral emphasis on the fate of the
soul by operating spirit homes in terms of ancestral temples
and spirit kingdoms—but with a multiple soul concept.

—*Firth 1955: 45*

Tablets and Graves

In the Chinese cult of the ancestors the personality of the dead is divided,
or better, multiplied in such a way that a man or woman may be worshiped for all time as an ancestor and yet undergo the experience of divine judgment and rebirth. Dead ancestors rely for their perennity on the
ritual memory of their descendants. Consequently, their number is constantly being reduced. They are given a place in the community of the
living by being located in wooden tablets and tended in shrines which
belong to domestic families and to lineages and their segments. At the
same time, they are given earthly abodes in their graves, where again they
are cared for by their agnatic descendants. In shrine and tomb the ancestors are allotted a continuing role in the lives of their issue. But, like all
men and women, ancestors at death are ushered through an underworld
from which, once they have accounted for their lives and been helped by
the prayers and sacrifices of their kin on earth, they pass on by reincarnation to a world of anonymity. (The exceptionally fortunate are sent to the
Western Paradise, the outstandingly miserable to the terrible suffering of
an inferno.) The screen of anonymity may be pierced soon after death to
allow the living a glimpse of the new identity of their late kinsman, but
it is an identity that has no direct connection with them and in which they

In Maurice Freedman, ed., *Social Organization: Essays Presented to Raymond Firth*
(London, 1967), 85–103.

will take no continuing interest. In this division of mortal fate we find our first important distinction. The morality of the individual life leads to the rapid extinction of the social personality. A chain of lives connects a man with his past and his future, but his kinsmen in one incarnation quickly lose sight of him as he slides over the horizon to his next. The social personality of the ancestor lives on because it is grounded, not in individual morality, but in the perpetual bond between men and their respected forebears.[1]

To be in the shrine, the grave, and (for a while) in the underworld, and to be treated ritually in all three places, a dead man must have three souls. They are provided in the analysis of the human personality into three *hun* and seven *p'o*. (But it is not necessary that this "theology" be present in the minds of all worshipers. From their point of view, there are three contexts in which the honored dead are approached, and it does not follow that the different contexts will be severally associated with defined metaphysical entities.) The *p'o* are *yin*; they emanate from and return to earth. If they form a continuing personality, it is *kuei* ("devil" or "ghost," as it is usually translated in the Western literature). The *hun* are *yang*, heavenly in their connections; they form *shen*. So that for his descendants a dead man is *shen* and offers three *hun* for their ritual attention. To people other than his descendants he may be *kuei*; and it is possible for me to speak of other people's ancestors as their *kuei*, but mine are *shen*. The dualism of *yang* and *yin* separates an ancestor as *shen* from a ghost as *kuei*; and an ancestor as he lives on in the shrine is unambiguously *yang*. Yet as he survives in his grave he is at one with earth, and it follows that he partakes of the nature of *yin*. *Yin-yang* makes a primary distinction between ghosts and ancestors; it goes on to discriminate between two aspects of one ancestor: his status in the tomb and his status in the shrine.

Ancestors in their shrines are attached to tablets. (Their *hun* are placed there by the rite of "dotting" which establishes the relationship between the tablet and the soul for which it stands. As a result, only one domestic tablet can exist for one person. But, as we shall see, independent worship before substitutes can be performed by people no longer members of the house where the tablets of their immediate ancestors are kept.) The ancestors are tended, reverenced, and fed. The living acknowledge them as their superiors, owing them a debt for their lives and the goodness of those lives; for the ancestors not only engendered their offspring but also now endow their descendants with the merit they themselves accumulated. In a very general sense the ancestors collectively embody the dignity and the authority of the groups over which they preside. Their due is gratitude and praise. And in paying them their due, the living are made conscious of their membership of the groups within which they worship.

The smallest of these groups is the domestic family, the largest, a higher-order lineage (Freedman 1966: 21ff) that may have a population of tens of thousands.[a] In the family the ancestors tended are rarely more than four generations distant from the living head; in a lineage the first ancestor may be forty generations away. In a finely segmented lineage, an individual (although not all individuals equally, given the uneven character of the segmentation—see Freedman 1958: 49–50, and Freedman 1966: 37ff) may be a member of a rising hierarchy of ancestor-worshiping groups, each with its own rites and sacrifices.

Something of the same sort may be said about the worship of ancestors in their tombs. Here too offerings are made and ancestors preside over groups of agnates worshiping together. But the ambiguity of the buried ancestor (as distinct from the ancestor in his tablet) enters at this point: he is not only a soul, discarnate and awesome, but also a corpse—*yin*. As a set of bones, an ancestor is no longer in command of his descendants; he is at their disposal. They no longer worship him; he serves their purposes. We have arrived at the subject of *feng-shui*. We shall see that it is, as it were, the reverse of ancestor worship.

Geomancy (for by an unfortunate convention *feng-shui* is translated so) delivers a man's ancestors into his hands. He may determine his own fortune by siting one or more of his ancestral graves in such a way that the geomantic influences (the "winds and waters") of the landscape are channeled through the bones of the ancestors to their agnatic descendants. (Cf. Freedman 1966: 118ff.) By geomancy a Chinese may seek riches and success for himself in order to outpace his agnates; he can do so by choosing ancestral graves that will give him the smallest number of fellow descendants with whom to share the benefit induced, and by procuring (through a geomancer) that the siting and orienting of the graves favor him among the descendants. It is for this reason that brothers will often wrangle long among themselves over the siting of their father's or mother's grave, each one seeking to ensure his private success at the expense of the others. Where *feng-shui* is carried to its highest degree of development (as appears to be the case in southeastern China), bones may be exhumed and reburied in the pursuit of good fortune. In all this

[a] On the other hand, domestic ancestor worship is not so unambiguously a form of group worship as is the ancestor worship by lineages and their segments. The ritual focus *par excellence* of a family as a domestic entity is the Kitchen God. Every family has its own hearth, and consequently a separate identity in the worship of that god. In ancestor worship, however, the members of two or more families may worship at the same tablets; units resulting from a recent division of a family may continue to pay their devotions to the ancestors represented in the altar retained by one of them. In domestic ancestor worship the relations between the dead and the living are more personal and individual than in the worship performed in ancestral halls.

seeking after riches, progeny, and success by the manipulation of their remains, the dead are virtually passive. They transmit the virtues of a site to their descendants, but they cannot initiate the flow of benefits or block it off. They may be dissatisfied with their position and uncomfortable in their graves; and so being ill at ease they may interfere with the process set going by geomantic technique; but, with the necessary readjustments made, they must continue to act as the channels through which their descendants seek to tap the benefits of their burial sites.

By geomancy, then, men use their ancestors as media for the attainment of worldly desires. And in doing so they have ceased to worship them and begun to use them as things. The authority implied in descent is ritualized in the worship of ancestors. In geomancy the tables are turned: descendants strive to force their ancestors to convey good fortune, making puppets of forebears and dominating the dominators. In ancestor worship, the ancestors are revered; in *feng-shui* they are subordinated. In the former, the ideal ties between the generations are reinforced; in the latter they are denied. In the first, men are brought together to underline their common group membership and solidarity; in the second, they seek to differentiate themselves one from another, each individualizing his fate within the common fate procured by the ancestors as *yang*.

The geomancy of graves is part of a large system of ideas and practices in which topography and man are made to interact. The Chinese have elaborated for all sorts of constructions (houses, government offices, villages, cities, and so on, as well as graves) a theory and set of practices which rest on the idea that men are, so to say, members of the universe. They do not walk the world as intruders. Changes made in the landscape are not (as we should say) simply modifications of nature; they are changes of man-in-the-world. As an important part of Chinese culture, *feng-shui* has gone where that culture has gone. We find it everywhere in China and in three great independent centers of the sinicized world: Japan, Korea, and Vietnam. Yet the distinction that the Chinese themselves make between the geomancy of *yang* (buildings for the living) and that of *yin* (graves) is at once relevant to the fashion in which *feng-shui* has spread. For while within the greater "Chinese" world we can everywhere find the geomancy of buildings, we do not always see that of graves. The geomancy of graves is present in Korea (see Osgood 1951: 149, 244) and Vietnam (Hickey 1964: 40), but not in Japan.[b] It is general in China it-

[b] Professor Smith told me what to read on geomancy in Japan. It is of course impossible for somebody who must confine himself to the Western literature on that country to get a clear picture of so complex an issue as geomancy; but I think I am right in asserting that the geomancy of graves does not appear in Japan. It is a matter of great interest to me

self, but not everywhere of equal importance. We may well suspect that the distribution is not accidental. Japan appears to supply the clue.

We might argue at great length about the precise nature of patriliny in Japan, but it is at least clear that we cannot find there the kind of agnatic descent system that we associate with China and which we can see also in Korea and Vietnam (cf. Nakane 1967). The Japanese kinship system, in which subordinate houses may be linked to main houses, not necessarily through agnatic ties, does not produce a regular hierarchy of agnatic ancestors marking out a hierarchy of nesting segments (cf. Nakane 1967: 105ff). Moreover, within China itself there is, I suggest (this must be stated as a hypothesis, not a fact, because the relevant ethnography has not yet been combed), a relation between the elaborateness of the geomancy of graves and the elaborateness of lineage structure. Deep and complex lineage organization is by no means universal in China, and it is probably no accident that in the southeastern part of the country (principally the two provinces of Fukien and Kwangtung) both lineages and the *feng-shui* of the tomb have been carried to extreme forms of development. Where (we may suggest) the authority of the past generations, as represented in the cult of the ancestors, weighs heaviest, there men redress the balance by recourse to the geomancy of the tomb. They take a kind of geomantic revenge, using as things what are otherwise symbols of autonomous virtue. As *yang* the ancestors are revered, as *yin* manipulated. Doubtless, in any system of ancestor worship, the ancestors honored must also be resented. In the Chinese case, men are conscious of deriving benefits both from ancestors in their shrines (through their merits and their blessings) and from ancestors as bones. They are free agents when they seek to use the *feng-shui* of graves, and can sometimes allow themselves to be cynical about their ancestors as *yang*. A French missionary working in Shun Te, Kwangtung, in the early 1930's, quotes a local saying: "Que la tombe soit bien orientée, que le vent du bonheur soit favorable. A quoi bon le culte rendu aux morts? Si la tombe est mal orientée, à quoi bon les vénérer?" (Fabre 1935: 132).[2]

---

that Plath (1964) in a paper on Japanese domestic ancestor worship says that when misfortune occurs "the usual first line of appeal is to geomancy: something is suspected to be wrong about the physical structure of the house itself" (p. 310). He then gives an informant's statement which speaks of the geomantic alterations carried out to a house, and adds in a note (p. 314 n. 12) that we "stand in need of a study of the social correlates of geomancy." May I, as an outsider to Japanese studies, raise the problem (which occurs to me as I read what little is readily available) of why the latrine is so important in Japanese geomancy? See Plath 1964: 314 and Dore 1958: 368. In commenting on this question, Professor Smith suggests that I had better ask "Why the latrine and the kitchen?," since both are considered "dirty" and therefore ideal entrances for evil. The kitchen of a Japanese house is its only dirt-floored room.

Benign Ancestors

Ancestors are worshiped in many different kinds of society, and we shall find the cult wider or more narrowly spread according to the meaning we give to the word "worship." And even if we start from the Chinese case, taking the tendance of forebears and their continuing interest in the affairs of their descendants as the basis of a definition, we shall be dealing with a very heterogeneous collection of societies. In some societies the ancestors worshiped serve as foci of determinate units constructed on a principle of unilineal descent. This is in fact the kind of ancestor worship that has traditionally captured the imagination and retained the interest of anthropologists. Radcliffe-Brown's exposition of this form (it will be recalled that he touched on the cases of ancient Greece and Rome—following Fustel de Coulanges—China, the Bakongo, and the Nayar) is the *locus classicus* (Radcliffe-Brown 1952b: 162ff). It is important to remember that Radcliffe-Brown defined ancestor worship in such a way as to limit the use of the term to those societies in which "the cult group . . . consists solely of persons related to one another by descent in one line from the same ancestor or ancestors" (p. 163). It is therefore unreasonable to object to his argument, as Evans-Pritchard has done (1965: 24), that "there are many societies with ancestor cults without a trace of a lineage system." By Radcliffe-Brown's definition such a cult would not fall within the range of the discussion.

It is now common ground among anthropologists (*pace* Evans-Pritchard) that there is a "fit" between a cult of ancestors and a system of unilineal descent groups. Professor Evans-Pritchard's colleague, Dr. Beattie, puts it fairly: "Societies which attach high value to unilineal descent . . . often have an ancestral cult" (Beattie 1964: 225–26). It does not follow that we should be surprised to find systems of ancestor worship in societies with non-unilineal systems of kinship or that we should be alarmed by not finding them in the kinds of society to which Radcliffe-Brown limited his argument. It may well be that we shall never get to the point of understanding why only some unilineally constituted kinship systems display cults of ancestors. Indeed, it may be pressing functionalist arguments too far to suggest that we ought ideally to be able to account over the globe for the presence of such a cult in some "suitable" societies and its absence from other such societies. But where the cult is found in a system of descent groups, there is surely no difficulty in seeing the appropriateness of a religion in which, either collectively or individually, as the case may be, ancestors stand at the center of the attention of the people descended from them. Every agnatically constituted unit in China stands out as a religious congregation worshiping its common forebears. Every lineage has its ancestral hall or shrine; in the most elaborate halls the rows of tablets on the altar and the honor boards hanging from beams and walls are a triumphant and awe-inspiring display of success. Every segment of a lineage has a hall or at least the tomb of a focal ancestor at which rites comparable to those in the main hall are performed. But the point hardly needs stressing; it has been so well treated in the context of other societies (cf. Fortes 1965: 123) that we can afford to pass on to a different aspect of ancestor worship.

Radcliffe-Brown's approach turned attention to ancestors as foci. In recent years (principally as a result of Fortes's work on the Tallensi) anthropologists have been studying the ritual aspect of the relationship between men and their proximate ancestors. In other words, they have been asking questions about the roles of ancestors among the people with whom they were once linked in life. In a first attempt to deal with this matter among the Chinese (Freedman 1957a: 218ff, and Freedman 1958: 84) I spoke of "memorialism"; more recently, trying to give a name to the thing that must be distinguished from the cult of descent group ancestors, I have written about the cult of immediate jural superiors (Freedman 1966: 144ff)—certainly an inelegant form of words, but I can think of no other. The two cults do not necessarily go together, since the latter can exist without the former. (In my earlier discussion on the point I instanced the case of the Manus.) But whether in isolation or in conjunction with a cult of descent group ancestors, the cult of immediate jural superiors raises some highly interesting questions about the relationship between domestic authority and the attitudes maintained to recently dead superiors.

The matter on which I think it profitable to concentrate is the general character of the intervention of which the ancestors are considered capable. Reading the general ethnography one may be struck not simply by the harshness of the behavior of ancestors but, more important, by its capriciousness. In very broad terms, we may say that it seems as though authority, once raised to the plane of the afterlife, is loosed of its fetters and may lash out at unfortunate mortals, even when their wrong-doing has been negligible or nonexistent.[c] Consider, as an example from the copious African data, the case of the Lovedu, as set out by the Kriges (Krige and Krige 1954: 63):

[c] On this point I find that what Fortes writes in the paper already cited leaves me somewhat puzzled. He says (1965: 135) that the "ancestors persecute in the etymological sense of persistently following and harrying their descendants; they do not punish for wickedness or reward for virtues, as these are defined by human standards. . . ." Yet on the next page he says: "In short, the persecuting ancestor is not a supernatural being capriciously punish-

Ancestors are capricious: their complaints . . . are usually about being neglected; but they may cause illness to those they most love in order to receive recognition, have their name perpetuated, or their beads worn. They are said to "hold" the woman experiencing difficult labour, to afflict children with sore eyes, and even to prevent the queen from making rain. Their complaints need imply no omission or neglect on the part of the afflicted descendant, but merely some special desire that could not have been anticipated.

Yet not all societies in which ancestors are worshiped credit dead fore-bears with behavior of this sort. The Chinese do not. In order to avoid going over ground I have covered before (Freedman 1958: 88–89, and Freedman 1966: 151), let me summarize what in my view is the charac-teristic behavior imputed to Chinese ancestors. While they will certainly punish their descendants if they suffer neglect or are offended by an act or omission which affects them directly (chiefly, the failure to secure for them a firm line of descent), they are essentially benign and considerate of their issue. Before taking action against their descendants they need to be provoked; capricious behavior is certainly alien to their benevolent and protective nature. (It may be worth adding, since I have referred to the Lovedu case, that the ancestors of the latter people also appear to be unconcerned about the general moral conduct of their descendants; but in respect of the personal offenses against themselves they are harsh in their reaction, while in general, as we have seen, their behavior is capri-cious—Krige and Krige 1954: 79.)

Now, it is possible to treat the problem (for such I take it to be) of the benign Chinese ancestor in different ways. From one point of view, and coming back to the question of authority, we may ask whether Chi-nese ancestors are kindly because, in making them ancestors, their de-scendants are not conscious of having displaced them from coveted posi-tions of power. The weight of the ethnographic evidence on ancestor worship seems to be in favor of the hypothesis that, by being displaced, a man-become-ancestor is thought at once to resent his successor and to endow that successor with the authority to rule in his place. Everything, then, turns on there being a man with domestic authority who, so to say,

---

ing wrong-doing or rewarding virtue. He is rather to be thought of as an ultimate judge and mentor whose vigilance is directed towards restoring order and discipline in compliance with the norms of right and duty, amity and piety, whenever transgressions threaten or occur. When misfortune occurs and is interpreted as a punitive, or to be more exact, cor-rective intervention by the ancestors, they are believed to have acted rightfully, not wan-tonly." In a society where many misfortunes are attributed to ancestral intervention, it must be difficult for men to avoid considering some of the behavior of their dead forebears as capricious. Doubtless, in a general and theoretical way ancestral conduct as a whole may be thought to be based on some underlying principle, but from an individual's point of view what his ancestor does to him must surely sometimes appear arbitrary.

has snatched it from the recently dead and who now reigns by virtue of that succession. At first sight it might well appear as though the Chinese case met these conditions. Is not the *chia-chang* (the family head) a powerful patriarch who yields his office only by dying? But the reality of the nature and the transfer of power in the Chinese family is different.

It is necessary, in the first place, to consider the constitution of the Chinese family and the place of primogeniture in it. An assumption is built into the official Chinese view of society that a family perpetuates itself through all time by means of the succession of the oldest son to the position of the father. There was a period in fact when primogeniture was a fully fledged institution in China: in the Chou dynasty (eleventh to third centuries B.C.). In noble families (we know little about the ordinary people) the oldest son stepped into his father's shoes to hold his property rights and exercise his authority. But when the "feudal" system of ancient China was superseded by the centralized state, the principle of equal inheritance among sons became established alongside the principle (essentially ritual, as we shall see) that the oldest son was to succeed his father. So that for the last two millennia there has existed in China a family system in which two apparently conflicting principles have been at work. From one point of view, the family can be seen as a corporation which passes down a senior line of descent; the oldest son succeeds his father, taking charge of the domestic stock of ancestor tablets, enjoying a prior right to the main part of the physical house, and, in this connection, often benefiting from the allocation to him of a share in the family property over and above that which is his due as one among several sons. The special position of his continuer of the main line of descent is ritually underlined by his unique role in the mourning for his parents and for his paternal grandfather if his father is already dead.

From another angle (and this the more realistic), the Chinese family is a property-owning estate which dissolves on the death of each senior generation to reform into successor-estates, none of which can be said to have the identity inhering in its predecessor. As each son is born (or adopted) he is automatically endowed with a potential share in the family estate. That estate is under the control of the *chia-chang*, and no son can realize his share against the opposition of living parents. But as soon as they are dead, the partible estate is divided, the family segmenting into new units which are residentially (they may partition the old dwelling or set up new quarters), economically, and ritually distinct. The new units may continue for some time to maintain a common ancestral shrine (which is in the keeping of the oldest son), but, since each is now endowed with a separate hearth, it is at liberty to establish its own shrine by setting up a board on which are inscribed the names of the ancestors individually represented in the original shrine by the several wooden tablets.

The so-called "joint" family (cf. Freedman 1966: 49 on the inappropriateness of the term) has a short life. If its head dies leaving a married and an unmarried son, they will continue to form one family until such time as the junior, now married, asserts his separate rights. (A *chia-chang* is privileged to prevent his own son taking out his share, but he cannot exercise a similar right vis-à-vis his brother or brother's sons.) Married brothers rarely continue in one family once the mourning period for their parents is over. The ritual precedence of the oldest son does not confer on him the authority to control his younger brothers, and indeed, the fragility of the fraternal bond in Chinese society is such that domestic harmony is improbable in the absence of the senior generation. Every new marriage inserts into the family a potential point of segmentation; a married son is potentially the head of the new *fang* (a term which, at all levels of the descent system, can be translated as segment), and he is not dissuaded from asserting his status as an independent *chia-chang* merely by reason of the ritually emphasized position of his oldest brother.

It follows that no one son can step effectively into his father's shoes to exercise authority over the same range of people. But there is more to it than that. Even during his life, a father as *chia-chang* may need to shed his authority—and sometimes well in advance of his death. If he fails (because of sickness, senility, or sheer incompetence) to maintain his position as ruler of his household, then he has in a way anticipated his death, and in handing over his authority to his oldest son he is likely to provoke the split which ideally should wait upon his being gathered to his ancestors.

The death of their father (or, more accurately, the end of the mourning period of the second parent to die) is the point at which most sons come fully into their inheritance. But they may, in reality, have advanced to their status as men well before that time. Marriage sets a man up as a mature human being; on his begetting a son he is unambiguously come to the fullness of life. And it is of the greatest significance that every Chinese father tries his best to marry off his sons as early as he possibly can. He does not see his married sons as a threat to his position. They, for their part, do not look upon him as a serious barrier to the attainment of their economic and ritual maturity. There is, in fact, a more gradual transfer of authority and a greater dispersion of it than is suggested by the rule of ritual primogeniture and the law which makes it an offense for men to take out their shares of family property against the wishes of their seniors by generation in the house.

Once installed as an ancestor in his tablet, a father does not in any precise sense support the authority of his sons over their juniors. He is wor-shiped (by acts of reverence and offerings of incense and food) but cannot be used as a major instrument of domestic discipline. True, he symbolizes ancestral authority and the honor of the family; and wayward juniors can be shamed before him. But there are no terrible ancestral sanctions that a *chia-chang* intent on maintaining his authority can call down on the people under his hand. No son effectively replaces his dead father; that father, now promoted to *shen*, cannot channel his supernatural authority through a true successor.

We have seen that the ritual primogeniture of modern China rests his-torically on the true primogeniture of a much older phase of Chinese society. It is extremely difficult to see, through the classical sources on this period, what view was taken by the ancients of their ancestors. Con-fucian orthodoxy (we may assume) has masked for us the nature of dead ancestral beings, for it tends markedly to set aside speculation about the world of the spirits. But consider the contrast between what we know to be the modern state of affairs and the kind of attitude implied in the fol-lowing statement in a text, supposedly of the first century A.D., which purports to be an official discussion of the Classics. In the section on marriage the *Po Hu T'ung* speaks of the sadness not only of the bride leaving her parental house (which could, of course, be paralleled from modern China) but also of the terrible significance of marriage for the groom's family. According to the *Li* ("rites"), the bride's family brood over their coming separation from their daughter. "'In the family of the man who takes the wife no music is made during three days: they think [of the fact that the son is going to] succeed his father.' They feel sad at [the thought that] the father has grown feeble and old in the course of years and that [the time of his] being replaced [by the son] has arrived. The *Li* says: 'The wedding is not [a case] for congratulations; it is [a case of] generations succeeding each other.'" And when the father sends off his son to meet his bride, he tells him to go that "thou mayst succeed me in the sacrifices to the ancestral temple" (Tjan 1949: 249). To realize the full implication of the text we need to know that the *Li* prescribes thirty as the age of marriage for men (p. 245); it is the very reverse of the modern situation in which men are to be married young and in joy.

We may well suspect that the aristocratic institutions of ancient China produced an array of stern and disciplinary ancestors. And (while I cer-tainly lack the scholarship to document such an assertion) I think it likely that over the course of Chinese history, the worship of ancestors in their shrines has been gradually overtaken by the attention paid to ancestral graves. This, indeed, appears to be Granet's conclusion in a remarkable passage in which (without mentioning the term) he relates the growth of *feng-shui* to a decline in the importance of the cult centering on the ancestral tablets. With the rise of imperial China, he writes, the cult of the ancestors assumed a new character: "it was a moral cult, completely symbolic, quite abstract"; whereas among the "feudal" nobility there had been an intimate and emotionally charged communion with the ancestors. And from the official point of view, at least, the cult became formalized, the ancestors being kept at a distance from their worshipers. Graves and funerals began to be elaborate.

More veneration was given to the tomb, public monument of filial piety, and less to the tablet, abstract centre of a completely domestic cult. The cult of the Ancestors tended to become a cult of tombs. In that, it once more moved nearer to the agrarian cults. Situated in a favourable landscape, arranged in a fashion to capture the influx of the sacred forces of Nature, visited and propitiated at the time of spring, the tombs transmitted to the living the good influences that had just been concretized in the bodies of the Ancestors. The Ancestral cult had only a symbolic and moral efficacy. ... The virtue of the graves and that of the bones were used for magic. ... What piety asked of the Ancestral tombs was never private favours but protection extended to the whole family. The religion of tombs kept up more concrete sentiments than the tablets could.[3]

There are two further aspects of this evolution. The noble cult of the ancestors in "feudal" times was tightly bound up with proximate forebears; the communion with the dead from whom authority immediately derived was intense. When ancestor worship became generalized in Chinese society, the elaborate hierarchies of tablets in halls entailed a distancing between the worshiper and the great host of his ancestors; and their comparative remoteness may perhaps have influenced domestic worship to make it a less personal and intimate traffic with the dead. In the second place, I think it could be argued that, as the domestic cult of the ancestors became popularized, it tended to be relegated in effect to the women of the house, the men concentrating their attention on the more recent dead in their tombs and the remote dead in the halls. When I studied Overseas Chinese in Singapore (many of them of very recent immigration from China) I was struck by the extent to which domestic worship was left in the hands of women, the adult men taking very little interest in it (Freedman 1957a: 45, 220). And in the fascinating paper by Fabre, to which I have already referred, we read that domestic ancestor worship is carried out by the women of the house, "en droit par la mère de famille, la belle-mère, parfois par l'une des brus. Mieux que les hommes, elles s'entendent à adresser leurs pétitions aux défunts, à leur exposer les besoins d'un mari, des enfants, de toute la famille. L'homme se désintéresse: il n'a un rôle actif dans les offrandes que lors de la fête du génie de l'âtre [the Kitchen God, as he is usually called in English].

... Il se dédommage enfin au temple des ancêtres et aux tombeaux" (Fabre 1935: 121).[4] Chinese women are transferred on marriage to the shadow of their husbands' ancestors; so much do these ancestors become their own that they assume the main responsibility for their tendance.

But they may do more than that. It is possible to argue that women are the main (perhaps sometimes the sole) means for bringing into play such hostile activity as is attributed to ancestors. The benignity of forebears springs from the relations to them of men; it may be that married women, standing in a different relation to these forebears, tend to perceive them as potentially hostile. And we may find on closer study that when, as sometimes happens, ancestors are credited with punitive behavior, the attribution of this behavior has been made by the women of the house. In Chinese domestic life married women are seen by men to be the ultimate source of trouble (cf. Freedman, 1958: 21–22; 1966: 46, 55–56); perhaps these women take their revenge on occasion by converting the kindly ancestors of their husbands into the originators of misfortune.

For modern China, then, we may argue that ancestors are kindly, at least from the point of view of men, because, in the absence of a corporate family, in the turnover of the generations a new head does not effectively displace his predecessor. But lest we imagine that the matter is quite as simple as that, we ought to glance at the comparative evidence from Japan. In that country too (and perhaps even more so than in China) the ancestors are benign. And yet in Japanese society the family is ideally a perpetual unit, each head of family being replaced by a single successor. The successor is not necessarily the oldest son; indeed, he may well be an adopted son (*yōshi*) or an adopted bridegroom (*muko-yōshi*). All sons failing to secure the succession must become members of other corporations or start their own. It might seem as though the situation were well designed to produce disciplinary ancestors. But: "So strong is the feeling that the household dead are friendly and supportive, that antagonism is not easily verbalized and must be glimpsed obliquely" (Plath 1964: 310).[5] In fact, the key to the benignity of the Japanese ancestors may lie in the manner in which the succession to family headship is effected. Ideally, succession should precede the death of the senior male in the family in order that he may, along with his wife, enjoy a period of retirement before he joins his ancestors (Plath 1964: 306, Dore 1958: 10). One recent writer puts the relevant points very succinctly: "Succession ... or retirement ... [is] ceremoniously observed when a successor's father reaches the age of sixty or when the successor's first son is born, at least in northern Japan, but becoming a gradual process there as elsewhere without the performance of ritual. The eldest (or chosen) son succeeds to leadership and, traditionally, supreme status in the household . . . , while the former house head attains the status of grandfather . . . or retired person . . . relieved of major responsibility." (Beardsley 1965: 110. And cf. Nakane 1967: 4, 16ff.) In other words, as in the Chinese case (but not now because the family is dispersed among a number of heirs), the death of one generation and the coming to majority of the next are not coincident events. There has been a transfer of authority *inter vivos*. One steps into a live man's shoes. I wish it were possible for me to pursue the inquiry within the same contexts as are necessary for the comparative study of geomancy; but I do not have at my command the necessary data on succession and attitudes to ancestors for Vietnam and Korea.

This is one possible approach to the problem posed. Another approach requires a broadening of the sociological framework. Can it be that Chinese and Japanese ancestors are typcially benign because their societies are highly differentiated? It seems to be characteristic of small-scale societies (in which individuals are bound together in complex webs of relationships) that evil and misfortune are seen to be embedded in personal ties. The things men fear—sickness, death, and barrenness of land, women, and beasts—tend to be ascribed to the actions or evil impulses of people with whom the sufferers are intimately connected. And it is along such lines that many anthropologists nowadays discuss the significance of witchcraft accusations and sorcery. (Cf. Gluckman 1965: esp. 242ff and Mair 1963: 160ff.) Of course, it may seem odd to put ancestor worship into the same class as witchcraft and sorcery, since it is the living human being who is thought to practice black arts or project evil, and a dead man who is said to inflict ancestral punishment. But we need to consider by what mechanisms the ancestors are able to affect their living descendants.

An ancestor may take punitive action either because he is invoked or on his own initiative. In the former case, the man who invokes him is calling down an ancestral sanction against the people over whom he himself has control. (And, as we have seen, no man in China derives his power from ancestors in such a fashion.) In the latter case, the punitive action taken by the ancestor is first a misfortune of which the cause is unknown and is then laid at the ancestor's door. Its origin must be divined, and the process of divining again asserts the relevance of relationships between persons closely linked, for the diagnosis must say that the afflicted man has misbehaved or failed in his duty either toward some kinsman or neighbor or toward the punishing ancestor himself. (The ancestor, though dead, is a person with rights and duties.) That witch-craft and ancestor worship can be seen to belong to the same religious universe is brought out vividly in Middleton's data on the Lugbara: here witchcraft is the unjustified calling down of the same evil that lineage elders can summon legitimately by an appeal to the ancestors. Lugbara use the same word for the "indignation" of the witch and that of the elder. Whether a particular case of misfortune caused by an elder is to be attributed to his witchcraft or to his invocation of the ancestors de-pends on the relationship to him of the interpreters: if the elder's au-thority is recognized he has invoked the ancestors; otherwise he is a witch (Middleton 1960: 34ff, 153, 225–26).

Chinese society does not in any marked way predispose its members to seek explanations for their misfortunes in the evil thoughts and mysti-cal malpractices of their kinsmen and neighbors. There are perhaps pro-fessional sorcerers, and sorcery is said sometimes to be practiced by ordi-nary people. (Cf. Groot 1907, pt. 3.) Accusations are sometimes made that one man or group has harmed another's *feng-shui*; and certainly brothers may quarrel because each is striving to promote his success by geomancy at the expense of the others. But the dominant mode of expla-nation is impersonal: misfortune is either the bitter reward for miscon-duct (in this or a previous incarnation) or the effect of some nonhuman power or entity undirected by men on earth. Except that the ancestors may in exceptional circumstances hit out at their descendants and in a very vague and general way be responsible for the ups and downs of their fortune, they are not automatically turned to when personal mis-chance must be explained. One may well divine the ancestors' satisfac-tion with the sacrifices made to them, but there is otherwise little attempt to make communication flow from them to men. It is instructive, in this connection, to consider the Chinese use of spirit-mediumship.

In the major form of spirit-mediumship clients bring their troubles to a medium (usually male) who, in a public or semipublic performance, provides advice and cures by speaking with the voice of a deity. It would appear that it is extremely rare for ancestors to be in question in such consultations. (Cf. Elliott 1955: 160–61.) On the other hand, communi-cation with the dead is the *raison d'être* of the minor form of spirit-mediumship. So far as the evidence on southeastern China goes, at any rate, in strictly private séances female mediums search out the dead in the underworld in order to bring them to speak with their clients. The most significant aspect of these séances, from the point of view of the present inquiry, is that not only are some of the souls raised those of kinsmen who are not ancestors, but all the souls brought to the séance belong to the recently dead. That is to say, if ancestors are contacted then they are conversing with their descendants in the short period between their death and the time when, having passed out of the underworld, they will be accessible to the living only in their tablets and graves.

The relatives who seek in this manner to communicate with their dead are concerned primarily to assure themselves that the dead in this phase of their other-world existence lack for nothing that the living can provide. Yet they may bring problems with them that are elicited in the course of the séance. Elliott's study of the subject is the best observed available, and although it was conducted in Singapore, I think we may safely assume that, in this regard at least, it reproduces what happens in southeastern China. He writes: "Some of the more susceptible members ask the ghost about particular problems that are worrying them. Some of these problems may involve personal antagonisms within the family or questions of rights to property. In each case the ghost gives a judgment which must be observed by those who hear it" (*ibid.*: 138–39). But, more important, there is a poignant passage in Elliott's account in which he tells us how, by gaining admission to a séance of this sort (no mean feat of fieldwork, as I can testify from my own experience),[d] he came to realize why séances are held in the strictest secrecy and seclusion. "A skilful soul raiser is capable of laying bare many of the skeletons in a family's cupboard and bringing to light some of the personal animosities of which an outsider might well remain ignorant" (*ibid.*: 136). A consultation with the recently dead may be allowed to bring out for their advice and adjudication the problems of the families they have left behind, but it is significant that there is no institution for continuing the conversation. Once the dead have gone from the underworld they are no longer capable of being invited to intervene so decisively in the affairs of the living.[e] It is as though Chinese society protected itself against too great an inter-

[d] And cf. Giles 1879: 244–45, where, referring to "dark séances," he says that he found it impossible to gain access to one, for, apart from anything else, such séances are almost, if not entirely, confined to women. Giles did not experience a similar difficulty in seeing other kinds of divination practiced. His account appears to be about Amoy.

[e] Cf. the account of the same institution given by de Groot (1886: 295–99, and 1910a: 1332ff). It is worth noting that de Groot (1910a: 1333) says that the séances are often held in "the private female rooms" of the house in order to exclude men. "Scepticism exercises an obstructive effect in spiritualism, and of scepticism menfolk are the only representatives." Another reference to this kind of séance in southeastern China is to be found in Kulp 1925: 288. Osgood (1963: 316–17) presents some comparable data for Yunnan, but Hsu (1948: 167ff), writing of sinicized Min Chia in that province, describes a very different kind of séance, which takes place in a temple. The séance is usually held within the mourning period of the person about whom the inquiry is to be made. It will be seen from the responses recorded by Hsu at pp. 173ff that only the vaguest information is given about the fate of the dead, and the dead are not consulted about the affairs of the living.

ference by the dead in the relations between kinsmen. And it would seem that it falls mainly to women to exploit what little opportunity there is to bring the ancestors actively into the lives of their descendants.

Conclusion

In writing about China one is forced to take the large view. Yet our knowledge of it (as anthropologists) is piecemeal, and every attempt to be systematic about a particular subject involves us in a scramble for bits of data to fit together. But data there are, and they are being rapidly increased by the new work in Taiwan and Hong Kong,[6] so that we are not forever condemned to the task of trying to extract meaning from facts collected by people with problems in mind very different from those which now drive us on. Yet as our understanding of Chinese society builds up, we shall find that the more consistent a picture we make of it, the less satisfied we shall be. It will become more apparent than it is now that the variations in institutions and beliefs are of greater importance than the consistencies. Well documented, China (or even a section of it) could provide an admirable framework for testing, by a study of variation, the validity of an analysis proposed for one small set of data.

In the second part of this essay I have raised the issue of the possible relationship between ancestor worship on the one side and the distribution of family authority and social differentiation on the other. Between town and country, farmer and merchant, peasant and official, rich and poor, landsman and fisherman (the simplified contrasts could be extended on and on) there must surely be crucial differences in the working out of domestic authority and in the nature of the social ties which bind individuals to those among whom they live out their lives. And these differences ought to be exploited in the effort to understand both the place of ancestor worship in the total system of control of Chinese behavior and the relation between that worship and the dynamics of family life. But the framework of comparison will not be kept down to that scale, for already it is clear that there are opportunities for fruitful comparative study in the institutions and beliefs of the various countries which share with China a common classical tradition. I have tried in the first part of the essay to show, for example, that it is meaningful to ask why Chinese geomancy differs between Japan on the one hand and China, Korea, and Vietnam on the other. And a systematic comparison between ancestor worship (especially perhaps as it is related to the transmission of domestic authority and the roles of married women) in all these countries would take us a step forward in our understanding of the social correlates of religious practices and ideas.

Geomancy

This address is about what we might go so far as to call mystical ecology. I am going to speak on the ritual aspect of the interaction between men and their physical environment, and I introduce my theme by quoting, not, as you might expect, from the Chinese evidence (there will be enough—perhaps too much—of that later),[1] but from an English master-piece on occult practices. In act one, scene three of *The Alchemist*, Abel Drugger the tobacco-man comes to consult Subtle, and, on being asked his business, replies:

> I am a young beginner, and am building
> Of a new shop, an't like your worship, just,
> At corner of a street. (Here's the plot on't.)
> And I would know, by art, sir, of your worship,
> Which way I should make my dore, by *necromancie*.[a]
> And, where my shelues. And, which should be for boxes.
> And, which for pots. I would be glad to thriue, sir.
> And, I was wish'd to your worship, by a gentleman,
> One Captaine Face, that say's you know mens *planets*,
> And their good *angels*, and their bad.

Subtle furnishes the advice he is asked for. He says:

> Make me your dore, then, south; your broad side, west:
> And, on the east-side of your shop, aloft,
> Write *Mathlai*, *Tarmiel*, and *Baraborat*;
> Vpon the north-part, *Rael*, *Velel*, *Thiel*,

Presidential Address, Royal Anthropological Institute, delivered 27 June 1968. *Proceedings of the Royal Anthropological Institute of Great Britain and Ireland 1968* (1969), 5–15.

[a] What that "necromancie" is by which Drugger would orient his door I cannot discover. The alchemy and astrology of the play have been much discussed, but nobody (as far as I can see) has commented on the magical technique of orientation. Nor have I managed to find any reference to it in the literature on Western magic. Geomancy there is, of course, in plenty in that literature, but it is a form of divination on the ground and is not concerned with orientation.

> They are the names of those *Mercurial* spirits,
> That doe fright flyes from boxes. . . . And
> Beneath your threshold, bury me a load-stone
> To draw in gallants, that weare spurres: The rest,
> They'll seeme to follow . . .
> And, on your stall, a puppet, with a vice,
> And a court-*fucus*, to call city-dames.
> You shall deale much, with *mineralls*.

But Drugger has a further request:

> But, to looke ouer, sir, my *almanack*,
> And crosse out my ill-dayes, that I may neither
> Bargaine, nor trust vpon them.[2]

Done into Chinese, and with just a little editing, these passages would make good sense to a Chinese audience—better sense than the original English makes to us. Chinese would recognize the *feng-shui* expert in Subtle, and commend the caution of the tradesman in wanting to orient his shop and to conduct his business on days favored in the almanac: a ritual treatment of space and time. But let us leave Ben Jonson.

Orientation is of the essence in *feng-shui* (i.e. Chinese geomancy) but its more dramatic feature is its concern with the forms of the landscape and buildings. Sir James Frazer's lively scissors snipped out two examples from de Groot's work to furnish Chinese illustrations of the magical maxim that like produces like. The first case deals with the city of Ch'üan-chou which, shaped like a carp, was thought in ancient times to have fallen victim to a neighboring town in the form of a fishing net. The inhabitants of Ch'üan-chou saved themselves by putting up two tall pagodas to intercept the net. The other story is of Shanghai in the mid-nineteenth century, where a rebellion was attributed by geomancers to the inauspicious nature of a temple shaped like a tortoise. The name of the temple was changed and its two eyes were put out (that is, the wells that stood before the door were filled up).[3]

As a final element in my introduction I shall cite the famous essay on primitive classification by Durkheim and Mauss—or should I say the essay made famous in this country by Dr. Rodney Needham's translation and critique (Durkheim and Mauss 1963)? The chapter written by Durkheim and Mauss on China, for all its poor scholarship and faults in reasoning, correctly sites geomancy within an enormous Chinese system of classificatory ideas and positional and temporal notions; and, by its determination to perceive a total system (even if in reality there is none such), balances the comical effect produced by the atomistic treatment of the subject found in *The Golden Bough*.

My references to Frazer and to Durkheim and Mauss show that Chinese geomancy has a place in the classical literature of anthropology; yet the subject did not until recent years seem to interest the anthropologists engaged in studies of China. They could hardly fail to notice the relevance of *feng-shui* for the orientation and disposition of graves[4] (although some appear to have managed even this degree of indifference); but the topic was quickly passed over, never to lead on to an inquiry into the significance of the roughly sketched-in ideas about the need for tombs to be pointed in the right direction. There is, in fact, some lesson for the historian of our discipline in this strange lacuna. The relevant facts, baldly stated, are as follows. In the nineteenth century, sinologues, missionaries, Western administrators and travelers found geomancy staring them in the face in China, and they published their impressions and researches. Frazer and Durkheim and Mauss drew on the writings of one such man, J. J. M. de Groot; there were many others. Now, to a large extent, these men of the last century were put on to geomancy by its emergence as a political force in the encounter between China and the West. The building of churches and European-style houses, the laying down of roads and railways, the digging of mines, and so on, were likely to be attended by Chinese protests that the *feng-shui* of villages, towns, or districts was being ruined. Sometimes the reactions blocked a proposed development; often they allowed projects to go forward in exchange for monetary compensation.[5] By the time the anthropologists came on stage these outbursts of resistance in geomancy had died down,[b] and moreover, the Chinese imperial system had disappeared. For the new kind of scholar-investigator the geomancers they came across seemed to be linked merely or predominantly with the siting of tombs, and the study of this ritual activity appeared tangential to the task of exploring social institutions. (Of course, it is in the nature of things that there are more tombs than houses; that fact alone goes some of the way to accounting for the one-sided treatment of *feng-shui*.) As for the literature of the nineteenth and early twentieth centuries, it was left to doze on its shelves.

But yet another kind of literature was overlooked. Some of the anthropologists were Chinese, yet they seem never to have bothered themselves with the handbooks of geomancy current in China. Indeed, it can be said

---

[b] Giles 1882: 71n: *feng-shui* "after having long been a serious obstacle to the introduction of telegraphs and railways, has in the last years been shaken to its centre, and is now destined very shortly to collapse." Yet earlier, Giles (1876: 145ff) had written: "Nothing less than years of contact with foreign notions and deep draughts of the real science which is even now stealing imperceptibly upon them, will bring the Chinese to see that Feng-shui is a vain shadow."

of this generation of Chinese anthropologists, as of many other kinds of Chinese intellectual of the period, that the most interesting aspects of Chinese religion and thought were closed off to them by their own ideological resistance to "superstition." Here is a version of their attitude in a book first published as recently as 1960 and intended to be a guide (published partly under the auspices of UNESCO) to Chinese tradition for Westerners.

While educated Chinese [the guide asserts] have paid homage only to Heaven and their ancestors, and sometimes to Confucius, Buddha, Lao Tzu, and a few other historical personages, the common people have believed in the existence of thirty-three Buddhist Heavens, eighty-one Taoist Heavens, and eighteen Buddhist hells, and put faith in astrology, almanacs, dream interpretation, geomancy, witchcraft, phrenology, palmistry, the recalling of the soul, fortune telling in all forms, charms, magic, and many other varieties of superstition [a dismal list!] (de Bary *et al.* 1960: 631).

How is the poor Westerner to know that the Confucian elite were involved in many of these practices and shared in many of these "superstitions"? Formulations of this sort may prevent us from seeing that geomancy (to stick to my subject) occupied a highly ambiguous status in the world of the educated. It was not part of the state cult and yet it was used by the imperial government for the siting and protection of important tombs and buildings (cf. C. K. Yang 1961: 263ff). It was often officially attacked for its harmful effects on public behavior,[c] especially in regard to its tendency to delay burial, and yet *feng-shui* lawsuits were entertained in the courts, and officialdom often responded to rebellion by smashing the ancestral tombs of the rebels.[6] As for the practitioners of *feng-shui*, the geomancers, we shall see a little later on that they were in one sense a part of the elite. De Groot, with a fine eye for the inconsistencies of Chinese attitudes, relates with great relish how anti-Buddhist dynasties in China made use of Buddhist monasteries for the effect they had on the *feng-shui* of their surroundings. He writes:

As for a conclusive proof of the influence of the Fung-shui system on the establishment and the preservation of Buddhistic monasteries and pagodas—it is a well-known fact, that even all around the Imperial metropolis, in the plains and on the hills, a great number are found, erected for the insurance or the improvement of the Fung-shui of the palace, and consequently of the Imperial family and the whole empire. And who were the founders? none others than the em-

---

[c] See the denunciation in "The sacred edict": "Moreover, there are the following capital offences, not reprieved at a time of general reprieve; . . . to destroy or remove from the place of interment the remains of either grandparents or parents, through belief in the sinister statements of geomancy" (Baller 1921: 90–91).

perors of the anti-buddhistic dynasties of Ming and Ts'ing; and who maintains them? the sovereigns of the last-named house (Groot 1903–4, vol. 1: 71; cf. Johnston 1913: 337ff).

I suggest that Chinese geomancy has come back into anthropological view for reasons that link up with what I have said about the past. In the first place, there is a political reason. Much of the recent anthropological research on Chinese society has been conducted in the British Crown Colony of Hong Kong, and there the massive economic development that has taken place since the early 1950's has led to the same kind of disturbance of the rural landscape as stimulated the *feng-shui* protests of the last century. I shall have more to say on that subject. The second reason lies partly in the general revival of anthropological interest in religion and ideas as systems, and partly in the fact that the most recent anthropological students of Chinese life, not being Chinese themselves, have failed to be blinded by radical prejudices about superstition. They have been able to search out and take the facts for what they are, being unfearful of the grotesque irrationality they might uncover, having no stake in the maintenance of a view of what Chinese society ought to be like.

I want very briefly to sketch the evolution of my own interest in the subject. I began by being fascinated by what I could find in de Groot and other older writers that bore on the *feng-shui* of graves as an aspect of competition among agnates and among rival lineages (Freedman 1958: 77ff). In 1963 I set out for a period of fieldwork in Hong Kong with geomancy high on my list of problems. There I found myself in an atmosphere in which *feng-shui* was much talked of, since, apart from anything else, it preoccupied government officials who were faced by reactions to the disturbance of graves, the construction of roads, and the movement of villages. My earlier one-sided interest was corrected, and I came away from Hong Kong not only with some information but, more important, a budget of questions to pose to the older literature. At this point I was fortunate enough to find that one of my sinologically trained graduate students, Mr. Stephan Feuchtwang, was eager to write a thesis on *feng-shui*, basing it for the greater part on the Chinese sources. I speak today from my brief experience in Hong Kong, from my knowledge of the literature, and from Mr. Feuchtwang's researches (Feuchtwang 1965).[7] Since I have invoked his splendid study of the subject, I ought to make it clear that Mr. Feuchtwang may very well not agree with all that I have to say today.

Writing on *feng-shui* in the last few years, I have confined myself for the most part to discussing the connections between the geomancy of tombs and ancestor worship, arguing (to compress a series of points) that they together form a system in which forebears are on the one hand looked up to and worshiped and on the other looked down on and manipulated. In ancestor worship Chinese express solidarity with their agnates; in the *feng-shui* of graves they give rein to their impulses to assert their independence of, and competition with, the same agnates (cf. Freedman 1966: 118–43; 1967a: 87ff). In this address I want to shift the focus of interest toward graves and houses as members of a single class. The Chinese distinguish between the two forms of construction as *yin* buildings and *yang* buildings respectively, at one and the same time distinguishing them as dwellings of darkness and dwellings of light and linking them together in one system. For *yin-yang* is a system of complementary opposites, not (as was sometimes thought in the past) a dualism of mutually antagonistic forces.

It is very important to grasp the idea that in the Chinese view a building is not simply something that sits upon the ground to serve as a convenient site for human activity. It is an intervention in the universe; and that universe is composed of the physical environment and men and the relationships among men. Men are bonded to the physical environment, working good or ill upon it and being done good or ill to by it. Moreover, when a man puts up a building he inserts something into the landscape and between him and his neighbors. It follows that risks attend his enterprise and he must take precautions. The physical universe is alive with forces that, on the one side, can be shaped and brought fruitfully to bear on a dwelling and those who live in it, and, on the other side, can by oversight or mismanagement be made to react disastrously. But the very act of siting and constructing a house to one's own advantage may be to the detriment of others. Modifications in the landscape reverberate. So that, in principle, every act of construction disturbs a complex balance of forces within a system made up of nature and society, and it must be made to produce a new balance of forces lest evil follow. Chinese are frightened by the act of building (cf. Ayscough 1925: 25; Hayes 1967: 22ff)—and they are wary, too, of the tricks that carpenters and masons can play on them (cf. Eberhard 1965: 77ff; 1966: 17ff and *passim*).

For the sake of simplicity I have spoken as though we were concerned only with individual buildings. In fact, *feng-shui* is applicable to any unit of habitation, so that from the single house at one end of the scale to the society as a whole there is a hierarchy of nesting units each with its *feng-shui* and subject also to the *feng-shui* of all the higher units to which it belongs. That is to say, localized lineages, villages, cities, districts, and provinces have each their geomancy; it may derive from the chief place (for example, the capital of an administrative unit) or the chief building (for example, the ancestral hall of a localized lineage) of the unit in question. Between coordinate units—between houses in one village, between villages, between towns, and so on—there may be rivalry issuing in geomantic quarrels, one side accusing the other of harming its *feng-shui* and taking countermeasures, as in the case cited by Frazer: you will remember that the city of Ch'üan-chou erected two pagodas to foil its netlike neighbor. But geomancy may also be involved in the relations between entities at different levels of the hierarchy, such that a capital city may harm one of the nearby villages in its jurisdiction.

Let me cite some examples. Here, to begin with, is a very simple one to reinforce Frazer's illustration of the significance of resemblances. Perhaps I should add that part of the interest of this case is that it originally appeared in a Hong Kong Chinese newspaper toward the end of the last century in response to a questionnaire sent out by the Folk-Lore Society, London.

In . . . the district of Shuntak, Kwangtung Province, there is a monumental gateway in an uninhabited part of the country which is said to resemble in shape a rat-trap. It is related that the crops in the neighborhood having failed for several seasons in succession, the aid of the geomancers was invoked in order to discover the reason. After carefully considering the surroundings of the place, they found that the hills opposite to where the crops were grown presented the appearance of a rat. This rat, they said, devoured the crops, so they advised the construction of a rat-trap to prevent its depredations. No sooner was the rat-trap erected than the crop yielded grain in abundance (Lockhart 1890a: 361).

To put such a case into perspective, we need to know that in modern times the dominant school of *feng-shui* (the so-called School of Forms, or Kiangsi School), while continuing to use the compass as a method of analyzing a landscape (of which more in a moment) has placed greater reliance on detecting conformations that can be identified as creatures or objects. Dragons, which are themselves the outward expression of the favorable mystical forces animating a landscape, are commonly and readily detectable—as I can testify to from my own experience after I had come to assimilate my perception of the countryside to that of the Chinese among whom I lived. By their eloquent and devious sinuosity dragons are apparent wherever a rise in the ground offers the imagination some purchase. Dragons apart, the shape of the landscape may suggest a great number of things and beings; some of them are the geomancer's standard symbols (as, for example, a writing-brush rest, which promises success in scholarship); others proliferate from the trained fancy of ordinary minds. In relation to either buildings or graves, what is read into the landscape presages good or ill fortune. I remember the ambiguous awe with which I was introduced to a grave said to be nestling comfortably between the raised thighs of a naked woman. (It took me a little while to be convinced.)

An alteration made or developing by itself in the landscape may well damage, but sometimes improve, the entities it embodies. The sinking of a well or the cutting of a road is likely to sever a dragon's artery or sinew (to take the commonest case) and release some terrible power of misfortune to issue in poverty, disease, or childlessness. A road made to lead straight to my door is an arrow against which I shall be able to protect myself only with difficulty, and perhaps at great expense. On the other hand, the good and bad forces in the landscape are by no means all represented in things and creatures; some are invisible, and yet may be concentrated upon or deflected by man-made devices: pools of water, stands of trees, buildings, and so on. For one building to rise above another or block its access to the *feng-shui* of its site is an infringement of a sort of geomantic ancient lights; and quarrels will ensue. The pagodas that have entered the Western spirit as pleasing (I had almost said quaint) monuments of Chinese taste are closely associated with attempts to procure a favorable *feng-shui*; and they illustrate two different mystical functions of man-made structures: they may be put up to remedy a geomantic defect in the landscape or to act as a symbol of some desirable feature or quality. In Ch'üan-chou they are supposed to have warded off the net. Pagodas shaped like writing brushes promise examination successes. The great pagoda of An-ching, the port in Anhwei province, is said to function as a mast for the port, which is said to resemble a junk. Two enormous anchors hang on the pagoda's walls, "their original purpose having been to prevent the city drifting away downstream" (Willetts 1965: 398). We are in a world of concrete poetry.

I draw my next example from an account in the 1870's of a typical kind of problem faced by foreigners in China. The story goes that some German missionaries in Kwangtung, in order to protect their schoolhouse from visits from thieves, added two watchtowers, a few feet high, to the ends of the building. Alas for them, one of the towers was just visible from a grave a quarter of a mile off.

The enraged descendants of the occupant of that tomb gathered the village together against the missionaries and threatened to burn down their establishment. In vain did the missionaries argue that so small a portion of their building could be seen from the tomb, that if, as was most reasonable, one supposed that the deceased spirit preferred to *sit* upon his semicircular armchair-like grave, instead of fatiguing himself by standing upon it, he then would not have the obnoxious projection within the field of vision at all. No matter, the offensive towers must be pulled down. As usual in China, it was found that even Feng-Shui could be propitiated by a gift; and the missionaries bought toleration of the disturbed spirit for a certain number of dollars, paid down to his representatives in the flesh (Turner 1874: 341).

There are two essential points to note in this jocularly told story. The first is that the *feng-shui* of a grave, and therefore the good fortune of the agnatic descendants of its occupant, could be said to be put at risk by a significant alteration in the landscape. The second point is that the villagers were seizing upon an opportunity to express their defiance of the missionaries. They were paid off, as villagers are being paid off to this day in similar circumstances in Hong Kong by the government and others. The annual accounts of the New Territories Administration in that colony show sums of money handed out as compensation payments relating to public works, two categories of the accounts being headed "*Ex Gratia* & Disturbance Allowance" and "Graves & Other Compensation." Some of these disbursements must certainly be connected with the damage done to *feng-shui*, and there can be no doubt about what lies behind the items labeled "tun fu," for they are rites (in these cases paid for by the government) for restoring peace, harmony, and luck to sites whose *feng-shui* has been disturbed.[d]

Now, the Hong Kong situation is an artificial one, in the sense that the government, not being Chinese, contends with the people on unequal terms. The people believe in *feng-shui*; the government does not, but thinks itself under an obligation to respect the religious beliefs and practices of those it governs. (I think, by the way, that in the early part of this century a tougher attitude was taken up to popular resistance by geomancy; since the Second World War the characteristic British colonial tolerance of exotic religions has been reinforced by the needs of a delicate political situation.) Were the government of Hong Kong to share the beliefs of the people it would be in a position to resist their consequences, for its officials would then be able to match their own *feng-shui* opinions against those of the objectors and, if necessary, call in professional geomancers to argue with those retained by the people.[8] There has, in fact, been a telling incident in the New Territories that rams home my point. At one time in the 1950's there was a Chinese District Officer (by a co-incidence he was the first pupil I ever taught at the London School of

---

[d] See Hong Kong, New Territories Administration 1962: 55ff, where *tun fu* to the value of HK$5,397 are shown for the year 1961–62. Note also the sum of HK$400 on p. 56 against the words "bamboo screens." These screens were put up outside a village to prevent the dragon's blood (the red earth in a road cutting) being visible from the ancestral hall. Hong Kong, New Territories Administration 1963: 43ff shows a total of HK$4,880 spent on *tun fu* in the year 1962–63.

Economics) who, when confronted by an irritating *feng-shui* case, took himself off to the library of Hong Kong University to read the subject up out of the Chinese handbooks. He then felt himself able to contradict and confound the geomancer retained by the complainants. The geomancer was floored and his clients withdrew in awe. In China itself a mandarin might well consult a geomancer in connection with the siting of a new building or well, bearing the interests and peace of his country in mind; but the people would never have been in a position to harass him with complaints about the geomantic effects of government action if he chose to talk back in their own language.

My last example comes from a conversation I had a couple of weeks ago with my friend Mr. Teh Cheang Wan, the chief architect of the Singapore Housing and Development Board. He told me that in some of the Singapore housing estates the officials have had to deal with complaints arising from the fact that the main doors of pairs of flats directly face each other. One nervous householder puts up a charm over his door to ward off the evil shooting out of the flat that confronts him, and the occupant of the latter flat then complains to the authorities that he is under attack by, so to say, reflection. I gather that, as a result, the plans of future blocks of flats are to be altered to prevent front doors facing one another. This simple piece of information illustrates, first, the survival of geomantic ideas in a modern city, and second, the Chinese fear of being deprived of one's fair share of good fortune. That fortune is a quantum; my neighbor's increment is my decrement. As a keen observer of nineteenth-century China pointed out, it was a common custom when a house was being built to hang up lanterns and beat gongs to attract luck. In self-defense the neighbors had then to do the same in order to prevent their luck being drawn away (Nevius 1869: 176).

The geomancer has appeared in several contexts in my account, and it is now necessary to speak about him in some detail. I shall begin with his skill and then deal with the question of his status. The best introduction to both matters is a sketch of the characteristic geomancer as he emerges from the nineteenth-century accounts and as, in some measure, he can still be seen today in Hong Kong. He stoops in a scholarly fashion, is long-gowned, and has large glasses perched upon his nose. He is borne to his work in a sedan chair, and in general affects the manner of a gentleman of leisure. In his hands he carries a compass and books; among the latter there may be a copy of the Classic of Changes (*I Ching*) and an almanac, as well as professional manuals (cf. Hubrig 1879: 35).

The magnetic compass is the geomancer's instrument *par excellence*. It always appears in professional geomancy, although its role there depends on whether we are dealing with the so-called Kiangsi School, in which the forms of the landscape are all-important, or the Fukien School, in which the compass dominates (cf. Needham 1962: 242). Yet, whichever the School, the compass serves as a sort of model of the universe, by means of which the features of heaven and earth can be brought into relation with a given site to analyze its potential over time and to predict of it what it will bring of good and bad. The floating needle of the compass stands at the center of a series of concentric rings of characters, such that a line drawn from the center provides a radius of characters to be read and interpreted together. The Chinese magnetic compass seems to have been invented as an instrument of divination (Needham 1962: 230, 293 ff) and, while assuming more scientific and practical functions, has remained part of the equipment of divination to this day.

Among the books he carries the geomancer uses the manuals for interpreting earthly shapes and currents and the almanac for calendric and astrological data: the divining process rests on the two axes of space and time. The third book, the Classic of Changes, is a link between *feng-shui* and all that is most respectable in Chinese thought. That ancient book of divination (in which the units are sixty-four hexagrams) has provided generation after generation of Chinese scholars and gentlemen with a basis—one can hardly say raw material—for moral and metaphysical speculation, as well as a means of deciding on a line of conduct within the framework of conditions ruling at a given time. It is the bridge between canonic metaphysics and divination, on the one hand, and the popular system of *feng-shui*, on the other.

Dressed in his long gown, spectacles rounding his eyes to impressive proportions, the geomancer is the scholar brought down into ordinary life, the one member—or pseudo-member—of the educated elite whose company and paid services are available to the common run of men. Whence his grand airs and literary pretensions. The basic metaphysic on which he works—a universe pulsing between *yin* and *yang*, permeated by *ch'i* (matter-energy), moved back and forth by the Five Agents of Water, Fire, Wood, Metal, and Earth—is the metaphysic of scholardom, the joint intellectual property of the Confucian literati. But the geomancer puts his metaphysic to common use. He mediates, then, between the two main strata of Chinese society, the learned (and therefore the bureaucratic) and the common; and occupies a status which is, in consequence, both hampered and advantaged by ambiguity. The true scholar, for whom the ideal is government service, may well join in respectable divining exercises with his intimates (consulting the *I Ching*, conducting sand-tray séances, the reading of faces, and so on), but he will not put his talents upon the open market. It follows that the geomancer is not quite the thing: he is a kind of gentleman and yet not entirely so; having a valence for both the literati and the common people (he serves both), he cannot clearly belong to either. From the point of view of the elite he is tainted by his attachment to the popular and the extra-bureaucratic; that same attachment, doubled by his airs and graces, is his strength with the common people. Alas, the sources are too vague for us to say exactly how the ranks of the geomancers were filled, but we may well suspect that the typical geomancer was either a failure of the imperial examination system (as was often the doctor, the schoolmaster, and the scribe) or the product of a literate family not yet ripe for the standing of the elite.[9] In contemporary Hong Kong, *mutatis mutandis*, we can find examples of both kinds.

That is the ideal type of geomancer. He stands contrasted with another such: the priest, the manipulator of the supernatural, the performer of rites. The geomancer need by no means confine himself to *feng-shui*; he may read fortunes and cast horoscopes in the marketplace, if he is forced to it by poverty, and yet not lose his special character by that humble activity. But to stay geomancer *pur sang*, he must not cross the line into the performance of rites or be party to the invocation of gods and spirits, for that is the terrain of the priest, a man who, mediating between humans and the supernatural, is unambiguously of the common people (except in a special case of certain Buddhists and Taoists), a low servant standing outside and at a great distance from the Confucian elite.

And yet in real life (as we can see from the literature and I have noted in Hong Kong today) geomancer and priest sometimes coincide in one man, in the sense that an expert who chooses and orients a site for a grave or house may also exorcise evil from the place and conduct prayers and offerings to the gods; whereas ideally the two groups of function should be kept clearly distinct. Doubtless, this merging of roles occurs most frequently in poor and isolated communities where the services of a "pure" geomancer are hard to come by and expensive.[10] But there is more than a mere sociological interest in the division between, and the occasional merging of, the two persons: there is a gulf in metaphysics between them, in that one deals in disembodied forces, being a kind of technical practitioner, and the other in anthropomorphous spirits. True, the geomancer of the School of Forms may point to beings in the landscape, but they are signs, not objects of worship. If they are to be treated as entities and not forces, then the geomancer (ideally) hands over to the priest; it is the latter who must conduct the rites and propitiate the offended spirit. I referred earlier on to the *tun fu* often paid for out of Hong Kong government funds to negate the consequences of a damaged *feng-shui*; they are rites to be carried out by priests.

Yet from another point of view this metaphysical gulf between geomancer and priest is no gulf at all, but rather a neat transformation. Most of the elements of *feng-shui* can be restated in the language of ordinary religion. Just as in Neo-Confucian philosophical writings the concretizing words *shen* and *kuei* (which are ordinarily translatable as gods and demons, respectively) are used for positive and negative spiritual forces, being stripped of their anthropomorphic connotations (cf. Chan 1967: 32, 366), so in popular religion a reverse transformation is worked by which the disembodied forces of the geomancer are turned into personal entities. For the expert in *feng-shui* a wall may need to be put up to shield a doorway from, and deflect, a baneful mystical force that, shooting straight up a road to the house, may bring its occupants to ruin; in religion that force becomes a demon to be baffled by the obstructing wall. For the geomancer the landscape is full of the signs of forces; for the priest it is inhabited by gods and spirits.

The geomancer stands outside the ordinary religious system, being counterposed to the priest. He looks like an observer of nature and he appeals to an orthodox Confucian metaphysic. And yet the fruits of his analysis and reasoning are expressible in popular religion. Is the geomancer in religion or out of it? The question may strike you as rather silly, but in fact it leads on to two interesting matters. The first matter we have already touched on: the standing of geomancy. It is respectable by virtue of its connection with respectable (i.e. orthodox) literacy, and in this fashion it is ordinarily exempt from the description "superstitious" in the eyes of respectable Chinese. For them there is something called religion, a debased and sometimes dirty thing, and there is *feng-shui* which rests on a kind of science of observation, backed up by a canonic literature and that impressive instrument, the compass. If they are misled by the geomancer, they are being dazzled by science, not bamboozled by religion. Atheists or Christians (to turn to the modern context in Hong Kong), they see no contradiction in believing in, and having recourse to geomancy. It is eminently reasonable—and of course it often works.

The second matter is one for us, the outside observers. Nearly a hundred years ago Eitel (1873) called his monograph *Feng-shui: or, the Rudiments of Natural Science in China*, and in our own day Dr. Joseph Needham has written about geomancy in the context of the development of Chinese science. He calls it a pseudo-science, a description clearly intended as a kind of compliment, and sees in it, as in many other Chinese magical and divinatory practices, the seeds of a more rational endeavor. Some of these magical practices, he writes, "led insensibly to important discoveries in the practical investigation of natural phenomena. Since magic and science both involve positive manual operations, the empirical element was never missing from Chinese 'proto-science'" (Needham 1956: 346). No doubt, just as in the history of alchemy and chemistry and of astrology and astronomy, there is some significant developmental connection between *feng-shui* and the Chinese understanding of the nature of the earth. (The term *ti-li*, another name for *feng-shui*, in modern times means geography.) But I think it is forcing the evidence to assert any stronger link between *feng-shui* and science. Chinese geomancy is a technique of divination; it states no unambiguous propositions; it foresees no rational comparison or experiment. For us it must be part of Chinese religion—when we take that word in its broadest sense—even though, from the point of view of the Chinese themselves, it is differentiated from what they think of as their religion.

We are now brought fact to face with *feng-shui* as divination. What is being divined? I argue that geomancy is essentially turned toward the future, a means for men to create their lives as they would have them, full of honor, riches, and progeny. It is the geomancer's job to point the way to the good future. He meddles with the past only to the extent of accounting for its failure as a prelude to designing what is to come. Yet at the same time, the ideas of *feng-shui*, as distinct from its techniques, furnish men with an opportunity to explain strange failures and successes; and Chinese folklore is full of stories that trace the origins of grandiose approaches to riches, high social standing, and illustrious and numerous issue. Many of the attempts are foiled by a Heaven (seen in its moral aspect) intervening to prevent the working out of an evil plot laid upon Earth by geomancy. I offer an example. I have drawn it from material on northwestern China in order to avoid giving the impression that *feng-shui* is something confined to the part of the country I know best, the southeast.[e]

In this story we are told that there once lived a family in which the profession of geomancy was hereditary. Toward the end of the Ming dynasty the family included two famous but poor geomancers, father and son. The father, wanting to ensure the success of his descendants, engaged in a long search for a grave site. Eventually he found one: whoever was buried in it would produce an emperor. To mark the site (or rather, to locate the exact spot in it that was crucial) the geomancer buried a cash in it. Not long afterward the son too set out in search of a grave site, and, finding one, stuck a needle in it to mark the spot. Reporting his discovery to his father, he told him that whoever was buried in the site

[e] I have argued (Freedman 1967a [Essay 17 below]: 89) that complex lineage organization and the *feng-shui* of graves are both carried to their highest point of development in the southeastern part of China. But geomancy, at the very least as an idea, is found everywhere in the country.

would have descendants who founded a dynasty. Father and son went off together to inspect the latter's find; it proved to be the same as the father's, the son's needle being stuck through the hole in the father's cash.

They set to work assiduously to acquire the land, keeping their secret even from the senior geomancer's other sons. After a few years the older man died, but before his death he admonished his geomancer son, saying that when he buried the body he was to pour ten bushels of rapeseed on the coffin. And the father handed over three magic arrows, instructing his son to observe the hundred days' mourning in strict seclusion at home and then, on the hundredth day, to shoot the arrows precisely at noon toward the south. On his father's death the son followed his instructions to the letter, except that on the ninety-ninth day of the mourning, being nagged by his wife to go out and buy the things needed for the feast on the morrow, he decided to shoot off his arrows a day earlier—to his great loss. The three arrows were to have killed the old Emperor: instead, they landed harmlessly in the palace.

That same day the three highest officials in the city all dreamed the same dream: they were the next day at dawn to go to the east gate where they would greet the new Emperor. They acted on the dream, and soon after their arrival at the east gate they saw a poorly dressed peasant approaching. The grand officials laughed and said that this could not be the Son of Heaven. They asked the poor man his name. He told them he was Chiang the geomancer. The officials waited a while longer and went back into the city, thinking that they had been duped by a ghost. They recounted their dream, and the Emperor was informed of the three arrows landing in the palace. The order went out to round up the whole lineage of Chiang. Many were taken and put to death. When he was seized the geomancer himself confessed his secret on the rack. The pursuers went to the father's grave and broke it open. As the coffin was removed a great cloud of paper people flew out; they were the rapeseeds; they darkened the sky. There came a thunderstorm. The corpse in the coffin was found to be burned, and from the dishonored grave there flowed out a stream of blood that grew to a river. People were aghast and wondered at the meaning of this astonishing event. It was said that a great misdeed had been committed which would have rooted out a dynasty established by Heaven. Heaven's curse had been drawn upon the evildoers. More blood would have to flow in China. The country would be long in a state of unrest (Kube 1952: 159–63).

This is a case of *feng-shui* as myth, and myth in a familiar form. My next example is a myth in modern dress and one which bridges past and future. I have taken it from an article on geomancy in a Chinese glossy magazine published in Hong Kong in 1962.[11] Here are a very few of the many points the author makes. . . . He has a friend who ten years ago opened a travel agency. At first business was very ordinary, but within a few years of his moving into a building in Queen's Road Central, it boomed. The friend made a fortune, and then after several years went bankrupt. *Feng-shui* explains why. The building was well sited, but a high government building was put up on its right corner; this was a White Tiger rearing its head and dominating the Azure Dragon on the opposite side. (Let me explain. Azure Dragon and White Tiger are the chief features flanking any geomantic site; they are respectively *yang* and *yin* and must be kept in the proper balance to ensure success.[12]) . . . *Feng-shui*, the account goes on, is a wonderful thing; it can affect an individual, a family, a city, a country. The reason why Hong Kong prospers is to be sought in geomancy, which shows how the dragon's arteries are successfully disposed in the landscape and how the cyclical movement of time brings in and takes out the Colony's prosperity. A major cycle opened in 1842 when the British took over the island of Hong Kong. The Japanese attack in 1941 came at an unfavorable point in a minor cycle, but within three years the cycle had moved on to lead into renewed good fortune. From its foundation as a colony Hong Kong has three cycles of sixty years (i.e. 180 years) of prosperity. One hundred and twenty of these years have passed, leaving sixty in which there will be nothing to worry about. When in this year (1962) hungry hordes streamed over the border from China, it looked like a disaster for Hong Kong, but in reality the good fortune of the Colony cannot be affected by events of this sort. Even if, at the end of the period of the ninety-nine year lease, the British hand back the New Territories to China and Hong Kong reverts to Chinese rule, the predetermined prosperity will last for the remainder of the cycle (Chou 1962).

With this example we are still, of course, in the realm of ideas, for no technique has been shown to be applied. It is to that aspect of the subject that we must now turn. People intent on securing the good fortune of their families or communities can take steps by retaining the services of a geomancer in connection with the siting of their tombs or buildings. Indeed, we may say that, in the traditional Chinese setting, there is more involved than a mere desire to procure good fortune; there is a moral obligation to seek a future of happiness for those for whom one is responsible. If I select my grave site in anticipation of my death, it is for the benefit of my sons and remoter agnatic issue. If my sons choose my grave, they are intent not only on their own prosperity but also on that of their descendants, each his own. If, as the head of a household, I build a new house, I look to the happiness of myself, my family, and those who will follow on from us. It is the geomancer's task to divine the potentialities of a given landscape and to bring them into relation with the future of the people who build in it.

The link between the general properties of a site and the fate of those who occupy it lies in the horoscope, which is a combination, for each man, of the eight characters expressing the time and date of his birth. Sites may be endowed with enormously favorable properties, but the precise times at which construction may begin, the exact orientation of graves and buildings on them, and their compatibility and their occupants narrow down in time and space the full range of potentialities to the needs of individuals. Horoscopes personalize geomancy (insofar as it is connected with graves and houses), marking out a separate future for separate men and their descendants. The geomancer charged with the job of finding and using sites for particular clients is engaged, on his client's behalf, in carving out their best possible future, in staking the best possible claim for them in a world of restricted opportunities. For happiness and prosperity are not limitless; they form a fixed fund from which each man must strive to draw for himself the maximum at the expense of others. It is for this reason that *feng-shui* is to be seen as an instrument of competition and the geomancer as an essential actor in a play in which Chinese strive to outdo one another in the struggle for the happy future. As I have explained elsewhere (Freedman 1966: 130ff), the competition can be seen most dramatically at work in the conduct of brothers seeking to find a grave site for their parent; they cannot all be equally advantaged by it (their inequality of benefit being built into the system by which the geomancer must orient the tomb); and they struggle among themselves, each for his own future and that of his own descendants. *Feng-shui* is a form of divination in which men set out, on the basis of occult knowledge, to make or remake their lives.

In the vast competition the geomancer is crucial because he alone commands the necessary level of knowledge. Ordinary men and women have a general grasp of the principles of *feng-shui* (especially in regard to the forms of landscape); indeed, if they did not, they would not find the geomancer credible, and he would then be too much like a priest, wrapped up in a mystery. Yet they cannot have the knowledge of the literature on which the geomancer's craft is supposed to rest. The geomancer is a kind of literatus; at least he is literate. Therefore he is raised above the common people and they need him. On his side, the geomancer is himself caught up in a different kind of competition, for, in order to maintain his standing as the professional supplier of a service, he must meet the challenge of rivals. There are no professional ethics to restrain competition between practitioners. One denigrates the other, gleefully condemning his work and proposing something better. In their strenuous search for the future, clients may call on a succession of geomancers, each contradicting his predecessor out of his superior knowledge. As Dr. Maurice Bloch has recently pointed out in his study of literacy in Madagascar (Bloch 1968: 294), a body of writings to which specialists have better access than laymen may promote the very elaboration of those writings to suit the competitive needs of the experts. Every geomancer in China is deeper read than his predecessor, has a better command of the literature, can interpret it with greater subtlety, and can apply his knowledge to better effect.

From our point of view, there is no objective test of a geomancer's success in his craft. In the course of a long career a man may have a run of luck in being the siter of tombs and houses that seem to have brought success. (*Feng-shui* works on a long time-scale; nobody expects quick results, although they are very pleased to have them, and everybody is prepared to put down to a geomancer's credit the happy consequences that follow many years after his labors.) I suppose that we should say that the successful geomancer is in reality the one who picks lucky clients. I mean that the man who starts off with the richest clientele (and therefore the people most likely to be happy, promoted, and blessed with progeny) is in the best position to gain for himself the reputation of a geomancer worth hiring. The persuasive geomancer working on rich clients can talk them into a number of projects (after all, every family has many tombs to be sited and resited), taking the credit for the one that succeeds and benefiting from the convenient memory that dismisses failures. There is another way in which the geomancer's success can be established; for he is judged not simply by results but also by the scale and grandeur of the works for which he is retained. A geomancer of little account picks up small jobs—the siting of a grave on which the owner can afford to spend little. The geomancer employed to site a magnificent house or tomb is by that fact an important man. It follows that the geomancer is not only after big fees and commission when he spurs on a client to lavish expense; he is trying to raise his own stock.

Yet in this, as in all aspects of his craft, the geomancer must be a very careful manipulator of men, for if he presses his clients too hard he may overreach himself and find himself replaced by the next geomancer to offer his services. I knew one such career-building geomancer in Hong Kong. He had acquired a respectable reputation as a geomancer of the old school, wanting only a long gown and a sedan chair to complete my picture of the nineteenth-century practitioner. But he came to a crisis in his affairs when he undertook to site a tomb for an industrialist's wife. The industrialist, remarried, wanted (according to my informant) to ensure the prosperity of his children by his first wife, and proposed to move her remains to a new grave. The geomancer picked the site, and work on the grave to the value of HK$4,000 was put in hand. But after the work had started the geomancer came along to complain that the grave was not large enough and to encourage the industrialist, a rich man, to build bigger. The work proposed would have raised the bill to some HK$10,000, at which sum the industrialist balked. He could not simply dismiss the geomancer and call in another for the same site. (It was explained to me that in such circumstances a geomancer may turn rogue and ruin the site by subterfuge.) The industrialist would have to pay off the contractor for the work done and retain a new geomancer to prospect for an entirely new site. My hitherto successful geomancer had put his career in jeopardy.

I hope I have made it clear that *feng-shui* cannot be treated entirely on its own, as though it were some independent feature of Chinese thought and life. Its basic ideas are those of a standard system of metaphysics; its elements are transposable into Chinese "religion"; it belongs as a form of divination with horoscopes, almanacs, face-reading, and so on. Indeed, a case can be made out for *feng-shui* as the most systematic statement of Chinese ideas about the constitution and working of the cosmos. But what I find particularly interesting is the way in which it brings all its elements to bear on the problem of adjusting men, through their habitations, to the physical environment. Men belong as of right in the universe. Heaven, Earth, and Man form a natural triad. But what men construct is an intrusion, and geomancy is preoccupied with the problem of allowing men to build what they need and want without destroying their natural relationships with the cosmos. Buildings are culture in a special sense; what men make for themselves in their constructions may be a challenge to the natural world, and *feng-shui* shows both the risks attending that challenge and the means of minimizing them.

I say "buildings" meaning to include tombs. We do not have in English a category to match the Chinese. For us, the habitations of the living and those of the dead belong to different worlds. The men who make our graves are not builders; gravediggers are not construction workers; tombs are not dwellings. In the Chinese view, as we have seen, the tomb is the *yin* habitation to match the *yang* habitation of the living. The two kinds form a system which turns out, on analysis, to be a grand classifier of men among themselves. In traditional China, men and their interrelations are grouped and arranged by buildings.

A house is a family, and its structure is the structure of a family.[13] For every domestic unit there is a hearth and for every conjugal pair a bedroom. When a family within one set of buildings grows more complex, it restructures its space to conform to new arrangements; wings are added or partitions put up to mark the nature of the new units. Houses clustered to form a hamlet or village group families to make a territorial community in relation to a temple or altar and one or more agnatic communities in relation to ancestral halls. Walled cities are dominated by the yamen, the government offices. The whole country is presided over by the capital city, the peak of the political and (from one point of view) the geomantic hierarchy. Men are sorted out by their family, agnatic, territorial, and political ties; those ties are expressible in the buildings that house or represent the units of different span. But we have not yet taken account of graves which, instead of grouping social relations within clearly bounded and structured units (as in the case of houses, villages, and so on), scatter them to underline the differentiation among agnates.

If we were inventing Chinese society all over again, we might very well provide it with orderly and compact graveyards on the principle that if *feng-shui* can provide a tidy arrangement for the living, it can be made to do so for the dead. If village houses can be lined up and cities laid out on grid plans, then tombs should be susceptible of regimentation. And indeed, there is evidence that Chinese have at times striven to impose this kind of order on the dead. Yet the general effect has been slight, because in geomancy there lies the inherent principle that tombs are a means of individualizing the fate of the living. The *feng-shui* of graves is a repudiation of the solidarity of agnates, each man seeking to procure his own success at the expense of those to whom he is closely related, such that brothers twist and turn to avoid the apparent truth that their like parenthood will entail for them a uniform future. The municipal cemetery which blocks off all opportunity for grand bids for fortune by its discipline of fixed plots is hateful to the Chinese. I have heard New Territories Chinese in Hong Kong, with all the marvelous mortuary resources of their hills at this disposal, express pity and contempt for the urban dead queueing up (as they put it) to be buried in the regimented grave plots prescribed by the government.

In the traditional disposition of tombs there is apparent anarchy and an open expression of the competition between agnates. In the arrangement of the buildings for the living there is orderliness and an apparent muting of competition. But the competition is there. Let one man in a village build a fraction too high; let him make a window or a door that can be interpreted as a threat; and he has a struggle on his hands. If one village appears to prosper at the expense of another, some alteration must be made (perhaps the erection of a pagoda) to redress the balance. We are dealing with a society in which the development of a sophisticated architecture has allowed men to classify their groupings and, so to say, objectify their relationship by means of constructions. *Feng-shui* is the ritual of a society not yet overborne by its architectural technology. In industrial societies we have lost the power of making our buildings conform to our social relations, and no amount of town planning seems to do any good. We can make very little social use of our cemeteries; we cannot fit our families to our flats and houses. We are not able neatly to order our social relations in space. The size, prominence, and style of our buildings seem to be out of step with their social, political, and religious significance. Think of a Chinese pagoda, and then remember the Post Office Tower.

Let us return to Abel Drugger and his consultation with Subtle. Ben Jonson was having his fun with the superstitions of his day and, while the abuse of alchemy was his chief butt, he has presented us (in the passages with which I opened this address) with a sketch of something extraordinarily like *feng-shui*. Here is a trader wanting to know how best to orient his door and arrange his wares in order to ensure success. And Jonson shows us a further parallel with the Chinese case in linking Drugger's request for this advice with one for guidance on bad days in the almanac. Subtle turns out to be something like a Chinese geomancer seen through the eyes of a Jacobean cynic. What have we here? I shall be cautious and suggest only that the world of *The Alchemist*, like that of traditional China, is one in which, before the days of victorious industrialism, civilized men were able to conceive of a systematic mystical relation between themselves and their environment and, by working on the assumption that the future was orderly, were determined to shape it.[f] We dominate our environment with increasing ferocity and have lost the power to make it speak about our future. Chinese I knew in Hong Kong used to say to me that, when you came down to it, what a good *feng-shui* really meant was that you were completely at ease in it. I think they implied that you were comfortable in a place because you could with confidence face the future. Space and time are interlocked.[14]

Will you allow me now to dedicate this address? I do so to an Institute searching for new premises and a new life within them.

[f] Cf. Eitel 1873: 60. "We see, therefore, it is left in great measure to man's foresight and energy to turn his fortunes into any channel he pleases, to modify and regulate the influences which heaven and earth bring to bear upon him, and it is the boast of the Feng-shui system that it teaches man how to rule nature and his own destiny by showing him how heaven and earth rule him."

The Politics of an Old State:
A View from the Chinese Lineage

The scholar for whom this book has been written is unique among social anthropologists in her capacity to relate the politics of the small-scale to the politics of the large-scale, treating both with high skill, and demonstrating that her brilliance as a social anthropologist springs from her being more than just that. This essay follows a common anthropological style in the study of the politics of complex societies, in that it gives most attention to the smaller-scale features of the Chinese polity, but, in honoring Lucy Mair, it tries at the end to rise above parochialism in order to suggest how anthropology and history may together produce a more convincing political analysis than either is able to offer on its own.

The study of lineage structure and organization is one of the main ways in which social anthropology has established itself within the general study of Chinese society. Up to quite recent times—in fact, up to five years ago or so—the Western writings on China normally made use of the term "clan" when referring to patrilineal kinship groups; and it was of course no *anthropological* discovery that throughout China, although in differing degrees of elaborateness in different parts of the country, groups formed on the ground which recruited their members on the basis of descent in the male line from common ancestors. The existence of "clans" was responsible in part for attracting anthropological attention to China, for the study of unilineal descent systems played a major role in a major phase of the discipline's development. If we ignore Marcel Granet's work, which is concerned with archaic forms of Chinese kinship, and has paradoxically had more influence upon the general study of kinship than upon the study of Chinese kinship (cf. Lévi-Strauss [1949] 1969: chaps. 19–21), we shall find the first attempt to be systematic

In John H. R. Davis, ed., *Choice and Change: Essays in Honor of Lucy Mair* (London, 1974), 68–88. London School of Economics and Political Science, Monographs on Social Anthropology, 50.

about the Chinese "clan" in Hu Hsien-chin, *The Common Descent Group in China and Its Functions* (1948). That book, written from within American anthropology, brought together a great deal of evidence from all over China on the functions (ritual, judicial, and economic) of the *tsu*, but it showed less interest in matters of morphology and was very reluctant to treat the *tsu* as one example of a form of kinship grouping widely distributed in the ethnographic record.[1]

The Chinese "clan"/*tsu* became a "lineage"—as every social anthropologist will at once guess—because of the diffusion of a category used by British students of African society. The term "lineage" was brought in to avoid the vagueness inherent in "clan" and to label those forms of unilineal kinship organization which were both corporate (in Maine's sense) and based upon the notion that the steps of descent back from the living generations to the apical ancestor could be spelled out. The African literature showed how lineages might form the basis of political life, by furnishing a series of articulated groups; it became clear that some analogies were to be found in China.

In a world of transient families[2] and kindreds an individual was, in many parts of China, a member of a corporation—or of a series of wider and wider corporations—based upon agnatic kinship. Lineages might be shallow or deep, small or large in their membership. They might be in one or more villages. What at one point in time might be small and simple might at another grow to be large and complex—and vice versa, for there was waning as well as waxing. Let us imagine a small nucleus of agnates (even perhaps those within one family) establishing itself in new terrain. (And because we are used to thinking of China as a crowded country, we need to remember that up to about the end of the eighteenth century there were opportunities for pioneers to expand at least to the southeast and the southwest of the country.) The nucleus may for some time continue to regard itself as part of the lineage it has left behind. If it is demographically and economically successful, the lapse of a few generations will see it composed of a number of families tracing their descent, so far as their male members are concerned, from a common ancestor. They are now a small lineage which either stands by itself or constitutes a segment of the lineage from which it sprang. A portion of land will have been set aside to finance the rites performed at the tomb of the local founding ancestor or the rites performed at a central ancestral shrine (or both). More time passes, and on the same assumption of success, the local lineage is now a large community which is segmented. Lesser agnatic groups have crystalized within it. The process by which the segments have come into being is the same as that by which the local lineage was created: an endowed ancestral grave or shrine is established to mark the segment and enable it to continue.[a] We shall see later on that this model of lineage growth and segmentation will not alone account for all the forms of agnatic grouping we can find in China; but it will do for our present purposes.

The property aspect of the process has an important consequence for the segmentary order. A sizable local lineage was unlikely to be composed of families at one level of prosperity, and differences in riches were reflected in differences in segmentation. New segments did not come into being in accordance with some rule that operated automatically upon the genealogical framework: a new segment was created when one small group of agnates were able to differentiate themselves from other members of their segment by financing their separation out—either by focusing on an ancestor in whose name the new property was to be held (and who would distinguish them from the descendants of other ancestors), or by a man entailing part of his estate to his agnatic descendants collectively to prevent his property being dispersed. The segmentary order, then, was uneven or asymmetrical (see Freedman 1958: 48f). Any family might be a member of a rising hierarchy of segments—a Chinese box within a set of Chinese boxes—benefiting from the resources of each, but different families might be members of a different number of such segments. The poorer the branch of the lineage to which any family belongs, the fewer the number of segments from which it is likely to benefit—and the higher its chance, as a consequence, of remaining poor.

The male agnates of each family (*chia*) were joint holders of an estate which, upon the death of the parental generation and the partition of the family, was divided equally among the sons, except that an extra share might go to the oldest of them in recognition of that primogeniture which in imperial China was a mere shadow of its feudal self. But the head of a family (as we have seen), or a group of brothers acting jointly, might decide to withhold from the division some portion of the property to form an ancestral estate or to be added to one already existing. Ancestral property, unlike family property, became (in theory) immune to division and acted as the anchor to which a segment was attached.[b] The

[a] Let me cite a literary source. In *The Dream of the Red Chamber* Ko Ching appears in a dream to Phoenix and explains that she is concerned for the future of the house of Chia. "True, the Chia clan had endured . . . for hundreds of years already, but blossoming is likely to be followed by decay. . . . Two things were on her mind: the consolidation of the family school and insurance of the perpetuity of the quarterly sacrifices to the ancestors. There was a need to buy family estates, thereby forming a lasting and inalienable family foundation. . . . A future dedicated to such cultural purposes would, even if the worst came to the worst, be safe from seizures by the State." (Ts'ao 1958: 93–94.)

[b] There appears to be another way in which ancestral estates sometimes came into being. There is reason to suppose that when new land was created by collective effort, as in the

estates of lineages and their segments might be agricultural land, and often were; but they might also take the form of rice mills or fishponds. They might be exploited in different ways. Small ancestral estates seem typically to have been passed round, year by year, among member families, the family for the time being holding an estate profiting by the difference between what they could extract from it and what they had to pay out to discharge the duties (providing the sacrifices and so on) that went with the privilege. Larger estates seem generally to have been subject to managements which rented them out and distributed the annual income to all members after paying for the appropriate sacrifices and other collective activities (which might include running a school).

Lineage relations in most cases stopped at the local community. That is to say, the commonest form of lineage we can see (in the literature and, as field-workers, on the ground) is the local lineage on its own: it may occupy a village or part of one. But a number of such local lineages might—as we should expect from the model set out earlier in the essay— be aggregated in a particular region to form a higher-order lineage which again was centered on an ancestral tomb or shrine. Those of us who have worked in the Hong Kong New Territories are familiar with the case of the Teng (Cantonese: Tang) local lineages which in pre-British days clearly formed a powerful higher-order lineage dominating the economic and political life of a large part of the county of Hsin-an. (Cf. Baker 1966.) Now, once we reach this level of organization we need to be careful about our terms and about the evidence for the existence of such agnatic groups. Local lineages might ally themselves temporarily for some political purpose (as in the pursuit of an interlineage struggle or against the county administration); they might be of the same surname, and therefore, in the Chinese view, of ultimate common descent, but they were not by that fact alone a single higher-order lineage. It is only when an alliance of that sort was made permanent and expressed by the establishment of an estate that we may say that a new higher-order lineage had come into being. Again, Chinese genealogists casting about for the ties which might be assumed historically to have linked lineages now widely separated might draw up accounts that made it seem as though groups of local lineages belonged together in one superordinate unit; but in reality these units were, and might well remain, artefacts of historiography and are not to be confused with organized entities.

Let us turn to the place of lineages within Chinese society. In what

---

reclamations along the southeastern coast, it might at once be established as an ancestral estate and kept out of the family mill which over the generations could grind property into smaller and smaller pieces. Cf. Wakeman 1966: 153.

sense were lineages treated as political entities and, perhaps, legal persons? We come up against an interesting feature of the Chinese political system: the relations between central power and individual subject were intended by the state to be mediated, up to a point, by his kinship ties. The *chia* (family) was, in the official view, a group of people owning a common estate and standing responsible for one another in some realms of conduct.[c] Beyond *chia* the state looked to the mourning grades (*wu-fu*) (cf. Freedman 1958: 41ff, 101ff) for a definition of the range within which an individual could be said to be involved in relationships such that his obligations to the state were modified. That is, we may say that at the levels of *chia* and *wu-fu* double loyalty was institutionalized. In the eyes of the state, a Confucian state, kinship was eminently respectable and could be held in some ways to cut across obligations to the sovereign. (Of course, the conflict between the two kinds of obligation could be rationalized away by asserting that a man who fulfilled his kinship obligations was by that fact a good and loyal subject.[d])

So far we can be carried along in the argument by the standard sources. But there is more to it than that. Confucianists did not usually philosophize about lineages (as against *chia* and kinship in general),[3] but when they were officers in the bureaucracy and had, especially in southeastern China, to deal with lineages, they treated them as respectable entities which embodied, on a larger scale than *chia* and *wu-fu*, the Confucian virtue of kinship solidarity. Moreover, the lineage could be looked to to police itself and help in the smooth collection of taxes. Whatever view we may take of the range of duties and functions of the Chinese county (*hsien*) mandarin, it is obvious that the maintenance of public order and tax-collecting were the two basic activities. His legal duties were defined in such a way as to make public peace to a large degree measurable by the absence of court business. Small-scale disorder which was contained within local units (villages or local lineages) and which could be prevented from being evidenced in the yamen (the mandarin's court) was no disorder;[4] and the administrator was not tempted to go out looking for trouble. Accordingly, lineages capable of managing their own affairs and

[c] There is a fascinating example in Bodde and Morris 1967: 193 of the way in which this official view could get worked into judicial reasoning. When two or more men were clearly not members of a single domestic group, but it was desirable to treat them as though they were in order to increase the penalty awardable to somebody who had wronged them, then the term *chia* might be stretched to cover even more or less temporary associations between men provided they could be said to have economic resources in common.

[d] See Fung 1949: 18–30 for some interesting observations on the relationship between *hsiao*, "filial piety" (and, by extension, duties to kin), and *chung*, loyalty to the sovereign. At pp. 29–30 he says that conflict might sometimes occur between the two classes of duty, and then "it was the duty of the son as a son that should receive first consideration."

blocking off attempts to raise disputes to the level of the yan
certainly a very good thing. In a like manner, while in theory
dividual owed a duty to the state to pay his taxes to its repres   ,
a well-organized lineage capable of producing the necessary yield from its
members was clearly an administrative convenience.

We shall have to go on from this point to consider the limits to the
state's tolerance of lineage organization, but for the moment we must
turn back to the internal order of the lineage to understand how it articulated with the external order. There has been a tendency (which in part
arises from a confusion of lineage with family) to speak of lineages in
China as though, when they were more than small groups, they were
characteristic of the rich and the powerful and not to be found among the
poor and the weak. That view shuts off a more rewarding one: the most
interesting feature of Chinese lineages is that they were often heterogeneous in their membership. While it makes good sense to speak of
some lineages being richer or stronger than others, the richer and the
stronger the lineage the more it was likely to be differentiated into rich
and poor, strong and weak. One must be careful to distinguish between
statements about the standing of lineages and statements about the
standing of families and individuals within lineages. Of course, many
individuals and families in rich and strong lineages were poorer than
individuals and families in poor and weak lineages. The differences within strong lineages were an aspect of the system of uneven (asymmetrical)
segmentation discussed earlier in the essay. Riches and power accumulated unevenly in the lineage. Members of rich segments had better access
to education and to the sources of power outside the lineage, and greater
opportunity to exercise control over lineage affairs as a whole.

We have now to make a distinction between political leaders and ritual
elders. Within a lineage and within each of its formal segments the oldest
man in the most senior generation was the ritual elder; that is, he took
the chief place in the performance of the periodic rites of ancestor worship, either at the ancestral hall altar (or shrine) or the key tomb. That
role was given genealogically. But the roles of political and economic
management were held by lineage and segment elites formed by men
whose standing rested, not upon genealogical position, but upon their
riches and their ties with the greater social world beyond the lineage. In
some lineages, the powerful political leaders belonged to what is often
nowadays referred to as the "gentry": the titled scholars, who had competed successfully in the state examinations or who had bought themselves equivalent titles. As soon as we picture to ourselves a lineage in
which there were both actual and potential mandarins on the one hand,

and uneducated farmers on the other, we realize that we are dealing with something very different from the homogeneous rich lineage that as a false stereotype sometimes infects the literature.

A very few lineages included in their ranks men who had attained the very highest positions in their society; and at once we see another crucial aspect of Chinese society. The study of lineage organization shows us, as does that of other features of the society, that no hard and fast distinction can be drawn between rural and urban society (cf. Cartier 1970). One does not expect lineage organization to take the same form in town and country (see Baker 1977 and Fried 1966), and it is obvious that urban conditions inhibit its development; but to move from country-side to town in traditional Chinese society was not to leave one social world and enter another. We are certainly not studying a society in which all that was rich and sophisticated was in the towns and all that was poor and naive in the villages. True, the richer and more educated a man, the more likely he was to have dealings in the towns, and even perhaps establish a house there. (Cf. Elvin 1970: 105f on cities as centers of "landlord power.") But he was not by those facts alienated from his rural home. On the contrary, home was in the village with which his ancestors were linked, and he was likely to spend a great part of his life there, even if, as an official, his work often took him elsewhere. Both through the hierarchy of administrative centers (from the county seat upward to the imperial capital) and the hierarchy of marketplaces (cf. Skinner 1964, 1965a, and 1971: 272ff), the lineage was linked into the wider society by its politically and economically more mobile members. These were the men through whom lineages could maintain their position and assert their rights vis-à-vis the county mandarin and those who stood above him. That county mandarin might have within his jurisdiction one or more lineages that included members who outranked him or, at any rate, who were strong enough to prevent him exercising fully the authority vested in him by the state.

It follows that a poor family in a powerful lineage was inferior and exploitable at home yet in a privileged position against the wider world. The riches, renown, and power that from one point of view were the prerogative of the lineage elite were from another the property of the lineage as a whole, all its members sharing in it. Whom the elite might oppress at home they might protect abroad. They might effectively rob the poor of their rightful share in the lineage estates and rig the rules about ritual privileges so as to monopolize them, but in his transactions with the members of other lineages the poor man in a strong lineage could stand with powerful co-members behind him.

Having to deal with organized lineages, led often by powerful men, the state found itself in a dilemma. Clearly, agnatic organization was to be approved; it demonstrated its orthodox virtue by the ceremonialized piety of the ancestral sacrifices and the lavish care of graves. At the level of ideas and ritual no exception could be taken. But say a lineage grew to be a great power on the local scene, engaging in acts of organized violence against other lineages and extending the area of its control; and say, even worse, that such a rising lineage began to form, along with other lineages of its surname in the area, a superordinate lineage by manipulating genealogies and setting up higher-order tombs and shrines; why then, the state took fright, and what had up to then been agnation respectable became at once agnation perilous. In other words, the Chinese state was responsible for creating a stick for beating its own back. It legitimated agnatic organization. It gave power to lineages by *de facto* recognition of their corporate nature; it fed the power of lineages by providing their elites with influence and prestige. And always the state ran the risk of that power being turned against its own interests—whence the screams against fraudulent genealogies and the sporadic attempts to put down interlineage fighting. On that last topic I have written a good deal (Freedman 1958: 105–12; 1966: 8f, 104–15) and I do not want to go over familiar ground, but I might add to the evidence a passage from Alabaster (1899), a source I have not before used.[5] he writes of the "clan fights" which "occur especially in Kwangtung and Fukien" that they are

the direct result of the clan system . . . and cause perpetual turbulence and often great loss of life. Many allusions to these occurrences appear in the Peking Gazette, and the evil seems to be an organised one, not capable of effective repression by the administration. Even where a case attains to judicial process, the employment of false witnesses, and assumption of responsibility by the whole clan, renders it a hard matter to reach a fair issue (p. 451). . . . In the south of China special provision is made for the repression of the clan fights which flourish there, and care has been taken when dealing with affrays to settle whether they come under these special clauses or not. That there are a number of people engaged, and that one side belongs to one part of the country and the other side to another, does not necessarily constitute a clan fight. The points to determine are whether there was a feud to start with, whether the fight was premeditated, whether men were hired to take part in it (there being regular professional fighters—free lances —open to engagement), and whether the factions went armed to the field. When it appears from these facts that it was a deliberate clan fight and not a chance or ordinary affair, the organiser will be held responsible as well as those actually taking part in the fight—the punishment being regulated by the number of men there were engaged upon the side of the organiser, and also by the number killed upon the other side. Nor are *both* sides to be brought under the clauses, unless the fight was prearranged between them—the attacking side ordinarily coming under the operation of the special statute (pp. 459f).

I would add only that the most bellicose lineages were the great ones (a fact still to be observed in the Hong Kong New Territories, although of course there the hostilities are more effectively restrained); and the great ones were precisely those most closely bonded to the state. What power the state gave them they could turn against it. In the field of lineage organization we are able to see in the clearest light the fact that political order in traditional Chinese society was based upon a tension between ties to the state and ties to kin. To make the most of both called for the exercise of great political skill.

I want now to turn to the big question of the uneven distribution of deep and large lineages in China. The first point to be made is that the evidence flies in the face of any theory that makes developed lineage organization the primeval pattern of Chinese society. (Since most writers on China recognize that the lineage as we now know it did not develop until the beginning of the imperial period and was not generalized within Chinese society for some centuries, it would perhaps be better to say that the evidence contradicts a theory that at some unspecified time in the past all Chinese were grouped in deep lineages, the smaller agnatic units now to be seen being taken as broken remnants.[6]) The fact is that developed lineage organization appears precisely where Chinese society is most recently established and appears to be largely absent where it is longest established. It is not for nothing that the provinces of Fukien and Kwangtung, on the southeastern border of the country and comparative late-comers to Chinese civilization, are singled out for mention whenever the subject comes up; they are not alone in presenting evidence of developed lineage organization on a wide scale, but they form the region where that model of organization has been most persistently followed. The lineages that we are still able to study (see especially Potter 1968 and Baker 1968) because of the academically happy accident that Britain acquired a 99-year lease of a large part of Hsin-an county in 1898 and made of that acquisition the New Territories of Hong Kong, are creations of the last 800 years, many of them tracing their points of origin to times much closer to the present day than that. Through the evidence we have accumulated, we can see them establishing themselves in unoccupied areas, expanding their agricultural lands, fortifying their settlements with formidable walls, watchtowers, and moats, and coming to dominate, politically and economically, the lesser lineages growing up around them. The southeast was a frontier area where new land could be brought into cultivation and where state control was weak. Lineages could build up large holdings, many of them entailed in lineage and segment estates, and at the same time amass huge local power. The area has one further feature that may be relevant to the problem under discussion: its agriculture is based upon wet rice, a highly productive crop that has allowed land to be set aside in inalienable estates—those estates which, as we have seen, lie at the heart of the segmentary system.

That argument I have set out before (Freedman 1966: 159–64). It has been taken up by Potter (1970): drawing upon his field data from the Ping Shan Tang lineage in the New Territories and other sources, he adds commercial development to the budget of factors (wealth created in trade being invested in land) and concludes, in his penultimate paragraph (p. 138), as follows:

> The evidence represented by the Ping Shan data would support a hypothesis that the strongest lineages would tend to be found in the agriculturally most productive two-crop rice regions of China, in frontier regions far from central government control, and especially in areas where industry and commerce were highly developed. The weakest lineages would tend to be located in North China's poorest agricultural areas, in long-settled areas where effective government control was present, and in regions characterized by subsistence agriculture and little commercial development. Moreover, in all areas lineage organization would tend to be weaker under strong dynasties and stronger in interregnal periods or under weak dynasties.

But the argument has come in for some comment from another quarter. The general view of the Chinese lineage I formed long before I had ever studied in the New Territories was confirmed (especially in regard to lineage segmentation) by the anthropologists who went to the New Territories with lineage organization at the center of their attention. The first was Potter (1968, 1969, 1970), the second Baker (1966, 1968); and other material collected in the New Territories has, along with data picked up here and there in the sources on the mainland of China, tended to reconfirm the general analysis. But there is another important group of anthropologists at work on Chinese society: the largely American group concentrating, so far as field study is concerned, on Taiwan; and from their researches, particularly those by M. L. Cohen (1969) and Pasternak (1968a, 1968b, 1969), there has emerged a significantly different picture. It is not that what they say controverts what has been said about lineage structure on the mainland of China (including of course the New Territories of Hong Kong); on the contrary, they accept it by and large as part of the historical background of the Chinese groups they have studied in the more recently settled Taiwan. The new element in their work lies in its tracing of a different process of lineage formation. Cohen and Pasternak, both working among Taiwan Hakkas, have pointed out that when lineages have emerged they have done so by the amalgamation of previously distinct agnatic groups. As I understand their argument, in the earlier phase of settlement of the island, and still today very generally, families proliferated and dispersed in such a way that they were unlikely to be included within some wider agnatic grouping. Local communities were composed of heterogeneous kinship elements. But in some cases a collection of groups of the same surname, scattered over an area, might be brought organizationally together within the framework of a lineage endowed with an estate, even though it was not possible to arrange the various agnatic components of the new unit in a coherent genealogical scheme. Whereas, therefore, the process of lineage formation on the mainland is seen as a matter of segmentation—a small agnatic group growing and gradually becoming differentiated internally by the emergence of new segments, and segments within segments, as in the simple model constructed earlier in this essay—in Taiwan, lineages appear to have come about by a process of fusion, independent units being welded together. To put the matter differently: if frontier conditions on the mainland encouraged small agnatic groups to grow into large ones, each such group striving to increase the territory under its control and maintaining its territorial compactness, frontier conditions in Taiwan (in a more recent movement of southern Chinese that took them over the water to new land) led families to disperse and then later to regroup themselves in fabricated lineage groups that tied together small units scattered over a large area. In mainland Fukien and in Kwangtung the association between agnatic grouping and local grouping was tight; emigrants from those same provinces moving to Taiwan built up a system in which agnatic ties and territorial ties cut across each other.

That is an interesting difference (although it is not clear to me yet how far the alternative model applies to non-Hakka in Taiwan). But it cannot escape our attention that the process of lineage formation in Taiwan, as Cohen and Pasternak have described it, corresponds closely to the process on the mainland by which local lineages were grouped into higher-order lineages by genealogical manipulation and the setting up of tombs and shrines. In other words, a process of lineage regrouping can be seen to have taken place both on the mainland and in Taiwan, but it appears to operate on localized lineages in the one case and on small groups of related families in the other. These two models of lineage formation having now been confronted, it will be found (I suggest) that they are both relevant to all parts of China, and that the closer we look at the evidence (the written genealogies and other sources), the more we shall discover that the Taiwan Hakka pattern is to be detected on the mainland, and that what I have described as the mainland pattern is also discernible in Taiwan. A more sophisticated model of the foundation and growth of the Chinese lineage than that set out earlier in this essay might then include, before the phase of elaborate internal differentiation, a phase during which scattered elements are brought together (territorially and genealogically, or at least genealogically) to form the lineage to begin with. If we reexamine the data on the Hong Kong New Territories (e.g. Aijmer 1967: 53–59 on Hakka, and Baker 1968: 28–30 on the early history of the Sheung Shui lineage) we may be able to benefit from the analyses made by M. L. Cohen and Pasternak.[7]

The latter's work also bears upon one of my earlier arguments—to knock it down. In *Chinese Lineage and Society* (1966: 159–62) I ventured to suggest that the establishment of irrigation works in pioneer conditions may have promoted large-scale lineage organization: dense populations were built up in small areas; the joint investment of labor in bringing new land into cultivation led to the setting up of undivided (lineage and segment) estates. In his 1969 paper Pasternak says that when a frontier area is being opened up and the population is heterogeneous (as it was in Taiwan), cooperative irrigation works will be undertaken by nonagnates, and the significant associations that people form will not of course be based upon agnation. Moreover, when government control is weak and the pioneers have to fend for themselves, the alliances created will be among nonagnates, since the population is agnatically heterogeneous to start with. He writes (p. 554):

It seems to me . . . that in the absence of effective state force, ethnic conflict in frontier situations might well encourage an initial articulation and cooperation of families and individuals among primarily territorial and ethnic lines rather than in terms of kinship. . . . Where the frontier situation involves an entrenched ethnic group, challenged by an initially less structural [*sic*] immigrant group, the emergence of multi-surname villges and non-kin associations of various sorts would be more likely than the formation of single-surname villages and large, highly corporate, localized lineages. For purposes of offense and defense, such communities might themselves be integrated into higher-order associations or alliances through the extension of kin (agnatic and affinal) and nonkin (e.g. ethnic, linguistic, or religious) affiliations.

And at the end of this interesting paper Pasternak suggests the possibility that the full realization of the patrilineal ideology (on which my own analysis has placed so much emphasis) may be part of the second, not the first, phase of settlement in a frontier area. He may well be right. I am particularly pleased that he has mounted his argument against me on the basis of field experience in Taiwan which, together with the Hong Kong New Territories, is all we have for the intensive field study of traditional Chinese society. It is reassuring to know that the opportunities are at last being used.

The view from Taiwan reinforces the need to keep the study of the lineage within the framework of the study of *all* groups and relationships.

Agnatic kinship is but one important axis along which Chinese society organized itself; and to understand its significance it must be taken in its full social context. The study of all modes of grouping and alignment—not only lineage but also village, marketing community, *hsiang*, secret society, cult, and so on—will show us how complex was the political system within which agnatic kinship played a role. But it is at this very point that the anthropologist, basing himself upon his own field study and those conducted by his colleagues in Hong Kong and Taiwan, finds himself checked in his progress by the nature of his evidence: much of the traditional political system is no longer there to be observed, and some of its remnants are tantalizingly obscure—unless the historian comes to the rescue.

I shall take an example from my own experience. In 1963 I carried out a field survey of the New Territories and wrote a report which contained, in the section dealing with political matters, an account of a system which, at the time of the British takeover in 1899, covered a large part of the area with a network of village groupings under the name of *yüeh* (Cantonese: *yeuk*), "compacts/treaties." I went on to show how one aggregate of such *yüeh* was involved in the foundation of a new market at Tai Po in the early 1890's and how it had persisted into modern life (Freedman 1963b [Essay 12 below]: 5–10; and cf. 1966: 82–89, and Groves 1964). *Yüeh* and another term for a local grouping, *tung* ("cave"), puzzled me greatly, but I was then in no position to start a historical inquiry that would show the extent to which the terms in these specialized uses were general in China, or the significance of the groupings in the nineteenth-century political system. But (1963b: 9) I linked up *yüeh* with *hsiang-yüeh* (the public lecture system) and sketched the interpenetration of *hsiang-yüeh*, *pao-chia*, and *li-chia* (the last two being governmental systems of grouping for security and taxation). I wrote:

It is on record that in places in Kwangtung the heads of "hsiang-yüeh" assumed roles of local leadership in such a way as to take command of local affairs. In addition, "hsiang-yüeh" were used as a setting for organising "regiment and drill corps" ("t'uan-lien") for local defence, and it is an interesting speculation that just as the "ke yüeh hsiang-yung," the village braves of the several *yeuk*, rallied to the defence of Canton against the British in 1842 [a slip for 1841], so we might find on closer inspection that some of the armed resistance to the first British in the New Territories was bound up with the Ts'at Yeuk [the seven *Yüeh*, the grouping associated with the founding of the new Tai Po market] and other *yeuk*-complexes.[8]

That was an anthropological guess, and later research, historical and anthropological, has shown it to be right. A few years after my New Territories Report was written, an American historian published a remarkable study of political developments in the Canton region in the middle of the last century (Wakeman 1966), and within another few years an anthropologist who had been at work in the Tai Po area of the New Territories produced a paper (Groves 1969) in which, basing himself on Wakeman's historical study and the recent anthropological work on Chinese lineage organization and marketing systems, he demonstrated from the British documents on the takeover of the New Territories in 1899 that the armed resistance to the British was merely one example of a nineteenth-century pattern in which lineage and local organizations were meshed to produce a social grouping able to mobilize sizable forces of village men for local defense.

The parallels with the Kwangtung militia of the 1840s and '50s are evident. Scarcely three weeks lapsed between the first meetings . . . and the final battle on 18 April [1899]. Within this time, over 2,000 armed men were mobilised and put into the field. As was the case half a century earlier, this was accomplished by means of well established and enduring sets of relationships that reflected the close-knit social structure and organisation of rural Kwangtung province (p. 58).

Wakeman, the historian, drew for his interpretation in part on the anthropological work on Chinese lineage organization; Groves, as we have just seen, drew upon Wakeman; since then, a further American historical work (Kuhn 1970), matching Wakeman's in its freshness and importance, builds upon both historical and (of course to a much lesser extent) anthropological research to treat the question of the militarization of Chinese society in the middle of the nineteenth century. The interaction between the history and the anthropology of Chinese society has been set going.[9]

From this new work, full to overflowing in its significance for our understanding of Chinese society, I want to extract one political point for comment. Looking at the British official papers on conditions in the New Territories at the time of the takeover, I was disturbed by Stewart Lockhart's account of local self-government, for it conflicted both with my general view of Chinese government at the local level and with my understanding of the hierarchy of local units in Chinese society. In 1899 Lockhart wrote:

The gentry and elders in the village council determined summarily cases of theft, disputes about land, domestic squabbles, and cases of debt. As a rule the decision of that council is accepted as final. But if either of the parties to a case is dissatisfied, he can appeal to a council of the Tung, or to a general council, made up of representatives of the different Tung. . . . In addition to a council of a Tung there is a general council for the whole of the Tung [= east] Lo or Eastern Sec-

tion ... styled the Tung [= east] P'ing Kuk [Mandarin: *Tung-p'ing Ch'ü*]. ...
If the decision of the council of the Tung, or of the General Council is not regarded as satisfactory, an appeal lies to the magistrate of the district (Hayes
1962: 9f).[10]

I confessed myself "sceptical about some of Lockhart's data on local
organisation and local tribunals, but I have not yet marshalled enough
historical material to be able to enter into a debate on these topics"
(Freedman 1963b: 10; and cf. Freedman 1966: 81f). Nor would I have
made any progress with the problem, try as I might, without the new
historical research by Wakeman and Kuhn.[11] In the event, Groves's
paper (1969: 40f) made the problem vanish: what Lockhart was clearly
describing—one can say "clearly" now that Groves has written his analysis—was the *t'uan-lien*, local militia system, which seems to have marked
a sharp turn in the political life of China from the 1840's onward.

Although its origins go further back in time (Wakeman 1966: 23f;
Kuhn 1970: 41ff, 64) a system of gentry-organized local militia was effectively begun by the Opium War.[12] The government feared this militia
and with good reason but, especially because of its role in the resistance
to the British in 1849 at Canton, to the rebels in the Red Turban rising
of 1854–55, and to the British and the French in the Arrow War (which
began in 1856), *t'uan-lien* seems to have established itself as a feature of,
and a mutation within, the political system of China. Up to that point in
Chinese history the control exercised by the government over the countryside rested, *inter alia*, upon the partial dissociation of the local gentry
from the people among whom they lived. That gentry had a political role
vis-à-vis the local representatives of the government (chiefly the county
mandarins) by its informal expression of local opinion and its mediation
between the governors and the mass of the governed;[13] but it was not
until the *t'uan-lien* system grew to be accepted as legitimate that the
gentry were permitted to engage actively and officially in the organization of local political life and to put themselves into offices within structures over which the government in effect had little control. As the historians have pointed out, the breakdown of national unity in the early
twentieth century had among its causes the weakening of government
control by the rise of the political power of the gentry in the middle of
the last century. (See, for example, Ichiko 1968: 299 for a succinct
statement.)

But who precisely were the local gentry? Scholars unfamiliar with the
historical and sociological writing on China need to be told that this
question cannot be answered from a general survey of sinological opinion; the definition of "gentry" is hotly debated (and an outsider might

well wonder why so much fuss is made over a label, and not even a Chinese one at that).[14] And, while the anthropologists sometimes intervene (cf. Fei 1953, and Freedman 1956, 1958: 53–60, 1966: 69f), they cannot regard themselves as authorities. But I think we may safely say that however difficult it may be in particular cases definitively to assign the members of a given population to one or other of the two groups "commoners and gentry," there was in traditional Chinese society a class of men who, by their close association with the literary values and their command of the literary skills upon which the governmental system was based, formed an elite in every largish area. Some of these *literati* were themselves officers of the government, but now resident at home because they were between postings or on (obligatory) mourning leave. Some were retired or about-to-be-appointed government officials. A much greater number were *sheng-yüan* or *chien-sheng*, that is to say, titled *literati* not yet of a status to qualify for government office. And of course one must take into account the members of *literati* families who for one reason or another had not attained even to the standing of *sheng-yüan* or *chien-sheng*, and the members of non-*literati* families who by their worldly success had in some way assimilated themselves to the gentry.[e]

The privileges and standing of the gentry within the communities where they lived were based historically on their constituting the pool of talent from which the bureaucracy was recruited. Their pursuits were gentlemanly,[f] even if at times commercial, and their general cultural style acted as a barrier which allowed them to live among and associate closely with "commoners" without losing their distinctiveness. There was social mobility; the style could be acquired; the many who did not have it could observe it at fairly close quarters. And because in this fashion the gentry were in but not entirely of their local communities they were no serious threat to the regime. But the extensive local militarization of Chinese society in the middle of the nineteenth century set the gentry up as local organizers;[g] hitherto the rule of "avoidance" had prevented them from

[e] And note Kuhn's view (1970: 66–67): "Leaders at the lowest level of defense organization in the *t'uan-lien* system, were often lower degree holders—*sheng-yuan* or *chien-sheng* —or those degree aspirants, the *t'ung-sheng*. Such leaders might also be holders of purchased brevet rank. But the leadership of simplex *t'uan* was by no means confined to men with formal degree status, and we can find in the record many examples of commoners who, by virtue of their wealth and community influence, were functionally indistinguishable from titled scholars in community defense."

[f] Moore (1966: 167) points out: "Though the scholar-landlords lived in the countryside, unlike their English and German counterparts (even *some* of their Russian and French ones), they seemed to have played no part whatever in the actual work of cultivation, not even a supervisory one."

[g] In Wakeman's view (1966: 115–16) the events of the 1840's in the Canton region led, via the creation of the system of local militia, to a slackening of the bonds holding rich

exercising authority where they were at home; the kind of local hierarchy described by Lockhart at the end of the century could now develop.

One other aspect of *t'uan-lien* is worth comment. Skinner's work on marketing systems (1964, 1965a, 1965b) has made us sensitive to the difference between what might be called the official and social topography of China: administrative maps drew their lines for marking out jurisdictions which might fit only roughly, if they fitted at all, with the conformation of communities and their groupings. The advent of a local militia system, based upon previous groupings of gentry and the local communities (lineages, villages, and aggregations of lineages and villages) to which they belonged, introduced the social map of China into the official map (cf. Kuhn 1970: 101f and 104).

The county (*hsien*) and its official subdivisions, *hsiang*, together with *pao-chia* and *li-chia* were now not the only legitimate political segments of the society. And I repeat what I said on an earlier occasion (only I had then no clear idea of the historical causes involved): when the British took over the island of Hong Kong as a result of the Opium War, they began by imitating the *pao-chia* system; when they assumed the administration of the New Territories fifty-seven years later they looked to the social map (*yüeh* included) which had by then clearly come to be taken as defining officially accepted areas. (Cf. Freedman 1966: 82 n. 2.)

As an anthropologist one starts from the Chinese lineage and one finishes up on the grand theme of the disintegration of the traditional Chinese political order. Lineage is but one form of organization and needs to be seen in the context of all other forms. One advances up to the limit of one's competence as an anthropologist and then turns for enlightenment to the historian. It is not of course for me to speak for the historians, but it is clear enough that they, symmetrically, are on the lookout for data, clues, and lessons from the anthropologists. As I write this essay (August 1971) hopes are being expressed for the resumption of anthropological field study in mainland China. If in that next phase of the social anthropology of China the field-workers become again, as they were in the 1930's, so intoxicated with the present that they forget that China has a past, they will slide back from the advance in sinological anthropology that has been made, doubtless improbably enough, by its being confined to Taiwan and the Hong Kong New Territories.[15]

---

and poor together in the same lineages. "As this process went on, the peasantry became disaffected. Greater and greater numbers began to join secret societies that transcended the clan." Kuhn 1970: 79 n. 32 challenges the truth of this analysis. It certainly would be difficult to test.

On the Sociological Study of Chinese Religion

Quand vous gémissez sur la politique de Mao Tse-toung à
l'égard des religions, vous montrez simplement que vous igno-
rez tout de l'histoire de la Chine.
—Etiemble, *Connaissons-nous la Chine?*

The character of this paper is in part explained by the purpose for which
its earlier version was composed. As the reader of this volume will by
now know, it arises from a conference on Chinese religion and ritual, one
of a series of meetings on the sociology and anthropology of China. In
ignorance of what my fellow contributors to the conference would say in
their papers, I took it upon myself to play the programist and in that
role to suggest some broad lines along which the sociological study of
Chinese religion might develop. As matters turned out, some of my ser-
monizing proved embarrassingly unnecessary, but in this revised version
of my paper I have retained its original spirit,[1] in order to reinforce what
I consider to be, in the present state of the sociology of China, the proper
trend it has taken.

I began the exercise of thinking myself into my subject by rereading,
among other standard works, C. K. Yang's *Religion in Chinese Society*.
That book is, after all, the latest of the very few works of its kind: an
attempt to characterize Chinese religion as a whole and in relation to the
society within which it was thought and practiced.[2] I then went back to

In Arthur P. Wolf, ed., *Religion and Ritual in Chinese Society* (Stanford, Calif., 1974),
19–41. The original version was prepared for the Conference on Religion and Ritual in
Chinese Society held at Asilomar, Pacific Grove, Calif., 11–15 Oct. 1971, under the auspices of the Subcommittee on Research on Chinese Society of the ACLS-SSRC Joint Committee on Contemporary China. A shortened version was read at a meeting of the University Association for the Sociology of Religion held at the London School of Economics and
Political Science on 15 Dec. 1971.

the review of the book I had written in 1962, to discover that I was now less in sympathy with the review than with the book it criticized. It seemed to me that in 1962 I was perched on an anthropological high horse (irritated by Yang's simpleminded treatment of ancestor worship) and skeptical about the possibility of making an advance in the study of Chinese religion without, as I put it, "a change in method and an accession of new data. One could argue that the next step would be to formulate a series of clearly defined problems and then tackle them on the basis of a detailed scrutiny of the literature and painstaking field investigations of Chinese behaving and expressing their beliefs in religious contexts." (Freedman 1962c: 534–35.) I do not now much care for the way in which the point is made, although I was not, I think, altogether wrong in making it. But I wish that in 1962 I had not passed so quickly over Yang's main achievement and the possibilities of our building upon it; I mean his interpretation of Chinese religion taken as a whole. And that is the topic upon which this essay effectively opens—and upon which it ends.

A Chinese religion exists; or, at any rate, we ought to begin with that assumption: the religious ideas and practices of the Chinese are not a congeries of haphazardly assembled elements, all appearances and the greater part of the extensive literature to the contrary. Consider, for example, Doré's and Wieger's compilations, which, precious sources of data though they unquestionably are, reduce the reader to a state of stunned resignation before a mass of nonaggregative facts.[3] Behind the superficial variety there is order of some sort. That order might be expressed by our saying that there is a Chinese religious system, both at the level of ideas (beliefs, representations, classifying principles, and so on) and at that of practice and organization (ritual, grouping, hierarchy, etc.). But it is easy to see that to use the word "system" systematically would be to run the constant risk of appearing to impute to Chinese religion a thoroughgoing unity and tightness that manifestly it does not have. The starting assumption made here is both more modest and more complex. It says that there is some order—of a kind that should allow us (if we take the trouble) to trace ruling principles of ideas across a vast field of apparently heterogeneous beliefs, and ruling principles of form and organization in an equally enormous terrain of varied action and association. Ideas and forms need not be uniform to be common; they may be reflections, perhaps misshapen reflections, or idiomatic translations of one another, as in their transmission back and forth between social strata, between sect and "church," between "church" and "church," between text and living language, between the cultivated and the popular. Their Chineseness lies in a basic stock upon which complex social and intellectual life works and elaborates variety. Chinese religion is not all of a piece, and in the end there may be much that we shall not be able to fit into any sort of order; but we should try to push out toward the limits so that we may know them.

One way in which to approach order—it is only a beginning—is to grasp the relations among the different parts of Chinese society. (I mean of course traditional Chinese society and its extensions into our own day and direct purview, especially in Taiwan and Hong Kong, from which areas of China my colleagues in this volume draw most of their data. I am not at all concerned here with modern changes as such.) We may start with two simple and connected propositions. First, Chinese religion entered into the unity of a vast polity. Second, it was an intrinsic part of a hierarchized society.

The narrowly political significance of Chinese religion can hardly have escaped the notice of early observers, but I can recall no study of it to compare with C. K. Yang's other than one first published in 1882 by Sir Arthur C. Lyall, the eminent Anglo-Indian scholar-bureaucrat (1835– 1911). I think his work so striking that I am giving him an honorary place among the small band of social scientists to whom I am limiting myself. (An odd thing about Lyall's essay is that it is generally unknown to people who write about China; I myself came across it only by accident.) Lyall knew about Chinese religion what he picked up from a very few sources: Edkins, de Groot, Giles, and above all the English translations of the so-called *Peking Gazette.*[a] What his study (Lyall 1907) demonstrates in the first place (and disenchantingly) is that the advances in our understanding of a society are not necessarily made by people who know a great deal about it. Lyall began from an interest in Indian government and comparative religion that prompted questions about, as he puts it (1907: 107), "that empire which at one time had attained, as a government, the highest level yet reached by purely Asiatic civilisation." He had earlier said that, to pass from the "intolerant monotheism" of Islam, it might be "more interesting . . . to examine the relations of the civil government to religion in a country where creeds and rituals still preserve their primitive multiformity, where they all have, nevertheless,

[a] This material is vivid. Here, for example, is a fine illustration of the religious foundations of bureaucratic practice, from the *Translation of the Peking Gazette for 1882* (1883: 110): it was reported in August that in a postscript to a memorial from the Censor of Kwangsi, an official "advocates a return to the practice of 'slaying the water-dragon . . .' in the sixth moon as recommended in the Monthly Rules (of the Records of Rites). This custom, though never enforced by law, is recollected by the farmers and aged country-folk. . . . The animal will always be discovered after digging to a depth of five feet or so. Would it not be better to destroy the hidden evil instead of merely providing against the floods it causes . . . ?"

free play, and where the ruler finds it possible and advantageous to preside over all of them" (p. 106).

I reproduce the following passages from Lyall to illustrate the quality of his argument. It will be noticed that he took much of the religious variety at its face value but saw it as being brought to the service of political unity.

China has attained this superiority over India, that she succeeded centuries ago in bringing her religious doctrines and worships [*sic*] into practical cooperation with her secular organisation. (P. 108.)

All this system harmonises with and favours the policy of associating religion with every department of the public service, and of identifying the laws of the Government with the decrees of Heaven. (P. 110.)

It becomes thus possible to form some trustworthy conception of the principles that underlie this vast organisation—unquestioned authority; lofty ostentation of public morality; the affectation of profound reverence for churches, rituals, and all things pertaining to divinity; deep respect for tradition and ancestral usage coupled with steady encouragement of classic learning; entire religious toleration conjoined with the peremptory assertion of civil supremacy; provincial home rule controlled, at least in form, by a despotic central executive; in short, the continuous experience of many ages applied to the management by a foreign dynasty of miscellaneous tribes and races, and an immense mixed population. (P. 118.)

It will be fairly obvious that Lyall's interest in China was that of somebody on the alert for solutions to the kind of problem faced by the British in India: how a foreign dynasty may succeed in reconciling religious toleration with effective rule. It follows that, from our point of view, Lyall may have seen the problem too narrowly (for in religious matters the Ch'ing rulers of China may not have differed substantially from their native predecessors); but I think it will be recognized that Lyall attained to an understanding of the politics of Chinese religion that was not to be matched until C. K. Yang wrote his first general study of Chinese religion (1957). The Englishman wrote as an outsider; Yang wrote as somebody brought up in China and sociologically formed in the United States. Somehow both encompassed a whole religio-political system, one of them by ignoring the details and proceeding unencumbered by specialist knowledge, the other by having that knowledge and transcending it. Nearly all other writers on Chinese religion either have lacked sociological insight or, if they have had it, have restricted its range to something less than the total system of religion-in-politics.[4]

Let us pass to the second proposition, that Chinese religion was part of the hierarchization of Chinese society. It is less obvious than the first proposition, and indeed more difficult to bring home, precisely because of the stratification that forms its subject. The great "discovery" by English-speaking social scientists in an earlier part of the century (say, from the thirties to the fifties) was that behind the Confucian smoke-screen there lay hidden a different way of life and a different set of values: roughly, the culture of the peasants. The second half of the century has seen the further "discovery" that the first was an illusion. That is to say, elite culture and peasant culture were not different things; they were versions of each other. To read much of what is still written about Chinese religion one might not realize that the second advance had been made. For example, C. P. FitzGerald tells us (1969: 389, 391):

> In broad general terms it might be said that the people were both Buddhist and followers of the old polytheism which came to be known as Taoism: the scholars were Confucian. . . . Popular religion was thus confused and inchoate, lacking any accepted overall theology, or central organization. . . . Agnosticism, instead of being a rare and unpopular attitude only safely adopted by the rich and powerful, was the acknowledged and proclaimed view of the ruling class, the basis of higher education, indeed of all education. Popular religion was not under the guidance and inspiration of dedicated men of learning, but left to persons of little education and often of less probity.[5]

But the newer view is firmly lodged in Yang's *Religion in Chinese Society*, and we may expect to find it more and more commonly expressed.[b]

Before dealing with Yang's book in some detail I think it may be instructive to go back in time and beyond the English-language social science tradition to consider the views taken of the interrelations between peasant and elite religion by the Dutchman J. J. M. de Groot (1854–1921) and the Frenchman Marcel Granet (1884–1940), in my opinion the two most important sociological-sinological contributors to the debate. I am not the first to give pride of place to these two writers or to see striking differences between them (cf. Eberhard 1971: 338ff, 362ff), but neither has yet been adequately studied, and I have thought it useful to sketch in here their significance as a complementary pair.[6] Both seek

---

[b] A more sophisticated version of the surviving and (as I think) mistaken view that popular and elite religions are divided by a gulf is to be found in B. E. Ward 1965: 131, where the author, pursuing her general thesis that areas of social conduct not governed by elite models show great variation, says: "Because formally the literati despised the popular cults we should perhaps expect the greatest variety of all to appear in this sphere. There is a good deal of evidence in support of this contention. In other words, there being no literati-derived model for religious behaviour outside the state and ancestral cults (which were uniform), the popular cults could develop to suit local fancy—and did." Is it really true that there was as great a variety in "popular cults" as is envisaged in this formulation? I think not. And it seems to me a mistake to imagine that there was not also variation between the elite and the common people in the sphere of the ancestor cult. But surface variation is in any case one thing, underlying similarity another.

the source of the various forms of Chinese religion and discuss their transmission through the hierarchy of Chinese society, but de Groot, in his maturer work, begins from an elite-classical version from which all others are, so to say, debased aberrations (unless they are spiritualized sectarian movements), whereas Granet appears to build up the elite-classical version from its alleged peasant origins. De Groot was during several crucial years of his career a field-worker—an official of the Netherlands Indies service sent to China to familiarize himself with Chinese life —who, as his studies developed, sought to anchor in the classical past what he saw of the present. Granet, the student of China's ancient past through her classical literature, aimed in much of his work at getting behind that past to a humbler origin that the classical literature was taken as trying to conceal. Both sought to explain at least in part by origins, but they moved in opposite social directions: de Groot, beginning as a field-worker, from the popular to the elite; Granet, starting from the Chinese classical texts, from the elite to the popular. Each was a sort of deflater, one diminishing the popular, the other the elite.

We know de Groot best for his unfinished monumental work in six volumes, *The Religious System of China* (1892–1910), which has as its subtitle *Its Ancient Forms, Evolution, History and Present Aspect. Manners, Customs and Social Institutions Connected Therewith*. Even if we were to take that work on its own, ignoring the rest of the author's considerable literary output (in English, Dutch, German and French), we should obviously be dealing with a man who set himself the task of producing a comprehensive study. It is important to understand how and why he came to compose that great work—and since nearly all writers on Chinese religion pick at his books (as I have myself done in the past) without an idea of his intellectual background,[7] I want to discuss it very briefly here. After studying Chinese at Leiden, in preparation for a career as a Chinese interpreter in the Indies service, in 1877 he went off to spend a year in China, chiefly in Amoy. During that 'prentice year he collected the data for the study that we usually consult in its French translation, *Les fêtes annuellement célébrées à Emoui (Amoy): Etude concernant la religion populaire des Chinois* (Groot 1886). That fruitful year of field study (in which, with no formal social science background, he invented a field method for himself)[8] was in fact the shorter of two stays in China; the career that he began in 1878 in the Indies as a civil servant specializing in Chinese affairs (and to which we owe, among other works, his important study [Groot 1885] of the "kongsis" of West Borneo) came prematurely to an end when, during sick leave in the Netherlands, he was granted a request to return to his investigations in China. His second sojourn lasted from June 1886 to April 1890, most of it again spent in the region of Amoy, the chief area of interest to the Dutch in connection with Chinese immigration to their eastern empire. In *Les fêtes* de Groot in at least one respect shows himself a true pupil of his teacher at Leiden, the sinologue Gustave Schlegel, who was, in his ideas, an extension of the eighteenth century into the second half of the nineteenth. The picture painted of China in *Les fêtes* is complimentary (more so in the original Dutch than in the French translation). China is an alternative civilization, having roots in common with Europe. It is to be compared with Europe, in some respects very favorably. The book expresses anti-Christian, especially anti-Catholic, sentiments, and emphasizes the religious tolerance prevailing in China. De Groot links the "three religions" with popular religion (the latter being the chief object of his study—he wanted to see how people behaved before committing himself to what was written in Chinese texts); and although he does not make a system of them, it seems to me that he was now ready to do so. But that system was to be achieved only after a break in his intellectual development and a complete transformation of his view of China. When exactly the change took place is difficult to pin down; but it must have occurred between 1886 and 1891, possibly as the joint result of his experience during his second stay in China and his switch to an academic career.

He returned to the Netherlands in 1890 to teach Chinese and Malay in Amsterdam, but he was soon called to occupy the chair at Leiden vacated by Wilken. He became Professor "in de Land- en Volkenkunde van Nederlansch-Indië." He was now a professor of ethnography not because he was an ethnographer (although of course he had written descriptively on the Chinese in both China and the Indies and drawn upon comparative ethnography ever since he had begun to write on them); he became an ethnographer because he undertook to profess the subject. And his manner of presenting China after his appointment to Leiden reflected the anthropology of the day. Spencerian evolution of a sort is present in his earliest work, but there countered by an eighteenth-century respect for China; de Groot now adopted a far less inhibited European view. In 1904 he reluctantly allowed himself to be translated to the Chair of Chinese vacated by Schlegel. His more narrowly sinological career was, so to say, confirmed when he finally accepted an invitation to a chair of Chinese in Berlin, where he installed himself in 1912. (One may amuse oneself by speculating about the turn Chinese studies might have taken in the United States if de Groot had accepted an invitation he received from Columbia University in 1902.) He saw the war through in Germany, and died there in 1921, broken by the tragedy of the country with which he had come closely to identify himself.

Although in both China and the Indies de Groot concerned himself with practical affairs (and wrote on them), it is clear that religion above all commanded his attention; and of course his greatest work falls in that field. In the General Preface to the first of the six volumes of *The Religious System of China* he points out (1892: vii) that Chinese religion had never up to then been studied as a whole and as it was lived: "Sinologists have never taken any serious pains to penetrate into the intimate Religious life of the nation." And he goes on to say (p. viii) that his aim in the work was precisely to depict "the Chinese Religion as it is really practised by the nation." But the social and religious matters he is to discuss, being "founded upon the past . . . rightly to understand them, a knowledge of Antiquity is necessary" (p. x). It is for that reason that a work of ethnography, based upon fieldwork (indeed, what must have been the first sustained and systematic fieldwork ever done in China), is —as it must seem to many readers—cluttered up with references to and quotations from the classical literature.[9]

De Groot's exposition has another aspect: he had always taken a vaguely evolutionary view of religion and culture, but the Chinese had now become for him a semicivilized people, and he thought himself obliged to try to relate his findings on the Chinese to those of comparative (or as we should now say, indiscriminate) ethnography. "Many rites and practices still flourish among the Chinese, which one would scarcely expect to find anywhere except among savages in a low state of culture" (Groot 1892: xi). (The alternative Europe has disappeared.) Happily, for editorial reasons, de Groot cut out nearly all the comparative references, but as he says himself, we shall "soon become aware that those references have left a distinct mark upon this work, a mark chiefly manifested by the fact that the author has followed the beaten track of Science for the study of Religions and Sociology in general" (1892: xi–xii). One might well wish that he had kept away from Science and been faithful to the humanism of his early work.

De Groot saw Chinese society from the top down. In the first place,

The customs described in the Book as observed by the Chinese of the present day are by no means conformed to by all classes of society. As has been remarked already by the ancient *Li-ki* . . . "the rites and ceremonies do not go down to the common people," whose means are small and manners rude. As a basis for our descriptions we have selected the well-to-do classes and families of fashionable standing, amongst whom, in China, we chiefly moved, and these may be said best to maintain the whole systems of the rites and ceremonies prescribed by the laws of custom (1892: 1–2).[c]

[c] One wonders of course how, having been sent to China to gain an understanding of the background (in its widest sense) of Chinese emigration overseas, de Groot justified his

Second, the customs seen and recorded for the well-to-do and the fashionable (slipping into de Groot's language one may have the pleasure of the snobbery without the responsibility for it), and mainly in one provincial corner of the Empire, are shown to be directly dependent upon the classical norms.

So determined is he to demonstrate this last connection that de Groot traps himself into contradicting his own field evidence when he comes to describe how tombs are arranged.

Down to this day, clan life and family life have undergone no change of any importance, the ancient method of burying the dead in family grave-yards or clan grave-grounds and of placing very near relations . . . in the same tomb, has probably remained in vogue uninterruptedly (1897: 831).

The current editions of the Rituals for Family Life generally contain an appendix, stating how the tombs should be arranged in family grave-grounds. . . . The Rituals for Family Life being the chief vademecum of the people for their domestic rites and ceremonies, we may assume that family grave-grounds certainly in most cases are laid out in accordance with those instructions (1897: 832).

Now, the arrangement prescribed in the Rituals involves a complicated pattern in which unmarried descendants of the apical ancestor are buried to the north of him, and his descendants with wives and children to the south; the latter group is so disposed that members of adjacent generations do not lie next to one another on the north-south axis (see diagram, Groot 1897: 833). How did de Groot come to imagine that the grave-yards of his day were usually so arranged unless he somehow persuaded himself that what was classical was right and therefore followed? All the other evidence we have contradicts his generalization for "modern" China, and, more important, he contradicts it himself when later he turns to discuss the influence of geomancy (*feng-shui*) upon burial (1897: 1017–18). What he there says implies dispersed burial and flies in the face of his earlier account. The passage quoted above is a telling example of the triumph of theoretical scheme over observed fact. Or consider what he says about mourning, which, though it illustrates his sensitivity to changes over time, shows him hard at work to justify his historical method. In Volume II (1894: 474–75) we are treated to a detailed account of ancient mourning practices. De Groot interrupts the flow of his exposition to remark (p. 533), "No doubt our readers will have had the question on their lips: Why weary us with these tedious mourning lists of

---

choice of the upper class as the one with which to associate and to investigate the most fully. From the ranks of the people he knew best, very few of the migrants to the Indies could have originated. The quotation from the *Li Chi* is a handy one for scholars wishing to stress the distinction between elite and people, or to show the difficulties experienced by the common people in conforming to elite ideals. For the latter, see Levy 1949: 99.

the ancients? Why fill up so many pages with such uninteresting stuff?"
It was to be expected that those questions were introduced in order to
justify answers at length. They culminate in the

chief reason, outweighing by far all the others . . . : that the mourning codex of
the *I li* . . . has through all the ages exercised a mighty influence upon Chinese
society and its organization, because, with modifications and revisions of more or
less importance, it has always been used by legislators in assigning to each individual a fixed place in the circle of his family (1894: 534).[d]

We are soon plunged into an exposition of the mourning regulations laid
down in the Ch'ing code, after which follows a section (pp. 585–602)
dealing with the "modern mourning attire at Amoy," showing

that, in this respect, the inveterate conservatism of the Chinese race abnegates
itself to no small degree. The nation's idiosyncrasy of closely imitating everything
bequeathed to posterity by the holy ancients has indeed not been strong enough
to prevent the people of the present day from indulging in considerable deviations
from the mourning dress of olden times, which cannot properly be ascribed to a
wrong understanding of the ancient works (1894: 586).[10]

Then why the deviations? That question is not answered, for it is not
posed. De Groot is saying throughout that the Chinese he knew followed
in the steps of their ancient forerunners—and if they did not, then they
were being irritatingly inconsistent.

It may be recalled that Lyall wrote of "entire religious toleration conjoined with the peremptory assertion of civil supremacy"; and the nature
and extent of religious tolerance in China are a theme that recurs in many
branches of the literature on that country. De Groot's view (that is, his
later view) of this important matter is interesting in part because it is of
a piece with his general attitude toward the Chinese in his later years. He
had come to disdain the people he had studied so long and so intensively.
And despite the sinological apparatus and learning he brought to his
work, one detects in him some of the less instructed arrogance of the late-
nineteenth-century Western European confronting an empire in collapse.
There is little of the Christian missionary about de Groot in most of his
writing,[11] but in one important context he springs to the defense of the
missionaries. In *Sectarianism and Religious Persecution in China: A
Page in the History of Religions* (Groot 1903–4) one kind of indignation
is made to do for both the imperial persecution of heterodox sects and
the harassment of Christian missions. De Groot then argued that intoler-

---

[d] De Groot's tracing of the kinship system of ancient China (1894: 507–11) is a flat
contradiction of the assertion quoted above, that "clan life and family life have undergone
no change of any importance" (1897: 831).

ance was built into China's system of political control, and in intemperate language expressed the hope that if ever Western politicians had again to consider whether, as during the Taiping Rebellion, they ought to "uphold the Confucian tyrant on his throne against his bloodily persecuted people rising in arms against him and his satraps," they would decide not to do so (1903–4: 565).[12] The Chinese society of this book is the nightmare version of the conservative, dull, and irrational China of *The Religious System*. In *Sectarianism* there are of course some heroes, the sectarians; but they are not enough to redeem China in de Groot's eyes. Evolutionary theory pushed de Groot toward an expectation of increasing civilization; that expectation was canceled by another theory embedded in his work: degeneration from antiquity. At times one detects yet a third contradictory theme: China never changes. The first theory de Groot clearly owed to European thought; the second and third, perhaps partly to different phases of that thought and partly to the Chinese self-image. It is just possible, I suppose, that his occasional messianic hopes for the triumph of both unorthodox Chinese and Christian religions were a way out of the impasse created by his two leading and mutually contradictory ideas.[13]

In turning from de Groot to Granet we enter an entirely new intellectual world, where we find so completely different a China that we must wonder at the outset whether the two sinologists were studying the same country. With Granet we are of course in the realm of Durkheim (who along with Chavannes was Granet's teacher), of Mauss (Granet's close friend), and of the *Année sociologique* in general. The China that Granet saw was remote, and it is not surprising that some of his readers regard him as an earlier Arthur Waley, never venturing to see for himself what China was like. In fact, after his sociological and sinological training in Paris (first at the Ecole Normale Supérieure and then at the Fondation Thiers), he went on a scholarship to Peking in 1911 and stayed there until 1913, having witnessed some of the events of the Revolution. And he passed a few months in China in 1919 on his way back to France from service with the Allied forces fighting the Bolsheviks in Siberia. But what he did in China was nothing approaching fieldwork, for his sociology was entirely Durkheimian, little touched by the Maussian version of it that moved up direct observation to a position of honor.

The China that engrossed his attention for nearly his whole career as student and teacher in Paris was the China that spanned the primitive and "feudal" and the beginnings of the imperial age. (At the end of his life, cut short by the events of 1940, he was doing research as far forward as the T'ang.) He was much preoccupied with the origins of imperial China, and with the peasant sources of high Chinese culture and social organization. Yet his sociological method was professedly anti-historical in one sense, and explanation merely by origin anathema.[14] Durkheimian method called for a rigorous dissection of a body of facts and an analysis of their connection. (What Granet meant by a fact is too complex a matter for discussion here.) In his first great book, *Fêtes et chansons anciennes de la Chine* (1919), he took "the most ancient facts of the religious history of China" (Granet 1932: 207) from the *Shih Ching* and, by an act of scholarly prestidigitation that still astonishes his readers, inferred a peasant way of life that he was later so to elaborate along with other forms of Chinese social order that it was to furnish models for students of society uninterested in China itself.[15]

So far as religion is concerned (I take the word in its broadest sense), the method was to be seen at work again chiefly in *La religion des Chinois* (1922), *Danses et légendes de la Chine ancienne* (1926), and two general works, *La civilisation chinoise: La vie publique et la vie privée* (1929b) and *La pensée chinoise* (1934). But I want to pay particular attention here to the first of those works, which, although it belongs among his early writings, states positions that he was for the most part to maintain. It is, moreover, the only one of his books in which he attempts to cover the whole span of Chinese history and all aspects of Chinese religion. Its brevity and comprehensiveness are due to its being written in response to a publisher's request for a short general study of Chinese religion to fit into a series.

The structure of the book implies a large part of its argument. It opens with peasant religion, moves to "feudal" religion, and thence proceeds to official religion. We are now two-thirds of the way through. The remainder is taken up with "religious revivals" (Taoism and Buddhism) and concluding remarks on religion in contemporary China.

Peasant religion and "feudal" religion together precede imperial religion; of the first two, peasant religion is prior. True enough, Granet sometimes writes as though peasants and nobles, rural and town life, were an aboriginal complementary pair. But in fact, he looks upon peasant life and thought as the ultimate foundation of all Chinese culture. It was the source from which "feudal" and imperial religion sprang, and from which many sectarian movements were later to derive. And were we to question the peasant mass, the very stuff of the country, in order to describe religious life as it is now, we should perhaps discover that common peasant base all over again (Granet 1951: xi). And for Granet, one might add, that peasant religion was essentially gentle, free of objectionable features of the religious forms to follow on from it (p. 107).

Peasant life and religion are described and analyzed with the assurance characteristic of Granet's writing—except when he briefly turns to present-day China. The closer we get, under his guidance, to the modern and the more fully documented, the remoter and more indefinite it seems to be. The peasants led their distinctive way of life, marked by the aristocratic ritual formula: the Rites do not go down to the common people (p. 1).[16] They lived in villages on high ground and enclosed within quickset hedges, and the men for part of the year in huts in the fields. The seasonal rhythm of work was different for men and women, the men at their labors during the warmer season, the women during the colder weather. Each village consisted of a homogeneous group barely differentiated by descent—sex and generation were the two chief organizing principles. (Descent began by being matrilineal.) Exogamy tied these close-knit communities one to another. And from this there arose the elaborate and colorful institutions of ritual centers ("Lieux Saints") and peasant festivals, marking the seasonal and social changes of the year and the crucial significance of sexual and marital relations. We are now in the presence of the origin of the calendar, destined of course to remain a key element in Chinese religion, and of the fundamental concept of *yin-yang*. The agrarian base of this early society provides the ritualization of the Earth and the first form of the ancestors (pp. 2–26). We know at once that we are in the same world as Durkheim's Australia (although paradoxically Granet, working on a literate civilization, had worse documentation than Durkheim upon which to draw); and we may well gasp at the vividness and richness of the description, wondering after the first impact whether it relates to very much outside Granet's superb sociological imagination.[17] Fortunately, that is a problem I am not obliged to consider here.

In the chapter on "feudal" religion (pp. 31–79) we are given the corresponding account of social life and its correlates in the towns, the seat of noble life. Here Granet's eloquence is devoted to expounding the agnatic and primogenitory kinship system and the concomitant elaborations of the ancestor cult; the worship of Heaven, a dynastic and official cult superimposed on the agrarian and ancestor cults; and the worship of Earth, which built upon and expanded the agrarian cult of Earth.

In the section on "La religion officielle" Granet reaches the climax of the book, for the remaining chapter and the conclusion slide down to a less arresting finish. Now both the peasant and the noble forms of religion are seen to be worked up into beliefs and cults serving the needs of an imperial state and its functionaries, the literati. China has become a unified country whose dominant system of ideas reaches down into all levels of society. In Granet's eyes, it was not a religion that was at all points commendable, but at least religious life remained dominated by a practical spirit that for the most part preserved China from mystical adventures (p. 99). Confucianism had triumphed even when it had at times to reckon with Taoism (pp. 88–120).

But Taoism began from the same source as its greater rival and, along with its "foreign" companion, Buddhism, complemented the official religion. Just as Taoism had to be called to the aid of the official religion in order that the forces of Nature might continue to render their services to the Chinese people, so Buddhism established its prestige by pacifying the world of the dead (p. 150). We have arrived at a synthesis in which beneath the surface variety and literate sophistication there lie a few simple and basic religious ideas, a heritage from the peasant past (pp. 121–75).[18]

De Groot and Granet, each in his own manner, have pointed the way to an understanding of how in modern times the vast hierarchized society of China might be seen to display a single underlying religion taking many guises. One of these sinologues thought (in his maturer work) that a classical tradition would account for nearly everything; the other assumed that by penetrating the literary deceptions practiced and the distortions worked in the name of the same tradition, we could reach a source from which all Chinese religion ultimately stems. We may now return to C. K. Yang and his analysis of the total religious system of China.

Yang opens the chapter of his book called "Political Role of Chinese Religion in Historical Perspective" by pointing out that the relation between the Chinese state and religion is an unsettled question: "in China the political role of religion was somewhat obscured by the dominance of Confucian orthodoxy in the function and structure of the state, for Confucianism had very prominent non-religious, secular features" (Yang 1961: 104). In fact, Yang says, religion in China has in recent times stood in every possible relation to the state—by suffusing and supporting it, by struggling against it (as in the case of the rebellions started by the sects), and by withdrawing into seclusion from it (as with the monasteries). To understand these three solutions, we need to survey the history of the relations between religion and state; and at the end of the survey Yang undertakes (pp. 105–26) we can see that by the modern period Buddhism and Taoism had adopted more or less passive roles, submitting to the state, but not submitting so far as to be incapable of acting on occasion as inspirers of rebellion.

The next chapter deals with the Mandate of Heaven, a topic which lends itself admirably to an analysis of the connections between the religious and the political, but which in Yang's hands turns into something more, for (on p. 134) he asks the key question: how did the common people come to believe in the idea of the Mandate of Heaven and to accept "the supremacy of imperial power partly on the ground that it was a predetermined course ordained by the gods? . . . The question is particularly pertinent in view of the relatively tenuous tie between the central imperial power and the intimate life of the common people." I think Yang slips into a phraseology uncongenial to his thought when he refers to "the magic-oriented common people" (p. 135), for his argument supposes a systematic coherence between elite ideas and those of what he calls the common people.

Observers have generally regarded these practices of divination and geomancy as a chaotic mass of ignorant superstitions. Actually they represented a well-coordinated system of religious concepts containing the belief in the power of Heaven and Earth to predetermine the course of all events, large and small, by controlling the time and space within which they occurred. . . . In this sense, the theology of Yin-yang and the Five Elements served as a link between the supernatural basis of the affairs of state and the intimate life of the people. (P. 136.)

Moreover, he goes on to argue:

The universal acceptance of the supreme power of Heaven over all gods and man provided the imperial power with an important religious basis for the political integration of a vast country. . . . Under this system the peasants in Chekiang or Kwangtung province might be intensely devoted to local gods and spirits stemming from a particular ethnic background, but these deities were a part of the hierarchy of supernatural powers subordinated to Heaven, the formal worship of which was monopolized by the central political power. (Pp. 136–37.)

The next chapter, "Ethicopolitical Cults," *inter alia* demonstrates the interlocking of official and popular cults (see especially p. 145), and brings out the untenability of a view such as Weber's, which makes official religion seem merely formal and conventional and so distanced from the religious fervor of the masses (pp. 178–79).

I jump to Chapter 10, "Religious Aspects of Confucianism . . . ," where we find a clear expression of a thesis I am holding up for approval:

Even taking into consideration the relative difference in the belief in magic and miracles, the Confucians did not constitute a group separate from the general current of religious life of traditional Chinese society. They shared with the rest of the population a basic system of religious belief in Heaven, fate, and other supernatural concepts. More important was the steady interflow of religious ideas between the Confucians and the general population. . . . The Confucians, therefore, cannot be regarded as a distinctively different group on religious grounds, but must be regarded as part of the general pattern of Chinese religious life with only relative differences due to their social and economic position. (Pp. 276–77.)[e]

Let us leave Yang at that point.

In what I have said so far I have tried to show that there is a sociological tradition, culminating for the moment in Yang's book, which takes Chinese religion to be one entity. When we survey the sociological work done on Chinese religion in the last thirty or forty years, Yang's book excepted, it is difficult to believe that there has been such a tradition to adhere to. I think we may in part trace the anomaly to two consequences of the fact that the adjective "sociological" in the last sentence in reality means "anthropological." Those consequences are, first, that some fragment of Chinese society and religion is studied, not Chinese society and religion as a whole,[f] second, that a special peasant's-eye view of China is promoted that inverts but otherwise reproduces the distortion of the Confucian's-eye view in the course of the wholly admirable effort to move from bookishness to fieldwork (see Li An-che 1938; Freedman 1963a: 9–10). We find ourselves in the rather tired intellectual world of the Great and Little Traditions.[19] For the field-worker is aware in a general way of the difference between the religious ideas and practices of the people he studies and those ascribed to the fully literate elite of the country—but in fact he does not know enough about the religious ideas and practices of that elite (for he does not study them)[20] to realize the extent to which elite and peasant religion rest upon a common base, representing two versions of one religion that we may see as idiomatic translations of each other. And so it comes about that field-workers in China are confident of having made a discovery in establishing that peasants do not belong to merely one of the Three Religions, but are heirs to a long syncretic tradition.[21]

[e] In chap. 8, "State Control of Religion," I think Yang errs on one point. He argues (1961: 192–93) that the persecution of religious heterodoxy by the Confucian state was due not to religious motives but to political ones. Certainly religious sects seemed often, perhaps usually, to be politically threatening, but there is more to it than that. Heterodoxy was also an affront to Confucian social principles, which in turn, of course, rested upon religious foundations. The best discussion I know of this point is in R. A. Stein, "*Les religions de la Chine*" (1957), a truly remarkable synthesis. Stein writes (pp. 54–55) that the *yin-ssu*, "immoral cults," implied a forbidden social promiscuity and a forbidden religious promiscuity—divinities incarnating and mixing with men.

[f] But I should really limit myself to anthropologists in the Anglo-American tradition. From other traditions of anthropological research, broader views might issue. Cf. the criticism by the eminent Russian S. M. Shirokogoroff of the choice of the "village" as a unit of study (Shirokogoroff 1942: 3). And note his remark at p. 6: "If one reads the works like that by *Hsiao-Tung Fei* or that by *D. H. Kulp* one may get quite a wrong impression of the ethnographical investigations in general."

Now, the question might be raised whether the fragmentary view of local religion obtained from anthropological studies is due solely to professional deformation. It may well be asked why it is that the Chinese anthropologists themselves, who presumably differ from their Western colleagues in knowing a great deal about the religion of the strata of Chinese society from which they come, seem to paint much the same distorted, or at any rate incomplete, picture as anyone else. I shall not presume to talk about scholars whose intellectual and social backgrounds I do not know well enough beyond observing that they may illustrate one aspect of that very polymorphism of Chinese elite religion to which I shall be referring presently: as literati they are licensed by their society to ignore or even to despise the religion of the common people by adopting one of the several positions open to them within their total religious field. That the religion of the masses was quaint, superstitious, or negligible was not an attitude suddenly produced by modern currents of thought. It is, of course, an old theme of elite Chinese culture—and one consistent with the fact of that culture's shared basis with peasant culture. But whatever the reason, Chinese intellectuals in this century have not shown any marked interest in the religion of ordinary people.[22]

But how precisely to consider Chinese religion as a whole? It is reasonable to assume (I think) that a country of China's extent and political cohesion would demonstrate a large measure of agreement on religious assumptions among all its people. And, more important, one might predict from first principles that a society so differentiated by social status and power would develop a religious system that allowed differences in beliefs and rites to complement one another—or, to put the point more provocatively, that allowed religious similarity to be expressed as though it were religious difference. When an educated Chinese, writing about Chinese religion as though from the outside, says that a rational agnosticism characterizes the elite and an indiscriminate superstition the masses, he is in reality writing from the *inside* and expressing the elite's view of the difference between the two great layers of his society. An example that springs to mind is one provided by Wing-tsit Chan, who, in his rightly celebrated *Religious Trends in Modern China*, says: "I have always urged that instead of dividing the religious life of the Chinese people into three compartments called Confucianism, Buddhism, and Taoism, it is far more accurate to divide it into two levels, the level of the masses and the level of the enlightened" (Chan 1953: 141).[23] He proceeds (p. 143) to distinguish the two levels above all by the differential vocabulary of religious service: *pai* and *chi*. "The masses *pai*, that is worship in the formal, orthodox, strictly religious sense, but the enlightened *chi*, that is, sacrifice or make offerings. . . . The idea of propitiation or expiation is never present." [24]

But the pragmatic-agnostic interpretation of elite religion is made possible by the very assumptions upon which that religion rests: there is an order in the universe presided over morally by *t'ien*, Heaven, whose workings may be analyzed by recourse to the ideas of yin-yang and the Five Elements. (See, for example, Topley 1967.) With all that simply taken for granted, it becomes possible to look upon the entities to which sacrifices must for official-political reasons be made as convenient fictions—if one chooses. But we, the outsiders, are not entitled to conclude that the pragmatic-agnostic interpretation was the common one among the elite. Apart from any other complicating factor, we would be hard put to distinguish between what a literatus believed qua official and what qua private citizen (cf. Welch 1970: 616; Stein 1957: 54–4). The polymorphism of Chinese religion allowed variation not only among the elite but also within the religious life of the individual literatus. With the exception of prophecy and ecstasy, every religious phenomenon to be found among the common people in China was susceptible of transformation into beliefs and rites among the cultivated elite. Heterodoxy might be a transformed version of orthodoxy, and vice versa. That is a point I made more narrowly a few years ago in the context of feng-shui. I said then that even though the geomancer and the priest are separated in function and the beliefs that surround their different roles, the "metaphysical" gulf between them

is no gulf at all, but rather a neat transformation. Most of the elements of *feng-shui* can be restated in the language of ordinary religion. Just as in the Neo-Confucian philosophical writings the concretising words *shen* and *kuei* . . . are used for positive and negative spiritual forces, being stripped of their anthropomorphic connotations . . . , so in popular religion a reverse transformation is worked by which the disembodied forces of the geomancer are turned into personal entities. (Freedman 1969: 10.)

At first sight, the baroque elaboration of popular feng-shui may seem to contrast sharply with the austere religious imagination of the elite; but on closer inspection it becomes evident that both sets of beliefs are products of the same assumptions and manipulate versions of the same concepts. I am suggesting now that similar transformations will be found in many other spheres of Chinese religion. [25]

How could China fail to constitute a community of ideas when the political center made itself responsible for disseminating its beliefs by the spoken and written word, when literacy, however thinly spread (Mote 1972: 110), was an institutionalized part of rural life, when the elite were based as much in the countryside as in the towns,[26] and when social mobility ensured a steady interchange of style between the common run of men and the high-literate? Members of the elite might stand by a puritanical version of Chinese religion, and in that posture deplore the antics of the superstitious masses; but the elite as a group was bound to the masses indissolubly by its religious beliefs and practices. Within that union of belief and ritual action, rebellion might occur, sects crystalize out, unorthodoxy provoke; Taoism might elaborate local community organization and Buddhism sanctify a withdrawal from the world. But let us take it as a working hypothesis that all religious argument and ritual differentiation were conducted within a common language of basic conceptions, symbols, and ritual forms.

And this great community of religion was achieved without a church, unless we choose to call the state itself a church, in which case one of the two terms becomes superfluous. Mandarins performed rites and commanded (or, as sometimes happened, pretended to command) spirits in their official capacity;[27] they were not priests. There were priests, Taoist and Buddhist; they were, generally speaking, men of low standing.[28] Among religious specialists only the geomancer seems consistently to have attracted the respect attaching to civil virtue, for religious practitioner though he was, he was a version of the literatus (Freedman 1969: 9–10). Chinese religion was in a sense a civil religion—not austere and cunningly calculated to serve political interests, but based upon a view of the interpenetration of society and the universe, and upon a conception of authority that in the last analysis would not allow the religious to separate off from the secular. Caesar was Pope, Pope Caesar. And if the sectaries were sometimes tempted, by turning away from normally constituted society, to introduce a sharp difference between the secular and the religious, they incurred a reaction from the state which, in killing and maiming them, should convince us, the outsiders, that the power-holding elite was not prepared to tolerate a bifurcation of authority. The Chinese state has on the whole been very successful—and to this day—in muting religious authority. That is one aspect of the religious unity of China.

PART FIVE

On the Study of Chinese Society

Sociology in China: A Brief Survey

In the general history of the social sciences we assume that the marriage between sociology and anthropology comes late, having been preceded by a long courtship. China does not fit this pattern. Almost as soon as the social sciences were established there anthropology and sociology were intertwined—to be disentangled in a strange way when the Communists arrived. To avoid a tedious recitation of evidence let me call just one witness, a scholar whose later career in the United States makes his testimony underline the Chinese paradox. Writing in China in 1944 Francis L. K. Hsu says: "In this paper the word sociology is used synonymously with the term social anthropology. Few serious Chinese scholars today maintain the distinction between the once separate disciplines. Sociologists teach anthropology in our universities as a matter of course, just as scholars with distinctively anthropological background lecture on sociology." [1]

It is customary to date the beginning of sociology in China by the publication of Yen Fu's translation of two chapters of Spencer's *The Study of Sociology* in 1898, but although from then on Chinese were able to read many European and American sociologists in translation, a few original works were produced in Chinese, and courses of instruction were introduced in the universities, it was not until about the 1920's that sociological investigations of any great weight began to be made. We realize how foreshortened is the history of Chinese sociology when we recognize that the names that have meaning for us belong to men working mainly in the two decades before the Communist regime: Wu Wen-

China Quarterly, no. 10 (1962), 166–73. A preliminary version was delivered at the Conference on Asian Sociology, London, 2 Dec. 1961, sponsored by the British Sociological Association. A version augmented by adding eight paragraphs to the end was published as "Sociology in and of China," *British Journal of Sociology*, 13, no. 2 (1962), 106–16. The text here substitutes for the final paragraph of the *China Quarterly* version the final paragraph of the *BJS* version. The omitted material concerns research in Taiwan and Hong Kong and among Overseas Chinese—all treated in more substantive form in papers subsequently published and reprinted below.

tsao, Ch'en Ta, Fei Hsiao-t'ung, Francis L. K. Hsu, Li Ching-han, Li An-che, Lin Yüeh-hua, Feng Han-yi, C. K. Yang, and T'ien Ju-k'ang.

What emerged from the labors of such men consisted partly of ethnographic studies of non-Han groups; these represent the purely anthropological stream, with which I shall not be concerned in this paper. The work which I shall in fact consider may be divided into three main kinds.

The first of these is survey-cum-demographic studies. Surveys setting out to answer questions relating directly to welfare problems go back a long way. A questionnaire inquiry into the living conditions of 302 rickshaw coolies in Peking was carried out as early as 1914–15.² Fact-finding for welfare, agricultural, medical, and educational purposes built up a mere fragment of the picture of Chinese society. The work was too sporadic, unsophisticated, and concerned with the poor. But in the famous Ting Hsien survey³ published by Franklin Lee (Li Ching-han) in 1933, in the voluminous reports on agriculture associated with the name of John Lossing Buck (1937 in particular) and in many lesser-known studies there are enough facts on demographic and near-demographic topics to justify someone going through them with care today. In some recent work on family structure I have found it rewarding to look carefully at the statistics tucked away in articles which are nowadays more referred to than read. The most ambitious attempt to write on the demography of China was, of course, Ch'en Ta's postwar study (1946), which reveals how far pre-Communist China was from understanding its dimensions.

The material to be culled from the Ting Hsien and other surveys takes on some real life if it is read into the framework established by the "community studies," the second kind of work I shall touch on. How these studies came to be made is an unwritten chapter in the history of sociology, although Morton H. Fried has supplied us with many of the necessary data.⁴ Community studies—notably by Fei Hsiao-t'ung, Lin Yüeh-hua, and F. L. K. Hsu—were set a precedent by the American D. H. Kulp's study of a Kwangtung village,⁵ written under the influence partly of American rural sociology.

Teaching sociology in Shanghai for a number of years, Kulp was in touch with, and his work affected by, Sergei Shirokogoroff, who lived in China for more than twenty years before his death in 1939. The Russian ethnologist and physical anthropologist was one of several men who promoted field studies by Chinese scholars. Among the other men were American and British teachers (some of them visited China) who shaped the theoretical preoccupations and methods of a small generation of Chinese field-workers. An interesting part of the influence wielded by visiting foreigners was that the Chinese tried to find a unity in what they severally taught, a point dramatically brought out by Hsu: "During many months between 1935 and 1936 Professor Radcliffe-Brown resided in Yenching University, Father Wilhelm Schmidt entrenched himself behind the castle-like structure of the Catholic University of Peking, while Professor S. M. Shirokogoroff was on the faculty of Tsing Hua University: but these three men could not be persuaded to see each other" (1944: 13).

The community studies made in China may be regarded as a kind of extension of Anglo-American rural sociology and anthropology, the fashions of foreign scholarship helping to shape the products of Chinese investigation. An idea of the effect of the outside influence may be got from a comparison of two different versions of his field study in Fukien put out by Lin Yüeh-hua. A paper in Chinese (1936) analyzes the village community in Radcliffe-Brownian structural terms; a book in English (1948) treats the village as a process of events arranged in accordance with ideas about equilibrium acquired by the author in the United States. The history of community studies may be said to have come to an end, so far as mainland China is concerned, with the publication of C. K. Yang's *A Chinese Village in Early Communist Transition* (1959).

It will be clear that the people I have so far mentioned were concerned with only a part of what sociologists take as their province. What of the larger issues, the grand analysis, the investigation of China as a whole? We at once come up against a practical problem which we should face in treating the sociology of any country: where to draw the boundary between sociology and the other disciplines which ask questions about the nature and course of society. In China, as elsewhere, the present and the recent past fascinated many historians. Some of them were concerned to fit what they saw around them into a general pattern of historical development. A few were Marxists, preoccupied with stages of development and economic institutions; their work has, of course, been extended in the last decade.

The Chinese concern with institutional history has many sources;[6] in the modern period Marxism was added to the older ones; while the fact that many of the leading historical writers were not historians by training, but lawyers, economists, and philosophers, gave their work an extra imaginative quality (see J. D. Gray 1961: 208–12). But if the historians were often sociological, the sociologists were—surprisingly, at first sight, in a society so historically minded—not very historical; and their work suffered in consequence (cf. Fried 1954: 33f).

But there were a few among the men we may more narrowly define as sociologists who asked big questions. One of the earliest general analyses of Chinese social institutions was written by two students of Hobhouse at the London School of Economics (Leong and Tao 1915). In the 1920's and 1930's certain institutions were fastened on because they seemed to represent practical problems and call for reform. They were treated in the grand manner, the results of small-scale inquiries sometimes being injected into the discussion. Family and marriage were very much in the air; let me mention the name of only Quentin Pan (P'an Kuang-tan).[7] Land tenure and other institutions of peasant life were treated generally; Tawney's work on China reflects a good deal of this work (Tawney 1932; and see Institute of Pacific Relations 1939). Somewhat later in the pre-Communist era sociologists began to write on social stratification; Fei Hsiao-t'ung's work on this subject (1946 and 1953) is well known in the West. Of course, what topics were taken up and how they were handled partly depended on the control on inquiry and publication exercised by the Nationalist regime.

Finally, under the head of work done before the advent of Communism I should like briefly to refer to research in the field of law. A spur for this branch of study was law reform and the efforts to give China a "modern" legal system. Attempts were made to collect and classify local customary law. A number of Chinese, especially those under the influence of French scholars, produced treatises which fall within the province of sociology.[8] The legal rules governing, or at least bearing on, many institutions were investigated historically (see esp. Ch'ü [1947] 1961).

I have not referred to several fields of Chinese sociological writing, the range of which may be suggested by the headlings used in the bibliography appended to Marsh's unpublished paper: biological aspects of society, population, and ecology, social psychological aspects, cultural aspects, kinship, family, and marriage, social stratification and mobility, minority ethnic groups and ethnic relations, social pathology and social problems, social movements and social change, social thought and social philosophy, and general works on Chinese society (cf. Fried 1958, Wang Yü-ch'üan 1936, and Newell 1952).

The year 1949, so close to us in time, is sociologically, as it were, very remote. The advent of a Communist regime produced two cleavages in the subject we are discussing. First, it broke up the sociologists into two camps between which there could be no communication. Second, it separated sociology, in the narrow sense, from anthropology by allotting a special task to practitioners of the latter subject and curbing the activities of the sociologists. The first cleavage was not in numerical terms so drastic as one might have imagined. Comparatively few intellectuals crossed the water to Taiwan; whatever they may think now, most sociologists in 1949 apparently foresaw some modus vivendi with the new regime.

The situation in Taiwan, as I understand it, is that of the sociologists and anthropologists now there, many were already in the island in 1949, and among them the Japanese-trained predominate. At the time of the Communist victory the social sciences including sociology looked as though they might survive, despite the lack of a precedent for sociology in the Soviet Russian model. A forced revaluation of the subject took place. The bourgeois history and background of the discipline were rejected; Marxist-Leninism was to give it a new form and purpose; departments of sociology were to be reformed.[9] The voice of Fei Hsiao-t'ung was loud in the inauguration of the new era.

How much teaching was carried on in fact, I have not been able to discover. As for research, while anthropologists were put on to studying the customs, languages, and folklore of the minority ethnic groups—a very practical high-pressure campaign in applied anthropology to win over the non-Han peoples and adjust them to a new society[10]—the sociologists were cut off from their subject matter. Indeed, they were cut off from the opportunity of reading books and, often, of teaching. While the study of history went ahead (producing work of some interest to sociologists, especially in such fields as the emergence of capitalism and peasant revolts),[11] the sociologists seem to have done virtually nothing up to the time of the Hundred Flowers.

In March 1957, Fei Hsiao-t'ung, having endured several years of the new sociology which he had helped to found, protested at the frustrations to which his colleagues had been subjected. Their talents had not been used. Ch'en Ta in the years since Liberation had published nothing. Li Ching-han had told Fei that in the past three years he had been asked to prepare three different courses of lectures, delivering none (C. J. Ch'en 1958: 511f).

Ch'en Ta, born in 1892, had taught at Tsing Hua University until 1951. Despite the fact that he was the most experienced demographer in China he took no part in the 1953 Census. According to an interview published in *Kuang-ming jih-pao*, 14 January 1957, he had in the last few years been studying the labor movements in China 1937–45 and was now Vice-Director of the Peking Labor Kanpu School of the Ministry of Labor. He was also now studying the 1953 Census and Peking birth and death rates, working alone and without the help of a single assistant.[12]

At the time of the Communist assumption of power Li Ching-han was Dean of Sociology at the Peking Fujen Catholic University. After "thought reform" he was sent to teach, first in the Central Government College of Economics and Finance and then in the People's University, as an "assistant teacher." He was obliged to teach subjects about which he knew nothing—machines and textile manufacture. Later he was sent to help a teacher of labor insurance to write his lectures, and was subsequently given tasks of his own in the field of labor. During the Hundred Flowers he came once more to notice and was asked by *Jen-min jih-pao* to make a survey of villages round Peking. He spent three months on this survey, the findings being published in the sponsoring newspaper (Li Ching-han 1957). In May 1957, a bureau of social survey had been newly established of which he had been made the head (see "Professor Li Ching-han" 1957: 7).

According to Fei, speaking in the spring of 1957, the scholars required a freer atmosphere in which to work and liberty to be critical (C. J. Ch'en 1958: 511f). The sociologists began to organize themselves. In June a working committee resolved to set up a Chinese Sociological Society and to reestablish sociological departments throughout the country (*ibid.*: 515).[a] But by this time the new freedom was in danger, and before long Fei and his colleagues were humbling themselves before the people as self-confessed rightists.

In the subsequent campaign the social sciences came under heavy fire. Fei, Wu Ching-ch'ao, and P'an Kuang-tan were attacked as rightists. "Bourgeois social science" was energetically opposed. Fei, a major Aunt Sally, was denounced in August 1957 by his colleague Lin Yüeh-hua as, *inter alia*, a "slave to imperialists" and a "betrayer of peasants." Ch'en Ta was held up as an example of the "reactionary, anti-scientific, and anti-Marxist social scientist" (T. H. E. Chen 1960: 191ff).

While the old sociologists now live on, having purged their deviation, their subject is buried in the ice. True, Chinese officialdom appears to carry out counts and inquiries of its own, but the fact that these give us little in the way of sociological data is well attested by the statement of a French sinologue whose own recent account of social change in China (Chesneaux 1960) is based largely on the Chinese press and foreigners' reports. During the very period when Chinese society has been undergoing its most radical transformation, the few men capable of illuminat-

[a] The Democratic League's academic program (as reported in *Kuang-ming jih-pao*, 9 June 1957) included the following: "Certain subjects have actually been dispensed with, or have ceased to be independent subjects; and a number of people who in the past specialized in sociology, political science and law have now changed their profession. A number of subjects have been dispensed with just because they do not appear in Soviet Russia's syllabuses. . . . Our attitude towards the traditional social sciences should be one of reform rather than abolition. Therefore we should take appropriate steps to reinstate these subjects where circumstances warrant it and lay emphasis where emphasis is due. . . . We deem it necessary to encourage social science research workers to lay stress upon investigation and research work and to submit proposals concerning the government's policies and statutes to further the search for truth."

ing the changes have been, except during the temporary release of the Hundred Flowers, blinkered and silenced.[13]

. . . .

It could be argued that before the Second World War, outside North America and Western Europe, China was the seat of the most flourishing sociology in the world, at least in respect of its intellectual quality. It is now only a frozen tradition. I argue that we should do something to keep the temperature up outside.

A Chinese Phase in Social Anthropology

Some twenty-six years ago Malinowski was visited by Professor Wu Wen-tsao of Yenching University. He learned from him, as he tells us, "that independently and spontaneously there had been organized in China a sociological attack on real problems of culture and applied anthropology, an attack which embodies all my dreams and desiderata." These words were written in 1938 in the Preface to Fei Hsiao-t'ung's *Peasant Life in China* (1939), a book which Malinowski thought would be counted "as a landmark in the development of anthropological fieldwork and theory." One reason for Malinowski's confidence in Fei's work was that it pushed the frontiers of anthropology outward from savagery to civilization. And Malinowski went on to quote a forecast he had made on another occasion: "'The anthropology of the future will be . . . as interested in the Hindu as in the Tasmanian, in the Chinese peasants as in the Australian aborigines, in the West Indian negro as in the Melanesian Trobriander, in the detribalized African of Haarlem [*sic*] as in the Pygmy of Perak.'"

We are now in the midst of the future of which Malinowski wrote. If we ignore the reference to the Trobrianders (who generously provide opportunities to present-day anthropologists for fruitful non-fieldwork), some of us might well say that the prophecy erred only in suggesting that we are *equally* interested in savagery and civilization. The bold ones among us might not be shy to confess that Hindus and Chinese seem rather more interesting than Australian aborigines. This is the point from which I start. Since the 1930's a number of Chinese, British, and American anthropologists—let us call them "social," most of them will not object—have tried to study Chinese society. What can we learn from their efforts to go beyond the older boundaries of their subject? I shall

Third Malinowski Memorial Lecture, delivered 30 Oct. 1962. *British Journal of Sociology*, 14, no. 1 (1963), 1–19. Reprinted in Robert A. Manners and David Kaplan, eds., *Theory in Anthropology: A Source Book* (Chicago, 1968), 145–56.

suggest some answers to this question which should enable us, like the eponym of my lecture in his time, to guess at the near future of social anthropology.[1]

The young Fei Hsiao-t'ung was one of several Chinese eager to study their own society by methods developed for investigating primitive social life. Francis L. K. Hsu, who followed Fei's example in taking his Ph.D. here at the School, belonged to this group, as did Lin Yüeh-hua, who will be known to you as the author of *The Golden Wing* (1948). After the war the next generation was represented in England by T'ien Ju-k'ang. The presence of determined Chinese scholars in Britain and the United States, as well as the potent attraction of a civilization which since the eighteenth century has had a special place in Western thinking, excited some of our number to interest themselves in China. Radcliffe-Brown taught at Yenching University in 1935, Dr. Fortune at Lingnan University in 1937–39. Professor Firth began to learn Mandarin but, unfortunately for Chinese studies, decided to go no further than the Malayan coast of the China Sea. It is said that Dr. Leach, during his earlier incarnation as a businessman in China, first began to dabble in the anthropology which he has since been acrobatically rethinking. By the time the war had been over a couple of years a good deal of anthropological energy was ready to be released in Chinese studies. In China Fei and his associates wanted to continue the fieldwork which they had bravely pursued during the war. W. H. Newell from Oxford, G. W. Skinner from Cornell, and M. H. Fried from Columbia established themselves in China, while Isabel Crook, having studied here at the School, returned to China, where, as Isabel Brown, she had earlier been at work. In 1948 Redfield went to teach at Fei's own university, Tsing Hua. But the potentialities of this talent could not be realized. Fei first butted his head against the political wall under the Kuomintang and then, as far as anthropology is concerned, succumbed to the alternating blandishments and severities of the Communists (cf. Freedman 1962b [Essay 21 above]). The coming of the People's Republic generally put an end to field studies by Western scholars; happily Professor Fried managed to complete a study of a county seat in Anhwei province in good time (Fried 1953); and Mrs. Crook, working under Communist auspices, produced some material on land reform (Crook and Crook 1959). For the period up to about 1950 there is little else to show. The outlook was unpromising. But since that time an encouraging lesson has been built into the history of our subject by the very handicap from which Chinese specialists thought they were suffering. The act which slammed the gates of China in the face of field anthropologists, cutting them off from the land for which they had studiously prepared themselves, turned them to other tasks which began by seeming to be inferior substitutes and are proving, as I shall contend, to be more and not less central to the social anthropology of the 1960's.

Three kinds of field study of Chinese social organization began to be undertaken. From both Britain and the United States a handful of people went off to study communities of Overseas Chinese, especially in Southeast Asia. A few British and American anthropologists carried out field investigations in the New Territories of Hong Kong. Finally, a small group of Americans, for the most part connected with Cornell University, turned their attention to Taiwan. This activity has been increasingly shaped by interests for which there are few precedents in the studies of China made by anthropologists before the coming of the Communists. Let me return to what Malinowski wrote in his Preface to Fei's book. He argued that Wu Wen-tsao and his pupils were on the right lines in striving to understand China by the study of "present reality." The anthropological approach was an indispensable supplement to historical research. There is nothing to quarrel with in that statement; it is a version of a common and defensible view of the contribution of anthropology to history. But the argument then proceeds to discuss how "present reality" was to be studied. The "methodological foundations of the modern Chinese School of Sociology" were sound, Malinowski wrote, as we could see from Fei's study of peasants. "By becoming acquainted with the life of a small village, we study, under a microscope as it were, the epitome of China at large." Malinowski then offers us a glimpse into Fei's future work which would include, sooner or later, "a wider synthesis of his own works and that of his colleagues, giving us a comprehensive picture of the cultural, religious and political systems of China." Now it is true that Fei did in fact later produce some general essays on the nature of his own society (see esp. 1953), but he never came near realizing the program expressed for him by his teacher. Nor could he have come near doing so as long as he was under the sway of the anthropological ideas of the 1930's. His expertise was too narrowly confined to villages. Of course, he was also interested in factories and other nonrural things, but his studies of them did not widen his competence to the extent envisaged by his British teacher.

The idea Malinowski was putting forward was part of the accepted dogma of the day—and it is by no means entirely extinct a quarter of a century later. A few years before Malinowski was introducing his Chinese pupil to Western readers, Radcliffe-Brown was speaking in China on the transfer to complex societies of anthropological methods of investigation. In China, he told his audiences, the most suitable unit of study was the village, both because most Chinese lived in villages and because it was possible for one or two fieldworkers to make a fairly detailed study in a year or so (Radcliffe-Brown 1936). According to Lin Yüeh-hua (1936), who sat at his feet in China, Radcliffe-Brown said that the best way to begin the study of Chinese social structure was to select a very small "social area," examine it meticulously, compare it with other specimens studied in the same manner, and then proceed to draw generalizations. It would seem that from this patient induction from studies of small social areas would emerge a picture of the social system of China. Of all the biases to which the anthropological approach has been subject this seems to me the most grievous. It is the anthropological fallacy *par excellence*. And it must strike us as a particularly ironical one if we remember that it springs directly from a preoccupation with totalities. When we study primitive societies we must take them in their entirety, but as soon as we turn to complex societies we find our instruments so adapted to the investigation of the small in scale that we must carve out from the unmanageable whole little social areas which, if I may make a pastiche of Malinowski and Radcliffe-Brown, are epitomes of convenient size.[2]

The anthropologists working on Chinese themes since about 1950 have wanted to catch some of the things which a miniaturizing method of this sort must let slip. Had China not gone Communist they might still today have been piling up samples of local communities; the ethnographic map of China would have had many more flags in it, but the anthropologists would probably have been no nearer that understanding of Chinese society of which Malinowski wrote than they were ten years ago. New experiences in the study of Chinese society outside mainland China have taught new lessons. Consider first the case of the anthropologists who have tried to study Overseas Chinese. There are few villages, at least in the traditional sense, to tempt them, while the towns for the most part lack that convenience of size which would allow a simple transfer of traditional technique. Social relationships among Overseas Chinese do not round themselves off neatly in suitable localities, and it is at once apparent that to delimit a "community" and confine one's attention to it would miss the very characteristic of the society which makes it interesting: its scale and its scatter. Trying to study the Overseas Chinese a man must find his anthropological prejudices corroded away. He must be mobile. He must learn to contain his impatience when he cannot see all his subjects acting out their many roles. He must be content with fragmentary direct observation. He must adjust his vision so that he may see behavior and ideas within the framework not only of the immediate locality but also of the society from which the migrants have come, of the largest territorial settlement within which they find themselves, and of the non-Chinese society in which they are embedded. All this imposes its own wearying discipline, but that it can be rewarding by bringing anthropological, linguistic, and historical talents to bear on interesting problems I can illustrate by referring you to Professor Skinner's splendid work on the Chinese in Thailand (1957 and 1958). Not the least important aspect of that work is its use of sociological techniques to lay bare the essential ties between individuals and corporations which constitute the channels of control and command in a heterogeneous, highly differentiated, and dispersed segment of Thailand society.

The case of those who have studied and those who are yet to study in Hong Kong is rather different. In the New Territories of that colony, as Barbara E. Ward and Jean A. Pratt have shown us by demonstration, Chinese villages can be studied by conventional anthropological methods to conventional anthropological benefit. The work they have pioneered is, I hope, the beginning of a long series of studies in the New Territories of problems of Chinese rural organization, especially since, by one of the practical jokes of history, a British Crown Colony has become the last refuge of a Chinese imperial administrative system. But to be in Hong Kong is also to have vividly before one's eyes a complex urban society reaching out, through two cities and many towns, into the life of the countryside. It offers a temptation, which surely cannot be resisted much longer, to remedy many of the lacunae in our understanding of urbanism in China.

The moral to be drawn from the experience of the anthropologists who have been at work in Taiwan is of yet another kind. Taiwan is China—that at least is not in dispute—but the anthropologists are able to seize on the benefit accruing from one important respect in which it is different from the rest of the country. It was for half a century a Japanese colonial possession, with the result that a remarkable descriptive and statistical documentation is here stored up which can hardly be matched elsewhere in China. This material is capable of answering questions independently of particular field studies and of providing information about the modern past of areas chosen for fieldwork.

One might say of all this work that it has carried Chinese specialists along a road also traveled in the 1950's by other anthropologists: toward a wider conception of the anthropological vocation. But I think that the people concerned with Chinese matters have been made especially sensitive to the challenge implied in the names "history" and "sociology."

Social anthropologists in Britain have swung round to commend historical studies when formerly they merely did them. (I think this summarizes a significant part of Professor Schapera's recent (1962) Presidential Address to the Royal Anthropological Institute.) At any rate, the case for the obvious has now been authoritatively made, and we have all a general license to sit in archives (or at least in libraries) and interview the dead. Good. But if we are to be fruitful in our historical researches we must talk to historians. What will the conversation be like? Listen to an eminent historian of China invoking the social scientists in an argument with another eminent historian of China. Professor Mary C. Wright of Yale is rebuking Professor John K. Fairbank of Harvard for telling the sinologues that they have been naughty historians for having been seduced into social science. The historians, Professor Wright says (1961), need to understand the social sciences more not less, but however far they succeed in this understanding,

they cannot themselves become social scientists of China, and not only because they haven't time. The historian's business, ideally, is to study all the varied and interrelated facets of some particular process of change in time. The social scientist's business, I take it, is to study similar facets abstracted from many varied phenomena, related not in origin but in type. Each approach can learn from the other, but the aims are quite different. Any one who supposes he is doing both understands neither. If the social sciences are to make their full contribution to our comprehension of the Chinese (or any other) historical record, social scientists must themselves do research in the primary sources.

The argument goes on: the historian must persuade "men of real skill in political science, economics, law, sociology and anthropology to apply these skills to the Chinese sources and tell us what they find." But there are few signs that the Chinese records are attracting the social scientists. The data are abundant and "the language can be learned." Are the social scientists going to abandon to the historians the "whole vast ranges of documented experiences to which [they] once laid formal claim"? And Professor Wright concludes with this provocation:

So far as I can ascertain . . . these questions have not attracted [the social scientists'] . . . attention. We must, therefore, now ask them whether the Chinese (or other non-Western) historical record is of professional interest to them. If so, do they intend to encourage their students to exploit it? If not, will they tell us why, so that we may understand more clearly what their professional interests are?

I am not "they" and cannot speak for them, but I shall try to give what I think is a reasonable anthropologist's reply, at least in the context of scholarship in this country. One may make many nice and valid distinctions between the respective aims of history and anthropology. In many cases the two disciplines require each other because they have a common interest in establishing and interpreting a body of facts relating to the past. Cooperation between them would, to take a simple example, prevent the historian making silly remarks about Chinese kinship in his ignorance of the properties of kinship systems, and the anthropologist perpetrating anachronisms for lack of an understanding of the changes in Chinese kinship over time. In my opinion, the problem raised by Professor Wright is much more practical than she seems to realize. She says the language can be learned. So it can, but who will teach it and how fast? The response to the Hayter report[3] should have convinced us that many of the orientalists are unhappy about accommodating the man whose interests are not engrossed by the civilization they teach. The young anthropologist with a technical literature to master which would have astonished even so recent a figure as Malinowski, and facing a mental discipline that makes great demands on him, cannot afford the time assumed by the traditional Chinese language training. On this score it is the sinologues who must make concessions if they are eager to have nonhistorians working on the records. But there is a practical difficulty which the anthropologists on their side could remove. Our profession is structured to produce field-workers, for if we are not field-workers are we anything? If the answer is no, then I think we are making poor use of our human resources and taking an excessively narrow view of our subject. Why should every young anthropologist have to be blooded in the field? Why should the field trip be the essential mark of the acceptable scholar? There are excellent grounds for saying that the tradition of fieldwork is the core of the profession, but it does not follow that absolutely everyone must be given a ticket to far places. An obsession which created a magnificent esprit de corps among a small band of worthies of the older generation is now degenerating in a much expanded profession into a snobbery which threatens to cut us off from a kind of scholarship which would benefit us as much as the historians for whom Professor Wright has spoken.[4]

I have tried to present what I consider a reasonable anthropologist's answer to Professor Wright's challenge. But not all anthropologists are reasonable; yet their views are influential. There appear to be some who think that their subject is fundamentally about primitive society, or at least about the kinds of thing that are best studied in primitive society. In the course of a general essay on, say, marriage, or feud, or ancestor worship, one may legitimately draw in scraps of information on civilized societies, but one must not stray too far from home ground. (Incidentally, how Frazerian this kind of comparative method sometimes looks is not clear to those who practice it.) Despite all the false rumors that the primitive world is shrinking to nothingness (circulated chiefly, I suspect, by jealous sociologists), the men who are for little anthropology were, are, and are likely to remain princes of the profession, however much they have belied Malinowski's prediction and however much of a nuisance they are to big anthropology.

On the other hand, there are some among us who, while they acknowledge the importance of venturing beyond the limits of the primitive, nevertheless are worried by the consequences of having too many institutional contacts with people like historians. They are in our ranks the analogues of the traditional orientalists who consider the Hayter report a subversive document. Both kinds of men can be goaded by the mention of area studies. What are such studies, they say, but an insipid dilution of several kinds of knowledge in the interests of current affairs, intelligence work, or, worst of all, imitating the Americans? The anthropological purist considers the historian a sort of temptress who will lure his young men away from the puritanical pleasures of disciplined inquiry and theory-building. To such an objection the reply is, in fact, very simple. If we set our pupils at the feet of the historians (or the geographers or the political scientists) in order to deepen their understanding of a particular part of the world, and they forget what we have taught them, then we have either taught them badly or they were no good anyway. If they fail to put our old questions to their new knowledge and cannot see in what their new teachers say ways of extending anthropology, then again the failure is in our subject or in those supposed to be carrying it on.

I turn to sociology. Like their fellows working in other complex situations, anthropologists studying the Overseas Chinese have found that the fieldwork tradition of their subject does not equip them fully for their inquiries. In circumstances for which sociologists have devised techniques of investigation the anthropologist at best takes them over, and at worst, in ignorance of their existence, laboriously and inefficiently invents them all over again. No anthropologist who has faced the difficulties of large-scale inquiries is likely to look down his nose at the sociologist's techniques for surveying and counting. On this I need say nothing further, because it seems to me that there is no intellectual question at stake. Either one uses appropriate sociological techniques or one does not.

The important question is whether we can learn ideas from the sociologists to help us in our efforts to study complex societies. We can, because their subject is constitutionally adapted to big issues and large phenomena. They, unlike us, have never made a virtue of narrowness. Of course, in reality many sociologists are as narrow as many anthropologists, and if sociologists can, in their casual way, sting anthropologists by asking them "Are you still talking about kinship?," the insult is repayable by the question whether they have got beyond thinking about social stratification. And if there are anthropologists who live, breathe, and talk Africa, there are sociologists similarly confined to Western Europe. There are failures of imagination all round. But as a discipline sociology knows about things which are essential to anthropologists striking out into the study of civilization. We must go to the sociologists whenever we have problems to tackle in, say, ideologies, population growth, urbanism, industrialization, education, communications, or social mobility. We must not imagine that because we are studying China and they are not (as is the case in Britain), we can dispense with their concepts and their experience.

It must seem strange to anyone unfamiliar with academic relations if, having spoken of the need for my profession to learn from sociology, I go on to say that most social anthropologists in this country appear to think of themselves as sociologists. (Some of them, I understand, are duly recognized by the sociologists, others not.) They are tempted to justify their continued existence as a separate profession, or a distinct branch of the larger profession, by appealing to that special interest in the small-scale which I earlier argued to have hampered the development of anthropological studies of China. We learned, when we were being brought up on savages—and Malinowski, of course, showed us brilliantly how it could be done—to examine small communities, subject them to minute observation, tease out the threads linking individual to individual, activity to activity, and idea to idea. As new and larger fields of inquiry open up we must look around for what, in terms of scale, are the equivalents of primitive societies. In 1938 Professor Firth sent a paper to the Chinese journal *The Sociological World*[5] which appeared in a special issue dedicated, charmingly, to "The London School of Anthropology." In that paper Firth used the term micro-sociology to describe the special contribution to be made by anthropologists to the study of Chinese society. Six years later, speaking at a forum in London on possible postwar developments in anthropology (1944), Professor Firth inserted the term into the British record. "Much of the anthropologist's work," he said, "has lain hitherto in what may be called micro-sociology—the study of small groups or of small units in larger groups; of how relationships operate on a small scale, in personal terms . . . I think that the most valuable contribution of the social anthropologist may well still lie in this micro-sociological field." He returned to the theme again in 1951 when he argued the many advantages of confining observation to a small unit (1951: 17—18).

Now these advantages are indeed impressive, and the fruits of micro-sociology bear witness to its virtues. In one of the most interesting discussions I have read of the relations between history and the social sciences Professor H. Stuart Hughes (1960: 42) referring to the aim of "the more imaginative historians of today . . . to grasp in a coherent pattern the economic, social and psychological manifestations of a given society," argues that it is primarily from the anthropologists that they can learn how to go about their tasks. And he goes on, citing Bloch's work and Wylie's study of a French village, to say that on-the-spot study of a small community seems to him "the best possible training ground for the historian whose mind is orientated toward social and psychological synthesis." (Cf. Benda 1962: 109.)

I remain suspicious of some of the implications of these statements. Professor Firth says that although our technique is micro-sociological, our theory is macro-sociological. We use "the microcosm to illumine the macrocosm, the particular to illustrate the general." But how do we, in fact, jump from microcosm to macrocosm? Professor Firth (1951: 18) warns anthropologists that they should be careful to show the representativeness of the small sample they select for study, but he does not seem in this statement to face the question of whether, be the sample as perfect as may be, it is anything more than a sample of like small units instead of a microcosm of a total society.[a]

There can be no quarrel with an argument which says that anthropologists are so good at firsthand observation of small units that they should do it whenever they have the chance. And it is undoubtedly true that, as a result of their habituation to the small-scale, anthropologists are especially skilled in certain kinds of institutional analysis, above all in the field of kinship. What needs to be disputed is the view that anthropologists should be chained by their virtues and made nervous of trying to do bigger things. Fei Hsiao-tung did his micro-sociology very well, and our knowledge of Chinese society would be vastly poorer if his books were expunged from the record. But he thought his understanding of his villages, coupled with his radical-mandarin insight into his society, gave

[a] In dealing summarily with the views of anthropologists on their possible contribution to the study of complex societies I have certainly not paid enough attention to the gap between general pronouncement and particular recommendation or practice. Firth, who gave us "micro-sociology," has been responsible for promoting a number of wide-ranging studies in Asia. His plans for research in Malaya (1948: esp. pp. 27–38), for example, show how he has balanced small-scale with large-scale inquiries in an attempt to provide for the study of an exceedingly complicated society. Malinowski, in his last fieldwork, seems to have tried to achieve something much broader than the work for which we remember him. Irving Rouse (1953: 61): ". . . there have also been attempts to record the nature of the culture during successive periods by combined use of historical documents, recollections of informants, and participant observation. This was Malinowski's objective in the study of Oaxaca markets which he was making at the time of his death." (Cf. Malinowsky [*sic*] and Fuente 1957.)

him privileged access to the social secrets of China. In my opinion he erred in his judgment because he lacked enough historical knowledge of China and a full understanding of its broader institutional framework. And I think that Fei's mistake illustrates a risk inherent in the anthropological preoccupation with the small in scale: the risk of speaking generally of a society with the confidence bred of an intimate acquaintance with local communities in it.

The big question of the anthropologist's contribution to the study of complex societies was taken up last year in an international parish magazine called *Current Anthropology*. Professor Eisenstadt (1961), the Israeli sociologist, who has for many years now taken a sympathetic interest in the doings of anthropologists, set out his estimate and appraisal of the contribution and was then given the "treatment" for which Professor Tax's journal is noted. The arguments and criticisms of which the "treatment" was composed show some of the intellectual and emotional barriers which need to be crossed before anthropologists really feel at home in the study of complex society. There is a suggestion that we have been studying it all along, for, after all, was not Nadel's Nupe society complex, and what does complex mean anyway? As for the difficulty that anthropologists turning their attention to complex society cannot cope with the total society, well, that is a false problem, because a total society cannot be studied, whether we call it complex or primitive. There is some resistance to the implication that anthropologists may have a special role to play in the study of the complex. There is support for the view that the frontiers between anthropology and certain other social sciences must be removed. And so on.

I stand by my earlier statements. There is a valid sense in which, however imperfectly they may in fact do it, anthropologists are able realistically to aim at observing and analyzing a total society when that society is small and relatively undifferentiated. And the statement remains true even when, as in the case of the Kachin and the Tallensi, the authors of the books describing them have only the vaguest notions of where the boundaries of the societies lie. The point is that Dr. Leach and Professor Fortes are able to convince us that there would be little to gain in our understanding of what they have discussed by our looking beyond the limits they themselves have imposed.

I am not sure that I myself know what a complex society is, or, more accurately, where along a continuum from most to least simple a complex society can be said to fall; but I think I know when I am in the presence of a civilization. In a civilization an ethnographer cannot do what ethnographers have done elsewhere; total society is beyond his individual grasp. And yet, if he is to be informative when he pronounces on his findings, he must have had access to material bearing on the total society and be able to bring his own work into relation with it. It is in this limited sense that anthropologists working on China must aim at the total society. Of course, the more competently they equip themselves in history and sociology, the larger the circuit they will be able to cover, although it is not necessary to assume that their activities as straightforward field ethnographers of the old type are of no use in the grand enterprise.

But today mainland China is closed to fieldwork. As a result, the thoughts of anthropologists sometimes turn to historical problems, and, casting about for ways to compensate for the loss of fieldwork opportunities, they consider the possibilities of reconstructing aspects of Chinese society from data collected in interviews with emigrés, by means of analogies drawn from Hong Kong and Overseas Chinese settlements, and by interpreting present-day official Chinese writings; and they often resort to torturing the existing information on nineteenth- and twentieth-century China to make it yield up answers to important questions. But in this very odd position they are automatically exempt, so far as the mainland is concerned, from conducting campaigns to endear themselves to the political controllers of the society and from adapting their activities to the wishes of its intellectual elite.

Elsewhere in Asia, where study on the spot is relatively free, the problem of accommodating scholarship to national interests already exists and may, I suggest, grow sterner. A price may have to be paid for the privilege of being a disinterested scholar, and paid in the coin of applied anthropology, so that the currency corrupts the purchase. In countries in which their leaders are struggling to assert national independence, cultural and political, and crying out for economic development, knowledge can easily come to be defined as that which is immediately useful. Some anthropological knowledge is immediately useful, and there is a case for giving advice in the post-colonial world just as there was in the days when Malinowski was enthusiastic about culture change and applied anthropology.[6] But there is a nasty booby trap in the new situation. In the classical colonial setting, when the anthropologists, as it was very natural for them to do, presented to their sponsors the circumstances and views of the underdogs, they were more or less liked and more or less believed. They were not, however, generally looked upon as subversive. The anthropologist nowadays may, by threatening the myths of determined elites, get himself seen as a national danger. He may, for example, demonstrate that peasants conduct their affairs in contravention of principles laid down for them in an ideological heaven; the peasants are individualists when the elite says they are collectivists. The exclusion of such an anthropologist is perhaps imminent, and he too ought to be thinking of doing historical research—although that also is not without its myth-breaking dangers.

But there is more to it than that. There can be no new generation of anthropologists in China, at least as we understand the name. In other countries of Asia we hope for a great expansion in our numbers and we look around eagerly for Asian students to come to us to be prepared and in their turn to set up centers of anthropological learning. And indeed in one or two places—outstandingly in India—there are signs that our hopes are not vain. But I suggest that there are reasons for moderating our optimism. New civil bureaucracies are great soakers-up of talent; little prestige, let alone income, is left for the unpractical scholar. In the press for political and economic development there is scant tolerance of fundamental scholarship in the social sciences. These in their theoretical aspects are easily damned as postponable luxuries and persecuted by "priorities." If I am right in this dark assessment, our own responsibilities become greater. We have to further the study of oriental civilizations among us, not simply because it is a matter of national security that we have people equipped in Asian languages and cultures, but because our own title to civilization must be kept alive by our capacity to view the world impartially.

I have spoken of developments in anthropological studies of China in the last decade or so as having marked a step forward from the traditional social anthropology. This is, of course, a very small phase in a much larger one in which our subject tries to cope with new circumstances and fresh ideas. The Indianists have done much better than their colleagues on the Chinese side; their field is open.[7] The Africanists for their part have not been slow to take the hint from the growth of towns, industry, trade unions, electoral systems, new states, and the Africans' awareness of their past (cf. Kaberry 1957: 86). The anthropological study of Asia, let alone that of China, can show nothing so grand as the panorama displayed by the International African Institute. But before the Chinese phase is dead—for who can say how long it will survive the attraction of talent to more accessible fields?—an interesting section will have been added to the annals of what Radcliffe-Brown liked to call comparative sociology.

The only study which Radcliffe-Brown himself attempted directly to sponsor during his stay in China was an investigation in the Yellow River region of "paired intermarrying clans." He was interested in the subject because he thought it was still possible to study in action a marriage system which, many centuries before, had been associated with the development of a philosophy of complementary opposites epitomized in the concepts of *yin* and *yang*. Speaking in 1951 Radcliffe-Brown ([1952a] 1958: 124) thought it might still not be too late for such a study to be done (it had been prevented in the 1930's by the Japanese attack); it would enable us, he said, "to evaluate more exactly the historical reconstruction of Marcel Granet." He was surely too optimistic to speak like this in 1951, but his recommendation still has a point in it for us. The historians, so they tell me, now know better than Granet; the anthropologists have moved on from Radcliffe-Brown in the study of marriage systems. It is possible to pose, in the light of theory as it now stands, many problems in Chinese marriage, affinity, and kinship which could be examined in the Chinese records for a great span of time, shifts in the proscription of marriage, in the scale of the marriage network, in the duties of affines, in the depth of lineage organization, and in the arrangement of the ancestor cult being brought into relation with one another and with changes in political and economic circumstances. As for the present, Hong Kong and Taiwan remain open.

My first example of what can be done is typically anthropological in the sense that it calls upon the traditional stock of interests and ideas. Take, then, towns and cities. The historians can tell us a little about them —I recommend to you Jacques Gernet's recent study (1962) of Hangchow in the second half of the thirteenth century. The anthropologists have in the last few years been looking at social organization in cities such as Bangkok and Singapore where great numbers of Chinese have come together. I have already referred to Professor Fried's study of a county seat in central China. Again, we have opportunities in Taiwan and Hong Kong. At least as far as the big cities are concerned, we begin to see some regularities. We notice that agnatic principles create solidarity between "clansmen" as well as "kinsmen"; that men adapt themselves to the city through loyalties built around the villages and regions from which they come; that political and economic order in the city is to a great extent a function of interlocking voluntary associations of a bewildering variety.

Consider too migration. Several of the anthropologists now working on Chinese themes are interested in the Hakka, a people identified in the first place by the dialect of Chinese they speak and widely dispersed in China. Much has been written on them, and a recent, as yet unpublished, historical study by a young American anthropologist, Mr. Myron Cohen, has raised the interesting question of how different kinds of Chinese maintained their several identities, competed and came into conflict with one another, and moved on to new places. Those who have studied Overseas Chinese have for long been asking about the reasons why particular villages in southeastern China specialized in sending their members abroad, and the consequences of the emigration for village economy and organization. Partial answers to these questions may be supplied by historical material, and a field study would certainly take us a long way to understanding, for example, the viability of village institutions in the absence of large numbers of men and the economic aspect of self-perpetuating migration such that, once well launched, the movement must continue, perhaps increase, because of the adaptation to external income. Now it happens that at this moment we have in Hong Kong and on our own doorstep the two ends of a classical Chinese village migration; for the owners of and waiters in the Chinese restaurants which have sprung up around us in this country are apparently recent emigrants from a few villages in the Hong Kong New Territories, villages which are themselves challenged by immigrants to Hong Kong who rent rice fields and turn them into intensively cultivated vegetable gardens.

A number of important works have been appearing in recent years on social mobility in China, a topic which, because of the nature of the imperial examination system and recruitment to the bureaucracy, lends itself to detailed historical treatment. An anthropological critique needs to be inserted into the discussion, not merely to help clarify, under sociological guidance, the technical apparatus for treating class and status, but also to work out the modes of life and structures of relationship which were transformed as individuals ceased to be peasants to become merchants, came first to be recognized as belonging to the gentry, or moved into higher officialdom.

The accumulation of wealth is an aspect of social mobility, but it needs to be taken with a different question, which has a history of its own in the social sciences: why did capitalist enterprise in China prove abortive? Students of Hong Kong and the Overseas Chinese know something of the way in which Chinese commerce and industry can thrive outside the framework of the Chinese state, and, with a friendly push from the economists, might succeed in describing how Chinese entrepreneurs manage their affairs (the account would certainly not be dull) and in throwing light on the factors which have favored and retarded Chinese economic innovation.

I shall take the themes of law and social control to illustrate in an especially acute form how the study of Chinese society challenges the anthropologist. He knows something of how rules are enforced in Chinese villages. The historians have mapped the formal legal apparatus of the state and the conceptions on which they rested. What is yet far from clear is the relationship between the various sets of norms operating in the society and between different mechanisms for producing conformity to any one set of them. In such an inquiry the anthropologist would need to range very widely, and in company; and his success would depend on his ability both to master an enormous mass of data and to encompass in his imagination the extent of a vast and complicated society.

If I were imprudent enough to try your patience further I should make similar comments on the study of such general questions as religious institutions and conceptions and such narrower matters as military organization and formal education. I shall in fact offer one more example, and I insist on it in order to make a case for the study of Communist China without necessarily getting involved in cold warfare. I refer to the communes. The fact-collecting is difficult; it calls for an ingenuity quite outside the normal repertory of anthropological talents; but here as elsewhere I lay less stress on techniques than on the importance of solving problems. The writings on the Chinese communes usually give pride of place to questions of economic efficiency and the fate of the family, but there are broader issues. What are the limits to massive "social engineering"? To what extent can preexisting modes of behavior reassert themselves within institutions deliberately designed to exclude them? (There is, in this connection, a lot to be said on the emergence of the "production brigade" as a possible retreat from the commune to former social units.) What consequences flow from the imposition of a mechanical social equality on systems previously relying for their order on social inequality? To what extent do the communes seal off local communities from the political centers of society? I believe that an anthropologist can properly ask and help to answer questions like these.

In studies of the sort I have sketched I suggest we can see some of the characteristics of the social anthropology of the 1960's. Our subject changes from year to year, although we may mask the gradual transformation by forgetting what we said ten years ago and by stressing the continuity from the founding fathers. British social anthropology is dissolving by being no longer exclusively British and by becoming more closely attuned to voices speaking from foreign lands. The French, who taught us much to begin with, are again reading us some lessons. The Americans, whom we thought we had domesticated in Chicago, are bombarding us with new kinds of studies and ideas. In the 1960's, taking up the problems springing from an expanding subject, we shall apply them more and more to complex societies. So that if a man says that he is interested in oriental civilization he is so far from being a deserter from the cause as to be an agent of its advancement. He is running ahead and not away. And in the process he will be engaged in activities unsanctioned by the sacred tradition which stretches all the way back to, say, 1922. One unconventional activity will be close cooperation with scholars in other fields, not because cooperation is a good thing in itself, but because it is a condition for the transfer to our subject of some of the intellectual excitement being aroused outside our frontiers (e.g. A. F. Wright 1960). To have caught a glimpse of the possibilities inherent in the Chinese record, to have sensed the opportunities stored up in local gazetteers and genealogy books, to know that the historians are looking for anthropological help in their attempt to analyze a vast and long-enduring civilization, is to recognize the early stage of a new venture in our subject.[b]

To come closer to the end of my oblique tribute to Malinowski I want briefly to discuss a different side of the expansion of social anthropology. If we think of ourselves not only as promoters of research and new ideas, but also as teachers, we shall discover, I suggest, that there are drawbacks in the way we have been going about our business. There is an honorable minority in our ranks (in which alas I cannot claim membership) which, during the last few years, has been pressing for a reappraisal of our educational role. Now, when university education seems about to expand, the majority must surely realize that our teaching must undergo some change. We have tended to treat the undergraduate reading social anthropology as though he were offering himself as a potential professional. We have been tempted to measure his achievements by the extent to which he could make himself resemble a research worker eager for the field. And we shall not be able to do better for the next generation of undergraduates unless we can plan for a subject to be taught which will give them an intellectually satisfying view of their world without leaving most of them, as they are capped and gowned, with the feeling that they are failed fieldworkers.

How this may be done I cannot discuss here, but I shall try to establish one principle by alluding to a subject with which social anthropology is held by some heretics to have a close connection. I mean anthropology. In this country anthropology as a teaching subject has lost its unity, although in professional circles kind words of solidarity are exchanged between what are called the branches. And we are characteristically astonished when, as is outstandingly the case with Professor Forde, we find

[b] It is clear that anthropological ideas have influenced sinology: American work sometimes bears Redfield's mark; Professor Wolfram Eberhard often writes on the basis of anthropological principles; Granet, to take an earlier example, acquired much through his Durkheimian connections. I am here looking forward to a closer correlation of interests. Of course, it could be objected to my line of reasoning that young anthropologists who are trained sinologically would, because of the nature of their investment, become less mobile than anthropologists are traditionally supposed to be—they would study no society other than China, and so fail to acquire that balance which is said to come from a close acquaintance with societies of different kind and region. While I agree that the danger exists and must be guarded against, I also think that it is not confined to oriental anthropology. Parochial concentration can develop in more conventional fields of anthropological study. A corner of Africa is no less stultifying than China.

a man with the encyclopaedic knowledge and mental stamina to contain the subject as a whole under one skull. In the United States, in contrast, anthropology flourishes in the undergraduate schools; it is thought of as a unity; people are trained to teach it as one subject; and it succeeds in doing what must be done for the education of American undergraduates: it provides them with a set of humanistic studies to help make up deficiencies in their high school education and prepare them intellectually both for the professional training of the graduate schools and for non-academic careers. The nature of our undergraduate schools is changing and we too shall need to consider groupings of subjects which will serve to educate rather than train. I can think of an ideal combination which would dissolve the present structure of anthropology and sociology at the undergraduate level in order to teach peole how to think about society and civilization both historically and sociologically.[8] In such a combination oriental societies would appear, and I would hope that some social anthropologists would be able to teach them. But in order to do so they would need to be better orientalists than we now are. In the case of China they would have to acquire a knowledge of the literature which went beyond an acquaintance with a few fieldwork monographs, the exploits of Judge Dee, and the more esoteric passages of the integral translation of *The Golden Lotus*.[9]

What Social Science Can Do for Chinese Studies

I am the joker in the pack—not simply for the obvious reason that I am not an American, but also, and much more significantly, because I have no right to sit on a platform with people learned in sinology. That I have been invited to join them says a great deal about American broadmindedness and something too about the underdeveloped state of Chinese studies in my own country. But in a way my disabilities qualify me: I am doubly an outsider (maybe that was why I was asked) and can therefore be relied on to be biased. Prejudice is a condition for argument.

The first point I want to make is that it might seem as though social science can do very little for Chinese studies. At the moment, the number and quality of social scientists working on Chinese themes are both so low that the sinologues have a good excuse for ignoring them. It is not that the sinologues are so numerous or brilliant themselves; but they have the advantage of being masters in their own house (and therefore know how to shut the door on unwanted guests) and the privilege of keeping their subject as dull as they think necessary to maintain academic standards and an empire. If, let us say—my example is purely imaginary—a sociologist writes a book on local grouping in China, the one sinologue who has read it can tell the others what they already assume to be true, namely, that the poor fellow is unhistorical, has failed to use all the relevant sources, has not understood the sources he has used, writes in an unintelligible jargon, and (the *coup de grâce*) cannot be much of a sociologist if he bothers with China (why is he not studying social class in Kansas or Camberwell?).

But perhaps the social scientists interested in China are not really knocking at the sinological door. They may be building a house of their own at the door of which the sinologues may soon be tapping. Then it

Paper delivered at a symposium on Chinese Studies and the Disciplines, 22 March 1964, at the 16th annual meeting of the Association for Asian Studies, Washington, D.C. The other participants were the late Joseph R. Levenson, F. W. Mote, G. William Skinner, and the late Mary C. Wright. *Journal of Asian Studies*, 23, no. 4 (1964), 523–29.

will be the social scientist's turn to look down his nose and ask what the fellow is up to. Why is he bothering about local groups when he should be worrying himself about the periodization of Chinese history? I have begun with this jolly nightmare of misunderstanding because I think that social science could do something useful for both sinology and sinologues. And I am confident that, given goodwill on both sides (of which this discussion is presumably an earnest) and the necessary level of incredulity, an interesting and sensible form of cooperation will soon be in sight.

"Area studies" are one reason for my moderate optimism. Of course, "area studies" may mean different things, some of which can be deservedly ridiculed. But where, as seems commonly to happen here in the United States, a young scholar is required to anchor himself in one discipline both before and during his exposure (if I may borrow an Americanism) to studies about one country or region, he is not likely to flounder in the nameless ocean which the critics of area studies predict to be their outcome. What I have seen of the results of attempts at area studies on China leads me to suppose that the new generation of social scientists working on that country are likely to have more standing in the eyes of the sinologues and an enhanced capacity to do good work.

For various reasons, not all of them academically very interesting, the appetite of the social scientists for China has been whetted and grows by what it feeds on. It is, at least on the face of it, absurd that just when we have a contingent of young men and women eager for the field, it is closed. Of course, there is Taiwan, there is Hong Kong, and there are the Overseas Chinese; but each of these is in its own way marginal and peculiar. Yet before we dismiss them as suitable fields, let us consider what use we may make of them. The relevance to sinology of Taiwan as a place for field study is less disputable than that of Hong Kong and the Overseas Chinese; after all, it *is* China, for all its (literal) insularity. Let me take the more contentious cases, on which, as it happens, I can speak from some personal knowledge. The social, political, and economic history of late Ch'ing is marked by a number of questions on which the field-worker in Hong Kong could have something interesting to say. Especially in regard to the New Territories of the Colony, there is a misconception, above all in the minds of grant-making bodies, about the extent to which something specifically Chinese survives in Hong Kong, both in memory and reality. If you are concerned to know for late Ch'ing times how market towns were formed and run; how villages were linked together in formal alliances; how leaders emerged and behaved; how religious ideas and practices were enmeshed in social and political life; how central government impinged on local communities; how disputes were resolved at different structural levels of society; how entrepreneurial roles were taken up—go, or if you lack the talent, send a young social scientist, to Hong Kong. The fieldwork, based on and amplifying documentary studies, should push knowledge and understanding a step further. Or if you are interested in city life in China, especially with regard to its texture of social ties, make for Hong Kong or one of the large Overseas Chinese settlements such as Singapore. If you think the development of Chinese agriculture an important subject, look at the way in which techniques of vegetable-farming built up in the neighborhood of cities in southeastern China have been spread to and elaborated in Malaya. These examples will have to do. Of course, not all that the young social scientist will set out to accomplish in peripheral China will be directly relevant to traditional sinological questions. He will have his own ideas and his own schemes to pursue. But on the other hand, if area studies in fact serve to correlate the interests of the new generation of social scientists with those of the people for whom the study of China is everything, then the sinologists are making a good investment.

It will not have escaped notice (and may well have caused resentment among my older colleagues) that I have spoken of the "young social scientist." The reason is not simply that I have for the moment been concentrating my attention on the products of the newer training; I have had at the back of my mind a characteristic of some of the social sciences, especially my own, which I must now make explicit. Fieldwork is looked upon by some social scientists as an indispensable test of the young professional; before it he is academically an adolescent, after it—provided he survives with honor—a man. He has been initiated, and the world of adult study, along with the privilege of never doing fieldwork again or of doing it only in small doses if he so chooses, is open to him. It follows that for the purposes I have so far been discussing, the sinologues can be advised to concentrate on the junior members of the subjects from which they seek help.

However, even maturer social scientists often want to do field research. For them too Taiwan, Hong Kong, and the Overseas Chinese are possible areas; but if they are really attached to the study of China, they are unlikely to be content for long with these margins or shadows of the great land. And it is at this point that we can begin to consider an advantage accruing from the handicap of a closed China. Consider first the case of the people interested in Communist China. For them fieldwork, at least in the ordinary sense of the term, is out. (And I might here stress a point I have taken the liberty of making before to American audiences: fieldwork in mainland China is out for everybody, including the mainland Chinese and the British. The denial to the Americans of the opportunity to do it is not, as some people seem to imagine in this country, an additional penalty exacted for the failure of the United States to enter into diplomatic relations with the People's Republic. True, in the last decade a few studies on Communist China have been published by both Chinese and foreigners which have been based on some sort of direct observation, but I do not see how they can fairly be classified as field studies when judged by the standards of research done before the coming of the Communists, let alone when measured against what is now expected of field research in other parts of the world.) If the social scientist is determined to study Communist China, he must do it at a distance, even if, taking up position in Hong Kong, the physical removal is a matter of a mere few miles. But while distance may lend disenchantment to the view, then at least the effort of making indirect observations has its rewards as well as its pains. It calls forth ingenuity and imagination—in the design and execution of refugee and emigré studies and in the interpretation of such materials as Communist China must or is willing to publish. A double service is being done to Chinese studies by people undertaking such tasks. First, they are doing as social scientists what others could not do, for they are professionally equipped with the interviewing, statistical, and other skills which, however much they may be undervalued outside the social science world, form an indispensable qualification for the work. Second, they are maintaining standards in the study of Communist China, refusing to allow the subject to become the monopoly of journalists, Pekinologists, and sinologues in their off-moments. Of course, they run the risk of being branded, and not only by the other side, as intelligence workers. When has the student of the present ever been completely free of suspicion? Academe has a built-in bias in favor of historical thinking. More honor, then, to our friends who try their hand at difficult and unpopular jobs.

The social scientists who study Communist China at a distance are, however, more conventional than the one or two social scientists whom exclusion from the promised land has turned to studies of the past. Precisely because they are a tiny minority and are apparently facing sinological historians on their own ground, they too are in a tricky position. Without being historians, they are doing something that looks like history. Everybody knows that just as anthropologists graze in the field, so historians feed on documents; the richest nourishment is thought to come in the one case from savages and in the other from primary sources. Imagine then an anthropologist who, having taken the first step out of line by devoting himself to the study of China, makes a further advance into unconventionality by deciding to spend a few of his years on China's past. Assume that he is very clever, has the necessary linguistic equipment, and all the right contacts—it will be obvious that my example is purely imaginary. If he now burrows into the primary sources, he will be encouraged by a few of the historians (see M. C. Wright 1961: 220) and perhaps even be given a fair hearing by all of them. But what if he should decide that, as an unconventional anthropologist, he should also be unconventional as a temporary historian to the extent of trying his hand with the secondary materials? Will he be received? I hope so.

I say this because it seems to me that we have now in fact come to the very heart of the social scientist's contribution to Chinese studies. All the field and other forms of empirical studies are important enough, for at the very least they bring in new material; but the best offering consists of ideas. And a good way to introduce social science ideas into sinology is to apply them to more or less ordinary sinological data. They need not, and probably will not, be original and great ideas, but they may well be new to sinology.

However, by no means all social science ideas are new to sinology, and if the traditional conceit of sinology consists in thinking of itself as an intellectually self-subsistent subject, then the arrogance of social science lies in imagining that only from its practitioners can sinology learn to analyze society. Chinese studies have in modern times been blessed by scholars sensitive enough to the intellectual world around them to take account of sociological ideas. Marcel Granet, as is well known, worked within a framework of ideas laid down by the Durkheimians; it is fairly obvious too that Granet read more widely in the social sciences than his scanty references would suggest; for example, in his treatment of Chinese kinship, he probably read both Radcliffe-Brown and Lloyd Warner on the Australian aborigines (cf. Leach 1961: 74). And in the present-day United States there is no lack of evidence that the sinologues scan the general social science literature in search of both comparative material and leading ideas. Occasionally the sinologue too soon reaches the limit of his curiosity, as in a remark I once heard (the speaker was not American) to the effect that comparison between China and certain African societies was grotesquely irrelevant. But on the whole there is probably a greater receptivity to social science ideas in sinology than many social scientists realize.[1] But at this point I exceed both my brief and my competence.

The sinologue may be in search of comparative material. What is comparison? All thinking about society is comparative, and the driest and narrowest account of Chinese history by a Western sinologue cannot avoid the imprint of the world from which the writer comes—in the topics chosen, the language used to expound them, and in the interpretations offered. A noncomparative study of Chinese society is an impossibility, unless it be written by a Chinese scholar who has never heard of any other society. People clearly have something else in mind when they say that sinological study should be comparative. They mean that when we examine some aspect of Chinese society we should make explicit comparisons with the corresponding aspects of other societies in order to deepen our understanding at the least and perhaps also to speed the coming of general explanatory principles. Then which societies are relevant to China for comparative purposes? The answer is—all, for the question has not been wisely put. Of course, in a general way the sinologue may think that a close study of Japan or Korea or Vietnam may help him get perspective on China; and he may well be right. But if he has a special problem to tackle (perhaps in the growth of cities, in bureaucratic processes, in the assimilation of aborigines, and so on) how is he, qua sinologue, to know which material is relevant and where to find it? It could become a matter for the social scientist who, if he knows nothing else, is likely to be able to find his way to the necessary comparative data— from Peru, so to say. And the beginning of an interesting inquiry may be in sight.

Comparison is all very well. It rests on some sort of social theory and its results may be comforting both to the sinologues and to the cooperating social scientists. But it is not enough if we are thinking of the total contribution of social science to Chinese studies. The social scientist gives most when he systematizes and analyzes. I earlier proposed the example of the anthropologist, now temporary historian, who turns to the Chinese past. He might generalize about a particular institution or problem from the secondary sources. But "generalize" is a misleading verb, for to use it plays into the hands of the censorious sinologue who will wish to take it as a synonym for oversimplify. The point of generalizing is not to make things seem simple but to reduce a large array of relevant facts to a system which is then amenable to analysis. Implicitly or explicitly, the social scientist is a builder of models, and it is partly for this reason that misunderstanding can arise between him and the sinological historian. For the latter, very properly, the pursuit of detail is a professional first duty, whatever other intellectual tasks he may set himself. A model-builder, working at one remove from the primary data by using secondary sources and at a second remove by "generalizing," looks at worst a charlatan and at best an inferior craftsman.

We must consider the question of models more closely. They may be of several kinds. It is possible to construct a model which does not begin from the examination of any one body of facts but draws its components from general knowledge and theory about society everywhere. The purpose of such a model is to explore the consequences that flow from the assumptions made and from modifications in the assumptions. The economists feel at home with this kind of model; other social scientists find it difficult to use because its basic components appear quickly to fall short of demands of any reality the model is called upon to illuminate, although in principle a satisfactory model could be made of the working of such restricted groups as the family.

More characteristically, models in the social sciences start from a particular concrete institution and are intended to tease out the implications of its rules and regularities. If the rules are clearly formulable, specifying a few possible modes of behavior, then, to use Lévi-Strauss's useful but misleadingly concrete terminology, a "mechanical" model can be built. Anthropologists play informative games with "mechanical" models of marriage rules. On the other hand, the components of the model may be found not in simple rules but in statistical regularities which result from the patterning of choices where the rules allow latitude: Lévi-Strauss's "statistical" model (1953: 530ff and 1958: 311ff). If a man is allowed to marry any one of a number of different relatives, what consequences flow and what regularities emerge, given certain other factors?

I am not asserting that, at least in any branch of social science of which I have intimate knowledge, models of this sophisticated form have been taken very far. Much more commonly, the model, often not even so called, is a complex of elements which the analyst manipulates in order to show what follows from different mixtures and weightings of elements. If the exercise works, then it helps to explain something: perhaps why an institution takes one particular form at one time and another at a different time, or why within one society a form of grouping emerges in this place and not that.

The social scientist's models, of whatever kind, will not by themselves solve any sinological problem. They assume, they reason, and they suggest answers. The value of the answers lies in their being based on systematic inquiry set going by imagination and carried through by a particular mental discipline. Social science applied to China is not a substitute for sinology; it is one way of being systematic about sinological matters. Social science is about society; sinology is about China; where they intersect, the system-building, theorizing, and general knowledge of the one can be made to put up alternative or supplementary answers to questions raised by the other. I realize that by putting my point in this fashion I have made social science seem to be merely a handmaiden to sinology; my excuse must be that, since Professor Skinner has spoken of what sinology can do for social science, I had better say what I think we can do for it.

The precise contribution to be made by social science to the solution of sinological problems depends on what we mean by social science (a term which, incidentally, in Britain suggests social administration and applied sociology: nothing could be further from my thoughts at the moment). It would be asking too much to expect me to speak for economists, political scientists, social psychologists, demographers, sociologists, anthropologists, social and economic geographers, and the members of the other disciplines conventionally grouped together, but not necessarily in harmony or unity, as the social sciences. From the outside they may seem to be a single subject; from the inside it is sometimes difficult to realize that they have anything in common. It is not simply that each subject concentrates on different things; they have different styles. (I teach at an institution the name of which is usually and unfairly abbreviated to the London School of Economics; its motto is *Rerum Cognoscere Causas*, and I daresay that each of the three Latin words would be differently glossed by members of the different subjects taught under its aegis.) If, on the other hand, I were to speak only for my own subject and what it can do, or could do, for Chinese studies, I should expose myself to the charge of parochialism, pretentiousness, or greed. I need to step warily.

But if I cannot allow myself to advertise anthropology, let me at least use it as a peg on which to hang two final and necessary points. The technique for which anthropologists are known (it will be clear that I am referring to social anthropologists here) is fieldwork in small communities and other restricted groupings by means of intensive and prolonged observation. Every first-year undergraduate gets that point very quickly, and like most points acquired early on in study, it turns out to be a half-truth. But for the sake of the present argument let the part stand for the whole. The technique of anthropology is in some measure at variance with its general aims, which are grander than a preoccupation with small social units would suggest.[2] Now, in one way or another, the sinologue looking to the social sciences for help with a specific problem is likely to find in all of them a partial disjunction between techniques and aims, between what people are equipped to do empirical research on and what the totality of research is supposed to add up to. It would be as well, therefore, for the sinologue to decide for himself whether he is looking for a specialist technique of investigation, and if so which one, or the intellectual aid characteristic of a particular discipline. I hope I have made it clear that, in my view, the social scientist's ideas are more relevant generally to Chinese studies than his techniques, but I recognize that practical, technical aid may in some situations be crucial.

The second point takes us back to the question of area studies and training. The better an anthropologist is sinologically, the more use he is to Chinese studies: granted. And if he can get himself up to the high standards required for doing basic documentary research, so much the better for everybody—or (for here comes the rub) everybody with the possible exception of himself. There is a case to be made against a sinological training that will distract a man in his formative years from pursuing his studies of societies and Society. It may be a capital idea to turn young anthropologists into sinologues, but they may then cease to be of use as anthropologists, being withdrawn from the developing tradition of their former subject and out of touch with the very sources of the imagination which made them desirable recruits to sinology in the first place. Cooperation which amounts to ingestion is cannibalism and not fraternity. The usefulness of social science to Chinese studies depends on its being allowed to be itself.

Why China?

Although I did not become aware of the fact until a day or so later, on 27 June last year, the date on which I gave my first Presidential Address, there appeared in *The Listener* an article which, treating of flying saucers and "the discovery that [they] . . . move in fixed and regular lines above the earth's surface," referred to "the beautiful Chinese geomantic system" (Michell 1968: 822). There is no need to go into details here. I was naturally struck by the coincidence. It was not to be the only occasion during the year that followed when China, an object of my anthropological interest, was presented to me in a new light.

The academic session 1968–69 has been a very Chinese year. It may be that the trials of a teacher at the London School of Economics have made me too sensitive to certain changing features of our lives; I am nonetheless sure that we run the risk of being at the beginning of a period about which books may need to be written (if the book survives) that bear such hauntingly familiar titles as *The Impact of China on the West*. By this act of gratuitous prophecy I draw your attention to the fact that the Great Proletarian Cultural Revolution is in some sense on your doorstep. At any rate, it is on my doorstep, and I propose, in the first part of my address today, to say why I find it interesting.

Allow me two autobiographical notes to start off with. The first goes back to the year of academic peace 1967–68. One of my pupils, a man of the far left, took it upon himself to chide me for my academic concern with institutions that appeared to be no longer relevant to Communist China. I gave what many of my British colleagues would regard as an orthodox anthropological reply, saying that I could not get to Communist China. It was a bad answer, for I should at once have repudiated the notion that we must justify what we study by its immediate relevance to some burning issue of the day. That young man has had his revenge,

Presidential address, Royal Anthropological Institute, delivered 26 June 1969. *Proceedings of the Royal Anthropological Institute of Great Britain and Ireland* 1969 (1970), 5–13.

for the antics of his successors, while certainly not turning me into a student of Communist China, have forced me to give it closer attention.

The second note relates to my qualifications as an observer of the local equivalent of the Red Guards. During one of the worst of my experiences this term, when I was arguing with a small group of people who had separated themselves off from a mass that had invaded and broken up one of my lectures. I suddenly caught sight of a serious-looking man making notes, his eyes darting from side to side, his pen lagging behind events. Presently he introduced himself to me amid the hubbub as—no, not an anthropologist—a writer come to observe the student troubles (although he thought of them as teacher troubles). The poignancy of the situation for me was that I was being recorded in the role of the doer, the anthropologist anthropologized. That is a sad fate for somebody who would prefer to take a dispassionate view of interesting events. I am not the best qualified of observers; that limits my usefulness; but I shall do my best.

It is often said, even by some sympathetic critics of the embattled academics, that they do not know how to handle political situations. That is as may be. But the criticism overlooks the point that what those wretched teachers often have to cope with—and what their experience as rational and skeptical men unfits them to cope with—is a religious movement. They were not bred in times that took religious enthusiasm for granted, and when they see it they are apt to mistake it for something else. The student of religion (cf. Martin 1969) or the anthropologist is more likely to put a true name to it. But to do so the anthropologist has first to jerk himself out of his setting. The slogan "We want everything, we want it now" is infuriating or comic if you believe that the people who utter it are starting from your premises. If they were of a different culture you would not bat an eyelid, for you have seen it all before, at least in the books on millenarian movements. It is an astonishing experience to find something like a cargo cult in W.C.2.

Least of all would you have expected it among students. A university is a place—one begins finally to believe one is parodying oneself—dedicated to the disinterested pursuit of learning; scholars reason, observe, contemplate. The students in revolt are often irrational, sometimes cruel, violent, and (not least reprehensibly) without humor. Much may be forgiven them in their religious mania, but the teacher finds it impossible to reconcile himself to the idea that his pupils are anti-intellectual. How can such a thing be?

Let us turn to the Great Proletarian Cultural Revolution. On that fantastic episode in Chinese history nobody, unless he be a charlatan, can speak with confidence. The strenuous extenders of charity to every strange turn in Communist Chinese affairs seem to be as surprised as the most professional ill-wishers. The two ends of the continuum of China-watchers join in lamenting the dearth of facts, but some facts there are, and I shall try to use a selection of them to illustrate what, without a trace of irony, I propose to call a juvenile millenarian movement.

The word "cultural" appears in the name of the "revolution" that began in 1966 for a reason that anthropologists should be quick to grasp. What was intended was a further stage in the total transformation of social and cultural life (cf. J. D. Gray and Cavendish 1968: 69), by a campaign directed against the remnants of "bourgeois" and "feudal" mentality and behavior—the Four Olds (to use the perverted English calqued on the Chinese original): old ideas, old culture, old customs, and old habits (e.g. Lifton 1968: 35). The offending values were most clearly institutionalized in seats of learning, and there the public assault began, opening apparently in Peking University in May and June 1966. A big-character poster attacking the President of the University was put up at the beginning of June; Mao Tse-tung commended it and ordered it to be published (cf. Lifton 1968: 35; Robinson 1969: 53). The poster campaign having opened, the universities, colleges, and schools entered the turbulence which virtually cut a year out of China's educational life and is only now dying down.

Under the heading "Educational Institutions, Peking and Shanghai" we find in Professor Joan Robinson's useful little book on the Cultural Revolution the following paragraph which illustrates the more rational side of the campaign—and which I invite you to edit in your minds to suit your experience of Anglo-American university problems:

The indictment of the rebel students against the teaching that they were receiving was, first, that the courses were too long, too formal and too little directed to practical application; second, that the object of education was to build up an elite, divorced from the mass of the people; and third, that students from worker and peasant families were discriminated against instead of being helped to make up for their lack of literary background (Robinson 1969: 138).

The Red Guards turned upon their teachers, abusing, reviling, and sometimes chasing them out. For obvious reasons, I shall not dwell on so painful a subject.

The millions of students and schoolchildren—ranging in age from about thirteen to the early twenties (Lifton 1968: 33)—mobilized within the framework of the various Red Guard groupings, were called to a political task which we may define as the (albeit temporary) undoing of the hierarchy and bureaucracy of Chinese Communist society. And they went about it with enthusiasm. They were not given the complete run of their society, for some areas were fenced off from their attacks, but they were allowed to make short work of many of their schools and colleges, and, joining in with workers and peasants, to take part in the dismantling of a large part of the Communist Party apparatus and a lesser part of the government machinery. Bliss was it in that dawn. . . .

The controlled chaos of the first period of the Cultural Revolution was, from the point of view of those who could exercise power, to throw into reverse the process which, as they saw it, was driving Chinese society toward the elitism and professionalism that it was the job of revolution to destroy. The formula "red and expert" is not a simple one and can be (in fact, must be) taken in different ways (e.g. Meisner 1968: 105–7); but in one of its senses it had earlier defined a compromise between, on the one hand, the ideological requirement of egalitarianism and non-professional leadership and, on the other, the needs of a society traveling the road of industrialization (cf. Schurmann 1968: 51–53, 164–67, 507). Now, redness was all, and expertness a dreaded breach of the principle that Communist man was a locus of a totality of roles no one of which was to be permitted to grow at the expense of the others (cf. Tsou 1969: 72–73; but see Schurmann 1968: 564–65 for a different view). Expertness, undue specialization, was a pathological distortion of the nature of man. In the end, the new Revolutionary Committees having been installed to give power to the lowly and the ideologically pure, and the corrupt bourgeois elements and "capitalist-roaders" having been gouged from the Party and governmental hierarchies, China was, as one might have expected, to shrink from the total logic of the revolutionary program and to begin to settle down to another compromise between the need for complementary specialization and the passion for equality. In the course of the Cultural Revolution Mao Tse-tung's charismatic authority was enhanced, his rivals were displaced, and the longest-lived bureaucratic society in the world was permitted to get back into gear.

But, for my purpose, the Red Guards must be given the center of the stage. It will not do simply to say that they were used as a tool by their powerful elders. What those old men did was to grant a license, and in temporarily freeing the young from the restraints of educational and communal discipline, they were releasing a passion for perfection that ran the risk of sacrificing the good on the altar of the best. In the end, the young had to be coaxed and ushered from the cities, where they had congregated, back to the schools, colleges, and communes where they belonged.[a]

[a] Millions of young people were on the move during the Cultural Revolution. Some of those who crowded into the cities had earlier been "sent down" (*hsia-fang*) into the countryside and now took the opportunity to absent themselves from rural life; and when the

While the going was good millions of young people were on the rampage, many of them fired by the moral passion to destroy—to destroy every last vestige of the old society and its culture, to destroy any authority not apparently springing from the central charismatic leader or from the masses. Intimidation, terror, unfettered abuse in speech and writing, violence, the occupation of buildings, the destruction of property: youth *en bloc* had been called to the banner of idealism. If you are young and summoned to implement the ideals that you consider to have been betrayed by your elders, your energy powers your ruthlessness. Bad manners and cruelty are not merely in order; they are overlegitimated, become great virtues. Intoxicated with rectitude, you are obliged to impose your desires on others whatever the cost to them. "So long as it is revolutionary, no action is a crime"; the words are those of a Red Guard (Lifton 1968: 59). If you are young and licensed to rebel, you will seek to drive all before you: people, ideas, institutions (cf. Israel 1967). I hope somebody in China got some amusement from the Red Guards' passion for symbolic consistency when it pushed them to demand that red and green in traffic lights be reversed in their significance (to make red mean go) and the command "eyes right!" be converted to "eyes left!"

The aim of this massive surge of passion was to produce the perfect society. But I think we may reasonably doubt that the detailed plans for such a society were in the head of any Red Guard. What the new society was *not* to be was clearer, to be sure. It was to be emptied of all content tainted by association with the naughty past—every scrap of superstition (read: religion), all feudal and bourgeois forms of thought and art were to be rooted out; nobody was to claim superiority by birth, skill, talent, or education; ideally, nobody was to be vested with other than temporary authority, subject to immediate withdrawal by mass demand. For the rest, one destroyed in the confidence that out of the ruins would rise the perfect state. It was a millenarian dream in action.[1]

I have called the Red Guards a juvenile millenarian movement, and I want now to return to our own affairs. There are two different ways of linking up what has gone on in China with the so-called revolt of the young in the West. In the first place there has been direct influence and imitation. We have seen the little red book of Chairman Mao's thought being flourished in London, and there is evidence all about that Maoism is a significant strand in the student radical movement. The London School of Economics has been nominated a Red Base, and for all I know the scurrilous slogans and wall newspapers that we have seen on univer-

---

new exodus into the countryside was ordered it included many urban boys and girls. See Mehnert 1969: 37–38, 41–42, 71.

sity walls are conscious imitations of Chinese models. But diffusion, fascinating though it be in its details, is not a very interesting process in the large. Let us turn to the second linkage.

At first sight, it may seem grotesque to compare our petty student uprisings with the monumental activity of the Red Guards. Even the troubles on the American and Japanese campuses look puny against the Chinese background. And the student movements have not been called into being by national leaders. But I think the comparison is justified by the resemblances between the internal connections in each case among revolt, ruthlessness, the passion for equality, the avid quest for the total (that is, unsegmented) life, and anti-intellectualism. Of course, there is no one student ideology in the West. I am concerned here with a class of pacemakers on the left who, on my reading, are caught up in a millenarian dream into which at moments of great tension numbers of other students are for a time drawn. In characteristic modes of behavior and in the pronouncements that go with them we may note "an emphasis on struggle rather than rationality, and on mass action rather than the technical and managerial elite"—those last words I have in fact taken from Professor Schram's recent statement about Mao's thought and policies since 1955 (Schram 1969: 25). If struggle is to replace reason, then argument is a mere slanging match and issues are to be settled by force. No room here for honest doubt and the respect for contrary opinion. What is it to the point that a man has thought long and hard about a problem? If his conclusions seem to block the path of an impetuous rush of passion, he must be summarily put out of the way. Scholars nowadays often deplore the politicization of university life; they would do well to consider whether they do not suffer as much from its moralization. I mean that process by which the burning moral concerns of the day (racialism, equality in education and housing, or whatever it happens to be) are thrust like firebrands into academic life—which is combustible.

The quest for equality, the denial of privilege, the rejection of elitism stand at the center. It is not a matter of equality of opportunity; men must be forced to be alike. Again, if one mistakes the religious tone of the anguished cries, one may giggle at the demands for parity among, and fusion of, "staff, students, and workers." But it is not a joke; it is a magical formula for healing the grievous wounds inflicted on the community by the sharp edges of the divisions that separate off man from man. To be fully human one must be every man's brother; and a division of labor ruins fraternity.

But I must not indulge myself further. As best I could, I have made the point that Communist China stands before us as a kind of working model on a gigantic scale of some of our anxieties and problems. It is startlingly relevant, and those who take the view that studies should be relevant (we know what they mean) ought to be good allies to scholars exerting themselves to promote the study of contemporary China. But let that pass. I want to ask the question, what role should the anthropologists play in that study?

In this country to date they have played no role to speak of, and even in the United States I can think of only a couple of anthropologists who have made other than superficial comments. If as anthropologists we classify ourselves as social scientists we can see that in the study of Communist China we have been put to shame by the economists, political scientists, social historians, and sociologists.

It is not of course that the anthropologists are uninterested in what is going on in Communist China. Before 1949 they were in the van in the study of contemporary Chinese society, and they might well have retained their lead if the Chinese civil war had had a different outcome. No: what has happened is that the tools of the anthropological trade (which I shall characterize by the word "fieldwork") have been applied to that residue of "China" left beyond the control of Peking. I refer to Taiwan, Hong Kong, and the Overseas Chinese. There is a sense in which loyalty to a technique of investigation has condemned its practitioners to provincialism. The economists, political scientists, and sociologists, always more ready to diversify their methods of collecting data, have seized upon the opportunities open to them. They have scrutinized the press, studied the polemical and official literature, interviewed émigrés, and weighed up the testimony of the handful of foreign eyewitnesses—exploiting every chance that offered itself to build up a body of facts and arrange them to answer important questions. Reading their work, I find myself enormously impressed, and correspondingly disheartened by the lack of an important anthropological presence in the enterprise. There is not, but there might have been, an anthropological voice to speak about the transformation of the institutions of kinship and marriage, the new norms governing interpersonal relationships, the reorganization of local groups, the change in the nature of property, the elaboration of techniques of social control, the reworking of ritual life, and (perhaps most important of all) the modes and conditions of mass mobilization. If Communist China is an experiment—or rather a series of experiments—then anthropologists should have been busy with it, testing their ideas about the transformability of society against attempts to transform it. Utopian ventures are not mere excrescences on the body of culture and so consignable to the category of the odd; they can be tests of our theories about the limits to the plasticity of social relations and to the organizations of activity. It is a matter I shall come back to later.

Against the loss I have just been deploring must be set the gain to anthropology brought by the concentration, since 1949, on "residual China." It is a remarkable fact (and one which I never tire of stating) that at precisely the point in time when the doors to mainland China were slammed, Anglo-American anthropology (and to some extent the same is true of Chinese anthropology itself) was poised for a great leap in Chinese studies. Since most of China has been inaccessible the anthropological talent for studying it has vastly increased. That talent has had to confine itself, so far as field study is concerned, to the residual areas. And I think there is some interest in tracing the process by which, during the last twenty years, different options within those areas have been taken up.

The first effect of the closure of mainland China to foreign scholarship was to promote a spurt in studies of the Overseas Chinese, primarily in southeast Asia. Indeed, during most of the decade 1949–58 Chinese studies conducted by anthropologists were almost entirely confined to that region, and within it to Thailand, the Malay peninsula, Sarawak, and Indonesia. Now that this interest in the Overseas Chinese has tailed off because of the opportunities to get closer, in Hong Kong and Taiwan, to the "real" China, it may be difficult to understand why in those earlier years southeast Asia seemed to be the most appropriate setting for study. Or, to put the matter another way, why did Hong Kong and Taiwan seem then so remote when now, a few years later, they appear so central? The answer to the question must be phrased in terms of changes in scholarly and political perception.

As a matter of fact, the first anthropological work in Hong Kong was begun in the early 1950's when Barbara E. Ward, after looking into a number of different projects, decided to devote herself to the study of a Tanka (i.e. boat people) fishing community in the New Territories. That remarkable study, carried out according to the canons of intensive fieldwork and since extended, ran the risk of being unique; in more recent years an American anthropologist has made a study of Tanka in another part of the New Territories.[2] But the two sets of work together could easily, but illegitimately, have been classed as exercises in the excessively exotic, for, despite Miss Ward's powerful argumentation, the Tanka are still regarded (not least by Chinese themselves) as being on the margins of Chinese society and culture, a sort of barbarian fringe.

Miss Ward's experience of Hong Kong, and perhaps too my memories of conversations with a Hong Kong Chinese whom I had helped to teach when I was myself a graduate student, fell to work upon an obsession I had developed during my study of Chinese in Singapore in 1949 and 1950. I had never been able to take them simply for what they were, a highly urbanized group of immigrants and their descendants, and had striven to see beyond them to the society from which they had come. During the early 1950's, in the midst of other preoccupations, I began to play with the notion of reconstructing traditional Chinese society (I mean the society of the nineteenth and early twentieth centuries) with special reference—as they say in the thesis titles—to its institutions of kinship and marriage. I used my knowledge of Singapore Chinese as background and whatever published material on China I was able to find in London. My dim perception of the possibility of studying that traditional society in action was turned into a startling vision when, by the accident of stopping off for a few days in Hong Kong in 1955 en route for the Philippines, I was confronted in the New Territories by the walled villages and localized lineages which hitherto had been merely the stuff of dreams.

I wrote my first book on Chinese lineage organization as an exercise in armchair anthropology, nervous of the possibility that I might have allowed my imagination too much license with the few facts at my disposal, confident that the Hong Kong countryside I had merely glimpsed would one day be the testing ground of my theorizing. In the light of the field research that has since been conducted in Hong Kong, it will seem almost incredible that in the second half of the 1950's I found it impossible to convince grant-making bodies that a British Colony was the ideal place for the study of traditional forms of Chinese society. But it is easy enough to trace the source of the resistance. Most people outside Hong Kong (and a good many people inside it) knew nothing of the great stretches of relatively untouched countryside in the New Territories. For them Hong Kong was urban Hong Kong, and the evidence of modernism all about was a guarantee that only a fanatical anthropologist would seek in the Colony for the traditional. In the end, I did not get to work in the New Territories until 1963.

By that time two other anthropologists had preceded me. One of them, diverted from the field of her choice in Oceania, settled in a Hakka village in the New Territories. Her study was over before mine began.[3] The other case touches me more nearly. During a second flying visit to Hong Kong in 1962 I discovered by accident that a young American anthropologist was at work in one of the great localized lineages. I sought him out with all speed. It was an act of generosity on his part to announce as we met that it had been my book that had persuaded him to go to the New Territories and that his study confirmed my analysis of the structure of the large-scale Chinese lineage (see Potter 1968; 1970).

My turn came, as I have said, in 1963. Since then the New Territories have become a standard training ground for anthropologists interested in China, and have begun to yield up great riches. I can count at least eleven anthropologists—British, American, and Swedish—who have, since 1963, chosen the New Territories as the setting for their research. Yet other anthropologists have been at work elsewhere in Hong Kong. In the space of seven years a dot on the map of continental China has come to stand for one of the two locations where Chinese society is now studied in the field.[4]

The other place is Taiwan. Now, if it is hard to understand why Hong Kong was slow in being exploited, we must be at least equally puzzled by Taiwan's late appearance on the scene. The first anthropological field study of Chinese society on that island of which I have definite knowledge was begun in 1957, although I think there may have been a slightly earlier one—it has been difficult to trace. The blindness to Taiwan parallels that to Hong Kong. The New Territories had not been under a Chinese government since 1898; Taiwan had emerged only in 1945 from half a century of Japanese rule. Colonialism in both cases, it was assumed, had abstracted the traditional. And although Taiwan was once again politically Chinese, it was, even more than Hong Kong, peripheral to China by standing well out to sea, an island of comparatively late Chinese settlement and doubtful Chinese cultural credentials. In retrospect, the characterization seems absurd. I do not think any British anthropologist gave Taiwan a second thought, but with some Americans the case was a little different: they knew more about it, but were restrained from going there by their reluctance to visit Nationalist China while, it seemed to them, there was hope of Communist China opening up. The years convinced them that they had been too hopeful, and the first anthropology students were dispatched from American universities in the late 1950's. I now know of some eight pieces of anthropological field research on Chinese topics in Taiwan conducted by foreigners; they include one carried out from this country.[5]

It would be a particular pleasure to me to be able to put all these Hong Kong and Taiwan studies together and assess their value as a set. After all, they now number a couple of dozen and excel in scope the anthropological work done in China before 1949. Since the Taiwan group also includes some work done by Chinese scholars,[6] a beginning that points to a kind of revival of a tradition that died on the mainland in the 1940's, one may feel reasonably secure in predicting that a good deal is yet to come and obliged to use the experience of the immediate past to guide the immediate future. But in fact only a small part of what has so far been achieved is available in published form, and it is too early to mount a proper exercise of evaluation. On the other hand, I do not want to let slip the opportunity of saying something about the way in which the work of the last ten years or so may have contributed both to our knowledge of China and to the development of the anthropological vocation.

Some of the studies undertaken in the New Territories have arisen from a plan of research devised in this country. Their joint findings, taken together with the results of other studies in "residual China," make it possible for us to recognize the advance on what now seems the rather crude understanding of Chinese rural society we had in the 1950's. That advance has been achieved not, needless to say, by the mere piling up of data. No amount of new facts would by themselves have helped us. Doubtless, a more thorough coordination of the research done (if we may ignore the possibility that on other grounds coordination might have been undesirable) would have produced a faster cumulation of knowledge: but even in the semihaphazard way in which things have gone on, it is possible to detect a profitable interplay between problem-stating and field inquiry, the critique of theory leading to new questions being put in the field. There is an impressive difference between the model of the Chinese family with which we were operating a mere decade ago and that which emerges from the new work in Taiwan and Hong Kong. Each formulation of the structure of the Chinese lineage and the dynamics of its segmentation has been revised in a series of field studies. Again, a great gulf exists between the earlier view of Chinese local organization above the level of the village and what we now understand to be the case. And a parallel statement can be made on ritual.

It is worth stressing that the advances do not spring merely from general progress in anthropological theory and the prosecution of field studies according to well-tried ethnographic principles. There are additional factors. I shall call one of them the interplay between the anthropologist as field-worker and the anthropologist as bookworm. Another is the role of what we might describe as history-in-the-field. I shall try to discuss both factors very briefly.

The great lack in the study of traditional Chinese society has never, all appearances to the contrary, lain in the dearth of facts. There are millions of them stored away in Chinese records (local gazetteers, written genealogies, compilations of customs, and so on) and in the Western and Japanese literature composed by sinologists, travelers, missionaries, and last and certainly least, social scientists. The problem is how to make use of the facts in their scattered and disorganized state. On the assumption that one has the necessary linguistic skills, one may read oneself silly and still not act to the profit of one's science. One has to carry to the written word the organizing ideas that one brings to the study of live societies. The point is obvious, and yet I shall be so discourteous to my colleagues as to suggest that they do not always recognize it. The people who tell you that, as a field-worker, you will only find what you are trained to look for (which is, roughly speaking, a valid proposition) will overlook the fact that, *mutatis mutandis*, the same is true of reading. No book is as versatile and variable as a human being, but it cannot be made to yield up at one go all that it has to say. It will say different things in response to the different questions in, and the receptivity of, the mind of the man reading it. It follows that no book can be read once for all; on each rereading it yields to a different frame of mind.

In the study of Chinese society the books have constantly to be re-shuffled and reexamined as new questions arise. The justification for fieldwork lies not simply in its production of new facts—of which, as we have seen, there is a superabundance—but in its capacity to generate the ideas to be taken home and applied to the ordering of old facts. It seems to be the case with most anthropologists—but there are some striking exceptions—that it is in their contact with their living subject matter that their imagination and creative faculty are most stimulated. That, it seems to me, is the best reason for doing field research, for if it were the routine affair of fact-collecting that an earlier generation of stay-at-home anthropologists thought it to be, it would be dreary beyond endurance.

In my last Address (Freedman 1969 [Essay 18 above]) I spoke on Chinese geomancy, and I want to try to show on that basis how the interplay of fieldwork and bookwork may develop. When I first got seriously interested in the subject I cannot now remember; it was certainly not during my field research in Singapore, although it was then that I must have read what J. J. M. de Groot has to say on the subject in his great work on Chinese religion (1892–1910).[7] While I was writing my first book on the Chinese lineage and thinking about competition between and within lineages, I fastened on the evidence in de Groot's books and other sources that seemed to suggest that Chinese played out their rivalry for social status within the system of *feng-shui* by competing for good grave sites (Freedman 1958: 77–78). It is clear from my notebooks that I had read a good deal of the relevant literature, and it astonishes me now that I made so little of what I read. It was the experience of a live system of geomancy in the New Territories in 1963 that forced me to think again and to formulate ideas on it to take back to London and to the books. The books began to yield (cf. Freedman 1966: 118). One important aspect of this re-view is that it suggested further problems which now await investigation in the field. The dialectic of fieldwork and book-work is, in principle, without end.

A vastly more important and striking example of the process is to be found in Professor Skinner's brilliant treatment of the Chinese market town, its significance as the center of a discrete segment of society, and the system by which all such segments are aggregated. It is clear from an account he once gave (10 February 1964) in a lecture at the London School of Economics that the seed of the idea was planted in his mind by his field experience in West China on the eve of the Communist takeover, an event which brought his fieldwork to an abrupt close. How that idea remained in its rudimentary form while he was busy with other things, and how it came, many years later, to bloom into the theorems he published (Skinner 1964–65), it is not for me to describe. The point I want to make is that the fantastically keen-minded and thorough exploitation of the Chinese and other documents that went to the making of his study of marketing areas and marketing communities in China was started off by an idea conceived in the field. And the study created from the library materials has in turn (as I think we shall see very clearly when more has been published of the recent studies in "residual China") furnished other people with ideas to take to and develop in their field research.

I turn now to what I have called history-in-the-field. Anybody coming fresh to the anthropological field studies of China made before the 1960's is bound to be unfavorably impressed by their preoccupation with the here and now—although, for reasons I cannot go into in this Address, the writing on the Overseas Chinese is less deserving of this sort of criticism. After all, what is the point of adapting anthropological method to the study of civilized societies if we ignore one of the great advantages offered by the new material: the access to data on the past? And I add hastily that the failure to make use of historical material is not to be accounted for simply by the linguistic handicaps of the investigators, for the same lack is to be seen in the work of the Chinese anthropologists themselves—men so dazzled by the novelty of the idea of fieldwork that they made of timelessness a virtue. I am not speaking here of the reluctance to write about China's past and to grapple with problems of historical sociology; I am talking about the failure to build facts about the past into the analysis of what is studied in the field—lineage, village, or small town. Again, my point is not simply concerned with the past as background to the present, but with the past as integral to the matter under study. If the data on the past are gathered, then it can be shown how families, lineages, villages, local alliances, marketing communities, cults, irrigation systems, and so on vary over time; and it may be possible in some cases to demonstrate that the changes follow regular patterns of linear or cyclical development.

Of course, the handling of material on the past—in land records, population registers, local histories, written genealogies, and the like—is not a task to be entrusted automatically to every anthropological field-worker; some special skills are called for. And it is not to be wondered at that the most successful examples to date of combining historical with field study are to be found in the work of an anthropologically minded sinologue and a historian who convinced herself of the desirability of studying documents in the setting of the living society to which they relate. I refer to Hugh Baker's research in a lineage-village in the New Territories (1968) and to Johanna Meskill's social-genealogical study in Taiwan (1970a and 1970b). Of Professor Meskill's work in particular it might well be said that it represents part of a neat inversion of roles: the historian takes to the field and the anthropologist to the archives. Sometimes, as they pass each other going in opposite directions, they stop and chat. I know that the conversation can be very instructive.

In this second part of my Address I have sketched out what seems to me to have been the main line of the advance made in recent time in anthropological studies of China by the exploitation of Hong Kong and Taiwan. As long as the mainland stays closed, those two residual territories will continue to be a magnet to anthropologists, and the impetus traceable to the late 1950's and early 1960's will, I imagine, be maintained. After all, only a fraction of the possibilities have yet been realized, and it is certainly clear that in the case of Hong Kong new and bolder directions in the urban field study by anthropologists are now beginning that will balance the earlier preoccupation with the countryside. The rhythm and pace of the anthropological studies of China never cease to fascinate me.

I deplored the absence of the anthropologists from the ranks of the students of Communist China, and I have now been crying up the value of field study. I have left the conflict between the two views just below the surface; it must now be brought into the open. If intensive fieldwork is to remain for anthropological students of China, as for all other social anthropologists, the sign of their guild and the hallmark of their product, then how are they to take part in the study of a society for which no fieldwork visas are issued? I wish there were a simple way out of the dilemma, but of course there is not. Yet there may be useful compromises to be made. We should certainly not rule out the possibility that some young anthropological scholar will prefer to devote himself to a long-distance study of society on the mainland—fieldwork may be a cult but it is not a religious duty (cf. Freedman 1963a [Essay 22 above]: 6–7). On the other hand, there is more to be said in favor of the man who has had some firsthand experience of Chinese society projecting himself, by imagination, into the Communist society he can know only by indirect methods of investigation (cf. Freedman 1964b [chap. 23 above]: 525).

If we make no such leaps in method we are condemning ourselves to ignorance of an unfolding series of radical and utopian experiments. Anthropologists are always busy stretching their awareness (and attempting to stretch the awareness of their pupils) to encompass the variety of solutions to human problems found in the ethnographic record. And the relevance of their contemplation of cultural variability is fairly obvious, even if it is not often made explicit. Social anthropology is not a mere search for scientific propositions, but an exploration of the realized possibilities of human action. That is why we range in our mental travels all the way from the simplest societies to the most complex, noting the constraints and liberties of each form as we pass it in review. We are not concerned directly with utopian visions, but once they enter into action they become part of the evidence bearing on the limits of social life. That is why Communist China is important to us.

Our role in regard to its study should, in fact, be part of a wider devotion to the assessment of social experiments, a point borne in upon me by my recent casual reading in the literature on real utopias—the bedside books of an embattled academic. I do not see why we should leave it to the historians to ask the anthropological questions. Let me take the example of the attempts to rework the family, purging it of its alleged defects and reshaping it to conform to the requirements of a remade society.

In Professor J. F. C. Harrison's new book on Robert Owen and the Owenites a few pages are given over to the discussion of the reasons why the utopians of whom he writes considered it necessary to reshape the family (Harrison 1969: 59–62). Of Christian marriage, Owen thought (in Harrison's résumé) that it "reinforced the isolation, privateness and secrecy of the family in relation to society, and within the family it strengthened prudery and false shame and prevented a happy, frank sexual relationship between the partners" (Harrison 1969: 61). Now, we can of course pick up an echo of this older view in the much quoted words of the anthropologist disguised as the Reith Lecturer: "Today the domestic household is isolated. The family looks inward upon itself . . . the family, with its narrow privacy and tawdry secrets, is the source of all our discontents" (Leach 1968: 44). And there is nothing surprising about Dr. Leach's adduction of the Israeli kibbutz and the Chinese commune as examples of communities where children might "grow up in larger, more relaxed domestic groups centered on the community rather than the mother's kitchen" (*ibid.*: 45). They are the first examples of family experiments that would spring to any anthropologist's mind; that is a pity, for there are more interesting cases recorded in the literature on communitarian ventures in the West.[8] I wonder, for instance, whether there is not something to be learned from the extreme case of the Oneida Perfectionists among whom an intelligent outside observer thought their so-called "complex marriage" system amounted to an "unprecedented combination of polygamy and polyandry," where what was aimed at was the abolition of "exclusiveness in regard to women and children," and where, under their striking leader, John Humphrey Noyes, a system of "scientific propagation" was practiced (Nordhoff 1966: 271, 272, 276).

Indeed, if we were to treat the reform of the family in Communist China as one among many ventures in social experimentation, we might well conclude that it has been a rather mild attempt at revolutionizing an institution, so mild in fact that, failing to keep pace with the changes induced in the other areas of social life, it has produced a conflict between the family and other institutions. Precisely because children have not been abstracted from domestic life the attempts thoroughly to commune-ize the society at large may have run up against serious difficulties (cf. Freedman 1964a and Chin 1970). That there have been such difficulties, we know; we may speculate—as a preliminary to study—on the extent to which they flow from an inadequate revolution in the family. It would be unsafe to assume that the Red Guards were made possible by a breakdown in family discipline; the maintenance of that discipline may be the reason why the movement is in the end containable. But I am speculating in the dark. . . .

I suppose that at the back of my mind when I chose "Why China?" as the title of my second and last Presidential Address was the idea that I might take the opportunity of doing some propaganda for a field of study that has not in fact attracted many members of the Institute. I have suggested a number of reasons why we may think China a profitable subject; but I confess that I did not foresee when I handed in my title early in 1969 that I should want to spend some of my time talking about the connection between Chinese studies and student unrest in this country. I hope you will not have resented the introduction into the Institute forum of matters that concern me in another role. As a matter of fact, the Institute cannot be immune to the influence of the universities, with which, through its members, it is increasingly linked. And if ever (which Heaven forbid) student idealism should be carried to the point at which scholarship became impossible in the universities, then it would fall to the Institute to harbor and succor the displaced anthropologists. It has already done so once—for my own department at the beginning of 1969.

Notes

Notes

1. The Chinese in Southeast Asia

1. The history of the Chinese in Southeast Asia is best approached through a remarkably concise and sophisticated pamphlet by Wang Gungwu (1959). A revised edition (1965) of Victor Purcell's standard work (1951) is soon to be published. On the key question of Chinese education in the Nanyang see Murray 1964 for a very useful survey.

2. In speaking about the Chinese in Malaya, I have drawn on my own experience as well as the considerable literature on the country. Gullick 1963 provides the best framework for understanding the present position of the Chinese: Le Page (1964) takes Malaya as one example of the linguistic problems it discusses. Some of the cultural questions mentioned are touched on in pieces I have published: Freedman 1957a, 1960 [Essay 5 below], and 1962a [Essay 6 below].

3. Important contributions to the study of the Chinese in Indonesia are to be found in the following works: L. E. Williams 1960, D. E. Willmott 1961, Skinner 1963, and Somers 1964.

4. It will have been obvious to anybody who knows the field that I have relied very heavily in this lecture on the shrewd analyses of the Thailand and Indonesian Chinese made by G. William Skinner. But my reliance on his work in no way involves him in any mistakes or interpretations I may have slipped into. In connection with the main theme of the lecture I may suggest the following of Skinner's works to the reader: 1957, 1960, and 1963.

2. The Handling of Money

1. Macgowan is of course here speaking generally of China, but he had special knowledge of the southeastern area. Among his works is a dictionary of the Amoy dialect.

2. This example is modeled on that given in Jacques 1931. Jacques is writing about Chinese loan societies in Sarawak, but he describes a system common in China.

3. On this last point cf. Freedman 1958: 18.

3. The Growth of a Plural Society in Malaya

1. See esp. Morris 1957, Rex 1959, and M. G. Smith 1960.

2. For guidance and comments, I am grateful to the members of the Seminar on Constitutional Problems of Multi-Racial Countries, Institute of Commonwealth Studies, University of London, and especially to the Chairman, Professor Kenneth Robinson.

3. The standard work on the Malayan population is T. E. Smith 1952.

4. For general historical background see Hall 1955.

5. On nationalism in Malaya see Silcock and Aziz 1950.

6. The general scene is described in Purcell 1948.

7. The best work known to me on this subject is Dobby 1953.

8. The latest published work on the secret societies in Comber 1959. In a recent paper

(Freedman 1960 [Essay 5 below]) I have attempted to give a sociological interpretation of secret societies and other forms of association in Singapore.

9. For a recent survey of economic questions see Silcock 1959.

4. An Epicycle of Cathay

1. For recent work showing the Chineseness of Vietnam see Woodside 1971 and Langlet (1970).

2. I have reviewed this book (Freedman 1972b) and assessed some of its arguments in my paper (1972a). Inevitably there is some considerable overlap between that paper and the present essay. I should like to thank Professor Myron L. Cohen for helpful comments.

3. See chaps. 5 and 6 of C. P. FitzGerald 1972 and, for other important recent work on the subject, Needham 1971 and Ma Huan 1970. Wang Gungwu 1970 furnishes the background of economic history.

4. As an example of the ineffective discovery in Ch'ing times of the past Chinese influences in the Nanyang, see Leonard 1972. The paper deals with a Chinese work that appeared in 1847.

5. The most comprehensive and convenient work on this general subject remains, alas, Purcell 1965. For a very useful survey of recent literature see Nevadomsky and Li 1970.

6. This argument is strengthened by S. A. FitzGerald 1972, an amazingly detailed account of the willed disengagement of China from the *hua-ch'iao*. And see Freedman 1972a. Purcell (1965: 567–68) argued against the thesis that the Overseas Chinese were a fifth column for China.

7. A good case can be made out for Nanyang studies precisely on the ground that they have contributed to our understanding of the homeland society. For examples see W. E. Willmott 1970: 160–74 and Crissman 1967: 200–203. Doubtless too a more thorough understanding of society in China, with particular, but not sole, reference to the provinces of Kwangtung and Fukien, would make for a clearer view of the society and culture of the Overseas Chinese. A more direct approach to the interaction between the two branches of study was pioneered in Ch'en Ta 1939—see also Hsu 1945—but it has never been taken very far. The most recent work along this line I know of is to be found in Chang Chen-ch'ien et al. 1957 and Chuang Wei-chi et al. 1958. The latter article is especially interesting. S. A. FitzGerald 1972, chap. 4, "Domestic Overseas Chinese Policy: 1949–1966," offers tantalizing glimpses, as when, for example (p. 62), we learn of a phase when the dependents of *hua-ch'iao* "were officially permitted to use their remittances on the upkeep of ancestral graves, geomancy, and other 'feudal superstitious practices.'" As a matter of fact, it might be pointed out that the decline in remittances from overseas to dependents at home must have followed fairly rapidly from the turnover of the generations, as we can see from the systematic analysis of the Chinese family and its economic arrangements. Cf. M. L. Cohen 1970a, esp. pp. 23–24.

8. Based upon the table in S. A. FitzGerald 1972: 196.

9. Go Gien Tjwan (1971: 564) speaks, surprisingly, of all the Overseas Chinese in Southeast Asia "sharing a common way of life distinct from the indigenous cultures of the host nations." But of course he shows himself sensitive to the differences from country to country. For an interesting attempt to isolate some organizational principles underlying the surface variety see Crissman 1967.

10. But see Metzger 1970 for a reappraisal of the attitude of the Confucian state to commercial activity.

11. On this matter see Skinner 1968 for a characteristically pointed paper.

12. Of course, the more personal element in the exercise of imperial power was not entirely lacking within the political system of the central, bureaucratically regulated, realm. See Wakeman 1970: 9. "A county official could, and sometimes did, receive instruction directly from the palace."

13. Fairbank 1968: 11. On the general matter see this book *passim* and cf. Ginsburg 1968.

14. Professor Wertheim has also published a paper entitled "Ahasverus in de Tropen" (see Nevadomsky and Li 1970: 8), but I have not seen it.

5. Immigrants and Associations

1. Namely Sarawak (see T'ien 1953) and Thailand (see Skinner 1957, 1958). For Indonesia see Cator 1936 and Ong 1943. Some forms of association in Singapore are discussed in Freedman 1957a. For the region as a whole see Purcell 1951. The general historical background to the material of this paper is to be found in the last work and in Purcell 1948. I should like to thank Mr. J. M. Gullick for criticizing an earlier draft of this paper and for making a number of historical and sociological comments, and Mr. W. L. Blythe, C.M.G., for his expert advice on a number of matters, especially those touching the secret societies. Part of the work on which this study is based was made possible by a grant from the Department of Sociological and Demographic Research, London School of Economics and Political Science.

2. See the sour comment of the Acting Protector of Chinese in Straits Settlements 1896: 166, and cf. Hare 1895, a fascinating monograph.

3. Among the more recent works on this topic are Blythe 1950 and Comber 1959.

4. The two societies mentioned here are the Hai San (i.e. M. Hai-shan) and Ghee Hin (i.e. M. I-hsing) of later writings.

5. Song 1923: 82ff. Cf. *SSGG*, 9 April 1880: 223, on secret-society hostility to Christian Chinese. Christianity did not make great headway among the Singapore Chinese.

6. Straits Settlements 1861–62: 3. See also Cavenagh 1884: 255. Cf. Read 1901: 105, 107–8.

7. *SSGG*, 28 Feb. 1878: 90.

8. *SSGG*, 21 Feb. 1879: 11, and Pickering 1879.

9. *SSGG*, 9 April 1880: 228. The romanization of the names of the secret societies was very erratic.

10. *SSGG*, 21 Feb. 1879: 111.

11. *SSGG*, 22 Feb. 1879: 90; 22 Feb. 1879: 111; 9 April 1880: 224; 29 April 1881: 355.

12. *SSGG*, 27 April 1888: 901–2.

13. Singapore Chinese played a prominent part in the Amoy uprising of 1853. See G. Hughes 1873.

14. See Song 1923 at many places for the details of the facts referred to in this paragraph.

15. E.g. *SSGG*, 9 April 1880: 223; 12 Feb. 1886: 129; 24 April 1890: 845.

16. *SSGG*, 22 Feb. 1878: 90.

17. E.g. *SSGG*, 12 Feb. 1886: 129.

18. Several texts of the ritual from Malaya, Java, and Sumatra have been published. See especially Ward and Stirling 1925 and Schlegel 1866.

19. *SSGG*, 9 April 1880: 224.

20. Cf. Siah 1848: 290 for occupational specialization by dialect groups in the middle of the century.

21. Straits Settlements 1898: 228, and cf. Straits Settlements 1896: 344.

22. See Purcell 1951: 221, 224ff; Lafargue 1909: 206ff; and Dubreuil 1910: 33ff.

23. Cf. the remarks by Hare (1895: 9) on Kwangtung.

6. Chinese Kinship and Marriage in Early Singapore

1. See, for example, Purcell 1948: 87n. 1 and S. W. Jones 1953: 3.

2. On *cin-cuĕ* cf. Freedman 1957a: 122–23.

3. Straits Settlements, Chinese Marriage Committee, 1926: 28, 34–37, 38–39, 82–86, 123–25.

4. Cf. Tan's poem "The Chinese Surnames, Some Moral Advices" (Tan 1924: 88).

5. Napier 1913: 146. For comparative material on this topic on Chinese in the Netherlands Indies see Vleming 1926: chap. 13.

6. Song (1923: 86) cites a newspaper report of 1853 that among the arrivals from Amoy "were the wives and families of several of the most respectable Chinese merchants," but he forgets that this unusual event was probably the effect of the fighting going on at Amoy at that time. Cf. Minchin 1870: 81 and Buckley 1902: 580.

7. Freedman 1950 [Essay 7 below]: 100. For a note on the law against perpetuities, see *ibid.*: 116.

8. This question is treated at length in Freedman 1958: 47ff, 129.

9. I have attempted elsewhere (Freedman 1960 [Essay 5 above]) to outline and discuss these groupings.

10. Cf. Ch'en Ta 1939: 8ff. There has been some historical study touching on this question in the People's Republic of China. See Chang Chen-ch'ien et al. 1957 and Chuang Wei-chi et al. 1958.

11. A Straits Chinese 1899: 45. On the matters touched on in this paragraph see Freedman 1960: 39ff.

7. *Colonial Law and Chinese Society*

1. For details of the development of the colonial legal system see Braddell 1931: 1–61.

2. "Colonial" and "colony" refer only since 1946 to the separate entity of Singapore. Before that year Singapore was one of three Settlements making up the Colony of the Straits Settlements. Statutes and case law valid for the Straits Settlements before 1946 are still valid in Singapore (unless, of course, canceled by subsequent legislation), but after that date Singapore stands alone.

3. For an account of the secret societies, see Purcell 1948: chap. 8. Freedman (1948: 171ff) discusses the legal and political significance of these organizations.

4. See, for example, Gilpatrick 1950: 39–44. Van der Valk (1939: 9–10) stresses the subordination of the written codes to the *li* "translated as the 'rites,' 'etiquette,' etc. They comprehend naturally what is understood by law, morals, law of nature, code of behaviour, etc."

5. See also Bryan 1925: chap. 2 for a brief account of family law in China between the founding of the Republic, and the introduction of the 1931 Code.

6. The article is in Chinese. I reproduce here the first and last paragraphs of a translation made by Mr. Toh Peng Koon, formerly Interpreter in the Department of Social Welfare, Singapore:

"Overseas Chinese living in the South Seas have never taken any great interest in local laws that concern themselves. They regard the changes and applicability of the law of China as no concern of theirs, without realising that they are making a great mistake. Any court, in deciding legal cases such as marriage, inheritance, and testament, must necessarily base its judgment on the native law of the individual concerned, even though the cases are tried within its jurisdiction. In trying criminal cases the law of the country from which the accused came is applied, and the same procedure is carried out in claims for inheritance and cases relating to contracts. Therefore, Overseas Chinese living in foreign countries must apply the law of China and not the law of the country in which they are resident in dealing with such matters as marriage, inheritance, and testament. This point is clearly understood by people living in Hong Kong and Macao. British courts in Hong Kong, in hearing cases such as those just mentioned, usually seek the advice of prominent Chinese and lawyers specialising in Chinese law in order to reach a decision. If such advice is not asked for by the court, the people involved in the suit will, of their own accord, engage Chinese lawyers to give evidence as witnesses on Chinese law. But it appears that such a procedure is completely overlooked in British Malaya, Siam, and Burma. Consequently, local law had been enforced in dealing with Overseas Chinese who regard it as matter of course. Many of them have suffered injustice, as nobody has come forward to remedy the situation. . . .

"From the above we can see, therefore, that there is a great difference between the Chinese and British laws in relation to these three classes of legal suits (i.e. marriage, inheritance, and testament). For instance, if a person comes from China to Malaya and establishes his business here, his property, according to the law of every nationality, should be dealt with in accordance with his native law (Chinese law) if he should die intestate. Therefore, if nobody paid attention to this matter and let it be handled in accordance with British law, the wife would then suffer greatly. Or if a will had been made, but not in accordance with Chinese law, the heirs could also claim by way of Chinese law. I consider, then, that there is a need for Overseas Chinese always to study carefully the administration of the law of China. It is the great responsibility of those engaged in cultural fields to imbue the minds of other Overseas Chinese with the knowledge of the system of the law in China." Of course, Chinese in the Colony have no choice as to the application of a particular system of law. In the matter of inheritance it is the law of the man's domicile which determines the division of his personal property, and real property is disposed of according to the law of the place in which it is situated. Kuan's confusion of domicile and nationality leads him to attack people who, "when faced with legal disputes, do not know how to make use of the law of China to protect their own legal interests, but rather put their affairs into the hands of foreign lawyers."

Kuan Ch'u-p'u, I am informed, was at one time on the editorial staff of one of Singapore's leading Chinese daily newspapers.

7. An earlier version of the new Communist code can be found in "Decree of the First Session of the Central Executive Committee of the Chinese Soviet Republic entitled 'Provisional Marriage Regulations'" (Chinese Soviet Republic, Laws, statutes, etc. 1934: 83–87). The decree was issued in 1931. The new version follows the older one very closely.

8. In the matter of the development of colonial law up to 1931, I have been guided by Braddell 1921 and 1931. I should like also to acknowledge the guidance which Sir Roland Braddell has given me personally. In reading case law I have used Payne 1936 and Mallal and Mallal 1940, and the various periodical compilations of reported cases which have appeared in Singapore.

9. E.g. Doolittle 1865: vol. 1, 98. This work describes the Chinese in Foochow, capital of Fukien province, in the middle of the last century.

10. *In re Lao Leong An, SSLR* 1893: 1–2.

11. *In the Matter of the Estate of Choo Eng Choon, decd., Choo Ang Chee v. Neo Chan Neo and others, SSLR* 1911: 148–49.

12. *Woon Kai Chiang v. Yeo Pak Wee and others, SSLR* 1893: 34. In the light of this prediction we may compare a recent decision by Chief Justice Murray-Aynsley (Singapore, Law Reports, 1949: 172): "The legal requirements for marriage with a *t'sai* and a *t'sip* are, I think, the same. This means that the law of this Colony merely requires a consensual marriage, that is, an agreement to form a relationship that comes within the English definition of marriage." I shall refer to this case again later.

13. *Rex v. Sim Boon Lip, SSLR* 1902–3: 4ff.

14. Braddell 1931: 85. This overseas institution of double principal wives also emerges from the evidence before the Chinese Marriage Committee. See Straits Settlements, Chinese Marriage Committee, 1926.

15. *Then Kang Chu, Respondent v. Tan Kim Hoe, Appellant, SSLR* 1926: 1.

16. The figures in both these tables were supplied by the Registry of Marriages, Singapore. The fluctuations during the Japanese Occupation, 1942–45, are interesting.

17. One has to realize, also, that some of the civil marriages are merely in fact subsequent registrations of earlier unions conducted under a traditional system.

18. The three poetic phrases which I have put in quotation marks appear to be adaptations of passages in the *Book of Odes*. See Karlgren 1950: Odes 6, 237, 300, at pp. 415, 189, 300. The "oath of red leaves" refers apparently to a T'ang story of the exchange of love pledges written on autumn leaves.

19. A description of an early new-style marriage in Singapore will be found in Stirling 1925.

20. *Soon Voon Sen v. Ang Kiong Hee, SSLR* 1933: 582–84. Note that the case carries the date 1924. The quotation appears at p. 582.

21. An interesting variation of modern Chinese marriage in the years since the war has been the Mass Wedding organized by the Mayfair Musical and Dramatic Society (now sup-

pressed by government). These weddings differ from others in the new style only in that they unite more than one couple at a time. (The numerical significance of "mass" has been about thirty-five.) The promoters affirm that they accept for marriage only those men who have not been married before and they point to their publication in the press, before each wedding, of a list of those about to be married, as a sanction against breach of this rule. The element of large scale publicity and the factor of political influence would have to be taken into account in an analysis of the popularity of the Mass Wedding.

22. Valk 1939: 66. I am relying on van der Valk for interpretation of the Code.

23. The Code computes degree of relationship by the Roman Law system, that is, in the case of collaterals, by adding the number of generations between ego and the common ancestor to the number of generations from that ancestor down to the relative. Thus, my clanswoman of the ninth degree is any of the following persons: father's father's brother's son's son's son's daughter; father's father's father's brother's son's son's son's daughter; father's father's father's father's brother's son's son's daughter. A clanswoman of the tenth degree and of my generation would be my father's father's father's father's brother's son's son's son's daughter.

24. Article 239 of the 1935 Criminal Code, setting up adultery as a crime for both husbands and wives, did not really attack concubinage. See Gilpatrick 1950: 53. And cf. Wang Tse-sin 1932: 129.

25. A few weeks before the appearance of the new laws, readers of the Chinese press in Singapore were startled by an account of a newfangled wedding ceremony in Shanghai. "Recently two employees of the Agricultural Department in Shanghai were married. The ceremony was quite unusual. . . . It took place in the Ching Hua Association. The guests did not make wedding presents, but each contributed $5,000 towards the expenses of the tea-party. Discussion was held during the ceremony. Subjects for discussion were printed on the invitation cards." The program was divided into four parts. In the first part the assembly was to criticize the old form of marriage ceremony and discuss the significance of the new. In the second part the topics turned upon "the new conception of marriage." Is marriage really a burden? What is the complete meaning of marriage? What is an ideal marriage? The third and fourth parts were divided between the guests and the bridal couple respectively. The former were to declare what they knew of the bride and groom and to express their hopes concerning the match, while the latter were to expound the theme "from friendship to marriage" and to discuss "the future struggle for the attainment of the common objective." *Hsin-chou jih-pao*, 24 March 1950. Singapore Chinese are familiar with the obtrusion of nationalist sentiments in wedding speeches, but were not quite prepared for the conversion of a wedding party into a political demonstration.

26. This is Hare's list (1904: 10); other compilations give the additional faults of jealousy and talkativeness.

27. *Nonia Cheah Yew* v. *Othmansaw Merican and another* (Straits Settlements, Supreme Court 1885: 160).

28. Ordinance No. 39 of 1939, p. 1. In the four years 1946–49 there was a total of 53 applications for divorce under this Ordinance by Chinese or by non-Chinese against Chinese spouses.

29. Cf. Straits Settlements, Chinese Marriage Committee 1926: 150.

30. That statutory backing does not exist is, of course, not realized generally by people who go to the Section. For them what is dispensed here is "government law."

31. There is no cost to "litigants."

32. See Hare 1904: 13–14. However Jamieson (1921: 5, 13, 23) is firm on the point that persons of different surnames cannot be legally adopted. And cf. Bryan (1925: 27): "If one adopts a son of a person outside of the adopter's lineage, then both the adopted father and the natural father must suffer punishment."

33. The Cantonese term *mui tsai* is used in all the official literature. The Hokkiens say *cā-bò-kân*.

34. I understand that a new Adoption Ordinance is in the course of preparation which will, firstly, make legal adoption a reasonably cheap and simple process, and, secondly, confer upon the adopted child the rights of inheritance of a begotten child.

35. For rules of inheritance by remoter next-of-kin see Payne 1936: 170–71.

36. E.g. *In the Matter of the Estate of Khoo Cheng Teow, decd. The British Malaya Trustee and Executor Coy. Ltd. v. Khoo Seng Seng (SSLR* 1932: 226ff).

37. The judges, of course, have not always been in agreement among themselves as to how far they have been obliged to go in accepting Chinese custom. See the judgments in *Ngai Lau Shias Low Hong Shiau* v. *Low Chee Neo (SSLR* 1921: 35–79), where three judges discuss the development of the legal treatment of Chinese marriage in the Straits Settlements.

38. For the purposes of this brief exposition I am dealing somewhat crudely with these entities. The significance of the labels ideally requires elaboration.

39. "Whoever marries his brother's widow is strangled" (Möllendorff 1896: 16–17).

40. And some of the few Christian Chinese were converts in China before migration. The effect of Islam (the religion of the Malays) has been negligible.

41. A term of abuse equivalent to "bourgeois" in similar political situations.

42. See Guardianship of Infants Ordinance.

43. A stormy debate centered about this problem in the middle 1930's in China. In 1934 the Article of the 1928 Criminal Code which said "Married women convicted of committing adultery shall be punished by imprisonment for not more than two years" came up for revision and was changed to read "Married spouses . . ." After debate in the Legislative Yüan the article was deleted.

But later it was reintroduced in the original version. There followed a series of protests by women's organizations who based their objections on Article 6 of the Provisional Constitution which lays down the principle of sexual equality before the law. The Central Political Council announced finally that it had decided to request the Legislative Yüan to revise the Article of the Criminal Code on the basis of sex equality. (See *China Weekly Review*, 24 Nov. 1934.) "Whereupon the Legislative Yuan adopted the suggestion of the Criminal Codification Commission and contented itself with a reduction of the maximum penalty from two to one year" (China [Republic], Laws, statutes, etc. 1936: IX).

44. This fact has been stressed in much of the literature dealing with Chinese village organization. De Groot (1892: 191) says: ". . . most villages of Fukien province . . . are inhabited by people of one clan name only."

45. Kulp (1925, esp. pp. 318–33), dealing with a single-surname Teochiu village supplying immigrants to Southeast Asia, has some interesting analyses of the relation between village and state justice.

46. I am ignoring the practice of justice in urbanized conditions.

8. *Chinese Family Law in Singapore*

1. I dealt fairly fully with this matter in an earlier paper (Freedman 1950 [Essay 7 above]), although, were I rewriting that article now, I should want to revise a number of the arguments in it. For other points touched on here, see Freedman 1953, 1957a, and 1962a [Essay 6 above]. For a recent survey of the treatment of Chinese family law in Singapore, see R. C. H. Lim 1961. I had the privilege of reading in prepublication draft Buxbaum 1966. In connection with the present paper, I should like to acknowledge the help I received in Singapore in July 1963 from the following people: Dr. Ahmad bin Mohamed Ibrahim, Mrs. Jennie Chee, Mr. E. H. D'Netto, Mr. Richard C. H. Lim, Mr. B. A. Mallal, Mr. L. Rayner, Mr. K. H. Tan, Mr. and Mrs. Harry Wee, and officers of the Marriage Registry and the Supreme Court. Both in Singapore in 1963 and during the writing of this paper I have greatly benefited from my wife's knowledge of the Singapore legal system. I am in debt to the Solicitor General, Singapore (Mr. Tan Boon Teik), for his courtesy in answering questions I put to him in a letter, and to the Singapore Trade Commissioner, London, for his making various official publications available to me. Finally, I have to thank Professor Morris Ginsberg, Mr. John M. Gullick, and Mr. David C. Buxbaum for their comments on the typescript of this paper.

2. Quoted in Purcell 1948: 49–50.

3. It would require a very detailed study to determine exactly how Muslim and Chinese

family law came to be treated differently in the courts. It is perhaps relevant that in the rules laid down by Raffles (the founder of modern Singapore) in 1823 it was stated that in all cases regarding the ceremonies of religion, and marriages, and the rules of inheritance, the laws and customs of the Malays will be respected, where they shall not be contrary to reason, justice, or humanity. Quoted in Ibrahim 1965b: 3. And cf. Sheridan 1961: 14–19.

4. *In re Lao Leong An, SSLR* 1893: 2.

5. *Woon Kai Chiang* v. *Yeo Pak Wee and others, SSLR* 1926: 34.

6. *Nonia Cheah Yew* v. *Othmansaw Merican and another.* Straits Settlements, Supreme Court, 1885: 160.

7. *Lew Ah Lui* v. *Choa Eng Wan and others, SSLR* 1935: 179.

8. The marriage figures given here and later in the paper have been extracted from *Monthly Digest of Statistics,* Singapore, and *Report on the Registration of Births and Deaths, Marriages and Persons,* Singapore, for various years.

9. *Singapore Legislative Assembly Debates,* 12, no. 7 (6 April 1960), cols. 442–43.

10. *Ibid.,* col. 454. Dr. Lee became chairman of the newly formed Barisan Socialis party in August 1961.

11. *Singapore Legislative Assembly Debates,* 12, no. 7 (6 April 1960), col. 458.

12. *Singapore Legislative Assembly Debates,* 14, no. 16 (27 March 1961), col. 1,199.

13. *Singapore Legislative Assembly Debates,* 14, no. 20 (24 May 1961), col. 1,546.

14. In 1962, 24 applications for legal aid were made in respect of Chinese customary marriages, all but two of them being allowed. They "produced" three decrees, 19 pending at the end of the year. In the first six months of 1963, 15 such applications were received, again all but two being granted.

15. For a fairly recent account of some relevant Chinese social institutions, see Wee 1963. See also Kaye 1960, B. E. Ward 1963, and Maris Stella Girls' School, Child Welfare and Social Work Section 1965.

9. Religion Among the Chinese in Singapore

1. Alan J. A. Elliott's field study was carried out in 1950–51 (see Elliott 1955). Marjorie Topley's field studies were carried out in 1951–52 and 1954–55 (see Topley 1951, 1952, 1954, 1955, 1956a, 1956b, 1957, 1961). Maurice Freedman's field work was carried out in 1949–50 (see Freedman 1957a, 1957b, 1958, 1959c, 1960 [Essay 5 above]). Barrington Kaye's study of a single Chinese street was carried out in 1954–56 (see Kaye 1960).

2. An earlier version of this paper, by Freedman alone, was published in French: Freedman 1959c. The dates given in the preceding note will show the reader that the present discussed here must not be taken literally. We are already separated from our field by a few significant years.

3. For the general historical background see Purcell 1948, 1951, and Freedman 1960.

4. On agnatic and local organization in Fukien and Kwangtung and its religious correlates see Freedman 1957a, 1957b, and 1958. A recent field study is briefly reported in Pratt 1960.

5. Freedman 1957a: 69 gives too low an estimate; see Swisher 1953. On Chinese names in Malaya see R. Jones 1959.

6. On the various types of religious institutions see Topley 1956a. Nobody has made a complete survey of Chinese temples and other religious places in Singapore; it would be an immense task. For general information see *Hsin-chia-p'o miao yü kai lan* 1951.

7. Groot 1886, vol. 11: 276–77, 283–84, 285–303; Groot 1910: 1269ff, 1295ff, 1332ff.

8. De Groot (1910: 1272) says that, although consultations through mediums may be of many kinds, they are principally concerned with "medical questions."

9. Cf. Granet 1951: chaps. 3 and 4; and Granet [1929a] 1953.

10. All information in this paper on syncretic religion is based, unless otherwise stated, on the field and documentary researches conducted by Marjorie Topley in Singapore. It will be presented in fuller form in later publications.

11. E.g. Newbold and Wilson 1841; Schlegel 1866; Stanton 1900; Ward and Stirling 1925; Favre 1933; and cf. Freedman 1958: 116ff.

12. In 1954 it was reported that there had been "anti-flood control" campaigns in Hankow and the surrounding area, in which the I-kuan Tao was involved. The news appeared in *Ch'ang-chiang jih-pao* 17 July and 2 Aug. 1954.

13. No detailed sociological analysis of the secret societies in Malaya and Singapore has yet been published. For historical data see Purcell 1948, Comber 1956 and 1959, and Wynne 1941. Freedman 1960 [Essay 5 above] makes some sociological points on the subject.

14. Sun Yat-sen established as his first revolutionary society the Hsing-Chung Hui in Honolulu in 1894. In 1905 this society was combined with other groupings under the name of T'ung-meng Hui, a branch of which was set up in Singapore in 1906. Purcell 1951: 354.

15. For an analysis of some aspects of the sect see De Korne 1941. De Korne is not aware of the connection between the sect and the Great Way. Topley hopes to publish more information on this subject at a later date.

16. Unfortunately, more precise figures cannot be given. The total number of halls is nowhere recorded. A survey of them would encounter considerable difficulty. They are spread out over the Island and, because they are architecturally various, are not easy to identify. The estimate offered here is based partly on records kept by private individuals concerned with the activities or management of halls, and partly on records kept by the religious organizations which include halls among their member organizations.

10. Chinese Geomancy in Hong Kong

1. Source: Lockhart's confidential correspondence, 1, 7, 8, and 14 May 1899.

2. Some slight indication of what can be got from genealogies is afforded by Hui-chen Wang Liu 1959: 168–69. See also C. K. Yang 1961: 264 for data drawn from genealogies and a Kwangtung gazetteer.

11. Shifts of Power in the Hong Kong New Territories

1. This paper draws on a general survey of the New Territories which I carried out during February to May 1963 under the auspices of the London-Cornell Project for East and Southeast Asian Studies.

2. A good deal can be learned about Hsin-an in the nineteenth century from a study of the British reports made in connection with the takeover in 1898, from the 1819 edition of the Hsin-an Gazetteer, and from a journal article written by an early missionary: Krone 1859.

3. On the general question see Chung-li Chang 1955 and Ch'ü 1961.

12. Emigration from the New Territories

1. See Barnett 1962: 25, Tables 110 and 111. Population figures, by sex, for individual villages and settlements are available from the 1861 census, although not included in the published census report; they provide a valuable guide on the communities from which male emigration has been heaviest, although again, the presence of new population in the figures often makes detection difficult.

13. The Chinese Domestic Family

1. Baller 1921: 9. [In the original Freedman quoted a different and unidentified translation. The Baller translation quoted here is closer to the Chinese original.—GWS]

14. The Family in China, Past and Present

1. A great deal of documentation bearing on these points is to be found in Hsiao 1960.

15. Rites and Duties, or Chinese Marriage

1. See China [Republic], Ssu fa hsing cheng pu [1930], 1965.
2. Serruys 1944 (no. 1): 82. This is one of the best sources among those I have used for this study. I cannot set out here all the sources I have consulted; I hope to publish a fuller account later on, and to print my bibliography there.
3. I have drawn this example from Cammann 1952: 103.

16. Ritual Aspects of Chinese Kinship and Marriage

1. Many of the ideas and formulations in this essay have been developed as a direct result of my participation in seminars at the London School of Economics and at Cornell University; in that regard I have particularly to thank my colleagues (above all Arthur P. Wolf) and the graduate students with whom I have worked. I am indebted to Hugh D. R. Baker for his work for me on some of the Chinese sources, and to Stephan Feuchtwang for his making available to me his notes from Chinese and Japanese published sources on marriage in Taiwan. Part of my research was made possible by the London-Cornell Project for East and Southeast Asian Studies, which is financed jointly by the Carnegie Corporation of New York and the Nuffield Foundation. I owe my wife a debt for her scrutiny of a draft of the essay.
2. I list the most interesting of the sources I have used: Buxbaum 1968: 30–60; Cormack 1935: 41–58; Dols 1915/16: 467–86; Doolittle 1865: vol. 1, 65–98; Doré 1914: 29–39; R. K. Douglas 1901: 192–204; Egerod 1959: 50–53; Feng and Shryock 1950; Fielde 1884: 48–58; Fielde 1894: 35–47; Frick 1952; Gamble 1954: 379–85; J. H. Gray 1878: vol. 1, 187–218; Grube 1901: 10–32; Highbaugh 1948: 46–51; Hsu 1948: 85–98; Hutson 1921: 14–21; Körner 1959: 8–14; Lin 1948: 39–49; Liu Wei-min 1936; Lockhart 1890b; Lynn 1928: 110–31; Osgood 1963: 277–84; Segers 1932: 91–117; Serruys 1944; Su 1966; Théry 1948–49; Wieger 1913: 451–87; S. W. Williams 1883: vol. 1, 785–91; A. P. Wolf 1964: 44–57; M. C. Yang 1945: 106–13. Also see Freedman 1957a: 126–58.
3. Other points are dealt with in Freedman 1967b [Essay 15 above]; I am planning a more comprehensive study of the subject.

17. Ancestor Worship

1. I have had the great advantage of listening to lectures by Professor Arthur P. Wolf and Robert J. Smith on Chinese and Japanese ancestor worship respectively; and I am in their debt for a number of valuable criticisms and suggestions. I am similarly indebted to Professor Lucy Mair, Dr. Burton Benedict, and my wife. [I have reproduced the text of this paragraph as it appeared in print, though it seems likely that the words "morality" in the third-to-last and last sentences should be either "mortality" in both places or "mortality" in the former and "immortality" in the latter—GWS.]
2. For a variation see Fabre 1937: 586.
3. Granet 1975: 114, 116. *Feng-shui*, under that name, is referred to again at p. 151.
4. And now cf. Gallin 1966: 148, 247 on this point.
5. I am greatly in debt to this paper not only for the insight it affords into Japanese ancestor worship but also for its discussion of many important problems.
6. See the impressive analysis of "Gods, Ghosts, and Ancestors" by Arthur P. Wolf (1974b), based on his field study in Taiwan.

18. Geomancy

1. I thought, when I began to outline this address in my mind, that I should be able to range more widely over the subject, taking non-Chinese data into account. (Cf. Danielli 1952 on Madagascar.) But I am not satisfied that I yet know enough about geomancy in other parts of the world. As far as East Asia is concerned, I have offered some prelimi-

nary remarks elsewhere (Freedman 1966: 141n; 1967a: 88ff) which I intend to develop into a fuller argument. A recent publication on Okinawa (Lebra 1966: 62, 85), which I had not read when I wrote my earlier analyses of Chinese geomancy, suggests some highly interesting questions that remain to be dealt with.

In connection with this address, I record with gratitude the fact that my field study in the Hong Kong New Territories in 1963 was made possible by the financial help of the London-Cornell Project for East and Southeast Asian Studies (which is financed jointly by the Carnegie Corporation of New York and the Nuffield Foundation) and the London School of Economics and Political Science (out of a Ford Foundation grant). I am greatly indebted to various officers of the New Territories Administration for their help and advice. I have to thank Dr. Hugh D. R. Baker for checking the translation of the article by Chou Ching to which I refer later on.

2. For notes on the passages quoted from Jonson, see Herford et al. 1950: 64ff; and on the character of Drugger see Herford and Simpson 1925: 103ff.

3. Frazer 1911a: 170. Frazer got these stories from de Groot (1897: 977, 1043ff). De Groot took the latter case from Yates (1868: 41). Frazer (1911b: 239) has another reference to *feng-shui* (again derived from Yates through de Groot).

4. E.g. Hsu 1948: 20, 47ff, 52; M. C. Yang 1945: 88; Lin 1948: 23. The last-named work, at p. 25, has an interesting reference to geomancy and house-siting.

5. Weber 1951: 199 has some remarks on *feng-shui* and economic development.

6. Cf. Eitel 1873: 80 on the last two points.

7. There has very recently appeared another study based on Chinese sources: March 1968. It is written by, and from the point of view of, a geographer.

8. Since I wrote this address a former District Officer in the Hong Kong New Territories has published some remarks on *feng-shui* from the administrator's point of view (see Coates 1968: 156, 169–74), and a geographer has produced a paper in which *feng-shui* is shown to enter into the relations between government and people in a part of the New Territories undergoing urbanization (see Boxer 1968: 231ff).

9. I owe Professor Wolfram Eberhard a debt for writing to me to draw my attention to the intermediate social status of the geomancer.

10. E.g. Graham 1961: 104ff, 112. Here (Szechwan) the geomancer and priest seem to be completely merged. For a Taiwan example see Gallin 1966: 288ff.

11. The article in question, written by Chou Ching, appears in *Hsing tao hua pao*, 19 June 1962, pp. 2–5. I have been unable to locate the issue to determine the title—GWS.

12. Cf. Freedman 1966: 122ff on the essentials of site analysis.

13. That, of course, is not a novel theme in anthropology. Cf., for example, Fortes 1967: 11 and notes 20, 21.

14. After this address went to press, Aijmer published a characteristically sensitive paper on *feng-shui*, based upon his fieldwork among Hakka in the Hong Kong New Territories (Aijmer 1968a). It treats geomancy from the point of view of what he calls "its communicative aspect": the natural world is made by geomancy symbolically to communicate messages.

19. The Politics of an Old State

1. For another American approach to the matter see Fried 1957 and 1970.

2. See Freedman 1967a [Essay 17 above]: 93ff for a discussion of the Chinese family as a unit constantly dividing into new units.

3. But note Chan 1967: 227ff, and Baller 1921: 19–25.

4. Cf. J. A. Cohen 1966: 1,215ff on "extrajudicial mediation."

5. I remember that I have Professor Lawrence Crissman (at the time a graduate student at the London School of Economics) to thank for drawing my attention to the relevance of Alabaster's book to my interest in this theme.

6. Ho (1968: 32) furnishes an exact date (1050) for the creation of the "modern type patrilineal clan . . . which became more and more common during the Ming and Ch'ing,

especially in the southern provinces." The historical reference is presumably to the institution of the Fan "charitable estate" about 1050. See Twitchett 1959. One might imagine a somewhat less abrupt incursion of the lineage into Chinese history.

7. Now (October 1973) see Pasternak 1972 and 1973, noting in the latter work, p. 261: "Our [i.e. his and M. L. Cohen's] more recent joint work in the Meinung [Taiwan] area (1971–72) has convinced me that the two processes, aggregative and fissive [i.e. segmentary], are by no means mutually exclusive."

8. I was relying for historical data mainly on Hsiao 1960; and I had consulted (by letter) Professor D. C. Twitchett, then at the School of Oriental and African Studies, London, and been advised in Hong Kong itself by Mr. James W. Hayes. Cf. the corresponding passage in Freedman 1966: 87 (with note 2) which shows a slightly later attempt to discover something about *hsiang-yüeh*. As for the mystifying *yüeh*, I was later to find brief but interesting information in Wakeman 1966: 144, 148, and Kuhn 1970: 95 (where, by the way, my own data on the subject are fed into the historical analysis), 169. Kuhn refers to *hsiang-yüeh* at pp. 136–37.

9. For another example of the influence of anthropology on history see the work of the historian Professor Johanna M. Meskill (1970a and 1970b).

10. Hayes (1962) presents the picture of the political system as Lockhart painted it.

11. Although a more careful reading of Lo 1965 (esp. pp. 89–90, 106) might have put me on the right track.

12. There is of course nothing very recent about military organization as such in rural China. M. L. Cohen (1970b), for example, refers to a Hakka system in south Taiwan that goes back to 1685; and Skinner (1971: 280) writes: "*The t'uan-lien or local militia . . . were normally formed in periods of dynastic crisis and disbanded in the wake of successful pacification by the succeeding dynasty.*"

13. Cf. Michael 1964: xxii–xxvi and Wakeman 1966: 29–31. And for a recent assessment of the role and functions of the local administrator see Watt 1970.

14. On the definition, status, and functions of the gentry cf. Ichiko 1968: 297ff and Fincher 1968: 187–88.

15. Cf. Freedman 1970 [Essay 24 below]: 10–11. I wish to thank Dr. Hugh D. R. Baker, Professor Myron L. Cohen, Mr. Robert G. Groves, and Professor Arthur P. Wolf for the comments they made on drafts of this essay. I have not been able to take all the comments they made into account here, and I hope to profit by them on another occasion.

20. On the Sociological Study of Chinese Religion

1. The present version reflects not only the discussion at the conference itself, but also comments made when a shortened version was read at the LSE in December 1971.

2. Yang's chief predecessors within sociology were Max Weber and Marcel Granet, to whom I shall be referring presently. One might consider the candidature of Edwin D. Harvey's *The Mind of Modern China* (1933), which was written by a sociologist with a long experience of China. But there is not enough sociology in Harvey's book, and although a case can be made for saying that he tried to see Chinese religious ideas as a whole, he does not appear to have considered Chinese society central to his inquiry. In method the book strikes me as a loosely aggregated assortment of facts from literary sources and rather unsystematically observed field data.

3. The recent (1970) republication of Doré's *Manuel* (1926) demonstrates the continuing usefulness of the data scattered over his many volumes on Chinese "superstitions," but while it classifies and systematizes, it does not analyze.

4. Max Weber does not, in my opinion, quite escape inclusion among "all other writers." True, he tried to deal with the whole religious system, and put his finger on a number of crucial points, e.g. when he discusses the imperial promotion and demotion of gods (Weber 1951: 29–32), drawing, though less extensively than Lyall, upon the *Peking Gazette* (*ibid.*: 260–61, notes 5, 60, 63); but, in his preoccupation with the nonemergence of capitalism in China, he fails to reach a satisfying synthesis. One might say that he threw away the advantage he enjoyed of writing totally from outside by a somewhat fussy atten-

tion to detail. And cf. Weber's remarks on China in *The Sociology of Religion* (1965), especially p. 95, where he gives "animism in China" as an example of religion among "the lower middle class, and particularly among the artisans." Cf. also C. K. Yang 1964 and Otto van der Sprenkel 1964.

5. For a similar view by a Chinese scholar, see Hsiao 1960: 225: "Crude polytheism was thus a way of life with the masses."

6. What follows on de Groot and Granet derives from a study in which I am now engaged. Since the first version of this paper was prepared I have carried out "field research" on the two men in Leiden and Paris, in connection with which I gratefully acknowledge the financial support of the Social Science Research Council (London). Given the complexity of the documentation, which I shall be discussing in later publications, I see no point in trying to justify my statements here with bibliographical references and citations of unpublished material. What appears here is the merest summary of one part of my researches as of August 1973. But in September 1973, after the present version of the paper was completed, I finally traced de Groot's manuscript journal, which will enable me to say more about, *inter alia*, his religious ideas, education, and reading.

7. Illustrated by C. K. Yang's astonishing description of de Groot as an "embittered Dutch missionary" (1964: xxxix).

8. De Groot may have attended lectures on the ethnography of the Dutch East Indies while studying at Leiden, but his time there was devoted primarily to learning Chinese. At Delft, before he went to Leiden, he certainly received some instruction in the ethnography of the Indies.

9. Large as it is, *The Religious System of China* realizes only six of the twelve to fourteen volumes planned; and of the six "Books" foreseen we have less than two, "Disposal of the Dead" being complete, and "On the Soul and Ancestral Worship" unfinished. On the other hand, much of the matter intended for the missing four Books was published elsewhere. For example, the yearly round of festivals we have in the form of *Les fêtes* (1886), while *Le code du Mahâyâna en Chine* (1893) probably represents part of the missing fifth Book. But whatever the possibilities open to us for reconstructing the unrealized work as a whole, we must be saddened by the thought of the enormous amount of information irretrievably lost to us.

10. As a matter of fact, one suspects that the mourning practices de Groot witnessed were still wider of the classical mark than he allowed. And it seems to me that a recent sinological writer has been misled by de Groot's exposition: Laurence G. Thompson says that in Volumes I and II of *The Religious System* "nearly every detail of late nineteenth-century practice is shown to conform to the scriptural injunctions" (Thompson 1969: 111).

11. He was brought up in a Catholic family but at the age of twenty left the Church. *Les fêtes* shows us his religious views during his early manhood; his later work demonstrates his respect for the missionaries in China. Religion was obviously something he took seriously.

12. The book is dedicated "To all missionaries of every Christian creed labouring in China." Cf. his Lamson Lectures, given at the Hartford Theological Seminary in Connecticut (Groot 1910a), in which he shows his contempt of Confucian materialism ("it is a religion of a lower order"; p. 131) and his assimilation of the Chinese sects to Christianity (pp. 222–23). The last words of the book (p. 223) are: "Is it too idle a suggestion that those humble sects are destined to be the precursors of Christianity in China?"

13. The line from *Les fêtes* to *The Religious System* is extended to de Groot's last great work on Chinese religion, *Universismus: Die Grundlage der Religion und Ethik, des Staatswesens und der Wissenchaften Chinas* (1918); we are now finally in the world of pure textual sinology, the field observations having vanished from sight; and China's single religion, "Universism," is cast in its final form.

14. In his first book on religion Granet castigates de Groot for writing in the tradition that seeks to explain current religious practice by a purpose ascribed to them by the Chinese themselves or by reference to some fashionable theory such as Naturism or Animism. "The search after the beginnings of things is generally misleading; particularly is this the case in

China, where native scholars devote their attention to discovering, not the actual beginnings of things, but only the date when the characters employed to denote these things were first used" (Granet 1932: 2–3).

15. Note the importance of Granet's work on Chinese kinship and marriage for Lévi-Strauss in chaps. 19–21 of *Les structures élémentaires de la parenté* (1949).

16. Granet contrives to put some life into this tired formula. Cf. fn. *c*, p. 358.

17. Most modern studies of ancient China are more restrained in their reconstructions, and Granet *as historian* seems to have been largely left behind. But we may note that one of his French successors takes some of his assertions about the ancient peasantry as though they were historically established facts: Jacques Gernet, *Ancient China from the Beginnings to the Empire* (1968), pp. 51–52. A parallel American study—Joseph R. Levenson and H. Franz Schurmann, *China: An Interpretive History, From the Beginnings to the Fall of Han* (1969)—does not even mention Granet.

18. Of the many crucial passages, let me quote just one example (from p. 170): "This religious life of the Chinese people is inspired by a few simple and deep-lying beliefs, the heritage of an ancient peasant past; they provide a meaning in life for the humblest Chinese; among the more cultivated, religious feeling is manifested in an effort of inner cultivation pursued within the framework of national traditions."

19. For some pertinent comments on the Redfieldian approach, see Tambiah 1970: 3–4, 367–77.

20. And if he were to confine himself to the texts he might be seriously misled. One can too easily slip into the fallacy: text-elite, oral culture-peasantry. The matter is, of course, vastly more complex.

21. For an early example see Kulp 1925: 308. More recently Norma Diamond has written (1969: 84–85): "The folk traditions and the literary traditions of China are inextricably combined in the total belief system. . . . The religious life of K'un Shen cannot be discussed in terms of a fixed and systematically elaborated doctrine; it can only be seen as a totality of eclectic practices and beliefs which to the villager's mind presents an integrated whole."

22. Note the passage in Chan 1953: 144, where he remarks upon the neglect by Chinese writers of the topic of the "religion of the masses": "Not a single book on Chinese folk religion has been published in the last five decades. . . . For information about the religion of the Chinese masses, we still have to rely on Maspero, Soothill, Hodous, Doré, Day, Shryock and Latourette." Certainly Francis L. K. Hsu has added considerably to our store of knowledge of popular Chinese religion in *Under the Ancestors' Shadow* (1948) and *Religion, Science, and Human Crises* (1952), but he appears up to recently to have been an exception.

23. But it must be noticed that Chan (*ibid.*: 142) defines "enlightened" and "masses" in an unconventional way. "By the masses is meant the 85 percent of the Chinese people who are devout but ignorant. By the enlightened is meant the intelligentsia and the illiterate farmers, fishermen and similar humble folks who may often use a smaller vocabulary but often express greater wisdom."

24. Note how this sort of characterization in turn affects the view formed by Western scholars. See, for example, H. Smith 1970: 109. "We must first distinguish between the views of the peasants and those of the intelligentsia. Peasants believed the unseen world to be peopled by innumerable spirits, both benign (*shen*) and malevolent (*kuei*), who could dwell in idols and natural objects and be used or warded off by magic and sacrifice."

25. Cf. the brief discussion on the possible connections between gentry thought and the ideas associated with such things as traditional Chinese "boxing" in Wakeman 1966: 27–28. And see Muramatsu 1960 and Dunstheimer 1972 for some relevant data.

26. The systematic interpenetration between town and country and the channels for the movement of ideas and practices back and forth between them are best seen in the work of G. William Skinner, in his articles "Marketing and Social Structure in Rural China, Part I" (1964, esp. p. 40), and "Chinese Peasants and the Closed Community: An Open and Shut Case" (1971, esp. pp. 272–74). See also Freedman 1974 [Essay 19 above].

27. Shryock (1931: 14) mentions the extension of the practice into the Republican pe-

riod. See also Ch'en Ta 1939: 239. On the implication of religion in administrative matters, see Balazs 1965: 63–64 (on Wang Hui-tsu) and Giles 1882: 163–68. And see Hsiao 1960: 22–35 and Bodde and Morris 1967: 271–78, 288–92.

28. The generalization is not meant to exclude the possibility of special contexts in which Taoist and Buddhist priests were held in high esteem and accorded high status.

21. *Sociology in China*

1. Hsu 1944: 12. The very next sentence shows the Chinese perspective: "The author is of the impression that these two terms are also merging into each other in the U.S.A."

2. Wang Yü-ch'üan 1936: 360. I have also been able to consult an unpublished paper, by Dr. Robert M. Marsh, entitled "The Development of Sociology in China." I am most grateful to Dr. Marsh.

3. The English version of the Ting Hsien materials is Gamble 1954.

4. See Fried 1954 and 1958. I have drawn heavily on these two papers.

5. Kulp 1925. Fried (1954: 18) seems to me to underestimate the influence exerted by Kulp on later studies.

6. See several of the papers in Beasley and Pulleyblank 1961.

7. On the literature on these topics see Levy 1949.

8. Some of these treatises were very naive. As an example of a good one see Hou You-ing 1933.

9. For a full account see Skinner 1951.

10. For a Norwegian anthropologist's account of this activity see Gjessing 1956. Gjessing visited China in mid-1954; at that time field research was only in its planning stage, but there was great activity in the Central Institute for National Minorities, Peking. Cf. Hsu 1961: 130.

11. See Feuerwerker and Cheng 1961, and *Revue bibliographique de sinologie*, 1 (1957) and 2 (1959). Before this article was in proof I had not managed to see Hawtin 1958. At p. 168 Mrs. Hawtin says that "social science as an accepted discipline at the universities . . . had been eliminated in 1952. . . ." This is an extremely valuable paper and could well provide the basis for a large-scale treatment of Fei and his part in contemporary Chinese intellectual life.

12. See "Professor Ch'en Ta" 1957: 6. And see the paper by Ch'en Ta (1957) sent to the 30th meeting of the International Institute of Statistics in Stockholm.

13. On the present position of the social sciences in the People's Republic of China, see Feinberg 1961: 93 and Lindbeck, 1961: 132. Cf. Hsu 1961. The only interesting work of a sociological character which I know to have been published in mainland China after the end of the Hundred Flowers is contained in the journal *Hsia-men ta-hsüeh hsüeh-pao, she-hui k'o-hsüeh pan*. No. 1 (1957), came out during the Hundred Flowers (it contains an important paper by Chang Chen-ch'ien et al.) but the two later issues, no. 2 (1957) and no. 1 (1958), fall within the most recent period of relative silence. No. 1 (1958) contains a paper by Chuang Wei-chi et al., which is remarkable for its being based upon field research (conducted in 1956–57). The approach is of course cautious. In the discussion on the clan and lineage registers collected in the field various objections which might be raised against using this feudal material (including the argument that reading it might be harmful) are countered. I have to thank Mrs. Hope M. Wright for work on this and other Chinese material. A considerable number of publications (mainly articles) have appeared in Communist China dealing with "survey research," which is largely of an economic character. I am not, alas, in a position to evaluate them, although it is clear from their titles that their sociological content is likely to be very limited. The people who have done the surveys have not been sociologists but party-men and administrators to some extent following a pattern of practically oriented rural research laid down by Mao Tse-tung's prewar studies. Having recently discussed this kind of writing with Professor G. William Skinner and Professor Morton H. Fried (to both of whom I am very grateful for information) I am under the impression that it would be worth somebody's while to collect all this material and submit it to a careful scrutiny.

22. *A Chinese Phase in Social Anthropology*

1. I am indebted to Mrs. Hope M. Wright for help with some of the Chinese sources to which I have referred and to Professor G. William Skinner and my wife for critical comments on early drafts of the lecture. I have not attempted in this published version to meet all the criticisms and answer all the questions raised by colleagues, but I have added a few afterthoughts in the notes.

2. In 1944 Radcliffe-Brown wrote (1958: 100): "In the last ten years, field studies by social anthropologists have been carried out on a town in Massachusetts, a town in Mississippi, a French Canadian community, County Clare in Ireland, villages in Japan and China. Such studies of communities in civilized countries, carried out by trained investigators, will play an increasingly large part in the social anthropology of the future." And cf. the famous passage in "On Social Structure" where communities emerge as societies (1952b: 193—94).

Professor Leslie White was another anthropological visitor and adviser to China in the 1930's. Since he spoke from an American platform his recommendations (1937) ranged very widely, but insofar as field research on Han Chinese was concerned (pp. 127, 131) he laid the emphasis on local communities. White refers to the possibilities of library studies, but they are of a vaguely cultural character and seem to bear little on the kinds of historical problems I touch on later in this lecture.

3. See Great Britain, Treasury, University Grants Committee 1961. Some of my sinological friends have suggested to me that it is important to make clear a distinction between two kinds of opposition to the Hayter report on the part of orientalists. Some orientalists spurn the advances of the social scientists. They will have none of them. Others, while welcoming cooperation, are worried lest the "training" in orientalism given, under the pressure of new fashions, to social scientists be superficial. My friends, needless to say, are in the second camp; I understand their anxiety, but I hope that it does not inhibit tendencies to experiment with the new human material being offered them.

4. For a sociologist's charitable view of the role of fieldwork in British social anthropology see MacRae 1961: 35.

5. Firth 1938. This volume also contains translations of some of Malinowski's writings on culture.

6. May I draw the attention of nonanthropologists to Mair 1957? This book offers the clearest statement I know of what social anthropologists can and cannot do when they give their minds to practical affairs. It is sometimes asserted (and in fact the statement was made by a sinologue immediately after this lecture was given) that anthropologists are free of the impulse to do good which sociologists have built into them by virtue of the history of their subject. Certainly, British social anthropology has always harbored ambitions to be of use. Malinowski and Radcliffe-Brown are vividly remembered by colonial administrators who know little of their theoretical work. I quote a mandarin of the present senior generation: ". . . the moral sense of the satisfaction it offers to the desire to make some addition to human welfare which every social scientist worth his salt carries within him" (Fortes 1953: 8).

7. Dr. Bailey (1962) and Dr. Mayer (1962) have kindly shown me how they see the role of the social anthropologist in the study of India. Their ambitions in the Indian context are certainly lower than mine in the Chinese, but they are thinking about a country in which other kinds of social scientist are also busily at work.

8. Cf. some similar remarks made in the Australian context in Barnes 1960.

9. Until I was on the point of sending this lecture to the printer I had not seen Clifford Geertz's paper "Studies in Peasant Life: Community and Society" (1962). Geertz touches on a number of the points I raise and provides a guide to what anthropologists have been writing in recent years on "peasant" organization and culture. It is useful to have an American statement of some of the problems involved in studying civilization from the anthropological standpoint. (Other American views are to be found in the discussion on S. N. Eisenstadt's paper referred to in the text.)

23. *What Social Science Can Do for Chinese Studies*

1. In moving into the modern world of scholarship, sinology had to free itself from "the incubus of Orientalism" by learning how to write history. See A. F. Wright 1960: 245ff. By the same token, it has had to take account of social science ideas (*ibid.*) and has shown itself willing to seek sociological help, as some of the volumes published under the auspices of the Committee on Chinese Thought of the Association for Asian Studies witness. See especially Fairbank 1957 and Nivison and Wright 1959.

2. On this and a number of other points touched on in this talk, cf. Freedman 1963a [Essay 22 above].

24. *Why China?*

1. I have had the advantage of discussing this point and a number of others with Mr. David Wilson of the *China Quarterly*, and I am beholden to him for his advice on the literature of the Cultural Revolution. My conclusions, however, are not always the same as his. There were Red Guards and Red Guards (see Mehnert 1969 for a fascinating analysis of a group of ultra-leftists), some more rationally political than others. I have tried to characterize the movement as a whole. Schurmann (1968: 522–23) says that it is "hard to find much of the positive side of utopianism, namely the promise of a bright future just in the offing, in the literature of the Cultural Revolution"; and he goes on to speculate that "the negative side of the utopianism, its hostility against an existing order, which is clearly present in the Cultural Revolution" may fit with the fact that that Revolution rested primarily on students (in the American sense of the term). "In many ways, the negative utopianism of the Cultural Revolution is similar to that of student movements throughout the world. . . . Such movements attack social orders but are incapable of projecting a new order."

2. See B. E. Ward 1965, 1966, and 1967. The American scholar is Eugene N. Anderson.

3. It has resulted in one paper (Pratt 1960); that paper is so rich that one regrets Miss Pratt's failure to publish more.

4. Topley 1969 is an indispensable guide to the research done in the New Territories and other parts of Hong Kong. And see Berkowitz and Poon 1969. The most important work so far published on the New Territories research is Aijmer 1967, Baker 1968, Potter 1968, Pratt 1960, and B. E. Ward 1965, 1966, 1967. See Topley 1969 for fuller bibliographical lists.

5. See M. L. Cohen 1967, 1968, 1969, and 1970a; Diamond 1969; Fried 1966; Gallin 1960, 1966, 1967, and 1968; Pasternak 1968a, 1968b, and 1969; A. P. Wolf 1966, 1968, and 1970; M. Wolf 1968 and 1970.

6. I am familiar with Wang Sung-hsing 1967.

7. In Singapore I saw some aspects of the geomancy of burial (Freedman 1957a: 206) but was incapable, in that urban setting, of penetrating the subject.

8. I wrote this before seeing Plath 1969, which indicates Japan as another source.

References Cited

References Cited

Addison, James Thayer. 1925. Chinese Ancestor Worship: A Study of Its Meaning and Its Relations with Christianity. Shanghai.

Ahern, Emily M. 1974. "Affines and the Rituals of Kinship," in Arthur P. Wolf, ed., Religion and Ritual in Chinese Society, 279–307. Stanford, Calif.

Aijmer, Lars Göran. 1964. The Dragon Boat Festival on the Hupeh-Hunan Plain, Central China: A Study in the Ceremonialism of the Transplantation of Rice. Stockholm (Ethnographical Museum of Sweden, Monograph Series, 9).

————. 1967. "Expansion and Extension in Hakka Society," Journal of the Hong Kong Branch of the Royal Asiatic Society, 7, 42–79.

————. 1968a. "Being Caught by a Fishnet: On Fengshui in Southeastern China," Journal of the Hong Kong Branch of the Royal Asiatic Society, 8, 74–81.

————. 1968b. "A Structural Approach to Chinese Ancestor Worship," Bijdragen tot de taal-, land- en volkenkunde van Nederlandsch-Indië, 124, no. 1, 91–98.

Alabaster, Ernest. 1899. Notes and Commentaries on Chinese Criminal Law and Cognate Topics, with Special Relation to Ruling Cases. London.

Annual Departmental Reports (Straits Settlements).

Athmulathmudali, L. W., and G. W. Bartholomew. 1961. "The Women's Charter," University of Malaya Law Review, 3, no. 2, 316–30.

Ayscough, Florence Wheelock. 1925. A Chinese Mirror: Being Reflections of the Reality Behind Appearances. Boston.

Bailey, Frederick G. 1962. "The Scope of Social Anthropology in the Study of Indian Society," in Triloki N. Madan and Gopāla Śarana, eds., Indian Anthropology: Essays in Memory of D. N. Majumdar, 254–65. Bombay and New York.

Baker, Hugh D. R. 1966. "The Five Great Clans of the New Territories," Journal of the Hong Kong Branch of the Royal Asiatic Society, 6, 25–48.

————. 1968. A Chinese Lineage Village: Sheung Shui [i.e. Shang-shui, Hong Kong]. Stanford, Calif.

————. 1977. "Extended Kinship in the Traditional City," in G. William Skinner, ed., The City in Late Imperial China, 499–518. Stanford, Calif.

Balazs, Etienne. 1965. Political Theory and Administrative Reality in Traditional China. London.

Ball, James Dyer. 1904. Things Chinese: or, Notes Connected with China, 4th ed. London.

Baller, Frederick W. 1921. (tr. and ed.) The Sacred Edict; with a Translation of the Colloquial Rendering, 5th ed. Shanghai.

Barnes, John A. 1960. "Future Developments in Anthropological Studies," *Australian Journal of Psychology*, 12, no. 1, 21–33.

Barnett, Kenneth M. A. 1962. Report on the 1961 Census, vol. 2. Hong Kong.

Beardsley, Richard K. 1965. "Cultural Anthropology: Prehistoric and Contemporary Aspects," in John Whitney Hall and R. K. Beardsley, eds., Twelve Doors to Japan, 48–120. New York.

Beasley, William Gerald, and Edwin George Pulleyblank. 1961. (eds.) Historians of China and Japan. London (University of London, School of Oriental and African Studies, Historical Writing on the Peoples of Asia, 3).

Beattie, John. 1964. Other Cultures: Aims, Methods and Achievements in Social Anthropology. London and New York.

Benda, Harry J. 1962. "The Structure of Southeast Asian History: Some Preliminary Observations," *Journal of Southeast Asian History*, 3, no. 1, 106–38.

Berkowitz, Morris Ira, and Eddie K. K. Poon (P'an Kuo-chü). 1969. Hong Kong Studies: A Bibliography. Hong Kong.

Beveridge, William Henry. 1949. "The London School of Economics and the University of London," in Margaret Isabel Cole, ed., The Webbs and Their Work, 41–53. London.

Bloch, Maurice. 1968. "Astrology and Writing in Madagascar," in Jack Goody, ed., Literacy in Traditional Societies, 277–97. Cambridge, Eng.

Blythe, Wilfred L. 1950. "The Interplay of Chinese Secret and Political Societies in Malaya, Parts 1 and 2," *Eastern World*, 4, no. 3, 14–15; 4, no. 4, 10–13.

Bodde, Derk, and Clarence Morris. 1967. Law in Imperial China. Cambridge, Mass. (Harvard Studies in East Asian Law, 1).

Bodman, Nicholas C. 1955. Spoken Amoy Hokkien. Kuala Lumpur.

Boxer, Baruch. 1968. "Space, Change and Feng-shui in Tsuen Wan's Urbanization [i.e. Ch'üan-wan, Hong Kong]," *Journal of Asian and African Studies*, 3, nos. 3/4, 226–40.

Braddell, Roland St. John. 1921. "Chinese Marriages, as Regarded by the Supreme Court of the Straits Settlements," *Journal of the Straits Branch of the Royal Asiatic Society*, no. 83, 153–65.

————. 1931. The Law of the Straits Settlements: A Commentary, 2d ed., vol. 1. Singapore.

Bredon, Juliet. 1930. Chinese New Year Festivals. Shanghai.

Bryan, Robert T., Jr. 1925. An Outline of Chinese Civil Law. Shanghai.

Buck, John Lossing. 1937. Land Utilization in China: A Study of 16,786 Farms in 168 Localities, and 32,256 Farm Families in Twenty-Two Provinces in China, 1929–1933, 3 vols. Nanking.

Buckley, Charles B. 1902. An Anecdotal History of Old Times in Singapore, 2 vols. Singapore.

Buxbaum, David C. 1963. "Freedom of Marriage in a Pluralistic Society: Re Loh Toh Met, Dec'd., Kong Lai Fong v. Loh Peng Heng," *Malaya Law Review*, 5, no. 2, 383–87.

————. 1966. "Chinese Family Law in a Common Law Setting: A Note on the Institutional Environment and the Substantive Family Law of the Chinese in Singapore and Malaysia," *Journal of Asian Studies*, 25, no. 4, 621–44.

————. 1968. Some Aspects of Substantive Family Law and Social Change in Rural China (1896–1967), with a Case Study of a North Taiwan Village. Ph.D. dissertation in Political Science, University of Washington [University Microfilms Publ. 69–1148].

Caine, Sydney. 1963. The History of the Foundation of the London School of Economics and Political Science. London.

Cammann, Schuyler. 1952. China's Dragon Robes. New York.

Campbell, Persia C. 1923. Chinese Coolie Emigration to Countries within the British Empire. London.

Cartier, Michel. 1970. "Une tradition urbaine: les villes dans la Chine antique et médiévale," *Annales: économies, sociétés, civilisations*, 25, no. 4, 831–41.

Cator, Writser J. 1936. The Economic Position of the Chinese in the Netherlands Indies. Oxford.

Cavenagh, Orfeur. 1884. Reminiscences of an Indian Official. London.

Chan, Wing-tsit (Ch'en Jung-chieh). 1953. Religious Trends in Modern China. New York (American Council of Learned Societies, Lectures on the History of Religions, new series 3).

————. 1967. (tr. and annot.) Reflections on Things at Hand: The Neo-Confucian Anthology, compiled by Chu Hsi and Lü Tsu-ch'ien. New York (Columbia University, Department of History, Records of Civilization: Sources and Studies, 75).

Chang Chen-ch'ien et al. 1957. "Fu-chien chu yao ch'iao ch'ü nung ts'un ching chi t'an lun: ch'iao ch'ü nung ts'un tiao ch'a chih i" (A study of the rural economy of the principal home districts of the Fukien Overseas Chinese), *Hsia-men ta hsüeh pao; she hui k'o hsüeh pan*, 1957, no. 1, 31–78.

Chang, Chung-li. 1955. The Chinese Gentry: Studies on Their Role in Nineteenth Century Chinese Society. Seattle.

Ch'ang-chiang jih-pao (Hankow).

Ch'en, C. J. 1958. "Chinese Social Scientists," *Twentieth Century*, 163, no. 976, 511–22.

Ch'en Chung-min. 1967. "Chin-chiang-ts'o ti tsu hsien tsung pai yü shih tsu tsu chih" (Ancestor worship and lineage organization in Chin-chiang-ts'o), *Chung yang yen chiu yüan, Min tsu hsüeh yen chiu so chi k'an*, 23, 192–224.

Ch'en Ta (Chen Ta). 1939. Emigrant Communities in South China: A Study of Overseas Migration and Its Influence on Standards of Living and Social Change, Bruno Lasker, ed. London.

———. 1946. Population in Modern China. Chicago.

———. 1957. "New China's Population Census of 1953 and Its Relations to National Reconstruction and Demographic Research," *Bulletin de l'Institut international de statistique*, 36, 2e livraison, 255–71.

Chen, Theodore H. E. (Ch'en Hsi-en). 1960. Thought Reform of the Chinese Intellectuals. Hong Kong.

Chesneaux, Jean. 1960. "Les transformations sociales" (Social transformations), in Université libre de Bruxelles, Institut de sociologie Solvay, Centre d'étude des pays de l'Est *with* Centre national pour l'étude des pays à régime communiste, joint eds., Le régime et les institutions de la République populaire chinoise (The government and institutions of the People's Republic of China), 97–114. Brussels.

Chia Cheng Sit. 1899. "The Language of the Babas," *Straits Chinese Magazine*, 3, no. 9, 11–15.

Chin, Ai-li Sung (Ch'en Shen Ai-li). 1970. "Family Relations in Modern Chinese Fiction," in Maurice Freedman, ed., Family and Kinship in Chinese Society, 87–120. Stanford, Calif.

China [Republic], Laws, statutes, etc. 1931. The Civil Code of the Republic of China, Ching-lin Hsia et al., trs. Shanghai.

———. 1936. The Criminal Code of the Republic of China, Ching-lin Hsia and Boyer P. H. Chu, trs. Shanghai.

China [Republic], Ssu fa hsing cheng pu (Ministry of Justice). [1930] 1965. Min shang shih hsi kuan tiao ch'a pao kao lu (Report on customary practices in civil and commercial affairs), 2 vols. Nanking. German version published 1965 as Die amtliche Sammlung chinesischer Rechtsgewohnheiten: Untersuchungsbericht über Gewohnheiten in Zivil- und Handelssachen (The collection of Chinese customary law: A research report on customary law in civil and commercial affairs), 3 vols., Eduard Josef M. Kroker, tr. and ed., Bergen-Enkheim.

China [Republic], Supreme Court Civil Cases. 1922. "In Reply to the High Court of Justice, Shangsi [*sic*], Supreme Court, August 11, 1919," *China Law Review* (English Side), 1, no. 3, 138–39.

China Mail (Hong Kong).

China Weekly Review (Shanghai).

"Chinese Emigrants." 1833. *Chinese Repository*, 2, no. 5, 230–32.

Chinese Soviet Republic, Laws, Statutes, etc. 1934. Fundamental Laws of the Chinese Soviet Republic, Bela Kun, ed. London and New York.

Chiu, Vermier Yantak (Chao P'ing). 1966. Marriage Laws and Customs of China. Hong Kong.

Chuang Wei-chi et al. 1958. "Fu-chien Chin-chiang chuan ch'ü hua ch'iao shih tiao ch'a pao kao" (Report on the history of overseas emigration from Chin-chiang special district in Fukien), *Hsia-men ta hsüeh hsüeh pao; she hui k'o hsüeh pan*, 1958, no. 1, 93–127.

Ch'ü T'ung-tsu. [1947] 1961. Chung-kuo fa lü yü Chung-kuo she hui. Shanghai. Rev. and enl. English version published 1961 as Law and Society in Traditional China, The Hague.

———. 1962. Local Government in China under the Ch'ing. Cambridge, Mass. (Harvard East Asian series, 9).

Coates, Austin. 1968. Myself a Mandarin. London.

Cohen, Jerome Alan. 1966. "Chinese Mediation on the Eve of Modernization," *California Law Review*, 54, no. 3, 1201–26.

Cohen, Myron L. 1967. "Variations in Complexity among Chinese Family Groups: The Impact of Modernization," *Transactions of the New York Academy of Sciences*, 2d series 29, no. 5, 638–44.

———. 1968. "A Case Study of Chinese Family Economy and Development," *Journal of Asian and African Studies*, 3, nos. 3/4, 161–80.

———. 1969. "Agnatic Kinship in South Taiwan," *Ethnology*, 8, no. 2, 167–82.

———. 1970a. "Developmental Process in the Chinese Domestic Group," in Maurice Freedman, ed., Family and Kinship in Chinese Society, 21–36. Stanford, Calif.

———. 1970b. The Politics of Religious Organizations in Rural China: A Case Study from South Taiwan. Paper presented at the 22d annual meeting of the Association for Asian Studies, San Francisco, 3–5 April 1970.

———. 1976. House United, House Divided: The Chinese Family in Taiwan. New York.

Comber, Leon. 1956. "Chinese Secret Societies in Malaya; an Introduction," *Journal of the Malayan Branch of the Royal Asiatic Society*, 29, pt. 1, 146–62.

———. 1959. Chinese Secret Societies in Malaya: A Survey of the Triad Society from 1800 to 1900. Locust Valley, N.Y. (Association for Asian Studies Monographs, 6).

Coppel, Charles. 1972. "The Position of the Chinese in the Philippines, Malaysia and Indonesia," in The Chinese in Indonesia, the Philippines and Malaysia, 16–29. London (Minority Rights Group Reports, 10).

[Cormack, Annie] Mrs. James G. Cormack. 1935. Everyday Customs in China, 4th ed. Edinburgh.

Coughlin, Richard J. 1960. Double Identity: The Chinese in Modern Thailand. Hong Kong.

Crissman, Lawrence W. 1967. "The Segmentary Structures of Urban Overseas Chinese Communities," *Man*, new (2d) series 2, no. 2, 185–204.

Crook, Isabel, and David Crook. 1959. Revolution in a Chinese Village: Ten Mile Inn [i.e. Shih-li-tien, She *hsien*, Hopei]. London.

Danielli, Mary. 1952. "The Geomancer in China, with Some Reference to Geomancy as Observed in Madagascar," *Folk-Lore*, 63, no. 4, 204–26.

Dawson, Raymond Stanley, 1967. The Chinese Chameleon: An Analysis of European Conceptions of Chinese Civilization. London and New York.

de Bary, William Theodore, et al. 1960. (comps.) Sources of Chinese Tradition. New York (Records of Civilization: Sources and Studies, 55).

De Korne, John Cornelius. 1941. The Fellowship of Goodness (T'ung shan she): A Study in Contemporary Chinese Religion. Grand Rapids, Mich.

Diamond, Norma J. 1969. K'un Shen, a Taiwan Village. New York.

Djamour, Judith. 1959. Malay Kinship and Marriage in Singapore. London (London School of Economics and Political Science, Monographs on Social Anthropology, 21).

——. 1966. The Muslim Matrimonial Court in Singapore. London (London School of Economics and Political Science, Monographs on Social Anthropology, 31).

Dobby, E. H. G. 1953. "Resettlement Transforms Malaya: A Case-History of Relocating the Population of an Asian Plural Society," *Economic Development and Cultural Change*, 1, no. 3, 163–89.

Dols, Joseph. 1915/16. "La vie chinoise dans la province de Kansou" (Chinese life in Kansu), *Anthropos*, 10/11, nos. 1/2, 68–74; 10/11, nos. 3/4, 466–503; 10/11, nos. 5/6, 726–57.

Doolittle, Justus. [1865] 1868. Social Life of the Chinese: With Some Account of Their Religious, Governmental, Educational, and Business Customs and Opinions, with Special but not Exclusive Reference to Fuhchau, 2 vols. New York. Rev. ed. published 1868 as Social Life of the Chinese: A Daguerreotype of Daily Life in China, Paxton Hood, ed. London.

Doré, Henri. 1914. Researches into Chinese Superstitions, vol. 1, M. Kennelly, tr. Shanghai.

——. 1926 [1970]. Manuel des superstitions chinoises; ou Petit indicateur des superstitions les plus communes en Chine. Shanghai. Reprinted 1970, Paris.

Dore, Ronald P. 1958. City Life in Japan: A Study of a Tokyo Ward. London.

Douglas, Robert Kennaway. 1901. Society in China. London.

Dubreuil, René. 1910. De la condition des Chinois et de leur rôle économique en Indo-Chine. Bar-sur-Seine.

Dunstheimer, Guillaume G. H. 1972. "Some Religious Aspects of Secret Societies," in Jean Chesneaux, ed., Popular Movements and Secret Societies in China, 1840–1950, 23–28. Stanford, Calif.

Durkheim, Emile, and Marcel Mauss. 1963. Primitive Classification, Rodney Needham, tr. and ed. Chicago and London.

Eberhard, Wolfram. 1958. Chinese Festivals. London and New York.

———. 1963. "Auspicious Marriages: A Statistical Study of a Chinese Custom," Sociologus, neue (2.) Folge 13, Heft 1, 49–55.

———. 1965. (tr. and ed.) Folktales of China, rev. ed. Chicago and London.

———. 1966. (ed.) Erzählungsgut aus Südost-China. Berlin (Fabula: Zeitschrift für Erzählforschung, Supplement-Serie, Reihe A: Texte, 6).

———. 1971. "Studies in Chinese Religion: 1920–1932," Alide Eberhard, tr., in Wolfram Eberhard, Moral and Social Values of the Chinese: Collected Essays, 335–99. Taipei (Chinese Materials and Research Aids Service Center, occasional series, 6).

Egerod, Søren. 1959. "A Sampling of Chungshan Hakka," in S. Egerod and Else Glahn, eds., Studia Serica Bernhard Karlgren Dedicata (Sinological studies dedicated to Bernhard Karlgren), 36–54. Copenhagen.

Eisenstadt, Schmuel N. 1961. "Anthropological Studies of Complex Societies." Current Anthropology, 2, no. 3, 201–22.

Eitel, Ernest John. 1873. Feng-shui: or, The Rudiments of Natural Science in China. Hong Kong.

Eitzen, D. Stanley, 1968. "Two Minorities: The Jews of Poland and the Chinese of the Philippines," Jewish Journal of Sociology, 10, no. 2, 221–40.

Elliott, Alan J. A. 1955. Chinese Spirit-Medium Cults in Singapore. London (London School of Economics and Political Science, Monographs on Social Anthropology, 14).

Elvin, Mark. 1970. "The Last Thousand Years of Chinese History: Changing Patterns in Land Tenure," Modern Asian Studies, 4, pt. 2, 97–114.

Etiemble, René. 1964. Connaissons-nous la Chine? Paris.

Evans-Pritchard, Edward Evan. 1965. The Position of Women in Primitive Societies, and Other Essays in Social Anthropology. London and New York.

Fabre, Alfred. 1935. "Avril au pays des aïeux," Collectanea Commissionis Synodalis, 8, 111–41.

———. 1937. Film de la vie chinoise: proverbes et locutions. Hong Kong.

Fairbank, John King. 1957. (ed.) Chinese Thought and Institutions. Chicago.

———. 1968. "A Preliminary Framework," in J. K. Fairbank, ed., The Chinese World Order: Traditional China's Foreign Relations, 1–19. Cambridge, Mass.

Favre, Benoît. 1933. Les sociétés secrètes en Chine: origine, rôle historique, situation actuelle (The origin, historical role, and present position of secret societies in China). Paris.

Fei Hsiao-tung (Fei Hsiao-t'ung). 1939. Peasant Life in China: A Field Study of Country Life in the Yangtze Valley. New York.

———. 1946. "Peasantry and Gentry: An Interpretation of Chinese Social Structure and Its Changes," *American Journal of Sociology*, 52, no. 1, 1–17.

———. 1953. China's Gentry: Essays in Rural-Urban Relations, rev. ed., Margaret Park Redfield, ed. Chicago.

Feinberg, Betty. 1961. "Report on the AAAS Symposium," *China Quarterly*, no. 6, 91–97.

Felix, Alfonso, Jr. 1966. "How We Stand," in A. Felix, Jr., ed., The Chinese in the Philippines, 1570–1770, vol. 1, 1–14. Manila.

Feng, Han-yi (Feng Han-chi), and John Knight Shryock. 1950. "Marriage Customs in the Vicinity of I-ch'ang [Hupeh]," *Harvard Journal of Asiatic Studies*, 13, nos. 3/4, 362–430.

Feuchtwang, Stephan. [1965] 1974. An Anthropological Analysis of Chinese Geomancy. M.A. dissertation in Anthropology, University of London [London School of Economics and Political Science]. Published 1974, Vientiane.

Feuerwerker, Albert, and Sally Cheng. 1961. Chinese Communist Studies of Modern Chinese History. Cambridge, Mass. (Harvard East Asian monographs, 11).

Fielde, Adele Marion. 1884. Pagoda Shadows: Studies from Life in China. Boston.

———. 1894. A Corner of Cathay: Studies from Life among the Chinese. New York.

Fincher, John Howard. 1968. "Political Provincialism and the National Revolution," in Mary Clabaugh Wright, ed., China in Revolution: The First Phase, 1900–1913, 185–226. New Haven, Conn.

Firth, Raymond W. 1938. "Chung-kuo nung ts'un she hui t'uan chieh hsing ti yen chiu; i ko fang fa lun ti chien i" (Social cohesion in rural Chinese society: A proposal concerning research methodology), Fei Hsiao-t'ung, tr., *She-hui-hsüeh chieh*, 10, 249–57.

———. 1944. "The Future of Social Anthropology," *Man*, 44, Article 8, 19–22.

———. 1948. Report on Social Science Research in Malaya. Singapore.

———. 1951. Elements of Social Organization. London.

———. 1955. The Fate of the Soul: An Interpretation of Some Primitive Concepts. Cambridge, Eng.

———. 1963–64. "A Brief History (1913–1963)," in London School of Economics and Political Science, Department of Anthropology, Programme of Courses, 1963–64. London.

FitzGerald, Charles Patrick. 1941. The Tower of Five Glories: A Study of the Min Chia of Ta Li, Yunnan. London.

————. 1965. The Third China: The Chinese Communities in South-East Asia. Melbourne.

————. 1969. "Religion in China," in Guy Wint, ed., Asia Handbook, rev. ed., 389–94. Harmondsworth, Eng.

————. 1972. The Southern Expansion of the Chinese People: "Southern Fields and Southern Ocean." Canberra, London, and New York.

FitzGerald, Stephen A. 1972. China and the Overseas Chinese: A Study of Peking's Changing Policy, 1949–1970. Cambridge, Eng.

Fortes, Meyer. 1953. "Preface," in Fernando Henriques, Family and Colour in Jamaica, 3–8. London.

————. 1958. "Introduction," in Jack Goody, ed., The Developmental Cycle in Domestic Groups, 1–14. Cambridge, Eng. (Cambridge Papers in Social Anthropology, 1).

————. 1965. "Some Reflections on Ancestor Worship in Africa," in Meyer Fortes and Germaine Dieterlen, eds., African Systems of Thought: Studies Presented and Discussed at the Third International African Seminar in Salisbury, December 1960, 122–44. London.

————. 1967. "Totem and Taboo" [Presidential Address 1966], *Proceedings of the Royal Anthropological Institute of Great Britain and Ireland for 1966, 5–22.*

Frazer, James George. 1911a. The Golden Bough: A Study in Magic and Religion. Part 1, The Magic Art and the Evolution of Kings, 3d ed., vol. 1. London.

————. 1911b. The Golden Bough: A Study in Magic and Religion. Part 2, Taboo and the Perils of the Soul, 3d ed. London.

Freedman, Maurice. 1948. The Sociology of Race Relations in South-East Asia with Special Reference to British Malaya. Unpublished M.A. thesis in Anthropology, University of London [London School of Economics and Political Science].

————. 1950. "Colonial Law and Chinese Society," *Journal of the Royal Anthropological Institute of Great Britain and Ireland, 80, pts. 1/2,* 97–126.

————. 1953. "The Penhas Case: Mixed and Unmixed Marriage in Singapore," *Modern Law Review, 16, no. 3, 366–68.*

————. 1956. *Review of* The Chinese Gentry: Studies on Their Role in Nineteenth-Century Chinese Society, by Chung-li Chang, *Pacific Affairs, 29, no. 1, 78–80.*

————. 1957a. Chinese Family and Marriage in Singapore. London (Colonial Office, Colonial Research Studies, 20).

————. 1957b. "Religion and Society in South-Eastern China," *Man, 57,* Article 62, 56–57.

————. 1958. Lineage Organization in Southeastern China. London (London School of Economics and Political Science, Monographs on Social Anthropology, 18).

————. 1959a. "The Handling of Money: A Note on the Background to the Economic Sophistication of Overseas Chinese," *Man*, 59, Article 89, 64–65.

———. 1959b. "Jews, Chinese and Some Others" [*Review of* The Jews: Social Patterns of an American Group, by Marshall Sklare; Chinese Society in Thailand: An Analytical History, by G. William Skinner; *and* Coloured Minorities in Britain, by Sydney Collins], *British Journal of Sociology*, 10, no. 1, 61–70.

———. 1959c. "Religion et adaptation sociale chez les Chinois de Singapour," *Archives de sociologie des religions*, 7, 89–103.

———. 1960. "Immigrants and Associations: Chinese in Nineteenth-Century Singapore," *Comparative Studies in Society and History*, 3, no. 1, 25–48.

———. 1962a. "Chinese Kinship and Marriage in Early Singapore," *Journal of Southeast Asian History*, 3, no. 2, 65–73.

———. 1962b. "Sociology in China: A Brief Survey," *China Quarterly*, no. 10, 166–73.

———. 1962c. Review of Religion in Chinese Society, by C. K. Yang, *Journal of Asian Studies*, 21, no. 4, 534–35.

———. 1963a. "A Chinese Phase in Social Anthropology," *British Journal of Sociology*, 14, no. 1, 1–19.

———. 1963b [1976]. A Report on Social Research in the New Territories. Hong Kong. Published 1976: *Journal of the Hong Kong Branch of the Royal Asiatic Society* 16, 191–261.

———. 1964a. "The Family under Chinese Communism," *Political Quarterly*, 35, no. 3, 342–50.

———. 1964b. "What Social Science Can Do for Chinese Studies," *Journal of Asian Studies*, 23, no. 4, 523–29.

———. [1965] 1969. The Chinese in South-East Asia: A Longer View. London (China Society Occasional Papers, 14). Reprinted 1969 in Robert O. Tilman, ed., Man, State and Society in Contemporary Southeast Asia, 431–49. New York.

———. 1966. Chinese Lineage and Society: Fukien and Kwangtung. London (London School of Economics and Political Science, Monographs on Social Anthropology, 33).

———. 1967a. "Ancestor Worship: Two Facets of the Chinese Case," in M. Freedman, ed., Social Organization: Essays Presented to Raymond Firth, 85–103. Chicago.

———. 1967b. Rites and Duties: or, Chinese Marriage. London.

———. 1969. "Geomancy" [Presidential Address 1968], *Proceedings of the Royal Anthropological Institute of Great Britain and Ireland for 1968*, 5–15.

———. 1970. "Why China?" [Presidential Address 1969], *Proceedings of the Royal Anthropological Institute of Great Britain and Ireland for 1969*, 5–13.

———. 1972a. "China South: Reflections on Two New Books" [*Review of* The Southern Expansion of the Chinese People: "Southern Fields and Southern Ocean," by Charles Patrick FitzGerald, *and* China and the Overseas Chinese: A Study of Peking's Changing Policy, by Stephen A. FitzGerald], *Round Table*, 62, no. 248, 425–40.

———. 1972b. *Review of* The Southern Expansion of the Chinese People: "Southern Fields and Southern Ocean," by Charles Patrick Fitz-Gerald, *China Quarterly*, no. 52, 742–45.

———. 1974. "The Politics of an Old State: A View from the Chinese Lineage," in John H. R. Davis, ed., Choice and Change: Essays in Honour of Lucy Mair, 68–88. London (London School of Economics and Political Science, Monographs on Social Anthropology, 50).

———. 1975. "Sinology and the Social Sciences: Some Reflections on the Social Anthropology of China," *Ethnos*, 40, 194–211.

———. 1979. "Social and Cultural Anthropology," in Main Trends of Research in the Social and Human Sciences, Part Two, Anthropological and Historical Sciences. The Hague.

Frick, Johannes. 1952. "Hochzeitssitten von Hei-tsuei-tzu in der Provinz Ch'ing-hai (China)" (Wedding customs in the village of Hei-tsui-tzu [Hsi-ning *hsien*], Tsinghai), in Ethnographische Beiträge aus der Ch'inghai Provinz (China) (Ethnographic reports from Tsinghai), 1–102. Peking (Catholic University of Peking, Museum of Oriental Ethnology, Folklore Studies supplements, 1).

Fried, Morton H. 1953. Fabric of Chinese Society: A Study of the Social Life of a Chinese County Seat. New York.

———. 1954. "Community Studies in China," *Far Eastern Quarterly*, 14, no. 1, 11–36.

———. 1957. "The Classification of Corporate Unilineal Descent Groups," *Journal of the Royal Anthropological Institute of Great Britain and Ireland*, 87, pt. 1, 1–29.

———. 1958. "China," in Joseph S. Roucek, ed., Contemporary Sociology, 993–1012. New York.

———. 1966. "Some Political Aspects of Clanship in a Modern Chinese City [Taipei]," in Marc J. Swartz et al., eds., Political Anthropology, 285–300. Chicago.

———. 1970. "Clans and Lineages: How to Tell Them Apart and Why, with Special Reference to Chinese Society," *Bulletin of the Institute of Ethnology, Academia Sinica*, 29, 11–36.

Fung Yu-lan (Feng Yu-lan). 1949. "The Philosophy at the Basis of Traditional Chinese Society," in Filmer S. C. Northrop, ed., Ideological Differences and World Order, 18–34. New Haven, Conn.

Furnivall, John S. 1939. Netherlands India: A Study of Plural Economy. Cambridge, Eng.

———. 1942. "The Political Economy of the Tropical Far East," *Journal of the Royal Central Asian Society*, 29, pts. 3/4, 195–210.

———. 1948. Colonial Policy and Practice: A Comparative Study of Burma and Netherlands India. Cambridge, Eng.

Gallin, Bernard. 1960. "Matrilineal and Affinal Relationships of a Taiwanese Village [Hsin-hsing, Chang-hua *hsien*]," *American Anthropologist*, 62, no. 4, 632–42.

———. 1966. Hsin Hsing [Chang-hua *hsien*], Taiwan: A Chinese Village in Change. Berkeley and Los Angeles.

———. 1967. "Mediation in Changing Chinese Society in Rural Taiwan," *Journal of Asian and African Studies*, 2, nos. 1/2, 77–90.

———. 1968. "Political Factionalism and Its Impact on Chinese Village Social Organization in Taiwan," in Marc J. Swartz, ed., Local-Level Politics: Social and Cultural Perspectives, 377–400. Chicago.

Gamble, Sidney D. 1954. Ting Hsien [Hopei], A North China Rural Community. New York.

Geertz, Clifford. 1962. "Studies in Peasant Life: Community and Society," in Bernard J. Siegel, ed., Biennial Review of Anthropology 1961, 1–41. Stanford, Calif.

Gernet, Jacques. [1959] 1962. La vie quotidienne en Chine à la veille de l'invasion mongole, 1250–1276. Paris. English version published 1962 as Daily Life in China on the Eve of the Mongol Invasion, 1250–1276, Hope M. Wright, tr. London and New York.

———. 1968. Ancient China from the Beginnings to the Empire, Raymond Rudorff, tr. Berkeley and London.

Giles, Herbert A. 1876. Chinese Sketches. London.

———. "Mesmerism, Planchette, and Spiritualism in China," *Fraser's Magazine*, new (2d) series 19, 238–45.

———. 1880. Freemasonry in China. Amoy.

———. 1882. Historic China, and Other Sketches. London.

Gilpatrick, Meredith P. 1950. "The Status of Law and Lawmaking Procedure under the Kuomintang, 1925–1946," *Far Eastern Quarterly*, 10, no. 1, 38–55.

Ginsburg, Norton S. 1968. "On the Chinese Perception of a World Order," in Tang Tsou, ed., China in Crisis, vol. 2, China's Policies in Asia and America's Alternatives, 73–91. Chicago.

Gjessing, Gutorm. 1956. "Chinese Anthropology and New China's Policy toward Her Minorities," *Acta Sociologica*, 2, fasc. 1, 45–68.

Gluckman, Max, ed. 1962. Essays on the Ritual of Social Relations. Manchester, Eng.

———. 1965. Politics, Law and Ritual in Tribal Society. Chicago and Oxford.

Go Gien Tjwan. 1971. "The Changing Trade Position of the Chinese in South-East Asia," *International Social Science Journal*, 23, no. 4, 564–75.

Graham, David Crockett. 1961. Folk Religion in Southwest China. Washington, D.C. (Smithsonian miscellaneous collections, vol. 142, 2).

Granet, Marcel. [1919, 1929] 1932. Fêtes et chansons anciennes de la Chine. Paris (Bibliothèque de la Fondation Thiers fascicules, 39). Rev.

ed. published 1929, Paris. English version published 1932 as *Festivals and Songs of Ancient China*, Evangeline D. Edwards, tr., London.

———. [1922, 1951] 1975. La religion des Chinois. Paris. Rev. ed. published 1951, Paris. English version published 1975 as *The Religion of the Chinese People*, Maurice Freedman, tr. and ed., New York and Oxford.

———. 1926. Danses et légendes de la Chine ancienne, 2 vols. Paris.

———. [1929a] 1953. "L'esprit de la religion chinoise" (The spirit of Chinese religion), *Scientia* (Milano), 45, no. 205, 329–37. Reprinted 1953 in M. Granet, Etudes sociologiques sur la Chine (Sociological studies on China), 251–60, Paris.

———. [1929b] 1930. La civilisation chinoise: La vie publique et la vie privée. Paris. English version published 1930 as *Chinese Civilization*, Kathleen E. Innes and Mabel R. Brailsford, trs., London and New York.

———. 1934. La pensée chinoise (Chinese thought). Paris.

Gray, Jack Douglas. 1961. "Historical Writing in Twentieth-Century China: Notes on its Background and Development," in William Gerald Beasley and Edwin George Pulleyblank, eds., Historians of China and Japan, 186–212. London (University of London, School of Oriental and African Studies, Historical Writing on the Peoples of Asia, 3).

Gray, Jack Douglas, and Patrick Cavendish. 1968. Chinese Communism in Crisis: Maoism and the Cultural Revolution. New York.

Gray, John Henry. 1878. China: A History of the Laws, Manners and Customs of the People, 2 vols., William Gow Gregor, ed. London.

Great Britain, Colonial Office, Mui Tsai Commission. 1937. Mui Tsai in Hong Kong and Malaya, Report of Commission, Wilfred Wentworth Woods, chairman. London (Colonial no. 125).

Great Britain, Parliament, House of Lords. 1930. Appeal Cases before the House of Lords . . . , Frederick Pollack, ed. London.

Great Britain, Treasury, University Grants Committee. 1961. Report of the Sub-Committee on Oriental, Slavonic, East European and African Studies. London.

Groot, Jan Jakob Maria de. [1881] 1886. Jaarlijksche feesten en gebruiken van de Emoy-Chineezen, 2 vols. Batavia (Bataviaasch Genootschap van Kunsten en Weetenschappen, Verhandelingen, Deel 42, 1–2). French version published 1886 as "Les fêtes annuelles célébrées à Emoui: Etude concernant la religion populaire des Chinois" (Annual festivals in Amoy: A study of Chinese folk religion), C. G. Chavannes, tr., *Annales du Musée Guimet*, 11, 1–399; 12, 400–830.

———. 1885. Het kongsiwezen van Borneo. Eene Verhandeling over den grondslag en den aard der Chineesche politieke vereenigingen in de koloniën; met eene Chineesche geschiedenis van de kongsi Lanfong. The Hague.

———. 1892. The Religious System of China: Its Ancient Forms, Evolution, History and Present Aspect. Manners, Customs, and Social Institutions Connected Therewith, vol. 1. Leiden.

———. 1893. Le code du Mahâyâna en Chine (The Mahayana code in China). Amsterdam (Koninklijke Akademie van Wetenschappen te Amsterdam, Verhandelingen, Afdeeling letterkunde, nieuwe reeks, Deel 1, 2).

———. 1894. The Religious System of China, vol. 2. Leiden.

———. 1897. The Religious System of China, vol 3. Leiden.

———. 1903–4. Sectarianism and Religious Persecution in China, 2 vols. Amsterdam (Koninklijke Akademie van Wetenschappen te Amsterdam, Verhandelingen, Afdeeling letterkunde, nieuwe reeks, Deel 4, 1–2).

———. 1907. The Religious System of China, vol. 5. Leiden.

———. 1910. The Religious System of China, vol. 6. Leiden.

———. 1910a. The Religion of the Chinese. New York.

———. 1918. Universismus: Die Grundlage der Religion und Ethik, des Staatswesens und der Wissenschaften Chinas (Universism, the basis of religion and ethics, state affairs, and sciences in China). Berlin.

Groves, Robert G. 1964. "The Origins of Two Market Towns in the New Territories," in Royal Asiatic Society, Hong Kong Branch, ed., Aspects of Social Organization in the New Territories, 16–20. Hong Kong.

———. 1969. "Militia, Market and Lineage: Chinese Resistance to the Occupation of Hong Kong's New Territories in 1899," *Journal of the Hong Kong Branch of the Royal Asiatic Society*, 9, 31–64.

Grube, Wilhelm. 1901. "Zur pekinger Volkskunde" (The folklore of Peking), *Veröffentlichungen aus dem königlichen Museum für Völkerkunde*, 7, 1–4 Heft, 1–160.

Gullick, John M. 1958. Indigenous Political Systems of Western Malaya. London (London School of Economics and Political Science, Monographs on Social Anthropology, 17).

———. 1963. Malaya. London and New York.

Hall, Daniel G. E. 1955. A History of South-East Asia. London and New York.

Hare, George T. 1895. The Wai Seng Lottery. Singapore (Straits Branch of the Royal Asiatic Society publications, 1).

———. 1904. (ed.) Notes on the Family Law and Usages and on the Criminal Code of the Chinese. Kuala Lumpur.

Harrison, John F. C. 1969. Robert Owen and the Owenites in Britain and America: The Quest for the New Moral World. London.

Harvey, Edwin D. 1933. The Mind of Modern China. New Haven, Conn.

Hawtin, Faye Elise. 1958. "The 'Hundred Flowers Movement' and the Role of the Intellectual in China: Fei Hsiao-t'ung, a Case History," *Papers on China*, 12, 147–98.

Hayes, James W. 1962. "The Pattern of Life in the New Territories in

1898," *Journal of the Hong Kong Branch of the Royal Asiatic Society*, 2, 75–102.

———. 1967. "Geomancy and the Village," in Marjorie D. Topley, ed., Some Traditional Chinese Ideas and Conceptions in Hong Kong Social Life Today, 22–30. Hong Kong.

Heidhues, Mary F. Somers. 1968. "Die chinesische Minderheit im politischen Leben Indonesiens," *Zeitschrift für Politik*, neue (2.) Folge 15, heft 3, 337–52.

Herford, Charles H., and Percy Simpson. 1925. (eds.) Ben Jonson, vol. 2. Oxford.

Herford, Charles H., et al. 1950. (eds.) Ben Jonson, vol. 10. Oxford.

Hickey, Gerald C. 1964. Village in Vietnam. London and New Haven, Conn.

Highbaugh, Irma. 1948. Family Life in West China. New York.

Hill, A. H. 1955. "The Hikayat Abdullah: An Annotated Translation," *Journal of the Malayan Branch of the Royal Asiatic Society*, 28, pt. 3, 1–354.

Ho, Ping-ti. 1968. "Salient Aspects of China's Heritage" [with comments by Arthur F. Wright et al.], in Ping-ti Ho and Tang Tsou, eds., China in Crisis, vol. 1, China's Heritage and the Communist Political System, 1–92. Chicago.

Hodder, Bramwell William. 1953. "Racial Groupings in Singapore," *Malayan Journal of Tropical Geography*, 1, 25–36.

Hong Kong, Legislative Council. 1912. Report on the New Territories, 1899–1912, Laid before the Legislative Council by Command of His Excellency the Governor, August 22nd 1912. Hong Kong.

Hong Kong, New Territories Administration. 1962. Annual Departmental Report by the District Commissioner, New Territories for the Financial Year 1961–62. Hong Kong.

———. 1963. Annual Departmental Report by the District Commissioner, New Territories for the Financial Year 1962–63. Hong Kong.

Hou Su-shuang. n.d. Tao Yüan at a Glance. Singapore.

Hou You-ing (Hu Yü-yin). 1933. Etude sur la parenté en droit chinois (A study of kinship in Chinese law). Paris.

Hsia-men ta hsüeh hsüeh pao; she hui k'o hsüeh pan (Universitatis Amoiensis, Acta Scientiarum Socialium) (Amoy).

Hsiao, Kung-chuan (Hsiao Kung-ch'üan). 1960. Rural China: Imperial Control in the Nineteenth Century. Seattle.

Hsin-chia-p'o miao yü kai lan (Chinese temples of Singapore). 1951. Singapore.

Hsin-chou jih pao [*Sin Chew Jit Poh*] (Singapore).

Hsu, Francis L. K. (Hsü Lang-kuang). 1944. "Sociological Research in China," *Quarterly Bulletin of Chinese Bibliography*, new (2d) series, 4, nos. 1–4, 12–26.

———. 1945. "Influence of South-Seas Emigration on Certain Chinese Provinces," *Far Eastern Quarterly*, 5, no. 1, 47–59.

————. [1948] 1971. Under the Ancestors' Shadow: Chinese Culture and Personality. New York. Rev. and enl. ed. published 1971 as Under the Ancestors' Shadow: Kinship, Personality, and Social Mobility in Village China, Stanford, Calif.

————. 1952. Religion, Science, and Human Crisis: A Study of China in Transition and Its Implications for the West [Study of Hsi-chou, Ta-li *hsien*, Yunnan]. London.

————. 1959. *Review of* Lineage Organization in Southeastern China, by Maurice Freedman, *American Anthropologist*, 61, no. 6, 1128–30.

————. 1961. "Anthropological Sciences," in Sidney [Sydney] Henry Gould, ed., Sciences in Communist China, 129–57. Washington, D.C. (American Association for the Advancement of Science publications, 68).

Hu, Hsien-chin. 1948. The Common Descent Group in China and Its Functions. New York (Viking Fund publications in anthropology, 10).

Hubrig, ————. 1879. "Fung Schui, oder chinesische Geomantie" (Feng-shui, or Chinese geomancy), *Zeitschrift für Ethnologie*, 11, 34–43 [Supplement: Verhandlungen der Berliner Gesellschaft für Anthropologie, Ethnologie und Urgeschichte].

Hughes, George. 1873. "The Small Knife Rebels: An Unpublished Chapter of Amoy History," *China Review*, 1, no. 4, 244–48.

Hughes, H. Stuart. 1960. "The Historian and the Social Scientist," *American Historical Review*, 66, no. 1, 20–46.

Hutson, James. 1921. Chinese Life in the Tibetan Foothills. Shanghai.

Ibrahim, Ahmad. 1965a. Islamic Law in Malaya, Shirle Gordon, ed. Singapore.

————. 1965b. The Legal Status of the Muslims in Singapore. Singapore.

Ichiko, Chūzō. 1968. "The Role of the Gentry: An Hypothesis," in Mary Clabaugh Wright, ed., China in Revolution: The First Phase, 1900–1913, 297–317. New Haven, Conn.

Institute of Pacific Relations. 1939. (comp.) Agrarian China. Chicago.

Israel, John W. 1967. "The Red Guards in Historical Perspective: Continuity and Change in the Chinese Youth Movement," *China Quarterly*, no. 30, 1–32.

Jacques, E. W. 1931. "A Chinese Loan Society," *Man*, 31, Article 216, 225–26.

Jamieson, George. 1921. Chinese Family and Commercial Law. Shanghai.

Johnston, Reginald Fleming. 1913. Buddhist China. New York.

Jones, Russell. 1959. "Chinese Names," *Journal of the Malayan Branch of the Royal Asiatic Society*, 32, pt. 3, 1–84.

Jones, Stanley W. 1953. Public Administration in Malaya. London and New York.

Kaberry, Phyllis. 1957. "Malinowski's Contribution to Field-work and the Writing of Ethnography," in Raymond W. Firth, ed., Man and Culture: An Evaluation of the Work of Bronislaw Malinowski, 71–91. London.

Karlgren, Bernhard. 1950. (tr. and ed.) The Book of Odes (Shih ching). Stockholm.

Kaye, Barrington. 1960. Upper Nankin Street, Singapore: A Sociological Study of Chinese Households Living in a Densely Populated Area. Singapore.

Körner, Brunhild. 1959. Die religiöse Welt der Bäuerin in Nordchina (The religious world of the peasant woman of North China [in the village of Huang-ts'un, Ta-hsing *hsien*, Hopei]). Stockholm (Reports from the Scientific Expedition to the North Western Provinces of China under the Leadership of Dr. Sven Hedin, publications, 43, Ethnography, 8).

Krige, Jacob D., and Eileen J. Krige. 1954. "The Lovedu of the Transvaal," in Cyril Daryll Forde, ed., African Worlds: Studies in the Cosmological Ideas and Social Values of African Peoples, 55–82. London.

Krone, Rudolf. 1859. "A Notice of the Sanon District [i.e. Hsin-an *hsien*, Kwangtung]," *Transactions of the China Branch of the Royal Asiatic Society*, 6, 71–105.

Kuan Ch'u-p'u (C. P. Kwan). 1940. "Nan-yang hua ch'iao yü wo kuo fa lü" (The Overseas Chinese in Southeast Asia and the law of China), *Nan-yang hsüeh pao* (Singapore), 1, no. 1, 75–78.

Kuang-ming jih-pao (Peking).

Kube, Josef. 1952. "Der Kaiser im Volksdenken" (The role of the emperor in the minds of the people), in Ethnographische Beiträge aus der Ch'inghai Provinz (China) (Ethnographic reports from Tsinghai), 157–66. Peking (Catholic University of Peking, Museum of Oriental Ethnology, Folklore Studies supplements, 1).

Kuhn, Philip A. 1970. Rebellion and Its Enemies in Late Imperial China: Militarization and Social Structure, 1796–1864. Cambridge, Mass. (Harvard East Asian series, 49).

Kulp, Daniel Harrison, II. 1925. Country Life in South China: The Sociology of Familism, vol. 1, Phenix Village [i.e. Feng-huang-ts'un, Ch'ao-an *hsien*], Kwangtung, China. New York.

Lafargue, Jean André. 1909. L'immigration chinoise en Indochine. Paris.

Lang, Olga. 1946. Chinese Family and Society. New Haven, Conn.

Langlet, Philippe, 1970. "La tradition vietnamienne: Un état national au sein de la civilisation chinoise," *Bulletin de la Société des études indo-chinoises de Saïgon*, nouvelle (2e) série 45, pte. 2/3, 1–395.

Lattimore, Owen. 1964. From China Looking Outward: An Inaugural Lecture. Leeds.

Leach, Edmund R. 1961. Rethinking Anthropology. London (London School of Economics and Political Science, Monographs on Social Anthropology, 22).

———. 1968. A Runaway World? The Reith Lectures 1967. London and New York.

Lebra, William P. 1966. Okinawan Religion: Belief, Ritual, and Social Structure. Honolulu.

Leonard, Jane Kate. 1972. "Chinese Overlordship and Western Penetration in Maritime Asia: A Late Ch'ing Reappraisal of Chinese Maritime Relations," *Modern Asian Studies*, 6, pt. 2, 151–74.

Leong, Y. K. (Liang Yü-kao), and L. K. Tao (T'ao Meng-ho). 1915. Village and Town Life in China. London (London School of Economics and Political Science, Monographs on Sociology, 4).

Le Page, Robert B. 1964. The National Language Question: Linguistic Problems of Newly Independent States. London and New York.

Levenson, Joseph R., and Herbert Franz Schurmann. 1969. China: An Interpretive History, from the Beginnings to the Fall of Han. Berkeley and Los Angeles.

Lévi-Strauss, Claude [1949] 1969. Les structures élémentaires de la parenté. Paris. Rev. English version published 1969 as The Elementary Structures of Kinship, James H. Bell and John R. von Sturmer, trs., Rodney Needham, ed., Boston and London.

———. 1953. "Social Structure," in Alfred L. Kroeber, ed., Anthropology Today: An Encyclopedic Inventory, 524–53. Chicago.

———. 1958. Anthropologie structurale. Paris.

Levy, Marion Jospeh, Jr. 1949. The Family Revolution in Modern China. Cambridge, Mass.

Li An-che. 1938. "Notes on the Necessity of Field Research in Social Science in China," *Yenching Journal of Social Studies*, 1, no. 1, 122–27.

Li Ching-han. 1957. "Pei-ching chiao ch'ü hsiang ts'un chia t'ing sheng huo ti chin hsi" (Family life in periurban Peking, past and present). *Jen-min jih-pao* 1 Feb., 3; 3 Feb., 3.

Lifton, Robert Jay. 1968. Revolutionary Immortality: Mao Tse-tung and the Chinese Cultural Revolution. New York.

Lim Boon Keng. 1897. "Our Enemies," *Straits Chinese Magazine*, 1, no. 2, 52–58.

Lim, Richard C. H. 1961. "Overseas Influence of English Law, Malaya and Singapore, Parts I and II," *Solicitors' Journal*, 105, no. 38, 794–96; 105, no. 39, 817–19.

Lin Yueh-hwa (Lin Yüeh-hua). 1936. "Ts'ung jen lei hsüeh ti kuan tien k'ao ch'a Chung-kuo tsung tsu hsiang ts'un" (An inquiry into the Chinese lineage village from the viewpoint of anthropology), *She hui hsüeh chieh*, 9, 125–42.

———. 1948. The Golden Wing: A Sociological Study of Chinese Familism. New York.

Lindbeck, John M. H. 1961. "The Organization and Development of Science," *China Quarterly*, no. 6, 98–132.

Liu, Hui-chen Wang. 1959. The Traditional Chinese Clan Rules. Locust Valley, N.Y. (Association for Asian Studies monographs, 7).

Liu Wei-min. 1936. "Tung-kuan hun su ti hsü shu chi yen chiu" (A study of marriage customs in Tung-kuan *hsien* [Kwangtung]), *Min su*, new (2d) series 1, no. 1, 81–99.

Lo, Winston Wan. 1965. "Communal Strife in Mid-Nineteenth Century Kwangtung: The Establishment of Ch'ih-ch'i [*t'ing*]," *Papers on China*, 19, 85–119.

Lockhart, James H. S. 1890a. "Notes on Chinese Folk-lore," *Folk-Lore*, 1, no. 3, 359–68.

———. 1890b. "The Marriage Ceremonies of the Manchus," *Folk-Lore*, 1, no. 4, 481–92.

Lyall, Arthur Comyn. 1882. "The Relations of Religion to Asiatic Studies," *Fortnightly Review* (London), 37, 137–54.

———. 1907. "On the Relations between the State and Religion in China," in A. C. Lyall, Asiatic Studies, Religious and Social, 2d ed., vol. 2, 101–75. London.

Lynn, Jermyn Chi-hung (Ling Ch'i-hung). 1928. Social Life of the Chinese, in Peking. Peking.

Ma Huan. 1970. Ying-yai Sheng-lan: "The Overall Survey of the Ocean's Shores," John V. G. Mills, tr. and ed. Cambridge, Eng. (Hakluyt Society, Extra Series, 42).

McAleavy, Henry. 1963. "Chinese Law in Hong Kong: The Choice of Sources," in James N. D. Anderson, ed., Changing Law in Developing Countries, 258–69. New York.

MacFarquhar, Roderick L. 1960. The Hundred Flowers Campaign and the Chinese Intellectuals. New York.

Macgowan, John. 1909. Lights and Shadows of Chinese Life. Shanghai.

MacRae, Donald G. 1961. "The British Tradition in Social Anthropology," in D. G. MacRae, Ideology and Society: Papers in Sociology and Politics, 30–37. London.

Mair, Lucy P. 1957. Studies in Applied Anthropology. London (London School of Economics and Political Science, Monographs on Social Anthropology, 16).

———. 1963. New Nations. Chicago and London.

Malayan Union. Supreme Court. 1950. Law Reports of the Malayan Union, 1947. Kuala Kumpur.

Malaysia. Law Reports. 1965. "Re Lee Gee Chong Deceased; Tay Geok Yap & Ors. vs. Tan Lian Cheow," *Malayan Law Journal*, 1965, no. 1, 102–16.

[Malinowski] Malinowsky, Bronislaw, and Julio de la Fuente. 1957. La Economía de un Sistema de Mercados en México: un ensayo de etnografía contemporanea y cambio social en un valle Mexicano. Mexico City (Acta Antropologica, Época 2, vol. 1, no. 2).

Mallal, Bashir A., and Nazir A. Mallal. 1940. Mallal's Digest of Malayan Case Law, Being a Comprehensive Digest of all Decisions of the Superior Courts of Malaya from 1808–1939. Singapore.

March, Andrew L. 1968. "An Appreciation of Chinese Geomancy," *Journal of Asian Studies*, 27, no. 2, 253–67.

Maris Stella Girls' School, Child Welfare and Social Work Section. 1965. Teen-Age Girls' Family Problems, Singapore. Singapore.

Martin, David. 1969. "The Dissolution of the Monasteries," in D. Martin, ed., Anarchy and Change: The Problem of the Contemporary University, 1–12. London.

Maspero, Henri. 1932. "The Mythology of Modern China," F. M. Atkinson, tr., in Joseph Hackin, ed., Asiatic Mythology, 252–84. New York.

Mayer, Adrian C. 1962. "System and Network: An Approach to the Study of Political Process in Dewas," in Triloki N. Madan and Gopāla Śarana, eds., Indian Anthropology: Essays in Memory of D. N. Majumdar, 266–78. Bombay and New York.

Mehnert, Klaus. 1969. Peking and the New Left, at Home and Abroad. Berkeley (University of California, Center for Chinese Studies, China Research Monographs, 4).

Meisner, Maurice J. 1968. "Utopian Goals and Ascetic Values in Chinese Communist Ideology," *Journal of Asian Studies*, 28, no. 1, 101–10.

Meskill, Johanna Menzel. 1970a. "The Chinese Genealogy as a Research Source," in Maurice Freedman, ed., Family and Kinship in Chinese Society, 139–61. Stanford, Calif.

——. 1970b. "The Lins of Wufeng [Chang-hua *hsien*]: The Rise of a Taiwanese Gentry Family," in Leonard H. D. Gordon, ed., Taiwan: Studies in Chinese Local History, 6–22. New York.

Metzger, Thomas A. 1970. "The State and Commerce in Imperial China," *Asian and African Studies* (Jerusalem), 6, 23–46 [Special issue: Martin Rudner, ed., Society and Development in Asia].

Michael, Franz H. 1964. "Introduction: Regionalism in Nineteenth-Century China," in Stanley Spector, Li Hung-chang and the Huai Army: A Study in Nineteenth-Century Chinese Regionalism, xxi–xliii. Seattle.

Michell, John. 1968. "Flying Saucers," *The Listener*, 79, no. 2048, 821–23.

Middleton, John F. M. 1960. Lugbara Religion: Ritual and Authority among an East African People. London and New York.

Mills, Lennox A. 1925. British Malaya, 1824–1867. Singapore.

Minchin, George. 1870. "Marriage Customs of Chinese, Residents in the Straits of Malacca," *Notes and Queries on China and Japan*, new (2d) series 4, no. 6, 81–86.

Miyakawa, Hisayuki. 1960. "The Confucianization of South China," in Arthur F. Wright, ed., The Confucian Persuasion, 21–46. Stanford, Calif.

Möllendorff, Paul Georg von. 1896. The Family Law of the Chinese. Shanghai.

Monthly Digest of Statistics (Singapore, Department of Statistics).

Moore, Barrington, Jr. 1966. Social Origins of Dictatorship and Democracy: Lord and Peasant in the Making of the Modern World. Boston.

Morris, Harold Stephen. 1957. "The Plural Society," *Man*, 57, Article 148, 124–25.

Mote, Frederick W. 1967. "Cities in North and South China," in Frederick S. Drake, ed., Symposium on Historical, Archeological and Linguistic Studies on Southern China, South-East Asia and the Hong Kong Region, 153–55. Hong Kong.

———. 1972. "China's Past in the Study of China Today: Some Comments on the Recent Work of Richard Solomon" [*Review of* Mao's Revolution and the Chinese Political Culture, by Richard H. Solomon], *Journal of Asian Studies*, 32, no. 1, 107–20.

Muramatsu, Yuji (Muramatsu Yūji). 1960. "Some Themes in Chinese Rebel Ideologies," in Arthur F. Wright, ed., The Confucian Persuasion, 241–67. Stanford, Calif.

Murray, Douglas P. 1964. "Chinese Education in South-East Asia," *China Quarterly*, no. 20, 67–95.

Nakane, Chie. 1967. Kinship and Economic Organization in Rural Japan. London (London School of Economics and Political Science, Monographs on Social Anthropology, 32).

Napier, Walter J. 1913. "The Application of English Law to Asiatic Races, with Special Reference to the Chinese," in Henry N. Ridley, ed., Noctes Orientales, being a Selection of Essays Read before the Straits Philosophical Society between the Years 1893 and 1910, 142–49. Singapore.

Needham, Joseph. 1956. Science and Civilization in China, vol. 2, History of Scientific Thought. Cambridge, Eng.

———. 1962. Science and Civilization in China, vol. 4, Physics and Physical Technology. Part 1, Physics. Cambridge, Eng.

———. 1971. Science and Civilization in China, vol. 4, Physics and Physical Technology. Part 3, Civil Engineering and Nautics. Cambridge, Eng.

Nevadomsky, Joseph-john, and Alice Li. 1970. The Chinese in Southeast Asia: A Selected and Annotated Bibliography of Publications in Western Languages, 1960 1970. Berkeley (University of California, Center for South and Southeast Asia Studies, Occasional Papers, 6).

Nevius, John Livingston. 1869. China and the Chinese: A General Description of the Country and its Inhabitants . . . London and New York.

Newbold, T. J., and F. W. Wilson. 1841. "The Chinese Secret Triad Society of the Tien-ti-huih," *Journal of the Royal Asiatic Society of Great Britain and Ireland*, 6, 120–58.

Newell, William H. 1952. "Modern Chinese Sociologists," *Sociological Bulletin* (Indian Sociological Society), 1, no. 2, 89–94.

Nivison, David S., and Arthur F. Wright. (eds.) 1959. Confucianism in Action. Stanford, Calif.

Nordhoff, Charles. [1875] 1966. The Communistic Societies of the United States; from Personal Visit and Observation . . . London and New York. Reissued 1966, New York.

Ong Eng Die. 1943. Chineezen in Nederlandsch-Indië: Sociografie van een Indonesische bevolkingsgroep. Assen (Sociografische monografieën, 2).

Osgood, Cornelius. 1951. The Koreans and Their Culture. New York.

———. 1963. Village Life in Old China: A Community Study of Kao Yao [K'un-ming *hsien*], Yunnan. New York.

Pan, Quentin (P'an Kuang-tan). 1928. "Familism and the Optimum Family," *China Critic*, 1, no. 20, 387–89.

Parker, Edward Harper, 1879. "Comparative Chinese Family Law," *China Review*, 8, no. 2, 67–107.

Pasternak, Burton. 1968a. "Agnatic Atrophy in a Formosan Village," *American Anthropologist*, 70, no. 1, 93–96.

———. 1968b. "Atrophy of Patrilineal Bonds in a Chinese Village in Historical Perspective," *Ethnohistory*, 15, no. 3, 293–327.

———. 1968c. "Social Consequences of Equalizing Irrigation Access," *Human Organization*, 27, no. 4, 332–43.

———. 1969. "The Role of the Frontier in Chinese Lineage Development," *Journal of Asian Studies*, 28, no. 3, 551–61.

———. 1972. Kinship and Community in Two Chinese Villages [Tat'ieh, P'ing-tung *hsien*, and Chung-she, T'ai-nan *hsien*, Taiwan]. Stanford, Calif.

———. 1973. "Chinese Tale-Telling Tombs," *Ethnology*, 12, no. 3, 259–73.

Payne, C. H. Withers. 1932. The Law of Administration of and Succession to Estates in the Straits Settlements. Singapore.

———. 1936. The Malayan Digest, Being a Complete Digest of Every Case in the Colony of the Straits Settlements and the Federated Malay States Reported from 1808 to the Present Day, Including Annotations and Full Index. Singapore.

Pickering, William A. 1876. "The Chinese in the Straits of Malacca," *Fraser's Magazine*, new (2d) series 14, 438–45.

———. 1879. "Chinese Secret Societies, Part II," *Journal of the Straits Branch of the Royal Asiatic Society*, no. 3, 1–18.

Plath, David W. 1964. "Where the Family of God Is the Family: The Role of the Dead in Japanese Households," *American Anthropologist*, 66, no. 2, 300–17.

———. 1969. "Modernization and Its Discontents: Japan's Little Utopias," *Journal of Asian and African Studies*, 4, no. 1, 1–17.

Potter, Jack M. 1968. Capitalism and the Chinese Peasant: Social and Economic Change in a Hong Kong Village. Berkeley and Los Angeles.

———. 1969. "The Structure of Rural Chinese Society in New Territories," in Ian C. Jarvie and Joseph Agassi, eds., Hong Kong: A Society in Transition, 3–28. London and New York.

———. 1970. "Land and lineage in Traditional China," in Maurice Freedman, ed., Family and Kinship in Chinese Society, 121–38. Stanford, Calif.

Pratt, Jean A. 1960. "Emigration and Unilineal Descent Groups: A Study of Marriage in a Hakka Village in the New Territories, Hong Kong," *Eastern Anthropologist*, 13, no. 4, 147–58.

"Professor Ch'en Ta." 1957. *China News Analysis*, no. 168 (15 Feb.), 6.

"Professor Li Ching-han." 1957. *China News Analysis*, no. 183 (31 May), 7.

Purcell, Victor. 1948. The Chinese in Malaya. London.

———. [1951] 1965. The Chinese in Southeast Asia. London. 2d ed. published 1965, London.

Radcliffe-Brown, Alfred R. 1936. "Tui yü Chung-kuo hsiang ts'un sheng huo she hui hsüeh tiao ch'a ti chien i" (A proposal for sociological surveys of village life in China), Wu Wen-tsao, tr., *She-hui-hsüeh chieh*, 9, 79–88.

———. [1944] 1958. "Meaning and Scope of Social Anthropology," *Nature*, 154, no. 3904 (26 Aug. 1944), 257–60. Reprinted 1958 in Mysore N. Srinivas, ed., Method in Social Anthropology: Essays by A. R. Radcliffe-Brown, 96–107, Chicago.

———. [1952a] 1958. "The Comparative Method in Social Anthropology," *Journal of the Royal Anthropological Institute*, 81 (1952), 15–22. Reprinted 1958 in Mysore N. Srinivas, ed., Method in Social Anthropology: Selected Essays by A. R. Radcliffe-Brown, 108–29, Chicago.

———. 1952b. Structure and Function in Primitive Society: Essays and Addresses. Chicago and London.

Read, William H. McL. 1901. Play and Politics: Recollections of Malaya by an Old Resident. London.

Report on the Registration of Births and Deaths, Marriages and Persons (Singapore. Registrar-General of Births and Deaths).

Revue bibliographique de sinologie (Paris and The Hague).

Rex, John. 1959. "The Plural Society in Sociological Theory," *British Journal of Sociology*, 10, no. 2, 114–24.

Robinson, Joan. 1969. The Cultural Revolution in China. Baltimore and Harmondsworth, Eng.

Rouse, Irving. 1953. "The Strategy of Culture History," in Alfred L. Kroeber, ed., Anthropology Today: An Encyclopedic Inventory, 57–76. Chicago.

Schapera, Isaac. 1962. "Should Anthropologists Be Historians?" [Presidential Address], *Journal of the Royal Anthropological Institute of Great Britain and Ireland*, 92, pt. 2, 143–56.

Schlegel, Gustaaf [Gustave]. 1866. Thian Ti Hwui, the Hung-League, or Heaven-Earth-League: A Secret Society with the Chinese in China and India. Batavia (Bataviaasch Genootschap van Kunsten en Weetenschappen, Verhandelingen, Deel 32).

———. 1885. Compte rendu de Het kongsiwezen van Borneo, par J. J. M. de Groot. *Revue Coloniale Internationale* (Amsterdam), 1, 448–65.

Schram, Stuart R. 1969. "The Party in Chinese Communist Ideology," *China Quarterly*, no. 38, 1–26.

Schurmann, Herbert Franz. 1968. Ideology and Organization in Communist China, 2d ed., enl. Berkeley and Los Angeles.

Segers, Arthur. 1932. La Chine: le peuple, sa vie quotidienne et ses cérémonies (The people, daily life, and ceremonies of China). Antwerp.

Serruys, Paul L. M. 1944. "Les cérémonies du mariage: usages populaires et textes dialectaux du sud de la préfecture de Ta-t'oung (Chansi)" (Wedding ceremonies: Popular customs and dialect texts from the southern part of Ta-t'ung *hsien*, Shansi), *Folklore Studies*, 3, no. 1, 73–154; 3, no. 2, 77–129.

Sharp, Lauriston. 1962. "Cultural Continuities and Discontinuities in Southeast Asia," *Journal of Asian Studies*, 22, no. 1, 3–11.

Shellabear, William G. 1913. "Baba Malay; an Introduction to the Language of the Straits-Born Chinese," *Journal of the Straits Branch of the Royal Asiatic Society*, no. 65, 49–63.

Sheridan, Lionel Astor, ed. 1961. Malaya and Singapore, the Borneo Territories: The Development of Their Laws and Constitutions. London.

Shirokogoroff [Shirokogorov], Sergei M. 1942. "Ethnographic Investigation of China," *Folklore Studies*, 1, 1–8.

Shryock, John Knight. 1931. The Temples of Anking and Their Cults: A Study of Modern Chinese Religion. Paris.

Siah U Chin. 1848. "The Chinese in Singapore, No. II, General Sketch of the Numbers, Tribes, and Avocations of the Chinese in Singapore," *Journal of the Indian Archipelago and Eastern Asia*, 2, 283–90.

Silcock, Thomas H. 1959. The Commonwealth Economy in Southeast Asia. Durham, N.C., and London (Duke University Commonwealth-Studies Center publications, 10).

Silcock, Thomas H., and Ungku Abdul Aziz. 1950. Nationalism in Malaya. New York (Institute of Pacific Relations, Secretariat papers, 8).

Singapore, Law Reports. 1949. "In the Estate of Yeow Kian Kee (deceased), Er Gek Cheng vs. Ho Ying Seng," *Malayan Law Journal*, 15, no. 7, 171–74.

Singapore, Legislative Assembly. 1957. Sessional Paper No. Cmd. 37 of 1957.

———. 1960. Report of the Select Committee on the Women's Charter Bill, L.A. 16 of 1960.

———. 1961. Report of the Select Committee on the Women's Charter Bill, L.A. 10 of 1961.

Singapore Legislative Assembly Debates (Singapore, Legislative Assembly).

Skinner, George William. 1951. "The New Sociology in China," *Far Eastern Quarterly*, 10, no. 4, 365–71.

———. 1957. Chinese Society in Thailand: An Analytical History. Ithaca, N.Y.

———. 1958. Leadership and Power in the Chinese Community of Thailand. Ithaca, N.Y. (Association for Asian Studies Monographs, 3).

————. 1960. "Change and Persistence in Chinese Culture Overseas: A Comparison of Thailand and Java," *Journal of the South Seas Society*, 16, pts. 1/2, 86–100.

————. 1963. "The Chinese Minority," in Ruth T. McVey, ed., Indonesia, 97–117. New Haven, Conn.

————. 1964. "Marketing and Social Structure in Rural China, Part I," *Journal of Asian Studies*, 24, no. 1, 3–43.

————. 1965a. "Marketing and Social Structure in Rural China, Part II," *Journal of Asian Studies*, 24, no. 2, 195–228.

————. 1965b. "Marketing and Social Structure in Rural China, Part III," *Journal of Asian Studies*, 24, no. 3, 363–99.

————. 1968. "Overseas Chinese Leadership: Paradigm for a Paradox," in Gehan Wijeyewardene, ed., Leadership and Authority, A Symposium, 191–207. Singapore.

————. 1971. "Chinese Peasants and the Closed Community: An Open and Shut Case," *Comparative Studies in Society and History*, 13, no. 3, 270–81.

Smith, Arthur Henderson. 1899. Village Life in China: A Study in Sociology. New York.

Smith, Huston. 1970. "Transcendence in Traditional China," in James T. C. Liu (Liu Tzu-chien) and Wei-ming Tu, eds., Traditional China, 109–22. Englewood Cliffs, N.J.

Smith, Michael G. 1960. "Social and Cultural Pluralism," *Annals of the New York Academy of Sciences*, 83, Article 5, 763–85.

Smith, Thomas Edward. 1952. Population Growth in Malaya: An Analysis of Recent Trends. London and New York.

Somers, Mary F. 1964. Peranakan Chinese Politics in Indonesia. Ithaca, N.Y. (Cornell University, Modern Indonesia Project, Interim Reports Series).

Song Ong Siang. 1923. One Hundred Years' History of the Chinese in Singapore. London.

South China Morning Post (Hong Kong).

SSGG, see *Straits Settlements Government Gazette*.

SSLR, see *Straits Settlements Law Reports*.

Stanton, William. 1900. The Triad Society, or Heaven and Earth Association. Hong Kong.

Staunton, George Thomas. 1810. (tr. and annot.) Ta Tsing Leu Lee; Being the Fundamental Laws, and a Selection from the Supplementary Statutes, of the Penal Code of China. London.

Stein, Rolf Alfred. 1957. "Les religions de la Chine," in Encyclopédie française, vol. 19, 54, 3–10. Paris.

Stirling, William G. 1925. "A Chinese Wedding in the Reform Style," *Journal of the Malayan Branch of the Royal Asiatic Society*, 3, pt. 3, 1–5.

A Straits Chinese. 1899. "Local Chinese Social Organisations," *Straits Chinese Magazine*, 3, no. 10, 43–47.

Straits Settlements. 1858–59. Administration Report, Orfeur Cavenagh, Governor.

———. 1861–62. Administration Report, Orfeur Cavenagh, Governor.

———. 1881. Census of the Straits Settlements. Singapore.

———. 1896. Annual Reports for the Year 1895. Singapore.

———. 1897. Annual Reports for the Year 1896. Singapore.

———. 1898. Annual Reports for the Year 1897. Singapore.

———. 1900. Annual Reports for the Year 1899. Singapore.

Straits Settlements, Chinese Marriage Committee. 1926. Proceedings of the Committee Appointed by His Excellency the Governor to Report on Matters Concerning Chinese Marriages. Singapore.

Straits Settlements, Supreme Court. 1869. A Selection of Oriental Cases Decided in the Supreme Courts of the Straits' Settlements, Robert Carr Woods, Jr., comp. Penang.

———. 1885. Cases Heard and Determined in Her Majesty's Supreme Court of the Straits Settlements, 1808–1884, vol. 1, Civil Cases, James William Norton-Kyshe, ed. Singapore.

Straits Settlements Government Gazette (Singapore).

Straits Settlements Law Reports, 1893–1927 (Singapore), 1928–(Singapore and/or London).

Su, Tina Han. 1966. A Thematic Study of Chinese Marriage Ritual and Symbolism. Unpublished B.A. Honors thesis in Anthropology. Cornell University.

Sung, Hok-p'ang. 1935–38. "Legends and Stories of the New Territories," *Hong Kong Naturalist*, 6, no. 1 (May 1935); 6, nos. 3/4 (Dec. 1935); 7, no. 1 (Apr. 1936); 7, no. 2 (June 1936); 7, nos. 3/4 (Dec. 1936); 8, nos. 3/4 (Mar. 1938).

Swisher, Earl. 1953. (comp.) Directory of Chinese Personal Names in Singapore. Washington, D.C.

Szczepanik, Edward F. 1960. The Economic Growth of Hong Kong, 2d ed. London.

Tambiah, Stanley J. 1970. Buddhism and the Spirit Cults in North-East Thailand. Cambridge, Eng. (Cambridge Studies in Social Anthropology, 2).

Tan Pow Teck [Ch'en Pao-te]. 1924. The Pek Kah Seng. Kuala Lumpur.

Tao Yüan, Singapore Branch. n.d. Explanatory Notes of "Tao Yüan." Singapore.

Tawney, Richard Henry. 1932. Land and Labor in China. London and New York.

Ternay, Johannes. 1952. "Familienjustiz im Trauerhaus" (Family justice in a household in mourning), in Ethnographische Beiträge aus der Ch'inghai Provinz (China) (Ethnographic reports from Tsinghai), 103–24. Peking (Catholic University of Peking, Museum of Oriental Ethnology, Folklore Studies supplements, 1).

Terrell, Arthur Koberwein à Beckett. 1932. Malayan Legislation and Its Future. Singapore.

Théry, François. 1948–49. "Les coutumes chinoises relatives au mariage" (Chinese customs relating to marriage), *Bulletin de l'université l'Aurore*, 3ᵉ série 9, no. 36, 367–400; 10, no. 37, 21–62; 10, no. 38, 255–97.

Thompson, Laurence G. 1969. Chinese Religion: An Introduction. Belmont, Calif.

T'ien, Ju-k'ang, 1953. The Chinese of Sarawak: A Study of Social Structure. London (London School of Economics and Political Science, Monographs on Social Anthropology, 12).

Tjan Tjoe Som. 1949. (tr. and ed.) Po Hu T'ung: The Comprehensive Discussions in the White Tiger Hall, vol. 1, Leiden.

Topley, Marjorie D. 1951. "Some Occasional Rites Performed by the Singapore Cantonese," *Journal of the Malayan Branch of the Royal Asiatic Society*, 24, pt. 3, 120–44.

———. 1952. "Chinese Rites for the Repose of the Soul; with Special Reference to Cantonese Custom," *Journal of the Malayan Branch of the Royal Asiatic Society*, 25, pt. 1, 149–60.

———. 1954. "Chinese Women's Vegetarian Houses in Singapore," *Journal of the Malayan Branch of the Royal Asiatic Society*, 27, pt. 1, 51–67.

———. 1955. "Ghost Marriages among the Singapore Chinese," *Man*, 55, Article 35, 29–30.

———. 1956a. "Chinese Religion and Religious Institutions in Singapore," *Journal of the Malayan Branch of the Royal Asiatic Society*, 29, pt. 1, 70–118.

———. 1956b. "Ghost Marriages among the Singapore Chinese: A Further Note," *Man*, 56, Article 63, 71–72.

———. 1957. "The Great Way of Former Heaven: A Chinese Semi-Secret Religion in Malaya," *New Malayan* (Singapore), 2, 13–23.

———. 1961. "The Emergence and Social Function of Chinese Religious Associations in Singapore," *Comparative Studies in Society and History*, 3, no. 3, 289–314.

———. 1964. "Capital, Saving and Credit among Indigenous Rice Farmers and Immigrant Vegetable Farmers in Hong Kong's New Territories," in Raymond W. Firth and Basil S. Yamey, eds., Capital, Saving and Credit in Peasant Societies, 157–86. Chicago.

———. 1967. "Some Basic Conceptions and Their Traditional Relationship to Society," in M. D. Topley, ed., Some Traditional Chinese Ideas and Conceptions in Hong Kong Social Life Today, 7–21. Hong Kong.

———. 1969. Anthropology and Sociology in Hong Kong: Field Projects and Problems of Overseas Scholars. Hong Kong.

Tracy, I. 1836. "Description of a Chinese Wedding: Containing Notices of the Ceremonies Performed on the Occasion. Extracted from a Journal at Singapore," *Chinese Repository*, 4, no. 12, 568–72.

Translation of the Peking Gazette for 1882. 1883. Shanghai.

Ts'ao Chan. 1958. The Dream of the Red Chamber: A Chinese Novel of the Early Ching Period, Florence McHugh and Isabel McHugh, trs. (based on Der Traum der roten Kammer: ein Roman aus der frühen Tsing-Zeit, Franz Kuhn, tr.). London.

Tsou, Tang. 1969. "The Cultural Revolution and the Chinese Political System," *China Quarterly*, no. 38, 63–91.

Tun Li-chen [Fu-ch'a Tun-ch'ung]. 1965. Annual Custom and Festivals in Peking, as Recorded in the "Yen-ching Sui-shih-chi," 2d ed., Derk Bodde, tr. and annot. Hong Kong.

T[urner], F. S. 1874. "Feng-shui," *Cornhill Magazine*, 29, 337–48.

Twitchett, Denis C. 1959. "The Fan Clan's Charitable Estate, 1050–1790," in David S. Nivison and Arthur F. Wright, eds., Confucianism in Action, 97–133. Stanford, Calif.

Valk, Marius Hendrikus van der. 1939. An Outline of Modern Chinese Family Law. Peiping (Monumenta Serica monograph series, 2).

van der Sprenkel, Otto P. N. Berkelbach. 1964. "Max Weber on China," *History and Theory*, 3, no. 3, 348–70.

Vaughan, Jonas Daniel. 1879. The Manners and Customs of the Chinese of the Straits Settlements. Singapore.

Vleming, J. L., Jr. 1926. Het chineesche Zakenlevan in Nederlandsch-Indië. Weltevreden.

Wakeman, Frederic E., Jr. 1966. Strangers at the Gate: Social Disorder in South China, 1839–1861. Berkeley and Los Angeles.

———. 1970. "High Ch'ing: 1683–1839," in James Buckley Crowley, ed., Modern East Asia: Essays in Interpretation, 1–28. New York.

Wang Gungwu (Wang Keng-wu). 1959. A Short History of the Nanyang Chinese. Singapore (Background to Malaya books, 13).

———. 1968. "Traditional Leadership in a New Nation: The Chinese in Malaya and Singapore," in Gehan Wijeyewardene, ed., Leadership and Authority, A Symposium, 208–22. Singapore.

———. 1970. "'Public' and 'Private' Overseas Trade in Chinese History," in Michel Mollat, ed., Sociétés et compagnies de commerce en Orient et dans l'océan Indien: Actes du huitième Colloque international d'histoire maritime (Beyrouth, 5–10 septembre 1966), 215–26. Paris.

Wang Sung-hsing. 1967. Kwei-shan Tao: A Study of a Chinese Fishing Community in Formosa. Taipei (Academia Sinica, Institute of Ethnology monographs, 13).

Wang Tse-sin (Wang Tsu-hsin). 1932. Le divorce en Chine (Divorce in China). Paris (Institut de droit comparé, Etudes de sociologie et d'ethnologie juridiques, 15).

Wang Yü-ch'üan. 1936. "Pacific Affairs, Bibliographies. No. 5, The Development of Modern Social Sciences in China," *Pacific Affairs*, 11, no. 3, 345–62.

Ward, Barbara E. 1954a. "A Hong Kong Fishing Village," *Journal of Oriental Studies*, 1, no. 1, 195–214.

———. 1954b. "A Hakka Kongsi in Borneo," *Journal of Oriental Studies*, 1, no. 2, 358–70.

———. 1959. "Floating Villages: Chinese Fishermen in Hong Kong," *Man*, 59, Article 62, 44–45.

———. 1963. "Men, Women and Change: An Essay in Understanding Social Roles in South and Southeast Asia," in B. E. Ward, ed., Women in the New Asia: The Changing Social Roles of Men and Women in South-East Asia, 25–99. Paris.

———. 1965. "Varieties of the Conscious Model: The Fishermen of South China," in Michael Banton, ed., The Relevance of Models for Social Anthropology, 113–37. New York (Association of Social Anthropologists Monographs, 1).

———. 1966. "Sociological Self-Awareness: Some Uses of the Conscious Models," *Man*, new (2d) series 1, no. 2, 201–15.

———. 1967. "Chinese Fishermen in Hong Kong: Their Post-Peasant Economy," in Maurice Freedman, ed., Social Organization: Essays Presented to Raymond Firth, 271–88. Chicago.

Ward, John S. M., and William G. Stirling. 1925. The Hung Society, or the Society of Heaven and Earth, vol. 1. London.

Watt, John R. 1970. "Leadership Criteria in Late Imperial China," *Ch'ing-shih wen-t'i*, 2, no. 3, 17–39.

Weber, Max. [1922a] 1951. "Die Wirtschaftsethik der Weltreligionen: Konfuzianismus und Religionssoziologie," in M. Weber, Gesammelte Aufsätze zur Religionssoziologie. Tübingen. English version published 1951 as The Religion of China: Confucianism and Taoism, Hans H. Gerth, tr. and ed., Glencoe, Ill.

———. [1922b] 1963. "Religionssoziologie: Typen der religiösen Vergemeinschaftung," in M. Weber, Wirtschaft und Gesellschaft, 227–363. Tübingen. English version published 1963 as The Sociology of Religion, Ephraim Fischoff, tr., Boston.

Wee, Ann E. 1963. "Chinese Women of Singapore: Their Present Status in the Family and in Marriage," in Barbara E. Ward, ed., Women in the New Asia: The Changing Social Roles of Men and Women in South and South-East Asia, 376–409. Paris.

Welch, Holmes H. 1970. "Facades of Religion in China," *Asian Survey*, 10, no. 7, 614–26.

Werner, Edward T. C. 1910. . . . Descriptive Sociology: or, Groups of Sociological Facts, No. 9, Chinese, Henry R. Tedder, ed. London (Div. III, Pt. 3-C).

Wertheim, Willem Frederik. 1960. "Exodus der Joden van het Oosten," *De Groene Amsterdammer*, 13 August, 5.

———. 1964. "The Trading Minorities in Southeast Asia," in W. F. Wertheim, East-West Parallels: Sociological Approaches to Modern Asia, 39–82. The Hague.

White, Leslie A. 1937. "Some Suggestions for a Program in Anthropology in China," *Chinese Social and Political Science Review*, 21, no. 1, 120–34.

Wickberg, Edgar B. 1965. The Chinese in Philippine Life, 1850–1898. New Haven, Conn. (Yale Southeast Asia Studies, 1).

Wieger, Léon. 1913. Dr. L. Wieger's Moral Tenets and Customs in China, Leo Davrout, tr. and annot. Ho-chien-fu, Chihli.

Wiens, Herold J. [1954] 1967. China's March toward the Tropics. Hamden, Conn. Reprinted 1967 as Han Chinese Expansion in South China, Hamden, Conn.

Willetts, William. 1965. Foundations of Chinese Art from Neolithic Pottery to Modern Architecture. London and New York.

Williams, Lea E. 1960. Overseas Chinese Nationalism: The Genesis of the Pan-Chinese Movement in Indonesia, 1900–1916. Glencoe, Ill.

Williams, Samuel Wells. 1883. The Middle Kingdom: A Survey of the Geography, Government, Literature, Social Life, Arts, and History of the Chinese Empire and its Inhabitants, rev. and enl. ed. New York.

Willmott, Donald E. 1961. The National Status of the Chinese in Indonesia, 1900–1958, rev. ed. Ithaca, N.Y. (Cornell University, Modern Indonesia Project, Monograph Series).

Willmott, William E. 1970. The Political Structure of the Chinese Community in Cambodia. London (London School of Economics and Political Science, Monographs on Social Anthropology, 42).

Wolf, Arthur P. 1964. Marriage and Adoption in a Hokkien Village [Hsia-chi-chou, T'ai-pei *hsien*, Taiwan]. Ph.D. dissertation in Anthropology, Cornell University [University Microfilms Publ. 65–4171].

———. 1966. "Childhood Association, Sexual Attraction and the Incest Taboo: A Chinese Case," *American Anthropologist*, 68, no. 4, 883–98.

———. 1968. "Adopt a Daughter-in-Law, Marry a Sister: A Chinese Solution to the Problem of the Incest Taboo," *American Anthropologist*, 70, no. 5, 864–74.

———. 1970. "Chinese Kinship and Mourning Dress," in Maurice Freedman, ed., Family and Kinship in Chinese Society, 189–207. Stanford, Calif.

———. 1974a. "Introduction," in A. P. Wolf, ed., Religion and Ritual in Chinese Society, 1–18. Stanford, Calif.

———. 1974b. "Gods, Ghosts, and Ancestors," in A. P. Wolf, ed., Religion and Ritual in Chinese Society, 131–82. Stanford, Calif.

———. 1974c. "Marriage and Adoption in Northern Taiwan," in Robert J. Smith, ed., Social Organization and the Applications of Anthropology, 128–60. Ithaca, N.Y.

Wolf, Arthur P., and Huang Chieh-shan. 1979. Marriage and Adoption in China, 1845–1945. Stanford, Calif.

Wolf, Margery. 1968. The House of Lim: A Study of a Chinese Farm Family. New York.

————. 1970. "Child Training and the Chinese Family," in Maurice Freedman, ed., Family and Kinship in Chinese Society, 37–62. Stanford, Calif.

————. 1972. Women and the Family in Rural Taiwan. Stanford, Calif.

Woodside, Alexander B. 1971. Vietnam and the Chinese Model: A Comparative Study of Nguyễn and Ch'ing Civil Government in the First Half of the Nineteenth Century. Cambridge, Mass. (Harvard East Asian Series, 52).

Wright, Arthur Frederick. 1959. Buddhism in Chinese History. Stanford, Calif.

————. 1960. "The Study of Chinese Civilization," *Journal of the History of Ideas*, 21, no. 2, 233–55.

Wright, Mary Clabaugh. 1961. "The Social Sciences and the Chinese Historical Record" [*Review of* Ch'ing Administration: Three Studies, by John King Fairbank and Ssu-yü Teng], *Journal of Asian Studies*, 20, no. 2, 218–21.

Wynne, Mervyn Llewelyn. 1941. Triad and Tabut: A Survey of the Origin and Diffusion of Chinese and Mohamedan Secret Societies in the Malay Peninsula, A.D. 1800–1935. Singapore.

Yang, C. K. (Yang Ch'ing-k'un). 1957. "The Functional Relationship between Confucian Thought and Chinese Religion," in John King Fairbank, ed., Chinese Thought and Institutions, 269–90. Chicago.

————. 1959. A Chinese Village in Early Communist Transition. Cambridge, Mass.

————. 1961. Religion in Chinese Society: A Study of Contemporary Social Functions of Religion and Some of Their Historical Factors. Berkeley and Los Angeles.

————. 1964. "Introduction," in Max Weber, The Religion of China: Confucianism and Taoism, Hans H. Gerth, tr. and ed., xiii–xliii. New York.

Yang, Lien-sheng. 1952. Money and Credit in China: A Short History. Cambridge, Mass. (Harvard-Yenching Institute, Monograph Series, 12).

Yang, Martin M. C. (Yang Mou-ch'un). 1945. A Chinese Village: Taitou [i.e., T'ai-t'ou, Chiao *hsien*], Shantung Province. New York.

Yang Pi-wang. 1963. "Ancient Bridal Laments," *China Reconstructs*, 12, no. 10, 42–44.

Yates, Matthew Tyson. 1868. "Ancestral Worship and Fung-shuy," *Chinese Recorder*, 1, no. 2, 23–28, 1, no. 3, 37–43.

Yeh, Stephen H. K. 1964. "Chinese Marriage Patterns in Singapore," *Malayan Economic Review*, 9, no. 1, 102–12.

Character List

Character List

Entries are categorized as follows: Mandarin (M), Cantonese (C), and Hokkien (H). The transcription systems followed are Wade-Giles for Mandarin, modified Eitel/Dyer Ball for Cantonese, and Bodman for Hokkien. Excluded from the list are the names of persons, major cities, and county- and higher-level administrative units.

bò (H) 婦

cā-bò-kân (H) 媕媒媕

cêk (H) 叔

chai (M) 齋

chai-t'ang (M) 齋堂

chi (C) 置

chi (M) 祭

chi-nien (M) 記念

ch'i (M) 氣

chia (M) 家

chia-chang (M) 家長

chien-sheng (M) 監生

Chin Chiang Ts'o (M) 晉江厝

Ch'ing-ming (M) 清明

chiū:-thaú (H) 上頭

chui-fu (M) 追夫

chung (M) 忠

Ch'ung-yang (M) 重陽

chü-jen (M) 舉人

cìn-cuĕ (H) 進做

fang (M) 房

Fanling (C) 粉嶺

feng-shui (M) 風水

fu-mu kuan (M) 父母官

fung shui (C) 風水

fung shui lo (C) 風水佬

fung shui sin shaang (C) 風水先生

hei (C) 氣

hiâ: (H) 兄

hsia-fang (M) 下放

hsiang (M) 鄉

hsiang-yung (M) 鄉勇

hsiang-yüeh (M) 鄉約

hsiao (M) 孝

hsien (M) 縣

Hsien-t'ien Ta-tao (M) 先天大道

Hsin Hsing (M) 新興

Hsing-Chung Hui (M) 興中會

hua-ch'iao (M) 華僑

hui-kuan (M) 會館

hun (M) 魂

I-kuan Tao (M) 一貫道

kǐ-liām (H) 記念

kongsi (C) 公司

kōng-sî (H) 公司

kou (H) 哥

kū (H) 舅

kǔ-à (H) 舅仔

kuei (M) 鬼

kung (M) 工

lap (C) 立

li (M) 禮

li-chia (M) 里甲

ling-p'ai (M) 靈牌

loi lung (C) 來龍

lung (C) 龍

mà (H) 媽

mai (C) 買

mui tsai (C) 妹仔

naam moh lo (C) 南巫佬

ng-cêk (H), *see* cêk 阿叔

ng-kou (H), *see* kou 阿哥

ng-kū (H), *see* kū 阿舅

nung (M) 農

paak fu (C) 白虎

pai (M) 拜

p'ai (M) 牌

pao-chia (M) 保甲

phièng-kîm (H) 聘金

Ping Shan (C) 屏山

p'o (M) 魄

Punti (C) 本地

Sai Kung (C) 西貢

sām-kǎi (H) 三界

San Tin (C) 新田

Sha Tau Kok (C) 沙頭角

shaat hei (C) 殺氣

shang (M) 商

Shap Sz Heung (C) 十四鄉

shen (M) 神

shen-chu (M) 神主

shen-wei (M) 神位

sheng-yüan (M) 生員

Sheung Shui (C) 上水

shih (M) 士

shue fuk (C) 舒服

sīm-pǔ-kià: (H) 媳婦囝

sīn-cù (H) 神主

sīn-khěq (H) 新客

Tai Po (C) 大埔

Tao Yüan (M) 道院

ti (M) 地

ti-li (M) 地理

ti-pao (M) 地保

t'ien (M) 天

t'ien-hsia (M) 天下

t'sai (C), *see* ts'ai

ts'ai (C) 妻

Tsao Chün (M) 灶君

Ts'at Yeuk (C) 七約

ts'ing lung (C) 青龍

t'sip (C), *see* ts'ip

ts'ip (C) 妾

tsu (M) 祖

ts'u/ts'ui (C) 娶

tuǎ-kū (H) 大舅

Tuan-wu (M) 端午

t'uan (M) 團

t'uan-lien (M) 團練

tun fu (C) 蘯符

tung (M) 洞

Tung Lo (C) 東路

Tung P'ing Kuk (C) 東平局

T'ung-meng Hui (M) 同盟會

T'ung-shan She (M) 同善社

t'ung-sheng (M) 童生

wu-fu (M) 五服

yang (M) 陽

yeuk (C) 約

yin (M) 陰

yin-ssu (M) 陰司

yin-yang (M) 陰陽

Yuen Long (C) 元朗

yüeh (M) 約

Index

Index

Adoption: in Singapore, 95, 120–24; and inheritance, 119f, 125, 141, 430*n*34; of sons, 120–21; of daughters, 121; of sons-in-law, 121–22, 134; of daughters-in-law, 122; of *mui tsai*, 122–24

Adoption of Children Ordinance (Singapore), 120

Aijmer, Lars G., 288

Altars: for ancestor worship, 275ff

Ancestors: and ancestor worship, 274, 278, 281–88 *passim*, 301–3, 306–7; relations with living, 283–86, 297–300, 305–6, 311; divided personalities of, 287–88, 296–97; souls of, 297; Chinese view of, 303–4; in Japan, 308–9; communication with, 310–11

Ancestor worship: among Babas, 88–89; trusts for, 88–90, 127, 132, 141; by lineages, 136, 242, 274, 277–82, 285–86, 298, 301–2, 307, 335, 339; tablets, 164, 275–85 *passim*, 296f, 307; in China, 164–65; in Singapore, 165; and geomancy, 208–11, 286–88, 298–300; and classes of ancestors, 274, 285; domestic, 274, 276f, 282–85, 298, 307; and ancestors, 274, 278, 281–88 *passim*, 301–3, 306–7; altars for, 275ff; inclusion in, 275–76; at graves, 282, 286–88; rites, 282–83, 297; and women, 283ff, 286, 307–8, 312; worship or commemoration, 284–85; and time, 289–90; and Chinese family, 304–6; evolution of, 306–7; and Chinese society, 309

Ancestral halls, 163, 208, 277–81, 285; in Singapore, 164; and geomancy, 201f, 206; as men's sphere, 285–86

Anthropology: in China, 380–83; post-1949, 381–83, 391f; village studies, 382–83; and history, 384–87; and fieldwork, 386, 413; and sociology, 387–90; of complex societies, 390–91; in Asia, 391–92; topics for study, 393–95; teaching of, 396–97; and China, 413–14, 420–22; and Overseas Chinese, 414; and Hong Kong, 414–17; and Taiwan, 416–17; use of written sources, 417–20; goals of, 421–22. *See also* Social sciences; Sociology

Associations: credit, 23–25, 77, 224; in Singapore, 33, 65, 74–80, 91, 135–37, 164; native-place, 33, 75f, 78; commercial, 33, 69, 76; and dialects, 71, 74f, 78ff; surname, 74ff, 79–80, 91, 135–37, 164; registration of, 76, 95; membership in, 76f; judicial activities of, 76f, 135–38; replace family, 77; welfare, 77–78; and immigrants, 78; reasons for, 79, 81–83; in Sarawak, 79–80; and economic relations, 79–80; in West Borneo, 79–82; and religion, 166, 175; charitable, 178, 180. *See also* Chambers of commerce; Guilds; Secret societies

Babas, 47, 162; history of, 8, 62–65, 84–85; and Chinese culture, 8–10, 33, 86–87, 162; population, 13, 85*n*; language of, 33, 50, 86ff; marriage among, 85–87; kinship terms, 87–88; ancestor worship among, 88–89

Baker, Hugh, 280f, 343, 420

Bangkok, 17

Banks, 225, 228

Baperki (association), 16

Betrothal, 98–99, 110, 263–64

Bigamy, 101, 110, 118, 147, 156*n*, 227

Boat people (Tanka), 213, 414

Borneo, 224f, 229. *See also* Brunei; Sabah; Sarawak; West Borneo

Brunei, 46

Buck, John L., 374

Buddhism, 17, 166–67, 169, 175–84 *passim*, 355, 364, 369

Burial practices, 195–96

Burma, 7, 46

Cambodia, 7, 46
Cantonese: in Singapore, 62, 66, 68, 71, 74, 85*n*, 180ff
Capitans China, 69, 94f
Cavenagh, Orfeur, 67
Chambers of commerce, 33, 69
Charter of Justice (Penang), 94, 141
Cheang Thye Pin v. *Tan Ah Loy*, 114
Chee Teang Why, 90
Ch'en Ta, 374, 377
Chiang Kai-shek, 200
Children: laws on, 123–24, 133–34
Children and Young Persons Ordinance (Singapore), 123–24
China: southward expansion of, 40–44, 48, 52; residual, 414, 417. *See also* Hong Kong; New Territories; Overseas Chinese; Taiwan
China bo, 85
Chin-choe (cin-cuě), 85f
Chinese Advisory Board (Singapore), 96
Chinese Chamber of Commerce (Singapore), 69
Chinese culture: in Southeast Asia, 8–12, 20, 33, 45, 86–87, 162
Chinese Marriage Committee (Singapore), 103–16 *passim*, 131, 143
Chinese Protectorate (Singapore), 69f
Ch'ing dynasty, 4–5, 43–44, 53
Choa Chong Long, 88
Choa Choon Neoh v. *Spottiswoode*, 94, 141
Christianity, 130, 162*n*, 175, 177
Christian Marriage Ordinance (Singapore), 106
Civil Code (ROC, 1931), 97, 120f; used in Singapore, 97–98; on marriage, 110–12; on divorce, 118; on inheritance, 125f; on family, 247–48
Civil Marriage Ordinance (Singapore), 106, 147
Clubs, 64, 77
Cohen, Myron L., 259, 343–44, 393
Colonialism: and Overseas Chinese, 5–6, 10f, 13, 15, 27
Compass: and geomancy, 322–23
Concubinage, 99–104, 111–12, 142, 159; and divorce, 113–15, 132, 144; and property rights, 142, 153
Confucianism, 168–69, 176ff, 242, 244, 355, 365–66
Coolies: in Southeast Asia, 5, 61f, 73, 95
Credit associations, 23–25

Daughters-in-law, 99, 122, 245
Department of Social Welfare (Singapore), 145, 157
Dialects: and associations, 71, 74f, 78ff
Divorce, 112–13; and property, 113, 116; of concubines, 113–15, 132, 144; laws, 113–18, 132, 149–50, 154–55; by government agency, 115–17, 134, 144–45; by announcement, 117–18; custody of children, 134; in Singapore, 144–45, 154–55, 157–58
Divorce Ordinance (Singapore), 115
Doolittle, Justus, 168
Dutch East Indies, 5, 224

E-ching-hwuy (secret society), 66
Eisenstadt, Schmuel N., 390
Emigration: from Fukien and Kwangtung, 5f, 44, 62, 91, 96, 129f, 223; of women, 181–82, 227, 229f; from New Territories, 219, 223–31; to Europe, 223f, 227, 231; to Americas, 224, 229; to Asia, 224, 229; financing of, 224f; restrictions on, 226; return to native place, 227f; for education, 228; age distribution, 229; reasons for, 229–30; consequences of, 229–30
Ethnicity: in Malaya, 36ff
Exogamy, 111f, 133

Family: in Peranakan society, 14; laws on, 95, 97, 128f, 132–41, 247–49; size of, 235, 244; variations in, 235–36; partition, 235–38, 258, 304; father-son relations, 236, 238; fraternal relations, 236, 238, 246, 305; and women, 236–37, 245–46, 258–60, 272, 305; and social classes, 237–39, 244–46; models, 238–39; as basic social unit, 240–41, 243; Republican reforms in, 246–48; in PRC, 248–52; and sinology, 252–54; and ancestor worship, 304–6; property, 336; and government, 338
Fei Hsiao-t'ung, 129, 136, 374–82 *passim*, 389–90
Feng Han-yi, 374
Feng shui, see Geomancy
Feuchtwang, Stephan, 317
Firecrackers, 266–67
Firth, Raymond, 381, 388f
Fitzgerald, C. P., 40–54 *passim*
Forest of Laymen, 178
Fried, Morton H., 252, 381
Fukien, 4, 23, 25*n*66, 73, 82, 130*n*, 172; emigration from, 5f, 44, 62, 91, 96,

129, 223–24; lineages in, 300, 341f, 344
Fung shui, see Geomancy

Gambier and Pepper Society, 77
Gambling, 77
Gentry, 129, 339, 347–50
Geomancy, 228, 359, 365, 368; and Hong
  Kong government, 189f, 197, 203–5,
  220–21, 321–22; belief in, 190–91,
  194f, 206–7; principles of, 191–94;
  terms used, 192f, 208; geomancers,
  194–95, 322–35, 329–31, 369; and
  success, 195–99, 209–11, 298–99, 310,
  318–19, 321f, 326–29, 332; and burial,
  195–201, 209–11; and morality, 198–
  99; and buildings, 200–203, 318–20,
  322, 331ff; and public works, 203–5;
  rituals, 207–8; and ancestor worship,
  208–11, 286–88, 298–300; in Japan,
  Korea, and Vietnam, 299–300; studies
  of, 314–17; Freedman's views, summarized, 317–18; Kiangsi School, 319,
  322–23; Fukien School, 323; as science,
  325–26; as divination, 326; and Chinese
  society, 331–33
Ghee Hin (secret society), 67f, 71, 72n, 82
Ghee Hok (secret society), 67f
Ghee Khee Kwang Hok (secret society), 67f
Ghee Sin (secret society), 67f
Government, local, 213–16, 349–50; local
  leaders, 215–16, 219
Granet, Marcel, 306–7, 334, 355–56,
  361–64, 393, 396n, 437n6, 437n11,
  437–38n14
Graves, 282, 286–88, 296–99, 359
Gray, John H., 168
Great Proletarian Cultural Revolution,
  408–12
Great Way of Former Heaven, 169n,
  170–83 *passim*
Groot, Jan J. M. de, 168ff, 315f, 355–61,
  364, 437n6–n10, 437n14
Groves, Robert G., 347f
Guilds, 76–77

Hae-shan-hwuy (secret society), 66
Hainanese: in Singapore, 62, 71, 74, 85n
Hai San (secret society), 67f, 71n, 72n
Hakka, 81, 230, 278, 343–45; in Singa-
  pore, 62, 66, 68, 71, 74, 85n
Heaven (deity), 354, 364–65, 368
Heaven and Earth League, 66, 174
Hok Hin (secret society), 67f
Hokkien: in Singapore, 62, 66f, 71, 74,
  85n, 87–88

Hong Kong, 5, 140, 212–13, 350, 414–16,
  420. *See also* New Territories
Horoscopes, 261, 291, 329
Hsiang-yüeh system, 346
Hsin-an county (Kwangtung), 213–16, 337
Hsu, Francis L. K., 237, 252, 373f, 381
Hui-kuan, 75. *See also* Native-place associ-
  ations
Hun (souls), 277, 286, 297

I-kuan-tao (sect), 169n, 177, 433n12
Illegitimacy, 103n, 112n, 118ff, 132, 134,
  142, 150
Incest, 133n
Indians: in Malaya, 28–37 *passim*
Indonesia: Chinese in, 5, 7, 13–17, 46, 51,
  55
Inheritance, 86; by women, 95, 100, 102f,
  106, 125–27, 132, 141f, 151, 153;
  laws, 97n, 119f, 124–27, 132, 141f; by
  adopted children, 119f, 125, 141,
  430n34
In re Chee Shang Leng's Estate, 119
Interest rates, 25
In the Estate of Sim Siew Guan Decd.,
  114
Islam, 8, 16, 28, 31, 34f, 175, 177

Japan, 224, 299–300, 308–9, 403

Khoo Hooi Leong v. Khoo Chong Yeok,
  114
*Khoo Tiong Bee and another v. Tan Beng
  Gwat*, 119
Kinship, 335; in Singapore, 76, 79, 87–88,
  90–91, 164–65; fictive, 183, 338n; and
  marriage, 237, 269–71, 294–95; laws
  on, 241–42, 248–49; and the state,
  241–43, 250, 338, 346; and the
  economy, 243. *See also* Family, Lineages
Kitchen God, 274–75, 283, 298n
Kong Fooy Sew (secret society), 67f
Kongsi (communities), 81f
Korea, 403
Kuei (ghosts), 297
Kuhn, Philip A., 348
Kulp, Daniel H., 374
Kwangtung, 4, 6, 25, 66, 77, 82, 172,
  181–82, 292, 320; emigration from, 5,
  44, 62, 91, 96, 129f, 223; lineages in,
  300, 341f, 344, 346f

Labour Code (Singapore), 95
Lamma Island, 224
Landsmannschaften, 33, 78. *See also*

Native-place associations; Surname associations
Lantan Island, 224
Laos, 7, 46
Law: Chinese v. British, 94–95, 127–29, 140f, 145, 155; and Chinese customs, 94–95; family, 95, 97, 128f, 132–41, 247–49; in Singapore, 95f, 132–35, 141, 145, 428n2, 428–29n6; Chinese, characterized, 96; on marriage, 97, 99–103, 110–12, 142–43, 147–49, 260–61; on inheritance, 97n, 119f, 124–27, 132, 141f; on illegitimacy, 103n, 112n, 118ff, 132, 134, 142, 150; on divorce, 113–18, 132, 149–50, 154–55; on adoption, 119–24; on children, 123–24, 133–34; and social classes, 129; and modernization, 130–31; customary v. formal, 138–39; on kinship, 241–42, 248–49
Lee Kuan Yew, 51, 146
Levy, Marion J., 252
Lew Ah Lui v. Choa Eng Wan and others, 114
Li An-che, 374
Li Ching-han (Franklin Lee), 374, 377–78
Li-chia system, 346, 350
Lin Yüeh-hua, 374f, 378, 381, 383
Lineages, 213, 278; and ancestor worship, 136, 242, 274, 277–82, 285–86, 298, 301–2, 307, 335, 339; in Hsin-an county, 214–15; leadership of, 215–18, 339–40; in Hong Kong, 216, 337, 342f, 347; and the family, 241; higher-order, 242, 337, 341, 344; and government, 242–43, 337–43; and geomancy, 300; in Kwangtung and Fukien, 300, 341f, 344, 346f; and the clan, 334–35; study of, 334–35; formation of, 335–36, 342, 344–45; heterogeneity of, 336, 339–40; property of, 336–37, 342f, 344; and villages, 337, 344; relations between, 337, 340f; and society, 340, 350; distribution of, 342ff, 345; and frontier areas, 342ff, 345; in Taiwan, 343–45; and irrigation, 345
Loan associations, 23–25, 77, 224
Local Communities Ordinance (Hong Kong), 217
Lyall, Arthur C., 353–54

McAleavey, Henry, 259
Maitreya, 171
Malacca, 5, 8, 33, 94, 140
Malaya: Chinese in, 5, 7–12, 31–35, 62, 224; population of, 27–28; immigration

into, 27–28; government of, 27–30, 35–37; Indians in, 28–37 *passim*; plural society, 35–38; economy of, 37. *See also* Singapore
Malayan Chinese Association (MCA), 35
Malays, 27, 30–31, 35, 141
Malaysia: Chinese in, 5, 7, 46. *See also* Malaya; Sabah; Sarawak; Singapore
Malinowski, Bronislaw, 42, 256, 380, 382f, 387f, 389n, 391
Mandarin (language): used in Southeast Asia, 6, 9–10, 33, 49
Mao Tse-tung, 200, 409f
Market towns, 214
Marketing systems, 350
Marriage: uxorilocal, 85–86, 104, 122; Chinese terminology, 85–86; among Babas, 85–87; ceremonies, 86–87, 98–99, 107ff, 111f, 257, 261–69, 272, 289–94, 429n21, 430n25; among Overseas Chinese, 89f; polygamy, 89, 99–103, 132, 141–42, 146f; laws on, 97, 99–103, 110–12, 142–43, 147–49, 260–61; 1950 PRC Marriage Law on, 98, 112; concubinage, 99–104, 111–12, 142–43, 159; bigamy, 101, 110, 118, 147, 156n, 227; in Singapore, 104, 106–8, 132; registration of, 106f, 109, 112, 143, 146ff, 152, 156–57; certificates, 107–8; by announcement, 109–10, 144; 1931 ROC Civil Code on, 110–12; prohibitions on, 110ff, 133, 148; numbers of, 146–47, 156; anti-marriage movement, 181–82; and kinship, 237, 269–71, 294–95; posthumous, 275; and movement in space, 290, 292–93
Marriage Law (PRC, 1950), 98, 112, 118, 120, 125, 127, 133, 145, 248–49.
Married Women and Children (Maintenance) Ordinance (Singapore), 103n, 115
Married Women's Property Ordinance (Singapore), 127
Meskill, Johanna, 420
MIC (political party), 35
Mining: and Chinese in Malaya, 5, 8, 27, 29, 32, 36
Minor Offenses Ordinance (Singapore), 115
Money loan associations, 23–25, 77, 224
Monogamy, 143, 146–47
Mui tsai, 122–24, 130ff
Munshi, Abdullah, 66, 73
Muslims Ordinance (Singapore), 146
Mutual credit clubs, 23–25, 77, 224

Nanchao kingdom, 42–43
Nanyang Chinese, *see* Overseas Chinese
Nan-Yang Sacred Union, 180
Nanyang University, 10
Nationalism: and Chinese in Southeast
  Asia, 6, 9–11, 14–15, 18, 33, 36, 48f
Native-place associations, 33, 75f, 78. *See
  also* Surname associations
Negri Sembilan, 29
New Territories: history of, 189–90, 212–
  13; and geomancy, 190, 203, 210, 321;
  under British, 203, 216–22, 347–48,
  350; during Ch'ing, 213–16; lineages in,
  216, 337, 342f, 347; population of,
  218–19; emigration from, 219, 223–31;
  population imbalances, 230; women in,
  230; study of, 382, 384, 394, 399–400,
  414–16, 420
New Villages: of Chinese in Malaya, 32, 35
Nyonya(h)s, 84n, 89

Overseas Chinese: in Southeast Asia, 4–5,
  44–45; in Indonesia, 5, 7, 13–17, 46, 51,
  55; in Thailand, 5, 7, 17–20, 41, 46, 51,
  224; anti-Chinese sentiments, 5, 16, 18f,
  55; and colonialism, 5–6, 10f, 13, 15,
  27; political activities of, 6, 35f, 40–41,
  54; education, 6, 9–18 *passim*, 49; and
  nationalism, 6, 9–11, 14–15, 18, 33, 36,
  48f; in Philippines, 7, 41–42, 46, 224;
  population, 7, 13, 27–28, 46–47; intermarriage with local peoples, 8, 14, 17f; in
  Malaya and Singapore, 8–12, 27–36,
  93–94, 161–63; assimilation of, 8–21
  passim, 47; and Chinese culture, 9–12,
  20, 48–51, 56; handling of money, 22,
  25–26; social classes, 22, 49–50; study
  of, 45, 382–84, 393–94, 400, 414f,
  426n7; Jewish analogy, 54–56; in
  Europe, 223–31 *passim*; in Americas,
  224, 229

P'an Kuang-tan (Quentin Pan), 246ff, 252,
  376, 378
Pan-Malayan Islamic Party, 36
Pao-chia system, 346, 350
Pasternak, Burton, 343ff
Penang, 5, 73, 94, 102n, 112f, 122, 140
People's Action Party (Singapore), 146
Perak, 36
Peranakans, 13–16

Philippines: Chinese in, 7, 41–42, 46, 224
Pickering, William A., 67f, 72ff, 95

"Pig business," 65, 73, 82
Pineapple Preservers' Guild, 77
P'o (soul), 297
Political parties, 35
Polygamy, 89, 99–103, 132, 141–42, 146f
Population: of Chinese in Southeast Asia, 7,
  13, 27–28, 46–47; of Singapore, 28,
  46–47, 61–62, 68, 85n, 140; of New
  Territories, 218–19; of Chinese in United
  Kingdom, 223
Portuguese Timor, 46
Potter, Jack M., 343, 415
Pratt, Jean, 384
Primogeniture, 304ff, 336
Property rights, 124; of concubines, 142,
  153; of women, 147, 150–51, 154
Prostitution, 89f
Protector of Chinese (Singapore), 67,
  95–96
Punti, 226, 230

Radcliffe-Brown, Alfred R., 256, 301f, 375,
  381ff, 392–93
Raffles, Stamford, 61, 65n, 66, 93
Red Guards, 409–12
Red Swastika Society, 177, 179–80
Religion: participation in, 166f; in Singapore, 168, 172–74, 178–85; state,
  168–69; and secret societies, 169; syn-
  cretism, 169f, 175, 177ff, 184; and salvation, 170, 182; and rebellion, 170–72,
  364; and sectarianism, 171, 175–78,
  179–84; and women, 173, 179, 181–84,
  311n; and modern politics, 175, 177–78,
  180–81, 185; in twentieth-century
  China, 175–78; lay organizations,
  178–79; as "family," 183; C. K. Yang on,
  351–52, 354f, 364–66; study of, 351–
  55, 366–69; Chinese, characterized,
  352–53; unity of, 352–53, 366, 368–
  69; Lyall on, 353–54; and government,
  353ff, 365, 369; as part of hierarchical
  society, 354–55; elite/popular, 355,
  362–69; Granet on, 355–56, 361–64;
  de Groot on, 355–61; toleration, 360–
  61, 369; Max Weber on, 436–37n4
Remittances, 223, 228–29
Rites: compared with laws, 294

Sabah, 7
Sago Dealers' Guild, 77
Sai Kung district (New Territories), 230
San Tin village (New Territories), 224
Sarawak, 7, 79–80

Schmidt, Wilhelm, 375
Schools: Chinese, in Southeast Asia, 6, 10–18 *passim*, 33–34
Secretariat for Chinese Affairs (Singapore), 145
Secret societies, 4, 33, 90; in Singapore, 65–74, 80, 172ff; coercion by, 66, 73; riots, 66–67; membership in, 66ff, 71ff; perform judicial functions, 67, 70, 95; government control of, 67f, 69, 174; leadership of, 67f, 73–74; suppression of, 68, 74, 91, 174; criminal activities, 68, 70, 74, 174; anti-Manchu sentiments, 69f, 169, 173f; and politics, 70, 73–74, 172, 174; connections between, 70f; rituals, 73; reasons for, 81–83; and religion, 169
Sha Tau Kok (area, New Territories), 224, 230
Shanghai, 5
Shap Sz Heung (area, New Territories), 224
Shen (spirits), 297, 306
Sheung Shui village (New Territories), 279–81, 285
Shirokogoroff, Sergei, 374f
Sĩm-pŭ-kià: (little daughters-in-law), 122
Singapore: Chinese in, 5, 7f, 10, 27, 69–70, 93–94, 96, 140, 161–63; population, 28, 46–47, 61–62, 68, 140; associations in, 33, 65, 74–80, 91, 135–37, 164; and Chinese culture, 51; economy, 63; social organization, 65; secret societies in, 65–74, 80, 172ff; laws of, 95f, 132–35, 141, 145, 428n2, 428–29n6; marriage laws, 98–112; marriage statistics, 106, 146–47; history of, 140–41, 146; religion in, 168, 172–74, 178–85
Singapore Chamber of Commerce, 69
Singapore Federation of Buddhists, 178–79
Sĩn-khĕq (greenhorns), 72f
Six Widows Case, 100ff, 113–14, 129, 142, 144
Skinner, G. William, 45, 216, 381, 384, 404, 418–19
Social classes, 129–30; of Overseas Chinese, 22, 49–50; and family, 237–39, 224–46
Social sciences: and China, 398–99, 404–6; area studies, 399; and fieldwork, 400–401; and the PRC, 400–401; and history, 401–2; comparative, 402–3; and sinology, 402–4; and models, 403–4. *See also* Anthropology; Sociology

Societies Ordinance (Singapore), 95
Sociology (in China): and anthropology, 373, 376, 387–90; under the Republic, 373–76; demography, 374; foreign influences, 374–75; community studies, 374f; Marxian, 375; on family, 376; on peasants, 376; on law, 376; under PRC, 376–79. *See also* Anthropology; Social sciences
Song Peh Kwan (secret society), 67f
Southeast Asia: Chinese in, 4–5, 20–21, 42–44, 47; anti-Chinese sentiments, 5, 16, 18f; takeover by Chinese, 44–45. *See also individual countries by name*
Spirit-mediums, 167–68, 184, 208, 310–11
Statute of Distributions (Singapore), 125–28
Straits Chinese, *see* Babas
Straits Settlements, 5, 9, 28, 140ff, 224. *See also* Malacca; Penang; Singapore
Sun Yat-sen, 6, 174, 199
Sung dynasty, 4
Surname associations: in Singapore, 74ff, 79–80, 91, 135–37, 164
Szechwan, 172

Tablets, ancestral, 164, 275–85 *passim*, 296f, 307
Tai Po (market town, New Territories), 230, 346f
Taiwan: lineages in, 343–45; study of, 382, 384, 399, 416–17, 420
Tali kingdom, 43
Tan Che Sang, 89–90
Taoism, 166, 169, 177, 355, 364, 369
Tao Yüan (sect), 177, 179–80, 184
Tean Tay Huey (secret society), 66
Temples, 163–64, 166
Teochiu: in Singapore, 62, 66f, 71, 74, 85n
Thailand: Chinese in, 5, 7, 17–20, 41, 46, 51, 224
Ti-pao (constables), 216, 221
T'ien Ju-k'ang, 374, 381
Ting Hsien survey, 374
Totoks, 13–16
Trade associations, 33
Triad society, 4, 66, 70, 73, 75, 82, 91, 174
Tuan Ch'i-jui, 178
T'uan-lien (local militias), 346, 348ff
Tun fu (rite), 207–8
T'ung (cave), 346ff
T'ung-shan She (Fellowship of Goodness), 169n, 176ff, 180, 184

UMNO (political party), 35
United Kingdom: Chinese in, 223–26, 229, 231
University of Malaya, 34

Vegetarian halls, 173, 176, 181–84
Vietnam, 299, 403; Chinese in, 7, 42–43, 46, 52
Village representatives (Hong Kong), 190, 219–21

Wakeman, Frederic E., 347f
Wang Gungwu, 45
Ward, Barbara E., 384, 414
Weber, Max, 436–37n4
Wertheim, Willem F., 55f
West Borneo, 79–82
White Lotus sect, 171–72
Wiens, Herold J., 41
Wills, C. A., 123
Wolf, Arthur P., 285
Women: inheritance by, 95, 100, 102f, 106, 125–27, 132, 141f, 151, 153; and property, 142, 147, 150–51, 153f, 258–60, 291; sexual equality, 158; and religion, 173, 179, 181–84, 311n; emigration, 181–82, 227, 229f; as labor force, 230; and family, 236–37, 245–46, 258–60, 272, 289; 1931 ROC Civil Code on, 248; and ancestor worship, 283ff, 286, 307–8, 312
Women and Girls Protection Ordinance (Singapore), 95, 151
Women and Girls Section (Singapore), 115–16, 134, 137–38
Women's Charter (Singapore), 140, 146; summary of, 147–51; debate over, 151–55; consequences of, 155–59
Woods, Wilfred, 122f
World Fellowship of Buddhists, 179
Wright, Mary C., 385–86
Wu Ching-ch'ao, 378
Wu Wen-tsao, 373–74, 380, 382

Yang, C. K., 252, 351f, 354f, 364–66, 374f
Yang, Martin M. C., 284
Yen Fu, 373
Yin-yang, 192, 286, 288, 297ff, 300, 323, 331
Yüan dynasty, 4
Yüeh (*yuek*, compacts, treaties), 346
Yunnan, 42–43, 48–49